# Diodorus Siculus

I

Temple of Zeus at Acragas
(From R. Koldewey–O. Puchstein, *Die griechischen Tempel in Unteritalien und Sicilien*)

# The Historical Library of DIODORUS the SICILIAN
in Forty Books

Edited by
Giles Laurén

## Volume One
Books 1-14

SOPHRON EDITOR
2014

Copyright 2014 by Giles Laurén

ISBN 13: 978-0-9897836-2-0
ISBN 10: 989783626

Design by Sophron Editor

# PREFACE

Once the serious reader of Greek history has gotten through the well-known historians like Herodotus, Xenophon and Thucydides, he soon comes across a reference to Diodorus Siculus. Indeed, for significant portions of Greek history Diodorus is our only source, and yet hitherto the only edition available to the reader in English is the twelve volume Loeb editions which is not readily accessible.

The purpose of this new edition is to bring Diodorus Siculus, historically complete, to English readers in an inexpensive two volume edition. It makes no pretence of providing new material or new insight; it is entirely based on the previous translations and introductory material of the Loeb editions.

An attempt has been made to provide useful dates in brackets [317/16] and some place names [Himera], personal names [brother of Helen], and so forth have been similarly made more identifiable. Instances of missing manuscript text are represented by the usual three periods . . . The Table of Contents has been expanded to make the many divisions and subsections of the text easy to locate. The Maps have been grouped at the end of the text for easier reference. The disjointed Fragments of the Diodorus Opus have been eliminated as superfluous. The Introduction consolidates the several previous introductions and has been greatly simplified: it now includes the entire work. Otherwise this edition is without critical or explanatory notes, bibliography or index.

Three modest objectives are gained by this simplification. **A.** an uncluttered and readable text for the general reader; **B.** an inexpensive paperback and digital ebook suitable for later enhancement; **C.** a desire to provide a reason and basis for some scholar to undertake a proper edition of Diodorus by making him better known.

Errors are unavoidable in such an undertaking and I can only promise to correct any I am advised of or discover as time goes by.

G. L.

# CONTENTS

| | |
|---|---|
| **MAPS** | xv |
| *Sigla* | xv |
| **INTRODUCTION** | xvi |
| General Introduction | xvi |
| The contents of the several Books: | xviii |
| Introduction to Books I - II, 34 | xx |
| Introduction Books II, 35-IV, 58 | xxi |
| Book XVI | xxii |
| Book XVII | xxiii |
| The Sources of Books 18-20 | xxvi |
| Introduction XXI | xxvi |
| Note on Chronology | xxvii |
| History of the Fragments | xxvii |
| **BOOK I** | 1 |
| Introduction to the entire work (1-5). | 1 |
| On the accounts given by the Egyptians about the origin of the universe (6-7). | 4 |
| On the first men and the earliest manner of life (8). | 6 |
| On the topography of the land of Egypt and the marvels related about the river Nile; the causes also of its flooding and the opinions thereupon of the historians and the philosophers (30 ff.). | 20 |
| On the first kings of Egypt and their deeds (ch. 44 ff.). | 32 |
| On the construction of the pyramids which are listed among the seven wonders of the world (63 ff.). | 43 |
| On the laws and the courts of law (69 ff.). | 48 |
| On the animals held sacred among the Egyptians (83 ff.). | 58 |
| On the customs of the Egyptians touching the dead (91 ff.). | 64 |
| On those Greeks, renowned for their learning, who visited Egypt and upon acquiring much useful knowledge brought it to Greece (96 ff.) | 67 |
| **BOOK II** | 71 |
| On Ninus, the first king in Asia, and his deeds (1-3). | 71 |
| On the birth of Semiramis and her rise (4-5). | 73 |
| How King Ninus married Semiramis because of her outstanding ability (6). | 74 |
| How Semiramis, ascending the throne on the death of Ninus, accomplished many great deeds. (7) The founding of Babylon and an account of its building (7-9). | 75 |
| On the hanging garden, as it is called, and the other astonishing things in Babylonia (10-13). | 78 |
| The campaign of Semiramis against Egypt, Ethiopia, and India (14-20). | 80 |
| On her descendants who were kings in Asia and their luxury and sluggishness (21-22). | 85 |
| How Sardanapallus, the last king, because of his luxuriousness lost his throne to Arbaces the Mede (23-28). | 87 |
| On the Chaldaeans and their observation of the stars (29-31). | 91 |
| On the kings of Media and the disagreement of historians upon them (32-34). | 93 |

*On the topography of India and the products of the land, and on the customs of the Indians 35-42).* 95
*On the Scythians, Amazons, and Hyperboreans (43-47).* 100
*On Arabia, and the products of the land and its legends (48-54).* 103
*On the islands which have been discovered to the south in the ocean (55-60).* 108

BOOK III 113
*On the Ethiopians who dwell beyond Libya and their antiquities (1-11).* 113
*On the gold mines on the farthest borders of Egypt and the working of the gold (12-14).* 119
*On the peoples who dwell upon the coast of the Arabian Gulf and, speaking generally, upon all the coast of the ocean as far as India. In this connection there is a discussion of the customs which each people follows and of the reasons why history records many things in connection with them which are entirely unique and are not believed because they are contrary to what one expects (15-48.* 120
*On the antiquities of Libya and the history of the Gorgons and Amazons, and of Amnion and Atlas (49-61).* 145
*On the myths related about Nysa, in connection with which there is also an account of the Titans and Dionysus and the Mother of the Gods (62-74).* 156

BOOK IV 167
*Introduction on the myths recounted by the historians (1).* 167
*On Dionysus, Priapus, Hermaphroditus, and the Muses (2-7).* 168
*On Heracles and the twelve Labours, and the other deeds of his up to the time of his deification (8-39).* 172
*On the Argonauts and Medea and the daughters of Pelias (40-56).* 196
*On the descendants of Heracles (57-58).* 209
*On Theseus and his labours (59-63)* 210
*On The Seven against Thebes (64-65)* 214
*On the Epigoni of The Seven against Thebes (66-67).* 215
*On Neleus and his descendants (68).* 217
*On the Lapiths and Centaurs (69-70).* 218
*On Asclepius and his descendants (71).* 219
*On the daughters of Asopus and the sons born to Aeacus (72).* 220
*On Pelops, Tantalus, Oenomaus, and Niobê (73-74).* 220
*On Dardanus and his descendants as far as Priam (75).* 221
*On Daedalus, the Minotaur, and the campaign cf Minos against the king Cocalus (76-80).* 222
*On Aristaeus, Daphnis, Eryx, and Orion (chaps. 81-85).* 226

BOOK V 231
*On the myths which are recounted about Sicily and the shape and size of the island (2).* 231
*On Demeter and Corê and the discovery of the fruit of wheat (3-6).* 232
*On Lipara and the other islands which are called the Aeolidcs (7-11).* 235
*On Melitê, Gaulus, and Cercina (12).* 238
*On Aethaleia, Cyrnus (Corsica), and Sardinia (13-15).* 238
*On Pityussa and the Gymnesiae islands, which some call the Baliarides (16-18).* 240

## Contents

*On the islands in the ocean which lie towards the west (19-20).*   *241*
*On the island of Britain and that called Basileia, where amber is found (21-23).*
  *243*
*On Gaul, Celtiberia, Iberia, Liguria, and Tyrrhenia, and on the inhabitants of these countries and the customs they observe (24-40).*   *245*
*On the islands in the ocean to the south, both the one called Hiera and that called Panchaea, and on what they are said to contain (41-46).*   *255*
*On Samothrace and the mysteries celebrated on the island (47-49).*   *259*
*On Naxos and Symê and Calydna (50-54).*   *261*
*On Rhodes and the myths which are recounted concerning it (55-59)*   *263*
*On the Cherronesus which lies over against the territory of Rhodes (60-63).*   *267*
*On Crete and the myths which are recounted about it, down to comparatively recent times (64-80).*   *269*
*On Lesbos and the colonies which were led by Macareus to Chios, Samos, and Cos (81-82).*   *280*
*On Tenedos, the colonisation of the island, and the fabulous tales told by the Tenedians about Tennes (83).*   *281*
*On the colonisation by Minos of the islands of the smaller Cyclades (84).*   *282*

**BOOK VI FRAGMENTS**   283
**BOOK VII FRAGMENTS**   287
    *From Eusebius, Chronicle*   *287*
    *From Eusebius, Chronicle*   *290*
    *From 11. Eusebius, Chronicle*   *291*
    *From 15. Eusebius, Chronicle*   *294*

**BOOK VIII FRAGMENTS**   296
**BOOK IX FRAGMENTS**   307
**BOOK X FRAGMENTS**   319
**FRAGMENTS OF UNCERTAIN PROVENIENCE**   331
**BOOK XI**   332
    *On the crossing of Xerxes into Europe (1-4).*   *332*
    *On the battle of Thermopylae (5-11).*   *335*
    *On the naval battle which Xerxes fought against the Greeks (12-13).*   *340*
    *How Themistocles outgeneralled Xerxes and the Greeks conquered the barbarians in the naval battle of Salamis (14-18).*   *341*
    *How Xerxes, leaving Mardonius behind as commander, withdrew with a portion of his army to Asia (19).*   *345*
    *How the Carthaginians with great armaments made war upon Sicily (20-21)345*
    *How Gelon, after outgeneralling the barbarians, slew some of them and took others captive (22-23).*   *347*
    *How Gelon, when the Carthaginians sued for peace, exacted money of them and then concluded the peace (24-26).*   *348*
    *Judgement passed on the Greeks who distinguished themselves in the war (27). The battle of the Greeks against Mardonius and the Persians about Plataea and the victory of the Greeks (27-39).*   *351*
    *The war which the Romans waged against the Aequi and the inhabitants of Tusculum (40).*   *359*
    *On the construction of the Peiraeus by Themistocles (41-50).*   *360*

*On the aid which king Hiero dispatched to the Cymaeans (51).* 366
*On the war which arose between the Tarantini and the Iapyges (52).* 366
*How Thrasydaeus, the son of Theron and tyrant of the Acragantini, was defeated by the Syracusans and lost his overlordship (53).* 366
*How Themistocles, who had fled for safety to Xerxes and was put on trial for his life, was set at liberty (54-59).* 367
*How the Athenians freed the Greek cities throughout Asia (60-62).* 371
*On the earthquake that occurred in Laconia (63). On the revolt of the Messenians and Helots against the Lacedaemonians (63-64).* 373
*How the Argives razed Mycenae to the ground and made the city desolate (65)* 374
*How the Syracusans overthrew the royal line of Gelon (67-68).* 376
*How Xerxes was slain by treachery and Artaxerxes became king (69).* 377
*On the revolt of the Egyptians against the Persians (71).* 379
*On the civil discords which took place among the Syracusans (72-73).* 379
*How the Athenians defeated in war the Aeginetans and Corinthians (78-79).* 383
*How the Phocians made war on the Dorians (79).* 383
*How Myronides the Athenian with a few soldiers defeated the Boeotians who far outnumbered them (81-82).* 385
*On the campaign of Tolmides against Cephallenia (84).* 386
*On the war in Sicily between the Egestaeans and Lilybaeans (86).* 388
*On the framing of the law of petalism by the Syracusans (87).* 388
*The campaign of Pericles against the Peloponnesus (88).* 389
*The campaign of the Syracusans against Tyrrhenia (88).* 389
*On the Palici, as they are called, in Sicily (89).* 390
*On the defeat of Ducetius and his astounding escape from death (91-92).* 391

BOOK XII 393
*On the campaign of the Athenians against Cyprus (1-4).* 393
*On the revolt of the Megarians from the Athenians (5).* 395
*On the battle at Coroneia between the Athenians and Boeotians (6).* 395
*On the campaign of the Athenians against Euboea (7).* 395
*The war in Sicily between the Syracusans and the Acragantini (8)* 395
*The founding in Italy of Thurii and its civil strife (9-11).* 396
*How Charondas, who was chosen lawgiver of Thurii, was responsible for many benefits to his native city (12-19).* 398
*How Zaleucus, the lawgiver in Locri, won for himself great fame (20-21).* 402
*How the Athenians expelled the Hestiaeans and sent there their own colonists (22).* 403
*On the war between the Thurians and the Tarantini (23).* 403
*On the civil strife in Rome (24-26).* 403
*On the war between the Samians and the Milesians (27-28).* 405
*How the Syracusans campaigned against the Picenians and razed their city (29).* 406
*How the Corinthian War, as it is called, broke out in Greece (30).* 406
*How the nation of the Campani was formed in Italy (31).* 407
*The naval battle between the Corinthians and the Cercyraeans (31-33).* 407

## Contents

*The revolt of Potidaea and the Chalcidians from the Athenians, and on the campaign of the Athenians against the Potidaeans (34).*    408

*On the civil strife which arose in Thurii (35).*    409

*How Meton of Athens was the first to expound the nineteen-year cycle (36).*    409

*How the Tarantini founded the city of Heracleia in Italy (36).*    409

*How in Rome Spurius Maelius attempted to seize the supreme power and was put to death (37).*    410

*On the Peloponnesian War, as it is called (38-41).*    410

*On the battle between the Boeotians and the Plataeans (42).*    413

*How, when Methone was being besieged by the Athenians, Brasidas the Spartan won distinction and fame (43).*    414

*How the Athenians campaigned against the Locrians and pillaged the city of Thronium (44).*    415

*How the Aeginetans, who had been expelled by the Athenians, colonised Thyreae, as it is called (44).*    415

*How the Lacedaemonians sent an army into Attica and destroyed the properties (45).*    415

*The second campaign of the Athenians against the Potidaeans (46).*    416

*The campaign of the Lacedaemonians against Acarnania and the naval battle with the Athenians (47-48).*    416

*The campaign of Sitalces against Macedonia, and of the Lacedaemonians against Attica (50-51).*    418

*On the embassy from Leontini to Athens and the powerful oratory of Gorgias their ambassador (53).*    419

*On the war between the Leontines and the Syracusans (54).*    420

*The revolt of the Lesbians from the Athenians and the seizure and destruction of Plataea by the Lacedaemonians (55-56).*    420

*The civil strife among the Cercyraeans (57).*    422

*How the Athenians were seized by a pestilential disease and lost many of their citizens (58).*    422

*How the Lacedaemonians founded Heracleia, a city in Trachis (59).*    423

*How the Athenians slew many of the Ambraciotes and laid waste their city (60).*    423

*On the Lacedaemonians who were made prisoners on the island of Sphacteria (61-63).*    424

*On the punishment inflicted by Postumius on his son because he left his place in the ranks (64).*    425

*On the war between the Lacedaemonians and Athenians over the Megarians (66).*    427

*The war between the Lacedaemonians and Athenians over the Chalcidians (67-68).*    428

*The battle in Boeotia between the Athenians and the Boeotians (69-70).*    429

*The campaign of the Athenians against the Lesbian exiles (72).*    430

*The expulsion of the Delians by the Athenians (73).*    431

*The capture and destruction of Toronê by the Athenians (73).*    431

*How, after the Athenians and Lacedaemonians had concluded an alliance between them, the rest of the cities were alienated from them (74-76).*    432

*How the Delians were restored by the Athenians to their native state (77).*    433

## Diodorus Siculus

*How the Lacedaemonians waged war upon the Mantineans and Argives (78-79).*    *434*

*The campaign of the Byzantians and Calchedonians against Bithynia (82).*    *437*

*On the reasons why the Athenians launched a campaign against Syracuse (83-84).*    *437*

# BOOK XIII    439

*The campaign of the Athenians against the Syracusans, with great armaments both land and naval (1-3).*    *439*

*The arrival of the Athenians in Sicily (4).*    *440*

*The recall of Alcibiades the general and his flight to Lacedaemon (5).*    *441*

*How the Athenians sailed through into the Great Harbour of the Syracusans and seized the regions about the Olympieum (6).*    *441*

*How the Athenians seized Epipolae and, after victories in battle in both areas, laid siege to Syracuse (7).*    *442*

*How, after the Lacedaemonians and Corinthians had sent them aid, the Syracusans took courage (8).*    *443*

*How the Syracusans, having gained control of Epipolae, compelled the Athenians to withdraw to the single camp before the Olympieum (8).*    *443*

*How the Athenians, after the death of their general Lamachus and the recall of Alcibiades, dispatched in their place as generals Eurymedon and Demosthenes with reinforcements and money (8).*    *443*

*The termination of the truce by the Lacedaemonians, and the Peloponnesian War, as it is called, against the Athenians (8).*    *443*

*The great battle about Epipolae and the victory of the Syracusans (8).*    *443*

*The battle between the Athenians and the Syracusans and the great victory of the Athenians (9).*    *444*

*The sea-battle between the Syracusans and the Athenians and the victory of the Athenians; the capture of the fortresses by the Syracusans and their victory on land (9).*    *444*

*The battle between the same opponents and the victory of the Syracusans (10).*    *445*

*How the Syracusans, having gained control of Epipolae, compelled the Athenians to withdraw to the single camp before the Olympieum (11-12).*    *445*

*The sea-battle of all the ships in the Great Harbour and the victory of the Syracusans (11-17).*    *445*

*The arrival from Athens of Demosthenes and Eurymedon with a strong force (11).*    *445*

*How the Syracusans prepared a naval force and decided to offer battle at sea (13).*    *447*

*The flight of the Athenians and the capture of the entire host (18-19).*    *449*

*How the Syracusans gathered in assembly and considered the question what disposition should be made of the captives (19).*    *450*

*The speeches which were delivered on both sides of the proposal (20-32).*    *451*

*The decrees which the Syracusans passed regarding the captives (33).*    *459*

*How, after the failure of the Athenians in Sicily, many of their allies revolted (34).*    *459*

*How the citizen-body of the Athenians, having lost heart, turned their back upon the democracy and put the government into the hands of four hundred men chaps. (34, 36).*    *459*

*How the Lacedaemonians defeated the Athenians in sea-battles (34).*    *459*

## Contents

*How the Syracusans honoured with notable gifts the men who had played a brave part in the war (34).* 459

*How Diocles was chosen law-giver and wrote their laws for the Syracusans (34-35).* 459

*How the Syracusans sent a notable force to the aid of the Lacedaemonians (34).* 459

*The sea-battle between the Athenians and Lacedaemonians off Sigeium and the victory of the Athenians (38-40).* 462

*How the Athenians overcame the Lacedaemonian admiral in a sea-fight and captured Cyzicus (39-40).* 462

*How, when the Lacedaemonians dispatched fifty ships from Euboea to the aid of the defeated, they together with their crews were all lost in a storm off Athos (41).* 464

*The return of Alcibiades and his election as a general (41-42).* 464

*The war between the Aegestaeans and the Seli-nuntians over the land in dispute (43-44).* 465

*How the Lacedaemonians filled up Euripus with earth and made Euboea a part of the mainland (47).* 467

*On the civil discord and massacre in Corcyra (48).* 468

*How Alcibiades and Theramenes won most notable victories over the Lacedaemonians on both land and sea (49-51).* 469

*How the Carthaginians transported great armaments to Sicily and took by storm Selinus and Himera (54-62).* 472

*How Alcibiades sailed into the Peiraeus with much booty and was the object of great acclaim (68-69).* 481

*How King Agis with a great army undertook to lay siege to Athens and was unsuccessful (72-73).* 483

*The banishment of Alcibiades and the founding of Thermae in Sicily (74, 79).* 485

*The sea-battle between the Syracusans and the Carthaginians and the victory of the Syracusans (80).* 489

*On the felicity of life in Acragas and the city's buildings (81-84).* 490

*How the Carthaginians made war upon Sicily with three hundred thousand soldiers and laid siege to Acragas (85-86).* 492

*How the Syracusans gathered their allies and went to the aid of the people of Acragas with ten thousand soldiers (86).* 493

*How, when forty thousand Carthaginians opposed them, the Syracusans gained the victory and slew more than six thousand of them (87).* 493

*How, when the Carthaginians cut off their supplies, the Acragantini were compelled, because of the lack of provisions, to leave their native city (88-89).* 494

*How Dionysius, after he was elected general, secured the tyranny over the Syracusans (92-96).* 497

*How the Athenians, after winning a most famous sea-battle at Arginusae, unjustly condemned their generals to death (97-103).* 500

*How the Athenians, after suffering defeat in a great sea-battle, were forced to conclude peace on the best terms they could secure, and in this manner the Peloponnesian War came to an end (104-107).* 505

*How the Carthaginians were struck by a pestilential disease and were compelled to conclude peace with Dionysius the tyrant (114).* 511

BOOK XIV 512

*The overthrow of the democracy in Athens and the establishment of the thirty men
(3-4).* 513
*The lawless conduct of the thirty men toward the citizens (5-6).* 514
*How the tyrant Dionysius prepared a citadel and distributed the city and its
territory among the masses (7).* 515
*How Dionysius, to the amazement of all, recovered his tyranny when it was
collapsing (8-9).* 516
*How the Lacedaemonians managed conditions in Greece (10).* 517
*The death of Alcibiades, and the tyranny of Clearchus the Lacedaemonian in
Byzantium and its overthrow (11-12).* 518
*How Lysander the Lacedaemonian undertook to overthrow the descendants of
Heracles and was unsuccessful (13).* 519
*How Dionysius sold into slavery Catane and Naxos and transplanted the
inhabitants of Leontini to Syracuse (14-15).* 520
*The founding of Halaesa in Sicily (16).* 521
*The war between the Lacedaemonians and the Eleians (17).* 521
*How Dionysius constructed the wall at the Hexapyli (18).* 522
*How Cyrus led an army against his brother and was slain (19-31).* 523
*How the Lacedaemonians came to the aid of the Greeks of Asia (35-36).* 534
*The founding of Adranum in Sicily and the death of Socrates the philosopher
(37).* 535
*The construction of the wall on the Chersonesus (38).* 536
*The preparations made by Dionysius for the war against the Carthaginians and
his manufacture of arms, in connection with which he invented the missile hurled
by a catapult (41-44).* 537
*How war broke out between the Carthaginians and Dionysius (45-47).* 540
*How Dionysius reduced by siege Motyê, a notable city of the Carthaginians
(48-53).* 542
*How the Aegestaeans set fire to the camp of Dionysius (54).* 545
*How the Carthaginians crossed over to Sicily with three hundred thousand
soldiers and made war upon Dionysius and the retreat of Dionysius to Syracuse
(55).* 546
*The Carthaginian expedition to the Straits and the capture of Messenê (56-58).*
546
*The great sea-battle between the Carthaginians and Dionysius and the victory of
the Carthaginians (59-62).* 548
*The plundering by the Carthaginians of the temples of both Demeter and Corê
(63).* 550
*The retribution by the gods upon the plunderers of the temples and the destruction
of the Carthaginian host by a pestilence (63, 70-71).* 550
*The sea-battle between the Syracusans and the Carthaginians and the victory of
the Syracusans (64).* 551
*The speech in the assembly on freedom by Theodoras (65-69).* 551
*The retribution by the gods upon the plunderers of the temples and the destruction
of the Carthaginian host by a pestilence (70-71).* 554
*How Dionysius outgeneralled the thousand most turbulent mercenaries of his and
caused them to be massacred (72).* 555
*How Dionysius laid siege to the outposts and camp of the Carthaginians (72).* 555

## Contents

*How Dionysius reduced the Carthaginians by siege and set fire to many ships of the enemy (73).* 556

*The defeat of the Carthaginians by land and also by sea (74).* 556

*The flight of the Carthaginians by night, Dionysius having co-operated with them without the knowledge of the Syracusans for a bribe of four hundred talents (75).* 557

*The difficulties which befell the Carthaginians because of their impiety against the deity (76-77).* 558

*The merging of the cities of Sicily which had been laid waste (78).* 559

*How Dionysius reduced by siege certain of the cities of Sicily and brought others into an alliance and how he established relations of friendship with the rulers Agyris of Agyrium and Nicodemus [Damon] of Centuripae (78).* 559

*How Agesilaüs, the Spartan king, crossed over into Asia with an army and laid waste the territory which was subject to the Persians (79).* 560

*How Agesilaüs defeated in battle the Persians, who were commanded by Pharnabazus (80).* 560

*On the Boeotian War and the actions comprised in it (81).* 561

*How Conon was appointed general by the Persians and rebuilt the walls of the Athenians (81, 85).* 561

*How Conon was appointed general by the Persians and rebuilt the walls of the Athenians (85).* 564

*How the Lacedaemonians defeated the Boeotians near Corinth and this war was called the Corinthian (86).* 564

*How Dionysius forced his way with much fighting into Tauromenium and then was driven out (87-88).* 565

*How the Carthaginians were defeated near the city of Bacaena [Abacaene] by Dionysius (90).* 566

*The expedition of the Carthaginians to Sicily and the settlement of the war (95-96).* 568

*How Thibrus, [Thibron] the Lacedaemonian general, was defeated by the Persians and slain (99).* 570

*How the Greeks of Italy joined to form a single political group and took the field against Dionysius (103).* 572

*How Dionysius, although he had been victorious in battle and had taken ten thousand prisoners, let them go without requiring ransom and allowed the cities to live under their own laws (105).* 573

*The capture and razing of Caulonia and Hipponium and the removal of their inhabitants to Syracuse (106-107).* 574

*How Dionysius laid siege to Rhegium (108, 111).* 574

*How the Greeks concluded the Peace of Antalcidas with Artaxerxes (110).* 576

*How Dionysius laid siege to Rhegium, the capture of Rhegium, and the disasters suffered by the city (111-112).* 576

*The capture of Rome, except for the Capitoline, by the Gauls (114-117).* 577

MAPS 581

DIODORUS SICULUS

# MAPS

### MAPS AT THE BACK OF VOLUME I

Frontispiece Temple of Zeus at Acragas
1. Asia
2. Egypt and Ethiopia
3. Greater Greece
4. Europe
5. Route of Xerxes
6. Thermopylae
7. Battle of Salamis
8. Sicily and Greece
9. Syracuse

### MAPS AT THE BACK OF VOLUME II

8a. Sicily and Greece
11. Conquests of Alexander West
12. Conquests of Alexander East
13. Conquest of Alexander
14. Hellenistic Monarchies
15. Italy, Sicily, North Africa
16. Sicily

### *Sigla*

Red Sea = Persian Gulf
lacunae . . . references to missing portions
Please refer to Wikipedia, *Ancient Greek units of Measurement* when necessary.

# INTRODUCTION

### *General Introduction*

With but one exception antiquity affords no further information on the life and work of Diodorus of Sicily than is to be found in his own *Library of History*. The exception is St. Jerome, who, in his *Chronology* under the Year of Abraham 1968 (= 49 B.C.), writes: "Diodorus of Sicily, a writer of Greek history, became illustrious."

Diodorus himself says (1. 4. 4) that the city of his birth was Agyrium in Sicily, one of the oldest settlements of the interior, which was visited even by Heracles (4. 24), whose cult was maintained by the inhabitants on a scale rivalling that of the Olympians, and this statement is rendered plausible by the importance accorded the city in his *History*. It is a striking coincidence that one of the only two Greek inscriptions from Agyrium (*IG*. XIV, 588) marked the final resting-place of a "Diodorus the son of Apollonius."

The earliest date at which Diodorus is known to have been gathering material for his history is the 180th Olympiad (60/59-57/6), in the course of which he visited Egypt (1. 44. 1). Diodorus records that while there he saw with his own eyes a mob of Egyptians demand, and apparently secure, the death of a man connected with a Roman embassy, because he had accidentally killed a cat, and this despite the fear which the Egyptians felt for the Romans, and despite the fact that Ptolemy their king had not as yet been given the appellation of 'friend' by the Romans (1. 83. 8). Ptolemy XI, "the Piper," had ascended the throne of the last nominally independent Hellenistic kingdom in 80, and after waiting twenty years, finally secured recognition by the Senate through the efforts of Caesar and Pompey in 59. The date of this recognition of Ptolemy by Rome clearly shows that Diodorus was in Egypt in the year 59, the length of his visit remains uncertain.

Diodorus had already commenced his work as early as 56. This is evident from the passage (1. 44. 1-4) in which he lists the number of years during which Egypt was under the control of foreigners. The last aliens to rule over Egypt, he says, are the Macedonians and their dynasty held the land for two hundred and seventy-six years; since the conquest of Egypt by Alexander is put by Diodorus (17. 49) in the year 331 he must have been at work upon the composition of his *Library of History* at least as early as 56.

The latest contemporary event mentioned by Diodorus is a reference to the city of Tauromenium in Sicily, when he records (16. 7. 1) that "Caesar removed the citizens from their native state and the city received a Roman colony." This likely took place in 36 B.C. or soon thereafter.

Diodorus informs us (1. 4. 1) that he had spent thirty years in the composition of his history, and it may justly be assumed that this period includes the travels which he made and the dangers which he met in visiting the most important sites about which he intended to write. The beginning of this period must surely be set some years before 59 B.C.

## INTRODUCTION

The task which Diodorus set himself was to write one of "the general histories", or "the general events" (1. 4. 6; 5. 1. 4); in other words, to compose a Universal, or World, History from the Creation to his day. The adjective "general" or "common" is used so much by him that it may be possible to find in its connotation the clue to his motive in taking upon himself so great a task. In the decade between 70 and 60 B.C. he had seen the entire Mediterranean shore brought under the control of Rome by Pompey; Egypt was still independent only in name, for its kings held their throne at the will of the Roman Senate; the sea swept clean of pirates, Roman supremacy extended "to the bounds of the inhabited world" (1. 4. 3). If Diodorus had not witnessed the celebration of this incorporation of the Eastern world in the Roman state, he had certainly heard from others of the great triumph of Pompey in 61. Under the dominion of Rome the Stoic idea of a cosmopolis was on the way to becoming an actuality. All mankind was coming to form a "common" civilisation, a "common" society, and Diodorus could speak of a "common life" in the sense that the whole Mediterranean world was now interested in the same things and what benefited one nation was of common value to all. If the term "Western civilisation" may properly include two cultures so different, for instance, as those of the United States and Spain, it is no exaggeration to say that by 60 Syrian, Greek, Iberian and Roman had become one. The limitations of the old city state, whereby a man was a stranger in any city but the one of his origin, were gone for ever. Surely, then, the history of each one of these nations was a matter of interest to all, since the past of every people was making its distinctive contribution to this most catholic of all civilisations, and he who would gather the records of all these peoples and present them in convenient form would have "composed a treatise of the utmost value to those who are studiously inclined" (1. 3. 6).

In preparation for his *History*, Diodorus states (1. 4. 1) that with much hardship and many dangers he visited all the most important regions of Europe and Asia. There is no evidence in his work that he travelled in any other land than Egypt, where he may have ascended the Nile as far as Memphis, in connection with which city he mentions a shrine of Isis which "is pointed out to this day in the temple-area of Hephaestus" (1. 22. 2); all the other details of his account of that marvellous land could have been gathered from his literary sources. The only other place where he claims to have stayed was Rome, which furnished him in abundance the materials necessary for his study (1. 4. 2).

Not only does Diodorus claim to have travelled widely in preparation for his *History*, but to have gained through his contact with the Romans in Sicily "considerable familiarity" (1. 4.4) with their language.

Diodorus commenced with the mythical period and brought his *History* down to 59 B.C. the year of Julius Caesar's first consulship. Of the forty Books only the first five and Books XI-XX are preserved, although fragments of the other twenty-five are found in different authors, notably in Eusebius and Byzantine excerptors. According to his own plan (1. 4. 6-7), Books I-VI embraced the period before the Trojan War, the first three treating of the history of the non-Greeks, the other three, of that of the Greeks. The next eleven, Books VII-XVII, were designed to form a Universal History from the Trojan War to the death of Alexander the Great, and the last twenty-three carried the account down to the

Archonship of Herodes in 60/59, *i.e.* to include the year 61/60. As for the years covered by his History, he makes no effort to estimate those which had elapsed before the Trojan War, since for that earlier period there existed no chronological table "that was trustworthy," but for the subsequent period he records that he followed the *Chronology* of Apollodorus of Athens in setting 80 years between the Trojan War (1184 B.C.) and the Return of the Heracleidae (1104 B.C.), thence 328 years to the First Olympiad (776/5 B.C.), and from the First Olympiad to the beginning of the Celtic War (60/59 B.C.), a date which Apollodorus did not reach, Diodorus counted 730 years. There can be no question about the correctness of these numbers of years, 80, 328, 730, because in the next sentence he makes the sum of them 1138; and yet 730 years after the First Olympiad is 46/5 B.C. just fifteen years later than the date at which he says his *History* closes. It is impossible to think that his work came down to so late a date, since his last book opened with the year 70 B.C. and he states specifically that his History closed before the year 60/59 B.C.

### *The contents of the several Books:*

Book I: The myths, kings and customs of Egypt.
Book II: History of Assyria, description of India, Scythia, Arabia, and the islands of the Ocean.
Book III: Ethiopia, the Amazons of Africa, the inhabitants of Atlantis and the origins of the first gods.
Book IV: The principal Greek gods, the Argonauts, Theseus, the Seven against Thebes.
Book V: The islands and peoples of the West, Rhodes and Crete.
Books VI-X: Fragments, from the Trojan War to 480 B.C.
Commencing with Book XI the *Library of History* covers:
Book XI: Years 480-451.
Book XII: Years 450-416.
Book XIII: Years 415-405.
Book XIV: Years 404-387.
Book XV: Years 386-361.
Book XVI: Years 360-336.
Book XVII: Years 335-324.
Book XVIII: Years 323-318.
Book XIX: Years 317-311.
Book XX: Years 310-302.
Books XXI-XL: Fragments, years 301-60 B.C.

To compose a history of the entire world down to his day was "an immense labour," as Diodorus says (1. 3. 6), looking back upon it, because the material for it lay scattered about in so many different authors, and because the authors themselves varied so widely. Perhaps this was his way of telling his readers that what they should expect of his history is no more than a compilation of what former writers had set down. The choice of so unusual a title, *Library of History* is further evidence that Diodorus made no pretence of doing anything more than giving a convenient summary of events which were to be found in greater detail in many works. It is generally held that while Diodorus probably leaned very

## INTRODUCTION

strongly upon a single author for one or another section of his work, he used at the same time other writers as well.

A brief discussion of the sources used by Diodorus is given in the Introductions to the several volumes.

One mistake of method made it almost impossible for Diodorus to write either a readable story or an accurate history. So soon as he entered the period which allowed precise dating he became an annalist, or, in other words, he endeavoured to present under one year the events which took place in Greece, Sicily, Africa and Italy, to write a synchronistic universal history. For a closely related series of incidents which covered several years this meant that he either had to break the story as many times as there were years, or crowd the events of several years into one. Moreover, he tried to synchronise the Roman consular year, which in his day commenced January 1st., and he uses this date even for the earlier period, with the Athenian archon year, which commenced about the middle of July. It should be observed to his credit that Diodorus recognised (20. 43. 7) the shortcomings of this annalistic arrangement, but he still felt that the recital of events in the order in which they were taking place gave a more truthful presentation of history.

It may be noted, in connection with this annalistic arrangement, that, although Diodorus says in his Preface to the First Book that he has brought his history down to 60/59 B.C. yet in three other places (3. 38. 2; 5. 21. 2; 5. 22. 1) he remarks that he will speak of Britain more in detail when he gives an account of the deeds of Gaius Caesar, and that, as observed above, in the *Chronology* which he gives of his entire work, 1138 years from the Trojan War brings his history down to 46/45 B.C. It seems more reasonable to suppose that, as Diodorus was engaged upon the writing of his earlier Books, he fully intended to bring his history down to include the year 46/45 B.C. which would make an excellent stopping-point. However, as Diodorus grew old and perhaps a little tired, he gave up his original plan. Since some of his Books, and presumably the earlier ones, came into the hands of the public before his final revision and the publication of his History as a whole, Diodorus may himself have overlooked the need of correcting that number in the final revision.

From scattered observations, which bear every mark of being from Diodorus himself and not from his sources, and from the emphasis upon certain phenomena or particular features of history, it is possible to get some idea of his views and interests. Again and again, and not alone in the Preface to the First Book, the Stoic doctrine of the *utilitas* of history is stressed, and nowhere does he demand that history be entertaining. It is obviously to this end that, as he states (11. 46. 1), he makes it his practice to increase the fame of good men by extolling them and to censure evil characters. More often than any extant ancient historian Diodorus stresses the view that history should instruct in the good life. He emphasises the qualities of the spirit, such as meekness, gentleness, kindliness, very much in the manner of Herodotus; but he thinks very little of democracy (1. 74. 7; 13. 95. 1), the natural counterpart of such a conviction being a great admiration for the strong man in history.

While characteristics such as these exclude Diodorus from a place among the abler historians of the ancient world, there is every reason to believe that he used the best sources and that he reproduced them faithfully. His First Book, which deals almost exclusively with Egypt, is the fullest literary account of the history and customs of that country after Herodotus. Books II-V cover a wide range, and because of their inclusion of much mythological material are of less value. In the period from 480 to 301, which he treats in annalistic fashion and in which his main source was the *Universal History* of Ephorus, his importance varies according as he is the sole continuous source, or again as he is paralleled by superior writers. To the fifty years from 480 to 430 Thucydides devotes only a little more than thirty chapters; Diodorus covers it more fully (11. 37-12. 38) and his is the only consecutive literary account for the chronology of the period. On the other hand, he is of less importance for the years 430-362 since the history of this period is covered in the contemporary accounts of Thucydides and Xenophon. For the years 362-302 Diodorus is again the only consecutive literary account, and although the *Epitome* by Justin of the *History of Philip* by Pompeius Trogus is preserved for the earlier period, and the *Anabasis* of Arrian and *The History of Alexander the Great* by Q. Curtius Rufus, more than half of which is extant, for the years 336-323, Diodorus offers the only chronological survey of the period of Philip, and supplements the writers mentioned and contemporary sources in many matters. For the period of the Successors to Alexander, 323-302, (Books XVIII-XX), he is the chief literary authority and his history of this period assumes, therefore, an importance which it does not possess for the other years. These three Books are based mainly upon the work of Hieronymus of Cardia, an historian of outstanding ability. As for Sicily, it has well been said that no history of that island could be written were it not for Diodorus, and as for Roman history, the *Fasti* of Diodorus are recognised in the most recent research to be by far the oldest and most trustworthy.

One merit even those critics who have dealt most severely with Diodorus accord him. Long speeches, happily used but unhappily introduced by Thucydides, Diodorus avoids, as he promises that he will do in the Preface to Book XX. With the exception of four instances he eliminates entirely that rhetorical device, which must have wearied even a contemporary audience. He gave great care to little details of writing, and when he errs in fact the fault is not so much his as that of his source.

One feature of the style of Diodorus calls for remark. A large part of his earlier Books is in indirect discourse, which is introduced with "they say" or "it is said" or "history records," and the like, or with the name of the writer he is following. Yet at times he inserts into this reported speech sentences of direct discourse which are presumably original with himself.

### *Introduction to Books I - II, 34*

After the Preface to his whole work Diodorus describes the origin of animal life, and then, "since Egypt is the country where mythology places the origin of the gods" (1. 9. 6), and since "animal life appeared first of all" (1. 10. 2) in that country, he devotes the entire First Book to the gods, kings, laws and customs of that land. His interest in religion causes him to pay more attention to that subject than to political institutions and military affairs, in contrast to his later Books. As for his literary sources, he is generally held to have drawn primarily upon Hecataeus of Abdera, who visited Egypt early in the 3rd century, for his account of the customs of the Egyptians, upon Agatharchides of Cnidus, an historian and geographer of the 2nd century, for his geographical data, and especially for the description of the Nile (cc. 32-41. 3), and upon Herodotus. He also mentions what is told by the priests of Egypt and natives of Ethiopia, and it is entirely possible that many a detail was picked up by personal observation and inquiry. By the time of his visit Greek had been the official language of the land for nearly three hundred years and was widely used in the better circles, and hence he was not in such danger of being imposed upon by guides and priests as was Herodotus.

In the opening chapters of the Second Book Diodorus moves to Asia and Assyrian affairs. Most of this material was drawn from Ctesias of Cnidus, who spent seventeen years as physician at the court of the Persian king, Artaxerxes Mnemon, returning to Greece some time after 390. Ctesias wrote a *Persica* in twenty-three Books, the first six of which dealt with Assyrian and Median history. He also used Cleitarchus and "certain of those who at a later time crossed into Asia with Alexander" (2. 7. 3). He also quotes from a particular Athenaeus, otherwise unknown, and "certain other historians" (2. 20. 3) to the effect that Semiramis was nothing more than a beautiful courtesan. While there is some shadowy outline of the long history of Egypt in Book I, what Diodorus (or rather Ctesias, Cleitarchus and others) offer on Babylonian history is of little value.

### *Introduction Books II, 35-IV, 58*

Book II, 35-42 is devoted to a brief description of India which was ultimately derived from Megasthenes, though Diodorus does not mention this author. The Scythians, the Amazons of Asia Minor, and the Hyperboreans are then briefly discussed, and Chapters 48-54 are devoted to Syria, Palestine, and Arabia. It is thought that this last section may go back to the Stoic philosopher, Poseidonius of Apameia. The Book closes with a description of a fabulous people living in a political Utopia on an island "in the ocean to the south," the account purporting to be the adventure of a certain Iambulus, which may indeed be the name of the author of the original tale.

The Third Book opens with an account of the Ethiopians on the upper Nile, then describes the working of the gold mines on the border between Egypt and Ethiopia, and includes a long discussion of the Red Sea and the peoples dwelling about it, with some mention of the tribes along the shores of the Indian Ocean and the Persian Gulf. Much of this material was drawn from the geographer Agatharchides and is quite reliable. With chapter 49 Diodorus turns to Libya and embarks upon the myths of the Libyans about the Gorgons and Amazons, this subject serving to lead him into Greek mythology, which is the theme of the entire Fourth Book.

Since, as Diodorus tells us, Ephorus, and Callisthenes and Theopompus, contemporaries of Ephorus, had not included the myths in their histories, Diodorus opens the Fourth Book with a defence of his exposition of Greek mythology. The gods were once kings and heroes who have been deified because of the great benefits which they conferred upon mankind; they have been the object of veneration by men of old and we "should not fail to cherish and maintain for the gods the pious devotion which has been handed down to us from our fathers" (ch. 8. 5); if their deeds appear superhuman it is because they are measured by the weakness of the men of Diodorus' day. Much of this material was drawn directly from Dionysius of Mitylenê who lived in Alexandria in the second century B.C. and composed, doubtless with the aid of the library in that city and certainly with considerable indulgence in the romantic, his *Kyklos,* a kind of encyclopaedia of mythology, which included accounts of the Argonauts, Dionysus, the Amazons, events connected with the Trojan War. It is generally held that for his account of Heracles Diodorus took generously from a *Praise of Heracles* by Matris of Thebes, who is otherwise unknown. Here and there, when he touched the western Mediterranean, Diodorus used Timaeus of Tauromenium, who, an exile in Athens for the best fifty years of his life, completed, not long before his death about 250 and almost altogether from literary sources, a history of Sicily and the western Mediterranean in thirty-eight Books.

## *Book XVI*

The second half of Book 16 contains two principal narratives, interspersed by two literary references (chaps. 71. 3; 76. 5-6) and a number of notes referring to other matters, chiefly of a chronological interest: the Molossians (chap. 72. 1), Caria (chap. 74. 2), Tarentum (chap. 88. 3-4), Heracleia Pontica (chap. 88. 5), Cius (chap. 90. 2) and Rome (chaps. 69-1; 90. 2). There are two references to Athenian activities (chaps. 74. 1; 88. 1-2). Otherwise the stories of Timoleon and of Philip are interwoven on a chronological basis (Timoleon: chaps. 66-69. 6; 70. 1-6; 72. 2-73. 3; 77. 4-83; 90. 1; Philip: chaps. 69. 7-8; 71. 1-2; 74. 2-76. 4; 77. 2-3; 84. 1-87. 3; 89; 91-95).

In one chapter (83), it is reasonable to suppose that Diodorus, the Siciliote, is writing from his own observation, as he expressly does of Alexandria in Book 17. 52. 6. Otherwise the problem of Diodorus's sources is complicated by the fact that we have very few specific fragments of earlier historians whom he may have used in this period.

In the case of Philip, the story of Diodorus differs sharply from that of Trogus-Justin. Diodorus's account of Philip is generally favourable. The Greeks joined Philip willingly out of gratitude and affection (chaps. 69. 8; 71. 2); Philip preferred to make friends rather than to defeat enemies (chap. 95. 3). In Justin, on the other hand, Philip is wily and treacherous. I make no suggestion as to the source of Justin, but it is not unreasonable to suppose that Diodorus's portrait is taken from Theopompus.

As to the narrative in the second part of Book 16 in general, Diodorus displays the unevenness for which he is well known. He indulges in vague generalities and often fails to get things quite right. On the other hand, he is capable of writing, or of repeating, dramatic and exciting stories. His account of the siege of Perinthus (chaps. 74-76), of the battle of the Crimisus (chaps. 79-80), of Chaeronea (chaps. 84-87), and of the death of Philip (chaps. 91-95) are good reading, all the more because in all but the second instance they are our only surviving account of these events. Diodorus is interested in the operation of Fortune and the reverses which that deity could produce (chap. 70. 2) and he is piously delighted when sacrilegious men meet their just deserts (chaps. 78-79. 1; 82. 1-2). We may be grateful that he has been preserved.

INTRODUCTION

## Book XVII

Diodorus does not name his source or sources in the Alexander History, nor does he anywhere cite any of the historians of Alexander except in Book 2. 7. 3, where Cleitarchus is quoted as his authority for the size of Babylon. Ptolemy, the future king and Arrian's principal source, is mentioned only as an actor in the story. Once he refers to his own observation in Alexandria and what was told him of the city and the country during his visit to Egypt (chap. 52. 6). Otherwise he tells a factual story on his own responsibility, rarely inserting an "it is said" or "they say" in support of a specific statement (chaps. 4. 8; 85. 2; 92. 1; 110. 7; 115. 5; 118. 1).

Our knowledge of the career of Alexander the Great is based primarily upon the surviving accounts of Diodorus, Quintus Curtius, Plutarch, and Arrian, and upon the excerpts of Pompeius Trogus made by Justin; the earliest of these belongs to the period of Augustus; behind them lie the narrators of the early Hellenistic period.

Completeness in assigning sources is impossible to attain, but instances may be cited where Diodorus seems to "follow" one or another of the primary historians of Alexander.

Crows guided Alexander on the road to Siwah (chap. 49; Callisthenes and Aristobulus).

The meaning of the oracle of Amnion was conveyed by nods and signs (chap. 50; Callisthenes).

Alexandria was founded after Alexander's return from Siwah (chap. 52; Aristobulus).

Thais incited Alexander to burn Persepolis (chap. 72; Cleitarchus).

Alexander found in Hyrcania a tree dripping honey (Onesicritus) and a ferocious bee (Cleitarchus; chap. 75).

The queen of the Amazons stayed with Alexander thirteen days in Hyrcania (chap. 77; Cleitarchus, Onesicritus, and others).

In northern India, Alexander found imitative monkeys (Cleitarchus), snakes sixteen cubits long (Cleitarchus) and small poisonous snakes (Nearchus), as well as huge banyan trees (chap. 90; Onesicritus and Aristobulus).

Alexander found the Adrestians practising suttee and the subjects of Sopithes admiring human beauty (chap. 91; Onesicritus).

Alexander killed 80,000 subjects of Sambus (chap. 102; Cleitarchus).

The Oreitae exposed their dead (Onesicritus), and the Gedrosians let their fingernails grow long (Cleitarchus) and built their houses out of whales' ribs (Nearchus; all chap. 105).

Alexander celebrated his own and Nearchus's safe completion of the journey from India (chap. 106; somewhat variously in Nearchus and Onesicritus).

Nearchus reported whales frightened by noise (chap. 106; Nearchus).

Harpalus kept various mistresses (chap. 108; Cleitarchus and Theopompus).

This is evidently not the material from which statistics are built, but it may be noted that Diodorus "follows" Cleitarchus eight times, Onesicritus six times, Nearchus and Aristobulus three times each, and Callisthenes twice. Since all of these authors wrote systematic histories, it is clear that they all must have told much the same story, differing in detail. Perhaps the later of them referred by name to their predecessors. Diodorus can be best supposed to have followed a single manuscript which contained all of this material.

Little more can be asserted positively, in view of our lack of certainty as to Diodorus's method of work in general. Probably he followed one source for any given subject, rewriting rather than excerpting, and adding additional material when it occurred to him.

Both Diodorus and Curtius give much which the other lacks and certainly add much of their own, especially Curtius: the long speeches with which his narrative abounds may be his own composition. Enough remains in Justin to suggest, although not to prove, that the history of Trogus was at least very similar.

In any event, the account of Diodorus is of interest and importance, although his conventional style of writing and his carelessness in abridgement often deprive him of the clarity and dramatic effect for which he aimed. His expression is turgid and laboured. True to his principles expressed in his introduction (Book 1. 1-5), he administers praise and blame and attempts to edify, calling attention to the reversals inflicted by Fortune. This has been thought to have a Stoic tone, but his enthusiasm as a narrator is called forth by valiant deeds of war, battles and sieges. This leads to a somewhat stereotyped pattern of engagement, combat with fluctuating success, and disengagement, and makes one suspect both that historical details have been blurred and that extraneous rhetorical material has been introduced. Nevertheless in more than one instance Diodorus preserves specific and statistical information which we should otherwise lack.

Without attempting completeness, I may list some of the incidents told by Diodorus which are lacking in the other preserved historians.

1. The removal of Attalus (chaps. 2, 5).
2. Description of Mt. Ida, and of Memnon's campaign in the Troad (chap. 7).
3. Appeal to Alexander by Antipater and Parmenion to beget an heir before crossing over to Asia (chap. 16).
4. Detailed figures of Alexander's army (chap. 17).
5. The fallen statue of Ariobarzanes (chap. 17).
6. The Persian order of battle at the Granicus (chap. 19).
7. Dispatch of Memnon's wife to the Great King (chap. 23).
8. Exploits of Ephialtes and Thrasybulus at Halicarnassus (chap. 25).
9. Suicide of the Marmares (chap. 28).
10. Alexander's substitution of the forged letter from the Great King (chap. 39).
11. Mechanisms of attack and defence at Tyre (chap. 43).
12. Description of Alexandria (chap. 52).
13. Revolt of Memnon in Thrace (chap. 62).
14. Reorganisation of the army (chap. 65).

## INTRODUCTION

15. Transport of fruit from the country of the Uxii to Babylon (chap. 67).
16. Description of Persepolis (chap. 71).
17. The institution of suttee (chap. 91).
18. Description of Ecbatana (chap. 110).
19. Description of Hephaestion's funeral pyre (chap. 115).

On other occasions, Diodorus gives a narrative differing from that of the other historians of Alexander. Sometimes, but by no means always, he is in error.

1. His account of the siege of Thebes is longer than that of Arrian; the Thebans fight well, and Alexander's victory is gained by a stratagem (chaps. 8-13).

2. The account of events at Athens is short, and emphasises the part of Demades; Phocion does not appear, and no one is exiled (chap. 15).

3. At the Granicus, Diodorus has Alexander cross the river unopposed in the morning, probably locating the battle downstream from Arrian (chap. 19).

4. Neoptolemus is killed while fighting on the Macedonian side at Halicarnassus (almost certainly wrong; chap. 25).

5. Alexander did not receive Parmenion's appeal for help at Gaugamela (chap. 60).

6. Alexander was wrecked on the Indus (chap. 97).

7. The Oreitae expose their dead to be eaten by wild beasts (Onesicritus in Strabo 11. 11. 3 tells a similar story of the Bactrians, but the victims were the sick and elderly; chap. 105).

At times, Diodorus omits elements which are traditional parts of the Alexander history.

1. The boyhood of Alexander.

2. The heroism of Timocleia of Thebes.

3. The sweating statue of Orpheus in Pieria and the visit to Diogenes at Corinth.

4. The adoption of Alexander by Ada, the Carian queen, and Alexander's attack on Myndus.

5. The miraculous passage of the Climax in Lycia and the episode of the Gordian knot.

6. There is no description of Babylon (already in Book 2. 7. 3) or of Susa.

7. Alexander feels no shame for the burning of Persepolis.

8. No real mutiny on the Hyphasis. Alexander saw and pitied his soldiers' weariness.

9. No voyage to the Rann of Kutch.

In these idiosyncrasies, of course, Diodorus invites comparison with Curtius and Justin, rather than with Plutarch and Arrian, whose sources were different. The Persian or Greek point of view which Diodorus reflects at times may have been lacking in Ptolemy and perhaps in Aristobulus also. On the other hand, taken in contrast with Curtius, Diodorus writes essentially sober history little coloured by rhetoric. Probably ancient as well as modern historians have tended to omit or to stress traditional stories depending on how these fitted their own concept of Alexander. Nevertheless there is a risk in our following this principle too enthusiastically in source criticism. How can we know, for example, that any given ancient would have regarded the burning of Persepolis (it was, of course, a little silly to burn your own property) or the massacre of 80,000 subjects of Sambus as unworthy of the great Macedonian?

For the manuscripts of these books, I may refer to the notes in the previous volumes of this series. My text is essentially that of C. Th. Fischer in the Teubner, and I have made no independent collation of the readings.

## *The Sources of Books 18-20*

The chief source of Diodorus in Books 18 through 20, except for the material dealing with Italy and Sicily, is the history of Hieronymus of Cardia, a friend and fellow countryman of Eumenes, and after Eumenes' death the companion of Antigonus, Demetrius, and Gonatas. Hieronymus was with Eumenes throughout the campaigns that followed the death of Alexander, took refuge with him on Nora, and was wounded in the final battle at Gabene. Antigonus placed Hieronymus in charge of the asphalt industry on the Dead Sea, and to this we owe the detailed account of that sea and of the Nabataean Arabs (Book 19. 94-100). That Diodorus tells more of the disposition of the troops of Demetrius at Gaza than of that of the enemy (Book 19. 82-83) is due to Hieronymus' presence by the side of Demetrius. Diodorus' treatment of Antigonus is, in general, sympathetic, but Antigonus is never presented as a hero as are both Eumenes and Demetrius; and here again we have a reflection of the attitude of Hieronymus.

There is general agreement that the major part of Diodorus' narrative of Sicilian affairs in this period rests on the *History of Agathocles* by Duris. The generally favourable treatment of Agathocles fit that author, a follower of the grand style and himself tyrant of Samos. It is also agreed that parts of the narrative rest upon Timaeus.

The theory has been advanced that for his brief notices of Roman affairs in Books 19 and 20 Diodorus used one of the earlier annalists, for example, Fabius Pictor, and thus preserves a purer tradition than that of Livy.

## *Introduction XXI*

The last twenty books (XXI-XL) of the *Library of History* begin with the battle of Ipsus, fought in 301, and in their original complete form carried the account down to the author's own day, closing with the events of 61/0. Though Diodorus is now held in scant esteem as a historian, in marked contrast to his high repute in the XVIth century, and though his work is admittedly derivative in character and hence of uneven worth, depending on the reliability of his sources, still the loss sustained by the disappearance of these books is scarcely to be measured in terms of their intrinsic merit. Had they survived intact, they would have given us, as nothing now does, a single, continuous, and detailed narrative of events in the whole Mediterranean world during two and a half crucial centuries, and a historical perspective that we now sadly lack. As it is, no more than a fraction of the original survives, mostly in brief excerpts or, occasionally, in longer but freely condensed paraphrase. Even these sorry fragments, however, preserve the record of many incidents otherwise unknown or give us a glimpse of historical traditions different from those that were destined to prevail.

## Introduction

By far the greater part of the fragments come from the historical anthologies compiled in the Xth century for Constantine VII Porphyrogenitus. Finally, there are the miscellaneous fragments drawn from the Church Fathers or from writers of the Byzantine period.

These sources preserve or reflect the text of Diodorus with varying degrees of fidelity. The most reliable are the Constantinian collections. The procedure followed by the excerptors was quite simple. From the complete text they selected the passages appropriate to their several rubrics, and these they copied out substantially as they stood, omitting whatever seemed irrelevant to their purpose and resorting occasionally to mere paraphrase of the original. As they had little interest in history as such, but only in the lessons of history, they would prefix to each selection no more than a summary indication of the situation, often with scant attention to grammatical niceties. For the reconstruction of the lost books it is of capital importance that in each of these collections the excerpts appear in proper sequence, according to the original.

### *Note on Chronology*

The dates given throughout this volume, both in the margin of the translation and in the notes, have been taken from the chronological table in the second edition of Beloch, *Griechische Geschickte,* 4. 2. 624 ff.

Hieronymus seems to have arranged his history by campaigning seasons, equivalent to the years of our calendar, clearly marking the end of each season by indicating the winter quarters of the various armies; and in general Diodorus followed this same plan, relating all the events of each year before passing to the next, and usually calling attention to the winter quarters of the chief leaders. For his own chronological framework, however, Diodorus used the Athenian archon years, and in fitting the campaigning seasons into these archon years he is not always consistent. As a rule he gives under each archon all the events of the year during which he took office; thus, under the archon of 318/17 he narrates all the events of 318. Quite naturally, in introducing a new character whose previous career has been outside the main course of the history, he goes back and tells what is necessary of that earlier career. Thus the whole story of Agathocles' rise to power is given at the beginning of Book 19 in connection with his successful *coup de main* in 317.

If the chronology of Diodorus is thus interpreted, it is reasonably accurate and consistent.

In equating the Roman and Greek systems of chronology, Diodorus used a list of Roman consuls to which the "dictator years" of 333, 324, 309, and 301 had not been added. In the period here in question he assigns the consuls to years that differ from those of the traditional (Varronian) chronology by two years.

### *History of the Fragments*

The unattached fragments are not included in a book for the general reader

# THE LIBRARY OF HISTORY

## OF

## DIODORUS OF SICILY

# BOOK I

The myths, kings and customs of Egypt. On the gods who founded cities in Egypt. On the honour paid to the immortals and the building of the temples to them.

## *Introduction to the entire work (1-5).*

**1.** It is only justice that we be grateful for those writers who have composed universal histories, for all of mankind has benefited from their individual labours. They offer us a schooling safe from the pitfalls of life through a presentation of events that have proved advantageous in the experience of others. For often that learning which is acquired

by real experience, with all the attendant toils and dangers, enables a man to discern in each instance where utility lies, and this is the reason why the most widely experienced of our heroes, Odyssey, suffered great misfortunes before he:

> Of many men the cities saw and learned
> Their thoughts;—

The understanding of the failures and successes of other men acquired by the study of history, affords a schooling that is free from the evils of experience. Furthermore, it has been the aspiration of these writers to marshal men separated by space and time into one orderly body of universal kinship. Such historians have shown themselves to be, as it were, ministers of Divine Providence, for just as Providence has brought the orderly arrangement of the visible stars and the natures of men together into one common relationship, so she continues to direct their courses through all eternity, apportioning to each that which falls to it by the direction of fate. So likewise the historians, in recording the common affairs of the inhabited world as though they were those of a single state, have made of their treatises a single reckoning of past events and a common storehouse of knowledge concerning them. It is an excellent thing to be able to use th' mistakes of others as warning examples for the correction of error, and, when w confront the vicissitudes of life, instead of having to re-investigate for ourselv' to be able to imitate the successes which have been achieved in the p' Certainly all men prefer the counsels of the oldest men to those who are youn because of the experience which has accrued to the former over time; but i' fact that any one man's experience is surpassed by the understanding wh' gained from history. For this reason one may hold that the acquisitior knowledge of history is of the greatest utility for every conceivable circun of life. It endows the young with the wisdom of the aged, while for th multiplies the experience which they already possess; citizens in private qualifies for leadership, their leaders it incites through the glory which i to undertake the noblest deeds; soldiers it prepares to face dangers in ( their country because of the public encomiums which they will re wicked men it turns aside from their impulses through the opprobrium to which it will condemn them.

**2.** In general it is because of the commemoration of good dee that some have been induced to founding cities, that others hav introduce laws improving man's social life with security, and that many have aspired to discover new sciences and arts in order to benefit the race of men. Since complete happiness can be attained only through the combination of all these activities, the foremost praise must be awarded to that which more than any other thing is the cause of them, that is, to history. History is guardian of the high achievements of illustrious men, the witness which testifies to the evil deeds of the wicked, and thus the benefactor of mankind. If it is true that the myths related about Hades, in spite of their fictitious nature, contribute greatly to piety and justice among men, how much more must we assume that history, the prophetess of truth and mother-city of philosophy, is still more potent to equip men's characters for noble living! All men live but an infinitesimal portion of eternity and are dead throughout all subsequent time; in the case of those who have done nothing of note, everything which pertained to them in life perishes when their bodies die, but in the case of those who have achieved virtuous fame, their deeds are remembered for evermore, heralded by history's voice most divine.

Is it not an excellent thing to receive in exchange for mortal labours an immortal fame? In the case of Heracles, for instance, it is agreed that during the time he spent among men he submitted to great and continuous labours and perils willingly, in order that he might confer benefits upon the race of men and thereby gain immortality. In the case of other great and good men, some have attained heroic honours and others honours equal to the divine, and all have been thought worthy of great praise; history immortalises their achievements. Whereas other memorials abide but a brief time, the power of history extends over the whole inhabited world and overcomes mortal time as a custodian that ensures perpetual transmission of events to posterity.

History also contributes to the power of speech, and a nobler thing may not easily be found. It is this that makes the Greeks superior to the barbarians, and the educated to the uneducated. It is by means of speech that one man is able to gain ascendancy over many; the impression made by every proposed measure corresponds to the power of the speaker who presents it. We describe great and good men as "worthy of speech," as though they had won the highest prize of excellence. When speech is resolved into its several kinds, we find that, poetry is more pleasing than profitable, the codes of law punish but do not instruct, and similarly the other kinds either contribute nothing to happiness or else contain a harmful element mingled with the beneficial. Some forms of speech even pervert the truth, while history alone, since therein word and fact are in perfect agreement, embraces in its narration all the other useful qualities; for it is ever urging men to justice, denouncing those who are evil, lauding the good, and laying up for its readers a mighty store of experience.

3. Observing that writers of history were accorded a merited approbation we were led to feel an enthusiasm for the subject, but when we turned our attention to the historians before our time, whose purpose we approved, we found that their treatises might have been improved upon. Although the profit which history affords its readers lies in its embracing a vast number and variety of circumstances, most writers have recorded no more than isolated wars waged by a single nation or a single state, and few have undertaken to record the events connected with all times and all peoples; and of the latter, some have not

attached to the several events their proper dates, and others have passed over the deeds of barbarian peoples; and some, again, have rejected the ancient legends because of the difficulties involved in their treatment, while others have failed to complete the plan which they had begun, their lives being cut short by fate. Of those who have undertaken an account of all peoples not one has continued his history beyond the Macedonian period. Some closed their accounts with the deeds of Philip, others with those of Alexander, and some with the Diadochi or the Epigoni. Despite the number and importance of the events subsequent to these and extending even to our own lifetime which have been neglected, no historian has essayed to treat of them within the compass of a single narrative, because of the magnitude of the undertaking. For this reason, since both the dates of the events and the events themselves lie scattered about in numerous treatises and in divers authors, knowledge of them becomes difficult for the mind to encompass and the memory to retain.

Consequently, after we had examined the composition of each of these authors' works, we resolved to write a history that would give its readers the greatest benefit with the smallest effort. If a man were to begin with the most ancient times and record to the best of his ability the affairs of the entire world down to his own day, so far as they were known, as though they were the affairs of a single city, he would obviously have to undertake an immense labour, yet his treatise would be of the utmost value to those who seek knowledge. From such a treatise every man will be able to take what is of use for his special purpose, drawing as it were from a great fountain. The reason for this is that, in the first place, it is not easy for those who propose to go through the writings of so many historians to procure the books which are needed, and, in the second place, because theses works vary so widely and are so numerous, that the recovery of past events becomes extremely difficult to encompass and attain; whereas, the treatise which keeps within the limits of a single narrative and contains a connected account of events, facilitates the reading and sets forth an exposition of the past in a form that is perfectly easy to follow. In general, a history of this nature must surpass all others to the same degree as the whole is more useful than the part and continuity than discontinuity, and, again, as an event whose date has been accurately determined is more useful than one which is undated.

**4.** Appreciating that an undertaking of this nature would require much labour and time, have been engaged upon it for thirty years, and with much hardship and many dangers we have visited a large portion of both Asia and Europe that we might see with our own eyes all the most important regions and as many others as possible; for many errors have been committed through ignorance of the sites, not only by the common run of historians, but even by some of the highest reputation. As for the resources which have availed us in this undertaking, they have been, first and foremost, enthusiasm for the work, and, in the second place, the abundant supply which Rome affords of the materials pertaining to the proposed study. The supremacy of this city, a supremacy so powerful that it extends to the bounds of the inhabited world, has provided us in the course of our long residence with copious resources in the most accessible form. The city of our origin was Agyrium in Sicily, and by our contact with the Romans in that island we gained a wide acquaintance with their language; we next acquired an accurate knowledge of all the events connected with this empire from the records which have been carefully preserved among them over a long period of time. Now we have begun our history with the legends of both Greeks and barbarians, after having first investigated to the best of our ability the accounts which each people records of its earliest times.

Since my undertaking is now complete, although the volumes are as yet unpublished, I wish to present a brief preliminary outline of the work as a whole. Our first six Books embrace the events and legends previous to the Trojan War: the first three set forth the antiquities of the barbarians, and the next three almost exclusively those of the Greeks; in the following eleven we have written a universal history of events from the Trojan War to the death of Alexander; and in the succeeding twenty-three Books we have given an orderly account of all subsequent events down to the beginning of the war between the Romans and the Celts, in the course of which the commander, Gaius Julius Caesar, who has been deified because of his deeds, subdued the most numerous and most warlike tribes of the Celts, and advanced the Roman Empire as far as the British Isles. The first events of this war occurred in the first year of the One Hundred and Eightieth Olympiad, [60-56] when Herodes was archon in Athens.

**5.** As for the periods included in this work, we do not attempt to fix with any strictness the limits of those before the Trojan War, because no trustworthy chronological table covering them has come into our hands. From the Trojan War [1184] we follow Apollodorus of Athens in setting the interval from then to the Return of the Heracleidae [1104] as eighty years, from then to the First Olympiad [776-5] three hundred and twenty-eight years, reckoning the dates by the reigns of the kings of Lacedaemon, and from the First Olympiad to the beginning of the Celtic War, which we have made the end of our history, seven hundred and thirty years; such that our whole treatise of forty Books embraces eleven hundred and thirty-eight years, exclusive of the periods which embrace the events before the Trojan War.

We have given this precise outline at the outset to inform our readers about the project as a whole, and at the same time to deter those who are accustomed to make their books by compilation, from mutilating works of which they are not the authors. Throughout our history it is to be hoped that what we have done well may not be the object of envy, and that the matters wherein our knowledge is defective may receive correction at the hands of more able historians.

Now that we have set forth the plan and purpose of our undertaking we shall attempt to make good our promise with such a treatise.

### *On the accounts given by the Egyptians about the origin of the universe (6-7).*

**6.** As to the various conceptions of the gods formed by those who were first to introduce the worship of the deities, and as to the myths which are told about each of the immortals, we shall refrain from setting them forth in great detail, since it would require a long account. Whatever of these subjects we feel to be pertinent to the several parts of our proposed history we shall present in a summary fashion, so that nothing worth hearing may be found missing. We shall give an accurate account of every race of men and all events that have taken place in the known parts of the inhabited world, so far as that is possible, beginning with the earliest times. As regards the first origin of mankind two opinions have arisen among the best authorities both on nature and on history. One group takes the position that the universe did not come into being and will not decay and that the race of men has existed from eternity; the other group holds that the universe came into being and will decay and maintains that men had their first origin at a definite time.

**7.** In the beginning, as their account runs, when the universe was being formed, both heaven and earth were indistinguishable in appearance and their elements were intermingled: then, when their bodies separated from one another, the universe took on in all its parts the ordered form which is now seen; the air was set in continual motion, the fiery element gathered into the highest regions, since anything of such a nature moves upward by reason of its lightness. It is for this reason that the sun and the multitude of other stars became involved in the universal whirl. All that was mud-like and thick and contained moisture sank because of its weight into one place, and as this continually turned about upon itself it became compressed, and out of the wet it formed the sea, and out of what was firmer, the land, which like potter's clay was entirely soft. Then, as the sun's fire shone upon the land, it first of all became firm, and then, since its surface was in a ferment because of the warmth, portions of the wet swelled up in masses in many places, and in these pustules covered with delicate membranes made their appearance. Such a phenomenon can be seen even yet in swamps and marshy places whenever, the ground having become cold, the air suddenly and without any gradual change becomes intensely warm. While the wet was being impregnated with life by reason of the warmth in the manner described, by night the living things forthwith received their nourishment from the mist that fell from the enveloping air, and by day were made solid by the intense heat; and finally, when the embryos had attained their full development and the membranes had been thoroughly heated and broken open, there was produced every form of animal life. Of these, such as had partaken of the most warmth became winged and set off to the higher regions, while such as retained an earthy consistency came to be numbered in the class of creeping things and of the other land animals, and those whose composition partook the most of the wet element gathered into the region congenial to them, receiving the name of water animals. As the earth constantly grew more solid through the action of the sun's fire and the winds, it was finally no longer able to generate any of the larger animals, but each kind of living creature was now begotten by breeding with one another.

Clearly Euripides, who was a pupil of Anaxagoras the natural philosopher, is not opposed to this account of the nature of the universe, for in his *Melanippe* he writes as follows:

> Tis thus that heav'n and earth were once one form;
> But since the two were sundered each from each,
> They now beget and bring to light all things,
> The trees and birds, the beasts, the spawn of sea,
> And race of mortals.

## DIODORUS SICULUS

### *On the first men and the earliest manner of life (8).*

**8.** Here follows the account we have received concerning the first generation of the universe. They say the first men led an undisciplined and bestial life, setting out one by one to secure their sustenance and taking for their food the tenderest herbs and the fruits of wild trees. Then, after they had been attacked by wild beasts, they learned to come to one another's aid, and by gathering together in this way from fear, they gradually came to recognise their mutual characteristics. The sounds they made were at first unintelligible and indistinct, yet gradually they came to give articulation to their speech, and by agreeing with one another upon symbols for each thing which presented itself to them, came to know among themselves the meaning attached to each term. Groups of this kind arose throughout the inhabited world and since each group organised its speech by mere chance, not all men had the same language. This explains the present existence of every conceivable kind of language. Out of these first groups came all of the original nations of the world.

Since none of the things useful for life had yet been discovered, the first men led a wretched existence; they had no clothing to cover them, they did not know the use of shelter and fire, and they were totally ignorant of cultivated food. Since they neglected harvesting wild food, they laid by no store of its fruits against their needs and consequently large numbers of them perished in the winter from cold and lack of food. Little by little, however, experience taught them to shelter in caves in the winter and to store such fruits as could be preserved, and bit by bit they become acquainted with fire and other useful things, capable of furthering man's social life. Indeed, in all things it was generally necessity that taught and supplied in appropriate fashion instruction to this creature which was well endowed by nature and had as assistants hands and speech and sagacity of mind.

As regards the origins of men and their earliest manner of life we shall be satisfied with what has been said, since we would keep due proportion in our account.

**9.** We shall now undertake to give a full account of all the events which have been handed down to memory and took place in the known regions of the inhabited world.

As to who were the first kings we are in no position to speak on our own authority, nor do we agree with those historians who profess to know; for it is impossible that the discovery of writing was of so early a date as to have been contemporary with the first kings. Once a man concedes this last point, it seems evident that writers of history are as a class a quite recent appearance in the society of man. When it comes to the antiquity of the human race, not only do Greeks, but many of the barbarians as well, put forth their claims that it is they who are autochthonous and the first to discover the things useful to life, and that it was their own history which was the first to be held worthy of record. For our purposes we shall make no attempt to determine with precision the antiquity of each nation or race or whose nations are prior in time to the rest and by how many years. Rather, we shall record summarily what each nation has to say of its antiquity and the early events in its history. The first peoples we shall discuss will be the barbarians, not that we consider them to be earlier than the Greeks, as

Ephorus has said, but because by setting out most of the facts about them at the outset, we will not have to interpolate them into the various accounts given by the Greeks of their relations with other peoples. Since Egypt is the country where mythology places the origin of the gods, where the earliest observations of the stars are said to have been made, and where, many noteworthy deeds of great men are recorded, we shall begin our history with the events connected with Egypt.

**10.** Now the Egyptians have an account like this: At the beginning the universe, men first came into existence in Egypt, because of the favourable climate of the land and because of the nature of the Nile. For this stream produces much life and provides a constant supply of food to support whatever living things it may engender. Both the root of the reed and the lotus, as well as the Egyptian bean and *corsaeum*, as it is called, and many other similar plants, supply mankind with nourishment ready for use. To prove that animal life first appeared in Egypt they argue that even at the present day the soil of the Thebaid generates mice in such numbers and of such size as to astonish all who see them, for some are fully formed as to the breast and front feet and are able to move although the rest of the body is unformed, a clod of earth retaining its natural character. From this they argue that, when the world was first taking shape, the land of Egypt was best suited for mankind to come into being because of the well-tempered nature of its soil. Even at the present time the soil of no other country generates any such things, while in it alone certain living creatures may be seen coming into being in a marvellous fashion.

They say that if the flood that occurred in the time of Deucalion destroyed most living things, it is more probable that the inhabitants of southern Egypt survived rather than others since their country is nearly rainless; or if, as others maintain, the destruction of living things was complete and the earth then brought forth new forms of animals, such a genesis most fittingly attaches to this country. For when the moisture from the abundant rains which fell among other peoples, was mingled with the intense heat which prevails in Egypt, it is reasonable to suppose that the air became very well tempered for the generation of all living things. Indeed, even in our day during the inundations of Egypt the generation of forms of animal life can clearly be seen taking place in the pools which remain the longest. When the river begins to recede and the sun dries the surface of the slime, they say living animals take shape, some fully formed, others only half so and still united with the earth.

**11.** They say that when the men of Egypt came into existence ages ago, they looked up at the firmament and being struck with awe and wonder at the nature of the universe conceived that two gods, the sun and the moon, were both eternal and first. They called them Osiris and Isis. These appellations were based upon the meanings in them, for when the names are translated into Greek Osiris meant "many-eyed," for by shedding his rays in every direction he surveys with many eyes all land and sea. The words of Homer are in agreement with this conception when he says:

> The sun, who sees all things and hears all things.

Of the ancient Greek writers of mythology, some call Osiris by the name Dionysus or, with a slight change in form, Sirius. One of them, Eumolpus, in his *Bacchic Hymn* speaks of

> Our Dionysus, shining like a star,
> With fiery eye in ev'ry ray;

while Orpheus says:

> And this is why men call him Shining One
> And Dionysus.

Some say that Osiris is also represented with the cloak of fawn-skin about his shoulders in imitation of the sky spangled with the stars. As for Isis, when translated the word means "ancient," the name given her because her birth was everlasting and ancient. They put horns on her head because of her appearance when the moon is crescent-shaped, and because among the Egyptians a cow is held sacred to her.

These two gods, they hold, regulate the universe, giving both nourishment and increase to all things by a system of three seasons which complete their full cycle through unobservable movements from spring to summer and to winter These seasons, by nature opposed to one another, complete the cycle of the year in full harmony. Moreover, practically all the physical matter essential to the generation of all things is furnished by these gods; the sun contributes the fiery element and the spirit while the moon contributes the wet and the dry, and both together the air. It is through these elements that all things are engendered and nourished. So it is out of the sun and moon that the whole physical body of the universe is made, and as for the five parts just named, the spirit, the fire, the dry, the wet, and, lastly, the air, just as in the case of a man we enumerate head and hands and feet and the other parts, so in the same way the body of the universe is composed of similar parts.

**12.** They regard each of these parts as a god and to each of them the first men in Egypt gave a distinct name appropriate to its nature. They named the spirit known to us as Zeus, and since he gave the spirit of life to animals they considered him the father of all things. They cite the most renowned of the Greek poets who seems to agree with this when he speaks of this god as:

> The father of men and of gods.

The fire they called Hephaestus, as it is translated, holding him to be a great god and one who contributes much both to the birth and full development of all things. The earth, again, they looked upon as a kind of vessel which holds all growing things and so gave it the name "mother"; and in like manner the Greeks also call it Demeter, the word having been slightly changed in the course of time; for in olden times they called her Gê Meter (Earth Mother), to which Orpheus bears witness when he speaks of:

> Earth the Mother of all, Demeter giver of wealth.

And the wet, according to them, was called by the men of old Oceanê, which means Fostering-mother; some of the Greeks have taken it to be Oceanus, of whom the poet also speaks:

> Oceanus source of gods and mother Tethys.

# Book I

For the Egyptians consider Oceanus to be their river Nile, on which their gods were born. They say, Egypt is the only country in the inhabited world where there are many cities which were founded by the first gods, such as Zeus, Helius, Hermes, Apollo, Pan, Eileithyia, and many more.

The air they called Athena, as the name is translated, and they considered her to be the daughter of Zeus and conceived of her as a virgin, because of the fact that the air is by its nature uncorrupted and occupies the highest part of the entire universe; for the latter reason also the myth arose that she was born from the head of Zeus. Another name given her was Tritogeneia (Thrice-born), because her nature changes three times in the course of the year, in the spring, summer, and winter. They add that she is also called Glaucopis (Blue-eyed), not because she has blue eyes, as some Greeks have held, a silly explanation, but because the air has a bluish cast.

These five deities, they say, visit all the inhabited world, revealing themselves to men in the form of sacred animals, and at times even appearing in the guise of men or in other shapes; nor is this a fabulous thing, but possible, if these are in truth the gods who give life to all things. The poet, who visited Egypt and became acquainted with such accounts from the priests, sets forth as fact what has been said:

> The gods, in strangers' form from alien lands,
> Frequent the cities of men in ev'ry guise,
> Observing their insolence and lawful ways.

So far as the celestial gods are concerned whose genesis is from eternity, this is the account given by the Egyptians.

**13.** Besides these there are other gods, they say, who were terrestrial, having once been mortals, but who, by reason of their sagacity and the good services which they rendered to all men, attained immortality, some of them having been kings in Egypt. Their names, when translated, are in some cases the same as those of the celestial gods, while others have a distinct appellation, such as Helius, Cronus, and Rhea, and also the Zeus who is called Ammon by some, and besides these Hera and Hephaestus, also Hestia, and, finally, Hermes. Helius was the first king of the Egyptians, his name being the same as that of the heavenly star. Some of the priests, however, say that Hephaestus was their first king, since he was the discoverer of fire and received the rule because of this service to mankind; once, when a tree on the mountains had been struck by lightning and the forest near by was ablaze, Hephaestus went up to it, for it was winter-time, and greatly enjoyed the heat; as the fire died down he kept adding fuel to it, and while keeping the fire going in this way he invited the rest of mankind to enjoy the advantage which came from it. Then Cronus became the ruler, and married his sister Rhea, he begat Osiris and Isis, according to some writers of mythology, but, according to the majority, Zeus and Hera, whose high achievements gave them dominion over the entire universe. From these last were sprung five gods, one born on each of the five days which the Egyptians intercalate; the names of these children were Osiris and Isis, and also Typhon, Apollo, and Aphrodite. Osiris when translated is Dionysus, and Isis is more similar to Demeter than to any other goddess; after Osiris married Isis and succeeded to the kingship he did many things of service to the social life of man.

**14.** Osiris was the first, they record, to make mankind give up cannibalism. After Isis had discovered the fruit of both wheat and barley, which grew wild over the land, along with the other plants, but was still unknown to man, Osiris devised the cultivation of these fruits. All men were glad to change their food, both because of the pleasing nature of the newly-discovered grains and because it seemed to their advantage to refrain from their butchery of one another. As proof of the discovery of these fruits they offer the following ancient custom which they still observe: At harvest time the people make a dedication of the first heads of the grain to be cut, and standing beside the sheaf beat themselves and call upon Isis, by this act rendering honour to the goddess for the fruits which she discovered, at the season when she first did this. Moreover in some cities, during the Festival of Isis, stalks of wheat and barley are carried among the other objects in the procession as a memorial of what the goddess so ingeniously discovered at the beginning. Isis also established laws, they say, in accordance with which the people regularly dispense justice to one another and are led to refrain through fear of punishment from illegal violence and insolence; it is for this reason also that the early Greeks gave Demeter the name Thesmophorus, [Lawgiver] acknowledging in this way that she had first established their laws.

**15.** Osiris, they say, founded in the Egyptian Thebaid a city with a hundred gates, which the men of his day named after his mother, though later generations called it Diospolis, [City of Zeus] and some named it Thebes. There is no agreement, however, as to when this city was founded, not only among the historians, but even among the priests of Egypt themselves; for many writers say that Thebes was not founded by Osiris, but many years later by a certain king of whom we shall give a detailed account in connection with his period. Osiris, they add, also built a temple to his parents, Zeus and Hera, which was famous both for its size and its costliness in general, and two golden chapels to Zeus, the larger one to him as god of heaven, the smaller one to him as former king and father of the Egyptians, in which role he is called by some Ammon. He also made golden chapels for the rest of the gods mentioned above, allotting honours to each of them and appointing priests to have charge over these. Special esteem at the court of Osiris and Isis was also accorded to those who should invent any of the arts or devise any useful process; consequently, since copper and gold mines had been discovered in the Thebaid, they fashioned implements with which they killed the wild beasts and worked the soil, and thus in eager rivalry brought the country under cultivation, and they made images of the gods and magnificent golden chapels for their worship.

Osiris, they say, was also interested in agriculture and was reared in Nysa, a city of Arabia Felix near Egypt, being a son of Zeus. The name which he bears among the Greeks is derived both from his father and from the birthplace, since he is called Dionysus. Mention is also made of Nysa by the poet in his Hymns, to the effect that it was in the vicinity of Egypt, when he says:

> There is a certain Nysa, mountain high,
> With forests thick, in Phoenicê afar,
> Close to Aegyptus' streams.

The discovery of the vine, they say, was made by him near Nysa, and that, having further devised the proper treatment of its fruit, he was the first to drink wine and taught mankind at large the culture of the vine and the use of wine, as well as the way to harvest the grape and to store the wine. The one most highly honoured by him was Hermes, who was endowed with unusual ingenuity for devising things capable of improving the social life of man.

**16.** It was by Hermes, for instance, according to them, that the common language of mankind was first further articulated, and that many objects which were still nameless received an appellation, that the alphabet was invented, and that ordinances regarding the honours and offerings due to the gods were duly established; he was the first also to observe the orderly arrangement of the stars and the harmony of the musical sounds and their nature, to establish a wrestling school, and to give thought to the rhythmical movement of the human body and its proper development. He made a lyre and gave it three strings, imitating the seasons of the year; for he adopted three tones, a high, a low, and a medium; the high from the summer, the low from the winter, and the medium from the spring. The Greeks also were taught by him how to expound (*hermeneia*) their thoughts, and it was for this reason that he was given the name Hermes. In a word, Osiris, taking him for his priestly scribe, communicated with him on every matter and used his counsel above that of all others. The olive tree also, they claim, was his discovery, not Athena's, as Greeks say.

**17.** Of Osiris they say that, being of a beneficent turn of mind, and eager for glory, he gathered together a great army, with the intention of visiting all the inhabited earth and teaching the race of men how to cultivate the vine and sow wheat and barley, for he supposed that if he made men give up their savagery and adopt a gentle manner of life he would receive immortal honours because of the magnitude of his benefactions. And this did in fact take place, since not only the men of his time who received this gift, but all succeeding generations as well, because of the delight which they take in the foods which were discovered, have honoured those who introduced them as gods most illustrious.

Now after Osiris had established the affairs of Egypt and turned the supreme power over to Isis his wife, they say that he placed Hermes at her side as counsellor because his prudence raised him above the king's other friends, and as general of all the land under his sway he left Heracles, who was both his kinsman and renowned for his valour and physical strength, while as governors he appointed Busiris over those parts of Egypt which lie towards Phoenicia and border upon the sea and Antaeus over those adjoining Ethiopia and Libya; then he himself left Egypt with his army to make his campaign, taking in his company also his brother, whom the Greeks call Apollo. And it was Apollo, they say, who discovered the laurel, a garland of which all men place about the head of this god above all others. The discovery of ivy is also attributed to Osiris by the Egyptians and made sacred to this god, just as the Greeks also do in the case of Dionysus. In the Egyptian language, they say, the ivy is called the "plant of Osiris" and for purposes of dedication it is preferred to the vine, since the latter sheds its leaves while the former ever remains green; the same rule, moreover, the ancients have followed in the case of other plants also which are perennially green, ascribing, for instance, the myrtle to Aphrodite and the laurel to Apollo.

**18.** Now Osiris was accompanied on his campaign, as the Egyptian account goes, by his two sons Anubis and Macedon, who were distinguished for their valour. Both of them carried the most notable accoutrements of war, taken from certain animals whose character was not unlike the boldness of the men; Anubis wearing a dog's skin and Macedon the fore-parts of a wolf; and it is for this reason that these animals are held in honour among the Egyptians. He also took Pan along on his campaign, who is held in special honour by the Egyptians; for the inhabitants of the land have not only set up statues of him at every temple but have also named a city after him in the Thebaid, called by the natives Chemmo, which when translated means City of Pan. In his company were also men who were experienced in agriculture, such as Maron in the cultivation of the vine, and Triptolemus in the sowing of grain and in every step in the harvesting of it. When all his preparations had been completed Osiris made a vow to the gods that he would let his hair grow until his return to Egypt and then made his way through Ethiopia; and this is the reason why this custom with regard to their hair was observed among the Egyptians until recent times, and why those who journeyed abroad let their hair grow until their return home.

While he was in Ethiopia, their account continues, the Satyr people were brought to him, who, they say, have hair upon their loins. As Osiris was laughter-loving and fond of music and the dance he consequently took with him a multitude of musicians among whom were nine maidens who could sing and were trained in the other arts; these maidens being those who among the Greeks are called the Muses, and their leader (*hegetes*), as the account goes, was Apollo, who was for that reason also given the name Musegetes. As for the Satyrs, they were taken along on the campaign because they were proficient in dancing and singing and every kind of relaxation and pastime. Osiris was not warlike, nor did he have to organise pitched battles or engagements, since every people received him as a god because of his benefactions. In Ethiopia he instructed the inhabitants in agriculture and founded some notable cities, and then left behind him men to govern the country and collect the tribute.

**19.** While Osiris and his army were thus employed, the Nile, they say, at the time of the rising of Sirius, which is the season when the river is usually at flood, breaking out of its banks inundated a large section of Egypt and covered especially that part where Prometheus was governor, and since practically everything in this district was destroyed, Prometheus was so grieved that he was on the point of quitting life wilfully. Because its water sweeps down so swiftly and with such violence the river was given the name Aëtus; [eagle] but Heracles, being ever intent upon great enterprises and eager for the reputation of a manly spirit, speedily stopped the flood at its breach and turned the river back into its former course. Consequently certain of the Greek poets worked the incident into a myth, to the effect that Heracles had killed the eagle which was devouring the liver of Prometheus. The river in the earliest period bore the name Oceanê, which in Greek is Oceanus; then because of this flood, they say, it was called Aëtus, and still later it was known as Aegyptus after a former king of the land. And the poet also adds his testimony to this when he writes:

> On the river Aegyptus my curved ships I stayed.

For it is at Thonis, as it is called, which in early times was the trading-port of Egypt, that the river empties into the sea. Its last name and that which the river now bears it received from the former king Nileus.

Now when Osiris arrived at the borders of Ethiopia, he curbed the river by dikes on both banks, so that at flood-time it might not form stagnant pools over the land to its detriment, but that the flood-water might be let upon the countryside, in a gentle flow as it might be needed, through gates which he had built. After this he continued his march through Arabia along the shore of the Red Sea [present Persian Gulf and Indian Ocean] as far as India and the limits of the inhabited world. He also founded not a few cities in India, one of which he named Nysa, wishing to leave there a memorial of that city in Egypt where he had been reared. He also planted ivy in the Indian Nysa, and throughout India and those countries which border upon it the plant to this day is still to be found only in this region. And many other signs of his stay he left in that country, which have led the Indians of a later time to lay claim to the god and say that he was by birth a native of India.

**20.** Osiris also took an interest in hunting elephants, and everywhere left behind him inscribed pillars telling of his campaign. He visited all the other nations of Asia as well and crossed into Europe at the Hellespont. In Thrace he slew Lycurgus, the king of the barbarians, who opposed his undertakings, and Maron, who was now old, he left there to supervise the culture of the plants which he introduced into that land and caused him to found a city to bear his name, which he called Maroneia. Macedon his son, moreover, he left as king of Macedonia, which was named after him, while to Triptolemus he assigned the care of agriculture in Attica. Finally, Osiris in this way visited all the inhabited world and advanced community life by the introduction of the fruits which are most easily cultivated. And if any country did not admit of the growing of the vine he introduced the drink prepared from barley, which is little inferior to wine in aroma and in strength. On his return to Egypt he brought with him the very greatest presents from every quarter and by reason of the magnitude of his benefactions received the gift of immortality with the approval of all men and honour equal to that offered to the gods of heaven. After this he passed from the midst of men into the company of the gods and received from Isis and Hermes sacrifices and every other highest honour. These also instituted rites for him and introduced many things of a mystic nature, magnifying in this way the power of the god.

**21.** Although the priests of Osiris had from the earliest times received the account of his death as a matter not to be divulged, in the course of years it came about that through some of their number this hidden knowledge was published to the many. This is the story as they give it: When Osiris was ruling over Egypt as its lawful king, he was murdered by his brother Typhon, a violent and impious man. Typhon then divided the body of the slain man into twenty-six pieces and gave one portion to each of the band of murderers, since he wanted all of them to share in the pollution and felt that in this way he would have in them steadfast supporters and defenders of his rule. But Isis, the sister and wife of Osiris, avenged his murder with the aid of her son Horus, and after slaying Typhon and his accomplices became queen over Egypt. The struggle between them took place on the banks of the Nile near the village now known as Antaeus, which, they say, lies on the Arabian side of the river and derives its name from that Antaeus, a contemporary of Osiris, who was punished by Heracles. Now Isis recovered all the pieces of the body except the privates, and wishing that the burial-place of her husband should remain secret and yet be honoured by all the inhabitants of Egypt, she fulfilled her purpose in somewhat the following manner. Over each piece of the body, as the account goes, she fashioned out of spices and wax a human figure about the size of Osiris; then summoning the priests group by group, she required of all of them an oath that they would reveal to no one the trust which she was going to confide to them, and taking each group of them apart privately she said that she was consigning to them alone the burial of the body, and after reminding them of the benefactions of Osiris she exhorted them to bury his body in their own district and pay honours to him as to a god, and to consecrate to him also someone that they might choose of the animals native to their district, pay to it while living the honours which they had formerly rendered to Osiris, and upon its death accord it the same kind of funeral as they had given to him. And since Isis wished to induce the priests to render these honours by the incentive of their own profit also, she gave them the third part of the country to defray the cost of the worship and service of the gods. And the priests, it is said, being mindful of the benefactions of Osiris and eager to please the queen who was petitioning them, and incited as well by their own profit, did everything just as Isis had suggested. It is for this reason that even to this day each group of priests supposes that Osiris lies buried in their district, pays honours to the animals which were originally consecrated to him, and, when these die, renews in the funeral rites for them the mourning for Osiris. The consecration to Osiris, however, of the sacred bulls, which are given the names Apis and Mnevis, and the worship of them as gods were introduced generally among all the Egyptians, since these animals had, more than any others, rendered aid to those who discovered the fruit of the grain, in connection with both the sowing of the seed and with every agricultural labour from which mankind profits.

**22.** Isis, they say, after the death of Osiris took a vow never to marry another man, and passed the remainder of her life reigning over the land with complete respect for the law and surpassing all sovereigns in benefactions to her subjects. And like her husband she also, when she passed from among men, received immortal honours and was buried near Memphis, where her shrine is pointed out to this day in the temple-area of Hephaestus. According to some writers, however, the bodies of these two gods rest, not in Memphis, but on the border between Egypt and Ethiopia, on the island in the Nile which lies near the city which is called Philae, but is referred to because of this burial as the Holy Field. In proof of this they point to remains which still survive on this island, both to the tomb constructed for Osiris, which is honoured in common by all the priests of Egypt, and to the three hundred and sixty libation bowls which are placed around it; for the priests appointed over these bowls fill them each day with milk, singing all the while a dirge in which they call upon the names of these gods. It is for this reason that travellers are not allowed to set foot on this island. And all the inhabitants of the Thebaid, which is the oldest portion of Egypt, hold it to be the strongest oath when a man swears "by Osiris who lieth in Philae."

Now the parts of the body of Osiris which were found were honoured with burial, they say, in the manner described above, but the privates, according to them, were thrown by Typhon into the Nile because no one of his accomplices was willing to take them. Yet Isis thought them as worthy of divine honours as the other parts, for, fashioning a likeness of them, she set it up in the temples, commanded that it be honoured, and made it the object of the highest regard and reverence in the rites and sacrifices accorded to the god. Consequently the Greeks too, inasmuch as they received from Egypt the celebrations of the orgies and the festivals connected with Dionysus, honour this member in both the mysteries and the initiatory rites and sacrifices of this god, giving it the name "phallus."

23. The number of years from Osiris and Isis, they say, to the reign of Alexander, who founded the city [331] which bears his name in Egypt, is over ten thousand, but, according to other writers, a little less than twenty-three thousand. And those who say that the god [Dionysus] was born of Semele and Zeus in Boeotian Thebes are, according to the priests, simply inventing the tale. For they say that Orpheus, upon visiting Egypt and participating in the initiation and mysteries of Dionysus, adopted them and as a favour to the descendants of Cadmus, since he was kindly disposed to them and received honours at their hands, transferred the birth of the god to Thebes; and the common people, partly out of ignorance and partly out of their desire to have the god thought to be a Greek, eagerly accepted his initiatory rites and mysteries. What led Orpheus to transfer the birth and rites of the god, they say, was something like this.

Cadmus, who was a citizen of Egyptian Thebes, begat several children, of whom one was Semelê; she was violated by an unknown person, became pregnant, and after seven months gave birth to a child whose appearance was such as the Egyptians hold had been that of Osiris. Now such a child is not usually brought into the world alive, either because it is contrary to the will of the gods or because the law of nature does not admit of it. But when Cadmus found out what had taken place, having at the same time a reply from an oracle commanding him to observe the laws of his fathers, he both gilded the infant and paid it the appropriate sacrifices, on the ground that there had been a sort of epiphany of Osiris among men. The fatherhood of the child he attributed to Zeus, in this way magnifying Osiris and averting slander from his violated daughter; this is the reason why the tale was given out among the Greeks to the effect that Semelê, the daughter of Cadmus, was the mother of Osiris by Zeus. Now at a later time Orpheus, who was held in high regard among the Greeks for his singing, initiatory rites, and instructions on things divine, was entertained as a guest by the descendants of Cadmus and accorded unusual honours in Thebes. Since he had become conversant with the teachings of the Egyptians about the gods, he transferred the birth of the ancient Osiris to more recent times, and, out of regard for the descendants of Cadmus, instituted a new initiation, in the ritual of which the initiates were given the account that Dionysus had been born of Semelê and Zeus. And the people observed these initiatory rites, partly because they were deceived through their ignorance, partly because they were attracted to them by the trustworthiness of Orpheus and his reputation in such matters, and most of all because they were glad to receive the god as a Greek, which, as has been said, is what he was considered to be. Later, after the writers of myths and poets had taken over this account of his ancestry, the theatres became filled with it and among following generations faith in the story grew stubborn and immutable.

In general, they say, the Greeks appropriate to themselves the most renowned of both Egyptian heroes and gods, and so also the colonies sent out by them.

**24.** Heracles, for instance, was by birth an Egyptian, who by virtue of his manly vigour visited a large part of the inhabited world and set up his pillar in Libya; and their proofs of this assertion they endeavour to draw from the Greeks themselves. For inasmuch as it is generally accepted that Heracles fought on the side of the Olympian gods in their war against the Giants, they say that it in no way accords with the age of the earth for the Giants to have been born in the period when, as the Greeks say, Heracles lived, which was a generation before the Trojan War, but rather at the time, as their own account gives it, when mankind first appeared on the earth; for from the latter time to the present the Egyptians reckon more than ten thousand years, but from the Trojan War less than twelve hundred. Likewise, both the club and the lion's skin are appropriate to their ancient Heracles, because in those days arms had not yet been invented, and men defended themselves against their enemies with clubs of wood and used the hides of animals for defensive armour. They also designate him as the son of Zeus, but about the identity of his mother they say that they know nothing. The son of Alcmenê, who was born more than ten thousand years later and was called Alcaeus at birth, in later life became known instead as Heracles, not because he gained glory (*kleos*) by the aid of Hera, as Matris says, but because, having avowed the same principles as the ancient Heracles, he inherited that one's fame and name as well.

The account of the Egyptians agrees also with the tradition which has been handed down among the Greeks since very early times, to the effect that Heracles cleared the earth of wild beasts, a story which is in no way suitable for a man who lived in approximately the period of the Trojan War, when most parts of the inhabited world had already been reclaimed from their wild state by agriculture and cities and the multitude of men settled everywhere over the land. Accordingly this reclamation of the land suits better a man who lived in early times, when men were still held in subjection by the vast numbers of wild beasts, a state of affairs which was especially true in the case of Egypt, the upper part of which is to this day desert and infested with wild beasts. Indeed it is reasonable to suppose that the first concern of Heracles was for this country as his birthplace, and that, after he had cleared the land of wild beasts, he presented it to the peasants, and for this benefaction was accorded divine honours. And they say that Perseus also was born in Egypt, and that the origin of Isis is transferred by the Greeks to Argos in the myth which tells of that Io who was changed into a heifer.

**25.** In general, there is great disagreement over these gods. For the same goddess is called by some Isis, by others Demeter, by others Thesmophorus, by others Selenê, by others Hera, while still others apply to her all these names. Osiris has been given the name Sarapis by some, Dionysus by others, Pluto by others, Ammon by others, Zeus by some, and many have considered Pan to be the same god; and some say that Sarapis is the god whom the Greeks call Pluto.

As for Isis, the Egyptians say that she was the discoverer of many health-giving drugs and was greatly versed in the science of healing; consequently, now that she has attained immortality, she finds her greatest delight in the healing of mankind and gives aid in their sleep to those who call upon her, plainly manifesting both her very presence and her beneficence towards men who ask her help. In proof of this, as they say, they advance not legends, as the Greeks do, but manifest facts; for practically the entire inhabited world is their witness, in that it eagerly contributes to the honours of Isis because she manifests herself in healing. For standing above the sick in their sleep she gives them aid for their diseases and works remarkable cures upon such as submit themselves to her; and many who have been despaired of by their physicians because of the difficult nature of their malady are restored to health by her, while numbers who have altogether lost the use of their eyes or of some other part of their body, whenever they turn for help to this goddess, are restored to their previous condition. Furthermore, she discovered also the drug which gives immortality, by means of which she not only raised from the dead her son Horus, who had been the object of plots on the part of the Titans and had been found dead under the water, giving him his soul again, but also made him immortal. And it appears that Horus was the last of the gods to be king after his father Osiris departed from among men. Moreover, they say that the name Horus, when translated, is Apollo, and that, having been instructed by his mother Isis in both medicine and divination, he is now a benefactor of the race of men through his oracular responses and his healing.

**26.** The priests of the Egyptians, reckoning the time from the reign of Helius to the crossing of Alexander into Asia, [334] say that it was in round numbers twenty-three thousand years. And, as their legends say, the most ancient of the gods ruled more than twelve hundred years and the later ones not less than three hundred. Since this great number of years surpasses belief, some men would maintain that in early times, before the movement of the sun had as yet been recognised, it was customary to reckon the year by the lunar cycle. Consequently, since the year consisted of thirty days, it was not impossible that some men lived twelve hundred years; for in our own time, when our year consists of twelve months, not a few men live over one hundred years. A similar explanation they also give regarding those who are supposed to have reigned for three hundred years; for at their time, namely, the year was composed of the four months which comprise the seasons of each year, that is, spring, summer, and winter; and it is for this reason that among some of the Greeks the years are called "seasons" (*horoi*) and that their yearly records are given the name "horographs."[records of the seasons]

Furthermore, the Egyptians relate in their myths that in the time of Isis there were certain creatures of many bodies, who are called by the Greeks Giants, but by themselves . . ., these being the men who are represented on their temples in monstrous form and as being cudgelled by Osiris. Now some say that they were born of the earth at the time when the genesis of living things from the earth was still recent, while some hold that they were only men of unusual physical strength who achieved many deeds and for this reason were described in the myths as of many bodies. It is generally agreed that when they stirred up war against Zeus and Osiris they were all destroyed.

**27.** The Egyptians also made a law, they say, contrary to the general custom of mankind, permitting men to marry their sisters, this being due to the success attained by Isis in this respect, for she had married her brother Osiris, and upon his death, having taken a vow never to marry another man, she both avenged the murder of her husband and reigned all her days over the land with complete respect for the laws, and, in a word, became the cause of more and greater blessings to all men than any other. It is for these reasons, in fact, that it was ordained that the queen should have greater power and honour than the king and that among private persons the wife should enjoy authority over her husband, the husbands agreeing in the marriage contract that they will be obedient in all things to their wives.

Now I am not unaware that some historians give the following account of Isis and Osiris: The tombs of these gods lie in Nysa in Arabia, and for this reason Dionysus is also called Nysaeus. And in that place there stands also a stele of each of the gods bearing an inscription in hieroglyphs. On the stele of Isis it runs: "I am Isis, the queen of every land, she who was instructed of Hermes, and whatsoever laws I have established, these can no man make void. I am the eldest daughter of the youngest god Cronus; I am the wife and sister of the king Osiris; I am she who first discovered fruits for mankind; I am the mother of Horus the king; I am she who riseth in the star that is in the Constellation of the Dog; by me was the city of Bubastus built. Farewell, farewell, O Egypt that nurtured me." And on the stele of Osiris the inscription is said to run: "My father is Cronus, the youngest of all the gods, and I am Osiris the king, who campaigned over every country as far as the uninhabited regions of India and the lands to the north, even to the sources of the river Ister, [Danube] and again to the remaining parts of the world as far as Oceanus. I am the eldest son of Cronus, and being sprung from a fair and noble egg I was begotten a seed of kindred birth to Day. There is no region of the inhabited world to which I have not come, dispensing to all men the things of which I was the discoverer." So much of the inscriptions on the stelae can be read, they say, but the rest of the writing, which was of greater extent, has been destroyed by time. However this may be, varying accounts of the burial of these gods are found in most writers by reason of the fact that the priests, having received the exact facts about these matters as a secret not to be divulged, are unwilling to give out the truth to the public, on the ground that perils overhang any men who disclose to the common crowd the secret knowledge about these gods.

**28.** Now the Egyptians say that also after these events a great number of colonies were spread from Egypt over all the inhabited world. To Babylon, for instance, colonists were led by Belus, who was held to be the son of Poseidon and Libya; and after establishing himself on the Euphrates river he appointed priests, called Chaldaeans by the Babylonians, who were exempt from taxation and free from every kind of service to the state, as are the priests of Egypt; they also make observations of the stars, following the example of the Egyptian priests, physicists, and astrologers. They say also that those who set forth with Danaus, from Egypt, settled what is practically the oldest city of Greece, Argos, and that the nation of the Colchi in Pontus and that of the Jews, which lies between Arabia and Syria, were founded as colonies by certain emigrants from their country; and this is the reason why it is a long-established institution among these two peoples to circumcise their male children, the custom having been brought over from Egypt. Even the Athenians, they say, are colonists from Saïs in Egypt, and they undertake to offer proofs of such a relationship; for the Athenians are the only Greeks who call their city "Asty," a name brought over from the city Asty in Egypt. Furthermore, their body politic had the same classification and division of the people as is found in Egypt, where the citizens have been divided into three orders: the first Athenian class consisted of the "eupatrids," as they were called, being those who were such as had received the best education and were held worthy of the highest honour, as is the case with the priests of Egypt; the second was that of the "geomoroi," who were expected to possess arms and to serve in defence of the state, like those in Egypt who are known as husbandmen and supply the warriors; and the last class was reckoned to be that of the "demiurgoi," who practise the mechanical arts and render only the most menial services to the state, this class among the Egyptians having a similar function.

Moreover, certain of the rulers of Athens were originally Egyptians, they say. Petes, [Peteus] for instance, the father of that Menestheus who took part in the expedition against Troy, having clearly been an Egyptian, later obtained citizenship at Athens and the kingship. . . . He was of double form, and yet the Athenians are unable from their own point of view to give the true explanation of this nature of his, although it is patent to all that it was because of his double citizenship, Greek and barbarian, that he was held to be of double form, that is, part animal and part man.

**29.** In the same way, they continue, Erechtheus also, who was by birth an Egyptian, became king of Athens, and in proof of this they offer the following considerations. Once when there was a great drought, as is generally agreed, which extended over practically all the inhabited earth except Egypt because of the peculiar character of that country, and there followed a destruction both of crops and of men in great numbers, Erechtheus, through his racial connection with Egypt, brought from there to Athens a great supply of grain, and in return those who had enjoyed this aid made their benefactor king. After he had secured the throne he instituted the initiatory rites of Demeter in Eleusis and established the mysteries, transferring their ritual from Egypt. And the tradition that an advent of the goddess into Attica also took place at that time is reasonable, since it was then that the fruits which are named after her were brought to Athens, and this is why it was thought that the discovery of the seed had been made again, as though Demeter had bestowed the gift. And the Athenians on their part agree that it was in the reign of Erechtheus, when a lack of rain had wiped out the crops, that Demeter came to them with the gift of grain. Furthermore, the initiatory rites and mysteries of this goddess were instituted in Eleusis at that time. And their sacrifices as well as their ancient ceremonies are observed by the Athenians in the same way as by the Egyptians; for the Eumolpidae were derived from the priests of Egypt and the Ceryces from the *pastophoroi*. They are also the only Greeks who swear by Isis, and they closely resemble the Egyptians in both their appearance and manners. By many other statements like these, spoken more out of a love for glory than with regard for the truth, as I see the matter, they claim Athens as a colony of theirs because of the fame of that city.

In general, the Egyptians say that their ancestors sent forth numerous colonies to many parts of the inhabited world, by reason of the pre-eminence of their former kings and their excessive population; but since they offer no precise proof whatsoever for these statements, and since no historian worthy of credence testifies in their support, we have not thought that their accounts merited recording.

So far as the ideas of the Egyptians about the gods are concerned, let what we have said suffice, since we are aiming at due proportion in our account, but with regard to the land, the Nile, and everything else worth hearing about we shall endeavour, in each case, to give the several facts in summary.

## On the topography of the land of Egypt and the marvels related about the river Nile; the causes also of its flooding and the opinions thereupon of the historians and the philosophers (30 ff.).

30. The land of Egypt stretches in a general way from north to south, and in natural strength and beauty of landscape is reputed to excel in no small degree all other regions that have been formed into kingdoms. For on the west it is fortified by the desert of Libya, which is full of wild beasts and extends along its border for a long distance, and by reason of its lack of rain and want of every kind of food makes the passage through it not only toilsome but even highly dangerous; while on the south the same protection is afforded by the cataracts of the Nile and the mountains flanking them, since from the country of the Trogodytes and the farthest parts of Ethiopia, over a distance of five thousand five hundred stades, it is not easy to sail by the river or to journey by land, unless a man is fitted out like a king or at least on a very great scale. As for the parts of the country facing the east, some are fortified by the river and some are embraced by a desert and a swampy flat called the Barathra. For between Coele-Syria and Egypt there lies a lake, quite narrow, but marvellously deep and some two hundred stades in length, which is called Serbonis and offers unexpected perils to those who approach it in ignorance of its nature. For since the body of the water is narrow, like a ribbon, and surrounded on all sides by great dunes, when there are constant south winds great quantities of sand are strewn over it. This sand hides the surface of the water and makes the outline of the lake continuous with the solid land and entirely indistinguishable from it. For this reason many who were unacquainted with the peculiar nature of the place have disappeared together with whole armies, when they wandered from the beaten road. For as the sand is walked upon it gives way but gradually, deceiving with a kind of malevolent cunning those who advance upon it, until, suspecting some impending mishap, they begin to help one another only when it is no longer possible to turn back or escape. For anyone who has been sucked in by the mire cannot swim, since the slime prevents all movement of the body, nor is he able to wade out, since he has no solid footing; for by reason of the mixing of the sand with the water and the consequent change in the nature of both it comes about that the place cannot be crossed either on foot or by boat. Consequently those who enter upon these regions are borne towards the depths and have nothing to

grasp to give them help, since the sand along the edge slips in with them. These flats have received a name appropriate to their nature as we have described it, being called Barathra. [devouring]

**31.** Now that we have set forth the facts about the three regions which fortify Egypt by land we shall add to them the one yet remaining. The fourth side, which is washed over its whole extent by waters which are practically harbourless, has for a defence before it the Egyptian Sea. The voyage along the coast of this sea is exceedingly long, and any landing is especially difficult; for from Paraetonium in Libya as far as Iopê [Joppa] in Coele-Syria, a voyage along the coast of some five thousand stades, there is not to be found a safe harbour except Pharos.[Alexandria] And, apart from these considerations, a sandbank extends along practically the whole length of Egypt, not discernible to any who approach without previous experience of these waters. Consequently those who think that they have escaped the peril of the sea, and in their ignorance turn with gladness towards the shore, suffer unexpected shipwreck when their vessels suddenly run aground; and now and then mariners who cannot see land in time because the country lies so low are cast ashore before they realise it, some of them on marshy and swampy places and others on a desert region.

The land of Egypt, then, is fortified on all sides by nature in the manner described, and is oblong in shape, having a coast-line of two thousand stades and extending inland about six thousand stades. In density of population it far surpassed of old all known regions of the inhabited world, and even in our own day is thought to be second to none other; for in ancient times it had over eighteen thousand important villages and cities, as can be seen entered in their sacred records, while under Ptolemy son of Lagus these were reckoned at over thirty thousand, this great number continuing down to our own time. The total population, they say, was of old about seven million and the number has remained no less down to our day. It is for this reason that, according to our historical accounts, the ancient kings of Egypt built great and marvellous works with the aid of so many hands and left in them immortal monuments to their glory. But these matters we shall set forth in detail a little later; now we shall tell of the nature of the river and the distinctive features of the country.

**32.** The Nile flows from south to north, having its sources in regions which have never been seen, since they lie in the desert at the extremity of Ethiopia in a country that cannot be approached because of the excessive heat. Being as it is the largest of all rivers as well as the one which traverses the greatest territory, it forms great windings, now turning towards the east and Arabia, now bending back towards the west and Libya; for its course from the mountains of Ethiopia to where it empties into the sea is a distance, inclusive of its windings, of some twelve thousand stades. In its lower stretches it is more and more reduced in volume, as the flow is drawn off to the two continents. Of the streams which thus break off from it, those which turn off into Libya are swallowed up by the sand, which lies there to an incredible depth, while those which pour in the opposite direction into Arabia are diverted into immense fens and large marshes on whose shores dwell many peoples. Where it enters Egypt it has a width of ten stades, sometimes less, and flows, not in a straight course, but in windings of every sort; for it twists now towards the east, now towards the west, and at times even towards the south, turning entirely back upon itself. For sharp hills extend along both sides of the river, which occupy much of the land bordering upon it and are cut through by precipitous ravines, in which are narrow defiles; and when it comes to these hills the stream rushes rapidly backward through the level country, and after being borne southward over an area of considerable extent resumes once more its natural course.

Distinguished as it is in these respects above all other streams, the Nile is also the only river which makes its way without violence or onrushing waves, except at the cataracts, as they are called. This is a place which is only about ten stades in length, but has a steep descent and is shut in by precipices so as to form a narrow cleft, rugged in its entire length and ravine-like, full, moreover, of huge boulders which stand out of the water like peaks. And since the river is split about these boulders with great force and is often turned back so that it rushes in the opposite direction because of the obstacles, remarkable whirlpools are formed; the middle space, moreover, for its entire length is filled with foam made by the backward rush of the water, and strikes those who approach it with great terror. And, in fact, the descent of the river is so swift and violent that it appears to the eye like the very rush of an arrow. During the flood-time of the Nile, when the peaked rocks are covered and the entire rapids are hidden by the large volume of the water, some men descend the cataract when they find the winds against them,[their sail check their speed] but no man can make his way up it, since the force of the river overcomes every human device. Now there are still other cataracts of this nature, but the largest is the one on the border between Ethiopia and Egypt.

**33.** The Nile also embraces islands within its waters, of which there are many in Ethiopia and one of considerable extent called Meroe, on which there also lies a famous city bearing the same name as the island, which was founded by Cambyses and named by him after his mother Meroë. This island, they say, has the shape of a long shield and in size far surpasses the other islands in these parts; for they state that it is three thousand stades long and a thousand wide. It also contains not a few cities, the most famous of which is Meroë. Extending the entire length of the island where it is washed by the river there are, on the side towards Libya, dunes containing an infinite amount of sand, and, on the side towards Arabia, rugged cliffs. There are also to be found in it mines of gold, silver, iron, and copper, and it contains in addition much ebony and every kind of precious stone. Speaking generally, the river forms so many islands that the report of them can scarcely be credited; for, apart from the regions surrounded by water in what is called the Delta, there are more than seven hundred other islands, of which some are irrigated by the Ethiopians and planted with millet, though others are so overrun by snakes and dog-faced baboons and other animals of every kind that human beings cannot set foot upon them.

Now where the Nile in its course through Egypt divides into several streams it forms the region which is called from its shape the Delta. The two sides of the Delta are described by the outermost branches, while its base is formed by the sea which receives the discharge from the several outlets of the river. It empties into the sea in seven mouths, of which the first, beginning at the east, is called the Pelusiac, the second the Tanitic, then the Mendesian, Phatnitic, and

Sebennytic, then the Bolbitine, and finally the Canopic, which is called by some the Heracleotic. There are also other mouths, built by the hand of man, about which there is no special need to write. At each mouth is a walled city, which is divided into two parts by the river and provided on each side of the mouth with pontoon bridges and guard-houses at suitable points. From the Pelusiac mouth there is an artificial canal to the Arabian Gulf and the Red Sea. The first to undertake the construction of this was Necho the son of Psammetichus, and after him Darius the Persian made progress with the work for a time but finally left it unfinished; for he was informed by certain persons that if he dug through the neck of land he would be responsible for the submergence of Egypt, for they pointed out to him that the Red Sea was higher than Egypt. At a later time the second Ptolemy [285-246]completed it and in the most suitable spot constructed an ingenious kind of a lock. This he opened, whenever he wished to pass through, and quickly closed again, a contrivance which usage proved to be highly successful. The river which flows through this canal is named Ptolemy, after the builder of it, and has at its mouth the city called Arsinoe.

**34.** The Delta is much like Sicily in shape, and its sides are each seven hundred and fifty stades long and its base, where it is washed by the sea, thirteen hundred stades. This island is intersected by many artificial canals and includes the fairest land in Egypt. For since it is alluvial soil and well watered, it produces many crops of every kind, inasmuch as the river by its annual rise regularly deposits on it fresh slime, and the inhabitants easily irrigate its whole area by means of a contrivance which was invented by Archimedes of Syracuse and is called, after its shape, a screw.

Since the Nile has a gentle current, carries down a great quantity of all kinds of earth, and, furthermore, gathers in stagnant pools in low places, marshes are formed which abound in every kind of plant. For tubers of every flavour grow in them and fruits and vegetables which grow on stalks, of a nature peculiar to the country, supplying an abundance sufficient to render the poor and the sick among the inhabitants self-sustaining. For not only do they afford a varied diet, ready at hand and abundant for all who need it, but they also furnish not a few of the other things which contribute to the necessities of life; the lotus, for instance, grows in great profusion, and from it the Egyptians make a bread which is able to satisfy the physical needs of the body, and the *ciborium,* which is found in great abundance, bears what is called the "Egyptian" bean.[*Nelumbium speciosum*] There are also many kinds of trees, of which that called *persea,* [*Mimusops Schimperi*] which was introduced from Ethiopia by the Persians when Cambyses conquered those regions, has an unusually sweet fruit, while of the fig-mulberry [*Ficus Sycamorus*] trees one kind bears the black mulberry and another a fruit resembling the fig; and since the latter produces throughout almost the whole year, the result is that the poor have a ready source to turn to in their need. The fruit called the blackberry is picked at the time the river is receding and by reason of its natural sweetness is eaten as a dessert. The Egyptians also make a drink out of barley which they call *zythos,* [beer] the bouquet of which is not much inferior to that of wine. Into their lamps they pour for lighting purposes, not the oil of the olive, but a kind which is extracted from a plant and called *kiki.* [castor oil] Many other plants, capable of supplying men with the necessities of life, grow in Egypt in great abundance, but it would be a long task to tell about them.

**35.** As for animals, the Nile breeds many of peculiar form, and two which surpass the others, the crocodile and what is called the "horse." [hippopotamus] Of these animals the crocodile grows to be the largest from the smallest beginning, since this animal lays eggs about the size of those of a goose, but after the young is hatched it grows to be as long as sixteen cubits. It is as long-lived as man, and has no tongue. The body of the animal is wondrously protected by nature; for its skin is covered all over with scales and is remarkably hard, and there are many teeth in both jaws, two being tusks, much larger than the rest. It devours the flesh not only of men but also of any land animal which approaches the river. The bites which it makes are huge and severe and it lacerates terribly with its claws, and whatever part of the flesh it tears it renders altogether difficult to heal. In early times the Egyptians used to catch these beasts with hooks baited with the flesh of pigs, but since then they have hunted them sometimes with heavy nets, as they catch some kinds of fish, and sometimes from their boats with iron spears which they strike repeatedly into the head. The multitude of them in the river and the adjacent marshes is beyond telling, since they are prolific and are seldom slain by the inhabitants; for it is the custom of most of the natives of Egypt to worship the crocodile as a god, while for foreigners there is no profit whatsoever in the hunting of them since their flesh is not edible. But against this multitude's increasing and menacing the inhabitants nature has devised a great help; for the animal called the *ichneumon,* which is about the size of a small dog, goes about breaking the eggs of the crocodiles, since the animal lays them on the banks of the river, and, what is most astonishing of all, without eating them or profiting in any way it continually performs a service which, in a sense, has been prescribed by nature and forced upon the animal for the benefit of men.

The animal called the "horse " is not less than five cubits high, and is four-footed and cloven-hoofed like the ox; it has tusks larger than those of the wild boar, three on each side, and ears and tail and a cry somewhat like those of the horse; but the trunk of its body, as a whole, is not unlike that of the elephant, and its skin is the toughest of almost any beast's. Being a river and land animal, it spends the day in the streams exercising in the deep water, while at night it forages about the countryside on the grain and hay, so that, if this animal were prolific and reproduced each year, it would entirely destroy the farms of Egypt. But even it is caught by the united work of many men who strike it with iron spears; for whenever it appears they converge their boats upon it, and gathering about it wound it repeatedly with a kind of chisel fitted with iron barbs, and then, fastening the end of a rope of tow to one of them which has become imbedded in the animal, they let it go until it dies from loss of blood. Its meat is tough and hard to digest and none of its inward parts is edible, neither the viscera nor the intestines.

**36.** Beside the beasts above mentioned the Nile contains every variety of fish and in numbers beyond belief; for it supplies the natives not only with abundant subsistence from the fish freshly caught, but it also yields an unfailing multitude for salting. Speaking generally, we may say that the Nile surpasses all the rivers of the inhabited world in its benefactions to mankind., for, beginning to rise at the summer solstice, it increases in volume until the autumnal equinox, and, since it is bringing down fresh mud all the time, it soaks both the fallow land and the seed land as well as the orchard land for so long a time as the farmers may wish. Since the water comes with a gentle flow, they easily divert the river from their fields by small dams of earth, and then, by cutting these, as easily let the river in again upon the land whenever they think this to be advantageous. In general the Nile contributes so greatly to the lightening of labour as well as to the profit of the inhabitants, that the majority of the farmers, as they begin work upon the areas of the land which are becoming dry, merely scatter their seed, turn their herds and flocks in on the fields, and after they have used these for trampling the seed in return after four or five months to harvest it; while some, applying light ploughs to the land, turn over no more than the surface of the soil after its wetting and then gather great heaps of grain without much expense or exertion. Generally speaking, every kind of field labour among other peoples entails great expense and toil, but among the Egyptians alone is the harvest gathered in with very slight outlay of money and labour. Also the land planted with the vine, being irrigated as are the other fields, yields an abundant supply of wine to the natives. Those who allow the land, after it has been inundated, to lie uncultivated and give it over to the flocks to graze upon, are rewarded with flocks which, because of the rich pasturage, lamb twice and are twice shorn every year.

The rise of the Nile is a phenomenon which appears wonderful enough to those who have witnessed it, but to those who have only heard of it, quite incredible. For while all other rivers begin to fall at the summer solstice and grow steadily lower and lower during the course of the following summer, this one alone begins to rise at that time and increases so greatly in volume day by day that it finally overflows practically all Egypt. And in like manner it afterwards follows precisely the opposite course and for an equal length of time gradually falls each day, until it has returned to its former level. And since the land is a level plain, while the cities and villages, as well as the farm-houses, lie on artificial mounds, the scene comes to resemble the Cyclades Islands. The wild land animals for the larger part are cut off by the river and perish in its waters, but a few escape by fleeing to higher ground; the herds and flocks, however, are maintained at the time of the flood in the villages and farm-houses, where fodder is stored up for them in advance. The masses of the people, being relieved of their labours during the entire time of the inundation, turn to recreation, feasting all the while and enjoying without hindrance every device of pleasure. And because of the anxiety occasioned by the rise of the river the kings have constructed a Nilometer at Memphis, where those who are charged with the administration of it accurately measure the rise and despatch messages to the cities, and inform them exactly how many cubits or fingers the river has risen and when it has commenced to fall. In this manner the entire nation, when it has learned that the river has ceased rising and begun to fall, is relieved of its anxiety, while at the same time all immediately know in advance how large the next harvest will be, since the Egyptians have kept an accurate record of their observations of this kind over a long period of terms.

**37.** Since there is great difficulty in explaining the swelling of the river, many philosophers and historians have undertaken to set forth the causes of it; regarding this we shall speak summarily, in order that we may neither make our digression too long nor fail to record that which all men are curious to know. For on the general subject of the rise of the Nile and its sources, as well as on the manner in which it reaches the sea and the other points in which this, the largest river of the inhabited world, differs from all others, some historians have actually not ventured to say a single word, although wont now and then to expatiate at length on some winter torrent or other, while others have undertaken to speak on these points of inquiry, but have strayed far from the truth. Hellanicus and Cadmus, for instance, as well as Hecataeus and all the writers like them, belonging as they do one and all to the early school, turned to the answers offered by the myths; Herodotus, who was a curious inquirer if ever a man was, and widely acquainted with history, undertook, it is true, to give an explanation of the matter, but is now found to have followed contradictory guesses; Xenophon and Thucydides, who are praised for the accuracy of their histories, completely refrained in their writings from any mention of the regions about Egypt; and Ephorus and Theopompus, who of all writers paid most attention to these matters, hit upon the truth the least. The error on the part of all these writers was due, not to their negligence, but to the peculiar character of the country. For from earliest times until Ptolemy who was called Philadelphus, not only did no Greeks ever cross over into Ethiopia, but none ascended even as far as the boundaries of Egypt; to such an extent were all these regions inhospitable to foreigners and altogether dangerous; but after this king had made an expedition into Ethiopia with an army of Greeks, being the first to do so, the facts about that country from that time forth have been more accurately learned.

Such, then, were the reasons for the ignorance of the earlier historians; and as for the sources of the Nile and the region where the stream arises, not a man, down to the time of the writing of this history, has ever affirmed that he has seen them, or reported from hearsay an account received from any who have maintained that they have seen them. The question, therefore, resolves itself into a matter of guesswork and plausible conjecture; and when, for instance, the priests of Egypt assert that the Nile has its origin in the ocean which surrounds the inhabited world, there is nothing sound in what they say, and they are merely solving one perplexity by substituting another, and advancing as proof an explanation which itself stands much in need of proof. On the other hand, those Trogodytes, known as the Bolgii, who migrated from the interior because of the heat, say that there are certain phenomena connected with those regions, from which a man might reason that the body of the Nile is gathered from many sources which converge upon a single place, and that this is the reason for its being the most fertile of all known rivers. But the inhabitants of the country about the island called Meroë, with whom a man would be most likely to agree, since they are far removed from the art of finding reasons in accordance with what is plausible and dwell nearest the regions under discussion, are so far from saying anything accurate about these problems that they even call the river Astapus, which means, when translated into Greek, "Water from Darkness."

# Book I

This people, then, have given the Nile a name which accords with the want of any first-hand information about those regions and with their own ignorance of them; but in our opinion the explanation nearest the truth is the one which is farthest from pure assumption. I am not unaware that Herodotus, when distinguishing between the Libya which lies to the east and that which lies to the west of this river, attributes to the Libyans known as the Nasamones the exact observation of the stream, and says that the Nile rises in a certain lake and then flows through the land of Ethiopia for a distance beyond telling; and yet assuredly no hasty assent should be given to the statements either of Libyans, even though they may have spoken truthfully, or of the historian when what he says does not admit of proof.

**38.** Now that we have discussed the sources and course of the Nile we shall endeavour to set forth the causes of its swelling. Thales, who is called one of the seven wise men, says that when the etesian [esesian] winds blow against the mouths of the river they hinder the flow of the water into the sea, and that this is the reason why it rises and overflows Egypt, which is low and a level plain. But this explanation, plausible as it appears, may easily be shown to be false. For if what he said were true, all the rivers whose mouths face the etesian winds would rise in a similar way; but since this is the case nowhere in the inhabited world the true cause of the swelling must be sought elsewhere. Anaxagoras the physical philosopher has declared that the cause of the rising is the melting snow in Ethiopia, and the poet Euripides, a pupil of his, is in agreement with him. At least he writes:

> He quit Nile's waters, fairest that gush from earth,
> The Nile which, drawn from Ethiop land, the black
> Man's home, flows with full flood when melts the snow.

But the fact is that this statement also requires but a brief refutation, since it is clear to everyone that the excessive heat makes it impossible that any snow should fall in Ethiopia; for, speaking generally, in those regions there is no frost or cold or any sign whatsoever of winter, and this is especially true at the time of the rising of the Nile. And even if a man should admit the existence of great quantities of snow in the regions beyond Ethiopia, the falsity of the statement is still shown by this fact: every river which flows out of snow gives out cool breezes, as is generally agreed, and thickens the air about it; but the Nile is the only river about which no clouds form, and where no cool breezes rise and the air is not thickened.

Herodotus says that the size of the Nile at its swelling is its natural one, but that as the sun travels over Libya in the winter it draws up to itself from the Nile a great amount of moisture, and this is the reason why at that season the river becomes smaller than its natural size; but at the beginning of summer, when the sun turns back in its course towards the north, it dries out and thus reduces the level of both the rivers of Greece and those of every other land whose geographical position is like that of Greece. Consequently there is no occasion for surprise, he says, in the phenomenon of the Nile; for, as a matter of fact, it does not increase in volume in the hot season and then fall in the winter, for the reason just given. Now the answer to be made to this explanation also is that it would follow that, if the sun drew moisture to itself from the Nile in the winter, it would also take some moisture from all the other rivers of Libya and reduce the flow of their waters. But since nowhere in Libya is anything like this to be seen taking place, it is clear that the historian is caught inventing an explanation; for the fact is that the rivers of Greece increase in winter, not because the sun is farther away, but by reason of the enormous rainfall.

**39.** Democritus of Abdera says that it is not the regions of the south that are covered with snow, as Euripides and Anaxagoras have asserted, but only those of the north, and that this is evident to everyone. The great quantities of heaped-up snow in the northern regions still remain frozen until about the time of the winter solstice, but when in summer its solid masses are broken up by the heat, a great melting sets up, and this brings about the formation of many thick clouds in the higher altitudes, since the vapour rises upwards in large quantities. These clouds are then driven by the etesian winds until they strike the highest mountains in the whole earth, which, he says, are those of Ethiopia; then by their violent impact upon these peaks, lofty as they are, they cause torrential rains which swell the river, to the greatest extent at the season of the etesian winds. But it is easy for anyone to refute this explanation also, if he will but note with precision the time when the increase of the river takes place; for the Nile begins to swell at the summer solstice, when the etesian winds are not yet blowing, and commences to fall after the autumnal equinox, when the same winds have long since ceased. Whenever, therefore, the precise knowledge derived from experience prevails over the plausibility of mere argumentation, while we should recognise the man's ingenuity, yet no credence should be given to his statements. Indeed, I pass over the further fact that the etesian winds can be seen to blow just as much from the west as from the north; since Borean and Aparctian [North winds] winds are not the only winds which are called etesian, but also the Argestean, which blow from the direction of the sun's summer setting. Also the statement that by general agreement the highest mountains are those of Ethiopia is not only advanced without any proof, but it does not possess, either, the credibility which is accorded to facts established by observation.

Ephorus, who presents the most recent explanation, endeavours to adduce a plausible argument, but, as may be seen, by no means arrives at the truth. For he says that all Egypt, being alluvial soil and spongy, and in nature like pumice-stone, is full of large and continuous cracks, through which it takes up a great amount of water; this it retains within itself during the winter season, but in the summer season it pours this out from itself everywhere like sweat, as it were, and by means of this exudation it causes the flood of the river. But this historian, as it appears to us, has not only never personally observed the nature of the country in Egypt, but has not even inquired with any care about it of those who are acquainted with the character of this land. For in the first place, if the Nile derived its increase from Egypt itself, it would then not experience a flood in its upper stretches, where it flow's through a stony and solid country; yet, as a matter of fact, it floods while flowing over a course of more than six thousand stades through Ethiopia before ever it touches Egypt. Secondly, if the stream of the Nile were, on the one hand, lower than the rifts in the alluvial soil, the cracks would then be on the surface and so great an amount of water could not possibly remain in them; and if, on the other hand, the river occupied a higher level than the rifts, there could not possibly be a flow of water from the lower hollows to the higher surface.

In general, can any man think it possible that the exudations from rifts in the ground should produce so great an increase in the waters of the river that practically all Egypt is inundated by it! For I pass over the false statements of Ephorus about the ground being alluvial and the water being stored up in the rifts, since the refutation of them is manifest. For instance, the Meander river in Asia has laid down a great amount of alluvial land, yet not a single one of the phenomena attending the flooding of the Nile is to be seen in its case. And like the Meander the river in Acarnania known as the Acheloüs, and the Cephisus in Boeotia, which flows out of Phocis, have built up not a little land, and in the case of both there is clear proof that the historian's statements are erroneous. However, under no circumstances would any man look for strict accuracy in Ephorus, when he sees that in many matters he has paid little regard to the truth.

**40.** Certain of the wise men in Memphis have undertaken to advance an explanation of the flooding, which is incapable of disproof rather than credible, and yet it is accepted by many. They divide the earth into three parts, and say that one part is that which forms our inhabited world, that the second is exactly opposed to these regions in its seasons, and that the third lies between these two but is uninhabited by reason of the heat. Now if the Nile rose in the winter, it would be clear that it was receiving its additional waters from our zone because of the heavy rains which fall with us in that season especially; but since, on the contrary, its flood occurs in the summer, it is probable that in the regions opposite to us the winter storms are being produced and that the surplus waters of those distant regions flow into our inhabited world. And it is for this reason that no man can journey to the sources of the Nile, because the river flows from the opposite zone through the uninhabited one. A further witness to this is the excessive sweetness of the water of the Nile; for in the course of the river through the torrid zone it is tempered by the heat, and that is the reason for its being the sweetest of all rivers, inasmuch as by the law of nature that which is fiery always sweetens what is wet.

But this explanation admits of an obvious rebuttal, for plainly it is quite impossible for a river to flow uphill into our inhabited world from the inhabited world opposite to ours, especially if one holds to the theory that the earth is shaped like a sphere. And indeed, if any man makes bold to do violence, by means of mere words, to facts established by observation, Nature at least will in no wise yield to him. For, in general, such men think that, by introducing a proposition incapable of being disproved and placing the uninhabited region between the two inhabited ones, they will in this way avoid all precise refutations of their argument; but the proper course for such as take a firm position on any matter is either to adduce the observed facts as evidence or to find their proofs in statements which have been agreed upon at the outset. But how can the Nile be the only river which flows from that inhabited world to our parts? For it is reasonable to suppose that other rivers as well are to be found there, just as there are many among us. Moreover, the cause which they advance for the sweetness of the water is altogether absurd. For if the river were sweetened by being tempered by the heat, it would not be so productive as it is of life, nor contain so many kinds of fishes and animals; for all water upon being changed by the fiery element is quite incapable of generating life. Therefore, since by the "tempering" process which they introduce they entirely change the real nature of the Nile, the causes which they advance for its flooding must be considered false.

**41.** Oenopides of Chios says that in the summer the waters under the earth are cold, but in the winter, on the contrary, warm; and that this may be clearly observed in deep wells, for in midwinter their water is least cold, while in the hottest weather the coldest water is drawn up from them. Consequently it is reasonable that the Nile should be small and should diminish in the winter, since the heat in the earth consumes the larger part of the moisture and there are no rains in Egypt; while in the summer, since there is no longer any consumption of the moisture down in the depths of the earth, the natural flow of the river is increased without hindrance. But the answer to be given to this explanation also is that there are many rivers in Libya, whose mouths are situated like those of the Nile and whose courses are much the same, and yet they do not rise in the same manner as the Nile; on the contrary, flooding as they do in the winter and receding in the summer, they refute the false statement of any man who tries to overcome the truth with specious arguments.

The nearest approach to the truth has been made by Agatharchides of Cnidus. His explanation is as follows: Every year continuous rains fall in the mountains of Ethiopia from the summer solstice to the autumnal equinox; and so it is entirely reasonable that the Nile should diminish in the winter when it derives its natural supply of water solely from its sources, but should increase its volume in the summer on account of the rains which pour into it. And just because no one up to this time has been able to set forth the causes of the origin of the flood waters, it is not proper, he urges, that his personal explanation be rejected; for nature presents many contradictory phenomena, the exact causes of which are beyond the power of mankind to discover. As to his own statement, he adds, testimony to its truth is furnished by what takes place in certain regions of Asia. For on the borders of Scythia which abut upon the Caucasus mountains, annually, after the winter is over, exceptionally heavy snowstorms occur over many consecutive days; in the northern parts of India at certain seasons hailstones come beating down which in size and quantity surpass belief; about the Hydaspes river continuous rains fall at the opening of summer; and in Ethiopia, likewise, the same thing occurs some days later, this climatical condition, in its regular recurrence, always causing storms in the neighbouring regions. He argues, it is nothing surprising if in Ethiopia as well, which lies above Egypt, continuous rains in the mountains, beating down during the summer, swell the river, especially since the plain fact itself is witnessed to by the barbarians who inhabit those regions. And if what has been said is of a nature opposite to what occurs among us, it should not be disbelieved on that score; for the south wind, for example, with us is accompanied by stormy weather, but in Ethiopia by clear skies, and in Europe the north winds are violent, but in that land they are gentle and light.

With regard, then, to the flooding of the Nile, though we are able to answer with more varied arguments all who have offered explanations of it, we shall rest

# Book I

content with what has been said, in order that we may not overstep the principle of brevity which we resolved upon at the beginning. And since we have divided this Book into two parts because of its length, inasmuch as we are aiming at due proportion in our account, at this point we shall close the first portion of our history, and in the second we shall set forth the facts in the history of Egypt which come next in order, beginning with the account of the former kings of Egypt and of the earliest manner of life among the Egyptians.

## PART TWO OF THE FIRST BOOK

**42.** The First Book of Diodorus being divided because of its length into two volumes, the first contains the preface to the whole treatise and the accounts given by the Egyptians of the genesis of the world and the first forming of the universe; then he tells of the gods who founded cities in Egypt and named them after themselves, of the first men and the earliest manner of life, of the honour paid to the immortals and the building of their temples to them, then of the topography of Egypt and the marvels related about the river Nile, and also of the causes of its flooding and the opinions thereupon of the historians and the philosophers as well as the refutation of each writer. In this volume we shall discuss the topics which come next in order after the foregoing. We shall begin with the first kings of Egypt and set forth their individual deeds down to King Amasis, [569-526] after we have first described in summary fashion the most ancient manner of life in Egypt.

**43.** As for their means of living in primitive times, the Egyptians, they say, in the earliest period got their food from herbs and the stalks and roots of the plants which grew in the marshes, making trial of each one of them by tasting it, and the first one eaten by them and the most favoured was that called Agrostis, [dog's tooth grass] because it excelled the others in sweetness and supplied sufficient nutriment for the human body; for they observed that this plant was attractive to the cattle and quickly increased their bulk. Because of this fact the natives, in remembrance of the usefulness of this plant, to this day, when approaching the gods, hold some of it in their hands as they pray to them; for they believe that man is a creature of swamp and marsh, basing this conclusion on the smoothness of his skin and his physical constitution, as well as on the fact that he requires a wet rather than a dry diet. A second way by which the Egyptians subsisted was, they say, by the eating of fish, of which the river provided a great abundance, especially at the time when it receded after its flood and dried up. They also ate the flesh of some of the pasturing animals, using for clothing the skins of the beasts that were eaten, and their dwellings they built out of reeds. Traces of these customs still remain among the herdsmen of Egypt, all of whom, they say, have no other dwelling up to this time than one of reeds, considering that with this they are well enough provided for. After subsisting in this manner over a long period of time they finally turned to the edible fruits of the earth, among which may be included the bread made from the lotus. The discovery of these is attributed by some to Isis, but by others to one of their early kings called Menas. The priests, however, have the story that the discoverer of the branches of learning and of the arts was Hermes, but that it was their kings who discovered such things as are necessary for existence; and that this was the reason why the kingship in early times was bestowed, not upon the sons of their former rulers, but upon such as conferred the greatest and most numerous benefits upon the peoples, whether it be that the inhabitants in this way sought to provoke their kings to useful service for the benefit of all, or that they have in very truth received an account to this effect in their sacred writings.

## On the first kings of Egypt and their deeds (*ch. 44 ff.*).

**44.** Some of them give the story that at first gods and heroes ruled Egypt for a little less than eighteen thousand years, the last of the gods to rule being Horus, the son of Isis; and mortals have been kings over their country, they say, for a little less than five thousand years down to the One Hundred and Eightieth Olympiad, [60-56] the time when we visited Egypt and the king was Ptolemy, who took the name of The New Dionysus. For most of this period the rule was held by native kings, and for a small pari of it by Ethiopians, Persians, and Macedonians. Now four Ethiopians held the throne, not consecutively but with intervals between, for a little less than thirty-six years in all; and the Persians, after their king Cambyses had subdued the nation by arms, ruled for one hundred and thirty-five years, including the periods of revolt on the part of the Egyptians which they raised because they were unable to endure the harshness of their dominion and their lack of respect for the native gods. Last of all the Macedonians and their dynasty held rule for two hundred and seventy-six years. For the rest of the time all the kings of the land were natives, four hundred and seventy of them being men and five women. About all of them the priests had records which were regularly handed down in their sacred books to each successive priest from early times, giving the stature of each of the former kings, a description of his character, and what he had done during his reign; as for us, however, it would be a long task to write of each of them severally, and superfluous also, seeing that most of the material included is of no profit. Consequently we shall undertake to recount briefly only the most important of the facts which deserve a place in history.

**45.** After the gods the first king of Egypt, according to the priests, was Menas, who taught the people to worship gods and offer sacrifices, and also to supply themselves with tables and couches and to use costly bedding, and, in a word, introduced luxury and an extravagant manner of life. For this reason when, many generations later, Tnephachthus, the father of Bocchoris the wise, was king and, while on a campaign in Arabia, ran short of supplies because the country was desert and rough, we are told that he was obliged to go without food for one day and then to live on quite simple fare at the home of some ordinary folk in private station, and that he, enjoying the experience exceedingly, denounced luxury and pronounced a curse on the king who had first taught the people their extravagant way of living; and so deeply did he take to heart the change which had taken place in the people's habits of eating, drinking, and sleeping, that he inscribed his curse in hieroglyphs on the temple of Zeus in Thebes; and this, in fact, appears to be the chief reason why the fame of Menas and his honours did not persist into later ages. And it is said that the descendants of this king, fifty-two in number all told, ruled in unbroken succession more than a thousand and forty years, but that in their reigns nothing occurred that was worthy of record.

Subsequently, when Busiris became king and his descendants in turn, eight in number, the last of the line, who bore the same name as the first, founded, they say, the city which the Egyptians call Diospolis [City of Zeus] the Great, though the Greeks call it Thebes. Now the circuit of it he made one hundred and forty stades, and he adorned it in marvellous fashion with great buildings and remarkable temples and dedicatory monuments of every other kind; in the same way he caused the houses of private citizens to be constructed in some cases four stories high, in other five, and in general made it the most prosperous city, not only of Egypt, but of the whole world. And since, by reason of the city's pre-eminent wealth and power, its fame has been spread abroad to every region, even the poet, we are told, has mentioned it when he says:

> Nay, not for all the wealth
> Of Thebes in Egypt, where in ev'ry hall
> There lieth treasure vast; a hundred are
> Her gates, and warriors by each issue forth
> Two hundred, each of them with car and steeds.

Some, however, tell us that it was not one hundred "gates" (*pulai*) which the city had, but rather many great propylaea in front of its temples, and that it was from these that the title "hundred-gated" was given it, that is, "having many gateways." Yet twenty thousand chariots did in truth, we are told, pass out from it to war; for there were once scattered along the river from Memphis to the Thebes which is over against Libya one hundred post-stations, each one having accommodation for two hundred horses, whose foundations are pointed out even to this day.

**46.** Not only this king, we have been informed, but also many of the later rulers devoted their attention to the development of the city. For no city under the sun has ever been so adorned by votive offerings, made of silver and gold and ivory, in such number and of such size, by such a multitude of colossal statues, and, finally, by obelisks made of single blocks of stone. Of four temples erected there the oldest is a source of wonder for both its beauty and size, having a circuit of thirteen stades, a height of forty-five cubits, and walls twenty-four feet thick. In keeping with this magnificence was also the embellishment of the votive offerings within the circuit wall, marvellous for the money spent upon it and exquisitely wrought as to workmanship. Now the buildings of the temple survived down to rather recent times, but the silver and gold and costly works of ivory and rare stone were carried off by the Persians when Cambyses burned the temples of Egypt; and it was at this time, they say, that the Persians, by transferring all this wealth to Asia and taking artisans along from Egypt, constructed their famous palaces in Persepolis and Susa and throughout Media. So great was the wealth of Egypt at that period, they declare, that from the remnants left in the course of the sack and after the burning the treasure which was collected little by little was found to be worth more than three hundred talents of gold and no less than two thousand three hundred talents of silver. There are also in this city, they say, remarkable tombs of the early kings and of their successors, which leave to those who aspire to similar magnificence no opportunity to outdo them.

Now the priests said that in their records they find forty-seven tombs of kings; but down to the time of Ptolemy son of Lagus, [323-383] they say, only fifteen remained, most of which had been destroyed at the time we visited those regions, in the One Hundred and Eightieth Olympiad. [60-56] Not only do the priests of Egypt give these facts from their records, but many also of the Greeks who visited Thebes in the time of Ptolemy son of Lagus and composed histories of Egypt, one of whom was Hecataeus, agree with what we have said.

**47.** Ten stades from the first tombs, he says, in which, according to tradition, are buried the concubines of Zeus, stands a monument of the king known as Osymandyas. At its entrance there is a pylon, constructed of variegated stone, two plethra in breadth and forty-five cubits high; passing through this one enters a rectangular peristyle, built of stone, four plethra long on each side; it is supported, in place of pillars, by monolithic figures sixteen cubits high, wrought in the ancient manner as to shape; and the entire ceiling, which is two fathoms wide, consists of a single stone, which is highly decorated with stars on a blue field. Beyond this peristyle there is yet another entrance and pylon, in every respect like the one mentioned before, save that it is more richly wrought with every manner of relief; beside the entrance are three statues, each of a single block of black stone from Syene, of which one, that is seated, is the largest of any in Egypt, the foot measuring over seven cubits, while the other two at the knees of this, the one on the right and the other on the left, daughter and mother respectively, are smaller than the one first mentioned. And it is not merely for its size that this work merits approbation, but it is also marvellous by reason of its artistic quality and excellent because of the nature of the stone, since in a block of so great a size there is not a single crack or blemish to be seen. The inscription upon it runs: "King of Kings am I, Osymandyas. If anyone would know how great I am and where I lie, let him surpass one of my works." There is also another statue of his mother standing alone, a monolith twenty cubits high, and it has three diadems on its head, signifying that she was both daughter and wife and mother of a king.

Beyond the pylon, he says, there is a peristyle more remarkable than the former one; in it there are all manner of reliefs depicting the war which the king waged against those Bactrians who had revolted; against these he had made a campaign with four hundred thousand foot-soldiers and twenty thousand cavalry, the whole army having been divided into four divisions, all of which were under the command of sons of the king.

**48.** On the first wall the king, he says, is represented in the act of besieging a walled city which is surrounded by a river, and of leading the attack against opposing troops; he is accompanied by a lion, which is aiding him with terrifying effect. Of those who have explained the scene some have said that in very truth a tame lion which the king kept accompanied him in the perils of battle and put the enemy to rout by his fierce onset; but others have maintained that the king, who was exceedingly brave and desirous of praising himself in a vulgar way, was trying to portray his own bold spirit in the figure of the lion. On the second wall, he adds, are wrought the captives as they are being led away by the king; they are without their privates and their hands, which apparently signifies that they were effeminate in spirit and had no hands when it came to the dread business of warfare. The third wall carries every manner of relief and excellent paintings, which portray the king performing a sacrifice of oxen and celebrating a triumph after the war. In the centre of the peristyle there had been constructed of the most beautiful stone an altar, open to the sky, both excellent in its workmanship and marvellous because of its size. By the last wall are two monolithic seated statues, twenty-seven cubits high, beside which are set three entrances from the peristyle; and by way of these entrances one comes into a hall whose roof was supported by pillars, constructed in the style of an Odeum, and measuring two plethra on each side. In this hall there are many wooden statues representing parties in litigation, whose eyes are fixed upon the judges who decide their cases; and these, in turn, are shown in relief on one of the walls, to the number of thirty and without any hands, and in their midst the chief justice, with a figure of Truth hanging from his neck and holding his eyes closed, and at his side a great number of books. And these figures show by their attitude that the judges shall receive no gift and that the chief justice shall have his eyes upon the truth alone.

**49.** Next to these courts, he says, is an ambulatory crowded with buildings of every kind, in which there are representations of the foods that are sweetest to the taste, of every variety. Here are to be found reliefs in which the king, adorned in colours, is represented as offering to the god the gold and silver which he received each year from the silver and gold mines of all Egypt; and an inscription below gives also the total amount, which, summed up according to its value in silver, is thirty-two million minas. Next comes the sacred library, which bears the inscription "Healing-place of the Soul," and contiguous to this building are statues of all the gods of Egypt, to each of whom the king in like manner makes the offering appropriate to him, as though he were submitting proof before Osiris and his assessors in the underworld that to the end of his days he had lived a life of piety and justice towards both men and gods. Next to the library and separated from it by a party wall is an exquisitely constructed hall, which contains a table with couches for twenty and statues of Zeus and Hera as well as of the king; here, it would seem, the body of the king is also buried. In a circle about this building are many chambers which contain excellent paintings of all the animals which are held sacred in Egypt. There is an ascent leading through these chambers to the tomb as a whole. At the top of this ascent there is a circular border of gold crowning the monument, three hundred and sixty-five cubits in circumference and one cubit thick; upon this the days of the year are inscribed, one in each cubit of length, and by each day the risings and settings of the stars as nature ordains them and the signs indicating the effects which the Egyptian astrologers hold that they produce. This border, they said, had been plundered by Cambyses and the Persians when he conquered Egypt.

Such, they say, was the tomb of Osymandyas the king, which is considered far to have excelled all others, not only in the amount of money lavished upon it, but also in the ingenuity shown by the artificers.

**50.** The Thebans say that they are the earliest of all men and the first people among whom philosophy and the exact science of the stars were discovered, since their country enables them to observe more distinctly than others the risings and settings of the stars. Peculiar to them also is their ordering of the months and years. For they do not reckon the days by the moon, but by the sun, making their month of thirty days, and they add five and a quarter days to the twelve months and in this way fill out the cycle of the year. But they do not intercalate months or subtract days, as most of the Greeks do. They appear to have made careful observations of the eclipses both of the sun and of the moon, and predict them, foretelling without error all the events which actually occur.

Of the descendants of this king, the eighth, known as Uchoreus, founded Memphis, the most renowned city of Egypt. For he chose the most favourable spot in all the land, where the Nile divides into several branches to form the "Delta," as it is called from its shape; and the result was that the city, excellently situated as it was at the gates of the Delta, continually controlled the commerce passing into upper Egypt. Now he gave the city a circumference of one hundred and fifty stades, and made it remarkably strong and adapted to its purpose by works of the following nature. Since the Nile flowed around the city and covered it at the time of inundation, he threw out a huge mound of earth on the south to serve as a barrier against the swelling of the river and also as a citadel against the attacks of enemies by land; and all around the other sides he dug a large and deep lake, which, by taking up the force of the river and occupying all the space about the city except where the mound had been thrown up, gave it remarkable strength. And so happily did the founder of the city reckon upon the suitableness of the site that practically all subsequent kings left Thebes and established both their palaces and official residences here. Consequently from this time Thebes began to wane and Memphis to increase, until the time of Alexander the king; for after he had founded the city on the sea which bears his name, all the kings of Egypt after him concentrated their interest on the development of it. Some adorned it with magnificent palaces, some with docks and harbours, and others with further notable dedications and buildings, to such an extent that it is generally reckoned the first or second city of the inhabited world. But a detailed description of this city we shall set forth in the appropriate period.

**51.** The founder of Memphis, after constructing the mound and the lake, erected a palace, which, while not inferior to those of other nations, yet was no match for the grandeur of design and love of the beautiful shown by the kings who preceded him. For the inhabitants of Egypt consider the period of this life to be of no account whatever, but place the greatest value on the time after death when they will be remembered for their virtue, and while they give the name of "lodgings" to the dwellings of the living, thus intimating that we dwell in them but a brief time, they call the tombs of the dead "eternal homes," since the dead spend endless eternity in Hades; consequently they give less thought to the furnishings of their houses, but on the manner of their burials they do not forgo any excess of zeal.

The aforementioned city was named, according to some, after the daughter of the king who founded it. They tell the story that she was loved by the river Nile, who had assumed the form of a bull, and gave birth to Egyptus, a man famous among the natives for his virtue, from whom the entire land received its name. For upon succeeding to the throne he showed himself to be a kindly king, just, and, in a word, upright in all matters; and so, since he was held by all to merit great approbation because of his goodwill, he received the honour mentioned.

Twelve generations after the king just named, Moeris succeeded to the throne of Egypt and built in Memphis itself the north propylaea, which far surpasses the others in magnificence, while ten schoeni [60 stades] above the city he excavated a lake which was remarkable for its utility and an undertaking of incredible magnitude. For its circumference, they say, is three thousand six hundred stades and its depth in most parts fifty fathoms; what man, accordingly, in trying to estimate the magnitude of the work, would not reasonably inquire how many myriads of men labouring for how many years were required for its completion? And as for the utility of this lake and its contribution to the welfare of all the inhabitants of Egypt, as well as for the ingenuity of the king, no man may praise them highly enough to do justice to the truth.

**52.** For since the Nile did not rise to a fixed height each year and yet the fruitfulness of the country depended on the constancy of the flood-level, he excavated the lake to receive the excess water, in order that the river might not, by an excessive volume of flow, immoderately flood the land and form marshes and pools, nor, by failing to rise to the proper height, ruin the harvests by the lack of water. He also dug a canal, eighty stades long and three plethra wide, from the river to the lake, and by this canal, sometimes turning the river into the lake and sometimes shutting it off again, he furnished the farmers with an opportune supply of water, opening and closing the entrance by a skilful device and yet at considerable expense; for it cost no less than fifty talents if a man wanted to open or close this work. The lake has continued to serve well the needs of the Egyptians down to our time, and bears the name of its builder, being called to this day the Lake of Moeris. Now the king in excavating it left a spot in the centre, where he built a tomb and two pyramids, a stade in height, one for himself and the other for his wife, on the tops of which he placed stone statues seated upon thrones, thinking that by these monuments he would leave behind him an imperishable commemoration of his good deeds. The income accruing from the fish taken from the lake he gave to his wife for her unguents and general embellishment, the value of the catch amounting to a talent of silver daily; for there are twenty-two different kinds of fish in the lake, they say, and they are caught in such abundance that the people engaged in salting them, though exceedingly many, can scarcely keep up with their task.

Now this is the account which the Egyptians give of Moeris.

**53.** Sesoösis, [Sesostris] they say, who became king seven generations later, performed more renowned and greater deeds than did any of his predecessors. And since, with regard to this king, not only are the Greek writers at variance with one another but also among the Egyptians the priests and the poets who sing his praises give conflicting stories, we for our part shall endeavour to give the most probable account and that which most nearly agrees with the monuments still standing in the land. Now at the birth of Sesoösis his father did a thing worthy of a great man and a king: Gathering together from over all Egypt the male children which had been born on the same day and assigning to them nurses and guardians, he prescribed the same training and education for them all, on the theory that those who had been reared in the closest companionship and had enjoyed the same frank relationship would be most loyal and as fellow-combatants in the wars most brave. He amply provided for their every need and then trained the youths by unremitting exercises and hardships; for no one of them was allowed to have anything to eat unless he had first run one hundred and eighty stades. Consequently upon attaining to manhood they were all veritable athletes of robustness of body, and in spirit qualified for leadership and endurance because of the training which they had received in the most excellent pursuits.

First of all Sesoösis, his companions also accompanying him, was sent by his father with an army into Arabia, where he was subjected to the laborious training of hunting wild animals and, after hardening himself to the privations of thirst and hunger, conquered the entire nation of the Arabs, which had never been enslaved before his day; and then, on being sent to the regions to the west, he subdued the larger part of Libya, though in years still no more than a youth. And when he ascended the throne upon the death of his father, being filled with confidence by reason of his earlier exploits he undertook to conquer the inhabited earth. There are those who say that he was urged to acquire empire over the whole world by his own daughter Athyrtis, who, according to some, was far more intelligent than any of her day and showed her father that the campaign would be an easy one, while according to others she had the gift of prophecy and knew beforehand, by means both of sacrifices and the practice of sleeping in temples, as well as from the signs which appear in the heavens, what would take place in the future. Some have also written that, at the birth of Sesoösis, his father had thought that Hephaestus had appeared to him in a dream and told him that the son who had been born would rule over the whole civilised world; and that for this reason, therefore, his father collected the children of the same age as his son and granted them a royal training, thus preparing them beforehand for an attack upon the whole world, and that his son, upon attaining manhood, trusting in the prediction of the god was led to undertake this campaign.

**54.** In preparation for this undertaking he first of all confirmed the goodwill of all the Egyptians towards himself, feeling it to be necessary, if he were to bring his plan to a successful end, that his soldiers on the campaign should be ready to die for their leaders, and that those left behind in their native lands should not rise in revolt. He therefore showed kindnesses to everyone by all means at his disposal, winning over some by presents of money, others by gifts of land, and others by remission of penalties, and the entire people he attached to himself by his friendly intercourse and kindly ways; for he set free unharmed everyone who was held for some crime against the king and cancelled the obligations of those who were in prison for debt, there being a great multitude in the gaols. And dividing the entire land into thirty-six parts which the Egyptians call nomes, he set over each a nomarch, who should superintend the collection of the royal revenues and administer all the affairs of his division. He then chose out the strongest of the men and formed an army worthy of the greatness of his undertaking; for he enlisted six hundred thousand foot-soldiers, twenty-four thousand cavalry, and twenty-seven thousand war chariots. In command of the several divisions of his troops he set his companions, who were by this time inured to warfare, had striven after a reputation for valour from their youth, and cherished with a brotherly love both their king and one another, the number of them being over seventeen hundred. And upon all these commanders he bestowed allotments of the best land in Egypt, in order that, enjoying sufficient income and lacking nothing, they might sedulously practise the art of war.

**55.** After he had made ready his army he marched first of all against the Ethiopians who dwell south of Egypt, and after conquering them he forced that people to pay a tribute in ebony, gold and the tusks of elephants. Then he sent out a fleet of four hundred ships into the Red Sea, [Persian Gulf & Indian Ocean] being the first Egyptian to build warships, and not only took possession of the islands in those waters, but also subdued the coast of the mainland as far as India, while he himself made his way by land with his army and subdued all Asia. Not only did he, in fact, visit the territory which was afterwards won by Alexander of Macedon, but also certain peoples into whose country Alexander did not cross. For he even passed over the river Ganges and visited all of India as far as the ocean, as well as the tribes of the Scythians as far as the river Tanais, which divides Europe from Asia; and it was at this time, they say, that some of the Egyptians, having been left behind near the Lake Maeotis, founded the nation of the Colchi. [Caucasus] And the proof which they offer of the Egyptian origin of this nation is the fact that the Colchi practise circumcision even as the Egyptians do, the custom continuing among the colonists sent out from Egypt as it also did in the case of the Jews. In the same way he brought all the rest of Asia into subjection as well as most of the Cyclades islands. And after he had crossed into Europe and was on his way through the whole length of Thrace he nearly lost his army through lack of food and the difficult nature of the land. Consequently he fixed the limits of his expedition in Thrace, and set up stelae in many parts of the regions which he had acquired; and these carried the following inscription in the Egyptian writing which is called "sacred": "This land the King of Kings and Lord of Lords, Sesoösis, subdued with his own arms." And he fashioned the stele with a representation, in case the enemy people were warlike, of the privy parts of a man, but in case they were abject and cowardly, of those of a woman, holding that the quality of the spirit of each people would be set forth most clearly to succeeding generations by the dominant member of the body. And in some places he also erected a stone statue of himself, armed with bow and arrows and a spear, in height four cubits and four palms, which was indeed his own stature. [7 feet] He dealt gently with all conquered peoples and, after concluding his campaign in nine years, commanded the nations to bring presents each year to Egypt according to their ability, while he himself, assembling a multitude of captives which has never been surpassed and a mass of other booty, returned to his country, having accomplished the greatest deeds of any king of Egypt to his day. All the temples of Egypt, moreover, he adorned with notable votive offerings and spoils, and honoured with gifts according to his merits every soldier who had distinguished himself for bravery. And in general, as a result of this campaign not only did the army, which had bravely shared in the deeds of the king and had gathered great wealth, make a brilliant homeward journey, but it also came to pass that all Egypt was filled to overflowing with benefits of every kind.

**56.** Sesoösis now relieved his peoples of the labours of war and granted to the comrades who had bravely shared in his deeds a care-free life in the enjoyment of the good things which they had won, while he himself, being ambitious for glory and intent upon everlasting fame, constructed works which were great and marvellous in their conception as well as in the lavishness with which their cost was provided, winning in this way immortal glory for himself and for the Egyptians security combined with ease for all time. For beginning with the gods first, he built in each city of Egypt a temple to the god who was held in special reverence by its inhabitants. On these labours he used no Egyptians, but constructed them all by the hands of his captives alone; and for this reason he placed an inscription on every temple to the effect that no native had toiled upon it. And it is said that the captives brought from Babylonia revolted from the king, being unable to endure the hardships entailed by his works; and they, seizing a strong position on the banks of the river, maintained a warfare against the Egyptians and ravaged the neighbouring territory, but finally, on being granted an amnesty, they established a colony on the spot, which they also named Babylon after their native land. For a similar reason, they say, the city of Troy likewise, which even to this day exists on the bank of the Nile, received its name: for Menelaus, on his voyage from Ilium with a great number of captives, crossed over into Egypt; and the Trojans, revolting from him, seized a certain place and maintained a warfare until he granted them safety and freedom, whereupon they founded a city, to which they gave the name of their native land. I am not unaware that regarding the cities named above Ctesias of Cnidus has given a different account, saying that some of those who had come into Egypt with Semiramis founded them, calling them after their native lands. But on such matters as these it is not easy to set forth the precise truth, and yet the disagreements among historians must be considered worthy of record, in order that the reader may be able to decide upon the truth without prejudice.

**57.** Now Sesoösis threw up many great mounds of earth and moved to them such cities as happened to be situated on ground that was not naturally elevated, in order that at the time of the flooding of the river both the inhabitants and their herds might have a safe place of retreat. And over the entire land from Memphis to the sea he dug frequent canals leading from the river, his purpose being that the people might carry out the harvesting of their crops quickly and easily, and that, through the constant intercourse of the peasants with one another, every district might enjoy both an easy livelihood and a great abundance of all things which minister to man's enjoyment. The greatest result of this work, however, was that he made the country secure and difficult of access against attacks by enemies; for practically all the best part of Egypt, which before this time had been easy of passage for horses and carts, has from that time on been very difficult for an enemy to invade by reason of the great number of canals leading from the river. He also fortified with a wall the side of Egypt which faces east, as a defence against inroads from Syria and Arabia; the wall extended through the desert from Pelusium to Heliopolis, and its length was some fifteen hundred stades. Moreover, he also built a ship of cedar wood, which was two hundred and eighty cubits long and plated on the exterior with gold and on the interior with silver. This ship he presented as a votive offering to the god who is held in special reverence in Thebes, as well as two obelisks of hard stone one hundred and twenty cubits high, upon which he inscribed the magnitude of his army, the multitude of his revenues, and the number of the peoples he had subdued; also in Memphis in the temples of Hephaestus he dedicated monolithic statues of himself and of his wife, thirty cubits high, and of his sons, twenty cubits high, the occasion of their erection being as follows. When Sesoösis had returned to Egypt after his great campaign and was tarrying at Pelusium, his brother, who was entertaining Sesoösis and his wife and children, plotted against them; for when they had fallen asleep after the drinking he piled great quantities of dry rushes, which he had kept in readiness for some time, around the tent in the night set them afire. When the fire suddenly blazed up, those who had been assigned to wait upon the king came to his aid in a churlish fashion, as would men heavy with wine, but Sesoösis, raising both hands to the heavens with a prayer to the gods for the preservation of his children and wife, dashed out safe through the flames. For this unexpected escape he honoured the rest of the gods with votive offerings, as stated above, and Hephaestus most of all, on the ground that it was by his intervention that he had been saved.

**58.** Although many great deeds have been credited to Sesoösis, his magnificence seems best to have been shown in the treatment which he accorded to the foreign potentates when he went forth from his palace. The kings whom he had allowed to continue their rule over the peoples which he had subdued and all others who had received from him the most important positions of command would present themselves in Egypt at specified times, bringing him gifts, and the king would welcome them and in all other matters show them honour and special preferment; but whenever he intended to visit a temple or city he would remove the horses from his four-horse chariot and in their place yoke the kings and other potentates, taking them four at a time, in this way showing to all men, as he thought, that, having conquered the mightiest of other kings and those most renowned for their excellence, he now had no one who could compete with him for the prize of excellence. This king is thought to have surpassed all former rulers in power and military exploits, and also in the magnitude and number of the votive offerings and public works which he built in Egypt. After a reign of thirty-three years he deliberately took his own life, his eyesight having failed him; and this act won for him the admiration not only of the priests of Egypt but of the other inhabitants as well, for it was thought that he had caused the end of his life to comport with the loftiness of spirit shown in his achievements.

So great became the fame of this king and so enduring through the ages that when, many generations later, Egypt fell under the power of the Persians and Darius, the father of Xerxes, was bent upon placing a statue of himself in Memphis before that of Sesoösis, the chief priest opposed it in a speech which he made in an assembly of the priests, to the effect that Darius had not yet surpassed the deeds of Sesoösis; and the king was far from being angered, but, on the contrary, being pleased at his frankness of speech, said that he would strive not to be found behind that ruler in any point when he had attained his years, and asked them to base their judgment upon the deeds of each at the same age, for that was the fairest test of their excellence.

As regards Sesoösis, then, we shall rest content with what has been said.

**59.** But his son, succeeding to the throne and assuming his father's appellation, did not accomplish a single thing in war or otherwise worthy of mention, though he did have a singular experience. He lost his sight, either because he shared in his father's bodily constitution or, as some fictitiously relate, because of his impiety towards the river, since once when caught in a storm upon it he had hurled a spear into the rushing current. Forced by this ill fortune to turn to the gods for aid, he strove over a long period to propitiate the deity by numerous sacrifices and honours, but received no consideration. But in the tenth year an oracular command was given to him to do honour to the god in Heliopolis and bathe his face in the urine of a woman who had never known any other man than her husband. Thereupon he began with his own wife and then made trial of many, but found not one that was chaste save a certain gardener's wife, whom he married as soon as he was recovered. All the other women he burned alive in a certain village to which the Egyptians because of this incident gave the name Holy Field; and to the god in Heliopolis, out of gratitude for his benefaction, he dedicated, in accordance with the injunction of the oracle, two monolithic obelisks, [One of these obelisks still stands, of red granite of Syene and 66 feet high. The largest obelisk in the world, that before the Lateran, is 100 feet high; the 150 feet of Diodorus seems a little too big.] eight cubits wide and one hundred high.

**60.** After this king a long line of successors on the throne accomplished no deed worth recording. But Amasis, who became king many generations later, ruled the masses of the people with great harshness; many he punished unjustly, great numbers he deprived of their possessions, and towards all his conduct was without exception contemptuous and arrogant. Now for a time his victims bore up under this, being unable in any way to protect themselves against those of greater power; but when Actisanes, the king of the Ethiopians, led an army against Amasis, their hatred seized the opportunity and most of the Egyptians revolted. As a consequence, since he was easily overcome, Egypt fell under the rule of the Ethiopians. But Actisanes carried his good fortune as a man should and conducted himself in a kindly manner towards his subjects. For instance, he had his own manner of dealing with thieves, neither putting to death such as were liable to that punishment, nor letting them go with no punishment at all; for after he had gathered together out of the whole land those who were charged with some crime and had held a thoroughly fair examination of their cases, he took all who had been judged guilty, and, cutting off their noses, settled them in a colony on the edge of the desert, founding the city which was called Rhinocolura [clipped nose] after the lot of its inhabitants.

This city, which lies on the border between Egypt and Syria not far from the sea-coast, is wanting in practically everything which is necessary for man's existence; for it is surrounded by land which is full of brine, while within the walls there is but a small supply of water from wells, and this is impure and very bitter to the taste. He settled them in this country in order that, in case they continued to practise their original manner of life, they might not prey upon innocent people, and also that they might not pass unrecognised as they mingled with the rest of mankind, and yet, despite the fact that they had been cast out into a desert country which lacked practically every useful thing, they contrived a way of living appropriate to the dearth about them, since nature forced them to devise every possible means to combat their destitution. For instance, by cutting down reeds in the neighbourhood and splitting them, they made long nets, which they set up along the beach for a distance of many stades and hunted quails; for these are driven in large coveys from the open sea, and in hunting them they caught a sufficient number to provide themselves with food.

**61.** After the death of this king the Egyptians regained the control of their government and placed on the throne a native king, Mendes, whom some call

# Book I

Marrus. So far as war is concerned this ruler did not accomplish anything at all, but he did build himself a tomb known as the Labyrinth, which was not so remarkable for its size as it was impossible to imitate in respect to its ingenious design; for a man who enters it cannot easily find his way out, unless he gets a guide who is thoroughly acquainted with the structure. Some say that Daedalus, visiting Egypt and admiring the skill shown in the building, also constructed for Minos, the king of Crete, a labyrinth like the one in Egypt, in which was kept, as the myth relates, the beast called Minotaur. However, the labyrinth in Crete has entirely disappeared, whether it be that some ruler razed it to the ground or that time effaced the work, but the one in Egypt has stood intact in its entire structure down to our lifetime.

**62.** After the death of this king there were no rulers for five generations, and then a man of obscure origin was chosen king, whom the Egyptians call Cetes, but who among the Greeks is thought to be that Proteus who lived at the time of the war about Ilium. Some tradition records that this Proteus was experienced in the knowledge of the winds and that he would change his body, sometimes into the form of different animals, sometimes into a tree or fire or something else, and it so happens that the account which the priests give of Cetes is in agreement with that tradition. For, according to the priests, from the close association which the king constantly maintained with the astrologers, he had gained experience in such matters, and from a custom which has been passed down among the kings of Egypt has arisen the myths current among the Greeks about the way Proteus changed his shape. For it was a practice among the rulers of Egypt to wear upon their heads the forepart of a lion, or bull, or snake as symbols of their rule; at times also trees or fire, and in some cases they even carried on their heads large bunches of fragrant herbs for incense, these last serving to enhance their comeliness and at the same time to fill all other men with fear and religious awe.

On the death of Proteus his son Remphis succeeded to the throne. This ruler spent his whole life looking after the revenues and amassing riches from every source, and because of his niggardly and miserly character spent nothing either on votive offerings to the gods or on benefactions to the inhabitants. Consequently, since he had been not so much a king as only an efficient steward, in the place of a fame based upon virtue he left a treasure larger than that of any king before him; for according to tradition he amassed some four hundred thousand talents of silver and gold.

### *On the construction of the pyramids which are listed among the seven wonders of the world (63 ff.).*

**63.** After Remphis died, kings succeeded to the throne for seven generations who were confirmed sluggards and devoted only to indulgence and luxury. Consequently, in the priestly records, no costly building of theirs nor any deed worthy of historical record is handed down in connection with them, except in the case of one ruler, Nileus, from whom the river came to be named the Nile, though formerly called Aegyptus. This ruler constructed a very great number of canals at opportune places and in many ways showed himself eager to increase the usefulness of the Nile, and therefore became the cause of the present appellation of the river.

The eighth king, Chemmis of Memphis, ruled fifty years and constructed the largest of the three pyramids, which are numbered among the seven wonders of the world. These pyramids, which are situated on the side of Egypt which is towards Libya, are one hundred and twenty stades from Memphis and forty-five from the Nile, and by the immensity of their structures and the skill shown in their execution they fill the beholder with wonder and astonishment. For the largest is in the form of a square and has a base length on each side of seven plethra and a height of over six plethra; it also gradually tapers to the top, where each side is six cubits long. [Including the facing, now almost entirely disappeared, the Great Pyramid was originally about 768 feet broad on the base and 482 feet high.] The entire construction is of hard stone, which is difficult to work but lasts for ever; for though no fewer than a thousand years have elapsed, as they say, to our lifetime, or, as some writers have it, more than three thousand four hundred, the stones remain to this day still preserving their original position and the entire structure un-decayed. It is said that the stone was conveyed over a great distance from Arabia and that the construction was effected by means of mounds, since cranes had not yet been invented at that time; and the most remarkable thing in the account is that, though the constructions were on such a great scale and the country round about them consists of nothing but sand, not a trace remains either of any mound or of the dressing of the stones, so that they do not have the appearance of being the slow handiwork of men but look like a sudden creation, as though they had been made by some god and set down bodily in the surrounding sand. Certain Egyptians would make a marvel out of these things, saying that, inasmuch as the mounds were built of salt and saltpetre, when the river was let in it melted them down and completely effaced them without the intervention of man's hand. However, there is not a word of truth in this, but the entire material for the mounds, raised as they were by the labour of many hands, was returned by the same means to the place from which it came; for three hundred and sixty thousand men, as they say, were employed on the undertaking, and the whole structure was scarcely completed in twenty years.

**64.** Upon the death of this king his brother Cephren succeeded to the throne and ruled fifty-six years; but some say that it was not the brother of Chemmis, but his son, named Chabryes, who took the throne. All writers, however, agree that it was the next ruler who, emulating the example of his predecessor, built the second pyramid, which was the equal of the one just mentioned in the skill displayed in its execution but far behind it in size, since its base length on each side is only a stade. An inscription on the larger pyramid gives the sum of money expended on it, since the writing sets forth that on vegetables and purgatives for the workmen there were paid out over sixteen hundred talents. The smaller bears no inscription but has steps cut into one side, and though the two kings built the pyramids to serve as their tombs, in the event neither of them was buried in them; for the multitudes, because of the hardships which they had endured in the building of them and the many cruel and violent acts of these kings, were filled with anger against those who had caused their sufferings and openly threatened to tear their bodies asunder and cast them in despite out of the tombs. Consequently each ruler when dying enjoined upon his kinsmen to bury his body secretly in an unmarked place.

After these rulers Mycerinus, to whom some give the name Mencherinus, a son of the builder of the first pyramid, became king. He undertook the construction of a third pyramid, but died before the entire structure had been completed. The base length of each side he made three plethra, and for fifteen courses he built the walls of black stone like that found about Thebes, but the rest of it he filled out with stone like that found in the other pyramids. In size this structure falls behind those mentioned above, but far surpasses them in the skill displayed in its execution and the great cost of the stone; and on the north side of the pyramid is an inscription stating that its builder was Mycerinus. This ruler, they say, out of indignation at the cruelty of his predecessors aspired to live an honourable life and one devoted to the welfare of his subjects; and he continually did many other things which might best help to evoke the goodwill of the people towards himself, and more especially, when he gave audiences, he spent a great amount of money, giving presents to such honest men as he thought had not fared in the courts of law as they deserved.

There are also three more pyramids, each of which is one plethrum long on each side and in general construction is like the others save in size; and these pyramids, they say, were built by the three kings named above for their wives.

It is generally agreed that these monuments far surpass all other constructions in Egypt, not only in their massiveness and cost but also in the skill displayed by their builders. And they say that the architects of the monuments are more deserving of admiration than the kings who furnished the means for their execution; for in bringing their plans to completion the former called upon their individual souls and their zeal for honour, but the latter only used the wealth which they had inherited and the grievous toil of other men. With regard to the pyramids there is no complete agreement among either the inhabitants of the country or the historians; for according to some the kings mentioned above were their builders, according to others they were different kings; for instance, it is said that Armaeus built the largest, Amosis the second, and Inaros the third. And this last pyramid, some say, is the tomb of the courtesan Rhodopis, for some of the nomarchs became her lovers, as the account goes, and out of their passion for her carried the building through to completion as a joint undertaking.

**65.** After the kings mentioned above Bocchoris succeeded to the throne, a man who was altogether contemptible in personal appearance but in sagacity far surpassed all former kings. Much later Egypt was ruled by Sabaco, [c.712-c799] who was by birth an Ethiopian and yet in piety and uprightness far surpassed his predecessors. A proof of his goodness may be found in his abolition of the severest one of the customary penalties (I refer to the taking of life); for instead of executing the condemned he put them in chains at forced labour for the cities, and by their services constructed many dykes and dug out not a few well-placed canals; for he held that in this way he had reduced for those who were being chastised the severity of their punishment, while for the cities he had procured, in exchange for useless penalties, something of great utility. The excessiveness of his piety may be inferred from a vision which he had in a dream and his consequent abdication of the throne, for he thought that the god of Thebes told him while he slept that he would not be able to reign over Egypt in happiness or for any great length of time, unless he should cut the bodies of all the priests in twain and accompanied by his retinue pass through the very midst of them. When this dream came again and again, he summoned the priests from all over the land and told them that by his presence in the country he was offending the god; for were that not the case such a command would not be given to him in his sleep, and so he would rather, he continued, departing pure of all defilement from the land, deliver his life to destiny than offend the Lord, stain his own life by an impious slaughter, and reign over Egypt. In the end he returned the kingdom to the Egyptians and retired again to Ethiopia.

**66.** There being no head of the government in Egypt for two years, and the masses betaking themselves to tumults and the killing of one another, the twelve most important leaders formed a solemn league among themselves, and after they had met together for counsel in Memphis and had drawn up agreements setting forth their mutual goodwill and loyalty they proclaimed themselves kings. After they had reigned in accordance with their oaths and promises and had maintained their mutual concord for a period of fifteen years, they set about to construct a common tomb for themselves, their thought being that, just as in their lifetime they had cherished a cordial regard for one another and enjoyed equal honours, so also after their death their bodies would all rest in one place and the memorial which they had erected would hold in one embrace the glory of those buried within. Being full of zeal for this undertaking they eagerly strove to surpass all preceding rulers in the magnitude of their structure. Selecting a site at the entrance to Lake Moeris in Libya they constructed their tomb of the finest stone, and made it in form a square but in magnitude a stade in length on each side; and in the carvings and, indeed, in all the workmanship they left nothing wherein succeeding rulers could excel them. [the Labyrinth] For as a man passed through the enclosing wall he found himself in a court surrounded by columns, forty on each side, and the roof of the court consisted of a single stone, which was worked into coffers and adorned with excellent paintings. This court also contained memorials of the native district of each king and of the temples and sacrificial rites therein, artistically portrayed in most beautiful paintings, and in general, the kings are said to have made the plan of their tomb on such an expensive and enormous scale that, had they not died before the execution of their purpose, they would have left no possibility for others to surpass them, so far as the construction of monuments is concerned.

After these kings had reigned over Egypt for fifteen years it came to pass that the sovereignty devolved upon one man for the following reasons. [663-609] Psammetichus of Sais, who was one of the twelve kings and in charge of the regions lying along the sea, furnished wares for all merchants and especially for the Phoenicians and the Greeks; and since in this manner he disposed of the products of his own district at a profit and exchanged them for those of other peoples, he was not only possessed of great wealth but also enjoyed friendly relations with peoples and rulers. This was the reason, they say, why the other kings became envious and opened war against him. Some of the early historians, however, tell this fanciful story: The generals had received an oracle to the effect that the first one of their number to pour a libation from a bronze bowl to the god in Memphis should rule over all Egypt, and when one of the priests brought out of the temple eleven golden bowls, Psammetichus took off his helmet and poured the libation from it. Now his colleagues, although suspecting his act, were not yet ready to put him to death, but drove him instead from public life, with orders that he should spend his days in the marshes along the sea. Whether they fell out for this reason or because of the envy which, as mentioned above, they felt towards him, at any rate Psammetichus, calling mercenaries from Caria and Ionia, overcame the others in a pitched battle near the city called Momemphis, and of the kings who opposed him some were slain in the battle and some were driven out into Libya and were no longer able to dispute with him for the throne.

**67.** After Psammetichus had established his authority over the entire kingdom he built for the god in Memphis the east propylon and the enclosure about the temple, supporting it with colossi twelve cubits high in place of pillars; and among the mercenaries he distributed notable gifts over and above their promised pay, gave them the region called *The Camps* to dwell in, and apportioned to them much land in the region lying a little up the river from the Pelusiac mouth; they being subsequently removed thence by Amasis, who reigned many years later, and settled by him in Memphis. Since Psammetichus had established his rule with the aid of the mercenaries, he henceforth entrusted these before others with the administration of his empire and regularly maintained large mercenary forces. Once in connection with a campaign in Syria, when he was giving the mercenaries a more honourable place in his order of battle by putting them on the right wing and showing the native troops less honour by assigning them the position on the left wing of the phalanx, the Egyptians, angered by this slight and being over two hundred thousand strong, revolted and set out for Ethiopia, having determined to win for themselves a country of their own. The king at first sent some of his generals to make excuse for the dishonour done to them, but since no heed was paid to these he set out in person after them by boat, accompanied by his friends, and when they still continued their march along the Nile and were about to cross the boundary of Egypt, he besought them to change their purpose and reminded them of their temples, their homeland, and of their wives and children. But they, all crying aloud and striking their spears against their shields, declared that so long as they had weapons in their hands they would easily find homelands; and lifting their garments and pointing to their genitals they said that so long as they had those they would never be in want either of wives or of children. After such a display of high courage and of utter disdain for what among other men is regarded as of the greatest consequence, they seized the best part of Ethiopia, and after apportioning much land among themselves they made their home there.

Although Psammetichus was greatly grieved over these things, he put in order the affairs of Egypt, looked after the royal revenues, and then formed alliances with both Athens and certain other Greek states. He also regularly treated with kindness any foreigners who sojourned in Egypt of their own free will, and was so great an admirer of the Hellenes that he gave his sons a Greek education, and, speaking generally, he was the first Egyptian king to open to other nations the trading-places throughout the rest of Egypt and to offer a large measure of security to strangers from across the seas. His predecessors in power had consistently closed Egypt to strangers, either killing or enslaving any who touched its shores. Indeed, it was because of the objection to strangers on the part of the people that the impiety of Busiris became a byword among the Greeks, although this impiety was not actually such as it was described, but was made into a fictitious myth because of the exceptional disrespect of the Egyptians for ordinary customs.

**68.** Four generations after Psammetichus, Apries was king for twenty-two years. [588-66] He made a campaign with strong land and sea forces against Cyprus and Phoenicia, took Sidon by storm, and so terrified the other cities of Phoenicia that he secured their submission; he also defeated the Phoenicians and Cyprians in a great sea-battle and returned to Egypt with much booty. After this he sent a strong native force against Cyrenê and Barcê and, when the larger part of it was lost, the survivors became estranged from him; for they felt that he had organised the expedition with a view to its destruction in order that his rule over the rest of the Egyptians might be more secure, and so they revolted. The man sent by the king to treat with them, one Amasis, a prominent Egyptian, paid no attention to the orders given him to effect a reconciliation, but, on the contrary, increased their estrangement, joined their revolt, and was himself chosen king. When a little later all the rest of the native Egyptians also went over to Amasis, the king was in such straits that he was forced to flee for safety to the mercenaries who numbered some thirty thousand men. A pitched battle accordingly took place near the village of Maria and the Egyptians prevailed in the struggle; Apries fell alive into the hands of the enemy and was strangled to death, and Amasis, arranging the affairs of the kingdom in whatever manner seemed to him best, ruled over the Egyptians in accordance with the laws and was held in great favour. He also reduced the cities of Cyprus and adorned many temples with noteworthy votive offerings. After a reign of fifty-five years he ended his days at the time when Cambyses, the king of the Persians, attacked Egypt, in the third year of the Sixty-third Olympiad, [526-5] that in which Parmenides of Camarina won the stadion.

### *On the laws and the courts of law (69 ff.).*

**69.** Now that we have discussed sufficiently the deeds of the kings of Egypt from the very earliest times down to the death of Amasis, we shall record the other events in their proper chronological setting; but at this point we shall give a summary account of the customs of Egypt, both those which are especially strange and those which can be of most value to our readers. Many of the customs that obtained in ancient days among the Egyptians have not only been accepted by the present inhabitants but have aroused no little admiration among the Greeks; and for that reason those men who have won the greatest repute in intellectual things have been eager to visit Egypt in order to acquaint themselves with its laws and institutions, which they considered to be worthy of note. For despite the fact that for the reasons mentioned above strangers found it difficult in early times to enter the country,it was nevertheless eagerly visited by Orpheus and the poet Homer in the earliest times and in later times by many others, such as Pythagoras of Samos and Solon the lawgiver. Now it is maintained by the Egyptians that it was they who first discovered writing and the observation of the stars, who also discovered the basic principles of geometry and most of the arts, and established the best laws. The best proof of all this, they say, lies in the fact that Egypt for more than four thousand seven hundred years was ruled over by kings of whom the majority were native Egyptians, and that the land was the most prosperous of the whole inhabited world; for these things could never have been true of any people which did not enjoy most excellent customs and laws and the institutions which promote culture of every kind. Now as for the stories invented by Herodotus and certain writers on Egyptian affairs, who deliberately preferred to the truth the telling of marvellous tales and the invention of myths for the delectation of their readers, these we shall omit, and we shall set forth only what appears in the written records of the priests of Egypt and has passed our careful scrutiny.

**70.** In the first place, then, the life which the kings of the Egyptians lived was not like that of other men who enjoy autocratic power and do in all matters exactly as they please without being held to account, but all their acts were regulated by prescriptions set forth in laws, not only their administrative acts, but also those that had to do with the way in which they spent their time from day to day, and with the food which they ate. In the matter of their servants, for instance, not one was a slave, such as had been acquired by purchase or born in the home, but all were sons of the most distinguished priests, over twenty years old and the best educated of their fellow-countrymen, in order that the king, by virtue of his having the noblest men to care for his person and to attend him throughout both day and night, might follow no low practices; for no ruler advances far along the road of evil unless he has those about him who will minister to his passions. The hours of both the day and night were laid out according to a plan, and at the specified hours it was absolutely required of the king that he should do what the laws stipulated and not what he thought best. For instance, in the morning, as soon as he was awake, he first of all had to receive the letters which had been sent from all sides, the purpose being that he might be able to despatch all administrative business and perform every act properly, being thus accurately informed about everything that was being done throughout his kingdom. Then, after he had bathed and bedecked his body with rich garments and the insignia of his office, he had to sacrifice to the gods.

When the victims had been brought to the altar it was the custom for the high priest to stand near the king, with the common people of Egypt gathered around, and pray in a loud voice that health and all the other good things of life be given the king if he maintains justice towards his subjects. And an open confession had also to be made of each and every virtue of the king, the priest saying that towards the gods he was piously disposed and towards men most kindly; for he was self-controlled and just and magnanimous, truthful, and generous with his possessions, and, in a word, superior to every desire, and that he punished crimes less severely than they deserved and rendered to his benefactors a gratitude exceeding the benefaction. And after reciting much more in a similar vein he concluded his prayer with a curse concerning things done in error, exempting the king from all blame therefor and asking that both the evil consequences and the punishment should fall upon those who served him and had taught him evil things. All this he would do, partly to lead the king to fear the gods and live a life pleasing to them, and partly to accustom him to a proper manner of conduct, not by sharp admonitions, but through praises that were agreeable and most conducive to virtue. After this, when the king had performed the divination from the entrails of a calf and had found the omens good, the sacred scribe read before the assemblage from out of the sacred books some of the edifying counsels and deeds of their most distinguished men, in order that he who held the supreme leadership should first contemplate in his mind the most excellent general principles and then turn to the prescribed administration of the several functions. For there was a set time not only for his holding audiences or rendering judgments, but even for his taking a walk, bathing, and sleeping with his wife, and, in a word, for every act of his life. And it was the custom for the kings to partake of delicate food, eating no other meat than veal and duck, and drinking only a prescribed amount of wine, which was not enough to make them unreasonably surfeited or drunken. Speaking generally, their whole diet was ordered with such continence that it had the appearance of having been drawn up, not by a lawgiver, but by the most skilled of their physicians, with only their health in view.

**71.** Strange as it may appear that the king did not have the entire control of his daily fare, far more remarkable still was the fact that kings were not allowed to render any legal decision or transact any business at random or to punish anyone through malice or in anger or for any other unjust reason, but only in accordance with the established laws relative to each offence, and in following the dictates of custom in these matters, so far were they from being indignant or taking offence in their souls, that, on the contrary, they actually held that they led a most happy life; for they believed that all other men, in thoughtlessly following their natural passions, commit many acts which bring them injuries and perils, and that oftentimes some who realise that they are about to commit a sin nevertheless do base acts when overpowered by love or hatred or some other passion, while they, on the other hand, by virtue of their having cultivated a manner of life which had been chosen before all others by the most prudent of all men, fell into the fewest mistakes. Since the kings followed so righteous a course in dealing with their subjects, the people manifested a goodwill towards their rulers which surpassed even the affection they had for their own kinsmen; for not only the order of the priests but, in short, all the inhabitants of Egypt were less concerned for their wives and children and their other cherished possessions than for the safety of their kings. Consequently, during most of the time covered by the reigns of the kings of whom we have a record, they maintained an orderly civil government and continued to enjoy a most felicitous life, so long as the system of laws described was in force; and, more than that, they conquered more nations and achieved greater wealth than any other people, and adorned their lands with monuments and buildings never to be surpassed, and their cities with costly dedications of every description.

**72.** Again, the Egyptian ceremonies which followed upon the death of a king afforded no small proof of the goodwill of the people towards their rulers; for the fact that the honour which they paid was to one who was insensible of it constituted an authentic testimony to its sincerity. For when any king died all the inhabitants of Egypt united in mourning for him, rending their garments, closing the temples, stopping the sacrifices, and celebrating no festivals for seventy-two days; and plastering their heads with mud and wrapping strips of linen cloth below their breasts, women as well as men went about in groups of two or three hundred, and twice each day, reciting the dirge in a rhythmic chant, they sang the praises of the deceased, recalling his virtues; nor would they eat the flesh of any living thing or food prepared from wheat, and they abstained from wine and luxury of any sort. No one would ever have seen fit to make use of baths or unguents or soft bedding, nay more, would not even have dared to indulge in sexual pleasures, but every Egyptian grieved and mourned during those seventy-two days as if it were his own beloved child that had died. But during this interval they had made splendid preparations for the burial, and on the last day, placing the coffin containing the body before the entrance to the tomb, they set up, as custom prescribed, a tribunal to sit in judgment upon the deeds done by the deceased during his life. And when permission had been given to anyone who so wished to lay complaint against him, the priests praised all his noble deeds one after another, and the common people who had gathered in myriads to the funeral, listening to them, shouted their approval if the king had led a worthy life, but if he had not, they raised a clamour of protest. And in fact many kings have been deprived of the public burial customarily accorded them because of the opposition of the people; the result was, consequently, that the successive kings practised justice, not merely for the reasons just mentioned, but also because of their fear of the despite which would be shown their body after death and of eternal obloquy.

Of the customs, then, touching the early kings these are the most important.

73. And since Egypt as a whole is divided into several parts which in Greek are called nomes, over each of these a nomarch is appointed who is charged with both the oversight and care of all its affairs. Furthermore, the entire country is divided into three parts, the first of which is held by the order of the priests, which is accorded the greatest veneration by the inhabitants both because these men have charge of the worship of the gods and because by virtue of their education they bring to bear a higher intelligence than others. With the income from these holdings of land they perform all the sacrifices throughout Egypt, maintain their assistants, and minister to their own needs; for it has always been held that the honours paid to the gods should never be changed, but should ever be performed by the same men and in the same manner, and that those who deliberate on behalf of all should not lack the necessities of life. Speaking generally, the priests are the first to deliberate upon the most important matters and are always at the king's side, sometimes as his assistants, sometimes to propose measures and give instructions, and they also, by their knowledge of astrology and of divination, forecast future events, and read to the king, out of the record of acts preserved in their sacred books, those which can be of assistance. For it is not the case with the Egyptians as it is with the Greeks, that a single man or a single woman takes over the priesthood, but many are engaged in the sacrifices and honours paid the gods and pass on to their descendants the same rule of life. They also pay no taxes of any kind, and in repute and in power are second after the king.

The second part of the country has been taken over by the kings for their revenues, out of which they pay the cost of their wars, support the splendour of their court, and reward with fitting gifts any who have distinguished themselves;

and they do not swamp the private citizens by taxation, since their income from these revenues gives them a great plenty.

The last part is held by the warriors, as they are called, who are subject to call for all military duties, the purpose being that those who hazard their lives may be most loyal to the country because of such allotment of land and thus may eagerly face the perils of war. For it would be absurd to entrust the safety of the entire nation to these men and yet have them possess in the country no property to fight for valuable enough to arouse their ardour. But the most important consideration is the fact that, if they are well-to-do, they will readily beget children and thus so increase the population that the country will not need to call in any mercenary troops. And since their calling, like that of the priests, is hereditary, the warriors are incited to bravery by the distinguished records of their fathers and, inasmuch as they become zealous students of warfare from their boyhood up, they turn out to be invincible by reason of their daring and skill.

**74.** There are three other classes of free citizens, namely, the herdsmen, the husbandmen, and the artisans. Now the husbandmen rent on moderate terms the arable land held by the king and the priests and the warriors, and spend their entire time in tilling the soil; and since from very infancy they are brought up in connection with the various tasks of farming, they are far more experienced in such matters than the husbandmen of any other nation; for of all mankind they acquire the most exact knowledge of the nature of the soil, the use of water in irrigation, the times of sowing and reaping, and the harvesting of the crops in general, some details of which they have learned from the observations of their ancestors and others in the school of their own experience. And what has been said applies equally well to the herdsmen, who receive the care of animals from their fathers as if by a law of inheritance, and follow a pastoral life all the days of their existence. They have received, it is true, much from their ancestors relative to the best care and feeding of grazing animals, but to this they add not a little by reason of their own interest in such matters; and the most astonishing fact is that, by reason of their unusual application to such matters, the men who have charge of poultry and geese, in addition to producing them in the natural way known to all mankind, raise them by their own hands, by virtue of a skill peculiar to them, in numbers beyond telling; for they do not use the birds for hatching the eggs, but, in effecting this themselves artificially by their own wit and skill in an astounding manner, they are not surpassed by the operations of nature. Furthermore, one may see that the crafts also among the Egyptians are very diligently cultivated and brought to their proper development; for they are the only people where all the craftsmen are forbidden to follow any other occupation or belong to any other class of citizens than those stipulated by the laws and handed down to them from their parents, the result being that neither ill-will towards a teacher nor political distractions nor any other thing interferes with their interest in their work. For whereas among all other peoples it can be observed that the artisans are distracted in mind by many things, and through the desire to advance themselves do not stick exclusively to their own occupation; for some try their hands at agriculture, some dabble in trade, and some cling to two or three crafts, and in states having a democratic form of government vast numbers of them, trooping to the meetings of the Assembly, ruin the work of the government, while they make a profit for themselves at the expense of others who pay them their wage, yet among the Egyptians if any artisan should take part in public affairs or pursue several crafts he is severely punished.

Such, then, were the divisions of the citizens, maintained by the early inhabitants of Egypt, and their devotion to their own class which they inherited from their ancestors.

**75.** In their administration of justice the Egyptians also showed no merely casual interest, holding that the decisions of the courts exercise the greatest influence upon community life, and this in each of their two aspects. For it was evident to them that if the offenders against the law should be punished and the injured parties should be afforded succour there would be an ideal correction of wrongdoing; but if, on the other hand, the fear which wrongdoers have of the judgments of the courts should be brought to naught by bribery or favour, they saw that the break-up of community life would follow. Consequently, by appointing the best men from the most important cities as judges over the whole land they did not fall short of the end which they had in mind. For from Heliopolis and Thebes and Memphis they used to choose ten judges from each, and this court was regarded as in no way inferior to that composed of the Areopagites at Athens or of the Elders at Sparta. And when the thirty assembled they chose the best one of their number and made him chief justice, and in his stead the city sent another judge. Allowances to provide for their needs were supplied by the king, to the judges sufficient for their maintenance, and many times as much to the chief justice. The latter regularly wore suspended from his neck by a golden chain a small image made of precious stones, which they called Truth; the hearings of the pleas commenced whenever the chief justice put on the image of Truth. The entire body of the laws was written down in eight volumes which lay before the judges, and the custom was that the accuser should present in writing the particulars of his complaint, namely, the charge, how the thing happened, and the amount of injury or damage done, whereupon the defendant would take the document submitted by his opponents in the suit and reply in writing to each charge, to the effect either that he did not commit the deed, or, if he did, that he was not guilty of wrongdoing, or, if he was guilty of wrongdoing, that he should receive a lighter penalty. After that, the law required that the accuser should reply to this in writing and that the defendant should offer a rebuttal. And after both parties had twice presented their statements in writing to the judges, it was the duty of the thirty at once to declare their opinions among themselves and of the chief justice to place the image of Truth upon one or the other of the two pleas which had been presented.

**76.** This was the manner, as their account goes, in which the Egyptians conducted all court proceedings, since they believed that if the advocates were allowed to speak they would greatly becloud the justice of a case; for they knew that the clever devices of orators, the cunning witchery of their delivery, and the tears of the accused would influence many to overlook the severity of the laws and the strictness of truth; at any rate they were aware that men who are highly respected as judges are often carried away by the eloquence of the advocates, either because they are deceived, or because they are won over by the speaker's charm, or because the emotion of pity has been aroused in them; but by having the parties to a suit present their pleas in writing, it was their opinion that the judgements would be strict, only the bare facts being taken into account. For in that case there would be the least chance that gifted speakers would have an advantage over the slower, or the well-practised over the inexperienced, or the audacious liars over those who were truth-loving and restrained in character, but all would get their just dues on an equal footing, since by the provision of the laws ample time is taken, on the one hand by the disputants for the examination of the arguments of the other side, and, on the other hand, by the judges for the comparison of the allegations of both parties.

77. Since we have spoken of their legislation, we feel that it will not be foreign to the plan of our history to present such laws of the Egyptians as were especially old or took on an extraordinary form, or, in general, can be of help to lovers of reading. Now in the first place, their penalty for perjurers was death, on the ground that such men are guilty of the two greatest transgressions — being impious towards the gods and overthrowing the mightiest pledge known among men. Again, if a man, walking on a road in Egypt, saw a person being killed or, in a word, suffering any kind of violence and did not come to his aid if able to do so, he had to die; and if he was truly prevented from aiding the person because of inability, he was in any case required to lodge information against the bandits and to bring an action against their lawless act; and in case he failed to do this as the law required, it was required that he be scourged with a fixed number of stripes and be deprived of every kind of food for three days. Those who brought false accusations against others had to suffer the penalty that would have been meted out to the accused persons had they been adjudged guilty. All Egyptians were also severally required to submit to the magistrates a written declaration of the sources of their livelihood, and any man making a false declaration or gaining an unlawful means of livelihood had to pay the death penalty. It is said that Solon, after his visit to Egypt, brought this law to Athens. If anyone intentionally killed a free man or a slave the laws enjoined that he be put to death; for they, in the first place, wished that it should not be through the accidental differences in men's condition in life but through the principles governing their actions that all men should be restrained from evil deeds, and, on the other hand, they sought to accustom mankind, through such consideration for slaves, to refrain all the more from committing any offence whatever against freemen.

In the case of parents who had slain their children, though the laws did not prescribe death, yet the offenders had to hold the dead body in their arms for three successive days and nights, under the surveillance of a state guard; for it was not considered just to deprive of life those who had given life to their children, but rather by a warning which brought with it pain and repentance to turn them from such deeds. For children who had killed their parents they reserved an extraordinary punishment; for it was required that those found guilty of this crime should have pieces of flesh about the size of a finger cut out of their bodies with sharp reeds and then be put on a bed of thorns and burned alive; for they held that to take by violence the life of those who had given them life was the greatest crime possible to man. Pregnant women who had been condemned to death were not executed until they had been delivered. The same law has also been enacted by many Greek states, since they held it entirely unjust that the innocent should suffer the same punishment as the guilty, that a penalty should be exacted of two for only one transgression, and, further, that, since the crime had been actuated by an evil intention, a being as yet without intelligence should receive the same correction, and, what is the most important consideration, that in view of the fact that the guilt had been laid at the door of the pregnant mother it was by no means proper that the child, who belongs to the father as well as to the mother, should be despatched; for a man may properly consider judges who spare the life of a murderer to be no worse than other judges who destroy that which is guilty of no crime whatsoever.

Of the laws dealing with murder these are those which are thought to have been the most successful.

**78.** Among their other laws one, which concerned military affairs, made the punishment of deserters or of any who disobeyed the command of their leaders, not death, but the uttermost disgrace; but if later on such men wiped out their disgrace by a display of manly courage, they were restored to their former freedom of speech. Thus the lawgiver at the same time made disgrace a more terrible punishment than death, in order to accustom all the people to consider dishonour the greatest of evils, and he also believed that, while dead men would never be of value to society, men who had been disgraced would do many a good deed through their desire to regain freedom of speech. In the case of those who had disclosed military secrets to the enemy the law prescribed that their tongues should be cut out, while in the case of counterfeiters or falsifiers of measures and weights or imitators of seals, and of official scribes who made false entries or erased items, and of any who adduced false documents, it ordered that both their hands should be cut off, to the end that the offender, being punished in respect of those members of his body that were the instruments of his wrongdoing, should keep until death his irreparable misfortune, and at the same time, by serving as a warning example to others, should turn them from the commission of similar offences.

Severe also were their laws touching women. If a man had violated a free married woman, they stipulated that he be emasculated, considering that such a person by a single unlawful act had been guilty of the three greatest crimes, assault, abduction, and confusion of offspring; but if a man committed adultery with the woman's consent, the laws ordered that the man should receive a thousand blows with the rod, and that the woman should have her nose cut off, on the ground that a woman who tricks herself out with an eye to forbidden licence should be deprived of that which contributes most to a woman's comeliness.

**79.** Their laws governing contracts they attribute to Bocchoris. These prescribe that men who had borrowed money without signing a bond, if they denied the indebtedness, might take an oath to that effect and be cleared of the obligation. The purpose was, in the first place, that men might stand in awe of the gods by attributing great importance to oaths, for, since it is manifest that the man who has repeatedly taken such an oath will in the end lose the confidence which others had in him, everyone will consider it a matter of the utmost concern not to have recourse to the oath lest he forfeit his credit. In the second place, the lawgiver assumed that by basing confidence entirely upon a man's sense of honour he would incite all men to be virtuous in character, in order that they might not be talked about as being unworthy of confidence; and, furthermore, he held it to be unjust that men who had been trusted with a loan without an oath should not be trusted when they gave their oath regarding the same transaction. And whoever lent money along with a written bond was forbidden to do more than double the principal from the interest.

In the case of debtors the lawgiver ruled that the repayment of loans could be exacted only from a man's estate, and under no condition did he allow the debtor's person to be subject to seizure, holding that whereas property should belong to those who had amassed it or had received it from some earlier holder by way of a gift, the bodies of citizens should belong to the state, to the end that the state might avail itself of the services which its citizens owed it, in times of both war and peace. It would be absurd, he felt, that a soldier, at the moment perhaps when he was setting forth to fight for his fatherland, should be haled to prison by his creditor for an unpaid loan, and that the greed of private citizens should in this way endanger the safety of all. It appears that Solon took this law also to Athens, calling it a "disburdenment," [*Seisachtheia*] when he absolved all the citizens of the loans, secured by their persons, which they owed. But certain individuals find fault, and not without reason, with the majority of the Greek lawgivers, who forbade the taking of weapons and ploughs and other quite indispensable things as security for loans, but nevertheless allowed the men who would use these implements to be subject to imprisonment.

**80.** The Egyptian law dealing with thieves was also a very peculiar one. For it bade any who chose to follow this occupation to enter their names with the Chief of the Thieves and by agreement to bring to him immediately the stolen articles, while any who had been robbed filed with him in like manner a list of all the missing articles, stating the place, the day, and the hour of the loss, and since by this method all lost articles were readily found, the owner who had lost anything had only to pay one-fourth of its value in order to recover just what belonged to him. As it was impossible to keep all mankind from stealing, the lawgiver devised a scheme whereby every article lost would be recovered upon payment of a small ransom.

In accordance with the marriage-customs of the Egyptians the priests have but one wife, but any other man takes as many as he may determine; and the Egyptians are required to raise all their children in order to increase the population, on the ground that large numbers are the greatest factor in increasing the prosperity of both country and cities. Nor do they hold any child a bastard, even though he was born of a slave mother; for they have taken the general position that the father is the sole author of procreation and that the mother only supplies the foetus with nourishment and a place to live, and they call the trees which bear fruit "male" and those which do not "female," exactly opposite to the Greek usage. They feed their children in a sort of happy-go-lucky fashion that in its inexpensiveness quite surpasses belief; for they serve them with stews made of any stuff that is ready to hand and cheap, and give them such stalks of the *byblos* plant as can be roasted in the coals, and the roots and stems of marsh plants, either raw or boiled or baked. Since most of the children are reared without shoes or clothing because of the mildness of the climate of the country, the entire expense incurred by the parents of a child until it comes to maturity is not more than twenty drachmas. These are the leading reasons why Egypt has such an extraordinarily large population, and it is because of this fact that she possesses a vast number of great monuments.

**81.** In the education of their sons the priests teach them two kinds of writing, that which is called "sacred" and that which is used in the more general instruction. Geometry and arithmetic are given special attention. For the river, by changing the face of the country each year in manifold ways, gives rise to many and varied disputes between neighbours over their boundary lines, and these disputes cannot be easily tested out with any exactness unless a geometer works out the truth scientifically by the application of his experience. Arithmetic is serviceable with reference to the business affairs connected with making a living and also in applying the principles of geometry, and likewise is of no small assistance to students of astrology as well. For the positions and arrangements of the stars as well as their motions have always been the subject of careful observation among the Egyptians, if anywhere in the world; they have preserved to this day the records concerning each of these stars over an incredible number of years, this subject of study having been zealously preserved among them from ancient times, and they have also observed with the utmost avidity the motions and orbits and stops of the planets, as well as the influences of each one on the generation of all living things - the good or the evil effects, namely, of which they are the cause. And while they are often successful in predicting to men the events which are going to befall them in the course of their lives, not infrequently they foretell destructions of the crops or, on the other hand, abundant yields, and pestilences that are to attack men or beasts, and as a result of their long observations they have prior knowledge of earthquakes and floods, of the risings of the comets, and of all things which the ordinary man looks upon as beyond all finding out. According to them the Chaldaeans of Babylon, being colonists from Egypt, enjoy the fame which they have for their astrology because they learned that science from the priests of Egypt.

As to the general mass of the Egyptians, they are instructed from their childhood by their fathers or kinsmen in the practices proper to each manner of life as previously described by us; but as for reading and writing, the Egyptians at large give their children only a superficial instruction in them, and not all do this, but for the most part only those who are engaged in the crafts. In wrestling and music, however, it is not customary among them to receive any instruction at all; they hold that from the daily exercises in wrestling their young men will gain, not health, but a vigour that is only temporary and in fact quite dangerous, while they consider music to be not only useless but even harmful, since it makes the spirits of the listeners effeminate.

**82.** In order to prevent sicknesses they look after the health of their bodies by means of drenches, fasting, and emetics, sometimes every day and sometimes at intervals of three or four days. They say that the larger part of the food taken into the body is superfluous and that it is from this superfluous part that diseases are engendered; consequently the treatment just mentioned, by removing the beginnings of disease, would be most likely to produce health. On their military campaigns and their journeys in the country they all receive treatment without the payment of any private fee; for the physicians draw their support from public funds and administer their treatments in accordance with a written law which was composed in ancient times by many famous physicians. If they follow the rules of this law as they read them in the sacred book and yet are unable to save their patient, they are absolved from any charge and go unpunished; but if they go contrary to the law's prescriptions in any respect, they must submit to a trial with death as the penalty, the lawgiver holding that but few physicians would ever show themselves wiser than the mode of treatment which had been closely followed for a long period and had been originally prescribed by the ablest practitioners.

### *On the animals held sacred among the Egyptians (83 ff.).*

**83.** As regards the consecration of animals in Egypt, the practice naturally appears to many to be extraordinary and worthy of investigation. For the Egyptians venerate certain animals exceedingly, not only during their lifetime but even after their death, such as cats, ichneumons and dogs, and, again, hawks and the birds which they call "ibis," as well as wolves and crocodiles and a number of other animals of that kind, and the reasons for such worship we shall undertake to set forth, after we have first spoken briefly about the animals themselves.

In the first place, for each kind of animal that is accorded this worship there has been consecrated a portion of land which returns a revenue sufficient for their care and sustenance; moreover, the Egyptians make vows to certain gods on behalf of their children who have been delivered from an illness, in which case they shave off their hair and weigh it against silver or gold, and then give the money to the attendants of the animals mentioned. These cut up flesh for the hawks and calling them with a loud cry toss it up to them, as they swoop by, until they catch it, while for the cats and ichneumons they break up bread into milk and calling them with a clucking sound set it before them, or else they cut up fish caught in the Nile and feed the flesh to them raw; and in like manner each of the other kinds of animals is provided with the appropriate food. As for the various services which these animals require, the Egyptians not only do not try to avoid them or feel ashamed to be seen by the crowds as they perform them, but on the contrary, in the belief that they are engaged in the most serious rites of divine worship, they assume airs of importance, and wearing special insignia make the rounds of the cities and the countryside. Since it can be seen from afar in the service of what animals they are engaged, all who meet them fall down before them and render them honour.

When one of these animals dies they wrap it in fine linen and then, wailing and beating their breasts, carry it off to be embalmed; and after it has been treated with cedar oil and such spices as have the quality of imparting a pleasant odour and of preserving the body for a long time, they lay it away in a consecrated tomb. Whoever intentionally kills one of these animals is put to death, unless it be a cat or an ibis that he kills; but if he kills one of these, whether intentionally or unintentionally, he is certainly put to death, for the common people gather in crowds and deal with the perpetrator most cruelly, sometimes doing this without waiting for a trial. Because of their fear of such a

## Book I

punishment any who have caught sight of one of these animals lying dead withdraw to a great distance and shout with lamentations and protestations that they found the animal already dead. So deeply implanted also in the hearts of the common people is their superstitious regard for these animals and so unalterable are the emotions cherished by every man regarding the honour due to them that once, at the time when Ptolemy their king had not as yet been given by the Romans the appellation of "friend" and the people were exercising all zeal in courting the favour of the embassy from Italy which was then visiting Egypt and, in their fear, were intent upon giving no cause for complaint or war, when one of the Romans killed a cat and the multitude rushed in a crowd to his house, neither the officials sent by the king to beg the man off nor the fear of Rome which all the people felt were enough to save the man from punishment, even though his act had been an accident. This incident we relate, not from hearsay, but we saw it with our own eyes on the occasion of the visit we made to Egypt.

**84.** If what has been said seems to many incredible and like a fanciful tale, what is to follow will appear far more extraordinary. Once, they say, when the inhabitants of Egypt were being hard pressed by a famine, many in their need laid hands upon their fellows, yet not a single man was even accused of having partaken of the sacred animals. Furthermore, whenever a dog is found dead in any house, every inmate of it shaves his entire body and goes into mourning, and what is more astonishing than this, if any wine or grain or any other thing necessary to life happens to be stored in the building where one of these animals has expired, they would never think of using it thereafter for any purpose; and if they happen to be making a military expedition in another country, they ransom the captive cats and hawks and bring them back to Egypt, and this they do sometimes even when their supply of money for the journey is running short. As for the ceremonies connected with the Apis of Memphis, the Mnevis of Heliopolis and the goat of Mendes, as well as with the crocodile of the Lake of Moeris, the lion kept in the City of Lions (Leontopolis), as it is called, and many other ceremonies like them, they could easily be described, but the writer would scarcely be believed by any who had not actually witnessed them. These animals are kept in sacred enclosures and are cared for by many men of distinction who offer them the most expensive fare; for they provide, with unfailing regularity, the finest wheaten flour or wheat-groats seethed in milk, every kind of sweetmeat made with honey, and the meat of ducks, either boiled or baked, while for the carnivorous animals birds are caught and thrown to them in abundance, and, in general, great care is given that they have an expensive fare. They are continually bathing the animals in warm water, anointing them with the most precious ointments, and burning before them every kind of fragrant incense; they furnish them with the most expensive coverlets and with splendid jewellery, and exercise the greatest care that they shall enjoy sexual intercourse according to the demands of nature; furthermore, with every animal they keep the most beautiful females of the same genus, which they call his concubines and attend to at the cost of heavy expense and assiduous service. When any animal dies they mourn for it as deeply as do those who have lost a beloved child, and bury it in a manner not in keeping with their ability but going far beyond the value of their estates. For instance, after the death of Alexander and just subsequently to the taking over of Egypt by Ptolemy the son of Lagus, it happened that the Apis in

Memphis died of old age; and the man who was charged with the care of him spent on his burial not only the whole of the very large sum which had been provided for the animal's maintenance, but also borrowed in addition fifty talents of silver from Ptolemy. And even in our own day some of the keepers of these animals have spent on their burial not less than one hundred talents.

**85.** There should be added to what has been said what still remains to be told concerning the ceremonies connected with the sacred bull called Apis. After he has died and has received a magnificent burial, the priests who are charged with this duty seek out a young bull which has on its body markings similar to those of its predecessor; and when it has been found the people cease their mourning and the priests who have the care of it first take the young bull to Nilopolis, where it is kept forty days, and then, putting it on a state barge fitted out with a gilded cabin, conduct it as a god to the sanctuary of Hephaestus at Memphis. During these forty days only women may look at it; these stand facing it and pulling up their garments show their genitals, but henceforth they are forever prevented from coming into the presence of this god. Some explain the origin of the honour accorded this bull in this way, saying that at the death of Osiris his soul passed into this animal, and therefore up to this day has always passed into its successors at the times of the manifestation of Osiris; but some say that when Osiris died at the hands of Typhon Isis collected the members of his body and put them in an ox (*bous*), made of wood covered over with fine linen, and because of this the city was called Bousiris. Many other stories are told about the Apis, but we feel that it would be a long task to recount all the details regarding them.

**86.** Since all the practices of the Egyptians in their worship of animals are astonishing and beyond belief, they occasion much difficulty for those who would seek out their origins and causes. Now their priests have on this subject a teaching which may not be divulged, as we have already stated in connection with their accounts of the gods, but the majority of the Egyptians give the following three causes, the first of which belongs entirely to the realm of fable and is in keeping with the simplicity of primitive times. They say, namely, that the gods who came into existence in the beginning, being few in number and overpowered by the multitude and the lawlessness of earth-born men, [the Giants] took on the forms of certain animals, and in this way saved themselves from the savagery and violence of mankind; afterwards, when they had established their power over all things in the universe, out of gratitude to the animals which had been responsible for their salvation at the outset, they made sacred those kinds whose form they had assumed, and instructed mankind to maintain them in a costly fashion while living and to bury them at death.

The second cause which they give is this: that the early Egyptians, after having been defeated by their neighbours in many battles because of the lack of order in their army, conceived the idea of carrying standards before the several divisions. Consequently, they say, the commanders fashioned figures of the animals which they now worship and carried them fixed on lances, and by this device every man knew where his place was in the array. And since the good order resulting therefrom greatly contributed to victory, they thought that the animals had been responsible for their deliverance; and so the people, wishing to show their gratitude to them, established the custom of not killing any one of the animals whose likeness had been fashioned at that time, but of rendering to them, as objects of worship, the care and honour which we have previously described.

**87.** The third cause which they adduce in connection with the dispute in question is the service which each one of these animals renders for the benefit of community life and of mankind. The cow [ox], for example, bears workers and ploughs the lighter soil; the sheep lamb twice in the year and provide by their wool both protection for the body and its decorous covering, while by their milk and cheese they furnish food that is both appetising and abundant. Again, the dog is useful both for the hunt and for man's protection, and this is why they represent the god whom they call Anubis with a dog's head, showing in this way that he was the bodyguard of Osiris and Isis. There are some, however, who explain that dogs guided Isis during her search for Osiris and protected her from wild beasts and wayfarers, and that they helped her in her search, because of the affection they bore for her, by baying; and this is the reason why at the Festival of Isis the procession is led by dogs, those who introduced the rite showing forth in this way the kindly service rendered by this animal of old. The cat is likewise useful against asps with their deadly bite and the other reptiles that sting, while the ichneumon keeps a look-out for the newly-laid seed of the crocodile and crushes the eggs left by the female, doing this carefully and zealously even though it receives no benefit from the act. Were this not done, the river would have become impassable because of the multitude of beasts that would be born. The crocodiles themselves are also killed by this animal in an astonishing and quite incredible manner; for the ichneumons roll themselves over and over in the mud, and when the crocodiles go to sleep on the land with their mouths open they jump down their mouths into the centre of their body; then, rapidly gnawing through the bowels, they get out unscathed themselves and at the same time kill their victims instantly. Of the sacred birds the ibis is useful as a protector against the snakes, the locusts, and the caterpillars, and the hawk against the scorpions, horned serpents, and the small animals of noxious bite which cause the greatest destruction of men. But some maintain that the hawk is honoured because it is used as a bird of omen by the soothsayers in predicting to the Egyptians events which are to come. Others, however, say that in primitive times a hawk brought to the priests in Thebes a book wrapped about with a purple band, which contained written directions concerning the worship of the gods and the honours due to them; and it is for this reason, they add, that the sacred scribes wear on their heads a purple band and the wing of a hawk. The eagle also is honoured by the Thebans because it is believed to be a royal animal and worthy of Zeus.

**88.** They have deified the goat, just as the Greeks are said to have honoured Priapus, because of the generative member; for this animal has a very great propensity for copulation, and it is fitting that honour be shown to that member of the body which is the cause of generation, being, as it were, the primal author of all animal life. In general, not only the Egyptians but not a few other peoples as well have in the rites they observe treated the male member as sacred, on the ground that it is the cause of the generation of all creatures; the priests in Egypt who have inherited their priestly offices from their fathers are initiated first into the mysteries of this god, and both the Pans and the Satyrs, they say, are worshipped by men for the same reason; and this is why most peoples set up in their sacred places statues of them showing the phallus erect and resembling a goat's in nature, since according to tradition this animal is most efficient in copulation; consequently, by representing these creatures in such fashion, the dedicants are returning thanks to them for their own numerous offspring.

The sacred bulls, I refer to the Apis and the Mnevis, are honoured like the gods, as Osiris commanded, both because of their use in farming and also because the fame of those who discovered the fruits of the earth is handed down by the labours of these animals to succeeding generations for all time. Red oxen, however, may be sacrificed, because it is thought that this was the colour of Typhon, who plotted against Osiris and was then punished by Isis for the death of her husband. Men also, if they were of the same colour as Typhon, were sacrificed, they say, in ancient times by the kings at the tomb of Osiris; however, only a few Egyptians are now found red in colour, but the majority of such are non-Egyptians, and this is why the story spread among the Greeks of the slaying of foreigners by Busiris, although Busiris was not the name of the king but of the tomb of Osiris, which is called that in the language of the land.

The wolves are honoured, they say, because their nature is so much like that of dogs, for the natures of these two animals are little different from each other and hence offspring is produced by their interbreeding. But the Egyptians offer another explanation for the honour accorded this animal, although it pertains more to the realm of myth; for they say that in early times when Isis, aided by her son Horus, was about to commence her struggle with Typhon, Osiris came from Hades to help his son and his wife, having taken on the guise of a wolf; and so, upon the death of Typhon, his conquerors commanded men to honour the animal upon whose appearance victory followed. But some say that once, when the Ethiopians had marched against Egypt, a great number of bands of wolves (*lykoi*) gathered together and drove the invaders out of the country, pursuing them beyond the city named Elephantine; and therefore that nome was given the name Lycopolite [City of Wolves] and these animals were granted the honour in question.

**89.** It remains for us to speak of the deification of crocodiles, a subject regarding which most men are entirely at a loss to explain how, when these beasts eat the flesh of men, it ever became the law to honour them like the gods. Their reply is, that the security of the country is ensured, not only by the river, but to a much greater degree by the crocodiles in it; that for this reason the robbers that infest both Arabia and Libya do not dare to swim across the Nile, because they fear the beasts, whose number is very great; and that this would never have been the case if war were continually being waged against the animals and they had been utterly destroyed by hunters dragging the river with nets. Still another account is given of these beasts, for some say that once one of the early kings whose name was Menas, being pursued by his own dogs, came in his flight to the Lake of Moeris, as it is called, where, strange as it may seem, a crocodile took him on his back and carried him to the other side. Wishing to show his gratitude to the beast for saving him, he founded a city near the place and named it City of the Crocodiles; and he commanded the natives of the region to worship these animals as gods and dedicated the lake to them for their sustenance; and in that place he also constructed his own tomb, erecting a pyramid with four sides, and built the Labyrinth which is admired by many.

A similar diversity of customs exists, according to their accounts, with regard to everything else, but it would be a long task to set forth the details concerning them. That they have adopted these customs for themselves because of the advantage accruing therefrom to their lives is clear to all from the fact that there are those among them who will not touch many particular kinds of food. Some, for instance, abstain entirely from lentils, others from beans, and some from cheese or onions or certain other foods, there being many kinds of food in Egypt, showing in this way that men must be taught to deny themselves things that are useful, and that if all ate of everything the supply of no article of consumption would hold out. Some adduce other causes and say that, since under the early kings the multitude were often revolting and conspiring against their rulers, one of the kings who was especially wise divided the land into a number of parts and commanded the inhabitants of each to revere a certain animal or else not to eat a certain food, his thought being that, with each group of people revering what was honoured among themselves but despising what was sacred to all the rest, all the inhabitants of Egypt would never be able to be of one mind, and this purpose, they declare, is clear from the results; for every group of people is at odds with its neighbours, being offended at their violations of the customs mentioned above.

**90.** Some advance some such reason as the following for their deification of the animals. When men, they say, first ceased living like the beasts and gathered into groups, at the outset they kept devouring each other and warring among themselves, the more powerful ever prevailing over the weaker; but later those who were deficient in strength, taught by expediency, grouped together and took for device upon their standards one of the animals which was later made sacred; then, when those who were from time to time in fear flocked to this symbol, an organised body was formed which was not to be despised by any who attacked it. When everybody else did the same thing, the whole people came to be divided into organised bodies, and in the case of each the animal which had been responsible for its safety it accorded honours like those belonging to the gods, as having rendered to them the greatest service possible. This is why to this day the several groups of the Egyptians differ from each other in that each group honours the animals which it originally made sacred.

In general, they say, the Egyptians surpass all other peoples in showing gratitude for every benefaction, since they hold that the return of gratitude to benefactors is a very great resource in life; for it is clear that all men will want to bestow their benefactions preferably upon those who they see will most honourably treasure up the favours they bestow, and it is apparently on these grounds that the Egyptians prostrate themselves before their kings and honour them as being in very truth gods, holding, on the one hand, that it was not without the influence of some divine providence that these men have attained to the supreme power, and feeling, also, that such as have the will and the strength to confer the greatest benefactions share in the divine nature.

Now if we have dwelt over-long on the topic of the sacred animals, we have at least thoroughly considered those customs of the Egyptians that men most marvel at.

### On the customs of the Egyptians touching the dead (91 ff.).

**91.** Not least will a man marvel at the peculiarity of the customs of the Egyptians when he learns of their usages with respect to the dead. Whenever anyone dies among them, all his relatives and friends, plastering their heads with mud, roam about the city lamenting, until the body receives burial. Nay more, during that time they indulge in neither baths, nor wine, nor in any other food worth mentioning, nor do they put on bright clothing. There are three classes of burial: the most expensive, the medium, and the most humble. If the first is used the cost, they say, is a talent of silver, if the second, twenty minae, and if the last, the expense is, they say, very little indeed. Now the men who treat the bodies are skilled artisans who have received this professional knowledge as a family tradition; and these lay before the relatives of the deceased a price-list of every item connected with the burial, and ask them in what manner they wish the body to be treated. When an agreement has been reached on every detail and they have taken the body, they turn it over to men who have been assigned to the service and have become inured to it. The first is the scribe, as he is called, who, when the body has been laid on the ground, circumscribes on the left flank the extent of the incision; then the one called the slitter cuts the flesh, as the law commands, with an Ethiopian stone and at once takes to flight on the run, while those present set out after him, pelting him with stones, heaping curses on him, and trying, as it were, to turn the profanation on his head; for in their eyes everyone he is an object of general hatred who applies violence to the body of a man of the same tribe or wounds him or, in general, does him any harm.

The men called embalmers, however, are considered worthy of every honour and consideration, associating with the priests and even coming and going in the temples without hindrance, as being undefiled. When they have gathered to treat the body after it has been slit open, one of them thrusts his hand through the opening in the corpse into the trunk and extracts everything but the kidneys and heart, and another one cleanses each of the viscera, washing them in palm wine and spices, and in general, they carefully dress the whole body for over thirty days, first with cedar oil and certain other preparations, and then with myrrh, cinnamon, and such spices as have the faculty not only of preserving it for a long time but also of giving it a fragrant odour. After treating the body they return it to the relatives of the deceased, every member of it having been so preserved intact that even the hair on the eyelids and brows remains, the entire appearance of the body is unchanged, and the cast of its shape is recognisable. This explains why many Egyptians keep the bodies of their ancestors in costly chambers and gaze face to face upon those who died many generations before their own birth, so that, as they look upon the stature and proportions and the features of the countenance of each, they experience a strange enjoyment, as though they had lived with those on whom they gaze.

**92.** When the body is ready to be buried the family announces the day of interment to the judges and to the relatives and friends of the deceased, and solemnly affirms that he who has just passed away, giving his name, "is about to cross the lake." Then, when the judges, forty-two in number, have assembled and have taken seats in a hemicycle which has been built across the lake, the *baris* is launched, which has been prepared in advance by men especially engaged in that service, and which is in the charge of the boatman whom the Egyptians in their language call *charon*. For this reason they insist that Orpheus, having visited Egypt in ancient times and witnessed this custom, merely invented his account of Hades, in part reproducing this practice and in part inventing on his own account; but this point we shall discuss more fully a little later. At any rate, after the *baris* has been launched into the lake but before the coffin containing the body is set in it, the law gives permission to anyone who wishes to arraign the dead person. Now if anyone presents himself and makes a charge, and shows that the dead man had led an evil life, the judges announce the decision to all and the body is denied the customary burial; but if it shall appear that the accuser has made an unjust charge he is severely punished. When no accuser appears or the one who presents himself is discovered to be a slanderer, the relatives put their mourning aside and laud the deceased. Of his ancestry, indeed, they say nothing, as the Greeks do, since they hold that all Egyptians are equally well born, but after recounting his training and education from childhood, they describe his righteousness and justice after he attained to manhood, also his self-control and his other virtues, and call upon the gods of the lower world to receive him into the company of the righteous. The multitude shouts its assent and extols the glory of the deceased, as one who is about to spend eternity in Hades among the righteous. Those who have private sepulchres lay the body in a vault reserved for it, but those who possess none construct a new chamber in their own home, and stand the coffin upright against the firmest wall. Any also who are forbidden burial because of the accusations brought against them or because their bodies have been made security for a loan they lay away in their own homes; it sometimes happens that their sons' sons, when they have become prosperous and paid off the debt or cleared them of the charges, give them later a magnificent funeral.

**93.** It is a most sacred duty, in the eyes of the Egyptians, that they should be seen to honour their parents or ancestors all the more after they have passed to their eternal home. Another custom of theirs is to put up the bodies of their deceased parents as security for a loan; and failure to repay such debts is attended with the deepest disgrace as well as with deprivation of burial at death. A person may well admire the men who established these customs, because they strove to inculcate in the inhabitants, so far as was possible, virtuousness and excellence of character, by means not only of their converse with the living but also of their burial and affectionate care of the dead. The Greeks have handed down their beliefs in such matters, in the honour paid to the righteous and the punishment of the wicked, by means of fanciful tales and discredited legends; consequently these accounts not only cannot avail to spur their people on to the best life, but, on the contrary, being scoffed at by worthless men, are received with contempt. Among the Egyptians, since these matters do not belong to the realm of myth but men see with their own eyes that punishment is meted out to the wicked and honour to the good, every day of their lives both the wicked and the good are reminded of their obligations and in this way the greatest and most profitable amendment of men's characters is effected. The best laws, in my opinion, must be held to be, not those by which men become most prosperous, but those by which they become most virtuous in character and best fitted for citizenship.

**94.** We must speak also of the lawgivers who have arisen in Egypt and who instituted customs unusual and strange. After the establishment of settled life in Egypt in early times, which took place, according to the mythical account, in the period of the gods and heroes, the first, they say, to persuade the multitudes to use written laws was Mneves, [Menas?] a man not only great of soul but also in his life the most public-spirited of all lawgivers whose names are recorded. According to the tradition he claimed that Hermes had given the laws to him, with the assurance that they would be the cause of great blessings, just as among the Greeks, they say, Minos did in Crete and Lycurgus among the Lacedaemonians, the former saying that he received his laws from Zeus and the latter his from Apollo. Also among several other peoples tradition says that this kind of a device was used and was the cause of much good to such as believed it. Thus it is recorded that among the Arians Zathraustes [Zarathustra / Zoroaster] claimed that the Good Spirit gave him his laws, among the people known as the Getae who represent themselves to be immortal Zalmoxis asserted the same of their common goddess Hestia, and among the Jews Moyses referred his laws to the god who is invoked as Iao. They all did this either because they believed that a conception which would help humanity was marvellous and wholly divine, or because they held that the common crowd would be more likely to obey the laws if their gaze were directed towards the majesty and power of those to whom their laws were ascribed.

A second lawgiver, according to the Egyptians, was Sasychis, a man of unusual understanding. He made sundry additions to the existing laws and, in particular, laid down with the greatest precision the rites to be used in honouring the gods, and he was the inventor of geometry and taught his countrymen both to speculate about the stars and to observe them. A third one, they tell us, was the king Sesoösis, who not only performed the most renowned deeds in war of any king of Egypt but also organised the rules governing the warrior class and, in conformity with these, set in order all the regulations that have to do with military campaigns. A fourth lawgiver, they say, was the king Bocchoris, a wise sort of a man and conspicuous for his craftiness. He drew up all the regulations which governed the kings and gave precision to the laws on contracts; and so wise was he in his judicial decisions as well, that many of his judgments are remembered for their excellence even to our day. And they add that he was very weak in body, and that by disposition he was the most avaricious of all their kings.

**95.** After Bocchoris, they say, their king Amasis [569-526] gave attention to the laws, who, according to their accounts, drew up the rules governing the nomarchs and the entire administration of Egypt. And tradition describes him as exceedingly wise and in disposition virtuous and just, for which reasons the Egyptians invested him with the kingship, although he was not of the royal line. They say also that the citizens of Elis, when they were giving their attention to the Olympic Games, sent an embassy to him to ask how they could be conducted with the greatest fairness, and that he replied, "Provided no man of Elis participates." Though Polycrates, the ruler of the Samians, had been on terms of friendship with him, when he began oppressing both citizens and such foreigners as put in at Samos, it is said that Amasis at first sent an embassy to him and urged him to moderation; and when no attention was paid to this, he wrote a letter in which he broke up the relations of friendship and hospitality that had existed between them; for he did not wish, as he said, to be plunged into grief in a short while, knowing right well as he did that misfortune is near at hand for the ruler who maintains a tyranny in such fashion, and he was admired, they say, among the Greeks both because of his virtuous character and because his words to Polycrates were speedily fulfilled.

A sixth man to concern himself with the laws of the Egyptians, [521-486] it is said, was Darius the father of Xerxes; for he was incensed at the lawlessness which his predecessor, Cambyses, had shown in his treatment of the sanctuaries of Egypt, and aspired to live a life of virtue and of piety towards the gods. Indeed he associated with the priests of Egypt themselves, and took part with them in the study of theology and of the events recorded in their sacred books; and when he learned from these books about the greatness of soul of the ancient kings and about their goodwill towards their subjects he imitated their manner of life. For this reason he was the object of such great honour that he alone of all the kings was addressed as a god by the Egyptians in his lifetime, while at his death he was accorded equal honours with the ancient kings of Egypt who had ruled in strictest accord with the laws.

The system, then, of law used throughout the land was the work, they say, of the men just named, and gained a renown that spread among other peoples everywhere; but in later times, they say, many institutions which were regarded as good were changed, after the Macedonians had conquered and destroyed once and for all the kingship of the native line.

### *On those Greeks, renowned for their learning, who visited Egypt and upon acquiring much useful knowledge brought it to Greece (96 ff.)*

**96.** Now that we have examined these matters, we must enumerate what Greeks, who have won fame for their wisdom and learning, visited Egypt in ancient times, in order to become acquainted with its customs and learning. For the priests of Egypt recount from the records of their sacred books that they were visited in early times by Orpheus, Musaeus, Melampus, and Daedalus, also by the poet Homer and Lycurgus of Sparta, later by Solon of Athens and the philosopher Plato, and that there also came Pythagoras of Samos and the mathematician Eudoxus, as well as Democritus of Abdera and Oenopides of Chios. As evidence for the visits of all these men they point in some cases to their statues and in others to places or buildings which bear their names, and they offer proofs from the branch of learning which each one of these men pursued, arguing that all the things for which they were admired among the Greeks were transferred from Egypt.

Orpheus, for instance, brought from Egypt most of his mystic ceremonies, the orgiastic rites that accompanied his wanderings, and his fabulous account of his experiences in Hades. For the rite of Osiris is the same as that of Dionysus and that of Isis very similar to that of Demeter, the names alone having been interchanged; and the punishments in Hades of the unrighteous, the Fields of the Righteous, and the fantastic conceptions, current among the many, which are figments of the imagination: all these were introduced by Orpheus in imitation of the Egyptian funeral customs. Hermes, for instance, the Conductor of Souls, according to the ancient Egyptian custom, brings up the body of the Apis to a certain point and then gives it over to one who wears the mask of Cerberus, and after Orpheus had introduced this notion among the Greeks, Homer followed it when he wrote:

> Cyllenian Hermes then did summon forth
> The suitors' souls, holding his wand in hand.

And again a little further on he says:

> They passed Oceanus' streams, the Gleaming Rock,
> The Portals of the Sun, the Land of Dreams;
> And now they reached the Meadow of Asphodel,
> Where dwell the Souls, the shades of men outworn.

Now he calls the river "Oceanus" because in their language the Egyptians speak of the Nile as Oceanus; the "Portals of the Sun" (*Heliopylai*) is his name for the city of Heliopolis; and "Meadows," the mythical dwelling of the dead, is his term for the place near the lake which is called Acherousia, which is near Memphis, and around it are fairest meadows, of a marsh-land and lotus and reeds. The same explanation also serves for the statement that the dwelling of the dead is in these regions, since the most and the largest tombs of the Egyptians are situated there, the dead being ferried across both the river and Lake Aeherousia and their bodies laid in the vaults situated there.

The other myths about Hades, current among the Greeks, also agree with the customs which are practised even now in Egypt, for the boat which receives the bodies is called *baris*, and the passenger's fee is given to the boatman, who in the Egyptian tongue is called *charon,* and near these regions, they say, are also the "Shades," which is a temple of Hecate, and "portals" of Cocytus and Lethe, which are covered at intervals with bands of bronze. There are, moreover, other portals, namely, those of Truth, and near them stands a headless statue of Justice.

**97.** Many other things as well, of which mythology tells, are still to be found among the Egyptians; the name being still preserved and the customs actually practised. In the city of Acanthi, for instance, across the Nile in the direction of Libya one hundred and twenty stades from Memphis, there is a perforated jar to which three hundred and sixty priests, one each day, bring water from the Nile; [daughters of Danaus] and not far from there the actual performance of the myth of Ocnus is to be seen in one of their festivals, where a single man is weaving at one end of a long rope and many others beyond him are unravelling it. Melampus also, they say, brought from Egypt the rites which the Greeks celebrate in the name of Dionysus, the myths about Cronus and the War with the Titans, and, in a word, the account of the things which happened to the gods. Daedalus, they relate, copied the maze of the Labyrinth which stands to our day and was built, according to some, by Mendes, but according to others, by king Marrus, many years before the reign of Minos. The proportions of the ancient statues of Egypt are the same as in those made by Daedalus among the Greeks.

The very beautiful propylon of the temple of Hephaestus in Memphis was also built by Daedalus, who became an object of admiration and was granted a statue of himself in wood, which was made by his own hands and set up in this temple; furthermore, he was accorded great fame because of his genius and, after making many discoveries, was granted divine honours; for on one of the islands off Memphis there stands even to this day a temple of Daedalus, which is honoured by the people of that region.

As proof of the presence of Homer in Egypt they adduce various pieces of evidence, and especially the healing drink which brings forgetfulness of all past evils, which was given by Helen to Telemachus in the home of Menelaüs. For it is manifest that the poet had acquired exact knowledge of the "nepenthic" [quieting pain] drug which he says Helen brought from Egyptian Thebes, given her by Polydamna the wife of Thon; for, they allege, even to this day the women of this city use this powerful remedy, and in ancient times, they say, a drug to cure anger and sorrow was discovered exclusively among the women of Diospolis; but Thebes and Diospolis, they add, are the same city. Again, Aphrodite is called "golden" by the natives in accordance with an old tradition, and near the city which is called Momemphis there is a plain "of golden Aphrodite." Likewise, the myths which are related about the dalliance of Zeus and Hera and of their journey to Ethiopia he also got from Egypt; for each year among the Egyptians the shrine of Zeus is carried across the river into Libya and then brought back some days later, as if the god were arriving from Ethiopia; and as for the dalliance of these deities, in their festal gatherings the priests carry the shrines of both to an elevation that has been strewn with flowers of every description.

**98.** Lycurgus also and Plato and Solon, they say, incorporated many Egyptian customs into their own legislation, and Pythagoras learned from Egyptians his teachings about the gods, his geometrical propositions and theory of numbers, as well as the transmigration of the soul into every living thing. Democritus also, as they assert, spent five years among them and was instructed in many matters relating to astrology. Oenopides likewise passed some time with the priests and astrologers and learned among other things about the orbit of the sun, that it has an oblique course and moves in a direction opposite to that of the other stars. Like the others, Eudoxus studied astrology with them and acquired a notable fame for the great amount of useful knowledge which he disseminated among the Greeks.

Also of the ancient sculptors the most renowned sojourned among them, namely, Telecles and Theodorus, the sons of Rhoecus, who executed for the people of Samos the wooden statue of the Pythian Apollo. One half of the statue, as the account is given, was worked by Telecles in Samos, and the other half was finished by his brother Theodorus at Ephesus; and when the two parts were brought together they fitted so perfectly that the whole work had the appearance of having been done by one man. This method of working is practised nowhere among the Greeks, but is followed generally among the Egyptians, for with them the symmetrical proportions of the statues are not fixed in accordance with the appearance they present to the artist's eye, as is done among the Greeks, but as soon as they lay out the stones and, after apportioning them, are ready to work on them, at that stage they take the proportions, from the smallest parts to the largest; by dividing the structure of the entire body into twenty-one parts and one-fourth in addition, they express in this way the complete figure in its symmetrical proportions. Consequently, so soon as the artisans agree as to the size of the statue, they separate and proceed to turn out the various sizes assigned to them, in such a way that they correspond, and they do it so accurately that the peculiarity of their system excites amazement. The wooden statue in Samos, in conformity with the ingenious method of the Egyptians, was cut into two parts from the top of the head down to the private parts and the statue was divided in the middle, each part exactly matching the other at every point. They say that this statue is for the most part rather similar to those of Egypt, as having the arms stretched stiffly down the sides and the legs separated in a stride.

Regarding Egypt, the events which history records and the things that deserve to be mentioned, this account is sufficient; and we shall present in the next Book, in keeping with our profession at the beginning of this Book, the events and legendary accounts next in order, beginning with the part played by the Assyrians in Asia.

# BOOK II

## *On Ninus, the first king in Asia, and his deeds (1-3).*

**1.** The preceding Book, being the first of the whole work, embraces the facts which concern Egypt, among which are included both the myths related by the Egyptians about their gods and about the nature of the Nile, and the other marvels which are told about this river, as well as a description of the land of Egypt and the acts of each of their ancient kings. Next in order came the structures known as the pyramids, which are listed among the seven wonders of the world. After that we discussed such matters connected with the laws and the courts of law, and also with the animals which are considered sacred among the Egyptians, as excite admiration and wonder, also their customs with respect to the dead, and then named such Greeks as were noted for their learning, who, upon visiting Egypt and being instructed in many useful things, thereupon transferred them to Greece. In this present Book we shall set forth the events which took place in Asia in the ancient period, beginning with the time when the Assyrians were the dominant power.

In the earliest age, then, the kings of Asia were native-born, and in connection with them no memory is preserved of either a notable deed or a personal name. The first to be handed down by tradition to history and memory for us as one who achieved great deeds is Ninus, king of the Assyrians, and of him we shall now endeavour to give a detailed account. For being by nature a warlike man and emulous of valour, he supplied the strongest of the young men with arms, and by training them for a considerable time he accustomed them to every hardship and all the dangers of war. And when now he had collected a notable army, he formed an alliance with Ariaeus, the king of Arabia, a country which in those times seems to have abounded in brave men. In general, this nation is one which loves freedom and under no circumstances submits to a foreign ruler; consequently neither the kings of the Persians at a later time nor those of the Macedonians, though the most powerful of their day, were ever able to enslave this nation, for Arabia is, in general, a difficult country for a foreign army to campaign in, part of it being desert and part of it waterless and supplied at intervals with wells which are hidden and known only to the natives. Ninus, however, the king.of the Assyrians, taking along the ruler of the Arabians as an ally, made a campaign with a great army against the Babylonians whose country bordered upon his; in those times the present city of Babylon had not yet been founded, but there were other notable cities in Babylonia, and after easily subduing the inhabitants of that region because of their inexperience in the dangers of war, he laid upon them the yearly payment of fixed tributes, while the king of the conquered, whom he took captive along with his children, he put to death. Then, invading Armenia in great force and laying waste some of its cities, he struck terror into the inhabitants; consequently their king Barzanes, realising that he was no match for him in battle, met him with many presents and announced that he would obey his every command. Ninus treated him with great magnanimity, and agreed that he should not only continue to rule over Armenia but should also, as his friend, furnish a contingent and supplies for the Assyrian army, and as his power continually increased, he made a campaign against Media. The king of this country, Pharnus, meeting him in battle with a formidable force, was defeated, and he both lost the larger part of his soldiers, and himself, being taken captive along with his seven sons and wife, was crucified.

**2.** Since the undertakings of Ninus were prospering in this way, he was seized with a powerful desire to subdue all of Asia that lies between the Tanais [the Don] and the Nile, for as a general thing, when men enjoy good fortune, the steady current of their success prompts in them the desire for more. Consequently he made one of his friends satrap of Media, while he himself set about the task of subduing the nations of Asia, and within a period of seventeen years he became master of them all except the Indians and Bactrians. No historian has recorded the battles with each nation or the number of all the peoples conquered, but we shall undertake to run over briefly the most important nations, as given in the account of Ctesias of Cnidus.

Of the lands which lie on the sea and of the others which border on these, Ninus subdued Egypt and Phoenicia, then Coele-Syria, Cilicia, Pamphylia, and Lycia, and also Caria, Phrygia, and Lydia; moreover, he brought under his sway the Troad, Phrygia on the Hellespont, Propontis, Bithynia, Cappadocia, and all the barbarian nations who inhabit the shores of the Pontus as far as the Tanaïs; he also made himself lord of the lands of the Cadusii, Tapyri, Hyrcanii, Drangi, of the Derbici, Carmanii, Choromnaei, and of the Borcanii, and Parthyaei; and he invaded both Persis and Susiana and Caspiana, as it is called, which is entered by exceedingly narrow passes, known for that reason as the Caspian Gates. Many other lesser nations he also brought under his rule, about whom it would be a long task to speak. But since Bactriana was difficult to invade and contained multitudes of warlike men, after much toil and labour in vain he deferred to a later time the war against the Bactriani, and leading his forces back into Assyria selected a place excellently situated for the founding of a great city.

**3.** For having accomplished deeds more notable than those of any king before him, he was eager to found a city of such magnitude, that not only would it be the largest of any which then existed in the whole inhabited world, but also that no other ruler of a later time should, if he undertook such a task, find it easy to surpass him. Accordingly, after honouring the king of the Arabians with gifts and rich spoils from his wars, he dismissed him and his contingent to return to their own country and then, gathering his forces from every quarter and all the necessary material, he founded on the Euphrates river a city [Nineveh] which was well fortified with walls, giving it the form of a rectangle. The longer sides of the city were each one hundred and fifty stades in length, and the shorter ninety. So, since the total circuit comprised four hundred and eighty stades, he was not disappointed in his hope, since a city its equal, in respect to either the length of its circuit or the magnificence of its walls, was never founded by any man after his time. For the wall had a height of one hundred feet and its width was sufficient for three chariots abreast to drive upon; and the sum total of its towers was one thousand five hundred, and their height was two hundred feet. He settled in it both Assyrians, who constituted the majority of the population and had the greatest power, and any who wished to come from all other nations.

To the city he gave his own name, Ninus, and he included within the territory of its colonists a large part of the neighbouring country.

### On the birth of Semiramis and her rise (4-5).

**4.** Since after the founding of this city Ninus made a campaign against Bactriana, where he married Semiramis, the most renowned of all women of whom we have any record, it is necessary first of all to tell how she rose from a lowly fortune to such fame.

Now there is in Syria a city known as Ascalon, and not far from it a large and deep lake, full of fish. On its shore is a precinct of a famous goddess whom the Syrians call Derceto; [Astarte] and this goddess has the head of a woman but all the rest of her body is that of a fish, the reason being something like this. The story as given by the most learned of the inhabitants of the region is as follows: Aphrodite, being offended with this goddess, inspired in her a violent passion for a certain handsome youth among her votaries; and Derceto gave herself to the Syrian and bore a daughter, but then, filled with shame of her sinful deed, she killed the youth and exposed the child in a rocky desert region, while she herself, from shame and grief, threw herself into the lake and was changed as to the form of her body into a fish; and it is for this reason that the Syrians to this day abstain from this animal and honour their fish as gods. About the region where the babe was exposed a great multitude of doves had their nests, and by them the child was nurtured in an astounding and miraculous manner; for some of the doves kept the body of the babe warm on all sides by covering it with their wings, while others, when they observed that the cowherds and the other keepers were absent from the nearby steadings, brought milk therefrom in their beaks and fed the babe by putting it drop by drop between its lips. When the child was a year old and in need of more solid nourishment, the doves, pecking off bits from the cheeses, supplied it with sufficient nourishment. Now when the keepers returned and saw that the cheeses had been nibbled about the edges, they were astonished at the strange happening; they accordingly kept a look-out, and on discovering the cause found the infant, which was of surpassing beauty. At once, then, bringing it to their steadings they turned it over to the keeper of the royal herds, whose name was Simmas; and Simmas, being childless, gave every care to the rearing of the girl, as his own daughter, and called her Semiramis, a name slightly altered from the word which, in the language of the Syrians, means "doves," birds which since that time all the inhabitants of Syria have continued to honour as goddesses.

**5.** Such, then, is in substance the story that is told about the birth of Semiramis. When she had already come to the age of marriage and far surpassed all the other maidens in beauty, an officer was sent from the king's court to inspect the royal herds; his name was Onnes, and he stood first among the members of the king's council and had been appointed governor over all Syria. He stopped with Simmas, and on seeing Semiramis was captivated by her beauty; consequently he earnestly entreated Simmas to give him the maiden in lawful marriage and took her off to Ninus, where he married her and begat two sons, Hyapates and Hydaspes. And since the other qualities of Semiramis were in keeping with the beauty of her countenance, it turned out that her husband became completely enslaved by her, and since he would do nothing without her advice he prospered in everything.

It was at just this time that the king, now that he had completed the founding of the city which bore his name, undertook his campaign against the Bactrians. Since he was well aware of the great number and the valour of these men, and realised that the country had many places which because of their strength could not be approached by an enemy, he enrolled a great host of soldiers from all the nations under his sway; for as he had come off badly in his earlier campaign, he was resolved on appearing before Bactriana with a force many times as large as theirs. Accordingly, after the army had been assembled from every source, it numbered, as Ctesias has stated in his history, one million seven hundred thousand foot-soldiers, two hundred and ten thousand cavalry, and slightly less than ten thousand six hundred scythe-bearing chariots.

On first hearing the great size of the army is incredible, but it will not seem at all impossible to any who consider the great extent of Asia and the vast numbers of the peoples who inhabit it. If a man, disregarding the campaign of Darius against the Scythians with eight hundred thousand men and the crossing made by Xerxes against Greece with a host beyond number, should consider the events which have taken place in Europe only yesterday or the day before, he would the more quickly come to regard the statement as credible. In Sicily, for instance, Dionysius led forth on his campaigns from the single city of the Syracusans one hundred and twenty thousand foot-soldiers and twelve thousand cavalry, and from a single harbour four hundred warships, some of which were quadriremes and quinqueremes; and the Romans, a little before the time of Hannibal, foreseeing the magnitude of the war, enrolled all the men in Italy who were fit for military service, both citizens and allies, and the total sum of them fell only a little short of one million; and yet as regards the number of inhabitants a man would not compare all Italy with a single one of the nations of Asia. Let these facts, then, be a sufficient reply on our part to those who try to estimate the populations of the nations of Asia in ancient times on the strength of inferences drawn from the desolation which at the present time prevails in its cities.

### How King Ninus married Semiramis because of her outstanding ability (6).

**6.** Now Ninus in his campaign against Bactriana with so large a force was compelled, because access to the country was difficult and the passes were narrow, to advance his army in divisions. The country of Bactriana, though there were many large cities for the people to dwell in, had one which was the most famous, this being the city containing the royal palace; it was called Bactra, and in size and in the strength of its acropolis was by far the first of them all. The king of the country, Oxyartes, had enrolled all the men of military age, and they had been gathered to the number of four hundred thousand, so taking this force with him and meeting the enemy at the passes, he allowed a division of the army of Ninus to enter the country. When he thought that a sufficient number of the enemy had debouched into the plain he drew out his own forces in battle-order and a fierce struggle then ensued in which the Bactrians put the Assyrians to flight, and pursuing them as far as the mountains which overlooked the field, killed about one hundred thousand of the enemy. Later, when the whole Assyrian force entered their country, the Bactrians, overpowered by the multitude of them, withdrew city by city, each group intending to defend its own homeland, and so Ninus easily subdued all the other cities, but Bactra, because of its strength and the equipment for war which it contained, he was unable to take by storm.

When the siege was proving a long affair the husband of Semiramis, who was enamoured of his wife and was making the campaign with the king, sent for the woman; she, endowed as she was with understanding, daring, and all the other qualities which contribute to distinction, seized the opportunity to display her native ability. First of all, since she was about to set out upon a journey of many days, she devised a garb which made it impossible to distinguish whether the wearer of it was a man or a woman. This dress was well adapted to her needs, as regards both her travelling in the heat, for protecting the colour of her skin, and her convenience in doing whatever she might wish to do, since it was quite pliable and suitable to a young person, and, in a word, was so attractive that in later times the Medes, who were then dominant in Asia, always wore the garb of Semiramis, as did the Persians after them. When Semiramis arrived in Bactriana and observed the progress of the siege, she noted that it was on the plains and at positions which were easily assailed that attacks were being made, but that no one ever assaulted the acropolis because of its strong position, and that its defenders had left their posts there and were coming to the aid of those who were hard pressed on the walls below. Consequently, taking with her such soldiers as were accustomed to clambering up rocky heights, and making her way with them up through a certain difficult ravine, she seized a part of the acropolis and gave a signal to those who were besieging the wall down in the plain. Thereupon the defenders of the city, struck with terror at the seizure of the height, left the walls and abandoned all hope of saving themselves. When the city had been taken in this way, the king, marvelling at the ability of the woman, at first honoured her with great gifts, and later, becoming infatuated with her because of her beauty, tried to persuade her husband to yield her to him of his own accord, offering in return for this favour to give him his own daughter Sosanê to wife. When the man took his offer with ill grace, Ninus threatened to put out his eyes unless he at once acceded to his commands; Onnes, partly out of fear of the king's threats and partly out of his passion for his wife, fell into a kind of frenzy and madness, put a rope about his neck, and hanged himself. Such, then, were the circumstances whereby Semiramis attained the position of queen.

## *How Semiramis, ascending the throne on the death of Ninus, accomplished many great deeds. (7) The founding of Babylon and an account of its building (7-9).*

7. Ninus secured the treasures of Bactra, which contained a great amount of both gold and silver, and after settling the affairs of Bactriana disbanded his forces. After this he begat by Semiramis a son Ninyas, and then died, leaving his wife as queen. Semiramis buried Ninus in the precinct of the palace and erected over his tomb a very large mound, nine stades high and ten wide, as Ctesias says. Consequently, since the city lay on a plain along the Euphrates, the mound was visible for a distance of many stades, like an acropolis; as this mound stands, they say, even to this day, though Ninus was razed to the ground by the Medes when they destroyed the empire of the Assyrians. [612]

Semiramis, whose nature made her eager for great exploits and ambitious to surpass the fame of her predecessor on the throne, set her mind upon founding a city in Babylonia, and after securing the architects of all the world and skilled artisans and making all the other necessary preparations, she gathered together from her entire kingdom two million men to complete the work. Taking the Euphrates river into the centre she threw about the city a wall with great towers set at frequent intervals, the wall being three hundred and sixty stades [40 miles] in circumference, as Ctesias of Cnidus says, but according to the account of Cleitarchus and certain of those who at a later time crossed into Asia with Alexander, three hundred and sixty-five stades; and these latter add that it was her desire to make the number of stades the same as the days in the year. Making baked bricks fast in bitumen she built a wall with a height, as Ctesias says, of fifty fathoms, but, as some later writers have recorded, of fifty cubits, and wide enough for more than two chariots abreast to drive upon; the towers numbered two hundred and fifty, their height and width corresponding to the massive scale of the wall. It need occasion no wonder that, considering the great length of the circuit wall, Semiramis constructed a small number of towers; since over a long distance the city was surrounded by swamps, she decided not to build towers along that space, the swamps offering a sufficient natural defence, and all along between the dwellings and the walls a road was left two plethra wide.

**8.** In order to expedite the building of these constructions she apportioned a stade to each of her friends, furnishing sufficient material for their task and directing them to complete their work within a year. And when they had finished these assignments with great speed she gratefully accepted their zeal, but she took for herself the construction of a bridge five stades long at the narrowest point of the river, skilfully sinking the piers, which stood twelve feet apart, into its bed. The stones, which were set firmly together, she bonded with iron cramps, and the joints of the cramps she filled by pouring in lead. Again, before the piers on the side which would receive the current she constructed cutwaters whose sides were rounded to turn off the water and which gradually diminished to the width of the pier, in order that the sharp points of the cutwaters might divide the impetus of the stream, while the rounded sides, yielding to its force, might soften the violence of the river. This bridge, then, floored as it was with beams of cedar and cypress and with palm logs of exceptional size and having a width of thirty feet, is considered to have been inferior in technical skill to none of the works of Semiramis. And on each side of the river she built an expensive quay of about the same width as the walls and one hundred and sixty stades long.

Semiramis also built two palaces on the very banks of the river, one at each end of the bridge, her intention being that from them she might be able both to look down over the entire city and to hold the keys, as it were, to its most important sections. And since the Euphrates river passed through the centre of Babylon and flowed in a southerly direction, one palace faced the rising and the other the setting sun, and both had been constructed on a lavish scale. In the case of the one which faced west she made the length of its first or outer circuit wall sixty stades, fortifying it with lofty walls, which had been built at great cost and were of burned brick, and within this she built a second, circular in form, in the bricks of which, before they were baked, wild animals of every kind had been engraved, and by the ingenious use of colours these figures reproduced the actual appearance of the animals themselves; this circuit wall had a length of forty stades, a width of three hundred bricks, and a height, as Ctesias says, of fifty fathoms; the height of the towers, however, was seventy fathoms. And she built within these two yet a third circuit wall, which enclosed an acropolis whose circumference was twenty stades in length, but the height and width of the structure surpassed the dimensions of the middle circuit wall. On both the towers and the walls there were again animals of every kind, ingeniously executed by the use of colours as well as by the realistic imitation of the several types; and the whole had been made to represent a hunt, complete in every detail, of all sorts of wild animals, and their size was more than four cubits. Among the animals, moreover, Semiramis had also been portrayed, on horseback and in the act of hurling a javelin at a leopard, and nearby was her husband Ninus, in the act of thrusting his spear into a lion at close quarters. In this wall she also set triple gates, two of which were of bronze and were opened by a mechanical device.

Now this palace far surpassed in both size and details of execution the one on the other bank of the river, for the circuit wall of the latter, made of burned brick, was only thirty stades long, and instead of the ingenious portrayal of animals it had bronze statues of Ninus and Semiramis and their officers, and one also of Zeus, whom the Babylonians call Belus; [Bel-Marduk] and on it were also portrayed both battle-scenes and hunts of every kind, which filled those who gazed thereon with varied emotions of pleasure.

**9.** After this Semiramis picked out the lowest spot in Babylonia and built a square reservoir, which was three hundred stades long on each side; it was constructed of baked brick and bitumen, and had a depth of thirty-five feet. Then, diverting the river into it, she built an underground passage-way from one palace to the other; and making it of burned brick, she coated the vaulted chambers on both sides with hot bitumen until she had made the thickness of this coating four cubits. The side walls of the passage-way were twenty bricks thick and twelve feet high, exclusive of the barrel-vault, and the width of the passage-way was fifteen feet. And after this construction had been finished in only seven days she let the river back again into its old channel, and so, since the stream flowed above the passageway, Semiramis was able to go across from one palace to the other without passing over the river. At each end of the passage-way she also set bronze gates which stood until the time of the Persian rule.

After this she built in the centre of the city a temple of Zeus whom, as we have said, the Babylonians call Belus. Now since with regard to this temple the historians are at variance, and since time has caused the structure to fall in ruins, it is impossible to give the exact facts concerning it. But all agree that it was exceedingly high, and that in it the Chaldaeans made their observations of the stars, whose risings and settings could be accurately observed by reason of the height of the structure. Now the entire building was ingeniously constructed at great expense of bitumen and brick, and at the top of the ascent Semiramis set up three statues of hammered gold, of Zeus, Hera, and Rhea. Of these statues that of Zeus represented him erect and striding forward, and, being forty feet high, weighed a thousand Babylonian talents; that of Rhea showed her seated on a golden throne and was of the same weight as that of Zeus; and at her knees stood two lions, while near by were huge serpents of silver, each one weighing thirty talents. The statue of Hera was also standing, weighing eight hundred talents, and in her right hand she held a snake by the head and in her left a sceptre studded with precious stones. A table for all three statues, made of hammered gold, stood before them, forty feet long, fifteen wide, and weighing five hundred talents. Upon it rested two drinking-cups, weighing thirty talents. And there were censers as well, also two in number but weighing each three hundred talents, and also three gold mixing bowls, of which the one belonging to Zeus weighed twelve hundred Babylonian talents and the other two six hundred each. But all these were later carried off as spoil by the kings of the Persians, [539] while as for the palaces and the other buildings, time has either entirely effaced them or left them in ruins; of Babylon itself but a small part is inhabited at this time, and most of the area within its walls is given over to agriculture.

## On the hanging garden, as it is called, and the other astonishing things in Babylonia (10-13).

**10.** There was also, beside the acropolis, the Hanging Garden, as it is called, which was built, not by Semiramis, but by a later Syrian king [Chaldaean Nebuchadrezzar, 605-562] to please one of his concubines; she, they say, being a Persian by race and longing for the meadows of her mountains, asked the king to imitate, through the artifice of a planted garden, the distinctive landscape of Persia. The park extended four plethra on each side, and since the approach to the garden sloped like a hillside and the several parts of the structure rose from one another tier on tier, the appearance of the whole resembled that of a theatre. When the ascending terraces had been built, there had been constructed beneath them galleries which carried the entire weight of the planted garden and rose little by little one above the other along the approach; and the uppermost gallery, which was fifty cubits high, bore the highest surface of the park, which was made level with the circuit wall of the battlements of the city. Furthermore, the walls, which had been constructed at great expense, were twenty-two feet thick, while the passage-way between each two walls was ten feet wide. The roofs of the galleries were covered over with beams of stone sixteen feet long, inclusive of the overlap, and four feet wide. The roof above these beams had first a layer of reeds laid in great quantities of bitumen, over this two courses of baked brick bonded by cement, and as a third layer a covering of lead, to the end that the moisture from the soil might not penetrate beneath. On all this again earth had been piled to a depth sufficient for the roots of the largest trees; and the ground, when levelled off, was thickly planted with trees of every kind that, by their great size or any other charm, could give pleasure to the beholder. And since the galleries, each projecting beyond another, all received the light, they contained many royal lodgings of every description; and there was one gallery which contained openings leading from the topmost surface and machines for supplying the garden with water, the machines raising the water in great abundance from the river, although no one outside could see it being done. Now this park, as I have said, was a later construction.

**11.** Semiramis founded other cities also along the Euphrates and Tigris rivers, in which she established trading-places for the merchants who brought goods from Media, Paraetacene, and all the neighbouring region. The Euphrates and Tigris, the most notable, one may say, of all the rivers of Asia after the Nile and Ganges, have their sources in the mountains of Armenia and are two thousand five hundred stades apart at their origin, and after flowing through Media and Paraetacene they enter Mesopotamia, which they enclose between them, thus giving this name to the country. ["region between the rivers"] After this they pass through Babylonia and empty into the Red Sea. Moreover, since they are great streams and traverse a spacious territory they offer many advantages to men who follow a merchant trade; and it is due to this fact that the regions along their banks are filled with prosperous trading-places which contribute greatly to the fame of Babylonia.

Semiramis quarried out a stone from the mountains of Armenia which was one hundred and thirty feet long and twenty-five feet wide and thick; and this she hauled by means of many multitudes of yokes of mules and oxen to the river and there loaded it on a raft, on which she brought it down the stream to Babylonia; she then set it up beside the most famous street, an astonishing sight to all who passed by. And this stone is called by some an obelisk from its shape, and they number it among the seven wonders of the world. [Obelisk is a diminutive of *obelos* ("a spit")].

**12.** Although the sights to be seen in Babylonia are many and singular, not the least wonderful is the enormous amount of bitumen which the country produces; so great is the supply of this that it not only suffices for their buildings, which are numerous and large, but the common people also, gathering at the place, draw it out without any restriction, and drying it burn it in place of wood. And countless as is the multitude of men who draw it out, the amount remains undiminished, as if derived from some immense source. Moreover, near this source there is a vent-hole, of no great size but of remarkable potency. For it emits a heavy sulphurous vapour which brings death to all living creatures that approach it, and they meet with an end swift and strange; for after being subjected for a time to a retention of the breath they are killed, as though the expulsion of the breath were being prevented by the force which has attacked the processes of respiration; and immediately the body swells and blows up, particularly in the region about the lungs. There is also across the river a lake whose edge offers solid footing, and if any man, unacquainted with it, enters it he swims for a short time, but as he advances towards the centre he is dragged down as though by a certain force; and when he begins to help himself and makes up his mind to turn back to shore again, though he struggles to extricate himself, it appears as if he were being hauled back by something else; and he becomes benumbed, first in his feet, then in his legs as far as the groin, and finally, overcome by numbness in his whole body, he is carried to the bottom, and a little later is cast up dead.

Now concerning the wonders of Babylonia let what has been said suffice.

**13.** After Semiramis had made an end of her building operations she set forth in the direction of Media with a great force. And when she had arrived at the mountain known as Bagistanus, [Behistun] she encamped near it and laid out a park, which had a circumference of twelve stades and, being situated in the plain, contained a great spring by means of which her plantings could be irrigated. The

Bagistanus mountain is sacred to Zeus and on the side facing the park has sheer cliffs which rise to a height of seventeen stades. The lowest part of these she smoothed off and engraved thereon a likeness of herself with a hundred spearmen at her side. She also put this inscription on the cliff in Syrian letters: "Semiramis, with the pack-saddles of the beasts of burden in her army, built up a mound from the plain and thereby climbed this precipice, even to its very ridge."

Setting forth from that place and arriving at the city of Chauon in Media, she noticed on a certain high plateau a rock both of striking height and mass. Accordingly, she laid out there another park of great size, putting the rock in the middle of it, and on the rock she erected, to satisfy her taste for luxury, some very costly buildings from which she used to look down both upon her plantings in the park and on the whole army encamped on the plain. In this place she passed a long time and enjoyed to the full every device that contributed to luxury; she was unwilling, however, to contract a lawful marriage, being afraid that she might be deprived of her supreme position, but choosing out the most handsome of the soldiers she consorted with them and then made away with all who had lain with her.

After this she advanced in the direction of Ecbatana and arrived at the mountain called Zarcaeus; [Zagros range] and since this extended many stades and was full of cliffs and chasms it rendered the journey round a long one. And so she became ambitious both to leave an immortal monument of herself and at the same time to shorten her way; consequently she cut through the cliffs, filled up the low places, and thus at great expense built a short road, which to this day is called the road of Semiramis. Upon arriving at Ecbatana, a city which lies on the plain, she built in it an expensive palace and in every other way gave rather exceptional attention to the region. For since the city had no water supply and there was no spring in its vicinity, she made the whole of it well watered by bringing to it with much hardship and expense an abundance of the purest water. For at a distance from Ecbatana of about twelve stades is a mountain, which is called Orontes and is unusual for its ruggedness and enormous height, since the ascent, straight to its summit, is twenty-five stades. And since a great lake, which emptied into a river, lay on the other side, she made a cutting through the base of this mountain. The tunnel was fifteen feet wide and forty feet high; and through it she brought in the river which flowed from the lake, and filled the city with water. Now this is what she did in Media.

### The campaign of Semiramis against Egypt, Ethiopia, and India (14-20).

**14.** After this she visited Persis and every other country over which she ruled throughout Asia. Everywhere she cut through the mountains and the precipitous cliffs and constructed expensive roads, while on the plains she made mounds, sometimes constructing them as tombs for those of her generals who died, and sometimes founding cities on their tops. It was also her custom, whenever she made camp, to build little mounds, upon which setting her tent she could look down upon all the encampment. As a consequence many of the works she built throughout Asia remain to this day and are called Works of Semiramis.

After this she visited all Egypt, and after subduing most of Libya she went also to the oracle of Ammon [in the Oasis of Siwah] to inquire of the god regarding her own end. And the account runs that the answer was given her that she would disappear from among men and receive undying honour among some of the peoples of Asia, and that this would take place when her son Ninyas should conspire against her. Then upon her return from these regions she visited most of Ethiopia, subduing it as she went and inspecting the wonders of the land. For in that country, they say, there is a lake, square in form, with a perimeter of some hundred and sixty feet, and its water is like cinnabar in colour and the odour of it is exceeding sweet, not unlike that of old wine; moreover, it has a remarkable power; for whoever has drunk of it, they say, falls into a frenzy and accuses himself of every sin which he had formerly committed in secret. However, a man may not readily agree with those who tell such things.

**15.** In the burial of their dead the inhabitants of Ethiopia follow customs peculiar to themselves; for after they have embalmed the body and have poured a heavy coat of glass over it they stand it on a pillar, so that the body of the dead man is visible through the glass to those who pass by. This is the statement of Herodotus. But Ctesias of Cnidus, declaring that Herodotus is inventing a tale, gives for his part this account. The body is indeed embalmed, but glass is not poured about the naked bodies, for they would be burned and so completely disfigured that they could no longer preserve their likeness. For this reason they fashion a hollow statue of gold and when the corpse has been put into this they pour the glass over the statue, and the figure, prepared in this way, is then placed at the tomb, and the gold, fashioned as it is to resemble the deceased, is seen through the glass. Now the rich among them are buried in this wise, he says, but those who leave a smaller estate receive a silver statue, and the poor one made of earthenware; as for the glass, there is enough of it for everyone, since it occurs in great abundance in Ethiopia and is quite current among the inhabitants. With regard to the customs prevailing among the Ethiopians and the other features of their country we shall a little later set forth those that are the most important and deserving of record, at which time we shall also recount their early deeds and their mythology.

**16.** After Semiramis had put in order the affairs of Ethiopia and Egypt she returned with her force to Bactra in Asia. Since she had great forces and had been at peace for some time she became eager to achieve some brilliant exploit in war. And when she was informed that the Indian nation was the largest one in the world and likewise possessed both the most extensive and the fairest country, she purposed to make a campaign into India. Stabrobates at that time was king of the country and had a multitude of soldiers without number; and many elephants were also at his disposal, fitted out in an exceedingly splendid fashion with such things as would strike terror in war. For India is a land of unusual beauty, and since it is traversed by many rivers it is supplied with water over its whole area and yields two harvests each year; consequently it has such an abundance of the necessities of life that at all times it favours its inhabitants with a bounteous enjoyment of them. It is said that because of the favourable climate in those parts the country has never experienced a famine or a destruction of crops. It also has an unbelievable multitude of elephants, which both in courage and in strength of body far surpass those of Libya, and likewise gold, silver, iron, and copper; furthermore, within its borders are to be found great quantities of precious stones of every kind and of practically all other things which contribute to luxury and wealth.

When Semiramis had received a detailed account of these facts she was led to begin her war against the Indians, although she had been done no injury by them. And realising that she needed an exceedingly great force in addition to what she had she despatched messengers to all the satrapies, commanding the governors to enrol the bravest of the young men and setting their quota in accordance with the size of each nation; and she further ordered them all to make new suits of armour and to be at hand, brilliantly equipped in every other respect, at Bactra on the third year thereafter. She also summoned shipwrights from Phoenicia, Syria, Cyprus, and the rest of the lands along the sea, and shipping thither an abundance of timber she ordered them to build river boats which could be taken to pieces. For the Indus river, by reason of its being the largest in that region and the boundary of her kingdom, required many boats, some for the passage across and others from which to defend the former from the Indians; and since there was no timber near the river the boats had to be brought from Bactriana by land.

Observing that she was greatly inferior because of her lack of elephants, Semiramis conceived the plan of making dummies like these animals, in the hope that the Indians would be struck with terror because of their belief that no elephants ever existed at all apart from those found in India. Accordingly she chose out three hundred thousand black oxen and distributed their meat among her artisans and the men who had been assigned to the task of making the figures, but the hides she sewed together and stuffed with straw, and thus made dummies, copying in every detail the natural appearance of these animals. Each dummy had within it a man to take care of it and a camel and, when it was moved by the latter, to those who saw it from a distance it looked like an actual animal. The artisans who were engaged in making these dummies for her worked at their task in a certain court which had been surrounded by a wall and had gates which were carefully guarded, so that no worker within could pass out and no one from outside could come in to them. This she did in order that no one from the outside might see what was taking place and that no report about the dummies might escape to the Indians.

**17.** When the boats and the beasts had been prepared in the two allotted years, on the third she summoned her forces from everywhere to Bactriana. And the multitude of the army which was assembled, as Ctesias of Cnidus has recorded, was three million foot-soldiers, two hundred thousand cavalry, and one hundred thousand chariots. There were also men mounted on camels, carrying swords four cubits long, as many in number as the chariots, and river boats which could be taken apart she built to the number of two thousand, and she had collected camels to carry the vessels overland. Camels also bore the dummies of the elephants, as has been mentioned; and the soldiers, by bringing their horses up to these camels, accustomed them not to fear the savage nature of the beasts. A similar thing was also done many years later by Perseus, the king of the Macedonians, before his decisive conflict with the Romans who had elephants from Libya. [Third Macedonian War, 171-167] But neither in his case did it turn out that the zeal and ingenuity displayed in such matters had any effect on the conflict, nor in that of Semiramis, as will be shown more precisely in our further account.

When Stabrobates, the king of the Indians, heard of the immensity of the forces mentioned and of the exceedingly great preparations which had been made for the war, he was anxious to surpass Semiramis in every respect. First of all, then, he made four thousand river boats out of reeds; for along its rivers and marshy places India produces a great abundance of reeds, so large in diameter that a man cannot easily put his arms about them; and it is said, furthermore, that ships built of these are exceedingly serviceable, since this wood does not rot. Moreover, he gave great care to the preparation of his arms and by visiting all India gathered a far greater force than that which had been collected by Semiramis. Furthermore, holding a hunt of the wild elephants and multiplying many times the number already at his disposal, he fitted them all out splendidly with such things as would strike terror in war; and the consequence was that when they advanced to the attack the multitude of them as well as the towers upon their backs made them appear like a thing beyond the power of human nature to withstand.

**18.** When he had made all his preparations for the war he despatched messengers to Semiramis, who was already on the road, accusing her of being the aggressor in the war although she had been injured in no respect; then, in the course of his letter, after saying many slanderous things against her as being a strumpet and calling upon the gods as witnesses, he threatened her with crucifixion when he had defeated her. Semiramis, however, on reading his letter dismissed his statements with laughter and remarked, "It will be in deeds that the Indian will make trial of my valour." When her advance brought her with her force to the Indus river she found the boats of the enemy ready for battle. Consequently she on her side, hastily putting together her boats and manning them with her best marines, joined battle on the river, while the foot-soldiers which were drawn up along the banks also participated eagerly in the contest. The struggle raged for a long time and both sides fought spiritedly, but finally Semiramis was victorious and destroyed about a thousand of the boats, taking also not a few men prisoners. Elated now by her victory, she reduced to slavery the islands in the river and the cities on them and gathered in more than one hundred thousand captives.

After these events the king of the Indians withdrew his force from the river, giving the appearance of retreating in fear, but actually with the intention of enticing the enemy to cross the river. Thereupon Semiramis, now that her undertakings were prospering as she wished, spanned the river with a costly and large bridge, by means of which she got all her forces across; and then she left sixty thousand men to guard the pontoon bridge, while with the rest of her army she advanced in pursuit of the Indians, the dummy elephants leading the way in order that the enemy's spies might report to the king the multitude of these animals in her army. Nor was she deceived in this hope; on the contrary, when those who had been despatched to spy her out reported to the Indians the multitude of elephants among the enemy, they were all at a loss to discover from where such a multitude of beasts as accompanied her could have come. However, the deception did not remain a secret for long; for some of Semiramis' troops were caught neglecting their night watches in the camp, and these, in fear of the consequent punishment, deserted to the enemy and pointed out to them their mistake regarding the nature of the elephants. Encouraged by this information, the king of the Indians, after informing his army about the dummies, set his forces in array and turned about to face the Assyrians.

**19.** Semiramis likewise marshalled her forces, and as the two armies neared each other Stabrobates, the king of the Indians, despatched his cavalry and chariots far in advance of the main body. But the queen stoutly withstood the attack of the cavalry, and since the elephants which she had fabricated had been stationed at equal intervals in front of the main body of troops, it came about that the horses of the Indians shied at them. For whereas at a distance the dummies looked like the actual animals with which the horses of the Indians were acquainted and therefore charged upon them boldly enough, yet on nearer contact the odour which reached the horses was unfamiliar, and then the other differences, which taken all together were very great, threw them into utter confusion. Consequently some of the Indians were thrown to the ground, while others, since their horses would not obey the rein, were carried with their mounts pell-mell into the midst of the enemy. Then Semiramis, who was in the battle with a select band of soldiers, made skilful use of her advantage and put the Indians to flight. But although these fled towards the battle-line, King Stabrobates, undismayed, advanced the ranks of his foot-soldiers, keeping the elephants in front, while he himself, taking his position on the right wing and fighting from the most powerful of the beasts, charged in terrifying fashion upon the queen, whom chance had placed opposite him. Since the rest of the elephants followed his example, the army of Semiramis withstood but a short time the attack of the beasts; for the animals, by virtue of their extraordinary courage and the confidence which they felt in their power, easily destroyed everyone who tried to withstand them. Consequently there was a great slaughter, which was effected in various ways, some being trampled beneath their feet, others ripped up by their tusks, and a number tossed into the air by their trunks. And since a great multitude of corpses lay piled one upon the other and the danger aroused terrible consternation and fear in those who witnessed the sight, not a man had the courage to hold his position any longer.

Now when the entire multitude turned in flight the king of the Indians pressed his attack upon Semiramis herself, and first he let fly an arrow and struck her on the arm, and then with his javelin he pierced the back of the queen, but only with a glancing blow; and since for this reason Semiramis was not seriously injured she rode swiftly away, the pursuing beast being much inferior in speed. Since all were fleeing to the pontoon bridge and so great a multitude was forcing its way into a single narrow space, some of the queen's soldiers perished by being trampled upon by one another and by cavalry and foot-soldiers being thrown together in unnatural confusion, and when the Indians pressed hard upon them a violent crowding took place on the bridge because of their terror, so that many were pushed to either side of the bridge and fell into the river. As for Semiramis, when the largest part of the survivors of the battle had found safety by putting the river behind them, she cut the fastenings which held the bridge together; and when these were loosened the pontoon bridge, having been broken apart at many points and bearing great numbers of the pursuing Indians, was carried down in haphazard fashion by the violence of the current and caused the death of many of the Indians, but for Semiramis it was the means of complete safety, the enemy now being prevented from crossing over against her. After these events the king of the Indians remained inactive, since heavenly omens appeared to him which his seers interpreted to mean that he must not cross the river, and Semiramis, after exchanging prisoners, made her way back to Bactra with the loss of two-thirds of her force.

**20.** Some time later her son Ninyas conspired against her through the agency of a certain eunuch; and remembering the prophecy given her by Ammon, she did not punish the conspirator, but, on the contrary, after turning the kingdom over to him and commanding the governors to obey him, she at once disappeared, as if she were going to be translated to the gods as the oracle had predicted. Some, making a myth of it, say that she turned into a dove and flew off in the company of many birds which alighted on her dwelling, and this, they say, is the reason why the Assyrians worship the dove as a god, thus deifying Semiramis. Be that as it may, this woman, after having been queen over all Asia with the exception of India, passed away in the manner mentioned above, having lived sixty-two years and having reigned forty-two.

Such, then, is the account that Ctesias of Cnidus has given about Semiramis; but Athenaeus and certain other historians say that she was a comely courtesan and because of her beauty was loved by the king of the Assyrians. Now at first she was accorded only a moderate acceptance in the palace, but later, when she had been proclaimed a lawful wife, she persuaded the king to yield the royal prerogatives to her for a period of five days, and Semiramis, upon receiving the sceptre and the regal garb, on the first day held high festival and gave a magnificent banquet, at which she persuaded the commanders of the military forces and all the greatest dignitaries to co-operate with her; and on the second day, while the people and the most notable citizens were paying her their respects as queen, she arrested her husband and put him in prison; and since she was by nature a woman of great designs and bold as well, she seized the throne and remained queen until old age and accomplished many great things. Such, then, are the conflicting accounts which may be found in the historians regarding the career of Semiramis.

### *On her descendants who were kings in Asia and their luxury and sluggishness (21-22).*

**21.** After her death Ninyas, the son of Ninus and Semiramis, succeeded to the throne and had a peaceful reign, since he in no wise emulated his mother's fondness for war and her adventurous spirit. In the first place, he spent all his time in the palace, seen by no one but his concubines and the eunuchs who attended him, and devoted his life to luxury and idleness and the consistent avoidance of any suffering or anxiety, holding the end and aim of a happy reign to be the enjoyment of every kind of pleasure without restraint. Moreover, having in view the safety of his crown and the fear he felt with reference to his subjects, he used to summon each year a fixed number of soldiers and a general from each nation and to keep the army, which had been gathered in this way from all his subject peoples, outside his capital, appointing as commander of each nation one of the most trustworthy men in his service; and at the end of the year he would summon from his peoples a second equal number of soldiers and dismiss the former to their countries. The result of this device was that all those subject to his rule were filled with awe, seeing at all times a great host encamped in the open and punishment ready to fall on any who rebelled or would not yield obedience. This annual change of the soldiers was devised by him in order that, before the generals and all the other commanders of the army should become well acquainted with each other, every man of them would have been separated from the rest and have gone back to his own country; for long service in the field both gives the commanders experience in the arts of war and fills them with arrogance, and, above all, it offers great opportunities for rebellion and for plotting against their rulers. The fact that he was seen by no one outside the palace made everyone ignorant of the luxury of his manner of life, and through their fear of him, as of an unseen god, each man dared not show disrespect of him even in word, so by appointing generals, satraps, financial officers, and judges for each nation and arranging all other matters as he felt at any time to be to his advantage, he remained for his lifetime in the city of Ninus.

The rest of the kings also followed his example, son succeeding father upon the throne, and reigned for thirty generations down to Sardanapallus; for it was under this ruler that the Empire of the Assyrians fell to the Medes, [612] after it had lasted more than thirteen hundred years, as Ctesias of Cnidus says in his Second Book.

22. There is no special need of giving all the names of the kings and the number of years which each of them reigned because nothing was done by them which merits mentioning. The only event which has been recorded is the despatch by the Assyrians to the Trojans of an allied force, which was under the command of Memnon the son of Tithonus. When Teutamus, they say, was ruler of Asia, being the twentieth in succession from Ninyas the son of Semiramis, the Greeks made an expedition against Troy with Agamemnon,[ca. 1190] at a time when the Assyrians had controlled Asia for more than a thousand years. And Priam, who was king of the Troad and a vassal of the king of the Assyrians, being hard pressed by the war, sent an embassy to the king requesting aid; and Teutamus despatched ten thousand Ethiopians and a like number of the men of Susiana along with two hundred chariots, having appointed as general Memnon the son of Tithonus. Now Tithonus, who was at that time general of Persis, was the most highly esteemed of the governors at the king's court, and Memnon, who was in the bloom of manhood, was distinguished both for his bravery and for his nobility of spirit. He also built the palace in the upper city of Susa which stood until the time of the Persian Empire and was called after him Memnonian; moreover, he constructed through the country a public highway which bears the name Memnonian to this time, but the Ethiopians who border upon Egypt dispute this, maintaining that this man was a native of their country, and they point out an ancient palace which to this day, they say, bears the name Memnonian. At any rate, the account runs that Memnon went to the aid of the Trojans with twenty thousand foot-soldiers and two hundred chariots; and he was admired for his bravery and slew many Greeks in the fighting, but was finally ambushed by the Thessalians and slain; whereupon the Ethiopians recovered his

body, burned the corpse, and took the bones back to Tithonus. Such is the account concerning Memnon that is given in the royal records, according to what the barbarians say.

### *How Sardanapallus, the last king, because of his luxuriousness lost his throne to Arbaces the Mede (23-28).*

**23.** Sardanapallus, the thirtieth in succession from Ninus, who founded the empire, and the last king of the Assyrians, outdid all his predecessors in luxury and sluggishness. For not to mention the fact that he was not seen by any man residing outside the palace, he lived the life of a woman, and spending his days in the company of his concubines and spinning purple garments and working the softest of wool, he had assumed the feminine garb and so covered his face and indeed his entire body with whitening cosmetics and the other unguents used by courtesans, that he rendered it more delicate than that of any luxury-loving woman. He also took care to make even his voice to be like a woman's, and at his carousals not only to indulge regularly in those drinks and viands which could offer the greatest pleasure, but also to pursue the delights of love with men as well as with women; he practised sexual indulgence of both kinds without restraint, showing not the least concern for the disgrace attending such conduct. To such an excess did he go of luxury and of the most shameless sensual pleasure and intemperance, that he composed a funeral dirge for himself and commanded his successors upon the throne to inscribe it upon his tomb after his death; it was composed by him in a foreign language but was afterwards translated by a Greek as follows:

> Knowing full well that thou wert mortal born,
> Thy heart lift up, take thy delight in feasts;
> When dead no pleasure more is thine. Thus I,
> Who once o'er mighty Ninus ruled, am naught
> But dust. Yet these are mine which gave me joy
> In life - the food I ate, my wantonness,
> And love's delights. But all those other things
> Men deem felicities are left behind.

Because he was a man of this character, not only did he end his own life in a disgraceful manner, but he caused the total destruction of the Assyrian Empire, which had endured longer than any other known to history.

**24.** The facts are these: A certain Arbaces, a Mede by race, and conspicuous for his bravery and nobility of spirit, was the general of the contingent of Medes which was sent each year to Ninus. And having made the acquaintance during this service of the general of the Babylonians, he was urged by him to overthrow the empire of the Assyrians. Now this man's name was Belesys, and he was the most distinguished of those priests whom the Babylonians call Chaldaeans. And since as a consequence he had the fullest experience of astrology and divination, he was wont to foretell the future unerringly to the people in general; therefore, being greatly admired for this gift, he also predicted to the general of the Medes, who was his friend, that it was certainly fated for him to be king over all the territory which was then held by Sardanapallus. Arbaces, commending the man, promised to give him the satrapy of Babylonia when the affair should be consummated, and for his part, like a man elated by a message from some god, both entered into a league with the commanders of the other nations and assiduously invited them all to banquets and social gatherings, establishing thereby a friendship with each of them. He was resolved also to see the king face to face and to observe his whole manner of life. Consequently he gave one of the eunuchs a golden bowl as a present and gained admittance to Sardanapallus; and when he had observed at close hand both his luxuriousness and his love of effeminate pursuits and practices, he despised the king as worthy of no consideration and was led all the more to cling to the hopes which had been held out to him by the Chaldaean. And the conclusion of the matter was that he formed a conspiracy with Belesys, whereby he should himself move the Medes and Persians to revolt while the latter should persuade the Babylonians to join the undertaking and should secure the help of the commander of the Arabs, who was his friend, for the attempt to secure the supreme control.

When the year's time of their service in the king's army had passed and, another force having arrived to replace them, the relieved men had been dismissed as usual to their homes, thereupon Arbaces persuaded the Medes to attack the Assyrian kingdom and the Persians to join in the conspiracy, on the condition of receiving their freedom from the Assyrians. Belesys too in similar fashion both persuaded the Babylonians to strike for their freedom, and sending an embassy to Arabia, won over the commander of the people of that country, a friend of his who exchanged hospitality with him, to join in the attack. After a year's time all these leaders gathered a multitude of soldiers and came with all their forces to Ninus, ostensibly bringing up replacements, as was the custom, but in fact with the intention of destroying the empire of the Assyrians. Now when these four nations had gathered into one place the whole number of them amounted to four hundred thousand men, and when they had assembled into one camp they took counsel together concerning the best plan to pursue.

**25.** As for Sardanapallus, so soon as he became aware of the revolt, he led forth against the rebels the contingents which had come from the rest of the nations, and at first, when battle was joined on the plain, those who were making the revolt were defeated, and after heavy losses were pursued to a mountain which was seventy stades distant from Ninus; but afterwards, when they came down again into the plain and were preparing for battle, Sardanapallus marshalled his army against them and despatched heralds to the camp of the enemy to make this proclamation: "Sardanapallus will give two hundred talents of gold to anyone who slays Arbaces the Mede, and will make a present of twice that amount to anyone who delivers him up alive and will also appoint him governor over Media." Likewise he promised to reward any who would either slay Belesys the Babylonian or take him alive. But since no man paid any attention to the proclamation, he joined battle, slew many of the rebels, and pursued the remainder of the multitude into their encampment in the mountains.

Arbaces, having lost heart because of these defeats, now convened a meeting of his friends and called upon them to consider what should be done. Now the majority said that they should retire to their respective countries, seize strong positions, and so far as possible prepare there whatever else would be useful for the war; but Belesys the Babylonian, by maintaining that the gods were promising them by signs that with labours and hardship they would bring their enterprise to a successful end, and encouraging them in every other way as much as he could, persuaded them all to remain to face further perils. So there was a third battle, and again the king was victorious, captured the camp of the rebels, and pursued the defeated foe as far as the boundaries of Babylonia; and it also happened that Arbaces himself, who had fought most brilliantly and had slain many Assyrians, was wounded. Now that the rebels had suffered defeats so decisive following one upon the other, their commanders, abandoning all hope of victory, were preparing to disperse each to his own country, but Belesys, who had passed a sleepless night in the open and had devoted himself to the observation of the stars, said to those who had lost hope in their cause, "If you will wait five days help will come of its own accord, and there will be a mighty change to the opposite in the whole situation; for from my long study of the stars I see the gods foretelling this to us." He appealed to them to wait that many days and test his own skill and the good will of the gods.

**26.** So after they had all been called back and had waited the stipulated time, there came a messenger with the news that a force which had been despatched from Bactriana to the king was near at hand, advancing with all speed. Arbaces, accordingly, decided to go to meet their generals by the shortest route, taking along the best and most agile of his troops, so that, in case they should be unable to persuade the Bactrians by arguments to join in the revolt, they might resort to arms to force them to share with them in the same hopes. The outcome was that the new-comers gladly listened to the call to freedom, first the commanders and then the entire force, and they all encamped in the same place.

It happened at this very time that the king of the Assyrians, who was unaware of the defection of the Bactrians and had become elated over his past successes, turned to indulgence and divided among his soldiers for a feast animals and great quantities of both wine and all other provisions. Consequently, since the whole army was carousing, Arbaces, learning from some deserters of the relaxation and drunkenness in the camp of the enemy, made his attack upon it unexpectedly in the night. As it was an assault of organised men upon disorganised and of ready men upon unprepared, they won possession of the camp, and after slaying many of the soldiers pursued the rest of them as far as the city. After this the king named for the chief command Galaemenes, his wife's brother, and gave his own attention to the affairs within the city. The rebels, drawing up their forces in the plain before the city, overcame the Assyrians in two battles, and they not only slew Galaemenes, but of the opposing forces they cut down some in their flight, while others, who had been shut out from entering the city and forced to leap into the Euphrates river, they destroyed almost to a man. So great was the multitude of the slain that the water of the stream, mingled with the blood, was changed in colour over a considerable distance. Furthermore, now that the king was shut up in the city and besieged there, many of the nations revolted, going over in each case to the side of liberty.

Sardanapallus, realising that his entire kingdom was in the greatest danger, sent his three sons and two daughters together with much of his treasure to Paphlagonia to the governor Cotta, who was the most loyal of his subjects, while he himself, despatching letter-carriers to all his subjects, summoned forces and made preparations for the siege. Now there was a prophecy which had come down to him from his ancestors: "No enemy will ever take Ninus by storm unless the river shall first become the city's enemy." Assuming, therefore, that this would never be, he held out in hope, his thought being to endure the siege and await the troops which would be sent from his subjects.

27. The rebels, elated at their successes, pressed the siege, but because of the strength of the walls they were unable to do any harm to the men in the city; for neither engines for throwing stones, nor shelters for sappers,[tortoises] nor battering-rams devised to overthrow walls had as yet been invented at that time. Moreover, the inhabitants of the city had a great abundance of all provisions, since the king had taken thought on that score. Consequently the siege dragged on, and for two years they pressed their attack, making assaults on the walls and preventing the inhabitants of the city from going out into the country; but in the third year, after there had been heavy and continuous rains, it came to pass that the Euphrates, running very full, both inundated a portion of the city and broke down the walls for a distance of twenty stades. At this the king, believing that the oracle had been fulfilled and that the river had plainly become the city's enemy, abandoned hope of saving himself. In order that he might not fall into the hands of the enemy, he built an enormous pyre in his palace, heaped upon it all his gold and silver as well as every article of the royal wardrobe, and then, shutting his concubines and eunuchs in the room which had been built in the middle of the pyre, he consigned both them and himself and his palace to the flames. The rebels, on learning of the death of Sardanapallus, took the city by forcing an entrance where the wall had fallen, and clothing Arbaces in the royal garb saluted him as king and put in his hands the supreme authority.

28. Thereupon, after the new king had distributed among the generals who had aided him in the struggle gifts corresponding to their several deserts, and as he was appointing satraps over the nations, Belesys the Babylonian, who had foretold to Arbaces that he would be king of Asia, coming to him, reminded him of his good services, and asked that he be given the governorship of Babylon, as had been promised at the outset. He also explained that when their cause was endangered he had made a vow to Belus that, if Sardanapallus were defeated and his palace went up in flames, he would bring its ashes to Babylon, and depositing them near the river and the sacred precinct of the god he would construct a mound which, for all who sailed down the Euphrates, would stand as an eternal memorial of the man who had overthrown the rule of the Assyrians. This request he made because he had learned from a certain eunuch, who had made his escape and come to Belesys and was kept hidden by him, of the facts regarding the silver and gold. Now since Arbaces knew nothing of this, by reason of the fact that all the inmates of the palace had been burned along with the king, he allowed him both to carry the ashes away and to hold Babylon without the payment of tribute. Thereupon Belesys procured boats and at once sent off to Babylon along with the ashes practically all the silver and gold; and the king, having been informed of the act which Belesys had been caught perpetrating, appointed as judges the generals who had served with him in the war. And when the accused acknowledged his guilt, the court sentenced him to death, but the king, being a magnanimous man and wishing to make his rule at the outset known for clemency, both freed Belesys from the danger threatening him and

allowed him to keep the silver and gold which he had carried off; likewise, he did not even take from him the governorship over Babylon which had originally been given to him, saying that his former services were greater than his subsequent misdeeds. When this act of clemency was noised about, he won no ordinary loyalty on the part of his subjects as well as renown among the nations, all judging that a man who had conducted himself in this wise towards wrongdoers was worthy of the kingship. Arbaces, however, showing clemency towards the inhabitants of the city, settled them in villages and returned to each man his personal possessions, but the city he levelled to the ground. Then the silver and gold, amounting to many talents, which had been left in the pyre, he collected and took off to Ecbatana in Media.

So the empire of the Assyrians, which had endured from the time of Ninus through thirty generations, for more than one thousand three hundred years, was destroyed by the Medes in the manner described above.

### *On the Chaldaeans and their observation of the stars (29-31).*

**29.** But to us it seems not inappropriate to speak briefly of the Chaldaeans of Babylon and of their antiquity, that we may omit nothing which is worthy of record. Now the Chaldaeans, belonging as they do to the most ancient inhabitants of Babylonia, have about the same position among the divisions of the state as that occupied by the priests of Egypt; for being assigned to the service of the gods they spend their entire life in study, their greatest renown being in the field of astrology. They occupy themselves largely with soothsaying as well, making predictions about future events, and in some cases by purifications, in others by sacrifices, and in others by some other charms they attempt to effect the averting of evil things and the fulfilment of the good. They are also skilled in soothsaying by the flight of birds, and they give out interpretations of both dreams and portents. They also show marked ability in making divinations from the observation of the entrails of animals, deeming that in this branch they are eminently successful.

The training which they receive in all these matters is not the same as that of the Greeks who follow such practices. For among the Chaldaeans the scientific study of these subjects is passed down in the family, and son takes it over from father, being relieved of all other services in the state. Since, therefore, they have their parents for teachers, they not only are taught everything ungrudgingly but also at the same time they give heed to the precepts of their teachers with a more unwavering trust. Furthermore, since they are bred in these teachings from childhood up, they attain a great skill in them, both because of the ease with which youth is taught and because of the great amount of time which is devoted to this study.

Among the Greeks, on the contrary, the student who takes up a large number of subjects without preparation turns to the higher studies only quite late, and then, after labouring upon them to some extent, gives them up, being distracted by the necessity of earning a livelihood; and but a few here and there really strip for the higher studies and continue in the pursuit of them as a profit-making business, and these are always trying to make innovations in connection with the most important doctrines instead of following in the path of their predecessors. The result of this is that the barbarians, by sticking to the same things always, keep a firm hold on every detail, while the Greeks, on the other hand, aiming at the profit to be made out of the business, keep founding new schools and, wrangling with each other over the most important matters of speculation, bring it about that their pupils hold conflicting views, and that their minds, vacillating throughout their lives and unable to believe anything at all with firm conviction, simply wander in confusion. It is at any rate true that, if a man were to examine carefully the most famous schools of the philosophers, he would find them differing from one another to the uttermost degree and maintaining opposite opinions regarding the most fundamental tenets.

**30.** Now, as the Chaldaeans say, the world is by its nature eternal, and neither had a first beginning nor will at a later time suffer destruction; furthermore, both the disposition and the orderly arrangement of the universe have come about by virtue of a divine providence, and to-day whatever takes place in the heavens is in every instance brought to pass, not at haphazard nor by virtue of any spontaneous action, but by some fixed and firmly determined divine decision. Since they have observed the stars over a long period of time and have noted both the movements and the influences of each of them with greater precision than any other men, they foretell to mankind many things that will take place in the future, but above all in importance, they say, is the study of the influence of the five stars known as planets, which they call "Interpreters" when speaking of them as a group, but if referring to them singly, the one named Cronus [Saturn] by the Greeks, which is the most conspicuous and presages more events and such as are of greater importance than the others, they call the star of Helius, whereas the other four they designate as the stars of Ares, Aphrodite, Hermes, and Zeus, [Mars, Venus, Mercury, Jupiter] as do our astrologers. The reason why they call them "Interpreters" is that whereas all the other stars are fixed and follow a single circuit in a regular course, these alone, by virtue of following each its own course, point out future events, thus interpreting to mankind the design of the gods. For sometimes by their risings, sometimes by their settings, and again by their colour, the Chaldaeans say, they give signs of coming events to such as are willing to observe them closely; at one time they show forth mighty storms of winds, at another excessive rains or heat, at times the appearance of comets, also eclipses of both sun and moon, and earthquakes, and in a word all the conditions which owe their origin to the atmosphere and work both benefits and harm, not only to whole peoples or regions, but also to kings and to persons of private station.

Under the course in which these planets move are situated, according to them, thirty stars, which they designate as "counselling gods"; of these one half oversee the regions above the earth and the other half those beneath the earth, having under their purview the affairs of mankind and likewise those of the heavens; and every ten days one of the stars above is sent as a messenger, so to speak, to the stars below, and again in like manner one of the stars below the earth to those above, and this movement of theirs is fixed and determined by means of an orbit which is unchanging for ever. Twelve of these gods, they say, hold chief authority, and to each of these the Chaldaeans assign a month and one of the signs of the zodiac, as they are called. And through the midst of these signs, they say, both the sun and moon and the five planets make their course, the sun completing his cycle in a year and the moon traversing her circuit in a month.

**31.** Each of the planets, according to them, has its own particular course, and its velocities and periods of time are subject to change and variation. These stars it is which exert the greatest influence for both good and evil upon the nativity of men; and it is chiefly from the nature of these planets and the study of them that they know what is in store for mankind. They have made predictions, they say, not only to numerous other kings, but also to Alexander, who defeated Darius, and to Antigonus and Seleucus Nicator who afterwards became kings, and in all their prophecies they are thought to have hit the truth. Of these things we shall write in detail on a more appropriate occasion. Moreover, they also foretell to men in private station what will befall them, and with such accuracy that those who have made trial of them marvel at the feat and believe that it transcends the power of man.

Beyond the circle of the zodiac they designate twenty-four other stars, of which one half, they say, are situated in the northern parts and one half in the southern, and of these those which are visible they assign to the world of the living, while those which are invisible they regard as being adjacent to the dead, and so they call them "Judges of the Universe." And under all the stars hitherto mentioned the moon, according to them, takes her way, being nearest the earth because of her weight and completing her course in a very brief period of time, not by reason of her great velocity, but because her orbit is so short. They also agree with the Greeks in saying that her light is reflected and that her eclipses are due to the shadow of the earth. Regarding the eclipse of the sun, however, they offer the weakest kind of explanation, and do not presume to predict it or to define the times of its occurrence with any precision. Again, in connection with the earth they make assertions entirely peculiar to themselves, saying that it is shaped like a boat and hollow, and they offer many plausible arguments about both the earth and all other bodies in the firmament, a full discussion of which we feel would be alien to our history. This point, however, a man may fittingly maintain, that the Chaldaeans have of all men the greatest grasp of astrology, and that they have bestowed the greatest diligence upon the study of it. As to the number of years which, according to their statements, the order of the Chaldaeans has spent on the study of the bodies of the universe, a man can scarcely believe them; for they reckon that, down to Alexander's crossing over into Asia, [334] it has been four hundred and seventy-three thousand years, since they began in early times to make their observations of the stars.

So far as the Chaldaeans are concerned we shall be satisfied with what has been said, that we may not wander too far from the matter proper to our history; and now that we have given an account of the destruction of the kingdom of the Assyrians by the Medes we shall return to the point at which we digressed.

### *On the kings of Media and the disagreement of historians upon them (32-34).*

**32.** Since the earliest writers of history are at variance concerning the mighty empire of the Medes, we feel that it is incumbent upon those who would write the history of events with a love for truth to set forth side by side the different accounts of the historians. Now Herodotus, who lived in the time of Xerxes, gives this account: After the Assyrians had ruled Asia for five hundred years they were conquered by the Medes, [612] and thereafter no king arose for many generations to lay claim to supreme power, but the city-states, enjoying a regimen of their own, were administered in a democratic fashion; finally, however, after many years a man distinguished for his justice, named Cyaxares, was chosen king among the Medes. He was the first to try to attach to himself the neighbouring peoples and became for the Medes the founder of their universal empire; and after him his descendants extended the kingdom by continually adding a great deal of the adjoining country, until the reign of Astyages who was conquered by Gyrus and the Persians. [549] We have for the present given only the most important of these events in summary and shall later give a detailed account of them one by one when we come to the periods in which they fall; for it was in the second year of the Seventeenth Olympiad, [711-10] according to Herodotus, that Cyaxares was chosen king by the Medes.

Ctesias of Cnidus, on the other hand, lived during the time when Cyrus made his expedition against Artaxerxes his brother, [401] and having been made prisoner and then retained by Artaxerxes because of his medical knowledge, he enjoyed a position of honour with him for seventeen years. Now Ctesias says that from the royal records, in which the Persians in accordance with a certain law of theirs kept an account of their ancient affairs, he carefully investigated the facts about each king, and when he had composed his history he published it to the Greeks. This, then, is his account: After the destruction of the Assyrian Empire the Medes were the chief power in Asia under their king Arbaces, who conquered Sardanapallus, as has been told before. When he had reigned twenty-eight years his son Maudaces succeeded to the throne and reigned over Asia fifty years. After him Sosarmus ruled for thirty years, Artycas for fifty, the king known as Arbianes for twenty-two, and Artaeus for forty years.

33. During the reign of Artaeus a great war broke out between the Medes and the Cadusii, for the following reasons. Parsondes, a Persian, a man renowned for his valour and intelligence and every other virtue, was both a friend of the king's and the most influential of the members of the royal council. Feeling himself aggrieved by the king in a certain decision, he fled with three thousand foot-soldiers and a thousand horsemen to the Cadusii, to one of whom, the most influential man in those parts, he had given his sister in marriage. Now that he had become a rebel, he persuaded the entire people to vindicate their freedom and was chosen general because of his valour. Then, learning that a great force was being gathered against him, he armed the whole nation of the Cadusii and pitched his camp before the passes leading into the country, having a force of no less than two hundred thousand men all told. Although the king Artaeus advanced against him with eight hundred thousand soldiers, Parsondes defeated him in battle and slew more than fifty thousand of his followers, and drove the rest of the army out of the country of the Cadusii. For this exploit he was so admired by the people of the land that he was chosen king, and he plundered Media without ceasing and laid waste every district of the country. After he had attained great fame and was about to die of old age, he called to his side his successor to the throne and required of him an oath that the Cadusii should never put an end to their enmity towards the Medes, adding that, if peace were ever

made with them, it meant the destruction of his line and of the whole race of the Cadusii. These, then, were the reasons why the Cadusii were always inveterate enemies of the Medes, and had never been subjected to the Median kings up to the time when Cyrus transferred the Empire of the Medes to the Persians.

**34.** After the death of Artaeus, Ctesias continues, Artynes ruled over the Medes for twenty-two years, and Astibaras for forty. During the reign of the latter the Parthians revolted from the Medes and entrusted both their country and their city to the hands of the Sacac. This led to a war between the Sacae and the Medes, which lasted many years, and after no small number of battles and the loss of many lives on both sides, they finally agreed to peace on the following terms, that the Parthians should be subject to the Medes, but that both peoples should retain their former possessions and be friends and allies for ever.

At that time the Sacae were ruled by a woman named Zarina, who was devoted to warfare and was in daring and efficiency by far the foremost of the women of the Sacae. Now this people, in general, have courageous women who share with their husbands the dangers of war, but she, it is said, was the most conspicuous of them all for her beauty and remarkable as well in respect to both her designs and whatever she undertook. For she subdued such of the neighbouring barbarian peoples as had become proud because of their boldness and were trying to enslave the people of the Sacae, and into much of her own realm she introduced civilised life, founded not a few cities, and, in a word, made the life of her people happier. Consequently her countrymen after her death, in gratitude for her benefactions and in remembrance of her virtues, built her a tomb which was far the largest of any in their land; for they erected a triangular pyramid, making the length of each side three stades and the height one stade, and bringing it to a point at the top; and on the tomb they also placed a colossal gilded statue of her and accorded her the honours belonging to heroes, and all the other honours they bestowed upon her were more magnificent than those which had fallen to the lot of her ancestors.

When, Ctesias continues, Astibaras, the king of the Medes, died of old age in Ecbatana, his son Aspandas, whom the Greeks call Astyages, succeeded to the throne. And when he had been defeated by Cyrus the Persian, the kingdom passed to the Persians. Of them we shall give a detailed and exact account at the proper time.

Concerning the kingdoms of the Assyrians and of the Medes, and concerning the disagreement in the accounts of the historians, we consider that enough has been said; now we shall discuss India and then, in turn, recount the legends of that land.

### *On the topography of India and the products of the land, and on the customs of the Indians 35-42).*

**35.** Now India is four-sided in shape and the side which faces east and that which faces south are embraced by the Great Sea, [Indian Ocean] while that which faces north is separated by the Emodus range of mountains from that part of Scythia which is inhabited by the Scythians known as the Sacae; and the fourth side, which is turned towards the west, is marked off by the river known as the Indus, which is the largest of all streams after the Nile. As for its magnitude, India as a whole, they say, extends from east to west twenty-eight thousand stades, and from north to south thirty-two thousand. Because it is of such magnitude, it is believed to take in a greater extent of the sun's course in summer than any other part of the world, and in many places at the Cape of India the gnomons of sundials may be seen which do not cast a shadow, while at night the Bears are not visible; in the most southerly parts not even Arcturus can be seen, and indeed in that region, they say, the shadows fall towards the south.

Now India has many lofty mountains that abound in fruit trees of every variety, and many large and fertile plains, which are remarkable for their beauty and are supplied with water by a multitude of rivers. The larger part of the country is well watered and for this reason yields two crops each year; and it abounds in all kinds of animals, remarkable for their great size and strength, land animals as well as birds. It also breeds elephants both in the greatest numbers and of the largest size, providing them with sustenance in abundance, and it is because of this food that the elephants of this land are much more powerful than those produced in Libya; consequently large numbers of them are made captive by the Indians and trained for warfare, and it is found that they play a great part in turning the scale to victory.

**36.** The same is true of the inhabitants also, the abundant supply of food making them of unusual height and bulk of body; and another result is that they are also skilled in the arts, since they breathe a pure air and drink water of the finest quality. The earth, in addition to producing every fruit which admits of cultivation, also contains rich underground veins of every kind of ore; for there are found in it much silver and gold, not a little copper and iron, and tin also and whatever else is suitable for adornment, necessity, and the trappings of war. In addition to the grain of Demeter [wheat] there grows throughout India much millet, which is irrigated by the abundance of running water supplied by the rivers, pulse in large quantities and of superior quality, rice also and the plant called *bosporos,* [a kind of millet] and in addition to these many more plants which are useful for food; and most of these are native to the country. It also yields not a few other edible fruits, that are able to sustain animal life, but to write about them would be a long task.

This is the reason, they say, why a famine has never visited India or, in general, any scarcity of what is suitable for gentle fare. For since there are two rainy seasons in the country each year, during the winter rains the sowing is made of the wheat crops as among other peoples, while in the second, which comes at the summer solstice, it is the general practice to plant the rice and *bosporos,* as well as sesame and millet; and in most years the Indians are successful in both crops, and they never lose everything, since the fruit of one or the other sowing comes to maturity. The fruits also which flourish wild and the roots which grow in the marshy places, by reason of their remarkable sweetness, provide the people with a great abundance of food. For practically all the plains of India enjoy the sweet moisture from the rivers and from the rains which come with astonishing regularity, in a kind of fixed cycle, every year in the summer, since warm showers fall in abundance from the enveloping atmosphere and the heat ripens the roots in the marshes, especially those of the tall reeds. Furthermore, the customs of the Indians contribute towards there never being any lack of food among them; for whereas in the case of all the rest of mankind their enemies ravage the land and cause it to remain uncultivated, yet among the Indians the workers of the soil are let alone as sacred and inviolable, and such of them as labour near the battle-lines have no feeling of the dangers. For although both parties to the war kill one another in their hostilities, yet they leave uninjured those who are engaged in tilling the soil, considering that they are the common benefactors of all, nor do they burn the lands of their opponents or cut down their orchards.

**37.** The land of the Indians has also many large navigable rivers which have their sources in the mountains lying to the north and then flow through the level country; and not a few of these unite and empty into the river known as the Ganges. This river, which is thirty stades in width, flows from north to south and empties into the ocean, forming the boundary towards the east of the tribe of the Gandaridae, which possesses the greatest number of elephants and the largest in size. Consequently no foreign king has ever subdued this country, all alien nations being fearful of both the multitude and the strength of the beasts. In fact even Alexander of Macedon, although he had subdued all Asia, refrained from making war upon the Gandaridae alone of all peoples; for when he had arrived at the Ganges river with his entire army, after his conquest of the. rest of the Indians, upon learning that the Gandaridae had four thousand elephants equipped for war he gave up his campaign against them.

The river which is nearly the equal of the Ganges and is called the Indus rises like the Ganges in the north, but as it empties into the ocean forms a boundary of India; and in its course through an expanse of level plain it receives not a few navigable rivers,the most notable being the Hypanis, Hydaspes, and Acesinus. In addition to these three rivers a vast number of others of every description traverse the country and bring it about that the land is planted in many gardens and crops of every description. Now for the multitude of rivers and the exceptional supply of water the philosophers and students of nature among them advance the following cause: The countries which surround India, they say, such as Scythia, Bactria, and Ariana, are higher than India, and so it is reasonable to assume that the waters which come together from every side into the country lying below them, gradually cause the regions to become soaked and to generate a multitude of rivers. A peculiar thing happens in the case of one of the rivers of India, known as the Silla, which flows from a spring of the same name; for it is the only river in the world possessing the characteristic that nothing cast into it floats, but that everything, strange to say, sinks to the bottom.

**38.** Now India as a whole, being of a vast extent, is inhabited, as we are told, by many peoples of every description, and not one of them had its first origin in a foreign land, but all of them are thought to be autochthonous; it never receives any colony from abroad nor has it ever sent one to any other people. According to their myths the earliest human beings used for food the fruits of the earth which grew wild, and for clothing the skins of the native animals, as was done by the Greeks. Similarly too the discovery of the several arts and of all other things which are useful for life was made gradually, necessity itself showing the way to a creature which was well endowed by nature and had, as its assistants for every purpose, hands and speech and sagacity of mind.

The most learned men among the Indians recount a myth which it may be appropriate to set forth in brief form. This, then, is what they say: In the earliest times, when the inhabitants of their land were still dwelling in scattered clan-villages, Dionysus came to them from the regions to the west of them with a notable army; and he traversed all India, since there was as yet no notable city which would have been able to oppose him. When an oppressive heat came and the soldiers of Dionysus were being consumed by a pestilential sickness, this leader, who was conspicuous for his wisdom, led his army out of the plains into the hill-country; here, where cool breezes blew and the spring waters flowed pure at their very sources, the army got rid of its sickness. The name of this region of the hill-country, where Dionysus relieved his forces of the sickness, is Meros; and it is because of this fact that the Greeks have handed down to posterity in their account of this god the story that Dionysus was nourished in a thigh (*meros*).

After this he took in hand the storing of the fruits and shared this knowledge with the Indians, and he communicated to them the discovery of wine and of all the other things useful for life. Furthermore, he became the founder of notable cities by gathering the villages together in well-situated regions, and he both taught them to honour the deity and introduced laws and courts; and, in brief, since he had been the introducer of many good works he was regarded as a god and received immortal honours. They also recount that he carried along with his army a great number of women, and that when he joined battle in his wars he used the sounds of drums and cymbals, since the trumpet had not yet been discovered. After he had reigned over all India for fifty-two years he died of old age. His sons, who succeeded to the sovereignty, passed the rule on successively to their descendants; but finally, many generations later, their sovereignty was dissolved and the cities received a democratic form of government.

**39.** As for Dionysus, then, and his descendants, such is the myth as it is related by the inhabitants of the hill-country of India. With regard to Heracles they say that he was born among them and they assign to him, in common with the Greeks, both the club and the lion's skin. Moreover, as their account tells us, he was far superior to all other men in strength of body and in courage, and cleared both land and sea of their wild beasts. And marrying several wives, he begot many sons, but only one daughter; and when his sons attained to manhood, dividing all India into as many parts as he had male children, he appointed all his sons kings, and rearing his single daughter he appointed her also a queen. Likewise, he became the founder of not a few cities, the most renowned and largest of which he called Palibothra. In this city he also constructed a costly palace and settled a multitude of inhabitants, and he fortified it with remarkable ditches which were filled with water from the river. When Heracles passed from among men he received immortal honour, but his descendants, though they held the kingship during many generations and accomplished notable deeds, made no campaign beyond their own frontiers and despatched no colony to any other people. Many years later most of the cities had received a democratic form of government, although among certain tribes the kingship endured until the time when Alexander crossed over into Asia. 334 B.C.

# Book II

As for the customs of the Indians which are peculiar to them, a man may consider one which was drawn up by their ancient wise men to be the most worthy of admiration; for the law has ordained that under no circumstances shall anyone among them be a slave, but that all shall be free and respect the principle of equality in all persons. For those, they think, who have learned neither to domineer over others nor to subject themselves to others will enjoy a manner of life best suited to all circumstances; since it is silly to make laws on the basis of equality for all persons, and yet to establish inequalities in social intercourse.

**40.** The whole multitude of the Indians is divided into seven castes, the first of which is formed of the order of the philosophers, which in number is smaller than the rest of the castes, but in dignity ranks first. For being exempt from any service to the state the philosophers are neither the masters nor the servants of the others. They are called upon by the private citizens both to offer the sacrifices which are required in their lifetime and to perform the rites for the dead, as having proved themselves to be most dear to the gods and as being especially experienced in the matters that relate to the underworld, and for this service they receive both notable gifts and honours. Moreover, they furnish great services to the whole body of the Indians, since they are invited at the beginning of the year to the Great Synod and foretell to the multitude droughts and rains, as well as the favourable blowing of winds, and epidemics, and whatever else can be of aid to their auditors. For both the common folk and the king, by learning in advance what is going to take place, store up from time to time that of which there will be a shortage and prepare beforehand from time to time anything that will be needed. The philosopher who has erred in his predictions is subjected to no other punishment than obloquy and keeps silence for the remainder of his life.

The second caste is that of the farmers, who, it would appear, are far more numerous than the rest. These, being exempt from war duties and every other service to the state, devote their entire time to labour in the fields; and no enemy, coming upon a farmer in the country, would think of doing him injury, but they look upon the farmers as common benefactors and therefore refrain from every injury to them.

Consequently the land, remaining as it does un-ravaged and being laden with fruits, provides the inhabitants with a great supply of provisions. The farmers spend their lives upon the land with their children and wives and refrain entirely from coming down into the city, for the land they pay rent to the king, since all India is royal land and no man of private station is permitted to possess any ground; and apart from the rental they pay a fourth part into the royal treasury.

The third division is that of the neat-herds and shepherds, and, in general, of all the herdsmen who do not dwell in a city or village but spend their lives in tents; and these men are also hunters and rid the country of both birds and wild beasts. And since they are practised in this calling and follow it with zest they are bringing India under cultivation, although it still abounds in many wild beasts and birds of every kind, which eat up the seeds sown by the farmers.

**41.** The fourth caste is that of the artisans; of these some are armorers and some fabricate for the farmers or certain others the things useful for the services they perform. They are not only exempt from paying taxes but they even receive rations from the royal treasury.

The fifth caste is that of the military, which is at hand in case of war; they are second in point of number and indulge to the fullest in relaxation and pastimes in the periods of peace. The maintenance of the whole multitude of the soldiers and of the horses and elephants for use in war is met out of the royal treasury.

The sixth caste is that of the inspectors. These men inquire into and inspect everything that is going on throughout India, and report back to the kings or, in case the state to which they are attached has no king, to the magistrates.

The seventh caste is that of the deliberators and councillors, whose concern is with the decisions which affect the common welfare. In point of number this group is the smallest, but in nobility of birth and wisdom the most worthy of admiration; for from their body are drawn the advisers for the kings and the administrators of the affairs of state and the judges of disputes, and, speaking generally, they take their leaders and magistrates from among these men.

Such in general terms are the groups into which the body politic of the Indians is divided. Furthermore, no one is allowed to marry a person of another caste or to follow another calling or trade, as, for instance, that one who is a soldier should become a farmer, or an artisan should become a philosopher.

**42.** The country of the Indians also possesses a vast number of enormous elephants, which far surpass all others both in strength and in size. Nor does this animal cover the female in a peculiar manner, as some say, but in the same way as horses and all other four-footed beasts; and their period of gestation is in some cases sixteen months at the least and in other cases eighteen months at the most. They bring forth, like horses, but one young for the most part, and the females suckle their young for six years. The span of life for most of them is about that of men who attain the greatest age, though some which have reached the highest age have lived two hundred years.

There are among the Indians also magistrates appointed for foreigners who take care that no foreigner shall be wronged; moreover, should any foreigner fall sick they bring him a physician and care for him in every other way, and if he dies they bury him and even turn over such property as he has left to his relatives. Again, their judges examine accurately matters of dispute and proceed rigorously against such as are guilty of wrongdoing.

As for India, then, and its antiquities we shall be satisfied with what has been said.

### On the Scythians, Amazons, and Hyperboreans (43-47).

**43.** But now, in turn, we shall discuss the Scythians who inhabit the country bordering upon India. This people originally possessed little territory, but later, as they gradually increased in power, they seized much territory by reason of their deeds of might and their bravery and advanced their nation to great leadership and renown. At first, then, they dwelt on the Araxes river, altogether few in number and despised because of their lack of renown; but since one of their early kings was warlike and of unusual skill as a general they acquired territory, in the mountains as far as the Caucasus, and in the steppes along the ocean and Lake Maeotis and the rest of that country as far as the Tanaïs [the Don] river.

At a later time, as the Scythians recount the myth, there was born among them a maiden sprung from the earth; the upper parts of her body as far as her waist were those of a woman, but the lower parts were those of a snake. With her Zeus lay and begat a son whose name was Scythes. This son became more famous than any who had preceded him and called the folk Scythians after his own name. Now among the descendants of this king there were two brothers who were distinguished for their valour, the one named Palus and the other Napes. Since these two performed renowned deeds and divided the kingship between them, some of the people were called Pali after one of them and some Napae after the other, but some time later the descendants of these kings, because of their unusual valour and skill as generals, subdued much of the territory beyond the Tanaïs river as far as Thrace, and advancing with their armies to the other side they extended their power as far as the Nile in Egypt. After enslaving many great peoples which lay between the Thracians and the Egyptians they advanced the empire of the Scythians on the one side as far as the ocean to the east, and on the other side to the Caspian Sea and Lake Maeotis; for this people increased to great strength and had notable kings, one of whom gave his name to the Sacae, another to the Massagetae, another to the Arimaspi, and several other tribes received their names in like manner. It was by these kings that many of the conquered peoples were removed to other homes, and two of these became very great colonies: the one was composed of Assyrians and was removed to the land between Paphlagonia and Pontus, and the other was drawn from Media and planted along the Tanaïs, its people receiving the name Sauromatae. Many years later this people became powerful and ravaged a large part of Scythia, and destroying utterly all whom they subdued they turned most of the land into a desert.

**44.** After these events there came in Scythia a period of revolutions, in which the sovereigns were women endowed with exceptional valour. For among these peoples the women train for war just as do the men and in acts of manly valour are in no wise inferior to the men. Consequently distinguished women have been the authors of many great deeds, not in Scythia alone, but also in the territory bordering upon it. For instance, when Cyrus the king of the Persians, the mightiest ruler of his day, made a campaign with a vast army into Scythia, the queen of the Scythians not only cut the army of the Persians to pieces but she even took Cyrus prisoner and crucified him; and the nation of the Amazons, after it was once organised, was so distinguished for its manly prowess that it not only overran much of the neighbouring territory but even subdued a large part of Europe and Asia. But for our part, since we have mentioned the Amazons, we feel that it is not foreign to our purpose to discuss them, even though what we shall say will be so marvellous that it will resemble a tale from mythology.

**45.** Now in the country along the Thermodon river, [in Pontus] as the account goes, the sovereignty was in the hands of a people among whom the women held the supreme power, and its women performed the services of war just as did the men. Of these women one, who possessed the royal authority, was remarkable for her prowess in war and her bodily strength, and gathering together an army of women she drilled it in the use of arms and subdued in war some of the neighbouring peoples. Since her valour and fame increased, she made war upon people after people of neighbouring lands, and as the tide of her fortune continued favourable, she was so filled with pride that she gave herself the appellation of Daughter of Ares; but to the men she assigned the spinning of wool and such other domestic duties as belong to women. Laws also were established by her, by virtue of which she led forth the women to the contests of war, but upon the men she fastened humiliation and slavery. As for their children, they mutilated both the legs and the arms of the males, incapacitating them in this way for the demands of war, and in the case of the females they seared the right breast that it might not project when their bodies matured and be in the way; and it is for this reason that the nation of the Amazons received the appellation it bears. In general, this queen was remarkable for her intelligence and ability as a general, and she founded a great city named Themiscyra at the mouth of the Thermodon river and built there a famous palace; furthermore, in her campaigns she devoted much attention to military discipline and at the outset subdued all her neighbours as far as the Tanaïs river. This queen, they say, accomplished the deeds which have been mentioned, and fighting brilliantly in a certain battle she ended her life heroically.

**46.** The daughter of this queen, the account continues, on succeeding to the throne emulated the excellence of her mother, and even surpassed her in some particular deeds. For instance, she exercised in the chase the maidens from their earliest girlhood and drilled them daily in the arts of war, and she also established magnificent festivals both to Ares and to the Artemis who is called Tauropolus. Then she campaigned against the territory lying beyond the Tanaïs and subdued all the peoples one after another as far as Thrace; and returning to her native land with much booty she built magnificent shrines to the deities mentioned above, and by reason of her kindly rule over her subjects received from them the greatest approbation. She also campaigned on the other side and subdued a large part of Asia and extended her power as far as Syria. After the death of this queen, as their account continues, women of her family, succeeding to the queenship from time to time, ruled with distinction and advanced the nation of the Amazons in both power and fame. Many generations after these events, when the excellence of these women had been noised abroad through the whole inhabited world, they say that Heracles, the son of Alcmenê and Zeus, was assigned by Eurystheus the Labour of securing the girdle of Hippolyte the Amazon. Consequently he embarked on this campaign, and coming off victorious in a great battle he not only cut to pieces the army of Amazons but also, after taking captive Hippolyte together with her girdle, completely crushed this nation. Consequently the neighbouring barbarians, despising the weakness of this people and remembering against them their past injuries, waged continuous wars against the nation to such a degree that they left in existence not even the name of the race of the Amazons. For a few years after the campaign of Heracles against them, they say, during the time of the Trojan War, Penthesileia, the queen of the surviving Amazons, who was a daughter of Ares and had slain one of her kindred, fled from her native land because of the sacrilege, and fighting as an ally of the Trojans after the death of Hector she slew many of the Greeks, and after gaining distinction in the struggle she ended her life heroically at the hands of Achilles. Now they say that Penthesileia was the last of the Amazons to win distinction for bravery and that for the future the race diminished more and more and then lost all its strength; consequently in later times, whenever any writers recount their prowess, men consider the ancient stories about the Amazons to be fictitious tales.

**47.** Now for our part, since we have seen fit to make mention of the regions of Asia which lie to the north, we feel that it will not be foreign to our purpose to discuss the legendary accounts of the Hyperboreans. Of those who have written about the ancient myths, Hecataeus and certain others say that in the regions beyond the land of the Celts [Gaul] there lies in the ocean an island no smaller than Sicily. This island, the account continues, is situated in the north and is inhabited by the Hyperboreans, who are called by that name because their home is beyond the point whence the north wind (Boreas) blows; and the island is both fertile and productive of every crop, and since it has an unusually temperate climate it produces two harvests each year. Moreover, the following legend is told concerning it: Leto [mother of Zeus, Apollo & Artemis] was born on this island, and for that reason Apollo is honoured among them above all other gods; and the inhabitants are looked upon as priests of Apollo, after a manner, since daily they praise this god continuously in song and honour him exceedingly. There is also on the island both a magnificent sacred precinct of Apollo and a notable temple which is adorned with many votive offerings and is spherical in shape. Furthermore, a city is there which is sacred to this god, and the majority of its inhabitants are players on the cithara; and these continually play on this instrument in the temple and sing hymns of praise to the god, glorifying his deeds.

The Hyperboreans also have a language, we are informed, which is peculiar to them, and are most friendly disposed towards the Greeks, and especially towards the Athenians and the Delians, who have inherited this good-will from most ancient times. The myth also relates that certain Greeks visited the Hyperboreans and left behind them there costly votive offerings bearing inscriptions in Greek letters. And in the same way Abaris, a Hyperborean, came to Greece in ancient times and renewed the goodwill and kinship of his people to the Delians. They say also that the moon, as viewed from this island, appears to be but a little distance from the earth and to have upon it prominences, like those of the earth, which are visible to the eye. The account is also given that the god visits the island every nineteen years, the period in which the return of the stars to the same place in the heavens is accomplished; and for this reason the nineteen-year period is called by the Greeks the "year of Meton." At the time of this appearance of the god he both plays on the cithara and dances continuously the night through from the vernal equinox until the rising of the Pleiades, expressing in this manner his delight in his successes. And the kings of this city and the supervisors of the sacred precinct are called Boreadae, since they are descendants of Boreas, and the succession to these positions is always kept in their family.

### On Arabia, and the products of the land and its legends (48-54).

**48.** But now that we have examined these matters we shall turn our account to the other parts of Asia which have not yet been described, and more especially to Arabia. This land is situated between Syria and Egypt, and is divided among many peoples of diverse characteristics. Now the eastern parts are inhabited by Arabs, who bear the name of Nabataeans and range over a country which is partly desert and partly waterless, though a small section of it is fruitful. They lead a life of brigandage, and overrunning a large part of the neighbouring territory they pillage it, being difficult to overcome in war., for in the waterless region, as it is called, they have dug wells at convenient intervals and have kept the knowledge of them hidden from the peoples of all other nations, and so they retreat in a body into this region out of danger. Since they themselves know about the places of hidden water and open them up, they have for their use drinking water in abundance; but such other peoples as pursue them, being in want of a watering-place by reason of their ignorance of the wells, in some cases perish because of the lack of water and in other cases regain their native land in safety only with difficulty and after suffering many ills. Consequently the Arabs who inhabit this country, being difficult to overcome in war, remain always unenslaved; furthermore, they never at any time accept a man of another country as their over-lord and continue to maintain their liberty unimpaired. Consequently neither the Assyrians of old, nor the kings of the Medes and Persians, nor yet those of the Macedonians have been able to enslave them, and although they led many great forces against them, they never brought their attempts to a successful conclusion.

There is also in the land of the Nabataeans a rock, [Petra] which is exceedingly strong since it has but one approach, and using this ascent they mount it a few at a time and thus store their possessions in safety. And a large lake [Dead Sea] is also there which produces asphalt in abundance, and from it they derive not a little revenue. It has a length of about five hundred stades and a width of about sixty, and its water is so ill-smelling and so very bitter that it cannot support fish or any of the other animals which commonly live in water. Although great rivers of remarkable sweetness empty into it, the lake gets the better of them by reason of its evil smell, and from its centre it spouts forth once a year a great mass of asphalt, which sometimes extends for more than three plethra, and sometimes for only two; and when this occurs the barbarians who live about the lake usually call the larger flow a "bull" and to the smaller one they give the name "calf." Since the asphalt floats on the surface of the lake, to those who view it from a distance it takes the appearance of an island. And the fact is that the emission of the asphalt is made known to the natives twenty days before it takes place; for to a distance of many stades around the lake the odour, borne on the wind, assails them, and every piece of silver and gold and brass in the locality loses its characteristic lustre. But this returns again as soon as all the asphalt has been spouted forth; and the region round about, by reason of its being exposed to fire and to the evil odours, renders the bodies of the inhabitants susceptible to disease and makes the people very short-lived. Yet the land is good for the growing of palms, wherever it happens to be traversed by rivers with usable water or to be supplied with springs which can irrigate it. And there is also found in these regions in a certain valley [the Jordan at Jericho] the balsam tree, as it is called, from which they receive a substantial revenue, since this tree is found nowhere else in the inhabited world and the use of it for medicinal purposes is most highly valued by physicians.

**49.** That part of Arabia which borders upon the waterless and desert country is so different from it that, because both of the multitude of fruits which grow

## Book II

therein and of its other good things, it has been called Arabia Felix. For the reed and the rush [ginger grass] and every other growth that has a spicy scent are produced in great abundance, as is also, speaking generally, every kind of fragrant substance which is derived from leaves, and the land is distinguished in its several parts by the varied odours of the gums which drip from them; for myrrh and that frankincense which is most dear to the gods and is exported throughout the entire inhabited world are produced in the farthest parts of this land. And *kostos* and *cassia* and cinnamon and all other plants of this nature grow there in fields and thickets of such depth that what all other peoples sparingly place upon the altars of the gods is actually used by them as fuel under their pots, and what is found among all other peoples in small specimens there supplies material for the mattresses of the servants in their homes. Moreover, the cinnamon, as it is called, which is exceptionally useful, and resin of the pine, and the terebinth, [turpentine] are produced in these regions in great abundance and of sweet odour. And in the mountains grow not only silver fir and pine in abundance, but also cedar and the Phoenician cedar in abundance and *boraton*, [Juniper] as it is called. There are also many other kinds of fruit-bearing plants of sweet odour, which yield sap and fragrances most pleasing to such as approach them. Indeed the very earth itself is by its nature full of a vapour which is like sweet incense. Consequently, in certain regions of Arabia, when the earth is dug up, there are discovered veins of sweet odour, in the working of which quarries of extraordinary magnitude are formed; and from these they gather stones and build their houses. As for their houses, whenever rain drops from the enveloping atmosphere, that part which is melted down by the moisture flows into the joints of the stones and hardening there makes the walls solid throughout.

**50.** There is also mined in Arabia the gold called "fireless," which is not smelted from ores, as is done among all other peoples, but is dug out directly from the earth; it is found in nuggets about the size of chestnuts, and is so fiery-red in colour that when it is used by artisans as a setting for the most precious gems it makes the fairest of adornments. There is also in the land such a multitude of herds that many tribes which have chosen a nomad life are able to fare right well, experiencing no want of grain but being provided for in abundance by their herds. That part of the country which borders upon Syria breeds a multitude of fierce wild beasts; for the lions and leopards there are far more numerous and larger and superior in ferocity as compared with those of Libya, and in addition to these there are the Babylonian tigers, as they are called, and it produces animals which are of double form and mingled in their natures, to which belong the struthocameli, which, as their name implies, embrace in their form the compound of a bird and of a camel. For in size they are like a newly-born camel, but their heads bristle with fine hair, and their eyes are large and black, indistinguishable in general appearance and colour from those of the camel. It is also long-necked and has a beak which is very short and contracted to a sharp point. And since it has wings with feathers which are covered with a fine hair, and is supported upon two legs and on feet with cloven hoofs, it has the appearance of a land animal as well as of a bird. But being unable by reason of its weight to raise itself in the air and to fly, it swiftly skims over the land, and when pursued by hunters on horseback with its feet it hurls stones as from a sling upon its pursuers, and with such force that they often receive severe wounds. Whenever it is overtaken and surrounded, it hides its head in a bush or some such shelter, not, as some men suppose, because of its folly and stupidity of spirit, as if it thought that since it could not see the others it could not itself be seen by others either, but because its head is the weakest part of its body it seeks a shelter for it in order to save its life; for Nature is an excellent instructor of all animals for the preservation not only of their own lives but also of their offspring, since by planting in them an innate love of life she leads successive generations into an eternal cycle of continued existence.

**51.** The camelopards, as they are called, represent the mixing of the two animals which are included in the name given to it. For in size they are smaller than the camel and have shorter necks, but in the head and the arrangement of the eyes they are formed very much like a leopard; and although they have a hump on the back like the camel, yet with respect to colour and hair they are like leopards; likewise in the possession of a long tail they imitate the nature of this wild beast. There are also bred *tragelaphoi* (goat-stags) and *bubali* and many other varieties of animals which are of double form and combine in one body the natures of creatures most widely different, about all of which it would be a long task to write in detail. For it would seem that the land which lies to the south breathes in a great deal of the sun's strength, which is the greatest source of life, and that, for that reason, it generates breeds of beautiful animals in great number and of varied colour; and that for the same reason there are produced in Egypt both the crocodiles and the river-horses, in Ethiopia and in the desert of Libya a multitude of elephants and of reptiles of every variety and of all other wild beasts and of serpents, which differ from one another in size and ferocity, and likewise in India the elephants of exceptional bulk and number and ferocity.

**52.** In these countries are generated not only animals which differ from one another in form because of the helpful influence and strength of the sun, but also outcroppings of every kind of precious stone which are unusual in colour and resplendent in brilliancy. The rock-crystals, so we are informed, are composed of pure water which has been hardened, not by the action of cold, but by the influence of a divine fire, and for this reason they are never subject to corruption and take on many hues when they are breathed upon. For instance *smaragdi* and *beryllia,* as they are called, which are found in the shafts of the copper mines, receive their colour by having been dipped and bound together in a bath of sulphur, and the chrysoliths, they say, which are produced by a smoky exhalation due to the heat of the sun, thereby get the colour they have. For this reason what is called "false gold," we are told, is fabricated by mortal fire, made by man, by dipping the rock crystals into it. And as for the natural qualities of the dark-red stones, it is the influence of the light, as it is compressed to a greater or less degree in them when they are hardening, which, they say, accounts for their differences. In like manner, it is reported, the different kinds of birds get their colouring, some kinds appearing to the eye as pure red, other kinds marked with colours of every variety one after the other; for some birds are naming red in appearance, others saffron yellow, some emerald green, and many of the colour of gold when they turn towards the light, and, in brief, hues are produced in great variety and difficult to describe; and this same thing can be seen taking place in the case of the rainbow in the heavens by reason of the light of the sun. It is from these facts that the students of nature draw their arguments when they affirm that the variety of colouring that is put forth by the things which we have mentioned above was caused by the heat coincident with their creation which dyed them, the sun, which is the source of life, assisting in the production of each several kind. It is generally true, they continue, that of the differences in the hues of the flowers and of the varied colours of the earth the sun is the cause and creator; and the arts of mortal men, imitating the working of the sun in the physical world, impart colouring and varied hues to every object, having been instructed in this by nature. For the colours, they continue, are produced by the light, and likewise the odours of the fruits and the distinctive quality of their juices, the different sizes of the animals and their several forms, and the peculiarities which the earth shows, all are generated by the heat of the sun which imparts its warmth to a fertile land and to water endowed with the generative power and thus becomes the creator of each separate thing as it is. Consequently, neither the white marble of Paros nor any other stone which men admire can be compared with the precious stones of Arabia, since their whiteness is most brilliant, their weight the heaviest, and their smoothness leaves no room for other stones to surpass them. The cause of the peculiar nature of the several parts of the country is, as I have said, the influence of the sun, which has hardened it by its heat, compressed it by its dryness, and made it resplendent by its light.

**53.** Hence it is that the race of birds also, having received the most warmth, became flying creatures because of their lightness, and of varied colour because of the influence of the sun, this being especially true in the lands which lie close to the sun. Babylonia, for instance, produces a multitude of peacocks which have blossomed out with colours of every kind, and the farthest parts of Syria produce parrots and purple coots and guinea-fowls and other kinds of animals of distinctive colouring and of every combination of hues. The same reasoning applies also to all the other countries of the earth which lie in a similar climate, such as India and the Red Sea and Ethiopia and certain parts of Libya. But the eastern part, being more fertile, breeds nobler and larger animals; and as for the rest of Libya, each animal is produced in form and characteristics corresponding to the quality of the soil.

Likewise as regards trees, the palms of Libya bear dry and small fruit, but in Coele-Syria dates called *caryoti* are produced which excel as to both sweetness and size and also as to their juices. Dates much larger than these can be seen growing in Arabia and Babylonia, six fingers in size and in colour either yellow like the quince, or dark red, or in some cases tending to purple, so that at the same time they both delight the eye and gratify the taste. The trunk of the palm stretches high in the air and its surface is smooth all over as far as its crown. Though they all have a tuft of foliage at the top, yet the arrangement of the foliage varies; for in some cases the fronds spread out in a complete circle and from the centre the trunk sends up, as if from out its broken bark, the fruit in a cluster like grapes, in other cases the foliage at the crown droops down on only one side so that it produces the appearance of a lamp from which the flame flares out, and occasionally they have their fronds bent down on both sides and by this double arrangement of the branches show a crown of foliage all about the trunk, thus presenting a picturesque appearance.

**54.** That part of Arabia as a whole which lies to the south is called Felix, but the interior part is ranged over by a multitude of Arabians who are nomads and have chosen a tent life. These raise great flocks of animals and make their camps in plains of immeasurable extent. The region which lies between this part and Arabia Felix is desert and waterless, as has been stated; and the parts of Arabia which lie to the west are broken by sandy deserts spacious as the air in magnitude, through which those who journey must, even as voyagers upon the seas, direct their course by indications obtained from the Bears. The remaining part of Arabia, which lies towards Syria, contains a multitude of farmers and merchants of every kind, who by a seasonable exchange of merchandise make good the lack of certain wares in both countries by supplying useful things which they possess in abundance. That Arabia which lies along the ocean is situated above Arabia Felix, and since it is traversed by many great rivers, many regions in it are converted into stagnant pools and into vast stretches of great swamps. And with the water which is brought into them from the rivers and that which comes with the summer rains they irrigate a large part of the country and get two crops yearly. This region also breeds herds of elephants and other monstrous land animals, and animals of double shape which have developed peculiar forms; and in addition to these it abounds in domestic animals of every kind, especially in cattle and in the sheep with large and fat tails.

This land also breeds camels in very great numbers and of most different kinds, both the hairless and the shaggy, and those which have two humps, one behind the other, along their spines and hence are called *dituloi*. Some of these provide milk and are eaten for meat, and so provide the inhabitants with a great abundance of this food, and others, which are trained to carry burdens on their backs, can carry some ten *medimni* [14.5 bushels, 900 lbs.]of wheat and bear up five men lying outstretched upon a couch. Others which have short legs and are slender in build are dromedaries and can go at full stretch a day's journey of a very great distance, especially in the trips which they make through the waterless and desert region. And also in their wars the same animals carry into battle two bowmen who ride back to back to each other, one of them keeping off enemies who come on them from in front, the other those who pursue in the rear.

With regard, then, to Arabia and the products of that land, even if we have written at too great length, we have at any rate reported many things to delight lovers of reading.

### On the islands which have been discovered to the south in the ocean (55-60).

**55.** But with regard to the island [Ceylon?] which has been discovered in the ocean to the south and the marvellous tales told concerning it, we shall now endeavour to give a brief account, after we have first set forth accurately the causes which led to its discovery. There was a certain Iambulus who from his boyhood up had been devoted to the pursuit of education, and after the death of his father, who had been a merchant, he also gave himself to that calling; and while journeying inland to the spice-bearing region of Arabia he and his companions on the trip were taken captive by some robbers. Now at first he and one of his fellow-captives were appointed to be herdsmen, but later he and his companion were made captive by certain Ethiopians and led off to the coast of Ethiopia. They were kidnapped in order that, being of an alien people, they might effect the purification of the land. For among the Ethiopians who lived in that place there was a custom, which had been handed down from ancient times, and had been ratified by oracles of the gods, over a period of twenty generations or six hundred years, the generation being reckoned at thirty years; and at the time when the purification by means of the two men was to take place, a boat had been built for them sufficient in size and strong enough to withstand the storms at sea, one which could easily be manned by two men; and then loading it with food enough to maintain two men for six months and putting them on board they commanded them to set out to sea as the oracle had ordered. Furthermore, they commanded them to steer towards the south; for, they were told, they would come to a happy island and to men of honourable character, and among them they would lead a blessed existence. In like manner, they stated, their own people, in case the men whom they sent forth should arrive safely at the island, would enjoy peace and a happy life in every respect throughout six hundred years; but if, dismayed at the extent of the sea, they should turn back on their course they would, as impious men and destroyers of the entire nation, suffer the severest penalties. Accordingly, the Ethiopians, they say, held a great festal assembly by the sea, and after offering costly sacrifices they crowned with flowers the men who were to seek out the island and effect the purification of the nation and then sent them forth. And these men, after having sailed over a vast sea and been tossed about four months by storms, were carried to the island about which they had been informed beforehand; it was round in shape and had a circumference of about five thousand stades.

**56.** But when they were now drawing near to the island, the account proceeds, some of the natives met them and drew their boat to land; and the inhabitants of the island, thronging together, were astonished at the arrival of the strangers, but they treated them honourably and shared with them the necessities of life which their country afforded. The dwellers upon this island differ greatly both in the characteristics of their bodies and in their manners from the men in our part of the inhabited world; for they are all nearly alike in the shape of their bodies and are over four cubits in height, but the bones of the body have the ability to bend to a certain extent and then straighten out again, like the sinewy parts. They are also exceedingly tender in respect to their bodies and yet more vigorous than is the case among us; for when they have seized any object in their hands no man can extract it from the grasp of their fingers. There is absolutely no hair on any part of their bodies except on the head, eyebrows and eyelids, and on the chin, but the other parts of the body are so smooth that not even the least down can be seen on them. They are also remarkably beautiful and well-proportioned in the outline of the body. The openings of their ears are much more spacious than ours and growths have developed that serve as valves, so to speak, to close them. And they have a peculiarity in regard to the tongue, partly the work of nature and congenital with them and partly intentionally brought about by artifice; among them, namely, the tongue is double for a certain distance, but they divide the inner portions still further, with the result that it becomes a double tongue as far as its base. Consequently they are very versatile as to the sounds they can utter, since they imitate not only every articulate language used by man but also the varied chattering of the birds, and, in general, they can reproduce any peculiarity of sound. And the most remarkable thing of all is that at one and the same time they can converse perfectly with two persons who fall in with them, both answering questions and discoursing pertinently on the circumstances of the moment; for with one division of the tongue they can converse with the one person, and likewise with the other talk with the second.

Their climate is most temperate, we are told, considering that they live at the equator, and they suffer neither from heat nor from cold. Moreover, the fruits in their island ripen throughout the entire year, even as the poet writes,

> Here pear on pear grows old, and apple close
> On apple, yea, and clustered grapes on grapes,
> And fig on fig.

And with them the day is always the same length as the night, and at midday no shadow is cast of any object because the sun is in the zenith.

57. These islanders, they go on to say, live in groups which are based on kinship and on political organisations, no more than four hundred kinsmen being gathered together in this way; and the members spend their time in the meadows, the land supplying them with many things for sustenance; for by reason of the fertility of the island and the mildness of the climate, food-stuffs are produced of themselves in greater quantity than is sufficient for their needs. For instance, a reed grows there in abundance, and bears a fruit in great plenty that is very similar to the white vetch. Now when they have gathered this they steep it in warm water until it has become about the size of a pigeon's egg; then after they have crushed it and rubbed it skilfully with their hands, they mould it into loaves, which are baked and eaten, and they are of surprising sweetness. There are also in the island, they say, abundant springs of water, the warm springs serving well for bathing and the relief of fatigue, the cold excelling in sweetness and possessing the power to contribute to good health. Moreover, the inhabitants give attention to every branch of learning and especially to astrology; and they use letters which, according to the value of the sounds they represent, are twenty-eight in number, but the characters are only seven, each one of which can be formed in four different ways. Nor do they write their lines horizontally, as we do, but from the top to the bottom perpendicularly. And the inhabitants, they tell us, are extremely long-lived, living even to the age of one hundred and fifty years, and experiencing for the most part no illness. Anyone also among them who has become crippled or suffers, in general, from any physical infirmity is forced by them, in accordance with an inexorable law, to remove himself from life. And there is also a law among them that they should live only for a stipulated number of years, and that at the completion of this period they should make away with themselves of their own accord, by a strange manner of death; for there grows among them a plant of a peculiar nature, and whenever a man lies down upon it, imperceptibly and gently he falls asleep and dies.

58. They do not marry, we are told, but possess their children in common, and maintaining the children who are born as if they belonged to all, they love them equally; and while the children are infants those who suckle the babes often change them around in order that not even the mothers may know their own

offspring. Consequently, since there is no rivalry among them, they never experience civil disorders and they never cease placing the highest value upon internal harmony.

There are also animals among them, we are told, which are small in size but the object of wonder by reason of the nature of their bodies and the potency of their blood; for they are round in form and very similar to tortoises, but they are marked on the surface by two diagonal yellow stripes, at each end of which, they have an eye and a mouth; consequently, though seeing with four eyes and using as many mouths, yet it gathers its food into one gullet, and down this its nourishment is swallowed and all flows together into one stomach; and in like manner its other organs and all its inner parts are single. It also has beneath it all around its body many feet, by means of which it can move in whatever direction it pleases. The blood of this animal, they say, has a marvellous potency; for it immediately glues on to its place any living member that has been severed; even if a hand or the like should happen to have been cut off, by the use of this blood it is glued on again, provided that the cut is fresh, and the same thing is true of such other parts of the body as are not connected with the regions which are vital and sustain the person's life. Each group of the inhabitants also keeps a bird of great size and of a nature peculiar to itself, by means of which a test is made of the infant children to learn what their spiritual disposition is; for they place them upon the birds, and such of them as are able to endure the flight through the air as the birds take wing they rear, but such as become nauseated and filled with consternation they cast out, as not likely either to live many years, and being, besides, of no account because of their dispositions.

In each group the oldest man regularly exercises the leadership, just as if he were a kind of king, and is obeyed by all the members; and when the first such ruler makes an end of his life in accordance with the law upon the completion of his one hundred and fiftieth year, the next oldest succeeds to the leadership. The sea about the island has strong currents and is subject to great flooding and ebbing of the tides and is sweet in taste. As for the stars of our heavens, the Bears and many more, we are informed, are not visible at all. The number of these islands was seven, and they are very much the same in size and at about equal distances from one another, and all follow the same customs and laws.

**59.** Although all the inhabitants enjoy an abundant provision of everything from what grows of itself in these islands, yet they do not indulge in the enjoyment of this abundance without restraint, but they practise simplicity and take for their food only what suffices for their needs. Meat and whatever else is roasted or boiled in water are prepared by them, but of all the other dishes ingeniously concocted by professional cooks, such as sauces and the various kinds of seasonings, they have no notion whatsoever. And they worship as gods that which encompasses all things and the sun, and, in general, all the heavenly bodies. Fishes of every kind in great numbers are caught by them by sundry devices and not a few birds. There is also found among them an abundance of fruit trees growing wild, and olive trees and vines grow there, from which they make both olive oil and wine in abundance. Snakes also, we are told, which are of immense size and yet do no harm to the inhabitants, have a meat which is edible and exceedingly sweet. And their clothing they make themselves from a certain reed which contains in the centre a downy substance [cotton?] that is bright to the eye and soft, which they gather and mingle with crushed sea-shells and thus make remarkable garments of a purple hue. As for the animals of the islands, their natures are peculiar and so amazing as to defy credence.

All the details of their diet, we are told, follow a prescribed arrangement, since they do not all take their food at the same time nor is it always the same; but it has been ordained that on certain fixed days they shall eat at one time fish, at another time fowl, sometimes the flesh of land animals, and sometimes olives and the most simple side-dishes. They also take turns in ministering to the needs of one another, some of them fishing, others working at the crafts, others occupying themselves in other useful tasks, and still others, with the exception of those who have come to old age, performing the services of the group in a definite cycle. At the festivals and feasts which are held among them, there are both pronounced and sung in honour of the gods hymns and spoken laudations, and especially in honour of the sun, after whom they name both the islands and themselves.

They inter their dead at the time when the tide is at the ebb, burying them in the sand along the beach, the result being that at flood-tide the place has fresh sand heaped upon it. The reeds, they say, from which the fruit for their nourishment is derived, being a span in thickness increase at the times of full-moon and again decrease proportionately as it wanes. And the water of the warm springs, being sweet and health-giving, maintains its heat and never becomes cold, save when it is mixed with cold water or wine.

**60.** After remaining among this people for seven years, the account continues, Iambulus and his companion were ejected against their will, as being malefactors and as having been educated to evil habits. Consequently, after they had again fitted out their little boat they were compelled to take their leave, and when they had stored up provisions in it they continued their voyage for more than four months. Then they were shipwrecked upon a sandy and marshy region of India; and his companion lost his life in the surf, but Iambulus, having found his way to a certain village, was then brought by the natives into the presence of the king at Palibothra, a city which was distant a journey of many days from the sea. And since the king was friendly to the Greeks and devoted to learning he considered Iambulus worthy of cordial welcome; and at length, upon receiving a permission of safe-conduct, he passed over first of all into Persia and later arrived safe in Greece.

Now Iambulus felt that these matters deserved to be written down, and he added to his account not a few facts about India, facts of which all other men were ignorant at that time. For our part, since we have fulfilled the promise made at the beginning of this Book, we shall bring it to a conclusion at this point.

# BOOK III

## *On the Ethiopians who dwell beyond Libya and their antiquities (1-11).*

**1.** Of the two preceding Books the First embraces the deeds in Egypt of the early kings and the accounts, as found in their myths, of the gods of the Egyptians; there is also a discussion of the Nile and of the products of the land, and also of its animals, which are of every kind, and a description of the topography of Egypt, of the customs prevailing among its inhabitants, and of its courts of law. The Second Book embraces the deeds performed by the Assyrians in Asia in early times, connected with which are both the birth and the rise to power of Semiramis, in the course of which she founded Babylon and many other cities and made a campaign against India with great forces; and after this is an account of the Chaldaeans and of their practice of observing the stars, of Arabia and the marvels of that land, of the kingdom of the Scythians, of the Amazons, and finally of the Hyperboreans. In this present Book we shall add the matters which are connected with what I have already narrated, and shall describe the Ethiopians and the Libyans and the people known as the Atlantians.

**2.** Now the Ethiopians, as historians relate, were the first of all men and the proofs of this statement, they say, are manifest. For that they did not come into their land as immigrants from abroad but were natives of it and so justly bear the name of "autochthones" [sprung from the soil] is, they maintain, conceded by practically all men; furthermore, that those who dwell beneath the noon-day sun were, in all likelihood, the first to be generated by the earth, is clear to all; since, inasmuch as it was the warmth of the sun which, at the generation of the universe, dried up the earth when it was still wet and impregnated it with life, it is reasonable to suppose that the region which was nearest the sun was the first to bring forth living creatures. And they say that they were the first to be taught to honour the gods and to hold sacrifices and processions and festivals and the other rites by which men honour the deity; and that in consequence their piety has been published abroad among all men, and it is generally held that the sacrifices practised among the Ethiopians are those which are the most pleasing to heaven. As witness to this they call upon the poet who is perhaps the oldest and certainly the most venerated among the Greeks; for in the *Iliad* he represents both Zeus and the rest of the gods with him as absent on a visit to Ethiopia to share in the sacrifices and the banquet which were given annually by the Ethiopians for all the gods together:

> For Zeus had yesterday to Ocean's bounds
> Set forth to feast with Ethiop's faultless men,
> And he was followed there by all the gods.

And they state that, by reason of their piety towards the deity, they manifestly enjoy the favour of the gods, inasmuch as they have never experienced the rule of an invader from abroad; for from all time they have enjoyed a state of freedom and of peace one with another, and although many and powerful rulers have made war upon them, not one of these has succeeded in his undertaking.

**3.** Cambyses, for instance, they say, who made war upon them with a great force, both lost all his army and was himself exposed to the greatest peril; Semiramis also, who through the magnitude of her undertakings and achievements has become renowned, after advancing a short distance into Ethiopia gave up her campaign against the whole nation; and Heracles and Dionysus, although they visited all the inhabited earth, failed to subdue the Ethiopians alone who dwell above Egypt, both because of the piety of these men and because of the insurmountable difficulties involved in the attempt.

They say also that the Egyptians are colonists sent out by the Ethiopians, Osiris having been the leader of the colony. For, speaking generally, what is now Egypt, they maintain, was not land but sea when in the beginning the universe was being formed; afterwards, however, as the Nile during the times of its inundation carried down the mud from Ethiopia, land was gradually built up from the deposit. The statement that all the land of the Egyptians is alluvial silt deposited by the river receives the clearest proof, in their opinion, from what takes place at the outlets of the Nile; for as each year new mud is continually gathered together at the mouths of the river, the sea is observed being thrust back by the deposited silt and the land receiving the increase. The larger part of the customs of the Egyptians are, they hold, Ethiopian, the colonists still preserving their ancient manners. For instance, the belief that their kings are gods, the very special attention which they pay to their burials, and many other matters of a similar nature are Ethiopian practices, while the shapes of their statues and the forms of their letters are Ethiopian; for of the two kinds of writing which the Egyptians have, that which is known as "popular" (demotic) is learned by everyone, while that which is called "sacred" [hieratic] is understood only by the priests of the Egyptians, who learn it from their fathers as one of the things which are not divulged, but among the Ethiopians everyone uses these forms of letters. Furthermore, the orders of the priests, they maintain, have much the same position among both peoples; for all are clean who are engaged in the service of the gods, keeping themselves shaven, like the Ethiopian priests, and having the same dress and form of staff, which is shaped like a plough and is carried by their kings, who wear high felt hats which end in a knob at the top and are circled by the serpents which they call asps; and this symbol appears to carry the thought that it will be the lot of those who shall dare to attack the king to encounter death-carrying stings. Many other things are also told by them concerning their own antiquity and the colony which they sent out that became the Egyptians, but about this there is no special need of our writing anything.

**4.** We must now speak about the Ethiopian writing which is called hieroglyphic among the Egyptians, in order that we may omit nothing in our discussion of their antiquities. Now it is found that the forms of their letters take the shape of animals of every kind, and of the members of the human body, and of implements and especially carpenters' tools; for their writing does not express the intended concept by means of syllables joined one to another, but by means of the significance of the objects which have been copied and by its figurative meaning which has been impressed upon the memory by practice. For instance, they draw the picture of a hawk, a crocodile, a snake, and of the members of the human body - an eye, a hand, a face, and the like. Now the hawk signifies to them everything which happens swiftly, since this animal is practically the swiftest of winged creatures, and the concept portrayed is then transferred, by the appropriate metaphorical transfer, to all swift things and to everything to which swiftness is appropriate, very much as if they had been named. The crocodile is a symbol of all that is evil, and the eye is the warder of justice and the guardian of the entire body. As for the members of the body, the right hand with fingers extended signifies a procuring of livelihood, and the left with the fingers closed, a keeping and guarding of property. The same way of reasoning applies also to the remaining characters, which represent parts of the body and implements and all other things; for by paying close attention to the significance which is inherent in each object and by training their minds through drill and exercise of the memory over a long period, they read from habit everything which has been written.

**5.** As for the customs of the Ethiopians, not a few of them are thought to differ greatly from those of the rest of mankind, this being especially true of those which concern the selection of their kings. The priests, for instance, first choose out the noblest men from their own number, and whichever one from this group the god may select, as he is borne about in a procession in accordance with a certain practice of theirs, him the multitude take for their king; and straightway it both worships and honours him like a god, believing that the sovereignty has been entrusted to him by Divine Providence. The king who has been thus chosen both follows a regimen which has been fixed in accordance with the laws and performs all his other deeds in accordance with the ancestral custom, according neither favour nor punishment to anyone contrary to the usage which has been approved among them from the beginning. It is also a custom of theirs that the king shall put no one of his subjects to death, not even if a man shall have been condemned to death and is considered deserving of punishment, but that he shall send to the transgressor one of his attendants bearing a token of death; and the guilty person, on seeing the warning, immediately retires to his home and removes himself from life. Moreover, for a man to flee from his own into a neighbouring country and thus by moving away from his native land to pay the penalty of his transgression, as is the custom among the Greeks, is permissible under no circumstances. Consequently, they say, when a man to whom the token of death had been sent by the king once undertook to flee from Ethiopia, and his mother, on learning of this, bound his neck about with her girdle, he dared not so much as raise his hands against her in any way but submitted to be strangled until he died, that he might not leave a greater disgrace to his kinsmen.

**6.** Of all their customs the most astonishing is that which obtains in connection with the death of their kings, for the priests at Meroe who spend their time in the worship of the gods and the rites which do them honour, being the greatest and most powerful order, whenever the idea comes to them, dispatch a messenger to the king with orders that he die. The gods, they add, have revealed this to them, and it must be that the command of the immortals should in no wise be disregarded by one of mortal frame, and this order they accompany with other arguments, such as are accepted by a simple-minded nature, which has been bred in a custom that is both ancient and difficult to eradicate and which knows no argument that can be set in opposition to commands enforced by no compulsion.

Now in former times the kings would obey the priests, having been overcome, not by arms nor by force, but because their reasoning powers had been put under a constraint by their very superstition; but during the reign of the second Ptolemy the king of the Ethiopians, [285-216] Ergamenes, who had had a Greek education and had studied philosophy, was the first to have the courage to disdain the command. For assuming a spirit which became the position of a king he entered with his soldiers into the unapproachable place where stood, as it turned out, the golden shrine of the Ethiopians, put the priests to the sword, and after abolishing this custom thereafter ordered affairs after his own will.

**7.** As for the custom touching the friends of the king, strange as it is, it persists, they said, down to our own time. The Ethiopians have the custom, they say, that if their king has been maimed in some part of his body through any cause whatever, all his companions suffer the same loss of their own choice; because they consider that it would be a disgraceful thing if, when the king had been maimed in his leg, his friends should be sound of limb, and if in their goings forth from the palace they should not all follow the king limping as he did; for it would be strange that steadfast friendship should share sorrow and grief and bear equally all other things both good and evil, but should have no part in the suffering of the body. They say also that it is customary for the comrades of the kings even to die with them of their own accord and that such a death is an honour able one and a proof of true friendship. It is for this reason, they add, that a conspiracy against the king is not easily raised among the Ethiopians, all his friends being equally concerned both for his safety and their own. These, then, are the customs which prevail among the Ethiopians who dwell in their capital [Napata] and those who inhabit both the island of Meroe and the land adjoining Egypt.

**8.** But there are also a great many other tribes of the Ethiopians, some of them dwelling in the land King on both banks of the Nile and on the islands in the river, others inhabiting the neighbouring country of Arabia, and still others residing in the interior of Libya. The majority of them, and especially those who dwell along the river, are black in colour and have flat noses and woolly hair. As for their spirit they are entirely savage and display the nature of a wild beast, not so much, however, in their temper as in their ways of living; for they are squalid all over their bodies, they keep their nails very long like the wild beasts, and are as far removed as possible from human kindness to one another; and speaking as they do with a shrill voice and cultivating none of the practices of civilised life as these are found among the rest of mankind, they present a striking contrast when considered in the light of our own customs.

As for their arms, some of them use shields of raw ox-hide and short spears, others javelins without a slinging-thong and sometimes bows of wood, four cubits in length, with which they shoot by putting their foot against them, and after their arrows are exhausted they finish the fight with wooden clubs. They also arm their women, setting an age limit for their service, and most of these observe the custom of wearing a bronze ring in the lip. As for clothing, certain of them wear none whatsoever, going naked all their life long and making for themselves of whatever comes to hand a rude protection from the heat alone; others, cutting off the tails and the ends of the hides of their sheep, cover their loins with them, putting the tail before them to screen, after a manner, the shameful part; and some make use of the skins of their domestic animals, while there are those who cover their bodies as far as the waist with shirts, which they weave of hair, since their sheep do not produce wool by reason of the peculiar nature of the land. For food some gather the fruits which are generated in their waters and which grow wild in both the lakes and marshy places, certain of them pluck off the foliage of a very tender kind of tree, with which they also cover their bodies in the midday and cool them in this way, some sow sesame and lotus, and there are those who are nourished by the most, tender roots of the reeds. Not a few of them are also well trained in the use of the bow and bring down with good aim many birds, with which they satisfy their physical needs; but the greater number live for their entire life on the meat and milk and cheese of their herds.

**9.** With regard to the gods, the Ethiopians who dwell above Meroë entertain two opinions: they believe that some of them, such as the sun and the moon and the universe as a whole, have a nature which is eternal and imperishable, but others of them, they think, share a mortal nature and have come to receive immortal honours because of their virtue and the benefactions which they have bestowed upon all mankind; for instance, they revere Isis and Pan, and also Heracles and Zeus, considering that these deities in particular have been benefactors of the race of men. A few of the Ethiopians do not believe in the existence of any gods at all; consequently at the rising of the sun they utter imprecations against it as being most hostile to them, and flee to the marshes of those parts.

Different also from those of other peoples are the customs they observe with respect to their dead; for some dispose of them by casting them into the river, thinking this to be the best burial; others, after pouring glass about the bodies, keep them in their houses, since they feel that the countenances of the dead should not be unknown to their kinsmen and that those who are united by ties of blood should not forget their near relations; and some put them in coffins made of baked clay and bury them in the ground in a ring about their temples, and they consider that the oath taken by them is the strongest possible.

The kingship some of them bestow upon the most comely, believing both supreme power and comeliness to be gifts of fortune, while others entrust the rule to the most careful keepers of cattle, as being the only men who would give the best thought to their subjects; some assign this honour to the wealthiest, since they feel that these alone can come to the aid of the masses because they have the means ready at hand; and there are those who choose for their kings men of unusual valour, judging that the most efficient in war are alone worthy to receive the meed of honour.

**10.** In that part of the country which lies along the Nile in Libya there is a section which is remarkable for its beauty; for it bears food in great abundance and of every variety and provides convenient places of retreat in its marshes where one finds protection against the excessive heat; consequently this region is a bone of contention between the Libyans and the Ethiopians, who wage unceasing warfare with each other for its possession. It is also a gathering-place for a multitude of elephants from the country lying above it because, as some say, the pasturage is abundant and sweet; for marvellous marshes stretch along the banks of the river and in them grows food in great plenty and of every kind. Consequently, whenever they taste of the rush and the reed, they remain there because of the sweetness of the food and destroy the means of subsistence of the human beings; and because of this the inhabitants are compelled to flee from these regions, and to live as nomads and dwellers in tents - in a word, to fix the bounds of their country by their advantage. The herds of the wild beasts which we have mentioned leave the interior of the country because of the lack of food, since every growing thing in the ground quickly dries up; for as a result of the excessive heat and the lack of water from springs and rivers it comes to pass that the plants for food are rough and scanty.

There are also, as some say, in the country of the wild beasts, as it is called, serpents which are marvellous for their size and multitude; these attack the elephants at the water-holes, pit their strength against them, and winding themselves in coils about their legs continue squeezing them tighter and tighter in their bands until at last the beasts, covered with foam, fall to the ground from their weight. Thereupon the serpents gather and devour the flesh of the fallen elephant, overcoming the beast with ease because it moves only with difficulty. Since it still remains a puzzle why, in pursuit of their accustomed food, they do not follow the elephants into the region along the river, which I have mentioned, they say that the serpents of such great size avoid the level part of the country and continually make their homes at the foot of mountains in ravines which are suitable to their length and in deep caves; consequently they never leave the regions which are suitable to them and to which they are accustomed, Nature herself being the instructor of all the animals in such matters.

As for the Ethiopians, then, and their land, this is as much as we have to say.

**11.** Concerning the historians, we must distinguish among them, to the effect that many have composed works on both Egypt and Ethiopia, of whom some have given credence to false report and others have invented many tales out of their own minds for the delectation of their readers, and so may justly be distrusted. For example, Agatharchides of Cnidus in the second Book of his work on Asia, and the compiler of geographies, Artemidorus of Ephesus, in his eighth Book, and certain others whose homes were in Egypt, have recounted most of what I have set forth above and are, on the whole, accurate in all they have written. Since, to bear witness ourselves, during the time of our visit to Egypt, we associated with many of its priests and conversed with not a few ambassadors from Ethiopia as well who were then in Egypt; and after inquiring carefully of them about each matter and testing the stories of the historians, we have composed our account so as to accord with the opinions on which they most fully agree.

Now as for the Ethiopians who dwell in the west, we shall be satisfied with what has been said, and we shall discuss in turn the peoples who live to the south and about the Red Sea. However, we feel that it is appropriate first to tell of the working of the gold as it is carried on in these regions.

# Book III

## *On the gold mines on the farthest borders of Egypt and the working of the gold (12-14).*

**12.** At the extremity of Egypt and in the contiguous territory of both Arabia and Ethiopia there lies a region which contains many large gold mines, where the gold is secured in great quantities with much suffering and at great expense. For the earth is naturally black and contains seams and veins of a marble which is unusually white and in brilliancy surpasses everything else which shines brightly by its nature, and here the overseers of the labour in the mines recover the gold with the aid of a multitude of workers. For the kings of Egypt gather together and condemn to the mining of the gold such as have been found guilty of some crime and captives of war, as well as those who have been accused unjustly and thrown into prison because of their anger, and not only such persons but occasionally all their relatives as well, by this means not only inflicting punishment upon those found guilty but also securing at the same time great revenues from their labours. And those who have been condemned in this way, and they are a great multitude and are all bound in chains, work at their task unceasingly both by day and throughout the entire night, enjoying no respite and being carefully cut off from any means of escape; since guards of foreign soldiers who speak a language different from theirs stand watch over them, so that not a man, either by conversation or by some contact of a friendly nature, is able to corrupt one of his keepers. The gold-bearing earth which is hardest they first burn with a hot fire, and when they have crumbled it in this way they continue the working of it by hand; and the soft rock which can yield to moderate effort is crushed with a sledge by myriads of unfortunate wretches. The entire operations are in charge of a skilled worker who distinguishes the stone and points it out to the labourers; and of those who are assigned to this unfortunate task the physically strongest break the quartz-rock with iron hammers, applying no skill to the task, but only force, and cutting tunnels through the stone, not in a straight line but wherever the seam of gleaming rock may lead. Now these men, working in darkness as they do because of the bending and winding of the passages, carry lamps bound on their foreheads; and since much of the time they change the position of their bodies to follow the particular character of the stone they throw the blocks, as they cut them out, on the ground; and at this task they labour without ceasing beneath the sternness and blows of an overseer.

**13.** The boys there who have not yet come to maturity, entering through the tunnels into the galleries formed by the removal of the rock, laboriously gather up the rock as it is cast down piece by piece and carry it out into the open to the place outside the entrance. Then those who are above thirty years of age take this quarried stone from them and with iron pestles pound a specified amount of it in stone mortars, until they have worked it down to the size of a vetch. Thereupon the women and older men receive from them the rock of this size and cast it into mills of which a number stand there in a row, and taking their places in groups of two or three at, the spoke or handle of each mill they grind it until they have worked down the amount given them to the consistency of the finest flour. Since no opportunity is afforded any of them to care for his body and they have no garment to cover their shame, no man can look upon the unfortunate wretches without feeling pity for them because of the exceeding hardships they suffer. No leniency or respite of any kind is given to any man who is sick, or maimed, or aged, or in the case of a woman for her weakness, but all without exception are compelled by blows to persevere in their labours, until through ill-treatment they die in the midst of their tortures. Consequently the poor unfortunates believe, because their punishment is so excessively severe, that the future will always be more terrible than the present and therefore look forward to death as more to be desired than life.

**14.** In the last steps the skilled workmen receive the stone which has been ground to powder and take it off for its complete and final working; for they rub the marble which has been worked down upon a broad board which is slightly inclined, pouring water over it all the while; whereupon the earthy matter in it, melted away by the action of the water, runs down the inclined board, while that which contains the gold remains on the wood because of its weight. And repeating this a number of times, they first of all rub it gently with their hands, and then lightly pressing it with sponges of loose texture they remove in this way whatever is porous and earthy, until there remains only the pure gold-dust. Then at last other skilled workmen take what has been recovered and put it by fixed measure and weight into earthen jars, mixing with it a lump of lead proportionate to the mass, lumps of salt and a little tin, and adding thereto barley bran; thereupon they put on it a close-fitting lid, and smearing it over carefully with mud they bake it in a kiln for five successive days and as many nights; and at the end of this period, when they have let the jars cool off, of the other matter they find no remains in the jars, but the gold they recover in pure form, there being but little waste. This working of the gold, as it is carried on at the farthermost borders of Egypt, is effected through all the extensive labours here described; for Nature herself, in my opinion, makes it clear that whereas the production of gold is laborious, the guarding of it is difficult, the zest for it very great, and that its use is half-way between pleasure and pain.

Now the discovery of these mines is very ancient, having been made by the early kings. But we shall undertake to discuss the peoples which inhabit the coast of the Arabian Gulf [Red Sea] and that of the Trogodytes and the part of Ethiopia that faces the noon-day sun and the south wind.

**On the peoples who dwell upon the coast of the Arabian Gulf and, speaking generally, upon all the coast of the ocean as far as India. In this connection there is a discussion of the customs which each people follows and of the reasons why history records many things in connection with them which are entirely unique and are not believed because they are contrary to what one expects (15-48.**

**15.** The first people we shall mention are the Ichthyophagi [fish-eaters] who inhabit the coast which extends from Carmania and Gedrosia to the farthest limits of the arm of the sea which is found at the Arabian Gulf, which extends inland an unbelievable distance and is enclosed at its mouth by two continents, on the one side by Arabia Felix and on the other by the land of the Trogodytes. As for these barbarians, certain of them go about entirely naked and have the women and children in common like their flocks and herds, and since they recognise only the physical perception of pleasure and pain they take no thought of things which are disgraceful and those which are honourable. They have their dwellings not far from the sea along the rocky shores, where there are not only deep valleys but also jagged ravines and very narrow channels which Nature has divided by means of winding side-branches. These branches being by their nature suited to their need, the natives close up the passages and outlets with heaps of great stones, and by means of these, as if with nets, they carry on the catching of the fish. For whenever the flood-tide of the sea sweeps violently over the land, which happens twice daily and usually about the third and ninth hour, the sea covers in its flood all the rocky shore and together with the huge and violent billow carries to the land an incredible multitude of fish of every kind, which at first remain along the coast, wandering in search of food among the sheltered spots and hollow places; but whenever the time of ebb comes, the water flows off little by little through the heaps of rocks and ravines, but the fish are left behind in the hollow places. At this moment the multitude of the natives with their children and women gather, as if at a single word of command, at the rocky shores. And the barbarians, dividing into several companies, rush in bands each to its respective place with a hideous shouting, as if they had come unexpectedly upon some prey. Thereupon the women and children, seizing the smaller fish which are near the shore, throw them on the land, and the men of bodily vigour lay hands upon the fish which are hard to overcome because of their size; for there are driven out of the deep creatures of enormous size, not only sea-scorpions and sea-eels and dog-fish, but also seals and many other kinds which are strange both in appearance and in name. These animals they subdue without the assistance of any skilful device of weapons but by piercing them through with sharp goat horns and by gashing them with the jagged rocks; for necessity teaches Nature everything, as Nature, in her own fashion, by seizing upon the opportunities which lie at hand adapts herself to their hoped-for utilisation.

**16.** Whenever they have collected a multitude of all kinds of fish they carry off their catch and bake the whole of it upon the rocks which are inclined towards the south. Since these stones are red-hot because of the very great heat, they leave the fish there for only a short time and then turn them over, and then, picking them up bodily by the tail, they shake them. And the meat, which has become tender by reason of the warmth, falls away, but the backbones are cast into a single spot and form a great heap, being collected for a certain use of which we shall speak a little later. Then placing the meat upon a smooth stone they carefully tread upon it for a sufficient length of time and mix with it the fruit of the Christ's thorn; for when this has been thoroughly worked into the meat the whole of it becomes a glutinous mass, and it would appear that this takes the place among them of a relish. Finally, when this has been well trodden, they mould it into little oblong bricks and place them in the sun; and after these have become thoroughly dry they sit down and feast upon them, eating not according to any measure or weight but according to every man's own wish, inasmuch as they make their physical desire the bounds of their indulgence. For they have at all times stores which are unfailing and ready for use, as though Poseidon had assumed the task of Demeter.

But at times a tidal wave of such size rolls in from the sea upon the land, a violent wave that for many days submerges the rocky shores, that no one can approach those regions. Consequently, being short of food at such times, they at first gather the mussels, which are of so great a size that some of them are found that weigh four minas; that is, they break their shells by throwing huge stones at them and then eat the meat raw, its taste resembling somewhat that of oysters. Whenever it comes to pass that the ocean is high for a considerable period because of the continued winds, and the impossibility of coping with that state of affairs prevents them from making their usual catch of fish, they turn, as has been said, to the mussels. If the food from the mussels fails them, they have recourse to the heap of backbones; that is, they select from this heap such backbones as are succulent and fresh and take them apart joint by joint, and then they grind some at once with their teeth, though the hard ones they first crush with rocks and thus prepare them before they eat them, their level of life being much the same as that of the wild beasts which make their homes in dens.

**17.** Now as for dry food they get an abundance of it in the manner described, but their use of wet food is astonishing and quite incredible. For they devote themselves assiduously for four days to the sea-food they have caught, the whole tribe feasting upon it merrily while entertaining one another with inarticulate songs; and furthermore, they lie at this time with any women they happen to meet in order to beget children, being relieved of every concern because their food is easily secured and ready at hand. But on the fifth day the whole tribe hurries off in search of drink to the foothills of the mountains, where there are springs of sweet water at which the pastoral folk water their flocks and herds. And their journey thither is like that of herds of cattle, all of them uttering a cry which produces, not articulate speech, but merely a confused roaring. As for their children, the women carry the babies continually in their arms, but the fathers do this after they have been separated from their milk, while those above five years of age lead the way accompanied by their parents, playing as they go and full of joy, as though they were setting out for pleasure of the sweetest kind. The nature of this people, being as yet un-perverted, considers the satisfying of their need to be the greatest possible good, desiring in addition none of the imported pleasures, and so soon as they arrive at the watering-places of the pastoral folk and have their bellies rilled with the water, they return, scarcely able to move because of the weight of it. On that day they taste no food, but everyone lies gorged and scarcely able to breathe, quite like a drunken man. The next day, however, they turn again to the eating of the fish; and their way of living follows a cycle after this fashion throughout their lives.

Now the inhabitants of the coast inside the Straits lead the kind of life which has been described, and by reason of the simplicity of their food they rarely are subject to attacks of disease, although they are far shorter-lived than the inhabitants of our part of the world.

**18.** As for the inhabitants of the coast outside the gulf, we find that their life is far more astonishing than that of the people just described, it being as though their nature never suffers from thirst and is insensible to pain. Although they have been banished by fortune from the inhabited regions into the desert, they fare quite well from their catch of the fish, but wet food they do not require.

Since they eat the fish while it is yet juicy and not far removed from the raw state, they are so far from requiring wet food that they have not even a notion of drinking, and they are content with that food which was originally allotted to them by fortune, considering that the mere elimination of that pain which arises from want (of food) is happiness.

But the most surprising thing of all is, that in lack of sensibility they surpass all men, and to such a degree that what is recounted of them is scarcely credible. Yet many merchants of Egypt, who sail, as is their practice, through the Red Sea down to this day and have often sailed as far as the land of the Ichthyophagi, agree in their accounts with what we have said about the human beings who are insensible to pain. The third Ptolemy [Ptolemy Euergetes I, 246-221] also, who was passionately fond of hunting the elephants which are found in that region, sent one of his friends named Simmias to spy out the land; and he, setting out with suitable supplies, made, as the historian Agatharchides of Cnidus asserts, a thorough investigation of the nations lying along the coast. Now he says that the nation of the "insensible" Ethiopians makes no use whatsoever of drink and that their nature does not require it for the reasons given above. As a general thing, he relates, they have no intercourse with other nations nor does the foreign appearance of people who approach their shores have any effect upon the natives, but looking at them intently they show no emotion and their expressions remain unaltered, as if there were no one present. Indeed when a man drew his sword and brandished it at them they did not turn to flight, nor, if they were subjected to insult or even to blows, would they show irritation, and the majority were not moved to anger in sympathy with the victims of such treatment; on the contrary, when at times children or women were butchered before their eyes they remained "insensible" in their attitudes, displaying no sign of anger or, on the other hand, of pity. In short, they remained unmoved in the face of the most appalling horrors, looking steadfastly at what was taking place and nodding their heads at each incident. Consequently, they say, they speak no language, but by movements of the hands which describe each object they point out everything they need. The most marvellous fact of all is that seals live with these tribes and catch the fish for themselves in a manner similar to that employed by the human beings. Likewise with respect to their lairs and the safety of their offspring these two kinds of beings place the greatest faith in one another; for the association with animals of a different species continues without any wrongdoing and with peace and complete observance of propriety. Now this manner of life, strange as it is, has been observed by these tribes from very early times, whether it has been fashioned by habit over the long space of time or by a need imposed by necessity because of stress of circumstances.

**19.** As for their dwelling-places, those used by these tribes are not all similar, but they inhabit homes modified to suit the peculiar nature of their surroundings. For instance, certain of them make their home in caves which open preferably towards the north and in which they cool themselves, thanks to the deep shade and also to the breezes which blow about them; since those which face the south, having as they do a temperature like that of an oven, cannot be approached by human beings because of the excessive heat. Others who can find no caves facing the north collect the ribs of the whales which are cast up by the sea; and then, since there is a great abundance of these ribs, they interweave them from either side, the curve outwards and leaning towards each other, and then weave fresh seaweed through them. Accordingly, when this vaulted structure is covered over, in it they gain relief from the heat when it is most intense, the necessity imposed by Nature suggesting to them a skill in which they were self-taught.

A third method by which the Ichthyophagi find a dwelling for themselves is as follows. Olive trees grow about these regions in very great numbers and their roots are washed by the sea, but they bear thick foliage and a fruit which resembles the sweet chestnut. These trees they interlace, forming in this way a continuous shade, and live in tents of this peculiar kind; for passing their days as they do on land and in the water at the same time, they lead a pleasurable life, since they avoid the sun by means of the shade cast by the branches and offset the natural heat of the regions with the continual washing of the waves against them, giving their bodies comfort and ease by the pleasant breezes which blow about them. We must speak also about the fourth kind of habitation. From time immemorial there has been heaped up a quantity of seaweed of tremendous proportions, resembling a mountain, and this has been so compacted by the unceasing pounding of the waves that it has become hard and intermingled with sand. Accordingly, the natives dig in these heaps tunnels of the height of a man, leaving the upper portion for a roof, and in the lower part they construct passage-ways connected with each other by borings. As they cool themselves in these tunnels they free themselves from all troubles, and leaping forth from them at the times when the waves pour over the shore they busy themselves with the catching of the fish; then, when the ebb-tide sets in, they flee back together into these same passage-ways to feast upon their catch. Their dead, moreover, they "bury" by leaving the bodies just as they are cast out at the ebb of the tide, and then when the flood-tide sets in they cast the bodies into the sea. Consequently, by making their own interment a nutriment of the fish, they have a life which follows in singular fashion a continuous cycle throughout all eternity.

**20.** One tribe of the Ichthyophagi has dwellings so peculiar that they constitute a great puzzle to men who take a pride in investigating such matters; for certain of them make their homes among precipitous crags which these men could not possibly have approached at the outset, since from above there overhangs a lofty rock, sheer at every point, while on the sides unapproachable cliffs shut off entrance, and on the remaining face the sea hems them in, which cannot be passed through on foot, and they do not use rafts at all, while of boats such as we have they have no notion. Such being the puzzle concerning them, the only solution left to us is that they are autochthonous, and that they experienced no beginning of the race they originally sprang from, but existed always from the beginning of time, as certain natural philosophers have declared to be true of all the phenomena of nature. Since the knowledge of such matters is unattainable by us, nothing prevents those who have the most to say about them from knowing the least, inasmuch as, while plausibility may persuade the hearing, it by no means discovers the truth.

**21.** We must speak also about the Chelonophagi, [turtle-eaters] as they are called, and the nature of their entire manner of life. There are islands in the ocean, which lie near the land, many in number, but small in size and low-lying, and bearing no food either cultivated or wild. Because these islands are so near to one another no waves occur among them, since the surf breaks upon the outermost islands, and so a great multitude of sea-turtles tarry in these regions, resorting thither from all directions to gain the protection offered by the calm. These animals spend the nights in deep water busied with their search for food, but during the days they resort to the sea which lies between the islands and sleep on the surface with their upper shells towards the sun, giving to the eye an appearance like that of overturned boats; for they are of extraordinary magnitude and not smaller than the smallest fishing skiffs. And the barbarians who inhabit the islands seize the occasion and swim quietly out to the turtles; and when they have come near the turtle on both sides, those on the one side push down upon it while those on the other side lift it up, until the animal is turned over on its back. Then the men, taking hold on both sides, steer the entire bulk of the creature, to prevent it from turning over and making its escape into the deep water by swimming with the means with which Nature has endowed it, and one man with a long rope, fastening it to its tail, swims towards the land, and drawing the turtle along after him he hauls it to the land, those who had first attacked it assisting him in bringing it in. When they have got the turtles upon the shore of their island, all the inside meat they bake slightly for a short time in the sun and then feast upon it, but the upper shells, which are shaped like a boat, they use both for sailing over to the mainland, as they do in order to get water, and for their dwellings, by setting them right side up upon elevations, so that it would appear that Nature, by a single act of favour, had bestowed upon these peoples the satisfaction of many needs; for the same gift constitutes for them food, vessel, house and ship.

Not far distant from these people the coast is inhabited by barbarians who lead an irregular life, for they depend for their food upon the whales which are cast up on the land, at times enjoying an abundance of food because of the great size of the beasts which they discover, but at times, when interruptions of the supply occur, they suffer greatly from the shortage; and when the latter is the case they are forced by the scarcity of food to gnaw the cartilages of old bones and the parts which grow from the ends of the ribs.

As for the Ichthyophagi, then this is the number of their tribes and such, speaking summarily, are the ways in which they live.

**22.** The coast of Babylonia borders on a land which is civilised and well planted and there is such a multitude of fish for the natives that the men who catch them are unable readily to keep ahead of the abundance of them. Along the beaches they set reeds close to one another and interwoven, so that their appearance is like that of a net which has been set up along the edge of the sea. And throughout the entire construction there are doors which are fixed close together and resemble basket-work in the way they are woven, but are furnished with hinges that easily yield to movements of the water in either direction. These doors are opened by the waves as they roll towards the shore at the time of flood-tide, and are closed at ebb-tide as they surge back. Consequently it comes about that every day, when the sea is at flood-tide, the fish are carried in from the deep water with the tide and pass inside through the doors, but when the sea recedes they are unable to pass with the water through the interwoven reeds. As a result it is possible at times to see beside the ocean heaps being formed of gasping fish, which are being picked up unceasingly by those who have been appointed to this work, who have from their catch subsistence in abundance as well as large revenues. Some of the inhabitants of these parts, because the country is both like a plain and low-lying, dig wide ditches leading from the sea over a distance of many stades to their private estates, and setting wicker gates at their openings they open these when the flood-tide is coming inland and close them when the tide changes to the opposite direction. Then, inasmuch as the sea pours out through the interstices of the gate but the fish are held back in the ditches, they have a controlled store of fish and can take of them as many as they choose and at whatever time they please.

**23.** Now that we have discussed the peoples who dwell on the coast from Babylonia to the Arabian Gulf, [Red Sea] we shall describe the nations who live next to them. In the Ethiopia which lies above Egypt there dwells beside the river Asa the nation of the Rhizophagi. [root-eaters] For the barbarians here dig up the roots of the reeds which grow in the neighbouring marshes and then thoroughly wash them; and after they have made them clean they crush them with stones until the stuff is without lumps and glutinous; and then, moulding it into balls as large as can be held in the hand, they bake it in the sun and on this as their food they live all their life long. Enjoying as they do the unfailing abundance of this food and living ever at peace with one another, they are nevertheless preyed upon by a multitude of lions; for since the air about them is fiery hot, lions come out of the desert to them in search of shade and in some cases in pursuit of the smaller animals. Consequently it comes to pass that when the Ethiopians come out of the marshy lands they are eaten by these beasts; for they are unable to withstand the might of the lions, since they have no help in the form of weapons, and indeed in the end the race of them would have been utterly destroyed had not Nature provided them with an aid which acts entirely of itself, for at the time of the rising of the dog-star, whenever a calm unexpectedly comes on, there swarms to these regions such a multitude of mosquitoes, surpassing in vigour those that are known to us, that while the human beings find refuge in the marshy pools and suffer no hurt, all the lions flee from those regions, since they not only suffer from their stings but are at the same time terrified by the sound of their humming.

**24.** Next to these people are the Hylophagi [wood-eaters] and the Spermatophagi, [seed-eaters] as they are called. The latter gather the fruit as it falls in great abundance from the trees in the summer season and so find their nourishment without labour, but during the rest of the year they subsist upon the most tender part of the plant which grows in the shady glens; for this plant, being naturally stiff and having a stem like the bounias, [French turnip] as we call it, supplies the lack of the necessary food. The Hylophagi, however, setting out with children and wives in search of food, climb the trees and subsist off the tender branches. And this climbing of theirs even to the topmost branches they perform so well as a result of their continued practice that a man can scarcely believe what they do; indeed they leap from one tree to another like birds and make their way up the weakest branches without experiencing dangers. Being in body unusually slender and light, whenever their feet slip they catch hold instead with their hands, and if they happen to fall from a height they suffer no hurt by reason of their light weight; and every juicy branch they chew so thoroughly with their teeth that their stomachs easily digest them. These men go naked all their life, and since they consort with their women in common they likewise look upon their offspring as the common children of all. They fight with one another for the possession of certain places, arming themselves with clubs, with which they also keep off enemies, and they dismember whomsoever they have overcome. Most of them die from becoming exhausted by hunger, when cataracts form upon their eyes and the body is deprived of the necessary use of this organ of sense.

**25.** The next part of the country of the Ethiopians is occupied by the Cynegi, [hunters] as they are called, who are moderate in number and lead a life in keeping with their name. For since their country is infested by wild beasts and is utterly worthless, and has few streams of spring water, they sleep in the trees from fear of the wild beasts, but early in the morning, repairing with their weapons to the pools of water, they secrete themselves in the woods and keep watch from their positions in the trees. At the time when the heat becomes intense, wild oxen and leopards and a multitude of every other kind of beast come to drink, and because of the excessive heat and their great thirst they greedily quaff the water until they are gorged, whereupon the Ethiopians, the animals having become sluggish and scarcely able to move, leap down from the trees, and by the use of clubs hardened in the fire and of stones and arrows easily kill them. They hunt in this way in companies and feed upon the flesh of their prey, and although now and then they are themselves slain by the strongest animals, yet for the most part they master by their cunning the superior strength of the beasts. If at any time they find a lack of animals in their hunt they soak the skins of some which they had taken at former times and then hold them over a low fire; and when they have singed off the hair they divide the hides among themselves, and on such fare as has been forced upon them they satisfy their want. Their boys they train in shooting at a mark and give food only to those who hit it. Consequently, when they come to manhood, they are marvellously skilled in marksmanship, being most excellently instructed by the pangs of hunger.

**26.** Far distant from this country towards the parts to the west are Ethiopians known as Elephant-fighters, hunters also, for dwelling as they do in regions covered with thickets and with trees growing close together, they carefully observe the places where the elephants enter and their favourite resorts, watching them from the tallest trees; and when they are in herds they do not set upon them, since they would have no hope of success, but they lay hands on them as they go about singly, attacking them in an astonishingly daring manner. As the beast in its wandering comes near the tree in which the watcher happens to be hidden, the moment it is passing the spot he seizes its tail with his hands and plants his feet against its left flank; he has hanging from his shoulders an axe, light enough so that a blow may be struck with one hand and yet exceedingly sharp, and seizing this in his right hand he hamstrings the elephant's right leg, raining blows upon it and maintaining the position of his own body with his left hand. And they bring an astonishing swiftness to bear upon the task, since there is a contest between the two of them for their very lives; for all that is left to the hunter is either to get the better of the animal or to die himself, the situation not admitting another conclusion. As for the beast which has been hamstrung, sometimes being unable to turn about because it is hard for it to move and sinking down on the place where it has been hurt, it falls to the ground and causes the death of the Ethiopian along with its own, and sometimes squeezing the man against a rock or tree it crushes him with its weight until it has killed him. In some cases, however, the elephant in the extremity of its suffering is far from thinking of turning on its attacker, but flees across the plain until the man who has set his feet upon it, striking on the same place with his axe, has severed the tendons and paralysed the beast. As soon as the beast has fallen they run together in companies, and cutting the flesh off the hind-quarters of the elephant while it is still alive they hold a feast.

**27.** Some of the natives who dwell nearby hunt the elephants without exposing themselves to dangers, overcoming their strength by cunning. It is the habit of this animal, whenever it has had its fill of grazing, to lie down to sleep, the manner in which it does this being different from that of all other four-footed animals; for it cannot bring its whole bulk to the ground by bending its knees, but leans against a tree and thus gets the rest which comes from sleep. Consequently the tree, by reason of the frequent leaning against it by the animal, becomes both rubbed and covered with mud, and the place about it, furthermore, shows both tracks and many signs, whereby the Ethiopians who search for such traces discover where the elephants take their rest. Accordingly, when they come upon such a tree, they saw it near the ground until it requires only a little push to make it fall; thereupon, after removing the traces of their own presence, they quickly depart in anticipation of the approach of the animal, and towards evening the elephant, filled with food, comes to his accustomed haunt. As soon as he leans against the tree with his entire weight he at once rolls to the ground along with the tree, and after his fall he remains there lying on his back the night through, since the nature of his body is not fashioned for rising. Then the Ethiopians who have sawn the tree gather at dawn, and when they have slain the beast without danger to themselves they pitch their tents at the place and remain there until they have consumed the fallen animal.

**28.** The parts west of these tribes are inhabited by Ethiopians who are called Simi, [flat-nosed] but those towards the south are held by the tribe of the Struthophagi. [bird-eaters] For there is found among them a kind of bird having a nature which is mingled with that of the land animal, and this explains the compound name it bears. This animal is not inferior in size to the largest deer and has been fashioned by Nature with a long neck and a round body, which is covered with feathers. Its head is weak and small, but it has powerful thighs and legs and its foot is cloven. It is unable to fly in the air because of its weight, but it runs more swiftly than any other animal, barely touching the earth with the tips of its feet; and especially when it raises its wings adown (sic.) the blasts of the wind it makes off like a ship under full sail; and it defends itself against its pursuers by means of its feet, hurling, as if from a sling, in an astonishing manner, stones as large as can be held in the hand. When it is pursued at a time of calm, its wings quickly collapse, it is unable to make use of the advantages

## Book III

given it by Nature, and being easily overtaken it is made captive. Since these animals abound in the land in multitude beyond telling, the barbarians devise every manner of scheme whereby to take them; moreover, since they are easily caught in large numbers, their meat is used for food and their skins for clothing and bedding. Being constantly warred upon by the Ethiopians known as "Simi," they are in daily peril from their attackers, and they use as defensive weapons the horns of gazelles; these horns, being large and sharp, are of great service and are found in abundance throughout the land by reason of the multitude of the animals which carry them.

**29.** A short distance from this tribe on the edge of the desert dwell the Acridophagi, [locust-eaters] men who are smaller than the rest, lean of body, and exceeding dark. Among them in the spring season strong west and south-west winds drive out of the desert a multitude beyond telling of locusts, of great and unusual size and with wings of an ugly, dirty colour. From these locusts they have food in abundance all their life long, catching them in a manner peculiar to themselves, for along the border of their land over many stades there extends a ravine of considerable depth and width; this they fill with wood from the forests, which is found in plenty in their land; and then, when the winds blow which we have mentioned and the clouds of the locusts approach, they divide among themselves the whole extent of the ravine and set fire to the brush in it. Since a great volume of pungent smoke rises, the locusts, as they fly over the ravine, are choked by the pungency of the smoke and fall to the ground after they have flown through it only a short space, and as the destruction of them continues over several days, great heaps of them are raised up; moreover, since the land contains a great amount of brine, all the people bring this to the heaps, after they have been gathered together, soak them to an appropriate degree with the brine and thus both give the locusts a palatable taste and make their storage free from rot and lasting for a long time. Accordingly, the food of this people, at the moment and thereafter, consists of these animals; for they possess no herds nor do they live near the sea nor do they have at hand any other resources; and light in body and very swift of foot as they are, they are also altogether short-lived, the oldest among them not exceeding forty years of age.

As for the manner in which they end their lives, not only is it astounding but extremely pitiful, for when old age draws near there breed in their bodies winged lice, which not only have an unusual form but are also savage and altogether loathsome in aspect. The affliction begins on the belly and the breast and in a short time spreads over the whole body. The person so affected is at first irritated by a kind of itching and insists on scratching himself a bit, the disease at this point offering a satisfaction combined with pain; but after this stage the animals, which have been continuously engendered more and more in the body, break out to the surface and there is a heavy discharge of a thin humour, the sting of which is quite unbearable. Consequently the man who is in the grip of the disease lacerates himself with his nails the more violently, groaning and moaning deeply. As his hands tear at his body, such a multitude of the vermin pours forth that those who try to pick them off accomplish nothing, since they issue forth one after another, as from a kind of vessel that is pierced throughout with holes, and so these wretches end their lives in a dissolution of the body after this manner, a miserable fate, meeting with such a sudden reversal of fortune either by reason of the peculiar character of their food or because of the climate.

**30.** Along the borders of this people there stretches a country great in size and rich in its varied pasturage; but it is without inhabitants and altogether impossible for man to enter; not that it has from the first never known the race of men, but in later times, as a result of an unseasonable abundance of rain, it brought forth a multitude of venomous spiders and scorpions. As historians relate, so great a multitude of these animals came to abound that, although at the outset the human beings dwelling there united in killing the natural enemy, yet, because the multitude of them was not to be overcome and their bites brought swift death to their victims, they renounced both their ancestral land and mode of life and fled from these regions. Nor is there any occasion to be surprised at this statement or to distrust it, since we have learned through trustworthy history of many things more astonishing than this which have taken place throughout all the inhabited world. In Italy, for instance, such a multitude of field-mice was generated in the plains that they drove certain people out of their native country; in Media birds, which came to abound beyond telling and made away with the seeds sown by the inhabitants, compelled them to remove into regions held by another people; and in the case of the Autariatae, [Illyrians] as they are called, frogs were originally generated in the clouds, and when they fell upon the people in place of the customary rain, they forced them to leave their native homes and to flee for safety to the place where they now dwell. Who indeed has not read in history, in connection with the Labours which Heracles performed in order to win his immortality, the account of the one Labour in the course of which he drove out of the Stymphalian Lake the multitude of birds which had come to abound in it? Moreover, in Libya certain cities have become depopulated because a multitude of lions came out of the desert against them.

Let these instances, then, suffice in reply to those who adopt a sceptical attitude towards histories because they recount what is astonishing; and now we shall in turn pass on to what follows the subjects we have been treating.

**31.** The borders of the parts to the south are inhabited by men whom the Greeks call "Cynamolgi," [milkers of bitches] but who are known in the language of the barbarians who live near them as Agrii. [savages] They wear great beards and maintain packs of savage dogs which serve to meet the needs of their life. From the time of the beginning of the summer solstice until midwinter, Indian cattle, in a multitude beyond telling, resort to their country, the reason for this being uncertain; for no man knows whether they are in flight because they are being attacked by a great number of carnivorous beasts, or because they are leaving their own regions by reason of a lack of food, or because of some other reversal of fortune which Nature, that engenders all astonishing things, devises, but which the mind of the race of men cannot comprehend. However, since they have not the strength of themselves to get the better of the multitude of the cattle, they let the dogs loose on them, and hunting them by means of the dogs they overcome a very great number of the animals; and as for the beasts which they have taken, some of them they eat while fresh and some they pack down with salt and store up. Many also of the other animals

## Book III

they hunt, thanks to the courage of their dogs, and so maintain themselves by the eating of flesh.

Now the most distant tribes of those peoples who live to the south have indeed the forms of men but their life is that of the beasts; however, it remains for us to discuss two peoples, the Ethiopians and the Trogodytes. But about the Ethiopians we have written in other connections, and so we shall now speak of the Trogodytes.

**32.** The Trogodytes, we may state, are called Nomads by the Greeks, and living as they do a nomadic life off their flocks, each group of them has its tyrant, and their women, like their children, they hold in common, with the single exception of the wife of the tyrant; but if any man goes in to this woman the ruler exacts of him a fine of a specified number of sheep. At the time of the etesian winds, when there are heavy rains in their country, they live off blood and milk which they mix together and seethe for a short while. But after this season the pasturage is withered by the excessive heat, and they retreat into the marshy places and fight with each other for the pasturage of the land. They eat the older animals of their flocks and such as are growing sick and maintain themselves on them at all times. Consequently they give the name of parents to no human being, but rather to a bull and a cow, and also to a ram and a sheep; these they call their fathers or their mothers, by reason of the fact that they ever secure their daily food from them, and not from those who had begotten them. As a drink the common people make use of juice from the plant Christ's-thorn, but for the rulers there is prepared from a certain flower a beverage like the vilest of our sweet new wines. Following after their herds and flocks they move about from one land to another, avoiding any stay in the same regions. And they are all naked as to their bodies except for the loins, which they cover with skins; moreover, all the Trogodytes are circumcised like the Egyptians with the exception of those who, because of what they have experienced, are called "colobi"; [mutilated] for these alone of all who live inside the Straits [to the Red Sea] have in infancy all that part cut completely off with the razor which among other peoples merely suffers circumcision.

**33.** As for the arms of the Trogodytes, those who bear the name of Megabari have round shields covered with raw ox-hide and a club with iron knobs, but the rest of them have bows and arrows and lances. Again, the burials practised by them differ entirely from all others; for after binding the bodies of the dead with withes of Christ's-thorn they tie the neck to the legs, and then placing the corpse upon a mound they cast at it stones as large as can be held in the hand, making merry the while, until they have built up a heap of stones and have hidden the bodies from sight; and finally they set up a goat's horn on the heap and separate, having shown no fellow-feeling for the dead. They fight with one another, not, as the Greeks do, for the possession of land or because of some alleged misdeeds, but for the pasturage as it comes up at one time and another. In their quarrels they at first hurl stones at each other, until some are wounded, and the rest of the time they resort to the struggle with bows and arrows. It is but a moment before many are dead, since they are accurate shooters by reason of their practice in archery and the object at which they are aiming is bare of protective armour. The fighting is terminated by the older women, who rush into the fray and offer themselves as a protection to the fighters, and are the object of respect; for it is a custom with these people that they shall in no wise strike one of these women, and so at their appearance they cease shooting. Those who can no longer accompany the flocks by reason of old age bind the tail of an ox about their own necks and so put an end to their lives of their own free will; and if a man postpones his death, anyone who wishes has the authority to fasten the noose about his neck, as an act of good-will, and, after admonishing the man, to take his life. Likewise it is a custom of theirs to remove from life those who have become maimed or are in the grip of incurable diseases; for they consider it to be the greatest disgrace for a man to cling to life when he is unable to accomplish anything worth living for. Consequently, a man can see every Trogodyte sound in body and of vigorous age, since no one of them lives beyond sixty years.

But we have said enough about the Trogodytes; and if anyone of our readers shall distrust our histories because of what is strange and astonishing in the different manners of life which we have described, when he has considered and compared the climate of Scythia and that of the Trogodyte country and has observed the differences between them, he will not distrust what has been here related.

**34.** So great, for instance, is the contrast between our climate and the climates which we have described that the difference, when considered in detail, surpasses belief. For example, there are countries where, because of the excessive cold, the greatest rivers are frozen over, the ice sustaining the crossing of armies and the passage of heavily laden wagons, the wine and all other juices freeze so that they must be cut with knives, yea, what is more wonderful still, the extremities of human beings fall off when rubbed by the clothing, their eyes are blinded, fire furnishes no protection, even bronze statues are cracked open, and at certain seasons, they say, the clouds are so thick that in those regions there is neither lightning nor thunder; and many other things, more astonishing than these, come to pass, which are unbelievable to such as are ignorant of them, but cannot be endured by any who have actually experienced them. On the farthermost bounds of Egypt and the Trogodyte country, because of the excessive heat from the sun at midday, men who are standing side by side are unable even to see one another by reason of the thickness of the air as it is condensed, and no one can walk about without foot-gear, since blisters appear at once on any who go barefoot. As for drink, unless it is ready to hand to satisfy the need of it, they speedily perish, since the heat swiftly exhausts the natural moistures in the body. Moreover, whenever any man puts any food into a bronze vessel along with water and sets it in the sun, it quickly boils without fire or wood. Nevertheless, the inhabitants of both the lands which we have mentioned, [Sythia and Trogodyte] far from desiring to escape from the excessive evils which befall them, actually, on the contrary, give up their lives of their own accord simply to avoid being compelled to make trial of a different fare and manner of life. Thus it is that every country to which a man has grown accustomed holds a kind of spell of its own over him, and the length of time which he has spent there from infancy overcomes the hardship which he suffers from its climate. Yet countries so different in both ways are separated by no great interval of space. For from Lake Maeotis, [Sea of Azof] near which certain Scythians dwell, living in the midst of frost and excessive cold, many sailors of merchant vessels, running before a favourable wind, have made Rhodes in ten days, from which they have reached Alexandria in four, and from that city many men, sailing by way of the Nile, have reached Ethiopia in ten, so that from the cold parts of the inhabited world to its warmest parts the sailing time is not more than twenty-four days, if the journey is made without a break. Consequently, the difference in climates in a slight interval being so great, it is nothing surprising that both the fare and the manners of life as well as the bodies of the inhabitants should be very different from such as prevail among us.

**35.** Now that we have discussed the principal facts concerning the nations and the manners of life which men consider astonishing, we shall speak in turn of the wild animals of the countries which we are considering. There is an animal, for instance, which is called, from its characteristic, rhinoceros; [nose-horn] in courage and strength it is similar to the elephant but not so high, and it has the toughest hide known and a colour like box-wood. [pale yellow] At the tip of its nostrils it carries a horn which may be described as snub and in hardness is like iron. Since it is ever contesting with the elephant about pasturage it sharpens its horn on stones, and when it opens the fight with this animal it slips under his belly and rips open the flesh with its horn as with a sword. By adopting this kind of fighting it drains the blood of the beasts and kills many of them. But if the elephant has avoided the attempt of the rhinoceros to get under his belly and has seized it beforehand with his trunk, he easily overcomes it by goring it with his tusks and making use of his superior strength.

These are also sphinxes [large baboon] in both the Trogodyte country and Ethiopia, and in shape they are not unlike those depicted in art save that they are more shaggy of hair, and since they have dispositions that are gentle and rather inclined towards cunning they yield also to systematic training.

The animals which bear the name cynocephali [dog-heads] are in body like misshapen men, and they make a sound like the whimpering of human beings. These animals are very wild and quite untameable, and their eyebrows give them a rather surly expression. A most peculiar characteristic of the female is that it carries the womb on the outside of its body during its entire existence.

The animal called the cepus [cebus] has received its name from the beautiful and pleasing grace which characterises its entire body, and it has a head like that of a lion, but the rest of its body is like that of a panther, save in respect to its size, in which it resembles a gazelle.

Of all the animals named the carnivorous bull is the wildest and altogether the hardest to overcome, for in bulk he is larger than the domestic bulls, in swiftness of foot he is not inferior to a horse, and his mouth opens clear back to the ears. His colour is a fiery red, his eyes are more piercing than those of a lion and shine at night, and his horns enjoy a distinctive property; for at all other times he moves them like his ears, but when fighting he holds them rigid. The direction of growth of his hair is contrary to that of all other animals. He is, again, a remarkable beast in both boldness and strength, since he attacks the boldest animals and finds his food in devouring the flesh of his victims. He also destroys the flocks of the inhabitants and engages in terrible combats with whole bands of the shepherds and packs of dogs. Rumour has it that their skin cannot be pierced; at any rate, though many men have tried to capture them, no man has ever brought one under subjection. If he has fallen into a pit or been captured by some other ruse he becomes choked with rage, and in no case does he ever exchange his freedom for the care which men would accord to him in domestication. It is with reason, therefore, that the Trogodytes hold this wild beast to be the strongest of all, since Nature has endowed it with the prowess of a lion, the speed of a horse, and the might of a bull, and since it is not subdued by the native strength of iron which is the greatest known.

The animal which the Ethiopians call the crocottas [hyena?] has a nature which is a mixture of that of a dog and that of a wolf, but in ferocity it is more to be feared than either of them, and with respect to its teeth it surpasses all animals; for every bone, no matter how huge in size, it easily crushes, and whatever it has gulped down its stomach digests in an astonishing manner. Among those who recount marvellous lies about this beast there are some who relate that it imitates the speech of men, but for our part they do not win our credence.

**36.** As for snakes, those peoples which dwell near the country which is desert and infested by beasts say that there is every kind of them, of a magnitude surpassing belief. When certain writers state that they have seen some one hundred cubits long, it may justly be assumed, not only by us but by everybody else, that they are telling a falsehood; indeed they add to this tale, which is utterly distrusted, things far more astonishing, when they say that, since the country is flat like a plain, whenever the largest of these beasts coil themselves up, they make, by the coils which have been wound in circles and rest one upon another, elevations which seen from a distance resemble a hill. Now a man may not readily agree as to the magnitude of the beasts of which we have just spoken; but we shall describe the largest beasts which have actually been seen and were brought to Alexandria in certain well-made receptacles, and shall add a detailed description of the manner in which they were captured.

The second Ptolemy, [Ptolemy Philadelphus, 285-246] who was passionately fond of the hunting of elephants and gave great rewards to those who succeeded in capturing against odds the most valiant of these beasts, expending on this hobby great sums of money, not only collected great herds of war-elephants, but also brought to the knowledge of the Greeks other kinds of animals which had never before been seen and were objects of amazement. Consequently certain of the hunters, observing the princely generosity of the king in the matter of the rewards he gave, rounding up a considerable number decided to hazard their lives and to capture one of the huge snakes and bring it alive to Ptolemy at Alexandria. Great and astonishing as was the undertaking, fortune aided their designs and crowned their attempt with the success which it deserved. For they spied one of the snakes, thirty cubits long, as it loitered near the pools in which the water collects; here it maintained for most of the time its coiled body motionless, but at the appearance of an animal which came down to the spot to quench its thirst it would suddenly uncoil itself, seize the animal in its jaws, and so entwine in its coil the body of the creature which had come into view that it could in no wise escape its doom. So, since the beast was long and slender and sluggish in nature, hoping that they could master it with nooses and ropes, they approached it with confidence the first time, having ready to hand everything which they might need; but as they drew near it they constantly grew more and more terrified as they gazed upon its fiery eye and its tongue darting out in every direction, caught the hideous sound made by the roughness of its scales as it made its way through the trees and brushed against them, and noted the extraordinary size of its teeth, the savage appearance of its mouth, and the astonishing height of its heap of coils. Consequently, after they had driven the colour from their cheeks through fear, with cowardly trembling they cast the nooses about its tail; but the beast, the moment the rope touched its body, whirled about with so mighty a hissing as to frighten them out of their wits, and raising itself into the air above the head of the foremost man it seized him in its mouth and ate his flesh while he still lived, and the second it caught from a distance with a coil as he fled, drew him to itself, and winding itself about him began squeezing his belly with its tightening bond; and as for all the rest, stricken with terror they sought their safety in flight.

**37.** Nevertheless, the hunters did not give up their attempt to capture the beast, the favour expected of the king and his reward outweighing the dangers which they had come to know full well as the result of their experiment, and by ingenuity and craft they did subdue that which was by force well-nigh invincible, devising a kind of contrivance like the following: They fashioned a circular thing woven of reeds closely set together, in general shape resembling a fisherman's creel and in size and capacity capable of holding the bulk of the beast. Then, when they had reconnoitred its hole and observed the time when it went forth to feed and returned again, so soon as it had set out to prey upon the other animals, as was its custom, they stopped the opening of its old hole with large stones and earth, and digging an underground cavity near its lair they set the woven net in it and placed the mouth of the net opposite the opening, so that it was in this way all ready for the beast to enter. Against the return of the animal they had made ready archers and slingers and many horsemen, as well as trumpeters and all the other apparatus needed, and as the beast drew near it raised its neck in air higher than the horsemen. Now the company of men who had assembled for the hunt did not dare to draw near it, being warned by the mishaps which had befallen them on the former occasion, but shooting at it from afar, and with many hands aiming at a single target, and a large one at that, they kept hitting it, and when the horsemen appeared and the multitude of bold fighting-dogs, and then again when the trumpets blared, they got the animal terrified. Consequently, when it retreated to its accustomed lair, they closed in upon it, but only so far as not to arouse it still more. When it came near the opening which had been stopped up, the whole throng, acting together, raised a mighty din with their arms and thus increased its confusion and fear because of the crowds which put in their appearance and of the trumpets. But the beast could not find the opening and so, terrified at the advance of the hunters, fled for refuge into the mouth of the net which had been prepared near by. When the woven net began to be filled up as the snake uncoiled itself, some of the hunters anticipated its movements by leaping forward, and before the snake could turn about to face the entrance they closed and fastened with ropes the mouth, which was long and had been shrewdly devised with such swiftness of operation in mind; then they hauled out the woven net and putting rollers under it drew it up into the air. The beast, enclosed as it was in a straitened place, kept sending forth an unnatural and terrible hissing and tried to pull down with its teeth the reeds which enveloped it, and by twisting itself in every direction created the expectation in the minds of the men who were carrying it that it would leap out of the contrivance which enveloped it. Consequently, in terror, they set the snake down on the ground, and by jabbing it about the tail they diverted the attention of the beast from its work of tearing with its teeth to its sensation of pain in the parts which hurt.

When they had brought the snake to Alexandria they presented it to the king, an astonishing sight which those cannot credit who have merely heard the tale. By depriving the beast of its food they wore down its spirit and little by little tamed it, so that the domestication of it became a thing of wonder. As for Ptolemy, he distributed among the hunters the merited rewards, and kept and fed the snake, which had now been tamed and afforded the greatest and most astonishing sight for the strangers who visited his kingdom. Consequently, in view of the fact that a snake of so great a size has been exposed to the public gaze, it is not fair to doubt the word of the Ethiopians or to assume that the report which they circulated far and wide was a mere fiction. For they state that there are to be seen in their country snakes so great in size that they not only eat both oxen and bulls and other animals of equal bulk, but even join issue in battle with the elephants, and by intertwining their coil about the elephants' legs they prevent the natural movement of them and by rearing their necks above their trunks they put their heads directly opposite the eyes of the elephants, and sending forth, by reason of the fiery nature of their eyes, brilliant flashes like lightning, they first blind their sight and then throw them to the ground and devour the flesh of their conquered foes.

**38.** But now that we have examined with sufficient care Ethiopia and the Trogodyte country and the territory adjoining them, as far as the region which is uninhabited because of excessive heat, and, beside these, the coast of the Red Sea [Persian Gulf] and the Atlantic deep which stretches towards the south, we shall give an account of the part which still remains, and I refer to the Arabian Gulf, [Red Sea] drawing in part upon the royal records preserved in Alexandria,and in part upon what we have learned from men who have seen it with their own eyes. This section of the inhabited world and that about the British Isles and the far north have by no means come to be included in the common knowledge of men. As for the parts of the inhabited world which lie to the far north and border on the area which is uninhabited because of the cold, we shall discuss them when we record the deeds of Gaius Caesar; for he it was who extended the Roman Empire the farthest into those parts and brought it about that all the area which had formerly been unknown came to be included in a narrative of history; but the Arabian Gulf, as it is called, opens into the ocean which lies to the south, [Indian Ocean] and its innermost recess, which stretches over a distance of very many stades in length, is enclosed by the farthermost borders of Arabia and the Trogodyte country. Its width at the mouth and at the innermost recess is about sixteen stades, but from the harbour of Panormus to the opposite mainland is a day's run for a warship. And its greatest width .is at the Tyrcaeus mountain and Macaria, an island out at sea, the mainlands there being out of sight of each other. But from this point the width steadily decreases more and more and continually tapers as far as the entrance. And as a man sails along the coast he comes in many places upon long islands with narrow passages between them, where the current runs full and strong. Such, then, is the setting, in general terms, of this gulf. For our part, we shall make our beginning with the farthest regions of the innermost recess and then sail along its two sides past the mainlands, in connection with which we shall describe what is peculiar to them and most deserving of discussion; and first of all we shall take the right side, the coast of which is inhabited by tribes of the Trogodytes as far inland as the desert.

**39.** In the course of the journey, then, from the city of Arsinoê along the right mainland, in many places numerous streams, which have a bitter salty taste, drop from the cliffs into the sea. And after a man has passed these waters, above a great plain there towers a mountain whose colour is like ruddle (sic.) and blinds the sight of any who gaze steadfastly upon it for some time. Moreover, at the edge of the skirts of the mountain there lies a harbour, known as Aphrodite's Harbour, which has a winding entrance. Above this harbour are situated three islands, two of which abound in olive trees and are thickly shaded, while one falls short of the other two in respect of the number of these trees but contains a multitude of the birds called *meleagrides*. [Guinea-fowl] Next there is a very large gulf which is called Acathartus, [foul] and by it is an exceedingly long peninsula, over the narrow neck of which men transport their ships to the opposite sea. As a man coasts along these regions he comes to an island which lies at a distance out in the open sea and stretches for a length of eighty stades; the name of it is Ophiodes [snaky] and it was formerly full of fearful serpents of every variety, which was in fact the reason why it received this name, but in later times the kings at Alexandria have laboured so diligently on the reclaiming of it that not one of the animals which were formerly there is any longer to be seen on the island.

However, we should not pass over the reason why the kings showed diligence in the reclamation of this island. For there is found on it the topaz, as it is called, which is a pleasing transparent stone, similar to glass, and of a marvellous golden hue. Consequently no unauthorised person may set foot upon the island and it is closely guarded, every man who has approached it being put to death by the guards who are stationed there. And the latter are few in number and lead a miserable existence. For in order to prevent any stone being stolen, not a single boat is left on the island; furthermore, any who sail by pass along it at a distance because of their fear of the king; and the provisions which are brought to it are quickly exhausted and there are absolutely no other provisions in the land. Consequently, whenever only a little food is left, all the inhabitants of the village sit down and await the arrival of the ship of those who are bringing the provisions, and when these are delayed they are reduced to their last hopes. The stone we have mentioned, being found in the rocks, is not discernible during the day because of the stifling heat, since it is overcome by the brilliance of the sun, but when night falls it shines in the dark and is visible from afar, in whatever place it may be. The guards on the island divide these places by lot among themselves and stand watch over them, and when the stone shines they put around it, to mark the place, a vessel corresponding in size to the chunk of stone which gives out the light; and when day comes and they go their rounds they cut out the area which has been so marked and turn it over to men who are able by reason of their craftsmanship to polish it properly.

**40.** After sailing past these regions one finds that the coast is inhabited by many nations of Ichthyophagi and many nomadic Trogodytes. Then there appear mountains of all manner of peculiarities until one comes to the Harbour of Soteria, [Safety] as it is called, which gained this name from the first Greek sailors who found safety there. From this region onwards the gulf begins to become contracted and to curve toward Arabia. And here it is found that the nature of the country and of the sea has altered by reason of the peculiar characteristic of the region; for the mainland appears to be low as seen from the sea, no elevation rising above it, and the sea, which runs to shoals, is found to have a depth of no more than three fathoms, while in colour it is altogether green. The reason for this is, they say, not because the water is naturally of that colour, but because of the mass of seaweed and tangle which shows from under water. For ships, then, which are equipped with oars the place is suitable enough, since it rolls along no wave from a great distance and affords, furthermore, fishing in the greatest abundance: but the ships which carry the elephants, being of deep draft because of their weight and heavy by reason of their equipment, bring upon their crews great and terrible dangers. Running as they do under full sail and often times being driven during the night before the force of the winds, sometimes they will strike against rocks and be wrecked or sometimes run aground on slightly submerged spits. The sailors are unable to go over the sides of the ship because the water is deeper than a man's height, and when in their efforts to rescue their vessel by means of their punting-poles they accomplish nothing, they jettison everything except their provisions; but if even by this course they do not succeed in effecting an escape, they fall into great perplexity by reason of the fact that they can make out neither an island nor a promontory nor another ship near at hand; for the region is altogether inhospitable and only at rare intervals do men cross it in ships. To add to these evils the waves within a moment's time cast up such a mass of sand against the body of the ship and heap it up in so incredible a fashion that it soon piles up a mound round about the place and binds the vessel, as if of set purpose, to the solid land.

Now the men who have suffered this mishap, at the outset bewail their lot with moderation in the face of a deaf wilderness, having as yet not entirely abandoned hope of ultimate salvation; for oftentimes the swell of the flood-tide has intervened for men in such a plight and raised the ship aloft, and suddenly appearing, as might a *deus ex machina,* has brought succour to men in the extremity of peril. When such god-sent aid has not been vouchsafed to them and their food fails, then the strong cast the weaker into the sea in order that for the few left the remaining necessities of life may last a greater number of days. Finally, when they have blotted out of their minds all their hopes, these perish by a more miserable fate than those who had died before; for whereas the latter in a moment's time returned to Nature the spirit which she had given them, these parcelled out their death into many separate hardships before they finally, suffering long-protracted tortures, were granted the end of life. As for the ships which have been stripped of their crews in this pitiable fashion, there they remain for many years, like a group of cenotaphs, embedded on every side in a

BOOK III

heap of sand, their masts and yard-arms still standing aloft, and they move those who behold them from afar to pity and sympathy for the men who have perished. It is the king's command to leave in place such evidences of disasters that they may give notice to sailors of the region which works their destruction, and among the Ichthyophagi who dwell near by has been handed down a tale which has preserved the account received from their forefathers, that once, when there was a great receding of the sea, the entire area of the gulf which has what may be roughly described as the green appearance became land, and that, after the sea had receded to the opposite parts and the solid ground in the depths of it had emerged to view, a mighty flood came back upon it again and returned the body of water to its former place.

**41.** The voyage along the coast, as one leaves these regions, from Ptolemais as far as the Promontories of the Tauri we have already mentioned, when we told of Ptolemy's hunting of the elephants; and from the Tauri the coast swings to the east, and at the time of the summer solstice the shadows fall to the south, opposite to what is true with us, at about the second hour of the day. The country also has rivers, which flow from the Psebaean mountains, as they are called. Moreover, it is checkered by great plains as well, which bear mallows, cress, and palms, all of unbelievable size; and it also brings forth fruits of every description, which have an insipid taste and are unknown among us. That part which stretches towards the interior is full of elephants and wild bulls and lions and many other powerful wild beasts of every description. The passage by sea is broken up by islands which, though they bear no cultivated fruit, support varieties of birds which are peculiar to them and marvellous to look upon. After this place the sea is quite deep and produces all kinds of sea-monsters of astonishing size, which, however, offer no harm to men unless one by accident falls upon their back-fins; for they are unable to pursue the sailors, since when they rise from the sea their eyes are blinded by the brilliance of the sun. These, then, are the farthest known parts of the Trogodyte country, and are circumscribed by the ranges which go by the name of Psebaean.

**42.** We shall now take up the other side, namely, the opposite shore which forms the coast of Arabia, and shall describe it, beginning with the innermost recess. This bears the name Poseideion, [Roman Posidium; Ras-Mohammed] since an altar was erected here to Poseidon Pelagius [of the sea] by that Ariston who was dispatched by Ptolemy to investigate the coast of Arabia as far as the ocean. Directly after the innermost recess is a region along the sea which is especially honoured by the natives because of the advantage which accrues from it to them. It is called the Palm-grove and contains a multitude of trees of this kind which are exceedingly fruitful and contribute in an unusual degree to enjoyment and luxury. But all the country round about is lacking in springs of water and is fiery hot because it slopes to the south; accordingly, it was a natural thing that the barbarians made sacred the place which was full of trees and, lying as it did in the midst of a region utterly desolate, supplied their food. And indeed not a few springs and streams of water gush forth there, which do not yield to snow in coldness; and these make the land on both sides of them green and altogether pleasing. Moreover, an altar is there built of hard stone and very old in years, bearing an inscription in ancient letters of an unknown tongue. The oversight of the sacred precinct is in the care of a man and a woman who hold the sacred office for life. The inhabitants of the place are long-lived and have their beds in the trees because of their fear of the wild beasts.

After sailing past the Palm-grove one comes to an island off a promontory of the mainland which bears the name Island of Phocae [seals] from the animals which make their home there; for so great a multitude of these beasts spend their time in these regions as to astonish those who behold them. The promontory which stretches out in front of the island lies over against Petra, as it is called, and Palestine; for to this country, as it is reported, both the Gerrhaeans and Minaeans convey from Upper Arabia, as it is called, both the frankincense and the other aromatic wares.

43. The coast which comes next was originally inhabited by the Maranitae, and then by the Garindanes who were their neighbours. The latter secured the country somewhat in this fashion: In the above-mentioned Palm-grove a festival was celebrated every four years, to which the neighbouring peoples thronged from all sides, both to sacrifice to the gods of the sacred precinct hecatombs of well-fed camels and also to carry back to their native lands some of the water of the place, since the tradition prevailed that this drink gave health to such as partook of it. When for these reasons, then, the Maranitae gathered to the festival, the Garindanes, putting to the sword those who had been left behind in the country, and lying in ambush for those who were returning from the festival, utterly destroyed the tribe, and after stripping the country of its inhabitants they divided among themselves the plains, which were fruitful and supplied abundant pasture for their herds and flocks. This coast has few harbours and is divided by many large mountains, by reason of which it shows every shade of colour and affords a marvellous spectacle to those who sail past it.

After one has sailed past this country the Laeanites Gulf comes next, about which are many inhabited villages of Arabs who are known as Nabataeans. This tribe occupies a large part of the coast and not a little of the country which stretches inland, and it has a people numerous beyond telling and flocks and herds in multitude beyond belief. Now in ancient times these men observed justice and were content with the food which they received from their flocks, but later, after the kings in Alexandria had made the ways of the sea navigable for their merchants, these Arabs not only attacked the shipwrecked, but fitting out pirate ships preyed upon the voyagers, imitating in their practices the savage and lawless ways of the Tauri of the Pontus; some time afterward, however, they were caught on the high seas by some quadriremes and punished as they deserved.

Beyond these regions there is a level and well-watered stretch of land which produces, by reason of springs which flow through its whole extent, dog's-tooth grass, lucerne, and lotus as tall as a man. And because of the abundance and excellent quality of the pasturage, not only does it support every manner of flocks and herds in multitude beyond telling, but also wild camels, deer, and gazelles. And against the multitude of animals which are nourished in that place there gather in from the desert bands of lions and wolves and leopards, against which the herdsmen must perforce battle both day and night to protect their charges; and in this way the land's good fortune becomes a cause of misfortune for its inhabitants, seeing that it is generally Nature's way to dispense to men along with good things what is hurtful as well.

**44.** Next after these plains as one skirts the coast comes a gulf of extraordinary nature. It runs, namely, to a point deep into the land, extends in length a distance of some five hundred stades, and shut in as it is by crags which are of wondrous size, its mouth is winding and hard to get out of; for a rock which extends into the sea obstructs its entrance and so it is impossible for a ship either to sail into or out of the gulf. Furthermore, at times when the current rushes in and there are frequent shiftings of the winds, the surf, beating upon the rocky beach, roars and rages all about the projecting rock. The inhabitants of the land about the gulf, who are known as Banizomenes, find their food by hunting the land animals and eating their meat. A temple has been set up there, which is very holy and exceedingly revered by all Arabians.

Next there are three islands which lie off the coast just described and provide numerous harbours. The first of these, history relates, is sacred to Isis and is uninhabited, and on it are stone foundations of ancient dwellings and stelae which are inscribed with letters in a barbarian tongue; the other two islands are likewise uninhabited and all three are covered thick with olive trees which differ from those we have. Beyond these islands there extends for about a thousand stades a coast which is precipitous and difficult for ships to sail past; for there is neither harbour beneath the cliffs nor roadstead where sailors may anchor, and no natural breakwater which affords shelter in emergency for mariners in distress. Parallel to the coast here runs a mountain range at whose summit are rocks which are sheer and of a terrifying height, and at its base are sharp undersea ledges in many places and behind them are ravines which are eaten away underneath and turn this way and that. Since these ravines are connected by passages with one another and the sea is deep, the surf, as it at one time rushes in and at another time retreats, gives forth a sound resembling a mighty crash of thunder. At one place the surf, as it breaks upon huge rocks, leaps on high and causes an astonishing mass of foam, at another it is swallowed up within the caverns and creates such a terrifying agitation of the waters that men who unwittingly draw near these places are so frightened that they die, as it were, a first death.

This coast, then, is inhabited by Arabs who are called Thamudeni; but the coast next to it is bounded by a very large gulf, off which lie scattered islands which are in appearance very much like the islands called the Echinades. [Kurtzolares] After this coast there come sand dunes, of infinite extent in both length and width and black in colour. Beyond them a neck of land is to be seen and a harbour, the fairest of any which have come to be included in history, called Charmuthas. Behind an extraordinary natural breakwater which slants towards the west there lies a gulf which not only is marvellous in its form but far surpasses all others in the advantages it offers; for a thickly wooded mountain stretches along it, enclosing it on all sides in a ring one hundred stades long; its entrance is two plethra wide, and it provides a harbour undisturbed by the waves sufficient for two thousand vessels. Furthermore, it is exceptionally well supplied with water, since a river, larger than ordinary, empties into it, and it contains in its centre an island which is abundantly watered and capable of supporting gardens. In general, it resembles most closely the harbour of Carthage, which is known as Cothon, of the advantages of which we shall endeavour to give a detailed discussion in connection with the appropriate time. A multitude of fish gather from the open sea into the harbour both because of the calm which prevails there and because of the sweetness of the waters which flow into it.

**45.** After these places, as a man skirts the coast, five mountains rise on high separated one from another, and their peaks taper into breast-shaped tips of stone which give them an appearance like that of the pyramids of Egypt. Then comes a circular gulf guarded on every side by great promontories, and midway on a line drawn across it rises a trapezium-shaped hill on which three temples, remarkable for their height, have been erected to gods, which indeed are unknown to the Greeks, but are accorded unusual honour by the natives. After this there is a stretch of dank coast, traversed at intervals by streams of sweet water from springs; on it there is a mountain which bears the name Chabinus and is heavily covered with thickets of every kind of tree. The land which adjoins the mountainous country is inhabited by the Arabs known as Debae. They are breeders of camels and make use of the services of this animal in connection with the most important needs of their life; for instance, they fight against their enemies from their backs, employ them for the conveyance of their wares and thus easily accomplish all their business, drink their milk and in this way get their food from them, and traverse their entire country riding upon their racing camels. And down the centre of their country runs a river which carries down such an amount of what is gold dust to all appearance that the mud glitters all over as it is carried out at its mouth. The natives of the region are entirely without experience in the working of the gold, but they are hospitable to strangers, not, however, to everyone who arrives among them, but only to Boeotians and Peloponnesians, the reason for this being the ancient friendship shown by Heracles for the tribe, a friendship which, they relate, has come down to them in the form of a myth as a heritage from their ancestors.

The land which comes next is inhabited by Ah'laei and Gasandi, Arab peoples, and is not fiery hot, like the neighbouring territories, but is often overspread by mild and thick clouds, from which come heavy showers and timely storms that make the summer season temperate. The land produces everything and is exceptionally fertile, but it does not receive the cultivation of which it would admit because of the lack of experience of the folk. Gold they discover in underground galleries which have been formed by nature and gather in abundance, not that which has been fused into a mass out of gold-dust, but the virgin gold, which is called, from its condition when found, "unfired" gold. As for size the smallest nugget found is about as large as the stone of fruit, and the largest not much smaller than a royal nut. This gold they wear about both their wrists and necks, perforating it and alternating it with transparent stones. Since this precious metal abounds in their land, whereas there is a scarcity of copper and iron, they exchange it with merchants for equal parts of the latter wares.

**46.** Beyond this people are the Carbae, as they are called, and beyond these the Sabaeans, who are the most numerous of the tribes of the Arabians. They inhabit that part of the country known as Arabia the Blest, [Arabia Felix] which produces most of the things which are held dear among us and nurtures flocks and herds of every kind in multitude beyond telling. A natural sweet odour pervades the entire land because practically all the things which excel in fragrance grow there unceasingly. Along the coast, for instance, grow balsam, as it is called, and cassia and a certain other herb possessing a nature peculiar to itself; for when fresh it is most pleasing and delightful to the eye, but when kept for a time it suddenly fades to nothing. Throughout the interior of the land there are thick forests, in which are great trees which yield frankincense and myrrh, as well as palms and reeds, cinnamon trees and every other kind which possesses a sweet odour such as these have; for it is impossible to enumerate both the peculiar properties and natures of each one severally because of the great volume and the exceptional richness of the fragrance as it is gathered from each and all. For a divine thing and beyond the power of words to describe seems the fragrance which greets the nostrils and stirs the senses of everyone. Indeed, even though those who sail along this coast may be far from the land, that does not deprive them of a portion of the enjoyment which this fragrance affords; for in the summer season, when the wind is blowing offshore, one finds that the sweet odours exhaled by the myrrh-bearing and other aromatic trees penetrate to the near-by parts of the sea; and the reason is that the essence of the sweet-smelling herbs is not, as with us, kept laid away until it has become old and stale, but its potency is in the full bloom of its strength and fresh, and penetrates to the most delicate parts of the sense of smell. Since the breeze carries the emanation of the most fragrant plants, to the voyagers who approach the coast there is wafted a blending of perfumes, delightful and potent, and healthful withal and exotic, composed as it is of the best of them, seeing that the product of the trees has not been minced into bits and so has exhaled its own special strength, nor yet lies stored away in vessels made of a different substance, but taken at the very prime of its freshness and while its divine nature keeps the shoot pure and undefiled. Consequently those who partake of the unique fragrance feel that they are enjoying the ambrosia of which the myths relate, being unable, because of the superlative sweetness of the perfume, to find any other name that would be fitting and worthy of it.

**47.** Nevertheless, fortune has not invested the inhabitants of this land with a felicity which is perfect and leaves no room for envy, but with such great gifts she has coupled what is harmful and may serve as a warning to such men as are wont to despise the gods because of the unbroken succession of their blessings. In the most fragrant forests is a multitude of snakes, the colour of which is dark-red, their length a span, and their bites altogether incurable; they bite by leaping upon their victim, and as they spring on high they leave a stain of blood upon his skin. And there is also something peculiar to the natives which happens in the case of those whose bodies have become weakened by a protracted illness. For when the body has become permeated by an undiluted and pungent substance and the combination of foreign bodies settles in a porous area, an enfeebled condition ensues which is difficult to cure: consequently at the side of men afflicted in this way they burn asphalt and the beard of a goat, combatting the excessively sweet odour by that from substances of the opposite nature. Indeed the good, when it is measured out in respect of quantity and order, is for human beings an aid and delight, but when it fails of due proportion and proper time the gift which it bestows is unprofitable.

The chief city of this tribe is called by them Sabae and is built upon a mountain. The kings of this city succeed to the throne by descent and the people accord to them honours mingled with good and ill. Though they have the appearance of leading a happy life, in that they impose commands upon all and are not accountable for their deeds, yet they are considered unfortunate, inasmuch as it is unlawful for them ever to leave the palace, and if they do so they are stoned to death, in accordance with a certain ancient oracle, by the common crowd. This tribe surpasses not only the neighbouring Arabs but also all other men in wealth and in their several extravagancies besides. In the exchange and sale of their wares they, of all men who carry on trade for the sake of the silver they receive in exchange, obtain the highest price in return for things of the smallest weight. Consequently, since they have never for ages suffered the ravages of war because of their secluded position, and since an abundance of both gold and silver abounds in the country, especially in Sabae, where the royal palace is situated, they have embossed goblets of every description, made of silver and gold, couches and tripods with silver feet, and every other furnishing of incredible costliness, and halls encircled by large columns, some of them gilded, and others having silver figures on the capitals. Their ceilings and doors they have partitioned by means of panels and coffers made of gold, set with precious stones and placed close together, and have thus made the structure of their houses in every part marvellous for its costliness; for some parts they have constructed of silver and gold, others of ivory and the most showy precious stones or of whatever else men esteem most highly. The fact is that these people have enjoyed their felicity unshaken since ages past because they have been entire strangers to those whose own covetousness leads them to feel that another man's wealth is their own godsend. The sea in these parts looks to be white in colour, so that the beholder marvels at the surprising phenomenon and at the same time seeks for its cause. And there are prosperous islands near by, containing unwalled cities, all the herds of which are white in colour, while no female has any horn whatsoever. These islands are visited by sailors from every part and especially from Potana, the city which Alexander founded on the Indus river, when he wished to have a naval station on the shore of the ocean.

Now as regards Arabia the Blest and its inhabitants we shall be satisfied with what has been said.

**48.** But we must not omit to mention the strange phenomena which are seen in the heavens in these regions. The most marvellous is that which, according to accounts we have, has to do with the constellation of the Great Bear and occasions the greatest perplexity among navigators. What they relate is that, beginning with the month which the Athenians call Maemacterion, [November ±]not one of the seven stars of the Great Bear is seen until the first watch, in Poseideon [December ±] none until the second, and in the following months they gradually drop out of the sight of navigators. As for the other heavenly bodies, the planets, as they are called, are, in the case of some, larger than they appear with us, and in the case of others their risings and settings are also not the same; and the sun does not, as with us, send forth its light shortly in advance of its actual rising, but while the darkness of night still continues, it suddenly and contrary to all expectation appears and sends forth its light. Because of this there is no daylight in those regions before the sun has become visible, and when out of the midst of the sea, as they say, it comes into view, it resembles a fiery red ball of charcoal which discharges huge sparks, and its shape does not look like a cone, as is the impression we have of it, but it has the shape of a column which has the appearance of being slightly thicker at the top; and furthermore it does not shine or send out rays before the first hour, appearing as a fire that gives forth no light in the darkness; but at the beginning of the second hour it takes on the form of a round shield and sends forth a light which is exceptionally bright and fiery. At its setting the opposite manifestations take place with respect to it; for it seems to observers to be lighting up the whole universe with a strange kind of ray for not less than two or, as Agatharchides of Cnidus has recorded, for three hours. And in the opinion of the natives this is the most pleasant period, when the heat is steadily lessening because of the setting of the sun.

As regards the winds, the west, the south-west, also the north-west and the east blow as in the other parts of the world; but in Ethiopia the south winds neither blow nor are known at all, although in the Trogodyte country and Arabia they are so exceptionally hot that they set the forests on fire and cause the bodies of those who take refuge in the shade of their huts to collapse through weakness. The north wind, however, may justly be considered the most favourable of all, since it reaches into every region of the inhabited earth and is ever cool.

## *On the antiquities of Libya and the history of the Gorgons and Amazons, and of Amnion and Atlas (49-61).*

**49**. But now that we have examined these matters, it will be appropriate to discuss the Libyans who dwell near Egypt and the country which borders upon them. The parts about Cyrene and the Syrtes as well as the interior of the mainland in these regions are inhabited by four tribes of Libyans; of these the Nasamones, as they are called, dwell in the parts to the south, the Auschisae in those to the west, the Marmaridae occupy the narrow strip between Egypt and Cyrene and come down to the coast, and the Macae, who are more numerous than their fellow Libyans, dwell in the regions about the Syrtis. Now of the Libyans whom we have just mentioned those are farmers who possess land which is able to produce abundant crops, while those are nomads who get their sustenance from the flocks and herds which they maintain; and both of these groups have kings and lead a life which is not entirely savage or different from that of civilised men. The third group, however, obeying no king and taking no account or even thought of justice, makes robbery its constant practice, and attacking unexpectedly from out of the desert it seizes whatever it has happened upon and quickly withdraws to the place from which it had set out. All the Libyans of this third group lead a life like that of the wild beasts, spending their days under the open sky and practising the savage in their mode of life; for they have nothing to do with civilised food or clothing, but cover their bodies with the skins of goats. Their leaders have no cities whatsoever, but only towers near the sources of water, and into these they bring and store away the excess of their booty. Of the peoples who are their subjects they annually exact an oath of obedience to their authority, and to any who have submitted to them they extend their protection as being allies, and such as take no heed of them they first condemn to death and then make war upon them as robbers. Their weapons are appropriate to both the country and their mode of life; for since they are light of body and inhabit a country which is for the most part a level plain, they face the dangers which beset them armed with three spears and stones in leather bags; and they carry neither sword nor helmet nor any other armour, since their aim is to excel in agility both in pursuit and again in withdrawal. Consequently they are expert in running and hurling stones, having brought to full development by practice and habit the advantages accorded them by nature. Speaking generally, they observe neither justice nor good faith in any respect in dealing with peoples of alien race.

**50.** That part of the country which lies near the city of Cyrene has a deep soil and bears products of many kinds; for not only does it produce wheat, but it also possesses large vineyards and olive orchards and native forests, and rivers which are of great utility; but the area which extends beyond its southern border where nitre is found, being uncultivated and lacking springs of water, is in appearance like a sea; and in addition to its showing no variety of landscape it is surrounded by desert land, the desert which lies beyond ending in a region from which egress is difficult. Consequently not even a bird is to be seen there nor any four-footed animal except the gazelle and the ox, nor indeed any plant or anything that delights the eye, since the land which stretches into the interior contains nearly continuous dunes throughout its length, and greatly as it is lacking in the things which pertain to civilised life, to the same degree does it abound in snakes of every manner of appearance and size, and especially in those which men call cerastes [horned serpents] the stings of which are mortal and their colour is like sand; and since for this reason they look like the ground on which they lie, few men discern them and the greater number tread on them unwittingly and meet with unexpected perils. Moreover, the account runs that in ancient times these snakes once invaded a large part of that section of Egypt which lies below this desert and rendered it uninhabitable.

And both in this arid land and in Libya which lies beyond the Syrtis there takes place a marvellous thing. For at certain times, and especially when there is no wind, shapes are seen gathering in the sky which assume the forms of animals of every kind; and some of these remain fixed, but others begin to move, sometimes retreating before a man and at other times pursuing him, and in every case, since they are of monstrous size, they strike such as have never experienced them with wondrous dismay and terror. For when the shapes which are pursuing overtake the persons they envelop their bodies, causing a chilling and shivering sensation, so that strangers who are unfamiliar with them are overcome with fear, although the natives, who have often met with such things, pay no attention to the phenomenon.

**51.** Now incredible though this effect may seem and like a fanciful tale, yet certain physical philosophers attempt to set forth the causes of it somewhat as follows: The winds, they say, either blow in this land not at all or else are altogether sluggish and without vigour; and often there prevails in the air a calm and wondrous lack of movement, because of the fact that neither wooded vales nor thickly-shaded glens lie near it nor are there any elevations that make hills; furthermore, these regions lack large rivers and, in general, the whole territory round about, being barren of plants, gives forth no vapour. Yet it is all these things which are wont, they explain, to generate beginnings, as it were, and gatherings of air-currents. Consequently, when so stifling an atmosphere extends over the arid land the phenomenon which we observe taking place now and then with respect to the clouds on humid days, when every kind of shape is formed, occurs likewise in Libya, they tell us, the air as it condenses assuming manifold shapes. Now this air is driven along by the weak and sluggish breezes, rising aloft and making quivering motions and impinging upon other bodies of similar character, but when a calm succeeds, it then descends towards the earth by reason of its weight and in the shape which it may chance to have assumed, whereupon, there being nothing to dissipate it, the air clings to such living creatures as accidentally come to be in the way. As for the movements which these shapes make in both directions, these, they say, indicate no volition on their part, since it is impossible that voluntary flight or pursuit should reside in a soulless thing. Yet the living creatures are, unknown to themselves, responsible for this movement through the air; for, if they advance, they push up by their violent motion the air which lies beneath them, and this is the reason why the image which has formed retreats before them and gives the impression of fleeing; whereas if the living creatures withdraw, they follow in the opposite direction, the cause having been reversed, since that which is empty and rarefied draws the shapes towards itself. Consequently it has the appearance of pursuing men who withdraw before it, for the image is drawn to the empty space and rushes forward in a mass under the influence of the backward motion of the living creature; and as for those who flee, it is quite reasonable that, whether they turn about or stand still, their bodies should feel the light touch of the image which follows them; and this is broken in pieces as it strikes upon the solid object, and as it pours itself out in all directions it chills the bodies of all with whom it comes in contact.

**52.** But now that we have examined these matters it will be fitting, in connection with the regions we have mentioned, to discuss the account which history records of the Amazons who were in Libya in ancient times. For the majority of mankind believe that the only Amazons were those who are reported to have dwelt in the neighbourhood of the Thermodon river on the Pontus; but the truth is otherwise, since the Amazons of Libya were much earlier in point of time and accomplished notable deeds. Now we are not unaware that to many who read this account the history of this people will appear to be a thing unheard of and entirely strange; for since the race of these Amazons disappeared entirely many generations before the Trojan War, whereas the women about the Thermodon river were in their full vigour a little before that time, it is not without reason that the later people, who were also better known, should have inherited the fame of the earlier, who are entirely unknown to most men because of the lapse of time. For our part, however, since we find that many early poets and historians, and not a few of the later ones as well, have made mention of them, we shall endeavour to recount their deeds in summary, following the account of Dionysius, [Skytobrachion] who composed a narrative about the Argonauts and Dionysus, and also about many other things which took place in the most ancient times.

Now there have been in Libya a number of races of women who were warlike and greatly admired for their manly vigour; for instance, tradition tells us of the race of the Gorgons, against whom, as the account is given, Perseus made war, a race distinguished for its valour; for the fact that it was the son of Zeus, the mightiest Greek of his day, who accomplished the campaign against these women, and that this was his greatest Labour may be taken by any man as proof of both the pre-eminence and the power of the women we have mentioned. Furthermore, the manly prowess of those of whom we are now about to write presupposes an amazing pre-eminence when compared with the nature of the women of our day.

**53.** We are told, namely, that there was once in the western parts of Libya, on the bounds of the inhabited world, a race which was ruled by women and followed a manner of life unlike that which prevails among us. For it was the custom among them that the women should practise the arts of war and be required to serve in the army for a fixed period, during which time they maintained their virginity; then, when the years of their service in the field had expired, they went in to the men for the procreation of children, but they kept in their hands the administration of the magistracies and of all the affairs of the state. The men, however, like our married women, spent their days about the house, carrying out the orders which were given them by their wives; and they took no part in military campaigns or in office or in the exercise of free citizenship in the affairs of the community by virtue of which they might become presumptuous and rise up against the women. When their children were born the babies were turned over to the men, who brought them up on milk and such cooked foods as were appropriate to the age of the infants; and if it happened that a girl was born, its breasts were seared that they might not develop at the time of maturity; for they thought that the breasts, as they stood out from the body, were no small hindrance in warfare; and in fact it is because they have been deprived of their breasts that they are called by the Greeks Amazons.

As mythology relates, their home was on an island which, because it was in the west, was called Hespera, and it lay in the marsh Tritonis. This marsh was near the ocean which surrounds the earth and received its name from a certain river Triton which emptied into it; and this marsh was also near Ethiopia and that mountain by the shore of the ocean which is the highest of those in the vicinity and impinges upon the ocean and is called by the Greeks Atlas. The island mentioned above was of great size and full of fruit-bearing trees of every kind, from which the natives secured their food. It contained also a multitude of flocks and herds, namely, of goats and sheep, from which the possessors received milk and meat for their sustenance; but grain the nation used not at all because the use of this fruit of the earth had not yet been discovered among them.

The Amazons, then, the account continues, being a race superior in valour and eager for war, first of all subdued all the cities on the island except the one called Mene, which was considered to be sacred and was inhabited by Ethiopian Ichthyophagi, and was also subject to great eruptions of fire and possessed a multitude of the precious stones which the Greeks call *anthrax, sardion,* and *smaragdos*; and after this they subdued many of the neighbouring Libyans and

## Book III

nomad tribes, and founded within the marsh Tritonis a great city which they named Cherronesus [peninsula] after its shape.

**54.** Setting out from the city of Cherronesus, the account continues, the Amazons embarked upon great ventures, a longing having come over them to invade many parts of the inhabited world. The first people against whom they advanced, according to the tale, was the Atlantians, the most civilised men among the inhabitants of those regions, who dwelt in a prosperous country and possessed great cities; it was among them, we are told, that mythology places the birth of the gods, in the regions which lie along the shore of the ocean, in this respect agreeing with those among the Greeks who relate legends, and about this we shall speak in detail a little later.

Now the queen of the Amazons, Myrina, collected, it is said, an army of thirty thousand foot-soldiers and three thousand cavalry, since they favoured to an unusual degree the use of cavalry in their wars. For protective devices they used the skins of large snakes, since Libya contains such animals of incredible size, and for offensive weapons, swords and lances; they also used bows and arrows, with which they struck not only when facing the enemy but also when in flight, by shooting backwards at their pursuers with good effect. Upon entering the land of the Atlantians they defeated in a pitched battle the inhabitants of the city of Cerne, as it is called, and making their way inside the walls along with the fleeing enemy, they got the city into their hands; and desiring to strike terror into the neighbouring peoples they treated the captives savagely, put to the sword the men from the youth upward, led into slavery the children and women, and razed the city. When the terrible fate of the inhabitants of Cerne became known among their fellow tribesmen, it is related that the Atlantians, struck with terror, surrendered their cities on terms of capitulation and announced that they would do whatever should be commanded them, and that the queen Myrina, bearing herself honourably towards the Atlantians, both established friendship with them and founded a city to bear her name in place of the city which had been razed; and in it she settled both the captives and any native who so desired. Whereupon the Atlantians presented her with magnificent presents and by public decree voted to her notable honours, and she in return accepted their courtesy and in addition promised that she would show kindness to their nation. Since the natives were often being warred upon by the Gorgons, as they were named, a folk which resided upon their borders, and in general had that people lying in wait to injure them, Myrina, they say, was asked by the Atlantians to invade the land of the afore-mentioned Gorgons. When the Gorgons drew up their forces to resist them a mighty battle took place in which the Amazons, gaining the upper hand, slew great numbers of their opponents and took no fewer than three thousand prisoners; and since the rest had fled for refuge into a certain wooded region, Myrina undertook to set fire to the timber, being eager to destroy the race utterly, but when she found that she was unable to succeed in her attempt she retired to the borders of her country.

**55.** Now as the Amazons, they go on to say, relaxed their watch during the night because of their success, the captive women, falling upon them and drawing the swords of those who thought they were conquerors, slew many of them; in the end, however, the multitude poured in about them from every side and the prisoners fighting bravely were butchered one and all. Myrina accorded a funeral to her fallen comrades on three pyres and raised up three great heaps of earth as tombs, which are called to this day "Amazon Mounds." The Gorgons, grown strong again in later days, were subdued a second time by Perseus, the son of Zeus, when Medusa was queen over them; and in the end both they and the race of the Amazons were entirely destroyed by Heracles, when he visited the regions to the west and set up his pillars in Libya, since he felt that it would ill accord with his resolve to be the benefactor of the whole race of mankind if he should suffer any nations to be under the rule of women. The story is also told that the marsh Tritonis disappeared from sight in the course of an earthquake, when those parts of it which lay towards the ocean were torn asunder.

As for Myrina, the account continues, she visited the larger part of Libya, and passing over into Egypt she struck a treaty of friendship with Horus, the son of Isis, who was king of Egypt at that time, and then, after making war to the end upon the Arabians and slaying many of them, she subdued Syria; but when the Cilicians came out with presents to meet her and agreed to obey her commands, she left those free who yielded to her of their free will and for this reason these are called to this day the "Free Cilicians." She also conquered in war the races in the region of the Taurus, peoples of outstanding courage, and descended through Greater Phrygia to the sea; then she won over the land lying along the coast and fixed the bounds of her campaign at the Caïcus River. Selecting in the territory which she had won by arms sites well suited for the founding of cities, she built a considerable number of them and founded one [in Mysia] which bore her own name, but the others she named after the women who held the most important commands, such as Cymê, Pitana, and Prienê.

These, then, are the cities she settled along the sea, but others, and a larger number, she planted in the regions stretching towards the interior. She seized also some of the islands, and Lesbos in particular, on which she founded the city of Mitylenê, which was named after her sister who took part in the campaign. After that, while subduing some of the rest of the islands, she was caught in a storm, and after she had offered up prayers for her safety to the Mother of the Gods, [Cybelê] she was carried to one of the uninhabited islands; this island, in obedience to a vision which she beheld in her dreams, she made sacred to this goddess, and set up altars there and offered magnificent sacrifices. She also gave it the name of Samothrace, which means, when translated into Greek, "sacred island." although some historians say that it was formerly called Samos and was then given the name of Samothrace by Thracians who at one time dwelt on it. However, after the Amazons had returned to the continent, the myth relates, the Mother of the Gods, well pleased with the island, settled in it certain other people, and also her own sons, who are known by the name of Corybantes, who their father was is handed down in their rites as a matter not to be divulged; and she established the mysteries which are now celebrated on the island and ordained by law that the sacred area should enjoy the right of sanctuary.

In these times, they go on to say, Mopsus the Thracian, who had been exiled by Lycurgus, the king of the Thracians, invaded the land of the Amazons with an army composed of fellow-exiles, and with Mopsus on the campaign was also Sipylus the Scythian, who had likewise been exiled from that part of Scythia which borders upon Thrace. There was a pitched battle, Sipylus and Mopsus gained the upper hand, and Myrina, the queen of the Amazons, and the larger part of the rest of her army were slain. In the course of the years, as the Thracians continued to be victorious in their battles, the surviving Amazons finally withdrew again into Libya. Such was the end, as the myth relates, of the campaign which the Amazons of Libya made.

**56.** But since we have made mention of the Atlantians, we believe that it will not be inappropriate in this place to recount what their myths relate about the genesis of the gods, in view of the fact that it does not differ greatly from the myths of the Greeks. Now the Atlantians, dwelling as they do in the regions on the edge of the ocean and inhabiting a fertile territory, are reputed far to excel their neighbours in reverence towards the gods and the humanity they showed in their dealings with strangers, and the gods, they say, were born among them. And their account, they maintain, is in agreement with that of the most renowned of the Greek poets when he represents Hera as saying:

> For I go to see the ends of the bountiful earth,
> Oceanus source of the gods and Tethys divine
> Their mother.

This is the account given in their myth: Their first king was Uranus, and he gathered the human beings, who dwelt in scattered habitations, within the shelter of a walled city and caused his subjects to cease from their lawless ways and their bestial manner of living, discovering for them the uses of cultivated fruits, how to store them up, and not a few other things which are of benefit to man; and he also subdued the larger part of the inhabited earth, in particular the regions to the west and the north. Since he was a careful observer of the stars he foretold many things which would take place throughout the world; and for the common people he introduced the year on the basis of the movement of the sun and the months on that of the moon, and instructed them in the seasons which recur year after year. Consequently the masses of the people, being ignorant of the eternal arrangement of the stars and marvelling at the events which were taking place as he had predicted, conceived that the man who taught such things partook of the nature of the gods, and after he had passed from among men they accorded to him immortal honours, both because of his benefactions and because of his knowledge of the stars; and then they transferred his name to the firmament of heaven, both because they thought that he had been so intimately acquainted with the risings and the settings of the stars and with whatever else took place in the firmament, and because they would surpass his benefactions by the magnitude of the honours which they would show him, in that for all subsequent time they proclaimed him to be the king of the universe.

**57.** To Uranus, the myth continues, were born forty-five sons from a number of wives, and, of these, eighteen, it is said, were by Titaea, each of them bearing a distinct name, but all of them as a group were called, after their mother, Titans. Titaea, because she was prudent and had brought about many good deeds for the peoples, was deified after her death by those whom she had helped and her name was changed to Ge. To Uranus were also born daughters, the two eldest of whom were by far the most renowned above the others and were called Basileia and Rhea, whom some also named Pandora. Of these daughters Basileia, who was the eldest and far excelled the others in both prudence and understanding, reared all her brothers, showing them collectively a mother's kindness; consequently she was given the appellation of "Great Mother;" and after her father had been translated from among men into the circle of the gods, with the approval of the masses and of her brothers she succeeded to the royal dignity, though she was still a maiden and because of her exceedingly great chastity had been unwilling to unite in marriage with any man. Later, because of her desire to leave sons who should succeed to the throne, she united in marriage with Hyperion, one of her brothers, for whom she had the greatest affection. When there were born to her two children, Helius and Selene, who were greatly admired for both their beauty and their chastity, the brothers of Basileia, they say, being envious of her because of her happy issue of children and fearing that Hyperion would divert the royal power to himself, committed an utterly impious deed; for entering into a conspiracy among themselves they put Hyperion to the sword, and casting Helius, who was still in years a child, into the Eridanus [Po] river, drowned him. When this crime came to light, Selene, who loved her brother very greatly, threw herself down from the roof, but as for his mother, while seeking his body along the river, her strength left her and falling into a swoon she beheld a vision in which she thought that Helius stood over her and urged her not to mourn the death of her children; for, he said, the Titans would meet the punishment which they deserve, while he and his sister would be transformed, by some divine providence, into immortal natures, since that which had formerly been called the "holy fire" in the heavens would be called by men Helius ("the sun") and that addressed as "mene" would be called Selene ("the moon"). When she was aroused from the swoon she recounted to the common crowd both the dream and the misfortunes which had befallen her, asking that they render to the dead honours like those accorded to the gods and asserting that no man should thereafter touch her body. After this she became frenzied, and seizing such of her daughter's playthings as could make a noise, she began to wander over the land, with her hair hanging free, inspired by the noise of the kettledrums and cymbals, so that those who saw her were struck with astonishment, and all men were filled

with pity at her misfortune and some were clinging to her body, when there came a mighty storm and continuous crashes of thunder and lightning; and in the midst of this Basileia passed from sight, whereupon the crowds of people, amazed at this reversal of fortune, transferred the names and the honours of Helius and Selene to the stars of the sky, and as for their mother, they considered her to be a goddess and erected altars to her, and imitating the incidents of her life by the pounding of the kettledrums and the clash of the cymbals they rendered unto her in this way sacrifices and all other honours.

**58.** However, an account is handed down also that this goddess [Magna Mater] was born in Phrygia. For the natives of that country have the following myth: In ancient times Melon became king of Phrygia and Lydia; and marrying Dindyme he begat an infant daughter, but being unwilling to rear her he exposed her on the mountain which was called Cybelus. There, in accordance with some divine providence, both the leopards and some of the other especially ferocious wild beasts offered their nipples to the child and so gave it nourishment, and some women who were tending the flocks in that place witnessed the happening,

## Book III

and being astonished at the strange event took up the babe and called her Cybele after the name of the place. The child, as she grew up, excelled in both beauty and virtue and also came to be admired for her intelligence; for she was the first to devise the pipe of many reeds and to invent cymbals and kettledrums with which to accompany the games and the dance, and in addition she taught how to heal the sicknesses of both flocks and little children by means of rites of purification; in consequence, since the babes were saved from death by her spells and were generally taken up in her arms, her devotion to them and affection for them led all the people to speak of her as the "mother of the mountain." The man who associated with her and loved her more than anyone else, they say, was Marsyas the Phrygian, who was admired for his intelligence and chastity; and a proof of his intelligence they find in the fact that he imitated the sounds made by the pipe of many reeds and carried all its notes over into the flute, and as an indication of his chastity they cite his abstinence from sexual pleasures until the day of his death.

Now Cybele, the myth records, having arrived at full womanhood, came to love a certain native youth who was known as Attis, but at a later time received the appellation Papas; with him she consorted secretly and became with child, and at about the same time her parents recognised her as their child.

**59.** Consequently she was brought up into the palace, and her father welcomed her at the outset under the impression that she was a virgin, but later, when he learned of her seduction, he put to death her nurses and Attis as well and cast their bodies forth to lie unburied; whereupon Cybele, they say, because of her love for the youth and grief over the nurses, became frenzied and rushed out of the palace into the countryside, and crying aloud and beating upon a kettledrum she visited every country alone, with hair hanging free, and Marsyas, out of pity for her plight, voluntarily followed her and accompanied her in her wanderings because of the love which he had formerly borne her. When they came to Dionysus in the city of Nysa they found there Apollo, who was being accorded high favour because of the lyre, which, they say, Hermes invented, though Apollo was the first to play it fittingly; and when Marsyas strove with Apollo in a contest of skill and the Nysaeans had been appointed judges, the first time Apollo played upon the lyre without accompanying it with his voice, while Marsyas, striking up upon his pipes, amazed the ears of his hearers by their strange music and in their opinion far excelled, by reason of his melody, the first contestant. But since they had agreed to take turn about in displaying their skill to the judges, Apollo, they say, added, this second time, his voice in harmony with the music of the lyre, whereby he gained greater approval than that which had formerly been accorded to the pipes. Marsyas, however, was enraged and tried to prove to the hearers that he was losing the contest in defiance of every principle of justice; for, he argued, it should be a comparison of skill and not of voice, and only by such a test was it possible to judge between the harmony and music of the lyre and of the pipes; and furthermore, it was unjust that two skills should be compared in combination against but one. Apollo, however, as the myth relates, replied that he was in no sense taking any unfair advantage of the other; in fact, when Marsyas blew into his pipes he was doing almost the same thing as himself; consequently the rule should be made either that they should both be accorded this equal privilege of combining their skills, or that neither of them should use his mouth in the contest but should display his special skill by the use only of his hands. When the hearers decided that Apollo presented the more just argument, their skills were again compared; Marsyas was defeated, and Apollo, who had become somewhat embittered by the quarrel, flayed the defeated man alive. Quickly repenting and being distressed at what he had done, he broke the strings of the lyre and destroyed the harmony of sounds which he had discovered. This harmony of the strings, however, was rediscovered, when the Muses added later the middle string, Linus the string struck with the forefinger, and Orpheus and Thamyras the lowest string and the one next to it. Apollo, they say, laid away both the lyre and the pipes as a votive offering in the cave of Dionysus, and becoming enamoured of Cybele joined in her wanderings as far as the land of the Hyperboreans

The myth goes on to say, a pestilence fell upon human beings throughout Phrygia and the land ceased to bear fruit, and when the unfortunate people inquired of the god how they might rid themselves of their ills he commanded them, it is said, to bury the body of Attis and to honour Cybele as a goddess. Consequently the Phrygians, since the body had disappeared in the course of time, made an image of the youth, before which they sang dirges and by means of honours in keeping with his suffering propitiated the wrath of him who had been wronged; and these rites they continue to perform down to our own lifetime. As for Cybele, in ancient times they erected altars and performed sacrifices to her yearly; and later they built for her a costly temple in Pisinus of Phrygia, and established honours and sacrifices of the greatest magnificence, Midas their king taking part in all these works out of his devotion to beauty; and beside the statue of the goddess they set up panthers and lions, since it was the common opinion that she had first been nursed by these animals.

Such, then, are the myths which are told about the Mother of the Gods both among the Phrygians and by the Atlantians who dwell on the coast of the ocean.

**60.** After the death of Hyperion, the myth relates, the kingdom was divided among the sons of Uranus, the most renowned of whom were Atlas and Cronus. Of these sons Atlas received as his part the regions on the coast of the ocean, and he not only gave the name of Atlantians to his peoples but likewise called the greatest mountain in the land Atlas. They also say that he perfected the science of astrology and was the first to publish to mankind the doctrine of the sphere; and it was for this reason that the idea was held that the entire heavens were supported upon the shoulders of Atlas, the myth darkly hinting in this way at his discovery and description of the sphere. There were born to him a number of sons, one of whom was distinguished above the others for his piety, justice to his subjects, and love of mankind, his name being Hesperus. This king, having once climbed to the peak of Mount Atlas, was suddenly snatched away by mighty winds while he was making his observations of the stars, and never was seen again; and because of the virtuous life he had lived and their pity for his sad fate the multitudes accorded to him immortal honours and called the brightest [Hesperus] of the stars of heaven after him.

Atlas, the myth goes on to relate, also had seven daughters, who as a group were called Atlantides after their father, but their individual names were Maea,

Electra, Taygete, Sterope, Merope, Halcyone, and the last Celaeno. These daughters lay with the most renowned heroes and gods and thus became the first ancestors of the larger part of the race of human beings, giving birth to those who, because of their high achievements, came to be called gods and heroes; Maea the eldest, for instance, lay with Zeus and bore Hermes, who was the discoverer of many things for the use of mankind; similarly the other Atlantides also gave birth to renowned children, who became the founders in some instances of nations and in other eases of cities. Consequently, not only among certain barbarians but among the Greeks as well, the great majority of the most ancient heroes trace their descent back to the Atlantides. These daughters were also distinguished for their chastity and after their death attained to immortal honour among men, by whom they were both enthroned in the heavens and endowed with the appellation of Pleiades. The Atlantides were also called "nymphs" because the natives of that land addressed their women by the common appellation of "nymph."

**61.** Cronus, the brother of Atlas, the myth continues, who was a man notorious for his impiety and greed, married his sister Rhea, by whom he begat that Zeus who was later called "the Olympian." There had been also another Zeus, the brother of Uranus and a king of Crete, who, however, was far less famous than the Zeus who was born at a later time. Now the latter was king over the entire world, whereas the earlier Zeus, who was lord of the above-mentioned island, begat ten sons who were given the name of Curetes; and the island he named after his wife Idaea, and on it he died and was buried, and the place which received his grave is pointed out to our day. The Cretans, however, have a myth which does not agree with the story given above, and we shall give a detailed account of it when we speak of Crete. Cronus, they say, was lord of Sicily and Libya, and Italy as well, and, in a word, established his kingdom over the regions to the west; and everywhere he occupied with garrisons the commanding hills and the strongholds of the regions, this being the reason why both throughout Sicily and the parts which incline towards the west many of the lofty places are called to this day after him "Cronia."

Zeus, however, the son of Cronus, emulated a manner of life the opposite of that led by his father, and since he showed himself honourable and friendly to all, the masses addressed him as "father." As for his succession to the kingly power, some say that his father yielded it to him of his own accord, but others state that, he was chosen as king by the masses because of the hatred they bore towards his father, and that when Cronus made war against him with the aid of the Titans, Zeus overcame him in battle, and on gaining supreme power visited all the inhabited world, conferring benefactions upon the race of men. He was pre-eminent also in bodily strength and in all the other qualities of virtue and for this reason quickly became master of the entire world. In general he showed all zeal to punish impious and wicked men and to show kindness to the masses. In return for all this, after he had passed from among men he was given the name of Zên, [to live] because he was the cause of right "living" among men, and those who had received his favours showed him honour by enthroning him in the heavens, all men eagerly acclaiming him as god and lord for ever of the whole universe.

These, then, are in summary the facts regarding the teachings of the Atlantians about the gods.

## On the myths related about Nysa, in connection with which there is also an account of the Titans and Dionysus and the Mother of the Gods (62-74).

**62.** Since we have previously made mention, in connection with our discussion of Egypt, of the birth of Dionysus and of his deeds as they are preserved in the local histories of that country, we are of the opinion that it is appropriate in this place to add the myths about this god which are current among the Greeks, but since the early composers of myths and the early poets who have written about Dionysus do not agree with one another and have committed to writing many monstrous tales, it is a difficult undertaking to give a clear account of the birth and deeds of this god. For some have handed down the story that there was but one Dionysus, others that there were three, and there are those who state that there was never any birth of him in human form whatsoever, and think that the word Dionysus means only "the gift of wine" (*oinou dosis*). For this reason we shall endeavour to run over briefly only the main facts as they are given by each writer.

Those authors, then, who use the phenomena of nature to explain this god and call the fruit of the vine "Dionysus" speak like this: The earth brought forth of itself the vine at the same time with the other plants and it was not originally planted by some man who discovered it, and they allege as proof of this the fact that to this day vines grow wild in many regions and bear fruit quite similar to that of plants which are tended by the experienced hand of man. Furthermore, the early men have given Dionysus the name of "Dimetor," [twice-born] reckoning it as a single and first birth when the plant is set in the ground and begins to grow, and as a second birth when it becomes laden with fruit and ripens its clusters, the god, therefore, being considered as having been born once from the earth and again from the vine. Though the writers of myths have handed down the account of a third birth as well, at which, as they say, the Sons of Gaia [Titans, sons of earth] tore to pieces the god, who was a son of Zeus and Demeter, and boiled him, but his members were brought together again by Demeter and he experienced a new birth as if for the first time, such accounts as this they trace back to certain causes found in nature. For he is considered to be the son of Zeus and Demeter, they hold, by reason of the fact that the vine gets its growth both from the earth and from rains and so bears as its fruit the wine which is pressed out from the clusters of grapes; and the statement that he was torn to pieces, while yet a youth, by the "earth-born" signifies the harvesting of the fruit by the labourers, and the boiling of his members has been worked into a myth by reason of the fact that most men boil the wine and then mix it, thereby improving its natural aroma and quality. Again, the account of his members, which the "earth-born" treated with despite, being brought together again and restored to their former natural state, shows forth that the vine, which has been stripped of its fruit and pruned at the yearly seasons, is restored by the earth to the high level of fruitfulness which it had before. For, in general, the ancient poets and writers of myths spoke of Demeter as Gê Metēr (Earth Mother). With these stories the teachings agree which are set forth in the Orphic poems and are introduced into their rites, but it is not lawful to recount them in detail to the uninitiated. In the same manner the account that Dionysus was born of Semele they trace back to natural beginnings, offering the explanation that Thuonê was the name which the ancients gave to the earth, and that this goddess received the appellation Semele because the worship and honour paid to her was dignified (semnê), and she was called Thuonê because of the sacrifices (thusiai) and burnt offerings (thuelai) which were offered (thuomenai) to her. Furthermore, the tradition that Dionysus was born twice of Zeus arises from the belief that these fruits also perished in common with all other plants in the flood at the time of Deucalion, and that when they sprang up again after the Deluge it was as if there had been a second epiphany of the god among men, and so the myth was created that the god had been born again from the thigh of Zeus. However this may be, those who explain the name Dionysus as signifying the use and importance of the discovery of wine recount such a myth regarding him.

**63.** Those mythographers, [mythographi] however, who represent the god as having a human form ascribe to him, with one accord, the discovery and cultivation of the vine and all the operations of the making of wine, although they disagree on whether there was a single Dionysus or several. Some, for instance, who assert that he who taught how to make wine and to gather "the fruits of the trees," as they are called, he who led an army over all the inhabited world, and he who introduced the mysteries and rites and Bacchic revelries were one and the same person; but there are others, as I have said, who conceive that there were three persons, at separate periods, and to each of these they ascribe deeds which were peculiarly his own.

This, then, is their account: The most ancient Dionysus was an Indian, and since his country, because of the excellent climate, produced the vine in abundance without cultivation, he was the first to press out the clusters of grapes and to devise the use of wine as a natural product, likewise to give the proper care to the figs and other fruits which grow upon trees, and, speaking generally, to devise whatever pertains to the harvesting and storing of these fruits. The same Dionysus is, furthermore, said to have worn a long beard, the reason for the report being that it is the custom among the Indians to give great care, until their death, to the raising of a beard. Now this Dionysus visited with an army all the inhabited world and gave instruction both as to the culture of the vine and the crushing of the clusters in the wine-vats (*lenoi*), which is the reason why the god was named Lenaeus. Likewise, he allowed all people to share in his other discoveries, and when he passed from among men he received immortal honour at the hands of those who had received his benefactions. Furthermore, there are pointed out among the Indians even to this day the place where it came to pass that the god was born, as well as cities which bear his name in the language of the natives; and many other notable testimonials to his birth among the Indians still survive, but it would be a long task to write of them.

**64.** The second Dionysus, the writers of myths relate, was born to Zeus by Persephone, though some say it was Demeter. He is represented by them as the first man to have yoked oxen to the plough, human beings before that time having prepared the ground by hand. Many other things also, which are useful for agriculture, were skilfully devised by him, whereby the masses were relieved of their great distress; and in return for this those whom he had benefited accorded to him honours and sacrifices like those offered to the gods, since all men were eager, because of the magnitude of his service to them, to accord to him immortality. And as a special symbol and token the painters and sculptors represented him with horns, at the same time making manifest thereby the other nature of Dionysus and also showing forth the magnitude of the service which he had devised for the farmers by his invention of the plough.

The third Dionysus, they say, was born in Boeotian Thebes of Zeus and Semele, the daughter of Cadmus. The myth runs as follows: Zeus had become enamoured of Semele and often, lured by her beauty, had consorted with her, but Hera, being jealous and anxious to punish the girl, assumed the form of one of the women who was an intimate of Semele's and led her on to her ruin; for she suggested to her that it was fitting that Zeus should lie with her while having the same majesty and honour in his outward appearance as when he took Hera to his arms. Consequently Zeus, at the request of Semelê that she be shown the same honours as Hera, appeared to her accompanied by thunder and lightning, but Semele, unable to endure the majesty of his grandeur, died and brought forth the babe before the appointed time. This babe Zeus quickly took and hid in his thigh, and afterwards, when the period which nature prescribed for the child's birth had completed its growth, he brought it to Nysa in Arabia. There the boy was reared by nymphs and was given the name Dionysus after his father (Dios) and after the place (Nysa); and since he grew to be of unusual beauty he at first spent his time at dances and with bands of women and in every kind of luxury and amusement, and after that, forming the women into an army and arming them with thyrsi, he made a campaign over all the inhabited world. He also instructed all men who were pious and cultivated a life of justice in the knowledge of his rites and initiated them into his mysteries, and, furthermore, in every place he held great festive assemblages and celebrated musical contests; [Dionysia] and, in a word, he composed the quarrels between the nations and cities and created concord and deep peace where there had existed civil strifes and wars.

**65.** Now since the presence of the god, the myth goes on to say, became noised abroad in every region, and the report spread that he was treating all men honourably and contributing greatly to the refinement of man's social life, the whole populace everywhere thronged to meet him and welcomed him with great joy. There were a few, however, who, out of disdain and impiety, looked down upon him and kept saying that he was leading the Bacchantes about with him because of his incontinence and was introducing the rites and the mysteries that he might thereby seduce the wives of other men, but such persons were punished by him right speedily. For in some cases he made use of the superior power which attended his divine nature and punished the impious, either striking them with madness or causing them while still living to be torn limb from limb by the hands of the women; in other cases he destroyed such as opposed him by a military device which took them by surprise. For he distributed to the women, instead of the thyrsi, lances whose tips of iron were covered with ivy leaves; consequently, when the kings in their ignorance disdained them because they were women and for this reason were unprepared, he attacked them when they did not expect it and slew them with the spears. Among those who were punished by him, the most renowned, they say, were Pentheus among the Greeks, Myrrhanus the king of the Indians, and Lycurgus among the Thracians. For the myth relates that when Dionysus was on the point of leading his force over from Asia into Europe, he concluded a treaty of friendship with Lycurgus, who was king of that part of Thrace which lies upon the Hellespont. Now when he had led the first of the Bacchantes over into a friendly land, as he thought, Lycurgus issued orders to his soldiers to fall upon them by night and to slay both Dionysus and all the Maenads, and Dionysus, learning of the plot from a man of the country who was called Charops, was struck with dismay, because his army was on the other side of the Hellespont and only a mere handful of his friends had crossed over with him. Consequently he sailed across secretly to his army, and then Lycurgus, they say, falling upon the Maenads in the city known as Nysium, slew them all, but Dionysus, bringing his forces over, conquered the Thracians in a battle, and taking Lycurgus alive put out his eyes and inflicted upon him every kind of outrage, and then crucified him. Thereupon, out of gratitude to Charops for the aid the man had rendered him, Dionysus made over to him the kingdom of the Thracians and instructed him in the secret rites connected with the initiations; and Oeagrus, the son of Charops, then took over both the kingdom and the initiatory rites which were handed down in the mysteries, the rites which afterwards Orpheus, the son of Oeagrus, who was the superior of all men in natural gifts and education, learned from his father; Orpheus also made many changes in the practices and for that reason the rites which had been established by Dionysus were also called "Orphic."

But some of the poets, one of whom is Antimachus, state that Lycurgus was king, not of Thrace, but of Arabia, and that the attack upon Dionysus and the Bacchantes was made at the Nysa which is in Arabia. However this may be, Dionysus, they say, punished the impious but treated all other men honourably, and then made his return journey from India to Thebes upon an elephant. The entire time consumed in the journey was three years, and it is for this reason, they say, that the Greeks hold his festival every other year. The myth also relates that he gathered a great mass of booty, such as would result from such a campaign, and that he was the first of all men to make his return to his native country in a triumph.

**66.** Now these accounts of the birth of Dionysus are generally agreed upon by the ancient writers; but rival claims are raised by not a few Greek cities to having been the place of his birth. The peoples of Elis and Naxos, for instance, and the inhabitants of Eleutherae and Teos and several other peoples, state that he was born in their cities. The Teans advance as proof that the god was born among them the fact that, even to this day, at fixed times in their city a fountain of wine, of unusually sweet fragrance, flows of its own accord from the earth; and as for the peoples of the other cities, they in some cases point out a plot of land which is sacred to Dionysus, in other cases shrines and sacred precincts which have been consecrated to him from ancient times. Speaking generally, since the god has left behind him in many places over the inhabited world evidences of his personal favour and presence, it is not surprising that in each case the people should think that Dionysus had had a peculiar relationship to both their city and country. And testimony to our opinion is also offered by the poet in his Hymns, when he speaks of those who lay claim to the birthplace of Dionysus and, in that connection, represents him as being born in the Nysa which is in Arabia:

> Some Dracanum, wind-swept Icarus some,
> Some Naxos, Zeus-born one, or Alpheius' stream
> Deep-eddied, call the spot where Semelê
> Bore thee, Eiraphiotes, unto Zeus
> Who takes delight in thunder; others still
> Would place thy birth, O Lord, in Thebes. Tis false;
> The sire of men and gods brought thee to light,
> Unknown to white-armed Hera, far from men.
> There is a certain Nysa, mountain high,
> With forests thick, in Phoenice afar,
> Close to Aegyptus' streams.

I am not unaware that also those inhabitants of Libya who dwell on the shore of the ocean lay claim to the birthplace of the god, and point out that Nysa and all the stories which the myths record are found among themselves, and many witnesses to this statement, they say, remain in the land down to our own lifetime; and I also know that many of the ancient Greek writers of myths and poets, and not a few of the later historians as well, agree with this in their accounts. Consequently, in order not to omit anything which history records about Dionysus, we shall present in summary what is told by the Libyans and those Greek historians whose writings are in accord with these and with that Dionysius who composed an account out of the ancient fabulous tales. For this writer has composed an account of Dionysus and the Amazons, as well as of the Argonauts and the events connected with the Trojan War and many other matters, in which he cites the versions of the ancient writers, both the composers of myths and the poets.

**67.** This, then, is the account of Dionysius: Among the Greeks Linus was the first to discover the different rhythms and song, and when Cadmus brought from Phoenicia the letters, as they are called, Linus was again the first to transfer them into the Greek language, to give a name to each character, and to fix its shape. Now the letters, as a group, are called "Phoenician" because they were brought to the Greeks from the Phoenicians, but as single letters the Pelasgians were the first to make use of the transferred characters and so they were called "Pelasgic." Linus also, who was admired because of his poetry and singing, had many pupils and three of greatest renown, Heracles, Thamyras, and Orpheus. Of these three Heracles, who was learning to play the lyre, was unable to appreciate what was taught him because of his sluggishness of soul, and once when he had been punished with rods by Linus he became violently angry and killed his teacher with a blow of the lyre. Thamyras, however, who possessed unusual natural ability, perfected the art of music and claimed that in the excellence of song his voice was more beautiful than the voices of the Muses. Whereupon the goddesses, angered at him, took from him his gift of music and maimed the man, even as Homer also bears witness when he writes:

> There met the Muses Thamyris of Thrace
> And made an end of his song;

and again:

> But him, enraged, they maimed, and from him took

# BOOK III

        The gift of song divine and made him quite
        Forget his harping.

About Orpheus, the third pupil, we shall give a detailed account when we come to treat of his deeds.

Now Linus, they say, composed an account in the Pelasgic letters of the deeds of the first Dionysus and of the other mythical legends and left them among his memoirs. In the same manner use was made of these Pelasgic letters by Orpheus and Pronapides who was the teacher of Homer and a gifted writer of songs; and also by Thymoetes, the son of Thymoetes, the son of Laomedon, who lived at the same time as Orpheus, wandered over many regions of the inhabited world, and penetrated to the western part of Libya as far as the ocean. He also visited Nysa, where the ancient natives of the city relate the myth that Dionysus was reared there, and, after he had learned from the Nysaeans of the deeds of this god one and all, he composed the "Phrygian poem," as it is called, wherein he made use of the archaic manner both of speech and of letters.

**68.** Dionysius, then, continues his account as follows: Ammon, the king of that part of Libya, married a daughter of Uranus who was called Rhea and was a sister of Cronus and the other Titans. Once when Ammon was going about his kingdom, near the Ceraunian Mountains, as they are called, he came upon a maiden of unusual beauty whose name was Amaltheia, and becoming enamoured of her he lay with the maiden and begat a son of marvellous beauty as well as bodily vigour, and Amaltheia herself he appointed mistress of all the region round about, which was shaped like the horn of a bull and for this reason was known as Hesperoukeras [horn of Hesperus]; and the region, because of the excellent quality of the land, abounds in every variety of the vine and all other trees which bear cultivated fruits. When the woman whom we have just mentioned took over the supreme power the country was named after her Amaltheias Keras [horn of Amaltheia]; consequently the men of later times, for the reason which we have just given, likewise call any especially fertile bit of ground which abounds in fruits of every kind "Amaltheia's Horn."

Now Ammon, fearing the jealousy of Rhea, concealed the affair and brought the boy secretly to a certain city called Nysa, which was at a great distance from those parts. This city lies on a certain island which is surrounded by the river Triton and is precipitous on all sides save at one place where there is a narrow pass which bears the name "Nysaean Gates." The land of the island is rich, is traversed at intervals by pleasant meadows and watered by abundant streams from springs, and possesses every kind of fruit-bearing tree and the wild vine in abundance, which for the most part grows up trees. The whole region, moreover, has a fresh and pure air and is furthermore exceedingly healthful; and for this reason its inhabitants are the longest lived of any in those parts. The entrance into the island is like a glen at its beginning, being thickly shaded by lofty trees growing close together, so that the sun never shines at all through the close-set branches but only the radiance of its light may be seen.

**69.** Everywhere along the lanes, the account continues, springs of water gush forth of exceeding sweetness, making the place most pleasant to those who desire to tarry there. Further in there is a cave, circular in shape and of marvellous size and beauty. For above and all about it rises a crag of immense height, formed of rocks of different colours; for the rocks lie in bands and send forth a bright gleam, some like that purple which comes from the sea, some bluish and others like every other kind of brilliant hue, the result being that there is not a colour to be seen among men which is not visible in that place. Before the entrance grow marvellous trees, some fruit-bearing, others evergreen, and all of them fashioned by nature for no other end than to delight the eye; and in them nest every kind of bird of pleasing colour and most charming song. Consequently the whole place is meet for a god, not merely in its aspect but in its sound as well, since the sweet tones which nature teaches are always superior to the song which is devised by art. When one has passed the entrance the cave is seen to widen out and to be lighted all about by the rays of the sun, and all kinds of flowering plants grow there, especially the cassia and every other kind which has the power to preserve its fragrance throughout the year; and in it are also to be seen several couches of nymphs, formed of every manner of flower, made not by hand but by the light touch of Nature herself, in manner meet for a god. Moreover, throughout the whole place round about not a flower or leaf is to be seen which has fallen. Consequently those who gaze upon this spot find not only its aspect delightful but also its fragrance most pleasant.

**70.** Now to this cave, the account runs, Ammon came and brought the child and gave him into the care of Nysa, one of the daughters of Aristaeus; and he appointed Aristaeus to be the guardian of the child, he being a man who excelled in understanding, and in self-control, and in all learning. The duty of protecting the boy against the plots of his stepmother Rhea he assigned to Athena, who a short while before had been born of the earth and had been found beside the river Triton, from which she had been called Tritonis. According to the myth this goddess, choosing to spend all her days in maidenhood, excelled in virtue and invented most of the crafts, since she was exceedingly ready of wit; she cultivated also the arts of war, and since she excelled in courage and in bodily strength she performed many other deeds worthy of memory and slew the Aegis, as it was called, a certain frightful monster which was a difficult antagonist to overcome. For it was sprung from the earth and in accordance with its nature breathed forth terrible flames of fire from its mouth, and its first appearance it made about Phrygia and burned up the land, which to this day is called "Burned Phrygia"; and after that it ravaged unceasingly the lands about the Taurus mountains and burned up the forests extending from that region as far as India. Thereupon, returning again towards the sea round about Phoenicia, it sent up in flames the forests on Mt. Lebanon, and making its way through Egypt it passed over Libya to the regions of the west and at the end of its wanderings fell upon the forests about Ceraunia. And since the country round about was going up in flames and the inhabitants in some cases were being destroyed and in others were leaving their native countries in their terror and removing to distant regions, Athena, they say, overcoming the monster partly through her intelligence and partly through her courage and bodily strength, slew it, and covering her breast with its hide bore this about with her, both as a covering and protection for her body against later dangers, and as a memorial of her valour and of her well-merited fame. Ge (Earth), however, the mother of the monster, was enraged and sent up the Giants, as they are called, to fight against the gods; but they were destroyed at a later time by Zeus, Athena and Dionysus and the rest of the gods taking part in the conflict on the side of Zeus.

Dionysus, however, being reared according to the account in Nysa and instructed in the best pursuits, became not only conspicuous for his beauty and bodily strength, but skilful also in the arts and quick to make every useful invention. For while still a boy he discovered both the nature and use of wine, in that he pressed out the clusters of grapes of the vine while it still grew wild, and such ripe fruits as could be dried and stored away to advantage, and how each one of them should be planted and cared for was likewise a discovery of his; also it was his desire to share the discoveries which he had made with the race of men, in the hope that by reason of the magnitude of his benefactions he would be accorded immortal honours.

**71.** When the valour and fame of Dionysus became spread abroad, Rhea, it is said, angered at Ammon, strongly desired to get Dionysus into her power; but being unable to carry out her design she forsook Ammon and, departing to her brothers, the Titans, married Cronus her brother. Cronus, then, upon the solicitation of Rhea, made war with the aid of the Titans upon Ammon, and in the pitched battle which followed Cronus gained the upper hand, whereas Ammon, who was hard pressed by lack of supplies, fled to Crete, and marrying there Crete, the daughter of one of the Curetes who were the kings at that time, gained the sovereignty over those regions, and to the island, which before that time had been called Idaea, he gave the name Crete after his wife. As for Cronus, the myth relates, after his victory he ruled harshly over these regions which had formerly been Ammon's, and set out with a great force against Nysa and Dionysus. Now Dionysus, on learning both of the reverses suffered by his father and of the uprising of the Titans against himself, gathered soldiers from Nysa, two hundred of whom were foster-brothers of his and were distinguished for their courage and their loyalty to him; and to these he added from neighbouring peoples both the Libyans and the Amazons, regarding the latter of whom we have already observed that it is reputed that they were distinguished for their courage and first of all campaigned beyond the borders of their country and subdued with arms a large part of the inhabited world. These women, they say, were urged on to the alliance especially by Athena, because their zeal for their ideal of life was like her own, seeing that the Amazons clung tenaciously to manly courage and virginity. The force was divided into two parts, the men having Dionysus as their general and the women being under the command of Athena, and coming with their army upon the Titans they joined battle. The struggle having proved sharp and many having fallen on both sides, Cronus finally was wounded and victory lay with Dionysus, who had distinguished himself in the battle. Thereupon the Titans fled to the regions which had once been possessed by Ammon, and Dionysus gathered up a multitude of captives and returned to Nysa. Here, drawing up his force in arms about the prisoners, he brought a formal accusation against the Titans and gave them every reason to suspect that he was going to execute the captives, but when he got them free from the charges and allowed them to make their choice either to join him in his campaign or to go scot free, they all chose to join him, and because their lives had been spared contrary to their expectation they venerated him like a god.

Dionysus, then, taking the captives singly and giving them a libation (*sponde*) of wine, required of all of them an oath that they would join in the campaign without treachery and fight manfully until death; consequently, these captives being the first to be designated as "freed under a truce" (*hypospondoi*), men of later times, imitating the ceremony which had been performed at that time, speak of the truces in wars as *spondai*.

72. Now when Dionysus was on the point of setting out against Cronus and his force was already passing out of Nysa, his guardian Aristaeus, the myth relates, offered a sacrifice and so was the first man to sacrifice to him as to a god. Companions of his on the campaign, they say, were also the most nobly born of the Nysaeans, those, namely, who bear the name Seileni. For the first man of all, they say, to be king of Nysa was Seilenus, but his ancestry was unknown to all men because of its antiquity. This man had a tail at the lower part of his back and his descendants also regularly carried this distinguishing mark because of their participation in his nature.

Dionysus, then, set out with his army, and after passing through a great extent of waterless land, no small portion of which was desert and infested with wild beasts, he encamped beside a city of Libya named Zabirna. Near this city an earth-born monster called Campe, which was destroying many of the natives, was slain by him, whereby he won great fame among the natives for valour. Over the monster which he had killed he also erected an enormous mound, wishing to leave behind him an immortal memorial of his personal bravery, and this mound remained until comparatively recent times. Then Dionysus advanced against the Titans, maintaining strict discipline on his journeyings, treating all the inhabitants kindly, and, in a word, making it clear that his campaign was for the purpose of punishing the impious and of conferring benefits upon the entire human race. The Libyans, admiring his strict discipline and high-mindedness, provided his followers with supplies in abundance and joined in the campaign with the greatest eagerness.

As the army approached the city of the Ammonians, Cronus, who had been defeated in a pitched battle before the walls, set fire to the city in the night, intending to destroy utterly the ancestral palace of Dionysus, and himself taking with him his wife Rhea and some of his friends who had aided him in the struggle, he stole unobserved out of the city. Dionysus, however, showed no such a temper as this; for though he took both Cronus and Rhea captive, not only did he waive the charges against them because of his kinship to them, but he entreated them for the future to maintain both the good-will and the position of parents towards him and to live in a common home with him, held in honour above all others. Rhea, accordingly, loved him like a son for all the rest of her life, but the good-will of Cronus was a pretence, and about this time there was born to both of these a son who was called Zeus, and he was honoured greatly by Dionysus and at a later time, because of his high achievements, was made king over all.

73. Since the Libyans had said to Dionysus before the battle that, at the time when Ammon had been driven from the kingdom, he had prophesied to the inhabitants that at an appointed time his son Dionysus would come, and that he would recover his father's kingdom and, after becoming master of all the

inhabited world, would be looked upon as a god, Dionysus, believing him to have been a true prophet, established there the oracle of his father, rebuilt the city and ordained honours to him as to a god, and appointed men to have charge of the oracle. Tradition also has recorded that the head of Ammon was shaped like that of a ram, since as his device he had worn a helmet of that form in his campaigns. There are some writers of myths who recount that in very truth there were little horns on both sides of his temples and that therefore Dionysus also, being Ammon's son, had the same aspect as his father and so the tradition has been handed down to succeeding generations of mankind that this god had horns. However this may be, after Dionysus had built the city and established the oracle he first of all, they say, inquired of the god with regard to his expedition, and he received from his father the reply that, if he showed himself a benefactor of mankind, he would receive the reward of immortality. Consequently, elated in spirit at this prophecy, he first of all directed his campaign against Egypt and as king of the country he set up Zeus, the son of Cronus and Rhea, though he was still but a boy in years, and at his side as his guardian he placed Olympus, by whom Zeus had been instructed and after whom he came to be called "Olympian," when he had attained pre-eminence in high achievements. As for Dionysus, he taught the Egyptians, it is said, both the cultivation of the vine and how to use and to store both wine and the fruits which are gathered from trees, as well as all others. Since a good report of him was spread abroad everywhere, no man opposed him as if he were an enemy, but all rendered him eager obedience and honoured him like a god with panegyrics and sacrifices. In like manner as in Egypt, they say, he visited the inhabited world, bringing the land under cultivation by means of the plantings which he made and conferring benefactions upon the people for all time by bestowing upon them great and valuable gifts. For this reason it comes about that, although not all men are of one belief with one another concerning the honours which they accord to the other gods, in the case of Dionysus alone we may almost say that they are in complete agreement in testifying to his immortality; for there is no man among Greeks or barbarians who does not share in the gift and favour which this god dispenses, nay, even those who possess a country which has become a wilderness or altogether unsuited to the cultivation of the vine learned from him how to prepare from barley a drink which is little inferior to wine in aroma.

Now Dionysus, they say, as he was marching out of India to the sea, learned that all the Titans had assembled their united forces together and had crossed over to Crete to attack Ammon. Already Zeus had passed over from Egypt to the aid of Ammon and a great war had arisen on the island, and forthwith Dionysus and Athena and certain others who had been considered to be gods rushed over in a body to Crete. In a great battle which followed Dionysus was victorious and slew all the Titans. When after this Ammon and Dionysus exchanged their mortal nature for immortality, Zeus, they say, became king of the entire world, since the Titans had been punished and there was no one whose impiety would make him bold enough to dispute with him for the supreme power.

**74.** As for the first Dionysus, the son of Ammon and Amaltheia, these, then, are the deeds he accomplished as the Libyans recount the history of them; the second Dionysus, as men say, who was born to Zeus by Io, the daughter of

Inachus, became king of Egypt and appointed the initiatory rites of that land; and the third and last was sprung from Zeus and Semele and became, among the Greeks, the rival of the first two. Imitating the principles of both the others he led an army over all the inhabited world and left behind him not a few pillars to mark the bounds of his campaign; the land he also brought under cultivation by means of the plantings which he made, and he selected women to be his soldiers, as the ancient Dionysus had done in the case of the Amazons. He went beyond the others in developing the orgiastic practices, and as regards the rites of initiation, he improved some of them, and others he introduced for the first time. Since in the long passage of time the former discoverers had become unknown to the majority of men, this last Dionysus fell heir to both the plan of life and the fame of his predecessors of the same name, and this Dionysus is not the only one to whom has happened that which we have related, but in later times Heracles likewise experienced the same fortune. For there had been two persons of an earlier period who had borne the same name, the most ancient Heracles who, according to the myths, had been born in Egypt, had subdued with arms a large part of the inhabited world, and had set up the pillar which is in Libya, and the second, who was one of the Idaean Dactyls of Crete and a wizard with some knowledge of generalship, was the founder of the Olympic Games; but the third and last, who was born of Alcmenê and Zeus a short time before the Trojan War, visited a large part of the inhabited world while he was serving Eurystheus and carrying out his commands. And after he had successfully completed all the Labours he also set up the pillar which is in Europe, but because he bore the same name as the other two and pursued the same plan of life as did they, in the course of time and upon his death he inherited the exploits of the more ancient persons of the name, as if there had been in all the previous ages but one Heracles.

To support the view that there were several of the name Dionysus the effort is made to cite, along with the other proofs, the battle waged against the Titans. For since all men agree that Dionysus fought on the side of Zeus in his war against the Titans, it will not do at all, they argue, to date the generation of the Titans in the time when Semele lived or to declare that Cadmus, the son of Agenor, was older than the gods of Olympus.

Such, their, is the myth which the Libyans recount concerning Dionysus; but for our part, now that we have brought to an end the plan which we announced at the beginning, we shall close the Third Book at this point.

# BOOK IV

*Introduction on the myths recounted by the historians (1).*

1. I am not unaware of the fact that those who compile the narratives of ancient mythology labour under many disadvantages in their composition. For, in the first place, the antiquity of the events they have to record, since it makes record difficult, is a cause of much perplexity to those who would compose an account of them; and again, inasmuch as any pronouncement they may make of the dates of events does not admit of the strictest kind of proof or disproof, a feeling of contempt for the narration is aroused in the mind of those who read it; furthermore, the variety and the multitude of the heroes, demigods, and men in general whose genealogies must be set down make their recital a difficult thing to achieve; but the greatest and most disconcerting obstacle of all consists in the fact that those who have recorded the deeds and myths of the earliest times are in disagreement among themselves. For these reasons the writers of greatest reputation among the later historians have stood aloof from the narration of the ancient mythology because of its difficulty, and have undertaken to record only the more recent events. Ephorus of Cymê, for instance, a pupil of Isocrates, when he undertook to. write his universal history, passed over the tales of the old mythology and commenced his history with a narration of the events which took place after the Return of the Heracleidae. Likewise Callisthenes and Theopompus, who were contemporaries of Ephorus, held aloof from the old myths. We, however, holding the opposite opinion to theirs, have shouldered the labour which such a record involves and have expended all the care within our power upon the ancient legends. For very great and most numerous deeds have been performed by the heroes and demigods and by many good men likewise, who, because of the benefits they conferred which have been shared by all men, have been honoured by succeeding generations with sacrifices which in some cases are like those offered to the gods, in other cases like such as are paid to heroes, and of one and all the appropriate praises have been sung by the voice of history for all time.

Now in the three preceding Books we have recorded the deeds of mythological times which are found among other nations and what their histories relate about the gods, also the topography of the land in every case and the wild beasts and other animals which are found among them, and, speaking generally, we have described everything which was worthy of mention and was marvellous to relate; and in the present Book we shall set forth what the Greeks in their histories of the ancient periods tell about their most renowned heroes and demigods and, in general, about all who have performed any notable exploit in war, and likewise about such also as in time of peace have made some useful discovery or enacted some good law contributing to man's social life. We shall begin with Dionysus because he not only belongs to a very ancient time but also conferred very great benefactions upon the race of men.

We have stated in the previous Books that certain barbarian peoples claim for themselves the birthplace of this god. The Egyptians, for example, say that the god who among them bears the name Osiris is the one whom the Greeks call

Dionysus. And this god, as their myths relate, visited all the inhabited world, was the discoverer of wine, taught mankind how to cultivate the vine, and because of this benefaction of his received the gift of immortality with the approval of all. The Indians likewise declare that this god was born among them, and that after he had ingeniously discovered how to cultivate the vine he shared the benefit which wine imparts with human beings throughout the inhabited world, but for our part, since we have spoken of these matters in detail, we shall at this point recount what the Greeks have to say about this god.

### On Dionysus, Priapus, Hermaphroditus, and the Muses (2-7).

**2.** The Greek account of Dionysus runs like this: Cadmus, the son of Agenor, was sent forth from Phoenicia by the king to seek out Europe, under orders either to bring him the maiden or never to come back to Phoenicia. After Cadmus had traversed a wide territory without being able to find her, he despaired of ever returning to his home; and when he had arrived in Boeotia, in obedience to the oracle which he had received he founded the city of Thebes. Here he made his home and marrying Harmonia, the daughter of Aphrodite, he begat by her Semelê, Ino, Autonoe, Agave, and Polydorus. Semelê was loved by Zeus because of her beauty, but since he had his intercourse with her secretly and without speech she thought that the god despised her; consequently she made the request of him that he come to her embraces in the same manner as in his approaches to Hera. Accordingly, Zeus visited her in a way befitting a god, accompanied by thundering and lightning, revealing himself to her as he embraced her; but Semelê, who was pregnant and unable to endure the majesty of the divine presence, brought forth the babe untimely and was herself slain by the fire. Thereupon Zeus, taking up the child, handed it over to the care of Hermes, and ordered him to take it to the cave in Nysa, which lay between Phoenicia and the Nile, where he should deliver it to the nymphs that they should rear it and with great solicitude bestow upon it the best of care. Consequently, since Dionysus was reared in Nysa, he received the name he bears from Zeus and Nysa. Homer bears witness to this in his Hymns, when he says:

> There is a certain Nysa, mountain high,
> With forests thick, in Phoenicê afar,
> Close to Aegyptus' streams

After he had received his rearing by the nymphs in Nysa, they say, he made the discovery of wine and taught mankind how to cultivate the vine. And as he visited the inhabited world almost in its entirety, he brought much land under cultivation and in return for this received most high honours at the hands of all men. He also discovered the drink made out of barley and called by some *zythos,* the bouquet of which is not much inferior to that of wine. The preparation of this drink he taught to those peoples whose country was unsuited to the cultivation of the vine. He also led about with himself an army composed not only of men but of women as well, and punished such men as were unjust and impious. In Boeotia, out of gratitude to the land of his birth, he freed all the cities and founded a city whose name signified independence, which he called Eleutherae. [City of Freedom].

**3.** Then he made a campaign into India, whence he returned to Boeotia in the third year, bringing with him a notable quantity of booty, and he was the first man ever to celebrate a triumph seated on an Indian elephant. The Boeotians and other Greeks and the Thracians, in memory of the campaign in India, have established sacrifices every other year to Dionysus, and believe that at that time the god reveals himself to human beings. Consequently in many Greek cities every other year Bacchic bands of women gather, and it is lawful for the maidens to carry the thyrsus and to join in the frenzied revelry, crying out "Euai!" and honouring the god; while the matrons, forming in groups, offer sacrifices to the god and celebrate his mysteries and, in general, extol with hymns the presence of Dionysus, in this manner acting the part of the Maenads who, as history records, were of old the companions of the god. He also punished here and there throughout all the inhabited world many men who were thought to be impious, the most renowned among the number being Pentheus and Lycurgus. Since the discovery of wine and the gift of it to human beings were the source of such great satisfaction to them, both because of the pleasure which derives from the drinking of it and because of the greater vigour which comes to the bodies of those who partake of it, it is the custom, they say, when unmixed wine is served during a meal to greet it with the words, "To the Good Deity!" but when the cup is passed around after the meal diluted with water, to cry out, "To Zeus Saviour!" For the drinking of unmixed wine results in a state of madness, but when it is mixed with the rain from Zeus the delight and pleasure continue, but the ill effect of madness and stupor is avoided. In general, the myths relate that the gods who receive the greatest approval at the hands of human beings are those who excelled in their benefactions by reason of their discovery of good things, namely, Dionysus and Demeter, the former because he was the discoverer of the most pleasing drink, the latter because she gave to the race of men the most excellent of the dry foods [wheat].

**4.** Some writers of myths, however, relate that there was a second Dionysus who was much earlier in time than the one we have just mentioned. For according to them there was born of Zeus and Persephone a Dionysus who is called by some Sabazius and whose birth and sacrifices and honours are celebrated at night and in secret, because of the disgrace resulting from the intercourse of the sexes. They state also that he excelled in sagacity and was the first to attempt the yoking of oxen and by their aid to effect the sowing of the seed, this being the reason why they also represent him as wearing a horn.

But the Dionysus who was born of Semelê in more recent times, they say, was a man who was effeminate in body and altogether delicate; in beauty, however, he far excelled all other men and was addicted to indulgence in the delights of love, and on his campaigns he led about with himself a multitude of women who were armed with lances which were shaped like thyrsi. They say also that when he went abroad he was accompanied by the Muses, who were maidens that had received an unusually excellent education, and that by their songs and dancing and other talents in which they had been instructed these maidens delighted the heart of the god. They also add that he was accompanied on his campaigns by a personal attendant and caretaker, Seilenus, who was his adviser and instructor in the most excellent pursuits and contributed greatly to the high achievements and fame of Dionysus. And in the battles which took place during his wars he arrayed himself in arms suitable for war and in the skins of panthers, but in assemblages and at festive gatherings in time of peace he wore garments which were bright-coloured and luxurious in their effeminacy. Furthermore, in order to ward off the headaches which every man gets from drinking too much wine he bound about his head, they report, a band (*mitra*), which was the reason for his receiving the name Mitrephorus [wearer of *mitra*]; and it was this head-band, they say, that in later times led to the introduction of the diadem for kings. He was also called Dimetor [of two mothers], they relate, because the two Dionysi were born of one father, but of two mothers. The younger one also inherited the deeds of the older, and so the men of later times, being unaware of the truth and being deceived because of the identity of their names, thought there had been but one Dionysus.

The *narthex* is also associated with Dionysus for the following reason. When wine was first discovered, the mixing of water with it had not as yet been devised and the wine was drunk unmixed; but when friends gathered together and enjoyed good cheer, the revellers, filling themselves to abundance with the unmixed wine, became like madmen and used their wooden staves to strike one another. Consequently, since some of them were wounded and some died of wounds inflicted in vital spots, Dionysus was offended at such happenings, and though he did not decide that they should refrain from drinking the unmixed wine in abundance, because the drink gave such pleasure, he ordered them hereafter to carry a *narthex* and not a wooden staff.

**5.** Many epithets, so we are informed, have been given him by men, who have found the occasions from which they arose in the practices and customs which have become associated with him. So, for instance, he has been called Baccheius from the Bacchic bands of women who accompanied him, Lenaeus from the custom of treading the clusters of grapes in a wine-tub (*lenos*), and Bromius from the thunder (*bromos*) which attended his birth; likewise for a similar reason he has been called Pyrigenes ("Born-of-Fire"). Thriambus is a name that has been given him, they say, because he was the first of those of whom we have a record to have celebrated a triumph (*thriambos*) upon entering his native land after his campaign, this having been done when he returned from India with great booty. It is on a similar basis that the other appellations or epithets have been given to him, but we feel that it would be a long task to tell of them and inappropriate to the history which we are writing.

He was thought to have two forms, men say, because there were two Dionysi, the ancient one having a long beard, because all men in early times wore long beards, the younger one being youthful and effeminate and young, as we have mentioned before. Certain writers say, however, that it was because men who become drunk get into two states, being either joyous or sullen, that the god has been called "two-formed." Satyrs also, it is reported, were carried about by him in his company and afforded the god great delight and pleasure in connection with their dancings and their goat-songs [tragedies]. In general, the Muses who bestowed benefits and delights through the advantages which their education gave them, and the Satyrs by the use of the devices which contribute to mirth, made the life of Dionysus happy and agreeable. There is general agreement also, they say, that he was the inventor of thymelic contests, and that he introduced places where the spectators could witness the shows and organised musical

## Book IV

concerts; furthermore, he freed from any forced contribution to the state those who had cultivated any sort of musical skill during his campaigns, and it is for these reasons that later generations have formed musical associations of the artists of Dionysus and have relieved of taxes the followers of this profession.

As for Dionysus and the myths which are related about him we shall rest content with what has been said, since we are aiming at due proportion in our account.

**6.** We shall at this point discuss Priapus and the myths related about him, realising that an account of him is appropriate in connection with the history of Dionysus. Now the ancients record in their myths that Priapus was the son of Dionysus and Aphrodite and they present a plausible argument for this lineage; for men when under the influence of wine find the members of their bodies tense and inclined to the pleasures of love. Certain writers say that when the ancients wished to speak in their myths of the sexual organ of males they called it Priapus. Some, however, relate that the generative member, since it is the cause of the reproduction of human beings and of their continued existence through all time, became the object of immortal honour, but the Egyptians in their myths about Priapus say that in ancient times the Titans formed a conspiracy against Osiris and slew him, and then, taking his body and dividing it into equal parts among themselves, they slipped them secretly out of the house, but this organ alone they threw into the river, since no one of them was willing to take it with him. Isis tracked down the murder of her husband, and after slaying the Titans and fashioning the several pieces of his body into the shape of a human figure, she gave them to the priests with orders that they pay Osiris the honours of a god, but since the only member she was unable to recover was the organ of sex she commanded them to pay to it the honours of a god and to set it up in their temples in an erect position. This is the myth about the birth of Priapus and the honour paid to him, as it is given by the ancient Egyptians.

This god is also called by some Ithyphallus, by others Tychon. Honours are accorded him not only in the city, in the temples, but also throughout the countryside, where men set up his statue to watch over their vineyards and gardens, and introduce him as one who punishes any who cast a spell over some fair thing which they possess. In the sacred rites, not only of Dionysus but of practically all other gods as well, this god receives honour to some extent, being introduced in the sacrifices to the accompaniment of laughter and sport.

A birth like that of Priapus is ascribed by some writers of myths to Hermaphroditus, as he has been called, who was born of Hermes and Aphrodite and received a name which is a combination of those of both his parents. Some say that this Hermaphroditus is a god and appears at certain times among men, and that he is born with a physical body which is a combination of that of a man and that of a woman, in that he has a body which is beautiful and delicate like that of a woman, but has the masculine quality and vigour of a man. There are some who declare that such creatures of two sexes are monstrosities, and coming rarely into the world as they do they have the quality of presaging the future, sometimes for evil and sometimes for good, but let this be enough for us on such matters.

7. As for the Muses, since we have referred to them in connection with the deeds of Dionysus, it may be appropriate to give the facts about them in summary. The majority of the writers of myths and those who enjoy the greatest reputation say that they were daughters of Zeus and Mnemosyne; but a few poets, among whose number is Alcman, state that they were daughters of Uranus and Gê. Writers similarly disagree also concerning the number of the Muses; for some say that they are three, and others that they are nine, but the number nine has prevailed since it rests upon the authority of the most distinguished men, such as Homer and Hesiod and others like them. Homer, for instance, writes:

> The Muses, nine in all, replying each
> To each with voices sweet;

and Hesiod even gives their names when he writes:

> Cleio, Euterpê, and Thaleia, Melpomenê,
> Terpsichorê and Erato, and Polymnia, Urania,
> Calliopê too, of them all the most comely.

To each of the Muses men assign her special aptitude for one of the branches of the liberal arts, such as poetry, song, pantomimic dancing, the round dance with music, the study of the stars, and the other liberal arts. They are also believed to be virgins, as most writers of myths say, because men consider that the high attainment which is reached through education is pure and uncontaminated. Men have given the Muses their name from the word *muein*, which signifies the teaching of those things which are noble and expedient and are not known by the uneducated. For the name of each Muse, they say, men have found a reason appropriate to her: Cleio is so named because the praise which poets sing in their encomia bestows great glory (*kleos*) upon those who are praised; Euterpê, because she gives to those who hear her sing delight (*terpein*) in the blessings which education bestows; Thaleia, because men whose praises have been sung in poems flourish (*thallein*) through long periods of time; Melpomene, from the chanting (*melodia*) by which she charms the souls of her listeners; Terpsichore, because she delights (*terpein*) her disciples with the good things which come from education; Erato [lovely one], because she makes those who are instructed by her men who are desired and worthy to be loved; Polymnia, because by her great (*polle*) praises (*humnesis*) she brings distinction to writers whose works have won for them immortal fame; Urania, because men who have been instructed of her she raises aloft to heaven (*ouranos*), for it is a fact that imagination and the power of thought lift men's souls to heavenly heights; Calliope, because of her beautiful (*kale*) voice (*ops*), that is, by reason of the exceeding beauty of her language she wins the approbation of her auditors.

But since we have spoken sufficiently on these matters we shall turn our discussion to the deeds of Heracles.

## On Heracles and the twelve Labours, and the other deeds of his up to the time of his deification (8-39).

8. I am not unaware that many difficulties beset those who undertake to give an account of the ancient myths, and especially is this true with respect to the myths about Heracles. For as regards the magnitude of the deeds which he accomplished it is generally agreed that Heracles has been handed down as one who surpassed all men of whom memory from the beginning of time has brought

down an account; consequently it is a difficult attainment to report each one of his deeds in a worthy manner and to present a record which shall be on a level with labours so great, the magnitude of which won for him the prize of immortality. Furthermore, since in the eyes of many men the very early age and astonishing nature of the facts which are related make the myths incredible, a writer is under the necessity either of omitting the greatest deeds and so detracting somewhat from the fame of the god, or of recounting them all and in so doing making the history of them incredible. Some readers set up an unfair standard and require in the accounts of the ancient myths the same exactness as in the events of our own time, and using their own life as a standard they pass judgment on those deeds the magnitude of which throw them open to doubt, and estimate the might of Heracles by the weakness of the men of our day, with the result that the exceeding magnitude of his deeds makes the account of them incredible. For, speaking generally, when the histories of myths are concerned, a man should by no means scrutinise the truth with so sharp an eye. In the theatres, for instance, though we are persuaded there have existed no Centaurs who are composed of two different kinds of bodies nor any Geryones with three bodies, we yet look with favour upon such products of the myths as these, and by our applause we enhance the honour of the god. And strange it would be indeed that Heracles, while yet among mortal men, should by his own labours have brought under cultivation the inhabited world, and that human beings should nevertheless forget the benefactions which he rendered them generally and slander the commendation he receives for the noblest deeds, and strange that our ancestors should have unanimously accorded immortality to him because of his exceedingly great attainments, and that we should nevertheless fail to cherish and maintain for the god the pious devotion which has been handed down to us from our fathers. However, we shall leave such considerations and relate his deeds from the beginning, basing our account on those of the most ancient poets and writers of myths.

**9.** This, then, is the story as it has been given us: Perseus was the son of Danae, the daughter of Acrisius, and Zeus. Now Andromeda, the daughter of Cepheus, lay with him and bore Electryon, and then Eurydice, the daughter of Pelops, married him and gave birth to Alcmenê, who in turn was wooed by Zeus, who deceived her, and bore Heracles. Consequently the sources of his descent, in their entirety, lead back, as is claimed, through both his parents to the greatest of the gods, in the manner we have shown. The prowess which was found in him was not only to be seen in his deeds, but was also recognised even before his birth. For when Zeus lay with Alcmenê he made the night three times its normal length and by the magnitude of the time expended on the procreation he presaged the exceptional might of the child which would be begotten, and, in general, he did not effect this union from the desire of love, as he did in the case of other women, but rather only for the sake of procreation. Consequently, desiring to give legality to his embraces, he did not choose to offer violence to Alcmenê, and yet he could not hope to persuade her because of her chastity; and so, deciding to use deception, he deceived Alcmenê by assuming in every respect the shape of Amphitryon.

When the natural time of pregnancy had passed, Zeus, whose mind was fixed upon the birth of Heracles, announced in advance in the presence of all the gods that it was his intention to make the child who should be born that day king over the descendants of Perseus; whereupon Hera, who was filled with jealousy, using as her helper Eileithyia her daughter, checked the birth-pains of Alcmenê and brought Eurystheus forth to the light before his full time. Zeus, however, though he had been outgeneralled, wished both to fulfil his promise and to take thought for the future fame of Heracles; consequently, they say, he persuaded Hera to agree that Eurystheus should be king as he had promised, but that Heracles should serve Eurystheus and perform twelve Labours, these to be whatever Eurystheus should prescribe, and that after he had done so he should receive the gift of immortality. After Alcmenê had brought forth the babe, fearful of Hera's jealousy she exposed it at a place which to this time is called after him the Field of Heracles. Now at this very time Athena, approaching the spot in the company of Hera and being amazed at the natural vigour of the child, persuaded Hera to offer it the breast, but when the boy tugged upon her breast with greater violence than would be expected at his age, Hera was unable to endure the pain and cast the babe from her, whereupon Athena took it to its mother and urged her to rear it. Anyone may well be surprised at the unexpected turn of the affair; for the mother whose duty it was to love her own offspring was trying to destroy it, while she who cherished towards it a stepmother's hatred, in ignorance saved the life of one who was her natural enemy.

**10.** After this Hera sent two serpents to destroy the babe, but the boy, instead of being terrified, gripped the neck of a serpent in each hand and strangled them both. Consequently the inhabitants of Argos, on learning of what had taken place, gave him the name Heracles because he had gained glory (*kleos*) by the aid of Hera, although he had formerly been called Alcaeus. Other children are given their names by their parents, this one alone gained his name by his valour.

After this time Amphitryon was banished from Tiryns and changed his residence to Thebes; and Heracles, in his rearing and education and especially in the thorough instruction which he received in physical exercises, came to be the first by far in bodily strength among all the rest and famed for his nobility of spirit. Indeed, while he was still a youth in age he first of all restored the freedom of Thebes, returning in this way to the city, as though it were the place of his birth, the gratitude which he owed it. For though the Thebans had been made subject to Erginus, the king of the Minyans, and were paying him a fixed yearly tribute, Heracles was not dismayed at the superior power of these overlords but had the courage to accomplish a deed of fame. Indeed, when the agents of the Minyans appeared to require the tribute and were insolent in their exactions, Heracles mutilated them and then expelled them from the city. Erginus then demanded that the guilty party be handed over to him, and Creon, the king of the Thebans, dismayed at the great power of Erginus, was prepared to deliver the man who was responsible for the crime complained of. Heracles, however, persuading the young men of his age to strike for the freedom of their fatherland, took out of the temples the suits of armour which had been affixed to their walls, dedicated to the gods by their forefathers as spoil from their wars; for there was not to be found in the city any arms in the hands of a private citizen, the Minyans having stripped the city of its arms in order that the inhabitants of Thebes might not entertain any thought of revolting from them. When Heracles learned that Erginus, the king of the Minyans, was advancing with troops against the city he went out to meet him in a certain narrow place, whereby he rendered the multitude of the hostile force of no avail, killed Erginus himself, and slew practically all the men who had accompanied him. Then appearing unawares before the city of the Orchomenians and slipping in at their gates he both burned the palace of the Minyans and razed the city to the ground.

After this deed had been noised about throughout the whole of Greece and all men were filled with wonder at the unexpected happening, Creon the king, admiring the high achievement of the young man, united his daughter Megara in marriage to him and entrusted him with the affairs of the city as though he were his lawful son; but Eurystheus, who was ruler of Argolis, viewing with suspicion the growing power of Heracles, summoned him to his side and commanded him to perform Labours. When Heracles ignored the summons Zeus despatched word to him to enter the service of Eurystheus; whereupon Heracles journeyed to Delphi, and on inquiring of the god regarding the matter he received a reply which stated that the gods had decided that he should perform twelve Labours at the command of Eurystheus and that upon their conclusion he should receive the gift of immortality.

**11.** At such a turn of affairs Heracles fell into despondency of no ordinary kind; for he felt that servitude to an inferior was a thing which his high achievements did not deserve, and yet he saw that it would be hurtful to himself and impossible not to obey Zeus, who was his father as well. While he was thus greatly at a loss, Hera sent upon him a frenzy, and in his vexation of soul he fell into a madness. As the affliction grew on him he lost his mind and tried to slay Iolaüs, and when Iolaüs made his escape but his own children by Megara were near by, he shot his bow and killed them under the impression that they were enemies of his. When he finally recovered from his madness and recognised the mistake he had made through a misapprehension, he was plunged in grief over the magnitude of the calamity, and while all extended him sympathy and joined in his grief, for a long while he stayed inactive at home, avoiding any association or meeting with men; at last, however, time assuaged his grief, and making up his mind to undergo the dangers he made his appearance at the court of Eurystheus.

The first Labour which he undertook was the slaying of the lion in Nemea. This was a beast of enormous size, which could not be wounded by iron or bronze or stone and required the compulsion of the human hand for his subduing. It passed the larger part of its time between Mycenae and Nemea, in the neighbourhood of a mountain which was called Tretus [perforated] from a peculiarity which it possessed; for it had a cleft at its base which extended clean through it and in which the beast was accustomed to lurk. Heracles came to the region and attacked the lion, and when the beast retreated into the cleft, after closing up the other opening he followed in after it and grappled with it, and winding his arms about its neck choked it to death. The skin of the lion he put about himself, and since he could cover his whole body with it because of its great size, he had in it a protection against the perils which were to follow.

The second Labour which he undertook was the slaying of the Lernaean hydra, springing from whose single body were fashioned a hundred necks, each bearing the head of a serpent. When one head was cut off, the place where it was severed put forth two others; for this reason it was considered to be invincible, and with good reason, since the part of it which was subdued sent forth a twofold assistance in its place. Against a thing so difficult to manage as this Heracles devised an ingenious scheme and commanded Iolaüs to sear with a burning brand the part which had been severed, in order to check the flow of the blood. So when he had subdued the animal by this means he dipped the heads of his arrows in the venom, in order that when the missile should be shot the wound which the point made might be incurable.

**12.** The third Command which he received was the bringing back alive of the Erymanthian boar which lived on Mount Lampeia in Arcadia. This Command was thought to be exceedingly difficult, since it required of the man who fought such a beast that he possess such a superiority over it as to catch precisely the proper moment in the very heat of the encounter. For should he let it loose while it still retained its strength he would be in danger from its tushes, and should he attack it more violently than was proper, then he would have killed it and so the Labour would remain unfulfilled. However, when it came to the struggle he kept so careful an eye on the proper balance that he brought back the boar alive to Eurystheus; and when the king saw him carrying the boar on his shoulders, he was terrified and hid himself in a bronze vessel.

About the time that Heracles was performing these Labours, there was a struggle between him and the Centaurs, as they are called, the reason being as follows. Pholus was a Centaur, from whom the neighbouring mountain came to be called Pholoe, and receiving Heracles with the courtesies due to a guest he opened for him a jar of wine which had been buried in the earth. This jar, the writers of myths relate, had of old been left with a certain Centaur by Dionysus, who had given him orders only to open it when Heracles should come to that place. So, four generations after that time, when Heracles was being entertained as a guest, Pholus recalled the orders of Dionysus. Now when the jar had been opened and the sweet odour of the wine, because of its great age and strength, came to the Centaurs dwelling near there, it came to pass that they were driven mad; consequently they rushed in a body to the dwelling of Pholus and set about plundering him of the wine in a terrifying manner. At this Pholus hid himself in fear, but Heracles, to their surprise, grappled with those who were employing such violence. He had indeed to struggle with beings who were gods on their mother's side, who possessed the swiftness of horses, who had the strength of two bodies, and enjoyed in addition the experience and wisdom of men. The Centaurs advanced upon him, some with pine trees which they had plucked up together with the roots, others with great rocks, some with burning firebrands, and still others with axes such as are used to slaughter oxen, but he withstood them without sign of fear and maintained a battle which was worthy of his former exploits. The Centaurs were aided in their struggle by their mother Nephelê [cloud], who sent down a heavy rain, by which she gave no trouble to those which had four legs, but for him who was supported upon two made the footing slippery. Despite all this Heracles maintained an astonishing struggle with those who enjoyed such advantages as these, slew the larger part of them, and forced the survivors to flee. Of the Centaurs which were killed the most renowned were Daphnis, Argeius, Amphion, also Hippotion, Oreius, Isoples, Melanchaetes, and Thereus, Doupon, and Phrixus. As for those who escaped the peril by flight, every one of them later received a fitting punishment: Homadus, for instance, was killed in Arcadia when he was attempting to violate Alcyone, the sister of Eurystheus. And for this feat it came to pass that Heracles was marvelled at exceedingly; for though he had private grounds for hating his enemy [Kurystheus], yet because he pitied her who was being outraged, he determined to be superior to others in humanity.

A peculiar thing also happened in the case of him who was called Pholus, the friend of Heracles. While he was burying the fallen Centaurs, since they were his kindred, and was extracting an arrow from one of them, he was wounded by the barb, and since the wound could not be healed he came to his death. Heracles gave him a magnificent funeral and buried him at the foot of the mountain, which serves better than a gravestone to preserve his glory; for Pholoê makes known the identity of the buried man by bearing his name and no inscription is needed. Likewise Heracles unwittingly by a shot from his bow killed the Centaur Cheiron, who was admired for his knowledge of healing. But as for the Centaurs let what we have said suffice.

**13.** The next Command which Heracles received was the bringing back of the hart which had golden horns and excelled in swiftness of foot. In the performance of this Labour his sagacity stood him in not less stead than his strength of body. For some say that he captured it by the use of nets, others that he tracked it down and mastered it while it was asleep, and some that he wore it out by running it down. One thing is certain, that he accomplished this Labour by his sagacity of mind, without the use of force and without running any perils.

Heracles then received a Command to drive the birds out of the Stymphalian Lake, and he easily accomplished the Labour by means of a device of art and by ingenuity. The lake abounded, it would appear, with a multitude of birds without telling, which destroyed the fruits of the country roundabout. Now it was not possible to master the animals by force because of the exceptional multitude of them, and so the deed called for ingenuity in cleverly discovering some device. Consequently he fashioned a bronze rattle whereby he made a terrible noise and frightened the animals away, and furthermore, by maintaining a continual din, he easily forced them to abandon their siege of the place and cleansed the lake of them.

Upon the performance of this Labour he received a Command from Eurystheus to cleanse the stables of Augeas, and to do this without the assistance of any other man. These stables contained an enormous mass of dung which had accumulated over a great period, and it was a spirit of insult which induced Eurystheus to lay upon him the command to clean out this dung. Heracles declined as unworthy of him to carry this out upon his shoulders, in order to avoid the disgrace which would follow upon the insulting command; and so, turning the course of the Alpheius river, as it is called, into the stables and cleansing them by means of the stream, he accomplished the Labour in a single day, and without suffering any insult. Surely, then, we may well marvel at the ingenuity of Heracles; for he accomplished the ignoble task involved in the Command without incurring any disgrace or submitting to something which would render him unworthy of immortality.

The next Labour which Heracles undertook was to bring back from Crete the bull of which, they say, Pasiphae had been enamoured, and sailing to the island he secured the aid of Minos the king and brought it back to Peloponnesus, having voyaged upon its back over so wide an expanse of sea.

**14.** After the performance of this Labour Heracles established the Olympic Games, having selected for so great a festival the most beautiful of places, which was the plain lying along the banks of the Alpheius river, where he dedicated these Games to Zeus the Father. And he stipulated that the prize in them should be only a crown, since he himself had conferred benefits upon the race of men without receiving any monetary reward. All the contests were won by him without opposition by anyone else, since no one was bold enough to contend with him because of his exceeding prowess. Yet the contests are very different one from another, since it is hard for a boxer or one who enters for the "Pankration" to defeat a man who runs the "stadion," and equally difficult for the man who wins first place in the light contests to wear down those who excel in the heavy. Consequently it was fitting that of all Games the Olympic should be the one most honoured, since they were instituted by a noble man. It would also not be right to overlook the gifts which were bestowed upon Heracles by the gods because of his high achievements. For instance, when he returned from the wars to devote himself to both relaxations and festivals, as well as to feasts and contests, each one of the gods honoured him with appropriate gifts; Athena with a robe, Hephaestus with a war-club and coat of mail, these two gods vying with one another in accordance with the arts they practised, the one with an eye to the enjoyment and delight afforded in times of peace, the other looking to his safety amid the perils of war. As for the other gods, Poseidon presented him with horses, Hermes with a sword, Apollo gave him a bow and arrows and taught him their use, and Demeter instituted the Lesser Mysteries in honour of Heracles, that she might purify him of the guilt he had incurred in the slaughter of the Centaurs.

A peculiar thing also came to pass in connection with the birth of this god. The first mortal woman, for instance, with whom Zeus lay was Niobe, the daughter of Phoroneus, and the last was Alcmenê, who, as the writers of myths state in their genealogies, was the sixteenth lineal descendant from Niobê. It appears, then, that Zeus began to beget human beings with the ancestors of this Alcmenê and ceased with her; that is, he stopped with her his intercourse with mortal women, since he had no hope that he would beget in after times one who would be worthy of his former children and was unwilling to have the better followed by the worse.

**15.** After this, when the Giants about Pallene chose to begin the war against the immortals, Heracles fought on the side of the gods, and slaying many of the Sons of Earth he received the highest approbation. For Zeus gave the name of "Olympian" only to those gods who had fought by his side, in order that the courageous, by being adorned by so honourable a title, might be distinguished by this designation from the coward; and of those who were born of mortal women he considered only Dionysus and Heracles worthy of this name, not only because they had Zeus for their father, but also because they had avowed the same plan of life as he and conferred great benefits upon the life of men.

And Zeus, when Prometheus had taken fire and given it to men, put him in chains and set an eagle at his side which devoured his liver. When Heracles saw him suffering such punishment because of the benefit which he had conferred upon men, he killed the eagle with an arrow, and then persuading Zeus to cease from his anger he rescued him who had been the benefactor of all.

The next Labour which Heracles undertook was the bringing back of the horses of Diomedes, the Thracian. The feeding-troughs of these horses were of brass because the steeds were so savage, and they were fastened by iron chains because of their strength, and the food they ate was not the natural produce of the soil but they tore apart the limbs of strangers and so got their food from the ill lot of hapless men. Heracles, in order to control them, threw to them their master Diomedes, and when he had satisfied the hunger of the animals by means of the flesh of the man who had taught them to violate human law in this fashion, he had them under his control. When the horses were brought to Eurystheus he consecrated them to Hera, and in fact their breed continued down to the reign of Alexander of Macedon.

When this Labour was finished Heracles sailed forth with Jason as a member of the expedition to the Colchi to get the golden fleece, but we shall give a detailed account of these matters in connection with the expedition of the Argonauts.

**16.** Heracles then received a Command to bring back the girdle of Hippolyte the Amazon and so made the expedition against the Amazons. Accordingly he sailed into the Pontus, which was named by him Euxeinus [hospitable top strangers], and continuing to the mouth of the Thermodon River he encamped near the city of Themiscyra, in which was situated the palace of the Amazons. First of all he demanded of them the girdle which he had been commanded to get; but when they would pay no heed to him, he joined battle with them. Now the general mass of the Amazons were arrayed against the main body of the followers of Heracles, but the most honoured of the women were drawn up opposite Heracles himself and put up a stubborn battle. The first, for instance, to join battle with him was Aella [whirlwind], who had been given this name because of her swiftness, but she found her opponent more agile than herself. The second, Philippis, encountering a mortal blow at the very first conflict, was slain. Then he joined battle with Prothoe, who, they said, had been victorious seven times over the opponents whom she had challenged to battle. When she fell, the fourth whom he overcame was known as Eriboea. She had boasted that because of the manly bravery which she displayed in contests of war she had no need of anyone to help her, but she found her claim was false when she encountered her better. The next, Celaeno, Eurybia, and Phoebe, who were companions of Artemis in the hunt and whose spears found their mark invariably, did not even graze the single target, but in that fight they were one and all cut down as they stood shoulder to shoulder with each other. After them Deïaneira, Asteria and Marpê, and Teemessa and Alcippê were overcome. The last-named had taken a vow to remain a maiden, and the vow she kept, but her life she could not preserve. The commander of the Amazons, Melanippê, who was also greatly admired for her manly courage, now lost her supremacy. Heracles, after thus killing the most renowned of the Amazons and forcing the remaining multitude to turn in flight, cut down the greater number of them, so that the race of them was utterly exterminated. As for the captives, he gave Antiopê as a gift to Theseus and set Melanippê free, accepting her girdle as her ransom.

**17.** Eurystheus then enjoined upon him as a tenth Labour the bringing back of the cattle of Geryones, which pastured in the parts of Iberia which slope towards the ocean. Heracles, realising that this task called for preparation on a large scale and involved great hardships, gathered a notable armament and a multitude of soldiers such as would be adequate for this expedition, for it had been noised abroad throughout all the inhabited world that Chrysaor [he of the golden sword], who received this appellation because of his wealth, was king over the whole of Iberia, and that he had three sons to fight at his side, who excelled in both strength of body and the deeds of courage which they displayed in contests of war; it was known, furthermore, that each of these sons had at his disposal great forces which were recruited from warlike tribes. It was because of these reports that Eurystheus, thinking any expedition against these men would be too difficult to succeed, had assigned to Heracles the Labour just described. But Heracles met the perils with the same bold spirit which he had displayed in the deeds which he had performed up to this time. His forces he gathered and brought to Crete, having decided to make his departure from that place; for this island is especially well situated for expeditions against any part of the inhabited world. Before his departure he was magnificently honoured by the natives, and wishing to show his gratitude to the Cretans he cleansed the island of the wild beasts which infested it. This is the reason why in later times not a single wild animal, such as a bear, or wolf, or serpent, or any similar beast, was to be found on the island. This deed he accomplished for the glory of the island, which, the myths relate, was both the birthplace and the early home of Zeus.

Setting sail, then, from Crete, Heracles put in at Libya, and first of all he challenged to a fight Antaeus, whose fame was noised abroad because of his strength of body and his skill in wrestling, and because he was wont to put to death all strangers whom he had defeated in wrestling, and grappling with him Heracles slew the giant. Following up this great deed he subdued Libya, which was full of wild animals, and large parts of the adjoining desert, and brought it all under cultivation, so that the whole land was filled with ploughed fields and such plantings in general as bear fruit, much of it being devoted to vineyards and much to olive orchards; and, speaking generally, Libya, which before that time had been uninhabitable because of the multitude of the wild beasts which infested the whole land, was brought under cultivation by him and made inferior to no other country in point of prosperity. He likewise punished with death such men as defied the law or arrogant rulers and gave prosperity to the cities. And the myths relate that he hated every kind of wild beast and lawless men and warred upon them because of the fact that it had been his lot that while yet an infant the serpents made an attempt on his life, and that when he came to man's estate he became subject to the power of an arrogant and unjust despot who laid upon him these Labours.

**18.** After Heracles had slain Antaeus he passed into Egypt and put to death Busiris, the king of the land, who made it his practice to kill the strangers who visited that country. Then he made his way through the waterless part of Libya, and coming upon a land which was well watered and fruitful he founded a city of marvellous size, which was called Hecatompylon [of a hundred gates], giving it this name because of the multitude of its gates. The prosperity of this city continued until comparatively recent times, when the Carthaginians made an expedition against it with notable forces under the command of able generals and made themselves its masters. After Heracles had visited a large part of Libya he arrived at the ocean near Gadeira [Cadiz], where he set up pillars on each of the two continents. His fleet accompanied him along the coast and on it he crossed over into Iberia. Finding there the sons of Chrysaor encamped at some distance from one another with three great armies, he challenged each of the leaders to single combat and slew them all, and then after subduing Iberia he drove off the celebrated herds of cattle. He then traversed the country of the Iberians, and since he had received honours at the hands of a certain king of the natives, a man who excelled in piety and justice, he left with the king a portion of the cattle as a present. The king accepted them, but dedicated them all to Heracles and made it his practice each year to sacrifice to Heracles the fairest bull of the herd; and it came to pass that the kine are still maintained in Iberia and continue to be sacred to Heracles down to our own time.

But since we have mentioned the pillars of Heracles, we deem it to be appropriate to set forth the facts concerning them. When Heracles arrived at the farthest points of the continents of Libya and Europe which lie upon the ocean, he decided to set up these pillars to commemorate his campaign. Since he wished to leave upon the ocean a monument which would be had in everlasting remembrance, he built out both the promontories, they say, to a great distance; consequently, whereas before that time a great space had stood between them, he now narrowed the passage, in order that by making it shallow and narrow he might prevent the great sea-monsters from passing out of the ocean into the inner sea, and that at the same time the fame of their builder might be held in everlasting remembrance by reason of the magnitude of the structures. Some authorities, however, say just the opposite, namely, that the two continents were originally joined and that he cut a passage between them, and that by opening the passage he brought it about that the ocean was mingled with our sea. On this question, however, it will be possible for every man to think as he may please.

A thing very much like this he had already done in Greece. For instance, in the region which is called Tempê, where the country is like a plain and was largely covered with marshes, he cut a channel through the territory which bordered on it, and carrying off through this ditch all the water of the marsh he caused the plains to appear which are now in Thessaly along the Peneius river. But in Boeotia he did just the opposite and damming the stream which flowed near the Minyan city of Orchomenus he turned the country into a lake [Copaïs] and caused the ruin of that whole region. But what he did in Thessaly was to confer a benefit upon the Greeks, whereas in Boeotia he was exacting punishment from those who dwelt in Minyan territory, because they had enslaved the Thebans.

**19.** Heracles, then, delivered over the kingdom of the Iberians to the noblest men among the natives and, on his part, took his army and passing into Celtica and traversing the length and breadth of it he put an end to the lawlessness and murdering of strangers to which the people had become addicted; and since a great multitude of men from every tribe flocked to his army of their own accord, he founded a great city which was named Alesia after the "wandering" (*alê*) on his campaign. He also mingled among the citizens of the city many natives, and since these surpassed the others in multitude, it came to pass that the inhabitants as a whole were barbarized. The Celts up to the present time hold this city in honour, looking upon it as the hearth and mother-city of all Celtica. For the entire period from the days of Heracles this city remained free and was never sacked until our own time; but at last Gaius Caesar, who has been pronounced a god because of the magnitude of his deeds, took it by storm and made it and the other Celts subjects of the Romans. Heracles then made his way from Celtica to Italy, and as he traversed the mountain pass through the Alps he made a highway out of the route, which was rough and almost impassable, with the result that it can now be crossed by armies and baggage-trains. The barbarians who inhabited this mountain region had been accustomed to butcher and to plunder such armies as passed through when they came to the difficult portions of the way, but he subdued them all, slew those that were the leaders in lawlessness of this kind, and made the journey safe for succeeding generations. After crossing the Alps he passed through the level plain of what is now called Galatia [Cissalpine Gaul] and made his way through Liguria.

**20.** The Ligurians who dwell in this land possess a soil which is stony and altogether wretched, and, in return for the labours and exceedingly great hardships of the natives, produces only scanty crops which are wrung from it. Consequently the inhabitants are of small bulk and are kept vigorous by their constant exercise; for since they are far removed from the care-free life which accompanies luxury, they are light in their movements and excel in vigour when it comes to contests of war. In general, the inhabitants of the region round about are inured to continuous work, and since the land requires much labour for its cultivation, the Ligurians have become accustomed to require the women to share in the hardships which the cultivation involves. Since both the men and the women work side by side for hire, it came to pass that a strange and surprising thing took place in our day in connection with a certain woman. She was with child, and while working for hire in company with the men she was seized by the labour-pains in the midst of her work and quietly withdrew into a thicket; here she gave birth to the child, and then, after covering it with leaves, she hid the babe there and herself rejoined the labourers, continuing to endure the same hardship as that in which they were engaged and giving no hint of what had happened. When the babe wailed and the occurrence became known, the overseer could in no wise persuade her to stop her work; and indeed she did not desist from the hardship until her employer took pity upon her, paid her the wages due her, and set her free from work.

**21.** After Heracles had passed through the lands of the Ligurians and of the Tyrrhenians [Etruscans] he came to the river Tiber and pitched his camp at the site where Rome now stands. This city was founded many generations afterwards by Romulus, the son of Ares, and at this time certain people of the vicinity had their homes on the Palatine Hill, as it is now called, and formed an altogether inconsiderable city. Here some of the notable men, among them Cacius and Pinarius, welcomed Heracles with marked acts of hospitality and honoured him with pleasing gifts; and memorials of these men abide in Rome to the present day. For, of the nobles of our time, the *gens* which bears the name Pinarii still exists among the Romans, being regarded as very ancient, and as for Cacius, there is a passage on the Palatine which leads downward, furnished with a stairway of stone, and is called after him the "Steps of Cacius" [scalae Caci], and it lies near the original house of Cacius. Now Heracles received with favour the good-will shown him by the dwellers on the Palatine and foretold to them that, after he had passed into the circle of the gods, it would come to pass that whatever men should make a vow to dedicate to Heracles a tithe of their goods would lead a more happy and prosperous life. In fact this custom did arise in later times and has persisted to our own day; for many Romans, and not only those of moderate fortunes but some even of great wealth, who have taken a vow to dedicate a tenth to Heracles and have thereafter become happy and prosperous, have presented him with a tenth of their possessions, which came to four thousand talents. Lucullus, for instance, who was perhaps the wealthiest Roman of his day, had his estate appraised and then offered a full tenth of it to the god, thus providing continuous feasting and expensive ones withal. Furthermore, the Romans have built to this god a notable temple on the bank of the Tiber, with the purpose of performing in it the sacrifices from the proceeds of the tithe.

Heracles then moved on from the Tiber, and as he passed down the coast of what now bears the name of Italy he came to the Cumaean Plain. Here, the myths relate, there were men of outstanding strength the fame of whom had gone abroad for lawlessness and they were called Giants. This plain was called Phlegraean ("fiery") from the mountain which of old spouted forth a huge fire as Aetna did in Sicily; at this time, however, the mountain is called Vesuvius and shows many signs of the fire which once raged in those ancient times. Now the Giants, according to the account, on learning that Heracles was at hand, gathered in full force and drew themselves up in battle-order against him. The struggle which took place was a wonderful one, in view of both the strength and the courage of the Giants, but Heracles, they say, with the help of the gods who fought on his side, gained the upper hand in the battle, slew most of the Giants, and brought the land under cultivation. The myths record that the Giants were sons of the earth because of the exceedingly great size of their bodies. With regard, then, to the Giants who were slain in Phlegra, this is the account of certain writers of myths, who have been followed by the historian Timaeus also.

**22.** From the Phlegraean Plain Heracles went down to the sea, where he constructed works about the lake which bears the name Lake of Avernus and is held sacred to Persephone. Now this lake lies between Misenum and Dicaearcheia [Puteoli] near the hot waters [Baiae], and is about five stades in circumference and of incredible depth; for its water is very pure and has to the eye a dark blue colour because of its very great depth. The myths record that in ancient times there had been on its shores an oracle of the dead which, they say, was destroyed in later days. Lake Avernus once had an opening into the sea, but Heracles is said to have filled up the outlet and constructed the road which runs at this time along the sea and is called after him the "Way of Heracles."

These, then, are the deeds of Heracles in the regions mentioned above. And moving on from there he came to a certain rock in the country of the people of Poseidonia [Paestum], where the myths relate that a peculiar and marvellous thing once took place. There was, that is, among the natives of the region a certain hunter, the fame of whom had gone abroad because of his brave exploits in hunting. On former occasions it had been his practice to dedicate to Artemis the heads and feet of the animals he secured and to nail them to the trees, but once, when he had overpowered a huge wild boar, he said, as though in contempt of the goddess, "The head of the beast I dedicate to myself," and bearing out his words he hung the head on a tree, and then, the atmosphere being very warm, at midday he fell asleep. While he was thus asleep the thong broke, and the head fell down of itself upon the sleeper and killed him. In truth there is no reason why anyone should marvel at this happening, for many actual occurrences are recorded which illustrate the vengeance this goddess takes upon the impious, but in the case of Heracles his piety was such that the opposite happened to him. For when he had arrived at the border between Rhegine and Locris and lay down to rest after his wearying journey, they say that he was disturbed by the crickets and that he prayed to the gods that the creatures which were disturbing him might disappear; whereupon the gods granted his petition, and not only did his prayer cause the insects to disappear for the moment, but in all later times as well not a cricket has ever been seen in the land.

When Heracles arrived at the strait where the sea is narrowest, he had the cattle taken over into Sicily, but as for himself, he took hold of the horn of a bull and swam across the passage, the distance between the shores being thirteen stades, as Timaeus says.

**23.** Upon his arrival in Sicily Heracles desired to make the circuit of the entire island and so set out from Pelorias in the direction of Eryx. While passing along the coast of the island, the myths relate, the Nymphs caused warm baths to gush forth so that he might refresh himself after the toil sustained in his journeying. There are two of these, called respectively Ilimeraea and Egestaea, each of them having its name from the place where the baths are. As Heracles approached the region of Eryx, he was challenged to a wrestling match by Eryx, who was the son of Aphrodite and Butas, who was then king of that country. The contest of the rivals carried with it a penalty, whereby Eryx was to surrender his land and Heracles the cattle. Now at first Eryx was displeased at such terms, maintaining that the cattle were of far less value as compared with the land; but when Heracles in answer to his arguments showed that if he lost the cattle he would likewise lose his immortality, Eryx agreed to the terms, and wrestling with him was defeated and lost his land. Heracles turned the land over to the natives of the region, agreeing with them that they should gather the fruits of it until one of his descendants should appear among them and demand it back; and this actually came to pass. For in fact many generations later Dorieus the Lacedaemonian came to Sicily, and taking back the land founded the city of Heracleia. Since the city grew rapidly, the Carthaginians, being jealous of it and also afraid that it would grow stronger than Carthage and take from the Phoenicians their sovereignty, came up against it with a great army, took it by storm, and razed it to the ground. This affair we shall discuss in detail in connection with the period in which it falls.

While Heracles was making the circuit of Sicily at this time he came to the city which is now Syracuse, and on learning what the myth relates about the Rape of Corê he offered sacrifices to the goddesses on a magnificent scale, and after dedicating to her the fairest bull of his herd and casting it in the spring Cyanê he commanded the natives to sacrifice each year to Corê and to conduct at Cyanê a festive gathering and a sacrifice in splendid fashion. He then passed with his cattle through the interior of the island, and when the native Sicani opposed him in great force, he overcame them in a notable battle and slew many of their number, among whom, certain writers of myths relate, were also some distinguished generals who receive the honours accorded to heroes even to this day, such as Leucaspis, Pediacrates, Buphonas, Glychatas, Bytaeas, and Crytidas.

**24.** After this Heracles, as he passed through the plain of Leontini, marvelled at the beauty of the land, and to show his affection for the men who honoured him he left behind him there imperishable memorials of his presence. And it came to pass that a peculiar thing took place near the city of Agyrium. Here he was honoured on equal terms with the Olympian gods by festivals and splendid sacrifices, and though before this time he had accepted no sacrifice, he then gave his consent for the first time, since the deity was giving intimations to him of his coming immortality. For instance, there was a road not far from the city which was all of rock, and yet the cattle left their tracks in it as if in a waxy substance. Since, then, this same thing happened in the case of Heracles as well and his tenth Labour was likewise coming to an end, he considered that he was already to a degree participating in immortality and so accepted the annual sacrifices which were offered him by the people of the city. Consequently, as a mark of his gratitude to the people who had found favour with him, he built before the city a lake, four stades in circumference, which he ordained should be called by his name; and he likewise gave his name to the moulds of the tracks which the cattle had left in the rock and dedicated to the hero Geryones a sacred precinct which is honoured to this day by the people of that region. To Iolaüs, his nephew, who was his companion on the expedition, he likewise dedicated a notable sacred precinct, and ordained that annual honours and sacrifices should be offered to him, as is done even to this day; for all the inhabitants of this city let the hair of their heads grow from their birth in honour of Iolaüs, until they have obtained good omens in costly sacrifices and have rendered the god propitious. And such a holiness and majesty pervade the sacred precinct that the boys who fail to perform the customary rites lose their power of speech and become like dead men. But so soon as anyone of them who is suffering from this malady takes a vow that he will pay the sacrifice and vouchsafes to the god a pledge to that effect, at once, they say, he is restored to health. Now the inhabitants, in pursuance of these rites, call the gate, at which they come into the presence of the god and offer him these sacrifices, "The Heracleian," and every year with the utmost zeal they hold games which include gymnastic contests and horse-races. Since the whole populace, both free men and slaves, unite in approbation of the god, they have commanded their servants, as they do honour to him apart from the rest, to gather in bands and when they come together to hold banquets and perform sacrifices to the god.

Heracles then crossed over into Italy with the cattle and proceeded along the coast; there he slew Lacinius as he was attempting to steal some of the cattle, and to Croton, whom he killed by accident, he accorded a magnificent funeral and erected for him a tomb; and he foretold to the natives of the place that also in after times a famous city would arise which should bear the name of the man who had died.

25. But when Heracles had made the circuit of the Adriatic, and had journeyed around the gulf on foot, he came to Epirus, whence he made his way to Peloponnesus. Now that he had performed the tenth Labour he received a Command from Eurystheus to bring Cerberus up from Hades to the light of day. Assuming that it would be to his advantage for the accomplishment of this Labour, he went to Athens and took part in the Eleusinian Mysteries, Musaeus, the son of Orpheus, being at that time in charge of the initiatory rites.

Since we have mentioned Orpheus it will not be inappropriate for us in passing to speak briefly about him. He was the son of Oeagrus, a Thracian by birth, and in culture and song-music and poesy he far surpassed all men of whom we have a record; for he composed a poem which was an object of wonder and excelled in its melody when it was sung. And his fame grew to such a degree that men believed that with his music he held a spell over both the wild beasts and the trees. After he had devoted his entire time to his education and had learned whatever the myths had to say about the gods, he journeyed to Egypt, where he further increased his knowledge and so became the greatest man among the Greeks both for his knowledge of the gods and for their rites, as well as for his poems and songs. He also took part in the expedition of the Argonauts, and because of the love he held for his wife he dared the amazing deed of descending into Hades, where he entranced Persephone by his melodious song and persuaded her to assist him in his desires and to allow him to bring up his dead wife from Hades, in this exploit resembling Dionysus; for the myths relate that Dionysus brought up his mother Semelê from Hades, and that, sharing with her his own immortality, he changed her name to Thyonê.

But now that we have discussed Orpheus, we shall return to Heracles.

26. Heracles, then, according to the myths which have come down to us, descended into the realm of Hades, and being welcomed like a brother by Persephone brought Theseus and Peirithoüs back to the upper world after freeing them from their bonds. This he accomplished by the favour of Persephone, and receiving the dog Cerberus in chains he carried him away to the amazement of all and exhibited him to men.

The last Labour which Heracles undertook was the bringing back of the golden apples of the Hesperides, and so he again sailed to Libya. With regard to these apples there is disagreement among the writers of myths, and some say that there were golden apples in certain gardens of the Hesperides in Libya, where they were guarded without ceasing by a most formidable dragon, whereas others assert that the Hesperides possessed flocks of sheep which excelled in beauty and were therefore called for their beauty, as the poets might do, "golden apples,"

## Book IV

just as Aphrodite is called "golden" because of her loveliness. There are some, however, who say that it was because the sheep had a peculiar colour like gold that they got this designation, and that Dracon (dragon) was the name of the shepherd of the sheep, a man who excelled in strength of body and courage, who guarded the sheep and slew any who might dare try to carry them off. With regard to such matters it will be every man's privilege to form such opinions as accord with his own belief. At any rate Heracles slew the guardian of the apples, and after he had duly brought them to Eurystheus and had in this wise finished his Labours he waited to receive the gift of immortality, even as Apollo had prophesied to him.

**27.** But we must not fail to mention what the myths relate about Atlas and about the race of the Hesperides. The account runs like this: In the country known as Hesperitis there were two brothers whose fame was known abroad, Hesperus and Atlas. These brothers possessed flocks of sheep which excelled in beauty and were in colour of a golden yellow, this being the reason why the poets, in speaking of these sheep as *mela,* called them golden *mela.* Now Hesperus begat a daughter named Hesperis, whom he gave in marriage to his brother and after whom the land was given the name Hesperitis; and Atlas begat by her seven daughters, who were named after their father Atlantides, and after their mother, Hesperides. And since these Atlantides excelled in beauty and chastity, Busiris the king of the Egyptians, the account says, was seized with the desire to get the maidens into his power; and consequently he dispatched pirates by sea with orders to seize the girls and deliver them into his hands.

About this time Heracles, while engaged in the performance of his last Labour, slew in Libya Antaeus, who was compelling all strangers to wrestle with him, and upon Busiris in Egypt, who was sacrificing to Zeus the strangers who visited his country, he inflicted the punishment which he deserved. After this Heracles sailed up the Nile into Ethiopia, where he slew Emathion, the king of the Ethiopians, who made battle with him unprovoked, and then returned to the completion of his last Labour. Meanwhile the pirates had seized the girls while they were playing in a certain garden and carried them off, and fleeing swiftly to their ships had sailed away with them. Heracles came upon the pirates as they were taking their meal on a certain strand, and learning from the maidens what had taken place he slew the pirates to a man and brought the girls back to Atlas their father; and in return Atlas was so grateful to Heracles for his kindly deed that he not only gladly gave him such assistance as his Labour called for, but he also instructed him quite freely in the knowledge of astrology. For Atlas had worked out the science of astrology to a degree surpassing others and had ingeniously discovered the spherical nature of the stars, and for that reason was generally believed to be bearing the entire firmament upon his shoulders. Similarly in the case of Heracles, when he had brought to the Greeks the doctrine of the sphere, he gained great fame, as if he had taken over the burden of the firmament which Atlas had borne, since men intimated in this enigmatic way what had actually taken place.

**28.** While Heracles was busied with the matters just described, the Amazons, they say, of whom there were some still left in the region of the Thermodon river, gathered in a body and set out to get revenge upon the Greeks for what Heracles had done in his campaign against them. They were especially eager to punish the Athenians because Theseus had made a slave of Antiopê, the leader of the Amazons, or, as others write, of Hippolyte. The Scythians had joined forces with the Amazons, and so it came about that a notable army had been assembled, with which the leaders of the Amazons crossed the Cimmerian Bosporus [Strait of Kertch] and advanced through Thrace. Finally they traversed a large part of Europe and came to Attica, where they pitched their camp in what is at present called after them "the Amazoneum." [Areopagus?] When Theseus learned of the oncoming of the Amazons he came to the aid of the forces of his citizens, bringing with him the Amazon Antiope, by whom he already had a son Hippolytus. Theseus joined battle with the Amazons, and since the Athenians surpassed them in bravery, he gained the victory, and of the Amazons who opposed him; some he slew at the time and the rest he drove out of Attica, and it came to pass that Antiope, who was fighting at the side of her husband Theseus, distinguished herself in the battle and died fighting heroically. The Amazons who survived renounced their ancestral soil, and returned with the Scythians into Scythia and made their homes among that people.

We have spoken enough about the Amazons, and shall return to the deeds of Heracles.

**29.** After Heracles had performed his Labours, the god revealed to him that it would be well if, before he passed into the company of the gods, he should despatch a colony to Sardinia and make the sons who had been born to him by the daughters of Thespius the leaders of the settlement, and so he decided to send his nephew Iolaüs with the boys, since they were still quite young. Now it seems to us indispensable that we should speak first of the birth of the boys, in order that we may be able to set forth more clearly what is to be said about the colony.

Thespius was by birth a distinguished man of Athens and son of Erechtheus, and he was king of the land which bears his name [Thespiae] and begot by his wives, of whom he had a great number, fifty daughters. And when Heracles was still a boy, but already of extraordinary strength of body, the king strongly desired that his daughters should bear children by him. Consequently he invited Heracles to a sacrifice, and after entertaining him in brilliant fashion he sent his daughters one by one in to him; and Heracles lay with them all, brought them all with child, and so became the father of fifty sons. These sons all took the same name after the daughters of Thespius [Thespiades], and when they had arrived at manhood Heracles decided to send them to Sardinia to found a colony, as the oracle had commanded. Since the expedition was under the general command of Iolaüs, who had accompanied Heracles on practically all of his campaigns, the latter entrusted him with the care of the Thespiadae and the planting of the colony. Of the fifty boys, two continued to dwell in Thebes, their descendants, they say, being honoured even to the present day, and seven in Thespiae, where they are called *demouchi* [protector of the people], and where their descendants, they say, were the chief men of the city until recent times. All the other Thespiadae and many more who wished to join in the founding of the colony Iolaüs took with him and sailed away to Sardinia. Here he overcame the natives in battle and divided the fairest part of the island into allotments, especially the land which was a level plain and is called to this day Iolaeium. When he had brought the land under cultivation and planted it with fruit-bearing trees he made of the island an object of contention; for instance, it gained such fame for the abundance of its fruits that at a later time the Carthaginians, when they had grown powerful, desired the island and faced many struggles and perils for possession of it. But we shall write of these matters in connection with the period to which they belong.

**30.** At the time we are considering, Iolaüs established the colony, and summoning Daedalus from Sicily he built through him many great works which stand to this day and are called "Daedaleia" after their builder. He also had large and expensive gymnasia constructed and established courts of justice and the other institutions which contribute to the prosperity of a state. Furthermore, Iolaüs named the folk of the colony Iolaüs, calling them after himself, the Thespiadae consenting to this and granting to him this honour as to a father. In fact his regard for them led them to entertain such a kindly feeling towards him that they bestowed upon him as a title the appellation usually given to the progenitor of a people; consequently those who in later times offer sacrifices to this god address him as "Father Iolaüs," as the Persians do when they address Cyrus. After this Iolaüs, on his return to Greece, sailed over to Sicily and spent a considerable time on that island. At this time several of those who were visiting the island in his company remained in Sicily because of the beauty of the land, and uniting with the Sicani they settled in the island, being especially honoured by the natives. Iolaüs also received a great welcome, and since he conferred benefits upon many men he was honoured in many of the cities with sacred precincts and with such distinctions as are accorded to heroes. And a peculiar and astonishing thing came to pass in connection with this colony in Sardinia. For the god had told them in an oracle that all who joined in this colony and their descendants should continually remain free men for evermore, and the event in their case has continued to be in harmony with the oracle even to our own times. For the people of the colony in the long course of time came to be barbarized, since the barbarians who took part in the colony about them outnumbered them, and so they removed into the mountainous part of the island and made their home in the rough and barren regions and there, accustoming themselves to live on milk and meat and raising large flocks and herds, they had no need of grain. They also built themselves underground dwellings, and by spending their lives in such dug-out homes they avoided the perils which wars entail. As a consequence both the Carthaginians in former days and the Romans later, despite the many wars which they waged with this people, did not attain their design.

As regards Iolaüs, then, and the Thespiadae and the colony which was sent to Sardinia, we shall rest satisfied with what has been said, and we shall continue the story of Heracles from the point at which our account left off.

**31.** After Heracles had completed his Labours he gave his own wife Megara in marriage to Iolaüs, being apprehensive of begetting any children by her because of the calamity which had befallen their other offspring, and sought another wife by whom he might have children without apprehension. Consequently he wooed Iole, the daughter of Eurytus who was ruler of Oechalia, but Eurytus was hesitant because of the ill fortune which had come in the case of

Megara and replied that he would deliberate concerning the marriage. Since Heracles had met with a refusal to his suit, because of the dishonour which had been shown him he now drove off the mares of Eurytus. Iphitus, the son of Eurytus, harboured suspicions of what had been done and came to Tiryns in search of the horses, whereupon Heracles, taking him up on a lofty tower of the castle, asked him to see whether they were by chance grazing anywhere; and when Iphitus was unable to discover them, he claimed that Iphitus had falsely accused him of the theft and threw him down headlong from the tower.

Because of his murder of Iphitus Heracles was attacked by a disease, and coming to Neleus at Pylus he besought him to purify him of the blood-guilt. Thereupon Neleus took counsel with his sons and found that all of them, with the exception of Nestor who was the youngest, agreed in advising him that he should not undertake the rite of purification. Heracles then went to Deïphobus, the son of Hippolytus, and prevailing upon him was given the rite of purification, but being still unable to rid himself of the disease he inquired of Apollo how to heal it. Apollo gave him the answer that he would easily rid himself of the disease if he should be sold as a slave and honourably pay over the purchase price of himself to the sons of Iphitus, and so, being now under constraint to obey the oracle, he sailed over to Asia in company with some of his friends. There he willingly submitted to be sold by one of his friends and became the slave of Omphale, the daughter of Iardanus, who was still unmarried and was queen of the people who were called at that time Maeonians, but now Lydians. The man who had sold Heracles paid over the purchase price to the sons of Iphitus, as the oracle had commanded, and Heracles, healed now of the disease and serving Omphale as her slave, began to mete out punishment upon the robbers who infested the land. As for the Cercopes, for instance, as they are called, who were robbing and committing many evil acts, some of them he put to death and others he took captive and delivered in chains to Omphale. Syleus, who was seizing any strangers who passed by and forcing them to hoe his vineyards, he slew by a blow with his own hoe; and from the Itoni, who had been plundering a large part of the land of Omphale, he took away their booty, and the city which they had made the base of their raids he sacked, and enslaving its inhabitants razed it to the ground. Omphale was pleased with the courage Heracles displayed, and on learning who he was and who had been his parents she marvelled at his valour, set him free, and marrying him bore him Lamus. Already before this, while he was yet a slave, there had been born to Heracles by a slave a son Cleodaeus.

**32.** After this Heracles, returning to Peloponnesus, made war against Ilium, since he had a ground of complaint against its king, Laomedon. For when Heracles was on the expedition with Jason to get the golden fleece and had slain the sea-monster, Laomedon had withheld from him the mares which he had agreed to give him and of which we shall give a detailed account a little later in connection with the Argonauts. At that time Heracles had not had the leisure, since he was engaged upon the expedition of Jason, but later he found an opportunity and made war upon Troy with eighteen ships of war, as some say, but, as Homer writes, with six in all, when he introduces Heracles' son Tlepolemus as saying:

> Aye, what a man, they say, was Heracles

# BOOK IV

> In might, my father he, steadfast, with heart
> Of lion, who once came here to carry off
> The mares of King Laomedon, with but
> Six ships and scantier men, yet sacked he then
> The city of proud Ilium, and made
> Her streets bereft.

When Heracles, then, had landed on the coast of the Troad, he advanced in person with his select troops against the city and left in command of the ships Oecles, the son of Amphiaraus. And since the presence of the enemy had not been expected, it proved impossible for Laomedon, on account of the exigencies of the moment, to collect a passable army, but gathering as many soldiers as he could he advanced with them against the ships, in the hope that if he could burn them he could bring an end to the war. Oecles came out to meet him, but when he, the general, fell, the rest succeeded in making good their flight to the ships and in putting out to sea from the land. Laomedon then withdrew and joining combat with the troops of Heracles near the city he was slain himself and most of the soldiers with him. Heracles then took the city by storm and after slaughtering many of its inhabitants in the action he gave the kingdom of the Iliadae to Priam because of his sense of justice; for Priam was the only one of the sons of Laomedon who had opposed his father and had counselled him to give the mares back to Heracles, as he had promised to do. Heracles crowned Telamon with the meed of valour by bestowing upon him Hesione the daughter of Laomedon, for in the siege he had been the first to force his way into the city, while Heracles was assaulting the strongest section of the wall of the acropolis.

**33.** After this Heracles returned to Peloponnesus and set out against Augeas, since the latter had defrauded him of his reward. It came to a battle between him and the Eleans, but on this occasion he had no success and so returned to Olenus [in Achaea] to Dexamenus. The latter's daughter Hippolyte was being joined in marriage to Azan, and when Heracles, as he sat at the wedding feast, observed the Centaur Eurytion acting in an insulting manner towards Hippolyte and endeavouring to do violence to her, he slew him. When Heracles returned to Tiryns, Eurystheus charged him with plotting to seize the kingdom and commanded that he and Alcmenê and Iphicles and Iolaüs should depart from Tiryns. Consequently he was forced to go into exile along with these just mentioned and made his dwelling in Pheneus in Arcadia. This city he took for his headquarters, and learning once that a sacred procession had been sent forth from Elis to the Isthmus in honour of Poseidon and that Eurytus, the son of Augeas, was at the head of it, he fell unexpectedly upon Eurytus and killed him near Cleonae, where a temple of Heracles still stands. After this he made war upon Elis and slew Augeas its king, and taking the city by storm he recalled Phyleus, the son of Augeas, and gave the kingdom into his hands; for the son had been exiled by his father at the time when he had served as arbitrator between his father and Heracles in the matter of the reward and had given the decision to Heracles.

After this Hippocoön exiled from Sparta his brother Tyndareüs, and the sons of Hippocoön, twenty in number, put to death Oeonus who was the son of Licymnius and a friend of Heracles; whereupon Heracles was angered and set out against them, and being victorious in a great battle he made a slaughter of every man of them. Then, taking Sparta by storm he restored Tyndareüs, who was the father of the Dioscori, to his kingdom and bestowed upon him the kingdom on the ground that it was his by right of war, commanding him to keep it safe for Heracles' own descendants. There fell in the battle but a very few of the comrades of Heracles, though among them were famous men, such as Iphiclus and Cepheus and seventeen sons of Cepheus, since only three of his twenty sons came out alive; whereas of the opponents Hippocoön himself fell, and ten sons along with him, and vast numbers of the rest of the Spartans. From this campaign Heracles returned into Arcadia, and as he stopped at the home of Aleos the king he lay secretly with his daughter Auge, brought her with child, and went back to Stymphalus. Aleos was ignorant of what had taken place, but when the bulk of the child in the womb betrayed the violation of his daughter he inquired who had violated her. When Auge disclosed that it was Heracles who had done violence to her, he would not believe what she had said, but gave her into the hands of Nauplius his friend with orders to drown her in the sea, but as Auge was being led off to Nauplia and was near Mount Parthenium, she felt herself overcome by the birth-pains and withdrew into a near-by thicket as if to perform a certain necessary act; here she gave birth to a male child, and hiding the babe in some bushes she left it there. After doing this Auge went back to Nauplius, and when she had arrived at the harbour of Nauplia in Argolis she was saved from death in an unexpected manner. Nauplius, that is, decided not to drown her, as he had been ordered, but to make a gift of her to some Carians who were setting out for Asia; and these men took Auge to Asia and gave her to Teuthras the king of Mysia. As for the babe that had been left on Parthenium by Auge, certain herdsmen belonging to Corythus the king came upon it as it was getting its food from the teat of a hind and brought it as a gift to their master. Corythus received the child gladly, raised him as if he were his own son, and named him Telephus after the hind (*elaphos*) which had suckled it. After Telephus had come to manhood, being seized with the desire to learn who his mother was, he went to Delphi and received the reply to sail to Mysia to Teuthras the king. Here he discovered his mother, and when it was known who his father was he received the heartiest welcome. Since Teuthras had no male children he joined his daughter Argiope in marriage to Telephus and named him his successor to the kingdom.

**34.** In the fifth year after Heracles had changed his residence to Pheneus, being grieved over the death of Oeonus, the son of Licymnius, and of Iphiclus his brother, he removed of his free will from Arcadia and all Peloponnesus. There withdrew with him a great many people of Arcadia and he went to Calydon in Aetolia and made his home there, and since he had neither legitimate children nor a lawful wife, he married Deianeira, the daughter of Oeneus, Meleager being now dead. In this connection it would not, in our opinion, be inappropriate for us to digress briefly and to speak of the reversal of fortune which befel Meleager.

The facts are these: Once when Oeneus had an excellent crop of grain, he offered sacrifices to the other gods, but neglected Artemis alone; and angered at him for this the goddess sent forth against him the famous Calydonian boar, a creature of enormous size. This animal harried the neighbouring land and damaged the farms; whereupon Meleager, the son of Oeneus, being then in the bloom of youth and excelling in strength and in courage, took along with himself many of the bravest men and set out to hunt the beast. Meleager was the first to plunge his javelin into it and by general agreement was accorded the reward of valour, which consisted of the skin of the animal, but Atalante, the daughter of Schoeneus, participated in the hunt, and since Meleager was enamoured of her, he relinquished in her favour the skin and the praise for the greatest bravery. The sons of Thestius, however, who had also joined in the hunt, were angered at what he had done, since he had honoured a stranger woman above them and set kinship aside. Consequently, setting at naught the award which Meleager had made, they lay in wait for Atalante, and falling upon her as she returned to Arcadia took from her the skin. Meleager, however, was deeply incensed both because of the love which he bore Atalante and because of the dishonour shown her, and espoused the cause of Atalante. First of all he urged the robbers to return to the woman the meed of valour which he had given her; and when they paid no heed to him he slew them, although they were brothers of Althaea. Consequently Althaea, overcome with anguish at the slaying of the men of her own blood, uttered a curse in which she demanded the death of Meleager; and the immortals, so the account runs, gave heed to her and made an end of his life.

Certain writers of myths give the following account: At the time of the birth of Meleager the Fates stood over Althaea in her sleep and said to her that her son Meleager would die at the moment when the brand in the fire had been consumed. Consequently, when she had given birth, she believed that the safety of her child depended upon the preservation of the brand and so she guarded the brand with every care. Afterward, however, being deeply incensed at the murder of her brothers, she burned the brand and so made herself the cause of the death of Meleager; but as time went on she grieved more and more over what she had done and finally made an end of her life by hanging.

**35.** At the time that these things were taking place, the myth continues, Hipponoiis in Olenus, angered at his daughter Periboea because she claimed that she was with child by Ares, sent her away into Aetolia to Oeneus with orders for him to do away with her at the first opportunity. Oeneus, however, who had recently lost his son and wife, was unwilling to slay Periboea, but married her instead and begat a son Tydeus. Such, then, is the way the story runs of Meleager and Althaea and Oeneus.

But Heracles, desiring to do a service to the Calydonians, diverted the river Achelotis, and making another bed for it he recovered a large amount of fruitful and which was now irrigated by this stream. Consequently certain poets, as we are told, have made this deed into a myth; for they have introduced Heracles as joining battle with Acheloüs, the river assuming the form of a bull, and as breaking off in the struggle one of his horns, which he gave to the Aetolians. This they call the "Horn of Amaltheia," and represent it as filled with a great quantity of every kind of autumn fruit, such as grapes and apples and the like, the poets signifying in this obscure manner by the horn of Acheloüs the stream which ran through the canal, and by the apples and pomegranates and grapes the fruitful land which was watered by the river and the multitude of its fruit-bearing plants. Moreover, they say that the phrase "Amaltheia's Horn" is used as of a quality incapable of being softened (*a-malakistia*), whereby is indicated the tense vigour of the man who built the work.

**36.** Heracles took the field with the Calydonians against the Thesprotians, captured the city of Ephyra by storm, and slew Phyleus the king of the Thesprotians, and taking prisoner the daughter of Phyleus he lay with her and begat Tlepolemus. Three years after his marriage to Deianeira Heracles was dining in the home of Oeneus and Eurynomus, and the son of Architeles, who was still a lad in years, was serving him, and when the boy made some slip in the service Heracles gave him a blow with his fist, and striking him too hard he unintentionally killed the lad. Overcome with grief at this misfortune he went again into voluntary exile from Calydonia along with his wife Deianeira and Hyllus, his son by her, who was still a boy in years. When in his journeying he arrived at the Euenus river he found there the Centaur Nessus who was conveying travellers across the river for a fee. Nessus carried Deianeira across first, and becoming enamoured of her because of her beauty he tried to assault her, but when she called to her husband for help Heracles shot the Centaur with an arrow, and Nessus, struck even while he was having intercourse with her and because of the sharpness of the blow being at once on the point of death, told Deianeira that he would give her a love-charm to the end that Heracles should never desire to approach any other woman. He urged her, accordingly, to take the seed which had fallen from him and, mixing it with olive oil and the blood which was dripping from the barb of the arrow, to anoint with this the shirt of Heracles. This counsel, then, Nessus gave Deianeira and at once breathed his last. She put the seed, as Nessus had enjoined upon her, into a jar and dipped in it the barb of the arrow and kept it all unknown to Heracles. He, after crossing the river, came to Ceyx, the king of Trachis, and made his dwelling with him, having with him the Arcadians who always accompanied him on his campaigns.

**37.** After this, when Phylas, the king of the Dryopes, had in the eyes of men committed an act of impiety against the temple of Delphi, Heracles took the field against him in company with the inhabitants of Melis, slew the king of the Dryopes, drove the rest of them out of the land, and gave it to the people of Melis; and the daughter of Phylas he took captive and lying with her begat a son Antiochus. By Deianeira he became the father of two sons, younger than Hyllus, Gleneus and Hodites. Of the Dryopes who had been driven from their land some passed over into Euboea and founded there the city Carystus, others sailed to the island of Cyprus, where they mixed with the natives of the island and made their home, while the rest of the Dryopes took refuge with Eurystheus and won his aid because of the enmity which he bore to Heracles; and with the aid of Eurystheus they founded three cities in Peloponnesus, Asinê, Hermionê, and Eïon.

After the removal of the Dryopes from their land a war arose between the Dorieis who inhabit the land called Hestiaeotis, whose king was Aegimius, and the Lapithae dwelling about Mount Olympus, whose king was Coronus, the son of Caeneus. And since the Lapithae greatly excelled in the number of their forces, the Dorieis turned to Heracles for aid and implored him to join with them, promising him a third part of the land of Doris and of the kingship, and when they had won him over they made common cause in the campaign against the Lapithae. Heracles had with him the Arcadians who accompanied him on his campaigns, and mastering the Lapithae with their aid he slew king Coronus himself, and massacring most of the rest he compelled them to withdraw from the land which was in dispute. After accomplishing these deeds he entrusted to Aegimius the third part of the land, which was his share, with orders that he keep it in trust in favour of Heracles' descendants. He now returned to Trachis, and upon being challenged to combat by Cycnus, the son of Ares, he slew the man; and as he was leaving the territory of Itonus and was making his way through Pelasgiotis he fell in with Ormenius the king and asked of him the hand of his daughter Astydameia. When Ormenius refused him because he already had for lawful wife Deianeira, the daughter of Oeneus, Heracles took the field against him, captured his city, and slew the king who would not obey him, and taking captive Astydameia he lay with her and begat a son Ctesippus. After finishing this exploit he set out to Oechalia to take the field against the sons of Eurytus because he had been refused in his suit for the hand of Iole. The Arcadians again fought on his side and he captured the city and slew the sons of Eurytus, who were Toxeus, Molion, and Clytius. And taking Iole captive he departed from Euboea to the promontory which is called Cenaeum.

**38.** At Cenaeon Heracles, wishing to perform a sacrifice, dispatched his attendant Lichas to Deianeira his wife, commanding him to ask her for the shirt and robe which he customarily wore in the celebration of sacrifices. But when Deianeira learned from Lichas of the love which Heracles had for Iole, she wished him to have a greater affection for herself and so anointed the shirt with the love-charm which had been given her by the Centaur, whose intention was to bring about the death of Heracles. Lichas, then, in ignorance of these matters, brought back the garments for the sacrifice; and Heracles put on the shirt which had been anointed, and as the strength of the toxic drug began slowly to work he met with the most terrible calamity. For the arrow's barb had carried the poison of the adder, and when the shirt for this reason, as it became heated, attacked the flesh of the body, Heracles was seized with such anguish that he slew Lichas, who had been his servant, and then, disbanding his army, returned to Trachis.

As Heracles continued to suffer more and more from his malady he dispatched Licymnius and Iolaüs to Delphi to inquire of Apollo what he must do to heal the malady, but Deianeira was so stricken by the magnitude of Heracles' misfortune that, being conscious of her error, she ended her life by hanging herself. The god gave the reply that Heracles should be taken, and with him his armour and weapons of war, unto Oete and that they should build a huge pyre near him; what remained to be done, he said, would rest with Zeus. Now when Iolaüs had carried out these orders and had withdrawn to a distance to see what would take place, Heracles, having abandoned hope for himself, ascended the pyre and asked each one who came up to him to put torch to the pyre. And when no one had the courage to obey him Philoctetes alone was prevailed upon; and he, having received in return for his compliance the gift of the bow and arrows of Heracles, lighted the pyre. And immediately lightning also fell from the heavens and the pyre was wholly consumed. After this, when the companions of Iolaüs came to gather up the bones of Heracles and found not a single bone anywhere, they assumed that, in accordance with the words of the oracle, he had passed from among men into the company of the gods.

**39.** These men, therefore, performed the offerings to the dead as to a hero, and after throwing up a great mound of earth returned to Trachis. Following their example Menoetius, the son of Actor and a friend of Heracles, sacrificed a boar and a bull and a ram to him as to a hero and commanded that each year in Opus Heracles should receive the sacrifices and honours of a hero. Much the same thing was likewise done by the Thebans, but the Athenians were the first of all other men to honour Heracles with sacrifices like as to a god, and by holding up as an example for all other men to follow their own reverence for the god they induced the Greeks first of all, and after them all men throughout the inhabited world, to honour Heracles as a god.

We should add to what has been said about Heracles, that after his apotheosis Zeus persuaded Hera to adopt him as her son and henceforth for all time to cherish him with a mother's love, and this adoption, they say, took place in the following manner. Hera lay upon a bed, and drawing Heracles close to her body then let him fall through her garments to the ground, imitating in this way the actual birth; and this ceremony is observed to this day by the barbarians whenever they wish to adopt a son. Hera, the myths relate, after she had adopted Heracles in this fashion, joined him in marriage to Hebe, regarding whom the poet speaks in the "Necyïa":

> I saw the shade of Heracles, but for
> Himself he takes delight of feasts among
> Th' immortal gods and for his wife he hath
> The shapely-ankled Hebê.

They report of Heracles further that Zeus enrolled him among the twelve gods but that he would not accept this honour; for it was impossible for him thus to be enrolled unless one of the twelve gods were first cast out; hence in his eyes it would be monstrous for him to accept an honour which involved depriving another god of his honour.

Now on the subject of Heracles if we have dwelt over-long, we have at least omitted nothing from the myths which are related concerning him.

### On the Argonauts and Medea and the daughters of Pelias (40-56).

**40.** As for the Argonauts, since Heracles joined them in their campaign, it may be appropriate to speak of them in this connection.

This is the account which is given: Jason was the son of Aeson and the nephew through his father of Pelias, the king of the Thessalians, and excelling as he did above those of his years in strength of body and nobility of spirit he was eager to accomplish a deed worthy of memory. Since he observed that of the men of former times Perseus and certain others had gained glory which was held in everlasting remembrance from the campaigns which they had waged in foreign lands and the hazard attending the labours they had performed, he was eager to follow the examples they had set. As a consequence he revealed his undertaking to the king and quickly received his approval. It was not so much that Pelias was eager to bring distinction to the youth as that he hoped that in the hazardous expeditions he would lose his life; for he himself had been deprived by nature of any male children and was fearful that his brother, with his son to aid him, would make an attempt upon the kingdom. Hiding, however, this suspicion and promising to supply everything which would be needed for the expedition, he urged Jason to undertake an exploit by sailing to Colchis after the renowned golden-fleeced skin of the ram. The Pontus at that time was inhabited on all its shores by nations which were barbarous and altogether fierce and was called "Axenos" [hostile to strangers], since the natives were in the habit of slaying the strangers who landed on its shores. Jason, who was eager for glory, recognising that the labour was difficult of accomplishment and yet not altogether impossible, and concluding that for this very reason the greater renown would attach to himself, made ready everything needed for the undertaking.

**41.** First of all, in the vicinity of Mount Pelion he built a ship which far surpassed in its size and in its equipment in general any vessel known in those days, since the men of that time put to sea on rafts or in very small boats. Consequently those who saw the ship at the time were greatly astonished, and when the report was noised about throughout Greece both of the exploit and of the enterprise of building the ship, no small number of the youths of prominence were eager to take part in the expedition. Jason, then, after he had launched the ship and fitted it out in brilliant fashion with everything which would astonish the mind, picked out the most renowned chieftains from those who were eager to share his plan, with the result that the whole number of those in his company amounted to fifty-four. Of these the most famous were Castor and Polydeuces, Heracles and Telamon, Orpheus and Atalante the daughter of Schoeneus, and the sons of Thespius, and the leader himself who was setting out on the voyage to Colchis. The vessel was called Argo after Argus, as some writers of myths record, who was the master-builder of the ship and went along on the voyage in order to repair the parts of the vessel as they were strained from time to time, but, as some say, after its exceeding great swiftness, since the ancients called what is swift *argos*. Now after the chieftains had gathered together they chose Heracles to be their general, preferring him because of his courage.

**42.** After they had sailed from Iolcus, the account continues, and had gone past Athos and Samothrace, they encountered a storm and were carried to Sigeium in the Troad. When they disembarked there, it is said, they discovered a maiden bound in chains upon the shore, the reason for it being as follows. Poseidon, as the story runs, became angry with Laomedon the king of Troy in connection with the building of its walls, according to the mythical story, and sent forth from the sea a monster to ravage the land. By this monster those who made their living by the seashore and the farmers who tilled the land contiguous to the sea were being surprised and carried off. Furthermore, a pestilence fell upon the people and a total destruction of their crops, so that all the inhabitants were at their wits' end because of the magnitude of what had befallen them. Consequently the common crowd gathered together into an assembly and sought for a deliverance from their misfortunes, and the king, it is said, dispatched a mission to Apollo to inquire of the god regarding what had befallen them. When the oracle, then, became known, which told that the cause was the anger of Poseidon and that only then would it cease when the Trojans should of their free will select by lot one of their children and deliver him to the monster for his food, although all the children submitted to the lot, it fell upon the king's daughter Hesione. Consequently Laomedon was constrained by necessity to deliver the maiden and to leave her, bound in chains, upon the shore. Here

Heracles, when he had disembarked with the Argonauts and learned from the girl of her sudden change of fortune, rent asunder the chains which were about her body and going up to the city made an offer to the king to slay the monster. When Laomedon accepted the proposal and promised to give him as his reward his invincible mares, Heracles, they say, did slay the monster and Hesione was given the choice either to leave her home with her saviour or to remain in her native land with her parents. The girl, then, chose to spend her life with the stranger, not merely because she preferred the benefaction she had received to the ties of kinship, but also because she feared that a monster might again appear and she be exposed by the citizens to the same fate as that from which she had just escaped. As for Heracles, after he had been splendidly honoured with gifts and the appropriate tokens of hospitality, he left Hesione and the mares in keeping with Laomedon, having arranged that after he had returned from Colchis, he should receive them again; he then set sail with all haste in the company of the Argonauts to accomplish the labour which lay before them.

43. But there came on a great storm and the chieftains had given up hope of being saved, when Orpheus, they say, who was the only one on shipboard who had ever been initiated in the mysteries of the deities of Samothrace [the Cabeiri], offered to these deities the prayers for their salvation. And immediately the wind died down and two stars fell over the heads of the Dioscori, and the whole company was amazed at the marvel which had taken place and concluded that they had been rescued from their perils by an act of Providence of the gods. For this reason, the story of this reversal of fortune for the Argonauts has been handed down to succeeding generations, and sailors when caught in storms always direct their prayers to the deities of Samothrace and attribute the appearance of the two stars to the epiphany of the Dioscori.

At that time, however, the tale continues, when the storm had abated, the chieftains landed in Thrace on the country which was ruled over by Phineus. Here they came upon two youths who by way of punishment had been shut within a burial vault where they were being subjected to continual blows of the whip; these were sons of Phineus and Cleopatra, who men said was born of Oreithyia, the daughter of Erechtheus, and Boreas, and had unjustly been subjected to such a punishment because of the unscrupulousness and lying accusations of their mother-in-law. For Phineus had married Idaea, the daughter of Dardanus the king of the Scythians, and yielding to her every desire out of his love for her he had believed her charge that his sons by an earlier marriage had insolently offered violence to their mother-in-law out of a desire to please their mother. When Heracles and his friends unexpectedly appeared, the youths who were suffering these tortures, they say, made supplication to the chieftains as they would to gods, and setting forth the causes of their father's unlawful conduct implored that they be delivered from their unfortunate lot.

44. Phineus, however, the account continues, met the strangers with bitter words and ordered them not to busy themselves with his affairs; for no father, he said, exacts punishment of his sons of his free will, unless they have overcome, by the magnitude of their crimes, the natural love which parents bear towards their children. Thereupon the young men, who were known as Boreadae [sons of Boreas] and were of the company which sailed with Heracles, since they were

brothers of Cleopatra, and because of their kinship with the: young men, were the first, it is said, to rush to their aid, and they tore apart the chains which encircled them and slew such barbarians as offered resistance. When Phineus hastened to join battle with them and the Thracian multitude ran together, Heracles, they say, who performed the mightiest deeds of them all, slew Phineus himself and no small number of the rest, and finally capturing the royal palace led Cleopatra forth from out the prison, and restored to the sons of Phineus their ancestral rule, but when the sons wished to put their stepmother to death under torture, Heracles persuaded them to renounce such a vengeance, and so the sons, sending her to her father in Scythia, urged that she be punished for her wicked treatment of them. This was done; the Scythian condemned his daughter to death, and the sons of Cleopatra gained in this way among the Thracians a reputation for equitable dealing.

I am not unaware that certain writers of myths say that the sons of Phineus were blinded by their father and that Phineus suffered the like fate at the hands of Boreas. Likewise certain writers have passed down the account that Heracles, when he went ashore once in Asia to get water, was left behind in the country by the Argonauts. As a general thing, we find that the ancient myths do not give us a simple and consistent story; consequently it should occasion no surprise if we find, when we put the ancient accounts together, that in some details they are not in agreement with those given by every poet and historian.

At any rate, according to these ancient accounts, the sons of Phineus turned over the kingdom to their mother Cleopatra and joined with the chieftains in the expedition. And after they had set sail from Thrace and had entered the Pontus, they put in at the Tauric Chersonese, being ignorant of the savage ways of the native people. For it is customary among the barbarians who inhabit this land to sacrifice to Artemis Tauropolus the strangers who put in there, and it is among them, they say, that at a later time Iphigeneia became a priestess of this goddess and sacrificed to her those who were taken captive.

**45.** Since it is the task of history to inquire into the reasons for this slaying of strangers, we must discuss these reasons briefly, especially since the digression on this subject will be appropriate in connection with the deeds of the Argonauts. We are told, that is, that Helius had two sons, Aeëtes and Perses, Aeëtes being king of Colchis and the other king of the Tauric Chersonese, and that both of them were exceedingly cruel. Perses had a daughter Hecate, who surpassed her father in boldness and lawlessness; she was also fond of hunting, and when she had no luck she would turn her arrows upon human beings instead of the beasts. Being likewise ingenious in the mixing of deadly poisons she discovered the drug called aconite and tried out the strength of each poison by mixing it in the food given to the strangers. Since she possessed great experience in such matters she first of all poisoned her father and so succeeded to the throne, and then, founding a temple of Artemis and commanding that strangers who landed there should be sacrificed to the goddess, she became known far and wide for her cruelty. After this she married Aeëtes and bore two daughters, Circe and Medea, and a son Aegialeus.

Although Circe also, it is said, devoted herself to the devising of all kinds of drugs and discovered roots of all manner of natures and potencies such as are difficult to credit, yet, notwithstanding that she was taught by her mother Hecate about not a few drugs, she discovered by her own study a far greater number, so that she left to the other woman no superiority whatever in the matter of devising uses of drugs. She was given in marriage to the king of the Sarmatians, whom some call Scythians, and first she poisoned her husband and after that, succeeding to the throne, she committed many cruel and violent acts against her subjects. For this reason she was deposed from her throne and, according to some writers of myths, fled to the ocean, where she seized a desert island, and there established herself with the women who had fled with her, though according to some historians she left the Pontus and settled in Italy on a promontory which to this day bears after her the name Circaeum.

**46.** Concerning Medea this story is related: From her mother and sister she learned all the powers which drugs possess, but her purpose in using them was exactly the opposite. For she made a practice of rescuing from their perils the strangers who came to their shores, sometimes demanding from her father by entreaty and coaxing that the lives be spared of those who were to die, and sometimes herself releasing them from prison and then devising plans for the safety of the unfortunate men. For Aeëtes, partly because . of his own natural cruelty and partly because he was under the influence of his wife Hecate, had given his approval to the custom of slaying strangers. Since Medea as time went on opposed the purpose of her parents more and more, Aeëtes, they say, suspecting his daughter of plotting against him consigned her to free custody; Medea, however, made her escape and fled for refuge to a sacred precinct of Helius on the shore of the sea. This happened at the very time when the Argonauts arrived from the Tauric Chersonese and landed by night in Colchis at this precinct. There they came upon Medea, as she wandered along the shore, and learning from her of the custom of slaying strangers they praised the maiden for her kindly spirit, and then, revealing to her their own project, they learned in turn from her of the danger which threatened her from her father because of the reverence which she showed to strangers. Since they now recognised that it was to their mutual advantage, Medea promised to co-operate with them until they should perform the labour which lay before them, while Jason gave her his pledge under oath that he would marry her and keep her as his life's companion so long as he lived. After this the Argonauts left guards to watch the ship and set off by night with Medea to get the golden fleece, concerning which it may be proper for us to give a detailed account, in order that nothing which belongs to the history which we have undertaken may remain unknown.

**47.** Phrixus, the son of Athamas, the myths relate, because of his stepmother's plots against him, took his sister Helle and fled with her from Greece. While they were making the passage from Europe to Asia, as a kind of Providence of the gods directed, on the back of a ram, whose fleece was of gold, the maiden fell into the sea, which was named after her Hellespont [Sea of Helle], but Phrixus continued on into the Pontus and was carried to Colchis, where, as some oracle had commanded, he sacrificed the ram and hung up its fleece as a dedicatory offering in the temple of Ares. After this, while Aeëtes was king of Colchis, an oracle became known, to the effect that he was to come to the end of his life whenever strangers should land there and carry off the golden fleece. For this

BOOK IV

reason and because of his own cruelty as well, Aeëtes ordained that strangers should be offered up in sacrifice, in order that, the report of the cruelty of the Colchi having been spread abroad to every part of the world, no stranger should have the courage to set foot on the land. He also threw a wall about the precinct and stationed there many guardians, these being men of the Tauric Chersonese, and it is because of these guards that the Greeks invented monstrous myths. For instance, the report was spread abroad that there were fire-breathing bulls (*tauroi*) round about the precinct and that a sleepless dragon (*drakon*) guarded the fleece, the identity of the names having led to the transfer from the men who were Taurians to the cattle because of their strength and the cruelty shown in the murder of strangers having been made into the myth of the bulls breathing fire; and similarly the name of the guardian who watched over the sacred precinct, which was Dracon, has been transferred by the poets to the monstrous and fear-inspiring beast, the dragon. Also the account of Phrixus underwent a similar working into a myth. For, as some men say, he made his voyage upon a ship which bore the head of a ram upon its bow, and Helle, being troubled with seasickness, while leaning far over the side of the boat for this reason, fell into the sea. Some say, however, that the king of the Scythians, who was a son-in-law of Aeëtes, was visiting among the Colchi at the very time when, as it happened, Phrixus and his attendant were taken captive, and conceiving a passion for the boy he received him from Aeëtes as a gift, loved him like a son of his own loins, and left his kingdom to him. The attendant, however, whose name was Crius (ram), was sacrificed to the gods, and when his body had been flayed the skin was nailed up on the temple, in keeping with a certain custom. When later an oracle was delivered to Aeëtes to the effect that he was to die whenever strangers would sail to his land and carry off the skin of Crius, the king, they say, built a wall about the precinct and stationed a guard over it; furthermore, he gilded the skin in order that by reason of its brilliant appearance the soldiers should consider it worthy of the most careful guarding. As for these matters, however, it rests with my readers to judge each in accordance with his own predilections.

**48.** Medea, we are told, led the way for the Argonauts to the sacred precinct of Ares, which was seventy stades distant from the city which was called Sybaris and contained the palace of the rulers of the Colchi. Approaching the gates, which were kept closed at night, she addressed the guards in the Tauric speech. And when the soldiers readily opened the gates to her as being the king's daughter, the Argonauts, they say, rushing in with drawn swords slew many of the barbarians and drove the rest, who were struck with terror by the unexpected happening, out of the precinct, and then, taking with them the fleece, made for the ship with all speed. Medea likewise, assisting the Argonauts, slew with poisons the dragon which, according to the myths, never slept as it lay coiled about the fleece in the precinct, and made her way with Jason down to the sea. The Tauri who had escaped by flight reported to the king the attack which had been made upon them, and Aeëtes, they say, took with him the soldiers who guarded his person, set out in pursuit of the Greeks, and came upon them near the sea. Joining battle on the first contact with them, he slew one of the Argonauts, Iphitus, the brother of that Eurystheus who had laid the Labours upon Heracles, but soon, when he enveloped the rest of them with the multitude of his followers and pressed too hotly into the fray, he was slain by Meleager. The moment the king fell, the Greeks took courage, and the Colchi turned in flight and the larger part of them were slain in the pursuit. There were wounded among the chieftains Jason, Laërtes, Atalantê, and the sons of Thespius, as they are called. However they were all healed in a few days, they say, by Medea by means of roots and certain herbs, and the Argonauts, after securing provisions for themselves, set out to sea, and they had already reached the middle of the Pontic sea when they ran into a storm which put them in the greatest peril, but when Orpheus, as on the former occasion, offered up prayers to the deities of Samothrace, the winds ceased and there appeared near the ship Glaucus the Sea-god, as he is called. The god accompanied the ship in its voyage without ceasing for two days and nights and foretold to Heracles his Labours and immortality, and to the Tyndaridae that they should be called Dioscori ("Sons of Zeus") and receive at the hands of all mankind honour like that offered to the gods. And, in general, he addressed all the Argonauts by name and told them that because of the prayers of Orpheus he had appeared in accordance with a Providence of the gods and was showing forth to them what was destined to take place; and he counselled them, accordingly, that so soon as they touched land they should pay their vows to the gods through the intervention of whom they had twice already been saved.

**49.** After this, the account continues, Glaucus sank back beneath the deep, and the Argonauts, arriving at the mouth of the Pontus, put in to the land, the king of the country being at that time Byzas, after whom the city of Byzantium was named. There they set up altars, and when they had paid their vows to the gods they sanctified the place, which is even to this day held in honour by the sailors who pass by. After this they put out to sea, and after sailing through the Propontis and Hellespont they landed at the Troad. Here, when Heracles dispatched to the city his brother Iphiclus and Telamon to demand back both the mares and Hesione, Laomedon, it is said, threw the ambassadors into prison and planned to lay an ambush for the other Argonauts and encompass their death. He had the rest of his sons as willing aids in the deed, but Priam alone opposed it; for he declared that Laomedon should observe justice in his dealings with the strangers and should deliver to them both his sister and the mares which had been promised. When no one paid any heed to Priam, he brought two swords to the prison, they say, and gave them secretly to Telamon and his companions, and by disclosing the plan of his father he became the cause of their deliverance. For immediately Telamon and his companions slew such of the guards as offered resistance, and fleeing to the sea gave the Argonauts a full account of what had happened. Accordingly, these got ready for battle and went out to meet the forces which were pouring out of the city with the king. There was a sharp battle, but their courage gave the chieftains the upper hand, and Heracles, the myths report, performed the bravest feats of them all; for he slew Laomedon, and taking the city at the first assault he punished those who were parties with the king to the plot, but to Priam, because of the spirit of justice he had shown, he gave the kingship, entered into a league of friendship with him, and then sailed away in company with the Argonauts. Certain of the ancient poets have handed down the account that Heracles took Troy, not with the aid of the Argonauts, but on a campaign of his own with six ships, in order to get the mares; and Homer also adds his witness to this version in the following lines:

> Aye, what a man, they say, was Heracles
> In might, my father he, steadfast, with heart
> Of lion, who once came here to carry off
> The mares of King Laomedon, with but
> Six ships and scantier men, yet sacked he then
> The city of proud Ilium, and made
> Her streets bereft.

The Argonauts, they say, set forth from the Troad and arrived at Samothrace, where they again paid their vows to the great gods and dedicated in the sacred precinct the bowls which are preserved there even to this day.

50. While the return of the chieftains was as yet not known in Thessaly, a rumour, they say, went the rounds there that all the companions of Jason in the expedition had perished in the region of the Pontus. Consequently Pelias, thinking that an occasion was now come to do away with all who were waiting for the throne, forced the father of Jason to drink the blood of a bull, and murdered his brother Promachus, who was still a mere lad in years. But Amphinome, his mother, they say, when on the point of being slain, performed a manly deed and one worthy of mention; for fleeing to the hearth of the king she pronounced a curse against him, to the effect that he might suffer the fate which his impious deeds merited, and then, striking her own breast with a sword, she ended her life heroically. As for Pelias, when he had utterly destroyed in this fashion all the relatives of Jason, he speedily received the punishment befitting his impious deeds. For Jason, who had sailed that night into a roadstead which lay not far from Iolcus and yet was not in sight of the dwellers in the city, learned from one of the country-folk of the misfortunes which had befallen his kinsmen. Now all the chieftains stood ready to lend Jason their aid and to face any peril on his behalf, but they fell into dispute over how they should make the attack; some, for instance, advised that they force their way at once into the city and fall upon the king while he was not expecting them, but certain others declared that each one of them should gather soldiers from his own birthplace and then raise a general war; since it was impossible, they maintained, for fifty-three men to overcome a king who controlled an army and important cities. While they were in this perplexity Medea, it is said, promised to slay Pelias all alone by means of cunning and to deliver to the chieftains the royal palace without their running any risk. When they all expressed astonishment at her statement and sought to learn what sort of a scheme she had in mind, she said that she had brought with her many drugs of marvellous potency which had been discovered by her mother Hecate and by her sister Circe; and though before this time she had never used them to destroy human beings, on this occasion she would by means of them easily wreak vengeance upon men who were deserving of punishment. Then, after disclosing beforehand to the chieftains the detailed plans of the attack she would make, she promised them that she would give them a signal from the palace during the day by means of smoke, during the night by fire, in the direction of the look-out which stood high above the sea.

51. Then Medea, the tale goes on, fashioning a hollow image of Artemis secreted in it drugs of diverse natures, and as for herself, she anointed her hair with certain potent ointments and made it grey, and filled her face and body so full of wrinkles that all who looked upon her thought that she was surely an old

woman, and finally, taking with her the statue of the goddess which had been so made as to strike with terror the superstitious populace and move it to fear of the gods, at daybreak she entered the city. She acted like one inspired, and as the multitude rushed together along the streets she summoned the whole people to receive the goddess with reverence, telling them that the goddess had come to them from the Hyperboreans to bring good luck to both the whole city and the king. While all the inhabitants were rendering obeisance to the goddess and honouring her with sacrifices, and the whole city, in a word, was, along with Medea herself, acting like people inspired, she entered the palace, and there she threw Pelias into such a state of superstitious fear and, by her magic arts, so terrified his daughters that they believed that the goddess was actually there in person to bring prosperity to the house of the king. For she declared that Artemis, riding through the air upon a chariot drawn by dragons, had flown in the air over many parts of the inhabited earth and had chosen out the realm of the most pious king in all the world for the establishment of her own worship and for honours which should be for ever and ever; and that the goddess had commanded her not only to divest Pelias, by means of certain powers which she possessed, of his old age and make his body entirely young, but also to bestow upon him many other gifts, to the end that his life should be blessed and pleasing to the gods.

The king was filled with amazement at these astonishing proposals, but Medea, we are informed, promised him that then and there, in the case of her own body, she would furnish the proof of what she had said. Then she told one of the daughters of Pelias to bring pure water, and when the maiden at once carried out her request, she shut herself up, they say, in a small chamber and washing thoroughly her whole body she made it clean of the potent influences of the drugs. Being restored, then, to her former condition, and showing herself to the king, she amazed those who gazed upon her. and they thought that a kind of Providence of the gods had transformed her old age into a maiden's youth and striking beauty. Also, by means of certain drugs, Medea caused shapes of the dragons to appear, which she declared had brought the goddess through the air from the Hyperboreans to make her stay with Pelias. Since the deeds which Medea had performed appeared to be too great for mortal nature, and the king saw fit to regard her with great approval and, in a word, believed that she was telling the truth, she now. they say, in private conversation with Pelias urged him to order his daughters to co-operate with her and to do whatever she might command them; for it was fitting, she said, that the king's body should receive the favour which the gods were according to him through the hands, not of servants, but of his own children. Consequently Pelias gave explicit directions to his daughters to do everything that Medea might command them with respect to the body of their father, and the maidens were quite ready to carry out her orders.

**52.** Medea then, the story relates, when night had come and Pelias had fallen asleep, informed the daughters that it was required that the body of Pelias be boiled in a cauldron. When the maidens received the proposal with hostility, she devised a second proof that what she said could be believed, for there was a ram full of years which was kept in their home, and she announced to the maidens that she would first boil it and thus make it into a lamb again. When they agreed to this, we are told that Medea severed it apart limb by limb, boiled the ram's body, and then, working a deception by means of certain drugs, she drew out of the cauldron an image which looked like a lamb. Thereupon the maidens were astounded, and were so convinced that they had received all possible proofs that she could do what she was promising that they carried out her orders. All the rest of them beat their father to death, but Alcestis alone, because of her great piety, would not lay hands upon him who had begotten her.

After Pelias had been slain in this way, Medea, they say, took no part in cutting the body to pieces or in boiling it, but pretending that she must first offer prayers to the moon, she caused the maidens to ascend with lamps to the highest part of the roof of the palace, while she herself took much time repeating a long prayer in the Colchian speech, thus affording an interval to those who were to make the attack. Consequently the Argonauts, when from their look-out they made out the fire, believing that the slaying of the king had been accomplished, hastened to the city on the run, and passing inside the walls entered the palace with drawn swords and slew such guards as offered opposition. The daughters of Pelias, who had only at that moment descended from the roof to attend to the boiling of their father, when they saw to their surprise both Jason and the chieftains in the palace, were filled with dismay at what had befallen them; for it was not within their power to avenge themselves on Medea, nor could they by deceit make amends for the abominable act which they had done. Consequently the daughters, it is related, were about to make an end of their lives. but Jason, taking pity upon their distress, restrained them, and exhorting them to be of good courage, showed them that it was not from evil design that they had done wrong but it was against their will and because of deception that they had suffered this misfortune.

53. Jason now, we are informed, promising all his kindred in general that he would conduct himself honourably and magnanimously, summoned the people to an assembly. After defending himself for what he had done and explaining that he had only taken vengeance on men who had wronged him first, inflicting a less severe punishment on them than the evils he himself had suffered, he bestowed upon Acastus, the son of Pelias, the ancestral kingdom, and as for the daughters of the king, he said that he considered it right that he himself should assume the responsibility for them. And ultimately he fulfilled his promise, they say, by joining them all in marriage after a time to the most renowned men. Alcestis, for instance, the eldest he gave in marriage to Admetus of Thessaly, the son of Pheres, Amphinome to Andraemon, the brother of Leonteus. Euadne to Canes, who was the son of Cephalus and king at that time of the Phocians. These marriages he arranged at a later period; but at the time in question, sailing together with the chieftains to the Isthmus of Peloponnesus, he performed a sacrifice to Poseidon and also dedicated to the god the ship Argo, and since he received a great welcome at the court of Creon, the king of the Corinthians, he became a citizen of that city and spent the rest of his days in Corinth.

When the Argonauts were on the point of separating and departing to their native lands, Heracles, they say, proposed to the chieftains that, in view of the unexpected turns fortune takes, they should exchange oaths among one another to fight at the side of anyone of their number who should call for aid; and that, furthermore, they should choose out the most excellent place in Greece, there to institute games and a festival for the whole race, and should dedicate the games to the greatest of the gods, Olympian Zeus. After the chieftains had taken their oath concerning the alliance and had entrusted Heracles with the management of the games, he, they say, picked the place for the festival on the bank of the Alpheius river in the land of the Eleans. Accordingly, this place beside the river he made sacred to the greatest of the gods and called it Olympia after his appellation. When he had instituted horse-races and gymnastic contests, he fixed the rules governing the events and then dispatched sacred commissioners to announce to the cities the spectacle of the games. Although Heracles had won no moderate degree of fame because of the high esteem in which he was held by the Argonauts throughout their expedition, to this was now added the glory of having founded the festival at Olympia, so that he was the most renowned man among all the Greeks and, known as he was in almost every state, there were many who sought his friendship and who were eager to share with him in every danger. Since he was an object of admiration because of his bravery and his skill as a general, he gathered a most powerful army and visited all the inhabited world, conferring his benefactions upon the race of men, and it was in return for these that with general approval he received the gift of immortality. The poets, following their custom of giving a tale of wonder, have recounted the myth that Heracles, single-handed and without the aid of armed forces, performed the Labours which are on the lips of all.

**54.** We have now recounted all the myths which are told about this god, and at this time must add what remains to be said about Jason. The account runs like this: Jason made his home in Corinth and living with Medea as his wife for ten years be begat children by her, the two oldest, Thessalus and Alcimenes, being twins, and the third, Tisandrus, being much younger than the other two. Now during this period, we are informed, Medea was highly approved by her husband, because she not only excelled in beauty but was adorned with modesty and every other virtue; but afterward, as time more and more diminished her natural comeliness, Jason, it is said, became enamoured of Glaucê, Creon's daughter, and sought the maiden's hand in marriage. After her father had given his consent and had set a day for the marriage, Jason, they say, at first tried to persuade Medea to withdraw from their wedlock of her free-will; for, he told her, he desired to marry the maiden, not because he felt his relations with Medea were beneath him, but because he was eager to establish a kinship between the king's house and his children. When his wife was angered and called upon the gods who had been the witnesses of their vows, they say that Jason, disdaining the vows, married the daughter of the king. Thereupon Medea was driven out of the city, and being allowed by Creon but one day to make the preparations for her exile, she entered the palace by night, having altered her appearance by means of drugs, and set fire to the building by applying to it a little root which had been discovered by her sister Circê and had the property that when it was once kindled it was hard to put out. Now when the palace suddenly burst into flames, Jason quickly made his way out of it, but as for Glaucê and Creon, the fire hemmed them in on all sides and they were consumed by it. Certain historians, however, say that the sons of Medea brought to the bride gifts which had been anointed with poisons, and that when Glaucê took them and put them about her body both she herself met her end and her father, when he ran to help her and embraced her body, likewise perished.

Although Medea had been successful in her first undertakings, yet she did not refrain, so we are told, from taking her revenge upon Jason. For she had come to such a state of rage and jealousy, yes, even of savageness, that, since he had escaped from the peril which threatened him at the same time as his bride, she determined, by the murder of the children of them both, to plunge him into the deepest misfortunes; for, except for the one son who made his escape from her, she slew the other sons and in company with her most faithful maids fled in the dead of night from Corinth and made her way safely to Heracles in Thebes. Her reason for doing so was that Heracles had acted as a mediator in connection with the agreements which had been entered into in the land of the Colchians and had promised to come to her aid if she should ever find them violated.

**55.** Meanwhile, they go on to say, in the opinion of everyone Jason, in losing children and wife, had suffered only what was just; consequently, being unable to endure the magnitude of the affliction, he put an end to his life. The Corinthians were greatly distressed at such a terrible reversal of fortune and were especially perplexed about the burial of the children. Accordingly, they dispatched messengers to Pytho to inquire of the god what should be done with the bodies of the children, and the Pythian priestess commanded them to bury the children in the sacred precinct of Hera and to pay them the honours which are accorded to heroes. After the Corinthians had performed this command, Thessalus, they say, who had escaped being murdered by his mother, was reared as a youth in Corinth and then removed to Iolcus, which was the native land of Jason; and finding on his arrival that Acastus, the son of Pelias, had recently died, he took over the throne which belonged to him by inheritance and called the people who were subject to himself Thessalians after his own name. I am not unaware that this is not the only explanation given of the name the Thessalians bear, but the fact is that the other accounts which have been handed down to us are likewise at variance with one another, and concerning these we shall speak on a more appropriate occasion.

Now as for Medea, they say, on finding upon her arrival in Thebes that Heracles was possessed of a frenzy of madness and had slain his sons, she restored him to health by means of drugs. But since Eurystheus was pressing Heracles with his commands, she despaired of receiving any aid from him at the moment and sought refuge in Athens with Aegeus, the son of Pandion. Here, as some say, she married Aegeus and gave birth to Medus, who was later king of Media, but certain writers give the account that, when her person was demanded by Hippotes, the son of Creon, she was granted a trial and cleared of the charges he raised against her. After this, when Theseus returned to Athens from Troezen, a charge of poisoning was brought against her and she was exiled from the city; but by the gift of Aegeus she received an escort to go with her to whatever country she might wish and she came to Phoenicia. From there she journeyed into the interior regions of Asia and married a certain king of renown, to whom she bore a son Medus; and the son, succeeding to the throne after the death of the father, was greatly admired for his courage and named the people Medes after himself.

**56.** Speaking generally, it is because of the desire of the tragic poets for the marvellous that so varied and inconsistent an account of Medea has been given out; and some indeed, in their desire to win favour with the Athenians, say that she took that Medus whom she bore to Aegeus and got off safe to Colchis; and at that time Aeëtes, who had been forcibly driven from the throne by his brother Perses, had regained his kingdom, Medus, Medea's son, having slain Perses; and that afterwards Medus, securing the command of an army, advanced over a large part of Asia which lies above the Pontus and secured possession of Media, which has been named after this Medus. Since in our judgment it is unnecessary and would be tedious to record all the assertions which the writers of myths have made about Medea, we shall add only those items which have been passed over concerning the history of the Argonauts.

Not a few both of the ancient historians and of the later ones as well, one of whom is Timaeus, say that the Argonauts, after the seizure of the fleece, learning that the mouth of the Pontus had already been blockaded by the fleet of Aeëtes, performed an amazing exploit which is worthy of mention. They sailed, that is to say, up the Tanais river [the Don] as far as its sources, and at a certain place they hauled the ship overland, and following in turn another river which flows into the ocean they sailed down it to the sea; then they made their course from the north to the west, keeping the land on the left, and when they had arrived near Gadeira (Cadiz) they sailed into our sea. The writers even offer proofs of these things, pointing out that the Celts who dwell along the ocean venerate the Dioscori above any of the gods, since they have a tradition handed down from ancient times that these gods appeared among them coming from the ocean. Moreover, the country which skirts the ocean bears, they say, not a few names which are derived from the Argonauts and the Dioscori. Likewise the continent this side of Gadeira contains visible tokens of the return voyage of the Argonauts. So, for example, as they sailed about the Tyrrhenian Sea, when they put in at an island called Aethaleia [Elba] they named its harbour, which is the fairest of any in those regions, Argoön [Portus Argous] after their ship, and such has remained its name to this day. In like manner to what we have just narrated a harbour in Etruria eight hundred stades from Rome was named by them Telamon, and also at Phormia [Formiae] in Italy the harbour Aeëtes, which is now known as Caeëtes [Gaeta]. Furthermore, when they were driven by winds to the Syrtes and had learned from Triton, who was king of Libya at that time, of the peculiar nature of the sea there, upon escaping safe out of the peril they presented him with the bronze tripod which was inscribed with ancient characters and stood until rather recent times among the people of Euhesperis [Berenicê].

We must not leave un-refuted the account of those who state that the Argonauts sailed up the Ister [Danube] river as far as its sources and then, by its arm which flows in the opposite direction, descended to the Adriatic Gulf. For time has refuted those who assumed that the Ister which empties by several mouths into the Pontus and the Ister which issues into the Adriatic flow from the same regions. As a matter of fact, when the Romans subdued the nation of the Istrians it was discovered that the latter river has its sources only forty stades from the sea. The cause of the error on the part of the historians was, they say, the identity in name of the two rivers.

### On the descendants of Heracles (57-58).

**57.** Since we have sufficiently elaborated the history of the Argonauts and the deeds accomplished by Heracles, it may be appropriate also to record, in accordance with the promise we made, the deeds of his sons.

Now after the deification of Heracles his sons made their home in Trachis at the court of Ceÿx the king, but later, when Hyllus and some of the others had attained to manhood, Eurystheus, being afraid lest, after they had all come of age, he might be driven from his kingdom at Mycenae, decided to send the Heracleidae into exile from the whole of Greece. Consequently he served notice upon Ceÿx, the king, to banish both the Heracleidae and the sons of Licymnius, and Iolaüs as well and the band of Arcadians who had served with Heracles on his campaigns, adding that, if he should fail to do these things, he must submit to war. The Heracleidae and their friends, perceiving that they were of themselves not sufficient in number to carry on a war against Eurystheus, decided to leave Trachis of their own free will, and going about among the most important of the other cities they asked them to receive them as fellow-townsmen. When no other city had the courage to take them in, the Athenians alone of all, such being their inborn sense of justice, extended a welcome to the sons of Heracles, and they settled them and their companions in the flight in the city of Tricorythus, which is one of the cities of what is called the Tetrapolis. After some time, when all the sons of Heracles had attained to manhood and a spirit of pride sprang up in the young men because of the glory of descent from Heracles, Eurystheus, viewing with suspicion their growing power, came up against them with a great army, but the Heracleidae, who had the aid of the Athenians, chose as their leader Iolaüs, the nephew of Heracles, and after entrusting to him and Theseus and Hyllus the direction of the war, they defeated Eurystheus in a pitched battle. In the course of the battle the larger part of the army of Eurystheus was slain and Eurystheus himself, when his chariot was wrecked in the flight, was killed by Hyllus, the son of Heracles; likewise the sons of Eurystheus perished in the battle to a man.

**58.** After these events all the Heracleidae, now that they had conquered Eurystheus in a battle whose fame was noised abroad and were well supplied with allies because of their success, embarked upon a campaign against Peloponnesus with Hyllus as their commander. Atreus, after the death of Eurystheus, had taken over the kingship in Mycenae, and having added to his forces the Tegeatans and certain other peoples as allies, he went forth to meet the Heracleidae. When the two armies were assembled at the Isthmus, Hyllus, Heracles' son, challenged to single combat any one of the enemy who would face him, on the agreement that, if Hyllus should conquer his opponent, the Heracleidae should receive the kingdom of Eurystheus, but that, if Hyllus were defeated, the Heracleidae would not return to Peloponnesus for a period of fifty years. Echemus, the king of the Tegeatans, came out to meet the challenge, and in the single combat which followed Hyllus was slain and the Heracleidae gave up, as they had promised, their effort to return and made their way back to Tricorythus. Some time later Licymnius and his sons and Tlepolemus, the son of Heracles, made their home in Argos, the Argives admitting them to citizenship of their own accord; but all the rest who had made their homes in Tricorythus, when the fifty-year period had expired, returned to Peloponnesus. Their deeds we shall record when we have come to those times.

Alcmene returned to Thebes, and when some time later she vanished from sight she received divine honours at the hands of the Thebans. The rest of the Heracleidae, they say, came to Aegimius, the son of Dorus, and demanding back the land which their father had entrusted to him made their home among the Dorians, but Tlepolemus, the son of Heracles, while he dwelt in Argos, slew Licymnius, the son of Electryon, we are told, in a quarrel over a certain matter, and being exiled from Argos because of this murder changed his residence to Rhodes. This island was inhabited at that time by Greeks who had been planted there by Triopas, the son of Phorbas. Accordingly, Tlepolemus, acting with the common consent of the natives, divided Rhodes into three parts and founded there three cities, Lindus, Ielysus (Ialysus), and Cameirus; and he became king over all the Rhodians, because of the fame of his father Heracles, and in later times took part with Agamemnon in the war against Troy.

## On Theseus and his labours (59-63)

**59.** But since we have set forth the facts concerning Heracles and his descendants, it will be appropriate in this connexion to speak of Theseus, since he emulated the Labours of Heracles. Theseus, then, was born of Aethra, the daughter of Pittheus, and Poseidon, and was reared in Troezen at the home of Pittheus, his mother's father, and after he had found and taken up the tokens which, as the myths relate, had been placed by Aegeus beneath a certain rock, he came to Athens. And taking the road along the coast, as men say, since he emulated the high achievements of Heracles, he set about performing Labours which would bring him both approbation and fame. The first, then, whom he slew was he who was called Corynetes [club-bearer] who carried a *korynê,* as it was called, or club, which was the weapon with which he fought, and with it killed any who passed by, and the second was Sinis who made his home on the Isthmus. Sinis, it should be explained, used to bend over two pines, fasten one arm to each of them, and then suddenly release the pines, the result being that the bodies were pulled asunder by the force of the pines and the unfortunate victims met a death of great anguish. For his third deed he slew the wild sow which had its haunts about Crommyon, a beast which excelled in both ferocity and size and was killing many human beings. Then he punished Sceiron who made his home in the rocks of Megaris which are called after him the Sceironian Rocks. This man, namely, made it his practice to compel those who passed by to wash his feet at a precipitous place, and then, suddenly giving them a kick, he would roll them down the crags into the sea at a place called Chelonê. Near Eleusis he slew Cercyon, who wrestled with those who passed by and killed whomever he could defeat. After this he put to death Procrustes, as he was called, who dwelt in what was known as Corydallus in Attica; this man compelled the travellers who passed by to lie down upon a bed, and if any were too long for the bed he cut off the parts of their body which protruded, while in the case of such as were too short for it he stretched (*prokrouein*) their legs, this being the reason why he was given the name Procrustes. After successfully accomplishing the deeds which we have mentioned, Theseus came to Athens and by means of the tokens caused

Aegeus to recognise him. Then he grappled with the Marathonian bull which Heracles in the performance of one of his Labours had brought from Crete to the Peloponnesus, and mastering the animal he brought it to Athens; this bull Aegeus received from him and sacrificed to Apollo.

**60.** It remains for us now to speak of the Minotaur which was slain by Theseus, in order that we may complete our account of the deeds of Theseus, but we must revert to earlier times and set forth the facts which are interwoven with this performance, in order that the whole narrative may be clear.

Tectamus, the son of Dorus, the son of Hellen, the son of Deucalion, sailed to Crete with Aeolians and Pelasgians and became king of the island, and marrying the daughter of Cretheus he begat Asterius. During the time when he was king in Crete Zeus, as they say, carried off Europe from Phoenicia, and carrying her across to Crete upon the back of a bull, he lay with her there and begat three sons, Minos, Rhadamanthys, and Sarpedon. After this Asterius, the king of Crete, took Europe to wife; and since he was without children by her he adopted the sons of Zeus and left them at his death to succeed to the kingdom. As for these children, Rhadamanthys gave the Cretans their laws, and Minos, succeeding to the throne and marrying Itone, the daughter of Lyctius, begat Lycastus, who in turn succeeded to the supreme power and marrying Ide, the daughter of Corybas, begat the second Minos, who, as some writers record, was the son of Zeus. This Minos was the first Greek to create a powerful naval force and to become master of the sea. And marrying Pasiphae, the daughter of Helius and Crete, he begat Deucalion and Catreus and Androgeos and Ariadnê and had other, natural, children more in number than these. As for the sons of Minos, Androgeos came to Athens at the time of the Panathenaic festival, while Aegeus was king, and defeating all the contestants in the games he became a close friend of the sons of Pallas. Thereupon Aegeus, viewing with suspicion the friendship which Androgeos had formed, since he feared that Minos might lend his aid to the sons of Pallas and take from him the supreme power, plotted against the life of Androgeos. Consequently, when the latter was on his way to Thebes in order to attend a festival there, Aegeus caused him to be treacherously slain by certain natives of the region in the neighbourhood of Oenoe in Attica.

**61.** Minos, when he learned of the fate which had befallen his son, came to Athens and demanded satisfaction for the murder of Androgeos. When no one paid any attention to him, he declared war against the Athenians and uttered imprecations to Zeus, calling down drought and famine throughout the state of the Athenians, and when drought quickly prevailed about Attica and Greece and the crops were destroyed, the heads of the communities gathered together and inquired of the god what steps they could take to rid themselves of their present evils. The god made answer to them that they should go to Aeacus, the son of Zeus and Aegine, the daughter of Asopus, and ask him to offer up prayers on their behalf. When they had done as they had been commanded, Aeacus finished offering the prayers and thereupon, among the rest of the Greeks, the drought was broken, but among the Athenians alone it continued; wherefore the Athenians were compelled to make inquiry of the god how they might be rid of their present evils. Thereupon the god made answer that they could do so if they would render to Minos such satisfaction for the murder of Androgeos as he might demand. The Athenians obeyed the order of the god, and Minos commanded them that they should give seven youths and as many maidens every nine years to the Minotaur for him to devour, for as long a time as the monster should live. When the Athenians gave them, the inhabitants of Attica were rid of their evils and Minos ceased warring on Athens.

At the expiration of nine years Minos came again to Attica accompanied by a great fleet and demanded and received the fourteen young people. Now Theseus was one of those who were to set forth, and Aegeus made the agreement with the captain of the vessel that, if Theseus should overcome the Minotaur, they should sail back with their sails white, but if he died, they should be black, just as they had been accustomed to do on the previous occasion. When they had landed in Crete, Ariadne, the daughter of Minos, became enamoured of Theseus, who was unusually handsome, and Theseus, after conversing with her and securing her assistance, both slew the Minotaur and got safely away, since he had learned from her the way out of the labyrinth. In making his way back to his native land he carried off Ariadne and sailed out unobserved during the night, after which he put in at the island which at that time was called Dia, but is now called Naxos.

At this same time, the myths relate, Dionysus showed himself on the island, and because of the beauty of Ariadne he took the maiden away from Theseus and kept her as his lawful wife, loving her exceedingly. Indeed, after her death he considered her worthy of immortal honours because of the affection he had for her, and placed among the stars of heaven the "Crown of Ariadnê." Theseus, they say, being vexed exceedingly because the maiden had been taken from him, and forgetting because of his grief the command of Aegeus, came to port in Attica with the black sails. Aegeus, we are told, witnessing the return of the ship and thinking that his son was dead, performed an act which was at the same time heroic and a calamity; for he ascended the acropolis and then, because he was disgusted with life by reason of his excessive grief, cast himself down the height. After Aegeus had died, Theseus, succeeding to the kingship, ruled over the masses in accordance with the laws and performed many deeds which contributed to the aggrandisement of his native land. The most notable thing which he accomplished was the incorporation of the demes, which were small in size but many in number, into the city of Athens; since from that time on the Athenians were filled with pride by reason of the importance of their state and aspired to the leadership of the Greeks. For our part, now that we have set forth these facts at sufficient length, we shall record what remains to be said about Theseus.

**62.** Deucalion, the eldest of the sons of Minos, while he was ruler of Crete, formed an alliance with the Athenians and united his own sister Phaedra in marriage to Theseus. After the marriage Theseus sent his son Hippolytus, who had been born to him by the Amazon, to Troezen to be reared among the brothers of Aethra, and by Phaedra he begat Acamas and Demophon. A short time after this Hippolytus returned to Athens for the celebration of the mysteries, and Phaedra, becoming enamoured of him because of his beauty, at that time, after he had returned to Troezen, erected a temple of Aphrodite beside the acropolis at the place whence one can look across and see Troezen, but at a later time, when she was stopping together with Theseus at the home of Pittheus, she asked

Hippolytus to lie with her. Upon his refusal to do so Phaedra, they say, was vexed, and on her return to Athens she told Theseus that Hippolytus had proposed lying with her. Since Theseus had his doubts about the accusation, he sent for Hippolytus in order to put him to the test, whereupon Phaedra, fearing the result of the examination, hanged herself; as for Hippolytus, who was driving a chariot when he heard of the accusation, he was so distraught in spirit that the horses got out of control and ran away with him, and in the event the chariot was smashed to bits and the youth, becoming entangled in the leathern thongs, was dragged along till he died. Hippolytus, then, since he had ended his life because of his chastity, received at the hands of the Troezenians honours equal to those offered to the gods, but Theseus, when after these happenings he was overpowered by a rival faction and banished from his native land, met his death on foreign soil. The Athenians, however, repenting of what they had done, brought back his bones and accorded him honours equal to those offered to the gods, and they set aside in Athens a sacred precinct which enjoyed the right of sanctuary and was called after him the Theseum.

**63.** Since we have duly set forth the story of Theseus, we shall discuss in turn the rape of Helen and the wooing of Persephone by Peirithoüs; for these deeds are interwoven with the affairs of Theseus. Peirithoüs, we are told, the son of Ixion, when his wife Hippodameia died leaving behind her a son Polypoetes, came to visit Theseus at Athens. Finding on his arrival that Phaedra, the wife of Theseus, was dead, he persuaded him to seize and carry off Helen, the daughter of Leda and Zeus, who was only ten years of age, but excelled all women in beauty. When they arrived in Lacedaemon with a number of companions and had found a favourable occasion, they assisted each other in seizing Helen and carrying her off to Athens. Thereupon they agreed among themselves to cast lots, and the one who had drawn the lot was to marry Helen and aid the other in getting another woman as wife, and in so doing to endure any danger. When they had exchanged oaths to this effect they cast lots, and it turned out that by the lot Theseus won her. Theseus, then, got the maiden for his own in the manner we have described; but since the Athenians were displeased at what had taken place, Theseus in fear of them got Helen off safely to Aphidna, one of the cities of Attica. With her he stationed his mother Aethra and the bravest men among his friends to serve as guardians of the maiden. Peirithoüs now decided to seek the hand of Persephone in marriage, and when he asked Theseus to make the journey with him Theseus at first endeavoured to dissuade him and to turn him away from such a deed as being impious; but since Peirithoüs firmly insisted upon it Theseus was bound by the oaths to join with him in the deed. When they had at last made their way below to the regions of Hades, it came to pass that because of the impiety of their act they were both put in chains, and although Theseus was later let go by reason of the favour with which Heracles regarded him, Peirithoüs because of the impiety remained in Hades, enduring everlasting punishment; but some writers of myths say that both of them never returned. While this was taking place, they say that Helen's brothers, the Dioscori, came up in arms against Aphidna, and taking the city razed it to the ground, and that they brought back Helen, who was still a virgin, to Lacedaemon and along with her, to serve as a slave, Aethra, the mother of Theseus.

## On The Seven against Thebes (64-65)

**64.** Since we have spoken on these matters at sufficient length, we shall now give the account of The Seven against Thebes, taking up the original causes of the war. Laius, the king of Thebes, married Jocastê, the daughter of Creon, and since he was childless for some time he inquired of the god regarding his begetting of children. The Pythian priestess made reply that it would not be to his interest that children should be born to him, since the son who should be begotten of him would be the murderer of his father and would bring great misfortunes upon all the house; but Laius forgot the oracle and begat a son, and he exposed the babe after he had pierced its ankles through with a piece of iron, this being the reason why it was later given the name Oedipus [swollen-footed], but the household slaves who took the infant were unwilling to expose it, and gave it as a present to the wife of Polybus, since she could bear no children. Later, after the boy had attained to manhood, Laius decided to inquire of the god regarding the babe which had been exposed, and Oedipus likewise, having learned from someone of the substitution which had been made in his case, set about to inquire of the Pythian priestess who were his true parents. In Phocis these two met face to face, and when Laius in a disdainful manner ordered Oedipus to make way for him, the latter in anger slew Laius, not knowing that he was his father.

At this very time, the myths go on to say, a sphinx, a beast of double form, had come to Thebes and was propounding a riddle to anyone who might be able to solve it, and many were being slain by her because of their inability to do so. Although a generous reward was offered to the man who should solve it, that he should marry Jocastê and be king of Thebes, yet no man was able to comprehend what was propounded except Oedipus, who alone solved the riddle. What had been propounded by the sphinx was this: What is it that is at the same time a biped, a triped, and a quadruped? While all the rest were perplexed, Oedipus declared that the animal proposed in the riddle was "man," since as an infant he is a quadruped, when grown a biped, and in old age a triped, using, because of his infirmity, a staff. At this answer the sphinx, in accordance with the oracle which the myth recounts, threw herself down a precipice, and Oedipus then married the woman who, unknown to himself, was his mother, and begat two sons, Eteocles and Polyneices, and two daughters, Antigone and Ismene.

**65.** When the sons had attained to manhood, they go on to say, and the impious deeds of the family became known, Oedipus, because of the disgrace, was compelled by his sons to remain always in retirement, and the young men, taking over the throne, agreed together that they should reign in alternate years. Eteocles, being the elder, was the first to reign, and upon the termination of the period he did not wish to give over the kingship. But Polyneices demanded of him the throne as they had agreed, and when his brother would not comply with his demand he fled to Argos to king Adrastus.

At the same time that this was taking place Tydeus, they say, the son of Oencus, who had slain his cousins Alcathoüs and Lycopeus in Calydon, fled from Aetolia to Argos. Adrastus received both the fugitives kindly, and in obedience to a certain oracle joined his daughters in marriage to them, Argeia to Polyneices, and Deipyle to Tydeus. And since the young men were held in high esteem and enjoyed the king's favour to a great degree, Adrastus, they say, as a mark of his good-will promised to restore both Polyneices and Tydeus to their native lands, and having decided to restore Polyneices first, he sent Tydeus as an envoy to Eteocles in Thebes to negotiate the return. While Tydeus was on his way thither, we are told, he was set upon from ambush by fifty men sent by Eteocles, but he slew every man of them and got through safe to Argos, to the astonishment of all, whereupon Adrastus, when he learned what had taken place, made preparations for the consequent campaign against Eteocles, having persuaded Capaneus and Hippomedon and Parthenopaeus, the son of Atalante, the daughter of Schoeneus, to be his allies in the war. Polyneices also endeavoured to persuade the seer Amphiaraüs to take part with him in the campaign against Thebes; and when the latter, because he knew in advance that he would perish if he should take part in the campaign, would not for that reason consent to do so, Polyneices, they say, gave the golden necklace which, as the myth relates, had once been given by Aphrodite as a present to Harmonia, to the wife of Amphiaraüs, in order that she might persuade her husband to join the others as their ally.

At the time in question Amphiaraüs, we are told, was at variance with Adrastus, striving for the kingship, and the two came to an agreement among themselves whereby they committed the decision of the matter at issue between them to Eriphyle, the wife of Amphiaraüs and sister of Adrastus. When Eriphyle awarded the victory to Adrastus and, with regard to the campaign against Thebes, gave it as her opinion that it should be undertaken, Amphiaraüs, believing that his wife had betrayed him, did agree to take part in the campaign, but left orders with his son Alcmaeon that after his death he should slay Eriphyle. Alcmaeon, therefore, at a later time slew his mother according to his father's injunction, and because he was conscious of the pollution he had incurred he was driven to madness, but Adrastus and Polyneices and Tydeus, adding to their number four leaders, Amphiaraüs, Capaneus, Hippomedon, and Parthenopaeus, the son of Atalantê the daughter of Schoeneus, set out against Thebes, accompanied by a notable army. After this Eteocles and Polyneices slew each other, Capaneus died while impetuously ascending the wall by a scaling-ladder, and as for Amphiaraüs, the earth opened and he together with his chariot fell into the opening and disappeared from sight. When the rest of the leaders, with the exception of Adrastus, had likewise perished and many soldiers had fallen, the Thebans refused to allow the removal of the dead and so Adrastus left them unburied and returned to Argos. So the bodies of those who had fallen at the foot of the Cadmeia remained unburied and no one had the courage to inter them, but the Athenians, who excelled all others in uprightness, honoured with funeral rites all who had fallen at the foot of the Cadmeia.

### On the Epigoni of The Seven against Thebes (66-67).

**66.** As for The Seven against Thebes, such, then, was the outcome of their campaign. Their sons, who were known as Epigoni [afterborn], being intent upon avenging the death of their fathers, decided to make common cause in a campaign against Thebes, having received an oracle from Apollo that they should make war upon this city, and with Alcmaeon, the son of Amphiaraüs, as their supreme commander. Alcmaeon, after they had chosen him to be their commander, inquired of the god concerning the campaign against Thebes and also concerning the punishment of his mother Eriphylê. Apollo replied that he should perform both these deeds, not only because Eriphylê had accepted the golden necklace in return for working the destruction of his father, but also because she had received a robe as a reward for securing the death of her son. For Aphrodite, as the tale is told, in ancient times had given both the necklace and a robe as presents to Harmonia, the daughter of Cadmus, and Eriphylê had accepted both of them, receiving the necklace from Polyneices and the robe from Thersandrus, the son of Polyneices, who had given it to her in order to induce her to persuade her son to make the campaign against Thebes. Alcmaeon, accordingly, gathered soldiers, not only from Argos but from the neighbouring cities as well, and so had a notable army as he set out on the campaign against Thebes. The Thebans drew themselves up against him and a mighty battle took place in which Alcmaeon and his allies were victorious; and the Thebans, since they had been worsted in the battle and had lost many of their citizens, found their hopes shattered. Since they were not strong enough to offer further resistance, they consulted the seer Teiresias, who advised them to flee from the city, for only in this way, he said, could they save their lives. Consequently the Cadmeans left the city, as the seer had counselled them to do, and gathered for refuge by night in a place in Boeotia called Tilphossaeum. Thereupon the Epigoni took the city and sacked it, and capturing Daphne, the daughter of Teiresias, they dedicated her, in accordance with a certain vow, to the service of the temple at Delphi as an offering to the god of the first-fruits of the booty. This maiden possessed no less knowledge of prophecy than her father, and in the course of her stay at Delphi she developed her skill to a far greater degree; moreover, by virtue of the employment of a marvellous natural gift, she also wrote oracular responses of every sort, excelling in their composition; and indeed it was from her poetry, they say, that the poet Homer took many verses which he appropriated as his own and with them adorned his own poesy. Since she was often like one inspired when she delivered oracles, they say that she was also called Sibylla, for to be inspired in one's tongue is expressed by the word *sibyllainein*.

67. The Epigoni, after they had made their campaign renowned, returned to their native lands, bear-, ing with them great booty. Of the Cadmeans who fled in a body to Tilphossaeum, Teiresias died there, and the Cadmeans buried him in state and accorded him honours equal to those offered to the gods; but as for themselves, they left the city and marched against the Dorians; and having conquered them in battle they drove out of their native lands the inhabitants of that country and they themselves settled there for some time, some of them remaining there permanently and others returning to Thebes when Creon, the son of Menoeceus, was king. Those who had been expelled from their native lands returned at some later period to Doris and made their homes in Erineus, Cytinium, and Boeum.

Before the period in which these things took place, Boeotus, the son of Arneê and Poseidon, came into the land which was then called Aeolis but is now called Thessaly, and gave to his followers the name of Boeotians. Concerning these inhabitants of Aeolis, we must revert to earlier times and give a detailed account of them. In the times before that which we are discussing the rest of the sons of Aeolus, who was the son of Hellen, who was the son of Deucalion, settled in the regions we have mentioned, but Mimas remained behind and ruled as king of Aeolis. Hippotes, who was born of Mimas, begat Aeolus by Melanippe, and Arne, who was the daughter of Aeolus, bore Boeotus by Poseidon, but Aeolus, not believing that it was Poseidon who had lain with Arnê and holding her to blame for her downfall, handed her over to a stranger from Metapontium who happened to be sojourning there at the time, with orders to carry her off to Metapontium. After the stranger had done as he was ordered, Arnê, while living in Metapontium, gave birth to Aeolus and Boeotus, whom the Metapontian, being childless, in obedience to a certain oracle adopted as his own sons. When the boys had attained to manhood, a civil discord arose in Metapontium and they seized the kingship by violence. Later, however, a quarrel took place between Arne and Autolyte, the wife of the Metapontian, and the young men took the side of their mother and slew Autolyte, but the Metapontian was indignant at this deed, and so they got boats ready and taking Arne with them set out to sea accompanied by many friends. Now Aeolus took possession of the islands in the Tyrrhenian Sea which are called after him "Aeolian" and founded a city to which he gave the name Lipara; but Boeotus sailed home to Aeolus, the father of Arne, by whom he was adopted and in succession to him he took over the kingship of Aeolis; and the land he named Arne after his mother, but the inhabitants Boeotians after himself. Itonus, the son of Boeotus, begat four sons, Hippalcimus, Electryon, Archilycus, and Alegenor. Of these sons Hippalcimus begat Peneleos, Electryon begat Leïtus, Alegenor begat Clonius, and Archilycus begat Prothoënor and Arcesilaüs, who were the leaders of all the Boeotians in the expedition against Troy.

### *On Neleus and his descendants (68).*

**68.** Now that we have examined these matters we shall endeavour to set forth the facts concerning Salmoneus and Tyro and their descendants as far as Nestor, who took part in the campaign against Troy. Salmoneus was a son of Aeolus, who was the son of Hellen, who was the son of Deucalion, and setting out from Aeolis with a number of Aeolians he founded a city in Eleia on the banks of the river Alpheius and called it Salmonia after his own name, and marrying Alcidice, the daughter of Aleus, he begat by her a daughter, her who was given the name Tyro, a maiden of surpassing beauty. When his wife Alcidice died Salmoneus took for a second wife Sidero, as she was called, who treated Tyro unkindly, as a step-mother would. Afterwards Salmoneus, being an overbearing man and impious, came to be hated by his subjects and because of his impiety was slain by Zeus with a bolt of lightning. As for Tyro, who was still a virgin when this took place, Poseidon lay with her and begat two sons, Pelias and Neleus. Then Tyro married Cretheus and bore Amythaon and Pheres and Aeson. At the death of Cretheus a strife over the kingship arose between Pelias and Neleus. Of these two Pelias came to be king over Iolcus and the neighbouring districts, but Neleus, taking with him Melampous and Bias, the sons of Amythaon and Aglaia, and certain other Achaeans of Phthiotis and Aeolians, made a campaign into the Peloponnesus. Melampous, who was a seer, healed the women of Argos of the madness which the wrath of Dionysus had brought upon them, and in return for this benefaction he received from the king of the Argives, Anaxagoras the son of Megapenthes, two-thirds of the kingdom; and he made his home in Argos and shared the kingship with Bias his brother. Marrying Iphianeira, the daughter of Megapenthes, he begat Antiphates and Manto, and also Bias and Pronoe; and of Antiphates and of Zeuxippe, the daughter of Hippocoon, the children were Oecles and Amphalces, and to Oecles and Hypermnestra, the daughter of Thespius, were born Iphianeira, Polyboea, and Amphiaraus. Now Melampous and Bias and their descendants shared in the kingship in Argos, as we have stated, but Neleus, when he had arrived in Messenê together with his companions, founded the city of Pylus, the natives of the region giving him the site, and while king of this city he married Chloris, the daughter of Amphion the Theban, and begat twelve sons, the oldest of whom was Periclymenus and the youngest the Nestor who engaged in the expedition against Troy.

As regards the ancestors of Nestor, then, we shall be satisfied with what has been said, since we are aiming at due proportion in our account.

## *On the Lapiths and Centaurs (69-70).*

**69.** We shall now discuss in turn the Lapiths and Centaurs. To Oceanus and Tethys, so the myths relate, were born a number of sons who gave their names to rivers, and among them was Peneius, from whom the river Peneius in Thessaly later got its name. He lay with the nymph named Creilsa and begat as children Hypseus and Stilbe, and with the latter Apollo lay and begat Lapithes and Centaurus. Of these two, Lapithes made his home about the Peneius river and ruled over these regions, and marrying Orsinome, the daughter of Eurynomus, he begat two sons, Phorbas and Periphas, and these sons became kings in this region and all the peoples there were called "Lapiths" after Lapithes. As for the sons of Lapithes, Phorbas went to Olenus, from which city Alector, the king of Eleia, summoned him to come to his aid, since he stood in fear of the overlordship of Pelops, and he gave him a share of the kingship of Elis; and to Phorbas were born two sons, Aegeus and Actor, who received the kingship over the Eleans. The other son of Lapithes, namely, Periphas, married Astyaguia, the daughter of Hypseus, and begat eight sons, the oldest of whom was Antion, who lay with Perimela, the daughter of Amythaon, and begat Ixion. He, the story goes, having promised that he would give many gifts of wooing to Eioneus, married Dia, the daughter of Eïoneus, by whom he begat Peirithoüs, but when afterward Ixion would not pay over the gifts of wooing to his wife, Eïoneus took as security for these his mares. Ixion thereupon summoned Eïoneus to come to him, assuring him that he would comply in every respect, but when Eïoneus arrived he cast him into a pit which he had filled with fire. Because of the enormity of this crime no man, we are informed, was willing to purify him of the murder. The myths recount, however, that in the end he was purified by Zeus, but that he became enamoured of Hera and had the temerity to make advances to her. Thereupon, men say, Zeus formed a figure of Hera out of a cloud and sent it to him, and Ixion, lying with the cloud (*Nephelê*) begat the Centaurs, as they are called, which have the shapes of men. The myths relate that in the end Ixion, because of the enormity of his misdeeds, was bound by Zeus upon a wheel and after death had to suffer punishment for all eternity.

**70.** The Centaurs, according to some writers, were reared by Nymphs on Mt. Pelion, and when they had attained to manhood they consorted with mares and brought into being the Hippocentaurs, as they are called, which are creatures of double form; but others say that it was the Centaurs born of Ixion and Nephelê who were called Hippocentaurs, because they were the first to essay the riding of horses, and that they were then made into a fictitious myth, to the effect that they were of double form. We are also told that they demanded of Peirithoüs, on the ground of kinship, their share of their father's kingdom, and that when Peirithoüs would not yield it to them they made war on both him and the Lapiths. At a later time, the account goes on to say, when they had made up their differences, Peirithoüs married Hippodameia, the daughter of Butes, and invited both Theseus and the Centaurs to the wedding. The Centaurs, however, becoming drunken assaulted the female guests and lay with them by violence, whereupon both Theseus and the Lapiths, incensed by such a display of lawlessness, slew not a few of them and drove the rest out of the city. Because of this the Centaurs gathered all their forces, made a campaign against the Lapiths, and slew many of them, the survivors fleeing into Mt. Pholoe in Arcadia and ultimately escaping from there to Cape Malea, where they made their home. And the Centaurs, elated by these successes, made Mt. Pholoe the base of their operations, plundered the Greeks who passed by, and slew many of their neighbours.

### *On Asclepius and his descendants (71).*

**71.** Now that we have examined these matters we shall endeavour to set forth the facts concerning Asclepius and his descendants. This, then, is what the myths relate: Asclepius was the son of Apollo and Coronis, and since he excelled in natural ability and sagacity of mind, he devoted himself to the science of healing and made many discoveries which contribute to the health of mankind. So far did he advance along the road of fame that, to the amazement of all, he healed many sick whose lives had been despaired of, and for this reason it was believed that he had brought back to life many who had died. Consequently, the myth goes on to say, Hades brought accusation against Asclepius, charging him before Zeus of acting to the detriment of his own province, for, he said, the number of the dead was steadily diminishing, now that men were being healed by Asclepius. So Zeus, in indignation, slew Asclepius with his thunderbolt, but Apollo, indignant at the slaying of Asclepius, murdered the Cyclopes who had forged the thunderbolt for Zeus; but at the death of the Cyclopes Zeus was again indignant and laid a command upon Apollo that he should serve as a labourer for a human being and that this should be the punishment he should receive from him for his crimes. To Asclepius, we are told further, sons were born, Machaon and Podaleirius, who also developed the healing art and accompanied Agamemnon in the expedition against Troy. Throughout the course of the war they were of great service to the Greeks, healing most skilfully the wounded, and because of these benefactions they attained to great fame among the Greeks; furthermore, they were granted exemption from the perils of battles and from the other obligations of citizenship, because of the very great service which they offered by their healing.

Now as regards Asclepius and his sons we shall be satisfied with what has been said.

## *On the daughters of Asopus and the sons born to Aeacus (72).*

**72.** We shall now recount the story of the daughters of Asopus and of the sons who were born to Aeacus. According to the myths there were born to Oceanus and Tethys a number of children who gave their names to rivers, and among their number were Peneius and Asopus. Now Peneius made his home in what is now Thessaly and called after himself the river which bears his name; but Asopus made his home in Phlius, where he married Metope, the daughter of Ladon, to whom were born two sons, Pelasgus and Ismenus, and twelve daughters, Corcyra and Salamis, also Aegina, Peirene, and Cleone, then Thebe, Tanagra, Thespeia, and Asopis, also Sinopê, and finally Ornia and Chalcis. One of his sons, Ismenus, came to Boeotia and settled near the river which received its name from him; but as for the daughters, Sinopê was seized by Apollo and carried off to the place where now stands the city of Sinopê, which was named after her, and to her and Apollo was born a son Syrus, who became king of the Syrians, who were named after him. Corcyra was carried off by Poseidon to the island which was named Corcyra after her; and to her and Poseidon was born Phaeax, from whom the Phaeacians afterwards received the name they bear. To Phaeax was born Alcinoüs, who brought about the return of Odysseus to Ithaca. Salamis was seized by Poseidon and taken to the island which was named Salamis after her; and she lay with Poseidon and bore Cychreus, who became king of this island and acquired fame by reason of his slaying a snake of huge size which was destroying the inhabitants of the island. Aegina was seized by Zeus and taken off by him from Phlius to the island which was named Aegina after her, and lying with Zeus on this island she gave birth to Aeacus, who became its king.

To Aeacus sons were born, Peleus and Telamon. Of these, Peleus, while hurling a discus, accidentally slew Phocus, who was his brother by the same father although born of another mother. Because of this slaying Peleus was banished by his father and fled to Phthia in what is now called Thessaly, where he was purified by Actor the king of the country and succeeded to the kingship, Actor being childless. To Peleus and Thetis was born Achilleus, who accompanied Agamemnon in the expedition against Troy. Telamon, being also a fugitive from Aegina, went to Salamis and marrying Glaucê, the daughter of Cychreus, the king of the Salaminians, he became king of the island. When his wife Glaucê died he married Eriboea of Athens, the daughter of Alcathus, by whom he begat Ajax, who served in the expedition against Troy.

## *On Pelops, Tantalus, Oenomaus, and Niobê (73-74).*

**73.** Now that we have examined these matters we shall endeavour to set forth the facts concerning Pelops and Tantalus and Oenomaüs, but to do so we must revert to earlier times and give in summary the whole story from the beginning. The account runs like this: In the city of Pisa in the Peloponnesus Ares lay with Harpinê, the daughter of Asopus, and begat Oenomaüs, who, in turn, begat a daughter, an only child, and named her Hippodameia, and once when he consulted an oracle about the end of his life the god replied to him that he should die whenever his daughter Hippodameia should marry. Consequently, we are told, he proceeded cautiously regarding the marriage of his daughter and decided to see that she was kept a virgin, assuming that only in this way could he escape from the danger which her marriage would entail. And so, since there were many

## BOOK IV

suitors for the girl's hand, he proposed a contest for any who wished to marry her, the conditions being that the defeated suitor must die, but whoever should win would have the girl in marriage. The contest he set was a chariot-race from Pisa to the altar of Poseidon on the Isthmus of Corinth, and the starting of the horses he arranged as follows: Oenomaüs was to be sacrificing a ram to Zeus, when the suitor should set out, driving a chariot drawn by four horses; then, when the sacrifice had been completed, Oenomaüs was to begin the race and make after the suitor, having a spear and Myrtilus as his driver, and if he should succeed in overtaking the chariot which he was pursuing he was to smite the suitor with the spear and slay him. By employing this method he kept overtaking the suitors as they appeared, his horses being swift, and was slaying them in great numbers; but when Pelops, the son of Tantalus, came to Pisa and looked upon Hippodameia, he set his heart upon marrying her, and by corrupting Myrtilus, the charioteer of Oenomaüs, and thus securing his co-operation toward winning the victory, he was the first to arrive at the altar of Poseidon on the Isthmus. And Oenomaüs, believing that the oracle had been fulfilled, was so disheartened by grief that he removed himself from life. In this way, then, Pelops got Hippodameia for his wife and succeeded to the sovereignty of Pisa, and increasing steadily in power by reason of his courage and his wisdom, he won over to himself the larger number of those who dwelt in the Peloponnesus and called the land after his own name "Peloponnesus" [island of Pelops].

74. Since we have made mention of Pelops, we must also relate the story concerning his father Tantalus, in order that we may omit nothing which deserves to be made known. Tantalus was a son of Zeus, and he possessed surpassing wealth and renown, dwelling in that part of Asia which is now called Paphlagonia. Because of his noble descent from Zeus his father he became, as men say, a very especial friend of the gods. At a later time, however, he did not bear as a human being should the good fortune which came to him, and being admitted to the common table of the gods and to all their intimate talk as well, he made known to men happenings among the immortals which were not to be divulged. For this reason he was chastened while yet in this life and after his death, as the myths relate, was condemned to eternal punishment by being rated in Hades among the impious. To him were born a son Pelops and a daughter Niobê, and Niobê became the mother of seven sons and an equal number of daughters, maids of exceeding beauty, and since she gave herself haughty airs over the number of her children, she frequently declared in boastful way that she was more blest in her children than was Leto. At this, so the myths tell us, Leto in anger commanded Apollo to slay with his arrows the sons of Niobê and Artemis the daughters. When these two hearkened to the command of their mother and slew with their arrows the children of Niobê at the same time, it came to pass that immediately, almost in a single moment, that woman was both blest with children and childless. But since Tantalus, after he had incurred the enmity of the gods, was driven out of Paphlagonia by Ilus, the son of Tros, we must also set forth all that relates to Ilus and his ancestors.

### On Dardanus and his descendants as far as Priam (75).

75. The first to rule as king over the land of Troy was Teucrus, the son of the river-god Scamandrus and a nymph of Mt. Ida [Idaea]; he was a distinguished

man and caused the people of the land to be called Teucrians, after his own name. To Teucrus was born a daughter Bateia, whom Dardanus, the son of Zeus, married, and when Dardanus succeeded to the throne he called the people of the land Dardanians after his own name, and founding a city on the shore of the sea he called it also Dardanus after himself. To him a son Erichthonius was born, who far excelled in good fortune and in wealth. Of him the poet Homer writes:

> The wealthiest was he of mortal men;
> Three thousand mares he had that grazed throughout
> His marshy pastures.

To Erichthonius was born a son Tros, who called the people of the land Trojans, after his own name. To Tros were born three sons, Ilus, Assaraeus, and Ganymedes. Ilus founded in a plain a city which was the most renowned among the cities in the Troad, giving it after himself the name Ilium. To Ilus was born a son Laomedon, who begat Tithonus and Priam; and Tithonus, after making a campaign against those parts of Asia which lay to the east of him and pushing as far as Ethiopia, begat by Eos, as the myths relate, Memnon, who came to the aid of the Trojans and was slain by Achilleus, whereas Priam married Hecabê and begat, in addition to a number of other sons, Hector, who won very great distinction in the Trojan War. Assaraeus became king of the Dardanians and begat Capys, whose son was Anchises, who by Aphrodite begat Aeneas, the most renowned man among the Trojans. Ganymedes, who excelled all men in beauty, was snatched up by the gods to serve as the cupbearer of Zeus.

But now that we have examined these matters we shall endeavour to set forth what relates to Daedalus, the Minotaur, and the expedition of Minos into Sicily against King Cocalus.

### On Daedalus, the Minotaur, and the campaign of Minos against the king Cocalus (76-80).

**76.** Daedalus was an Athenian by birth and was known as one of the clan named Erechthids, since he was the son of Metion, the son of Eupalamus, the son of Erechtheus. In natural ability he towered far above all other men and cultivated the building art, the making of statues, and the working of stone. He was also the inventor of many devices which contributed to the advancement of his art and built works in many regions of the inhabited world which arouse the wonder of men. In the carving of his statues he so far excelled all other men that later generations invented the story about him that the statues of his making were quite like their living models; they could see, they said, and walk and, in a word, preserved so well the characteristics of the entire body that the beholder thought that the image made by him was a being endowed with life. Since he was the first to represent the open eye and to fashion the legs separated in a stride and the arms and hands as extended, it was a natural thing that he should have received the admiration of mankind; for the artists before his time had carved their statues with the eyes closed and the arms and hands hanging and attached to the sides.

Though Daedalus was an object of admiration because of his technical skill, yet he had to flee from his native land, since he had been condemned for murder for the following reason: Talos, a son of the sister of Daedalus, was receiving his education in the home of Daedalus, while he was still a lad in years; being more gifted than his teacher he invented the potter's wheel, and then, when once he had come by chance upon a jawbone of a snake and with it had sawn through a small piece of wood, he tried to imitate the jaggedness of the serpent's teeth. Consequently he fashioned a saw out of iron, by means of which he would saw the lumber which he used in his work, and for this accomplishment he gained the reputation of having discovered a device which would be of great service to the art of building. He likewise discovered also the tool for describing a circle and certain other cunningly contrived devices whereby he gained for himself great fame. Daedalus, becoming jealous of the youth and feeling that his fame was going to rise far above that of his teacher, treacherously slew the youth, and being detected in the act of burying him, he was asked what he was burying, whereupon he replied, "I am inhuming a snake." Here a man may well wonder at the strange happening, that the same animal that led to the thought of devising the saw should also have been the means through which the murder came to be discovered. Daedalus, having been accused and adjudged guilty of murder by the court of the Areopagites, at first fled to one of the demes of Attica, the inhabitants of which, we are told, were named after him Daedalidae.

**77.** Afterwards Daedalus made his escape out of Attica to Crete, where, being admired because of the fame of his art, he became a friend of Minos who was king there. Now according to the myth which has been handed down to us Pasiphaê, the wife of Minos, became enamoured of the bull, and Daedalus, by fashioning a contrivance in the shape of a cow, assisted Pasiphaê to gratify her passion. In explanation of this the myths offer the following account: Before this time it had been the custom of Minos annually to dedicate to Poseidon the fairest bull born in his herds and to sacrifice it to the god; but at the time in question there was born a bull of extraordinary beauty and he sacrificed another from among those which were inferior, whereupon Poseidon, becoming angry at Minos, caused his wife Pasiphaê to become enamoured of the bull. By means of the ingenuity of Daedalus Pasiphaê had intercourse with the bull and gave birth to the Minotaur, famed in the myth. This creature, they say, was of double form, the upper parts of the body as far as the shoulders being those of a bull and the remaining parts those of a man. As a place in which to keep this monstrous thing Daedalus, the story goes, built a labyrinth, the passage-ways of which were so winding that those unfamiliar with them had difficulty in making their way out; in this labyrinth the Minotaur was maintained and here it devoured the seven youths and seven maidens which were sent to it from Athens, as we have already related.

Daedalus, they say, on learning that Minos had made threats against him because he had fashioned the cow, became fearful of the anger of the king and departed from Crete, Pasiphaê helping him and providing a vessel for his escape. With him fled also his son Icarus and they put in at a certain island which lay in the open sea, but when Icarus was disembarking onto the island in a reckless manner, he fell into the sea and perished, and in memory of him the sea was named the Icarian and the island was called Icaria. Daedalus, however, sailing away from this island, landed in Sicily near the territory over which Cocalus reigned as king, who courteously received Daedalus and because of his genius and his renown made him his close friend.

Certain writers of myths have the following account: Daedalus remained a while longer in Crete, being kept hidden by Pasiphaê, and king Minos, desiring to wreak vengeance upon him and yet being unable to find him, caused all the boats which were on the island to be searched and announced that he would give a great sum of money to the man who should discover Daedalus. Thereupon Daedalus, despairing of making his escape by any boat, fashioned with amazing ingenuity wings which were cleverly designed and marvellously fitted together with wax; and fastening these on his son's body and his own he spread them out for flight, to the astonishment of all, and made his escape over the open sea which lies near the island of Crete. As for Icarus, because of the ignorance of youth he made his flight too far aloft and fell into the sea when the wax which held the wings together was melted by the sun, whereas Dardalus, by flying close to the sea and repeatedly wetting the wings, made his way in safety, marvellous to relate, to Sicily. Now as for these matters, even though the myth is a tale of marvel, we none the less have thought it best not to leave it unmentioned.

**78.** Daedalus spent a considerable time with Cocalus and the Sicani, being greatly admired for his very great skill in his art. And on this island he constructed certain works which stand even to this day. For instance, near Megaris he ingeniously built a *kolumbethra* [swimming bath], as men have named it, from which a great river, called the Alabon, empties into the sea which is not far distant from it. Also in the present territory of Acragas on the Camicus river, as it is called, he built a city which lay upon a rock and was the strongest of any in Sicily and altogether impregnable to any attack by force; for the ascent to it he made narrow and winding, building it in so ingenious a manner that it could be defended by three or four men. Consequently Cocalus built in this city the royal residence, and storing his treasures there he had them in a city which the inventiveness of its designer had made impregnable. A third construction of his, in the territory of Selinus, was a grotto where he so successfully expelled the steam caused by the fire which burned in it that those who frequented the grotto got into a perspiration imperceptibly because of the gentle action of the heat, and gradually, and actually with pleasure to themselves, they cured the infirmities of their bodies without experiencing any annoyance from the heat. Also at Eryx, where a rock rose sheer to an extraordinary height and the narrow space, where the temple of Aphrodite lay, made it necessary to build it on the precipitous tip of the rock, he constructed a wall upon the very crag, by this means extending in an astonishing manner the overhanging ledge of the crag. Moreover, for the Aphrodite of Mt. Eryx, they say, he ingeniously constructed a golden ram, working it with exceeding care and making it the perfect image of an actual ram. Many other works as well, men say, he ingeniously constructed throughout Sicily, but they have perished because of the long time which has elapsed.

**79.** Minos, the king of the Cretans, who was at that time the master of the seas, when he learned that Daedalus had fled to Sicily, decided to make a campaign against that island. After preparing a notable naval force he sailed forth from Crete and landed at a place in the territory of Acragas which was called after him Minoa. Here he disembarked his troops and sending messengers to King Cocalus he demanded Daedalus of him for punishment. Cocalus invited Minos to a conference, and after promising to meet all his demands he brought him to his home as his guest, and when Minos was bathing Cocalus kept him too long in the hot water and thus slew him; the body he gave back to the Cretans, explaining his death on the ground that he had slipped in the bath and by falling into the hot water had met his end. Thereupon the comrades of Minos buried the body of the king with magnificent ceremonies, and constructing a tomb of two storeys, in the part of it which was hidden underground they placed the bones, and in that which lay open to gaze they made a shrine of Aphrodite. Here Minos received honours over many generations, the inhabitants of the region offering sacrifices there in the belief that the shrine was Aphrodite's; but in more recent times, after the city of the Acragantini had been founded and it became known that the bones had been placed there, it came to pass that the tomb was dismantled and the bones were given back to the Cretans, this being done when Theron [d.472] was lord over the people of Acragas.

However, the Cretans of Sicily, after the death of Minos, fell into factious strife, since they had no ruler, and, since their ships had been burned by the Sicani serving under Cocalus, they gave up any hope they had had of returning to their native land; and deciding to make their home in Sicily, a part of them established on that island a city to which they gave the name Minoa after their king, and others, after wandering about through the interior of the island, seized a place which was naturally strong and founded a city to which they gave the name Engyum after the spring which flowed forth within the city. At a later time, after the capture of Troy, when Meriones the Cretan came to shore in Sicily, they welcomed, because of their kinship to them, the Cretans who landed with him and shared with them their citizenship; and using as their base a well-fortified city and having subdued certain of the neighbouring peoples, they secured for themselves a fairly large territory. Growing steadily stronger all the while they built a temple to the Mothers and accorded these goddesses unusual honours, adorning their temple with many votive offerings. The cult of these goddesses, so men say, they moved from their home in Crete, since the Cretans also hold these goddesses in special honour.

**80.** The account which the myths preserve of the Mothers runs like this: They nurtured Zeus of old without the knowledge of his father Cronus, in return for which Zeus translated them into the heavens and designated them as a constellation which he named the Bears. Aratus agrees with this account when he states in his poem on the stars:

> Turned backwards then upon their shoulders are
> The Bears; if true it be that they from Crete
> Into the heavens mounted by the will
> Of mighty Zeus, for that when he was babe
> In fragrant Dicton near th' Idaean mount
> They set him in a cave and nurtured him
> A year, the while Curetes Dictaean
> Practised deceit on Cronus.

There is no reason why we should omit to mention the sanctity of these goddesses and the renown which they enjoy among mankind. They are honoured, indeed, not only by the inhabitants of this city, but certain of the neighbouring peoples also glorify these goddesses with magnificent sacrifices and every other kind of honour. Some cities were indeed commanded by oracles from the Pythian god to honour the goddesses, being assured that in this way the lives of their private citizens would be blessed with good fortune and their cities would flourish. And in the end the renown of the goddesses advanced to such a degree that the inhabitants of this region have continued to honour them with many votive offerings in silver and gold down to the time of the writing of this history. For instance, a temple was built there for them which not only excels in size but also occasions wonder by reason of the expense incurred in its construction; for since the people had no suitable stone in their own territory they brought it from their neighbours, the inhabitants of Agyrium, though the cities were nearly one hundred stades apart and the road by which they had to transport the blocks were rough and altogether hard to traverse. For this reason they constructed wagons with four wheels and transported the stone by the use of one hundred span of oxen. Indeed, because of the vast quantity of the sacred properties of the temple they were so plentifully supplied with means that, by reason of their abundant prosperity, they took no account of the expense; for only a short time before our day the goddesses possessed three thousand head of sacred cattle and vast holdings of land, so that they were the recipients of great revenues.

### *On Aristaeus, Daphnis, Eryx, and Orion (chaps. 81-85).*

81. But now that we have discoursed upon these matters at sufficient length, we shall next undertake to write about Aristaeus. Aristaeus was the son of Apollo and Cyrenê, the daughter of Hypseus the son of Peneius, and the manner of his birth is given by certain writers of myths as follows: Apollo became enamoured of a maiden by the name of Cyrenê, who was reared in the neighbourhood of Mt. Pelion and was of surpassing beauty, and he carried her off from there to that part of the land of Libya where in later times he founded a city and named it, after her, Cyrenê. Now Apollo begat by Cyrenê in that land a son Aristaeus and gave him while yet a babe into the hands of the Nymphs to nurture, and the latter bestowed upon him three different names, calling him, that is, Nomius, Aristaeus, and Agreus. He learned from the Nymphs how to curdle milk, to make bee-hives, and to cultivate olive-trees, and was the first to instruct men in these matters. And because of the advantage which came to them from these discoveries the men who had received his benefactions rendered to Aristaeus honours equal to those offered to the gods, even as they had done in the case of Dionysus.

After this, they say, Aristaeus went to Boeotia, where he married one of the daughters of Cadmus, Autonoe, to whom was born Acteon, who, as the myths relate, was torn to pieces by his own dogs. The reason for this bad turn of fortune of his, as some explain it, was that, presuming upon his dedication to Artemis of the first-fruits of his hunting, he purposed to consummate the marriage with Artemis at the temple of the goddess, but according to others, it was because he represented himself as superior to Artemis in skill as a hunter. It is not incredible that it was for both these reasons that the goddess became angry; for whether Acteon made an improper use of the spoils of his hunting to satisfy his own desire upon her who has no part in marriage, or whether he was so bold as to assert that as a hunter he was to be preferred above her before whom even gods withdraw from rivalry in the chase, all would agree that the goddess was justified in having become indignant at him. Speaking generally, we may well believe that, when he had been changed into the form of one of the animals which he was wont to hunt, he was slain by the dogs which were accustomed to prey upon the other wild beasts.

**82.** As for Aristaeus, after the death of Acteon, we are told, he went to the oracle of his father, Apollo, who prophesied to him that he was to change his home to the island of Ceos and told him likewise of the honours which would be his among the Ceans. To this island he sailed, but since a plague prevailed throughout Greece the sacrifice he offered there was on behalf of all the Greeks. And since the sacrifice was made at the time of the rising of the star Sirius, which is the period when the etesian winds customarily blow, the pestilential diseases, we are told, came to an end. Now the man who ponders upon this event may reasonably marvel at the strange turn which fortune took; for the same man who saw his son done to death by the dogs likewise put an end to the influence of that star which, of all the stars of heaven, bears the same name and is thought to bring destruction upon mankind, and by so doing was responsible for saving the lives of the rest.

We are further informed that Aristaeus left descendants behind on the island of Ceos and then returned to Libya, from where he set forth with the aid of his mother, a Nymph, and put ashore on the island of Sardinia. Here he made his home, and since he loved the island because of its beauty, he set out plantings in it and brought it under cultivation, whereas formerly it had lain waste. Here he begat two sons, Charmus and Callicarpus. After this he visited other islands and spent some time in Sicily, where, because of the abundance of the fruits on the island and the multitude of flocks and herds which grazed there, he was eager to display to its inhabitants the benefactions which were his to bestow. Consequently among the inhabitants of Sicily, as men say, Aristaeus received especial honour as a god, in particular by those who harvested the fruit of the olive-tree. And finally, as the myths relate, he visited Dionysus in Thrace and was initiated into his secret rites, and during his stay in the company of the god he learned from him much useful knowledge. And after dwelling some time in the neighbourhood of Mount Haemus he never was seen again of men, and became the recipient of immortal honours not only among the barbarians of that region but among the Greeks as well.

**83.** But as regards Aristaeus we shall rest content with what has been said, and we shall next endeavour to set forth what relates to Daphnis and Eryx. This is what is told of them: Eryx was a son of Aphrodite and Butas, a certain native king of Sicily of very great fame, and he was admired by the natives because of his noble birth on his mother's side and became king over a part of the island. He also founded a notable city which bore his name; it was set upon a lofty place, and on the highest point within the city he established a shrine of his mother, which he embellished not only with a beautifully built temple, but also with the multitude of his dedications. The goddess, both because of the reverence which the inhabitants of the region paid to her and because of the honour which she received from the son whom she had borne, displayed an exceptional love for the city, and for this reason she came to be called Erycinian Aphrodite. A man may well be filled with wonder when he stops to sum up the fame which has gathered about this shrine; all other sanctuaries have indeed enjoyed a flush of fame, but frequently sundry happenings have brought them low, whereas this is the only temple which, founded as it was at the beginning of time, not only has never failed to be the object of veneration but, on the contrary, has as time went on ever continued to enjoy great growth. For after Eryx has bestowed upon it the honours we have described, Aeneas, the son of Aphrodite, when at a later time he was on his way to Italy and came to anchor off the island, embellished the sanctuary, since it was that of his own mother, with many votive offerings; after him the Sicanians paid honour to the goddess for many generations and kept continually embellishing it with both magnificent sacrifices and votive offerings; and after that time the Carthaginians, when they had become the masters of a part of Sicily, never failed to hold the goddess in special honour. Last of all the Romans, when they had subdued all Sicily, surpassed all people who had preceded them in the honours they paid to her, and it was with good reason that they did so, for since they traced back their ancestry to her and for this reason were successful in their undertakings, they were but requiting her who was the cause of their aggrandisement with such expressions of gratitude and honours as they owed to her. The consuls and praetors, for instance, who visit the island and all Romans who sojourn there clothed with any authority, whenever they come to Eryx, embellish the sanctuary with magnificent sacrifices and honours, and laying aside the austerity of their authority, they enter into sports and have conversation with women in a spirit of great gaiety, believing that only in this way will they make their presence there pleasing to the goddess. Indeed the Roman senate has so zealously concerned itself with the honours of the goddess that it has decreed that the seventeen cities of Sicily which are most faithful to Rome shall pay a tax in gold to Aphrodite, and that two hundred soldiers shall serve as a guard of her shrine.

Now if we have dwelt over-long on the topic of Eryx, we have at least given an account of the goddess such as was rightly her due.

**84.** At this time we shall endeavour to set forth what the myths relate concerning Daphnis. There are in Sicily, namely, the Heraean Mountains, which, men say, are naturally well suited, by reason of the beauty and nature and special character of the region round about, to relaxation and enjoyment in the summer season. For they possess many springs of exceptionally sweet water and are full of trees of every description. On them also is a multitude of great oak-trees which bear fruit of extraordinary size, since it is twice as large as any that grows in other lands, and they possess as well some of the cultivated fruits, which have sprung up of their own accord, since the vine is found there in profusion and tree-fruits in quantities beyond telling. Consequently the area once supported a Carthaginian army when it was facing starvation, the mountains supplying many tens of thousands of soldiers with sources of food for their unfailing sustenance.

It was in this region, where there were glens filled with trees and meet for a god and a grove consecrated to the Nymphs, that, as the myths relate, he who was known as Daphnis was born, a son of Hermes and a Nymph, and he, because of the sweet bay (*daphne*) which grew there in such profusion and so thick, was given the name Daphnis. He was reared by Nymphs, and since he possessed very many herds of cattle and gave great attention to their care, he was for this reason called by the name Bucolus or "Neatherd." Being endowed with an unusual gift of song, he invented the bucolic or pastoral poem and the bucolic song which continues to be so popular throughout Sicily to the present day. The myths add that Daphnis accompanied Artemis in her hunting, serving the goddess in an acceptable manner, and that with his shepherd's pipe and singing of pastoral songs he pleased her exceedingly. The story is also told that one of the Nymphs became enamoured of him and prophesied to him that if he lay with any other woman he would be deprived of his sight; and indeed, when once he had been made drunken by a daughter of a king and had lain with her, lie was deprived of his sight in accordance with the prophecy delivered by the Nymph. As for Daphnis, then, let what we have said suffice.

**85.** We shall now recount what the myths relate about Orion. The story runs like this: Orion, far surpassing in size and strength of body all the heroes of whom we have record, was a lover of the chase and the builder of mighty works by reason of his great strength and love of glory. In Sicily, for instance, for Zanclus, who was king at that time of the city which was called at that time after him Zancle, but now Messenê, he built certain works, and among them he formed the harbour by throwing up a mole and made the Acte [promontory], as it is called. Since we have mentioned Messenê we think it will not be foreign to our purpose to add to what has been set forth thus far what men have written about the Strait. The ancient mythographers, that is, say that Sicily was originally a peninsula, and that afterward it became an island, the cause being somewhat as follows. The isthmus at its narrowest point was subjected to the dash of the waves of the sea on its two sides and so a gap (*rhegma*) was made (*anarrhegnusthai*), and for this reason the spot was named *Rhegion,* and the city which was founded many years later received the same appellation as the place. Some men say, however, that mighty earthquakes took place and the neck of what was the mainland was broken through, and in this way the Strait was formed, since the sea now separated the mainland from the island. The poet Hesiod states the very opposite, namely, that when the sea extended itself in between, Orion built out the headland which lies at Peloris and also erected there the sanctuary of Poseidon which is held in special honour by the natives; after he had finished these works he removed to Euboea and made his home there; and then, because of his fame, he was numbered among the stars of heaven and thus won for himself immortal remembrance. And he is also mentioned by the poet Homer in his "Necuia " when he says:

> And after him I marked Orion huge,
> Driving wild beasts together o'er the mead
> Of asphodel, the beasts that he himself
> Had slain on lonely hills; and in his hands
> He held a mace, ever unbroken, all
> Of bronze.

Likewise, to show forth also his great size, whereas he had spoken before of the Aloiadae [Otus and Ephialtes], that at nine years of age they were nine cubits in breadth and an equal number of fathoms in height, he adds:

> These were the tallest men that ever earth,
> Giver of grain, did rear, and goodliest
> By far, save for Orion, famed abroad.

But for our part, since we have spoken, in accordance with the plan which we announced at the beginning, at sufficient length about the heroes and demigods, at this point we shall close the present Book.

# BOOK V

1. It should be the special care of historians, when they compose their works, to give attention to everything which may be of utility, and especially to the arrangement of the varied material they present. This eye to arrangement, for instance, is not only of great help to persons in the disposition of their private affairs if they would preserve and increase their property, but also, when men come to writing history, it offers them not a few advantages. Some historians indeed, although they are worthy objects of praise in the matter of style and in the breadth of experience derived from the events which they record, have nevertheless fallen short in respect of the way in which they have handled the matter of arrangement, with the result that, whereas the effort and care which they expended receive the approbation of their readers, yet the order which they gave to the material they have recorded is the object of just censure. Timaeus, for example, bestowed, it is true, the greatest attention upon the precision of his chronology and had due regard for the breadth of knowledge gained through experience, but he is criticised with good reason for his untimely and lengthy censures, and because of the excess which he went in censuring he has been given by some men the name Epitimaeus or Censurer. Ephorus, on the other hand, in the universal history which he composed has achieved success, not alone in the style of his composition, but also as regards the arrangement of his work; for each one of his Books is so constructed as to embrace events which fall under a single topic. Consequently we also have given our preference to this method of handling our material, and, in so far as it is possible, are adhering to this general principle.

### On the myths which are recounted about Sicily and the shape and size of the island (2).

2. And since we have given this Book the title "On the Islands," in accordance with this heading the first island we shall speak about will be Sicily, since it is both the richest of the islands and holds first place in respect of the great age of the myths related concerning it. The island in ancient times was called, after its shape, Trinacria [three capes], then Sicania after the Sicani who made their home there, and finally it has been given the name Sicily after the Siceli who crossed over in a body to it from Italy. Its circumference is some four thousand three hundred and sixty stades; for of its three sides, that extending from Pelorias to Lilybaeum is one thousand seven hundred stades, that from Lilybaeum to Pachynus in the territory of Syracuse is a thousand five hundred, and the remaining side is one thousand one hundred and forty stades. The Siceliotae who dwell in the island have received the tradition from their ancestors, the report having ever been handed down successively from earliest time by one generation to the next, that the island is sacred to Demeter and Core; although there are certain poets who recount the myth that at the marriage of Pluton and Persephone Zeus gave this island as a wedding present to the bride. That the ancient inhabitants of Sicily, the Sicani, were indigenous, is stated by the best authorities among historians, and also that the goddesses we have mentioned made their first appearance on this island, and that it was the first,

because of the fertility of the soil, to bring forth the fruit of the corn, facts to which the most renowned of the poets also bears witness when he writes:

> But all these things grow there for them unsown
> And e'en untilled, both wheat and barley, yea,
> And vines, which yield such wine as fine grapes give,
> And rain of Zeus gives increase unto them.

Indeed, in the plain of Leontini, we are told, and throughout many other parts of Sicily the wheat men call "wild " grows even to this day, and, speaking generally, before the corn was discovered, if one were to raise the question, what manner of land it was of the inhabited earth where the fruits we have mentioned appeared for the first time, the meed of honour may reasonably be accorded to the richest land; and in keeping with what we have stated, it is also to be observed that the goddesses who made this discovery are those who receive the highest honours among the Siceliotae.

### On Demeter and Corê and the discovery of the fruit of wheat (3-6).

**3.** Again, the fact that the Rape of Core took place in Sicily is, men say, proof most evident that the goddesses made this island their favourite retreat because it was cherished by them before all others. And the Rape of Core, the myth relates, took place in the meadows in the territory of Enna. The spot lies near the city, a place of striking beauty for its violets and every other kind of flower and worthy of the goddess. And the story is told that, because of the sweet odour of the flowers growing there, trained hunting dogs are unable to hold the trail, because their natural sense of smell is balked. The meadow we have mentioned is level in the centre and well watered throughout, but on its periphery it rises high and falls off with precipitous cliffs on every side, and it is conceived of as lying in the very centre of the island, which is the reason why certain writers call it the navel of Sicily. Near to it also are sacred groves, surrounded by marshy flats, and a huge grotto which contains a chasm which leads down into the earth and opens to the north, and through it, the myth relates, Pluton, coming out with his chariot, effected the Rape of Core. The violets, we are told, and the rest of the flowers which supply the sweet odour continue to bloom, to one's amazement, throughout the entire year, and so the whole aspect of the place is one of flowers and delight. Both Athena and Artemis, the myth goes on to say, who had made the same choice of maidenhood as had Core and were reared together with her, joined with her in gathering the flowers, and all of them together wove the robe for their father Zeus, and because of the time they had spent together and their intimacy they all loved this island above any other, and each one of them received for her portion a territory, Athena receiving hers in the region of Himera, where the Nymphs, to please Athena, caused the springs of warm water to gush forth on the occasion of the visit of Heracles to the island, and the natives consecrated a city to her and a plot of ground which to this day is called Athena's. Artemis received from the gods the island at Syracuse which was named after her, by both the oracles and men, Ortygia [quail-island]. On this island likewise these Nymphs, to please Artemis, caused a great fountain to gush forth to which was given the name Arethusa. Not only in ancient times did this fountain contain large fish in great numbers, but also in our own day we find these fish still there, considered to be holy and not to be touched by men; and on many occasions, when certain men have eaten them amid stress of war, the deity has shown a striking sign, and has visited with great sufferings such as dared to take them for food. Of these matters we shall give an exact account in connection with the appropriate period of time.

**4.** Like the two goddesses whom we have mentioned Core, we are told, received as her portion the meadows round about Enna; but a great fountain was made sacred to her in the territory of Syracuse and given the name Cyane or "Azure Fount." For the myth relates that it was near Syracuse that Pluton effected the Rape of Core and took her away in his chariot, and that after cleaving the earth asunder he himself descended into Hades, taking along with him the bride whom he had seized, and that he caused the fountain named Cyane to gush forth, near which the Syracusans each year hold a notable festive gathering; and private individuals offer the lesser victims, but when the ceremony is on behalf of the community, bulls are plunged in the pool, this maimer of sacrifice having been commanded by Heracles on the occasion when he made the circuit of all Sicily, while driving off the cattle of Geryones.

After the Rape of Core, the myth goes on to recount, Demeter, being unable to find her daughter, kindled torches in the craters of Mt. Aetna and visited many parts of the inhabited world, and upon the men who received her with the greatest favour she conferred benefactions, rewarding them with the gift of the fruit of the wheat. Since a more kindly welcome was extended the goddess by the Athenians than by any other people, they were the first after the Siceliotae to be given the fruit of the wheat; and in return for this gift the citizens of that city in assembly honoured the goddess above all others with the establishment both of most notable sacrifices and of the mysteries of Eleusis, which, by reason of their very great antiquity and sanctity, have come to be famous among all mankind. From the Athenians many peoples received a portion of the gracious gift of the corn, and they in turn, sharing the gift of the seed with their neighbours, in this way caused all the inhabited world to abound with it. The inhabitants of Sicily, since by reason of the intimate relationship of Demeter and Core with them they were the first to share in the corn after its discovery, instituted to each one of the goddesses sacrifices and festive gatherings, which they named after them, and by the time chosen for these made acknowledgment of the gifts which had been conferred upon them. In the case of Core, for instance, they established the celebration of her return at about the time when the fruit of the corn was found to come to maturity, and they celebrate this sacrifice and festive gathering with such strictness of observance and such zeal as we should reasonably expect those men to show who are returning thanks for having been selected before all mankind for the greatest possible gift; but in the case of Demeter they preferred that time for the sacrifice when the sowing of the corn is first begun, and for a period of ten days they hold a festive gathering which bears the name of this goddess and is most magnificent by reason of the brilliance of their preparation for it, while in the observance of it they imitate the ancient manner of life. It is their custom during these days to indulge in coarse language as they associate one with another, the reason being that by such coarseness the goddess, grieved though she was at the Rape of Core, burst into laughter.

**5.** That the Rape of Core took place in the manner we have described is attested by many ancient historians and poets. Carcinus the tragic poet, for instance, who often visited in Syracuse and witnessed the zeal which the inhabitants displayed in the sacrifices and festive gatherings for both Demeter and Core, has the following verses in his writings:

> Demeter's daughter, her whom none may name,
> By secret schemings Pluton, men say, stole,
> And then he dropped into earth's depths, whose light
> Is darkness. Longing for the vanished girl
> Her mother searched and visited all lands
> In turn. And Sicily's land by Aetna's crags
> Was filled with streams of fire which no man could
> Approach, and groaned throughout its length; in grief
> Over the maiden now the folk, beloved
> Of Zeus, was perishing without the corn.
> Hence honour they these goddesses e'en now.

But we should not omit to mention the very great benefaction which Demeter conferred upon mankind; for beside the fact that she was the discoverer of corn, she also taught mankind how to prepare it for food and introduced laws by obedience to which men became accustomed to the practice of justice, this being the reason, we are told, why she has been given the epithet Thesmophoros or Lawgiver. Surely a benefaction greater than these discoveries of hers one could not find; for they embrace both living and living honourably. However, as for the myths which are current among the Siceliotae, we shall be satisfied with what has been said.

**6.** We must now write briefly about the Sicani who were the first inhabitants of Sicily, in view of the fact that certain historians are not in agreement about this people. Philistus, for instance, says that they removed from Iberia and settled the island, having got the name they bore from a certain river in Iberia named Sicanus, but Timaeus adduces proof of the ignorance of this historian and correctly declares that they were indigenous; and inasmuch as the evidences he offers of the antiquity of this people are many, we think that there is no need for us to recount them. The Sicani, then, originally made their homes in villages, building their settlements upon the strongest hills because of the pirates; for they had not yet been brought under the single rule of a king, but in each settlement there was one man who was lord. At first they made their home in every part of the island and secured their food by tilling the land; but at a later time, when Aetna sent up volcanic eruptions in an increasing number of places and a great torrent of lava was poured forth over the land, it came to pass that a great stretch of the country was ruined, and since the fire kept consuming a large area of the land during an increasing number of years, in fear they left the eastern parts of Sicily and removed to the western. Last of all, many generations later, the people of the Siceli crossed over in a body from Italy into Sicily and made their home in the land which had been abandoned by the Sicani. Since the Siceli steadily grew more avaricious and kept ravaging the land which bordered on theirs, frequent wars arose between them and the Sicani, until at last they struck covenants and set up boundaries, upon which they had agreed, for the territory. With regard to the Sicani we shall give a detailed account in connection with the appropriate period of time. The colonies of the Greeks, and notable ones they were, were the last to be made in Sicily, and their cities were founded on the sea. All the inhabitants mingled with one another, and since the Greeks came to the island in great numbers, the natives learned their speech, and then, having been brought up in the Greek ways of life, they lost in the end their barbarian speech as well as their name, all of them being called Siceliotae.

## *On Lipara and the other islands which are called the Aeolidcs (7-11).*

7. But since we have spoken about these matters at sufficient length we shall turn our discussion to the islands known as the Aeolides [Lipari islands]. These islands are seven in number and bear the following names: Strongyle, Euonymus, Didyme, Phoenicodes, Encodes, Hiera Hephaestu, and Lipara, on which is situated a city of the same name. They lie between Sicily and Italy in a straight line from the Strait, extending from east to west. They are about one hundred and fifty stades distant from Sicily and are all of about the same size, and the largest one of them is about one hundred and fifty stades in circumference. All of them have experienced great volcanic eruptions, and the resulting craters and openings may be seen to this day. On Strongyle and Hiera even at the present time there are sent forth from the open mouths great exhalations accompanied by an enormous roaring, and sand and a multitude of red-hot stones are erupted, as may also be seen taking place on Aetna. The reason is, as some say, that passages lead under the earth from these islands to Aetna and are connected with the openings at both ends of them, and this is why the craters on these islands usually alternate in activity with those of Aetna.

We are told that the islands of Aeolus were uninhabited in ancient times, but that later Liparus, as he was called, the son of Auson the king, was overcome by his brothers who rebelled against him, and securing some warships and soldiers he fled from Italy to the island, which received the name Lipara after him; on it he founded the city which bears his name and brought under cultivation the other islands mentioned before. When Liparus had already come to old age, Aeolus, the son of Hippotes, came to Lipara with certain companions and married Cyane, the daughter of Liparus; and after he had formed a government in which his followers and the natives shared equally he became king over the island. To Liparus, who had a longing for Italy, Aeolus gave his aid in securing for him the regions about Surrentum, where he became king and, after winning great esteem, ended his days; and after he had been accorded a magnificent funeral he received at the hands of the natives honours equal to those offered to the heroes. This is the Aeolus to whom, the myth relates, Odysseus came in the course of his wanderings. He was, they say, pious and just and kindly as well in his treatment of strangers; furthermore, he introduced sea-farers to the use of sails and had learned, by long observation of what the fire foretold, to predict with accuracy the local winds, this being the reason why the myth has referred to him as the "keeper of the winds"; and it was because of his very great piety that he was called a friend of the Gods.

8. To Aeolus, we are told, sons were born to the number of six, Astyoehus, Xuthus, and Androcles, and Pheraemon, Jocastus, and Agathyrnus, and they every one received great approbation both because of the fame of their father and because of their own high achievements. Of their number Jocastus held fast to

Italy and was king of the coast as far as the regions about Rhegium, but Pheraemon and Androcles were lords over Sicily from the Strait as far as the regions about Lilybaeum. Of this country the parts to the east were inhabited by Siceli and those to the west by Sicani. These two peoples quarrelled with each other, but they rendered obedience of their own free will to the sons of Aeolus we have mentioned, both because of the piety of their father Aeolus, which was famed afar, and because of the fair-dealing of the sons themselves. Xuthus was king over the land in the neighbourhood of Leontini, which is known after him as Xuthia to this day. Agathyrnus, becoming king of the land now called Agathyrnitis, founded a city which was called after him Agathyrnus; and Astyoehus secured the lordship over Lipara. All these men followed the example which their father had set for both piety and justice and hence were accorded great approbation. Their descendants succeeded to their thrones over many generations, but in the end the kings of the house of Aeolus were overthrown throughout Sicily.

**9.** After this the Siceli put the leadership in each case in the hands of the ablest man, but the Sicani quarrelled over the lordship and warred against each other during a long period of time. But many years later than these events, when the islands again were becoming steadily more destitute of inhabitants, certain men of Cnidus and Rhodes, being aggrieved at the harsh treatment they were receiving at the hands of the kings of Asia, resolved to send out a colony. Consequently, having chosen for their leader Pentathlus of Cnidus, who traced his ancestry back to Hippotes, who was a descendant of Heracles, in the course of the Fiftieth Olympiad [580-576], that in which Epitelidas of Sparta won the "stadion," these settlers, then, of the company of Pentathlus sailed to Sicily to the regions about Lilybaeum, where they found the inhabitants of Egesta and of Selinus at war with one another. Being persuaded by the men of Selinus to take their side in the war, they suffered heavy losses in the battle, Pentathlus himself being among those who fell. Consequently the survivors, since the men of Selinus had been defeated in the war, decided to return to their homes; and choosing for leaders Gorgus and Thestor and Epithersides, who were relatives of Pentathlus, they sailed off through the Tyrrhenian Sea. When they put in at Lipara and received a kindly reception, they were prevailed upon to make common cause with the inhabitants of Lipara in forming a single community there, since of the colony of Aeolus there remained only about five hundred men. At a later time, because they were being harassed by the Tyrrheni who were carrying on piracy on the sea, they fitted out a fleet, and divided themselves into two bodies, one of which took over the cultivation of the islands which they had made the common property of the community, whereas the other was to fight the pirates; their possessions also they made common property, and living according to the public mess system, they passed their lives in this communistic fashion for some time. At a later time they apportioned among themselves the island of Lipara, where their city also lay, but cultivated the other islands in common. In the final stage they divided all the islands among themselves for a period of twenty years, and then they cast lots for them again at every expiration of this period. After effecting this organisation they defeated the Tyrrhenians in many sea-fights, and from their booty they often made notable dedications of a tenth part, which they sent to Delphi.

## Book V

**10.** It remains for us now, as regards the city of the Liparians, to give an explanation of the causes why in later times it grew to a position, not only of prosperity, but even of renown. These, then, are the reasons: The city is adorned by nature with excellent harbours and springs of warm water which are famed far and wide; for not only do the baths there contribute greatly to the healing of the sick, but they also, in keeping with the peculiar property of such warm springs, provide pleasure and enjoyment of no ordinary kind. Consequently many people throughout Sicily who are afflicted by illnesses of a peculiar nature come to the city and by taking the baths regain their health in a marvellous manner. And this island contains the far-famed mines of styptic earth [*alumen*], from which the Liparians and Romans derive great revenues. For since styptic earth is found nowhere else in the inhabited world and is of great usefulness, it stands to reason that, because they enjoy a monopoly of it and can raise the price, they should get an unbelievable amount of money; for on the island of Melos alone is there found a deposit of styptic earth, but a small one, which cannot suffice for many cities. The island of the Liparians is also small in extent but sufficiently fruitful and, so far as the wants of men are concerned, it supports even a high degree of luxury; for it supplies the inhabitants with a multitude of fish of every kind and contains those fruit trees which can offer the most pleasure when one enjoys them. As regards Lipara and the rest of the islands of Aeolus, as they are called, we shall be satisfied with what has been said.

**11.** Beyond Lipara, toward the west, lies an island in the open sea which is small in extent and uninhabited and bears the name Osteodes [bony] because of the following strange occurrence. During the time when the Carthaginians were waging many great wars with the Syracusans they were employing notable forces on both land and sea, and on the occasion in question they had many mercenaries who were gathered from every people; such troops are always trouble-makers and make it their practice to cause many and serious mutinies, especially on occasions when they do not get their pay promptly, and at the time of which we are speaking they practised their accustomed knavishness and audacity. For being in number about six thousand and not receiving their pay, they at first massed together and inveighed against the generals, and since the latter were without funds and time after time kept deferring payment, they threatened that they would take up arms and wreak vengeance upon the Carthaginians, and they even laid violent hands upon the commanders. Though the senate admonished them, the quarrel always blazed forth the more, whereupon the senate gave secret orders to the generals to do away with all the recalcitrants; and the generals then, acting upon the commands, embarked the mercenaries upon ships and sailed off as if upon some mission of war. Putting in at the island we have mentioned they disembarked all the mercenaries upon it and then sailed away, leaving the recalcitrants upon the island. The mercenaries, being in deep distress at the condition in which they found themselves and yet unable to wreak vengeance upon the Carthaginians, perished from hunger, and since it was a small island on which so many confined men died, it came to pass that the place, little as it was, was tilled with their bones; and this is the reason why the island received the name it bears. In this way, then, did the mercenaries, who were guilty of crime in the manner we have described, suffer the greatest misfortune, perishing from lack of food.

### On Melitê, Gaulus, and Cercina (12).

12. But for our part, since we have set forth the facts concerning the islands of the Aeolides, we shall consider it appropriate to make mention in turn of the islands which lie on the other side. For off the south of Sicily three islands lie out in the sea, and each of them possesses a city and harbours which can offer safety to ships which are in stress of weather. The first one is that called Melitê [Malta], which lies about eight hundred stades from Syracuse, and it possesses many harbours which offer exceptional advantages, and its inhabitants are blest in their possessions; for it has artisans skilled in every manner of craft, the most important being those who weave linen, which is remarkably sheer and soft, and the dwellings on the island are worthy of note, being ambitiously constructed with cornices and finished in stucco with unusual workmanship. This island is a colony planted by the Phoenicians, who, as they extended their trade to the western ocean, found in it a place of safe retreat, since it was well supplied with harbours and lay out in the open sea; and this is the reason why the inhabitants of this island, since they received assistance in many respects through the sea-merchants, shot up quickly in their manner of living and increased in renown.

After this island there is a second which bears the name of Gaulus [Gozo], lying out in the open sea and adorned with well-situated harbours, a Phoenician colony. Next comes Cercina [Kerkenna], facing Libya, which has a modest city and most serviceable harbours which have accommodations not only for merchant vessels but even for ships of war.

But now that we have spoken of the islands which are to the south of Sicily, we shall turn back to those which follow upon Lipara and lie in the sea which is known as the Tyrrhenian.

### On Aethaleia, Cyrnus (Corsica), and Sardinia (13-15).

13. Off the city of Tyrrhenia known as Poplonium there is an island which men call Aethaleia [Elba]. It is about one hundred stades distant from the coast and received the name it bears from the smoke (*aithalos*) which lies so thick about it. For the island possesses a great amount of iron-rock, which they quarry in order to melt and cast and thus to secure the iron, and they possess a great abundance of this ore. For those who are engaged in the working of the ore crush the rock and burn the lumps which have thus been broken in certain ingenious furnaces; and in these they smelt the lumps by means of a great fire and form them into pieces of moderate size which are in their appearance like large sponges. These are purchased by merchants in exchange either for money or for goods and are then taken to Dicaearcheia [Puteoli] or the other trading-stations, where there are men who purchase such cargoes and who, with the aid of a multitude of artisans in metal whom they have collected, work it further and manufacture iron objects of every description. Some of these are worked into the shape of armour, and others are ingeniously fabricated into shapes well suited for two-pronged forks and sickles and other such tools; and these are then carried by merchants to every region and thus many parts of the inhabited world have a share in the usefulness which accrues from them.

After Aethaleia there is an island, some three hundred stades distant, which is called Cyrnus by the Greeks, but Corsica by the Romans and who dwell upon it.

This island, being easy to land on, has a most excellent harbour which is called Syracosium. There are also on it two notable cities, the one being known as Calaris and the other as Nicaea. Calaris [Aleria] was founded by Phocaeans, who made their home there for a time and were then driven out of the island by Tyrrhenians; but Nicaea was founded by Tyrrhenians at the time they were masters of the sea and were taking possession of the islands lying off Tyrrhenia. They were lords of the cities of Cyrnus for a considerable period and exacted tribute of the inhabitants in the form of resin, wax, and honey, since these things were found in the island in abundance. Slaves from Cyrnus are reputed to be superior to all others for every service which the life of man demands, nature herself giving them this characteristic. The entire island, which is of great extent, has mountainous land over much of its area, which is thickly covered with continuous forests and traversed by small rivers.

**14.** The inhabitants of Cyrnus use for their food milk and honey and meat, the land providing all these in abundance, and among themselves they live lives of honour and justice, to a degree surpassing practically all other barbarians. Any honeycomb, for instance, which may be found in the trees on the mountainside belongs to the first man to find it, no one disputing his claim; their cattle are distinguished by brands, and even though no man may watch over them, they are still kept safe for their owners; and in their other ways of living one and all it is astonishing how they revere uprightness before everything else. The most amazing thing which takes place among them is connected, with the birth of their children; for when the wife is about to give birth she is the object of no concern as regards her delivery, but it is her husband who takes to his bed, as though sick, and he practises couvade for a specified number of days, feigning that his body is in pain. There also grows in this island box-wood in great abundance and of excellent quality, and it is due to it that the honey of the island is altogether bitter. The island is inhabited by barbarians who have a language which is different from others and hard to understand, and they are in number more than thirty thousand.

**15.** Adjoining Cyrnus is an island which is called Sardinia, and in size it is about the equal of Sicily and is inhabited by barbarians who bear the name of Iolaes and are thought to be descendants of the men who settled there along with Iolaüs and the Thespiadae. For at the time when Heracles was accomplishing his famous Labours he had many sons by the daughters of Thespius, and these Heracles dispatched to Sardinia, in accordance with a certain oracle, sending along with them a notable force composed of both Greeks and barbarians, in order to plant a colony. Iolaüs, the nephew of Heracles, was in charge of the undertaking, and taking possession of the island he founded in it notable cities, and when he had divided the land into allotments he called the folk of the colony Iolaës after himself; and he also constructed gymnasia and temples to the gods and everything else which contributes to making happy the life of man, memorials of this remaining even to this day; since the fairest plains there derive their name from him and are called "Iolaeia," and the whole body of the people preserve to the present the name which they took from Iolaüs.

Now the oracle regarding the colony contained also the promise that the participants in this colony should maintain their freedom for all time, and it has indeed come to pass that the oracle, contrary to what one would expect, has preserved autonomy for the natives unshaken to this day. Thus the Carthaginians, though their power extended far and they subdued the island, were not able to enslave its former possessors, but the Iolaes fled for safety to the mountainous part of the island and built underground dwellings, and here they raised many flocks and herds which supplied them with food in abundance, so that they were able to maintain themselves on a diet of milk and cheese and meat; and since they had retired from the plain country, they avoided the hardship which accompanies labour, but ranged over the mountainous part of the island and led a life which had no share in hardship, in that they continued to use the foods mentioned above. Although the Carthaginians made war upon them many times with considerable armies, yet because of the rugged nature of the country and the difficulty of dealing with their dug-out dwellings the people remained unenslaved. Last of all, when the Romans conquered the island and oftentimes made war on them, they remained unsubdued by the troops of an enemy for the reasons we have mentioned. In the early period, however, Iolaüs, after helping to establish the affairs of the colony, returned to Greece, but the Thespiadae were the chief men of the island for many generations, until finally they were driven out into Italy, where they settled in the region of Cymê [Cumae]; the mass of the colonists who were left behind became barbarized, and choosing the best among the natives to be their chieftains, they have maintained their freedom down to our own day.

## On Pityussa and the Gymnesiae islands, which some call the Baliarides (16-18).

**16.** But now that we have spoken about Sardinia at sufficient length we shall discuss the islands in the order in which they lie. After those we have mentioned there comes first an island called Pityussa [Ibiza & Formentera], the name being due to the multitude of pine-trees (*pityes*) which grow throughout it. It lies out in the open sea and is distant from the Pillars of Heracles a voyage of three days and as many nights, from Libya a day and a night, and from Iberia one day; and in size it is about as large as Corcyra. The island is only moderately fertile, possessing little land that is suitable for the vine, but it has olive trees which are engrafted upon the wild olive. Of all the products of the island, they say that the softness of its wool stands first in excellence. The island is broken up at intervals by notable plains and highlands and has a city named Eresus, a colony of the Carthaginians, and it also possesses excellent harbours, huge walls, and a multitude of well-constructed houses. Its inhabitants consist of barbarians of every nationality, but Phoenicians preponderate. The date of the founding of the colony falls one hundred and sixty years after the settlement of Carthage.

**17.** There are other islands lying opposite Iberia, which the Greeks call Gymnesiae because the inhabitants go naked (*gymnoi*) of clothing in the summer time, but which the inhabitants of the islands and the Romans call Baliarides because in the hurling (*ballein*) of large stones with slings the natives are the most skilful of all men. The larger of these is the largest of all islands after the seven, Sicily, Sardinia, Cyprus, Crete, Euboea, Cyrnus, and Lesbos, and it is a day's voyage distant from Iberia; the smaller lies more to the east and maintains great droves and flocks of every kind of animal, especially of mules, which stand very high and are exceptionally strong. Both islands have good land which produces fruits, and a multitude of inhabitants numbering more than thirty thousand, but as for their food products they raise no wine whatsoever; consequently the inhabitants are one and all exceedingly addicted to indulgence in wine because of the scarcity of it among them; and they are altogether lacking in olive-oil and therefore prepare an oil from the mastich-tree, which they mix with the fat from pigs, and with this they anoint their bodies.

The Baliares are of all men the most fond of women and value them so highly above everything else that, when any of their women are seized by visiting pirates and carried off, they will give as ransom for a single woman three and even four men. Their dwellings they make under hollow rocks, or they dig out holes along the faces of sharp crags, in general putting many parts of them underground, and in these they pass their time, having an eye both to the shelter and to the safety which such homes afford. Silver and gold money is not used by them at all, and as a general practice its importation into the island is prevented, the reason they offer being that of old Heracles made an expedition against Geryones, who was the son of Chrysaor and possessed both silver and gold in abundance. Consequently, in order that their possessions should consist in that against which no one would have designs, they have made wealth in gold and silver alien from themselves, and so, in keeping with this decision of theirs, when in early times they served once in the campaigns of the Carthaginians, they did not bring back their pay to their native land but spent it all upon the purchase of women and wine.

**18.** The Baliares have also an amazing custom which they observe in connection with their marriages; for during their wedding festivities the relatives and friends lie with the bride in turn, the oldest first and then the next oldest and the rest in order, and the last one to enjoy this privilege is the bridegroom. Peculiar also and altogether strange is their practice regarding the burial of the dead; for they dismember the body with wooden knives, and then they place the pieces in a jar and pile upon it a heap of stones. Their equipment for fighting consists of three slings, and of these they keep one around the head, another around the belly, and the third in the hands. In the business of war they hurl much larger stones than do any other slingers, and with such force that the missile seems to have been shot, as it were, from a catapult; consequently, in their assaults upon walled cities, they strike the defenders on the battlements and disable them, and in pitched battles they crush both shields and helmets and every kind of protective armour, and they are so accurate in their aim that in the majority of cases they never miss the target before them. The reason for this is the continual practice which they get from childhood, in that their mothers compel them, while still young boys, to use the sling continually; for there is set up before them as a target a piece of bread fastened to a stake, and the novice is not permitted to eat until he has hit the bread, whereupon he takes it from his mother with her permission and devours it.

*On the islands in the ocean which lie towards the west (19-20).*

**19.** But now that we have discussed what relates to the islands which lie within the Pillars of Hercules, we shall give an account of those which are in the ocean. For there lies out in the deep off Libya an island of considerable size, and situated as it is in the ocean it is distant from Libya a voyage of a number of days to the west. Its land is fruitful, much of it being mountainous and not a little being a level plain of surpassing beauty. Through it flow-navigable rivers which are used for irrigation, and the island contains many parks planted with trees of every variety and gardens in great multitudes which are traversed by streams of sweet water; on it also are private villas of costly construction, and throughout the gardens banqueting houses have been constructed in a setting of flowers, and in them the inhabitants pass their time during the summer season, since the land supplies in abundance everything which contributes to enjoyment and luxury. The mountainous part of the island is covered with dense thickets of great extent and with fruit-trees of every variety, and, inviting men to life among the mountains, it has cozy glens and springs in great number. In a word, this island is well supplied with springs of sweet water which not only makes the use of it enjoyable for those who pass their life there but also contribute to the health and vigour of their bodies. There is also excellent hunting of every manner of beast and wild animal, and the inhabitants, being well supplied with this game at their feasts, lack of nothing which pertains to luxury and extravagance; for in fact the sea which washes the shore of the island contains a multitude of fish, since the character of the ocean is such that it abounds throughout its extent with fish of every variety. Speaking generally, the climate of this island is so altogether mild that it produces in abundance the fruits of the trees and the other seasonal fruits for the larger part of the year, so that it would appear that the island, because of its exceptional felicity, were a dwelling-place of a race of gods and not of men.

20. In ancient times this island remained undiscovered because of its distance from the entire inhabited world, but it was discovered at a later period for the following reason. The Phoenicians, who from ancient times on made voyages continually for purposes of trade, planted many colonies throughout Libya and not a few as well in the western parts of Europe. And since their ventures turned out according to their expectations, they amassed great wealth and essayed to voyage beyond the Pillars of Heracles into the sea which men call the ocean. First of all, upon the Strait itself by the Pillars they founded a city on the shores of Europe, and since the land formed a peninsula they called the city Gadeira [Cadiz]; in the city they built many works appropriate to the nature of the region, and among them a costly temple of Heracles [Melkart], and they instituted magnificent sacrifices which were conducted after the manner of the Phoenicians. It has come to pass that this shrine has been held in an honour beyond the ordinary, both at the time of its building and in comparatively recent days down even to our own lifetime. Also many Romans, distinguished men who have performed great deeds, have offered vows to this god, and these vows they have performed after the completion of their successes. The Phoenicians, then, while exploring the coast outside the Pillars for the reasons we have stated and while sailing along the shore of Libya, were driven by strong winds a great distance out into the ocean, and after being storm-tossed for many days they were carried ashore on the island we mentioned above, and when they had observed its felicity and nature they caused it to be known to all men. Consequently the Tyrrhenians, at the time when they were masters of the sea, purposed to dispatch a colony to it; but the Carthaginians prevented their doing so, partly out of concern lest many inhabitants of Carthage should remove there

because of the excellence of the island, and partly in order to have ready in it a place in which to seek refuge against an incalculable turn of fortune, in case some total disaster should overtake Carthage. For it was their thought that, since they were masters of the sea, they would thus be able to move, households and all, to an island which was unknown to their conquerors.

### On the island of Britain and that called Basileia, where amber is found (21-23).

**21.** But since we have set forth the facts concerning the ocean lying off Libya and its islands, we shall now turn our discussion to Europe. Opposite that part of Gaul which lies on the ocean and directly across from the Hercynian Forest, as it is called, which is the largest of any in Europe of which tradition tells us, there are many islands out in the ocean of which the largest is that known as Britain. In ancient times this island remained unvisited by foreign armies; for neither Dionysus, tradition tells us, nor Heracles, nor any other hero or leader made a campaign against it; in our day, however, Gaius Caesar, who has been called a god because of his deeds, was the first man of whom we have record to have conquered the island, and after subduing the Britains he compelled them to pay fixed tributes. But we shall give a detailed account of the events of this conquest in connection with the appropriate period of time, and at present we shall discuss the island and the tin which is found in it.

Britain is triangular in shape, very much as is Sicily, but its sides are not equal. This island stretches obliquely along the coast of Europe, and the point where it is least distant from the mainland, we are told, is the promontory which men call Cantium [Forelands and Kent], and this is about one hundred stades from the land, at the place where the sea has its outlet, whereas the second promontory, known as Belerium [Land's End], is said to be a voyage of four days from the mainland, and the last, writers tell us, extends out into the open sea and is named Orca [Dunnet Head]. Of the sides of Britain the shortest, which extends along Europe, is seven thousand five hundred stades, the second, from the Strait to the (northern) tip, is fifteen thousand stades, and the last is twenty thousand stades, so that the entire circuit of the island amounts to forty-two thousand five hundred stades. Britain, we are told, is inhabited by tribes which are autochthonous and preserve in their ways of living the ancient manner of life. They use chariots, for instance, in their wars, even as tradition tells us the old Greek heroes did in the Trojan War, and their dwellings are humble, being built for the most part out of reeds or logs. The method they employ of harvesting their grain crops is to cut off no more than the heads and store them away in roofed granges, and then each day they pick out the ripened heads and grind them, getting in this way their food. As for their habits, they are simple and far removed from the shrewdness and vice which characterise the men of our day. Their way of living is modest, since they are well clear of the luxury which is begotten of wealth. The island is also thickly populated, and its climate is extremely cold, as one would expect, since it actually lies under the Great Bear. It is held by many kings and potentates, who for the most part live at peace among themselves.

**22.** But we shall give a detailed account of the customs of Britain and of the other features which are peculiar to the island when we come to the campaign which Caesar undertook against it, and at this time we shall discuss the tin which the island produces. The inhabitants of Britain who dwell about the promontory known as Belerium [Cornwall] are especially hospitable to strangers and have adopted a civilised manner of life because of their intercourse with merchants of other peoples. They it is who work the tin, treating the bed which bears it in an ingenious manner. This bed, being like rock, contains earthy seams and in them the workers quarry the ore, which they then melt down and cleanse of its impurities. Then they work the tin into pieces the size of knuckle-bones and convey it to an island which lies off Britain and is called Ictis [St. Michael's Mount]; for at the time of ebb-tide the space between this island and the mainland becomes dry and they can take the tin in large quantities over to the island on their wagons. (A peculiar thing happens in the case of the neighbouring islands which lie between Europe and Britain, for at flood-tide the passages between them and the mainland run full and they have the appearance of islands, but at ebb-tide the sea recedes and leaves dry a large space, and at that time they look like peninsulas.) On the island of Ictis the merchants purchase the tin of the natives and carry it from there across the Strait to Galatia or Gaul; and finally, making their way on foot through Gaul for some thirty days, they bring their wares on horseback to the mouth of the river Rhone.

**23.** But as regards the tin of Britain we shall rest content with what has been said, and we shall now discuss the *electron,* as it is called (amber). Directly opposite the part of Scythia which lies above Galatia there is an island out in the open sea which is called Basileia [Heligoland]. On this island the waves of the sea cast up great quantities of what is known as amber, which is to be seen nowhere else in the inhabited world; and about it many of the ancient writers have composed fanciful tales, such as are altogether difficult to credit and have been refuted by later events. For many poets and historians give the story that Phaethon, the son of Helius, while yet a youth, persuaded his father to retire in his favour from his four-horse chariot for a single day; and when Helius yielded to the request Phaethon, as he drove the chariot, was unable to keep control of the reins, and the horses, making light of the youth, left their accustomed course; and first they turned aside to traverse the heavens, setting it afire and creating what is now called the Milky Way, and after that they brought the scorching rays to many parts of the inhabited earth and burned up not a little land. Consequently Zeus, being indignant because of what had happened, smote Phaethon with a thunderbolt and brought back the sun to its accustomed course. Phaethon fell to the earth at the mouths of the river which is now known as the Padus (Po), but in ancient times was called the Eridanus, and his sisters vied with each other in bewailing his death and by reason of their exceeding grief underwent a metamorphosis of their nature, becoming poplar trees. These poplars, at the same season each year, drip tears [sap], and these, when they harden, form what men call amber, which in brilliance excels all else of the same nature and is commonly used in connection with the mourning attending the death of the young. But since the creators of this fictitious tale have one and all erred, and have been refuted by what has transpired at later times, we must give ear to the accounts which are truthful; for the fact is that amber is gathered on the island we have mentioned and is brought by the natives to the opposite continent, and that it is conveyed through the continent to the regions known to us, as we have stated.

**On Gaul, Celtiberia, Iberia, Liguria, and Tyrrhenia, and on the inhabitants of these countries and the customs they observe (24-40).**

**24.** Since we have set forth the facts concerning the islands which lie in the western regions, we consider that it will not be foreign to our purpose to discuss briefly the tribes of Europe which lie near them and which we failed to mention in our former Books. Now Celtica was ruled in ancient times, so we are told, by a renowned man who had a daughter who was of unusual stature and far excelled in beauty all the other maidens, but she, because of her strength of body and marvellous comeliness, was so haughty that she kept refusing every man who wooed her in marriage, since she believed that no one of her wooers was worthy of her. Now in the course of his campaign against Geryones, Heracles visited Celtica and founded there the city of Alesia, and the maiden, on seeing Heracles, wondered at his prowess and his bodily superiority and accepted his embraces with all eagerness, her parents having given their consent. From this union she bore to Heracles a son named Galates, who far surpassed all the youths of the tribe in quality of spirit and strength of body. And when he had attained to man's estate and had succeeded to the throne of his fathers, he subdued a large part of the neighbouring territory and accomplished great feats in war. Becoming renowned for his bravery, he called his subjects Galatae or Gauls after himself, and these in turn gave their name to all of Galatia or Gaul.

**25.** Since we have explained the name by which the Gauls are known, we must go on to speak about their land. Gaul is inhabited by many tribes of different size; for the largest number some two hundred thousand men, and the smallest fifty thousand, one of the latter [Aedui] standing on terms of kinship and friendship with the Romans, a relationship which has endured from ancient times down to our own day. The land, lying as it does for the most part under the Bears, has a wintry climate and is exceedingly cold. For during the winter season on cloudy days snow falls deep in place of rain, and on clear days ice and heavy frost are everywhere and in such abundance that the rivers are frozen over and are bridged by their own waters; for not only can chance travellers, proceeding a few at a time, make their way across them on the ice, but even armies with their tens of thousands, together with their beasts of burden and heavily laden wagons, cross upon it in safety to the other side. Many large rivers flow through Gaul, and their streams cut this way and that through the level plain, some of them flowing from bottomless lakes and others having their sources and affluents in the mountains, and some of them empty into the ocean and others into our sea. The largest one of those which flow into our waters is the Rhone, which has its sources in the Alps and empties into the sea by five mouths. Of the rivers which flow into the ocean the largest are thought to be the Danube and the Rhine, the latter of which the Caesar who has been called a god spanned with a bridge in our own day with astonishing skill, and leading his army across on foot he subdued the Gauls who lived beyond it. There are also many other navigable rivers in Celtica, but it would be a long task to write about them, and almost all of them become frozen over by the cold and thus bridge their own streams, and since the natural smoothness of the ice makes the crossing slippery for those who pass over, they sprinkle chaff on it and thus have a crossing which is safe.

**26.** A peculiar thing and unexpected takes place over the larger part of Gaul which we think we should not omit to mention. For from the direction of the sun's summer setting and from the north winds are wont to blow with such violence and force that they pick up from the ground rocks as large as can be held in the hand together with a dust composed of coarse gravel; and, generally-speaking, when these winds rage violently they tear the weapons out of men's hands and the clothing off their backs and dismount riders from their horses. Furthermore, since temperateness of climate is destroyed by the excessive cold, the land produces neither wine nor oil, and as a consequence those Gauls who are deprived of these fruits make a drink out of barley which they call *zythos* or beer, and they also drink the water with which they cleanse their honeycombs. The Gauls are exceedingly addicted to the use of wine and fill themselves with the wine which is brought into their country by merchants, drinking it unmixed, and since they partake of this drink without moderation by reason of their craving for it, when they are drunken they fall into a stupor or a state of madness. Consequently many of the Italian traders, induced by the love of money which characterises them, believe that the love of wine of these Gauls is their own godsend. For these transport the wine on the navigable rivers by means of boats and through the level plain on wagons, and receive for it an incredible price; for in exchange for a jar of wine they receive a slave, getting a servant in return for the drink.

**27.** Throughout Gaul there is found practically no silver, but there is gold in great quantities, which Nature provides for the inhabitants without their having to mine for it or to undergo any hardship. For the rivers, as they course through the country, having as they do sharp bends which turn this way and that and dashing against the mountains which line their banks and bearing off great pieces of them, are full of gold-dust. This is collected, by those who occupy themselves in this business, and these men grind or crush the lumps which hold the dust, and after washing out with water the earthy elements in it they give the gold-dust over to be melted in the furnaces. In this manner they amass a great amount of gold, which is used for ornament not only by the women but also by the men. For around their wrists and arms they wear bracelets, around their necks heavy necklaces of solid gold, and huge rings they wear as well, and even corselets of gold. And a peculiar and striking practice is found among the upper Celts, in connection with the sacred precincts of the gods; for in the temples and precincts made consecrate in their land, a great amount of gold has been deposited as a dedication to the gods, and not a native of the country ever touches it because of religious scruple, although the Celts are an exceedingly covetous people.

**28.** The Gauls are tall of body, with rippling muscles, and white of skin, and their hair is blond, and not only naturally so, but they also make it their practice by artificial means to increase the distinguishing colour which nature has given it. For they are always washing their hair in lime-water, and they pull it back from the forehead to the top of the head and back to the nape of the neck, with the result that their appearance is like that of Satyrs and Pans, since the treatment of their hair makes it so heavy and coarse that it differs in no respect from the mane of horses. Some of them shave the beard, but others let it grow a little; and the nobles shave their cheeks, but they let the moustache grow until it covers the mouth. Consequently, when they are eating, their moustaches become entangled in the food, and when they are drinking, the beverage passes, as it were, through a kind of a strainer. When they dine they all sit, not upon chairs, but upon the ground, using for cushions the skins of wolves or of dogs. The service at the meals is performed by the youngest children, both male and female, who are of suitable age; and near at hand are their fireplaces heaped with coals, and on them are caldrons and spits holding whole pieces of meat. Brave warriors they reward with the choicest portions of the meat, in the same manner as the poet introduces Ajax as honoured by the chiefs after he returned victorious from his single combat with Hector:

> To Ajax then were given of the chine
> Slices, full-length, unto his honour.

They invite strangers to their feasts, and do not inquire until after the meal who they are and of what things they stand in need. It is their custom, even during the course of the meal, to seize upon any trivial matter as an occasion for keen disputation and then to challenge one another to single combat, without any regard for their lives; for the belief of Pythagoras prevails among them, that the souls of men are immortal and that after a prescribed number of years they commence upon a new life, the soul entering into another body. Consequently, we are told, at the funerals of their dead some cast letters upon the pyre which they have written to their deceased kinsmen, as if the dead would be able to read these letters.

**29.** In their journeyings and when they go into battle the Gauls use chariots drawn by two horses, which carry the charioteer and the warrior; and when they encounter cavalry in the fighting they first hurl their javelins at the enemy and then step down from their chariots and join battle with their swords. Certain of them despise death to such a degree that they enter the perils of battle without protective armour and with no more than a girdle about their loins. They bring along to war also their free men to serve them, choosing them out from among the poor, and these attendants they use in battle as charioteers and as shield-bearers. It is also their custom, when they are formed for battle, to step out in front of the line and to challenge the most valiant men from among their opponents to single combat, brandishing their weapons in front of them to terrify their adversaries. When any man accepts the challenge to battle, they then break forth into a song in praise of the valiant deeds of their ancestors and in boast of their own high achievements, reviling all the while and belittling their opponent, and trying, in a word, by such talk to strip him of his bold spirit before the combat. When their enemies fall they cut off their heads and fasten them about the necks of their horses; and turning over to their attendants the arms of their opponents, all covered with blood, they carry them off as booty, singing a paean over them and striking up a song of victory, and these first-fruits of battle they fasten by nails upon their houses, just as men do, in certain kinds of hunting, with the heads of wild beasts they have mastered. The heads of their most distinguished enemies they embalm in cedar-oil and carefully preserve in a chest, and these they exhibit to strangers, gravely maintaining that in exchange for this head some one of their ancestors, or their father, or the man himself, refused the offer of a great sum of money. Some men among them, we are told, boast that they have not accepted an equal weight of gold for the head they show, displaying a barbarous sort of greatness of soul; for not to sell that which constitutes a witness and proof of one's valour is a noble thing, but to continue to fight against one of our own race, after he is dead, is to descend to the level of beasts.

**30.** The clothing they wear is striking; shirts which have been dyed and embroidered in varied colours, and breeches, which they call in their tongue *bracae;* and they wear striped coats, fastened by a buckle on the shoulder, heavy for winter wear and light for summer, in which are set checks, close together and of varied hues. For armour they use long shields, as high as a man, which are wrought in a manner peculiar to them, some of them even having the figures of animals embossed on them in bronze, and these are skilfully worked with an eye not only to beauty but also to protection. On their heads they put bronze helmets which have large embossed figures standing out from them and give an appearance of great size to those who wear them; for in some cases horns are attached to the helmet so as to form a single piece, in other cases images of the fore-parts of birds or four-footed animals. Their trumpets are of peculiar nature and such as barbarians use, for when they are blown upon they give forth a harsh sound, appropriate to the tumult of war. Some of them have iron cuirasses, chain-wrought, but others are satisfied with the armour which Nature has given them and go into battle naked. In place of the short sword they carry long broadswords which are hung on chains of iron or bronze and are worn along the right flank, and some of them gather up their shirts with belts plated with gold or silver. The spears they brandish, which they call *lanciae,* have iron heads a cubit in length and even more, and a little under two palms in breadth; for their swords are not shorter than the javelins of other peoples, and the heads of their javelins are larger than the swords of others. Some of these javelins come from the forge straight, others twist in and out in spiral shapes for their entire length, the purpose being that the thrust may not only cut the flesh, but mangle it as well, and that the withdrawal of the spear may lacerate the wound.

**31.** The Gauls are terrifying in aspect and their voices are deep and altogether harsh; when they meet together they converse with few words and in riddles, hinting darkly at things for the most part and using one word when they mean another; and they like to talk in superlatives, to the end that they may extol themselves and depreciate all other men. They are also boasters and threateners and are fond of pompous language, and yet they have sharp wits and are not without cleverness at learning. Among them are also to be found lyric poets whom they call Bards. These men sing to the accompaniment of instruments which are like lyres, and their songs may be either of praise or of obloquy. Philosophers, as we may call them, and men learned in religious affairs are unusually honoured among them and are called by them Druids. The Gauls likewise make use of diviners, accounting them worthy of high approbation, and these men foretell the future by means of the flight or cries of birds and of the slaughter of sacred animals, and they have all the multitude subservient to them. They also observe a custom which is especially astonishing and incredible, in case they are taking thought with respect to matters of great concern; for in such cases they devote to death a human being and plunge a dagger into him in the region above the diaphragm, and when the stricken victim has fallen they read the future from the manner of his fall and from the twitching of his limbs, as well as from the gushing of the blood, having learned to place confidence in an ancient and long-continued practice of observing such matters. It is a custom of theirs that no one should perform a sacrifice without a "philosopher"; for thank-offerings should be rendered to the gods, they say, by the hands of men who are experienced in the nature of the divine, and who speak, as it were, the language of the gods, and it is also through the mediation of such men, they think, that blessings likewise should be sought. Nor is it only in the exigencies of peace, but in their wars as well, that they obey, before all others, these men and their chanting poets, and such obedience is observed not only by their friends but also by their enemies; many times, for instance, when two armies approach each other in battle with swords drawn and spears thrust forward, these men step forth between them and cause them to cease, as though having cast a spell over certain kinds of wild beasts. In this way, even among the wildest barbarians, does passion give place before wisdom, and Ares stands in awe of the Muses.

**32.** And now it will be useful to draw a distinction which is unknown to many: The peoples who dwell in the interior above Massalia, those on the slopes of the Alps, and those on this side the Pyrenees mountains are called Celts, whereas the peoples who are established above this land of Celtica in the parts which stretch to the north, both along the ocean and along the Hercynian Mountain, and all the peoples who come after these, as far as Scythia, are known as Gauls; the Romans, however, include all these nations together under a single name, calling them one and all Gauls.

The women of the Gauls are not only like the men in their great stature but they are a match for them in courage as well. Their children are usually born with greyish hair, but as they grow older the colour of their hair changes to that of their parents. The most savage peoples among them are those who dwell beneath the Bears and on the borders of Scythia, and some of these, we are told, eat human beings, even as the Britains do who dwell on Iris [Ireland], as it is called. Since the valour of these peoples and their savage ways have been famed abroad, some men say that it was they who in ancient times overran all Asia and were called Cimmerians, time having slightly corrupted the word into the name of Cumbrians, as they are now called. For it has been their ambition from old to plunder, invading for this purpose the lands of others, and to regard all men with contempt. For they are the people who captured Rome [c.390], who plundered the sanctuary at Delphi [279], who levied tribute upon a large part of Europe and no small part of Asia, and settled themselves upon the lands of the peoples they had subdued in war, being called in time Greco-Gauls, because they became mixed with the Greeks, and who, as their last accomplishment, have destroyed many large Roman armies. In pursuance of their savage ways they manifest an outlandish impiety also with respect to their sacrifices; for their criminals they keep prisoner for five years and then impale in honour of the gods, dedicating them together with many other offerings of first-fruits and constructing pyres of great size. Captives also are used by them as victims for their sacrifices in honour of the gods. Certain of them likewise slay, together with the human beings, such animals as are taken in war, or burn them or do away with them in some other vengeful fashion.

Although their wives are comely, they have very little to do with them, but rage with lust, in outlandish fashion, for the embraces of males. It is their practice to sleep upon the ground on the skins of wild beasts and to tumble with a catamite on each side. The most astonishing thing of all is that they feel no concern for their proper dignity, but prostitute to others without a qualm the flower of their bodies; nor do they consider this a disgraceful thing to do, but rather when anyone of them is thus approached and refuses the favour offered him, this they consider an act of dishonour.

**33.** Now that we have spoken at sufficient length about the Celts we shall turn our history to the Celtiberians who are their neighbours. In ancient times these two peoples, namely, the Iberians and the Celts, kept warring among themselves over the land, but when later they arranged their differences and settled upon the land altogether, and when they went further and agreed to intermarriage with each other, because of such intermixture the two peoples received the appellation given above, and since it was two powerful nations that united and the land of theirs was fertile, it came to pass that the Celtiberians advanced far in fame and were subdued by the Romans with difficulty and only after they had faced them in battle over a long period. This people, it would appear, provide for warfare not only excellent cavalry but also foot-soldiers who excel in prowess and endurance. They wear rough black cloaks, the wool of which resembles the hair of goats. As for their arms, certain of the Celtiberians carry light shields like those of the Gauls, and certain carry circular wicker shields as large as an *aspis,* and about their shins and calves they wind greaves made of hair and on their heads they wear bronze helmets adorned with purple crests. The swords they wear are two-edged and wrought of excellent iron, and they also have dirks a span in length which they use in fighting at close quarters. A peculiar practice is followed by them in the fashioning of their defensive weapons; for they bury plates of iron in the ground and leave them there until in the course of time the rust has eaten out what is weak in the iron and what is left is only the most unyielding, and of this they then fashion excellent swords and such other objects as pertain to war. The weapon which has been fashioned in the manner described cuts through anything which gets in its way, for no shield or helmet or bone can withstand a blow from it, because of the exceptional quality of the iron. Able as they are to fight in two styles, they first carry on the contest on horseback, and when they have defeated the cavalry they dismount, and assuming the role of foot-soldiers they put up marvellous battles. A peculiar and strange custom obtains among them: careful and cleanly as they are in their ways of living, they nevertheless observe one practice which is low and partakes of great uncleanness; for they consistently use urine to bathe the body and wash their teeth with it, thinking that in this practice is constituted the care and healing of the body.

**34.** As for the customs they follow toward malefactors and enemies the Celtiberians are cruel, but toward strangers they are honourable and humane. Strangers, for instance, who come among them they one and all entreat to stop at their homes and they are rivals one of another in their hospitality, and any among them who are attended by strangers are spoken of with approval and regarded as beloved of the gods. For their food they use meats of every description, of which they enjoy an abundance, and a drink of honey mixed with wine, since the country supplies them with a great quantity of honey, although the wine they purchase from merchants who sail over the seas to them. Of the tribes neighbouring upon the Celtiberians the most advanced is the people of the Vaccaei, as they are called; for this people each year divides among its members the land which it tills and making the fruits the property of all they measure out his portion to each man, and for any cultivators who have appropriated some part for themselves they have set the penalty as death. The most valiant among the Iberians are those who are known as Lusitanians, who carry in war very small shields which are interwoven with cords of sinew and are able to protect the body unusually well, because they are so tough; and shifting this shield easily as they do in their fighting, now here, now there, they cleverly ward off from their person every blow which comes at them. They also use barbed javelins made entirely of iron, and wear helmets and swords very much like those of the Celtiberians. They hurl the javelin with good effect, even over a long distance, and, in fine, are doughty in dealing their blows. Since they are nimble and wear light arms, they are swift both in flight and in pursuit, but when it comes to enduring the hardships of a stiff fight they are far inferior to the Celtiberians. In time of peace they practise a kind of elfin dance which requires great nimbleness of limb, and in their wars they march into battle with even step and raise a battle-song as they charge upon the foe. A peculiar practise obtains among the Iberians and particularly among the Lusitanians; for when their young men come to the bloom of their physical strength, those who are the very poorest among them in worldly goods and yet excel in vigour of body and daring equip themselves with no more than valour and arms and gather in the mountain fastnesses, where they form into bands of considerable size and then descend upon Iberia and collect wealth from their pillaging. This brigandage they continually practise in a spirit of complete disdain; for using as they do light arms and being altogether nimble and swift, they are a most difficult people for other men to subdue, and, speaking generally, they consider the fastnesses and crags of the mountains to be their native land and to these places, which large and heavily equipped armies find hard to traverse, they flee for refuge. Consequently, although the Romans in their frequent campaigns against the Lusitanians rid them of their great spirit of disdain, they were nevertheless unable, often as they eagerly set about it, to put a complete end to their plundering.

**35.** Since we have set forth the facts concerning the Iberians, we think that it will not be foreign to our purpose to discuss the silver mines of the land; for this land possesses, we may venture to say, the most abundant and most excellent known sources of silver, and to the workers of this silver it returns great revenues. Now in the preceding Books which told of the achievements of Heracles we have mentioned the mountains in Iberia which are known as the Pyrenees. Both in height and in size these mountains are found to excel all others; for they stretch from the southern sea practically as far as the northern ocean and extend for some three thousand stades, dividing Gaul from Iberia and Celtiberia. And since they contain many thick and deep forests, in ancient times, we are told, certain herdsmen left a fire and the whole area of the mountains was entirely consumed; and due to this fire, since it raged continuously day after day, the surface of the earth was also burned and the mountains, because of what had taken place, were called the Pyrenees; furthermore, the surface of the burned land ran with much silver and, since the elementary substance out of which the silver is worked was melted down, there were formed many streams of pure silver. Now the natives were ignorant of the use of the silver, and the Phoenicians, as they pursued their commercial enterprises and learned of what had taken place, purchased the silver in exchange for other wares of little if any worth. This was the reason why the Phoenicians, as they transported this silver to Greece and Asia and to all other peoples, acquired great wealth. So far indeed did the merchants go in their greed that, in case their boats were fully laden and there still remained a great amount of silver, they would hammer the lead off the anchors and have the silver perform the service of the lead. The result was that the Phoenicians, as in the course of many years they prospered greatly, thanks to commerce of this kind, sent forth many colonies, some to Sicily and its neighbouring islands, and others to Libya, Sardinia, and Iberia.

36. At a much later time the Iberians, having come to know the peculiar qualities possessed by silver, sunk notable mines, and as a consequence, by working the most excellent and, we may say, the most abundant silver to be found, they received great revenues. The manner, then, in which the Iberians mine and work the silver is in part as follows. The mines being marvellous in their deposits of copper and gold and silver, the workers of the copper mines recover from the earth they dig out a fourth part of pure copper, and among the unskilled workers in silver there are some who will take out a Euboic talent in three days; for all the ore is full of solid silver-dust which gleams forth from it. Consequently a man may well be filled with wonder both at the nature of the region and at the diligence displayed by the men who labour there. Now at first unskilled labourers, whoever might come, carried on the working of the mines, and these men took great wealth away with them, since the silver-bearing earth was convenient at hand and abundant; but at a later time, after the Romans had made themselves masters of Iberia, a multitude of Italians have swarmed to the mines and taken great wealth away with them, such was their greed. For they purchase a multitude of slaves whom they turn over to the overseers of the working of the mines; and these men, opening shafts in a number of places and digging deep into the ground, seek out the seams of earth which are rich in silver and gold; and not only do they go into the ground a great distance, but they also push their diggings many stades in depth and run galleries off at every angle, turning this way and that, in this manner bringing up from the depths the ore which gives them the profit they are seeking.

37. Great also is the contrast these mines show when they are compared with those of Attica. The men, that is, who work the Attic mines, although they have expended large sums on the undertakings, yet "Now and then, what they hoped to get, they did not get, and what they had, they lost," so that it would appear that they met with misfortune in a kind of riddle; but the exploiters of the mines of Spain, in their hopes, amass great wealth from their undertakings. For their first labours are remunerative, thanks to the excellent quality of the earth for this sort

of thing, and they are ever coming upon more splendid veins, rich in both silver and gold; for all the ground in that region is a tangled network of veins which wind in many ways. Now and then, as they go down deep, they come upon flowing subterranean rivers, but they overcome the might of these rivers by diverting the streams which flow in on them by means of channels leading off at an angle. For being urged on as they are by expectations of gain, which indeed do not deceive them, they push each separate undertaking to its conclusion, and what is the most surprising thing of all, they draw out the waters of the streams they encounter by means of what is called by men the Egyptian screw, which was invented by Archimedes of Syracuse at the time of his visit to Egypt; and by the use of such screws they carry the water in successive lifts as far as the entrance, drying up in this way the spot where they are digging and making it well suited to the furtherance of their operations. Since this machine is an exceptionally ingenious device, an enormous amount of water is thrown out, to one's astonishment, by means of a trifling amount of labour, and all the water from such rivers is brought up easily from the depths and poured out on the surface. And a man may well marvel at the inventiveness of the craftsman, in connection not only with this invention but with many other greater ones as well, the fame of which has encompassed the entire inhabited world and of which we shall give a detailed and precise account when we come to the period of Archimedes.

**38.** To continue with the mines, the slaves who are engaged in the working of them produce for their masters revenues in sums defying belief, but they themselves wear out their bodies both by day and by night in the diggings under the earth, dying in large numbers because of the exceptional hardships they endure. For no respite or pause is granted them in their labours, but compelled beneath blows of the overseers to endure the severity of their plight, they throw away their lives in this wretched manner, although certain of them who can endure it, by virtue of their bodily strength and their persevering souls, suffer such hardships over a long period; indeed death in their eyes is more to be desired than life, because of the magnitude of the hardships they must bear. Although many are the astounding features connected with the mining just described, a man may wonder not the least at the fact that not one of the mines has a recent beginning, but all of them were opened by the covetousness of the Carthaginians at the time when Iberia was among their possessions. It was from these mines, that is, that they drew their continued growth, hiring the ablest mercenaries to be found and winning with their aid many and great wars. For it is in general true that in their wars the Carthaginians never rested their confidence in soldiers from among their own citizens or gathered from their allies, but that when they subjected the Romans and the Sicilians and the inhabitants of Libya to the greatest perils it was by money, thanks to the abundance of it which they derived from their mines, that they conquered them in every instance. For the Phoenicians, it appears, were from ancient times clever men in making discoveries to their gain, and the Italians are equally clever in leaving no gain to anyone else.

Tin also occurs in many regions of Iberia, not found, however, on the surface of the earth, as certain writers continually repeat in their histories, but dug out of the ground and smelted in the same manner as silver and gold. For there are many mines of tin in the country above Lusitania and on the islets which lie off Iberia out in the ocean and are called because of that fact the Cassiterides [*kassiteros* = tin]. Tin is brought in large quantities also from the island of Britain to the opposite Gaul, where it is taken by merchants on horses through the interior of Celtica both to the Massalians and to the city of Narbo, as it is called. This city is a colony of the Romans, and because of its convenient situation it possesses the finest market to be found in those regions.

**39.** Since we have discussed the Gauls, the Celt-iberians, and the Iberians, we shall pass on to the Ligurians. The Ligurians inhabit a land which is stony and altogether wretched, and the life they live is, by reason of the toils and the continuous hardships they endure in their labour, a grievous one and unfortunate. For the land being thickly wooded, some of them fell the wood the whole day long, equipped with efficient and heavy axes, and others, whose task it is to prepare the ground, do in fact for the larger part quarry out rocks by reason of the exceeding stoniness of the land; for their tools never dig up a clod without a stone. Since their labour entails such hardship as this, it is only by perseverance that they surmount Nature and that after many distresses they gather scanty harvests, and no more. By reason of their continued physical activity and minimum of nourishment the Ligurians are slender and vigorous of body. To aid them in their hardships they have their women, who have become accustomed to labour on an equal basis with the men. They are continually hunting, whereby they get abundant game and compensate in this way for the lack of the fruits of the field. Consequently, spending their lives as they do on snow-covered mountains, where they are used to traversing unbelievably rugged places, they become vigorous and muscular of body. Some of the Ligurians, because of the lack among them of the fruits of the earth, drink nothing but water, and they eat the flesh of both domestic and wild animals and fill themselves with the green things which grow in the land, the land they possess being untrodden by the most kindly of the gods, namely, Demeter and Dionysus.

The nights the Ligurians spend in the fields, rarely in a kind of crude shanty or hut, more often in the hollows of rocks and natural caves which may offer them sufficient protection. In pursuance of these habits they have also other practices wherein they preserve the manner of life which is primitive and lacking in implements. Speaking generally, in these regions the women possess the vigour and might of men, and the men those of wild beasts. Indeed, they say that oftentimes in campaigns the mightiest warrior among the Gauls has been challenged to single combat by a quite slender Ligurian and slain. The weapons of the Ligurians are lighter in their structure than those of the Romans; for their protection is a long shield, worked in the Gallic fashion, and a shirt gathered in with a belt, and about them they throw the skins of wild animals and carry a sword of moderate size; but some of them, now that they have been incorporated in the Roman state, have changed the type of their weapons, adapting themselves to their rulers. They are venturesome and of noble spirit, not only in war, but in those circumstances of life which offer terrifying hardships or perils. As traders, for instance, they sail over the Sardinian and Libyan seas, readily casting themselves into dangers from which there is no succour; for although the vessels they use are more cheaply fashioned than make-shift boats and their equipment is the minimum of that usual on ships, yet to one's astonishment and terror they will face the most fearful conditions which storms create.

**40.** It remains for us now to speak of the Tyrrhenians. This people, excelling as they did in manly vigour, in ancient times possessed great territory and founded many notable cities. Likewise, because they also availed themselves of powerful naval forces and were masters of the sea over a long period, they caused the sea along Italy to be named Tyrrhenian after them; and because they also perfected the organisation of land forces, they were the inventors of the *salpinx,* as it is called, a discovery of the greatest usefulness for war and named after them the "Tyrrhenian trumpet." They were also the authors of that dignity which surrounds rulers, providing their rulers with lictors and an ivory stool and a toga with a purple band; and in connection with their houses they invented the peristyle, a useful device for avoiding the confusion connected with the attending throngs; and these things were adopted for the most part by the Romans, who added to their embellishment and transferred them to their own political institutions. Letters, and the teaching about Nature and the gods they also brought to greater perfection, and they elaborated the art of divination by thunder and lightning more than all other men; and it is for this reason that the people who rule practically the entire inhabited world show honour to these men even to this day and employ them as interpreters of the omens of Zeus as they appear in thunder and lightning.

The land the Tyrrhenians inhabit bears every crop, and from the intensive cultivation of it they enjoy no lack of fruits, not only sufficient for their sustenance but contributing to abundant enjoyment and luxury. For example, twice each day they spread costly tables and upon them everything that is appropriate to excessive luxury, providing gay-coloured couches and having ready at hand a multitude of silver drinking-cups of every description and servants-in-waiting in no small number; and these attendants are some of them of exceeding comeliness and others are arrayed in clothing more costly than befits the station of a slave. Their dwellings are of every description and of individuality, those not only of their magistrates but of the majority of the free men as well. Speaking generally, they have now renounced the spirit which was emulated by their forebears from ancient times, and passing their lives as they do in drinking-bouts and unmanly amusements, it is easily understood how they have lost the glory in warfare which their fathers possessed. Not the least of the things which have contributed to their luxury is the fertility of the land; for since it bears every product of the soil and is altogether fertile, the Tyrrhenians lay up great stores of every kind of fruit. In general, indeed, Tyrrhenia, being altogether fertile, lies in extended open fields and is traversed at intervals by areas which rise up like hills and yet are fit for tillage; and it enjoys moderate rainfall not only in the winter season but in the summer as well.

**On the islands in the ocean to the south, both the one called Hiera and that called Panchaea, and on what they are said to contain (41-46).**

**41.** Now that we have described the lands which lie to the west and those which extend toward the north, and also the islands in the ocean, we shall in turn discuss the islands in the ocean to the south which lie off that portion of Arabia which extends to the east and borders upon the country known as Cedrosia. Arabia contains many villages and notable cities, which in some cases are situated upon great mounds and in other instances are built upon hillocks or in plains; and the largest cities have royal residences of costly construction, possessing a multitude of inhabitants and ample estates. The entire land of the Arabians abounds with domestic animals of every description, and it bears fruits as well and provides no lack of pasturage for the fatted animals; and many rivers flow through the land and irrigate a great portion of it, thus contributing to the full maturing of the fruits. Consequently that part of Arabia which holds the chief place for its fertility has received a name appropriate to it, being called Arabia the Blest [Yemen].

On the farthest bounds of Arabia the Blest, where the ocean washes it, there lie opposite it a number of islands, of which there are three which merit a mention in history, one of them bearing the name Hiera or Sacred, on which it is not allowed to bury the dead, and another lying near it, seven stades distant, to which they take the bodies of the dead whom they see fit to inter. Now Hiera has no share in any other fruit, but it produces frankincense in such abundance as to suffice for the honours paid to the gods throughout the entire inhabited world; and it possesses also an exceptional quantity of myrrh and every variety of all the other kinds of incense of highly fragrant odour. The nature of frankincense and the preparing of it is like this: In size it is a small tree, and in appearance it resembles the white Egyptian Acacia, its leaves are like those of the willow, as it is called, the bloom it bears is in colour like gold, and the frankincense which comes from it oozes forth in drops like tears, but the myrrh-tree is like the mastich-tree, although its leaves are more slender and grow thicker. It oozes myrrh when the earth is dug away from the roots, and if it is planted in fertile soil this takes place twice a year, in spring and in summer; the myrrh of the spring is red, because of the dew, but that of the summer is white. They also gather the fruit of the Christ's thorn, which they use both for meat and for drink and as a drug for the cure of dysentery.

**42.** The land of Hiera is divided among its inhabitants, and the king takes for himself the best land and likewise a tithe of the fruits which the island produces. The width of the island is reputed to be about two hundred stades, and the inhabitants of the island are known as Panchaeans, and these men take the frankincense and myrrh across to the mainland and sell it to Arab merchants, from whom others in turn purchase wares of this kind and convey them to Phoenicia and Coele-Syria and Egypt, and in the end merchants convey them from these countries throughout all the inhabited world. And there is yet another large island, thirty stades distant from the one we have mentioned, lying out in the ocean to the east and many stades in length; for men say that from its promontory which extends toward the east one can descry India, misty because of its great distance.

As for Panchaea itself, the island possesses many things which are deserving to be recorded by history. It is inhabited by men who were sprung from the soil itself, called Panchaeans, and the foreigners there are Oceanites and Indians and Scythians and Cretans. There is also a notable city on the island, called Panara, which enjoys unusual felicity; its citizens are called "suppliants of Zeus

Triphylius," [Zeus of the three tribes] and they are the only inhabitants of the land of Panchaea who live under laws of their own making and have no king over them. Each year they elect three chief magistrates; these men have no authority over capital crimes, but render judgment in all other matters; and the weightiest affairs they refer of their own accord to the priests.

Some sixty stades distant from the city of Panara is the temple of Zeus Triphylius, which lies out on a level plain and is especially admired for its antiquity, the costliness of its construction, and its favourable situation.

**43.** Thus, the plain lying around the temple is thickly covered with trees of every kind, not only such as bear fruit, but those also which possess the power of pleasing the eye; for the plain abounds with cypresses of enormous size and plane-trees and sweet-bay and myrtle, since the region is full of springs of water. Indeed, close to the sacred precinct there bursts forth from the earth a spring of sweet water of such size that it gives rise to a river on which boats may sail, and since the water is led off from the river to many parts of the plain and irrigates them, throughout the entire area of the plain there grow continuous forests of lofty trees, wherein a multitude of men pass their time in the summer season and a multitude of birds make their nests, birds of every kind and of various hues, which greatly delight the ear by their song; therein also is every kind of garden and many meadows with varied plants and flowers, so that there is a divine majesty in the prospect which makes the place appear worthy of the gods of the country. There were palm trees there with mighty trunks, conspicuous for the fruits they bore, and many varieties of nut-bearing trees, which provide the natives of the place with the most abundant subsistence. In addition to what we have mentioned, grape-vines were found there in great number and of every variety, which were trained to climb high and were variously intertwined so that they presented a pleasing sight and provided an enjoyment of the season without further ado.

**44.** The temple was a striking structure of white marble, two plethra in length and the width proportionate to the length; it was supported by large and thick columns and decorated at intervals with reliefs of ingenious design; and there were also remarkable statues of the gods, exceptional in skill of execution and admired by men for their massiveness. Around about the temple the priests who served the gods had their dwellings, and the management of everything pertaining to the sacred precinct was in their hands. Leading from the temple an avenue had been constructed, four stades in length and a plethrum in width. On each side of the avenue are great bronze vessels which rest upon square bases, and at the end of the avenue the river we mentioned above has its sources, which pour forth in a turbulent stream. The water of the stream is exceedingly clear and sweet and the use of it is most conducive to the health of the body; and the river bears the name "Water of the Sun." The entire spring is surrounded by an expensive stone quay, which extends along each side of it four stades, and no man except the priests may set foot upon the place up to the edge of the quay. The plain lying below the temple has been made sacred to the gods, for a distance of two hundred stades, and the revenues which are derived from it are used to support the sacrifices.

Beyond the above-mentioned plain there is a lofty mountain which has been made sacred to the gods and is called the "Throne of Uranus" and also "Triphylian Olympus." For the myth relates that in ancient times, when Uranus was king of the inhabited earth, he took pleasure in tarrying in that place and in surveying from its lofty top both the heavens and the stars therein, and that at a later time it came to be called Triphylian Olympus because the men who dwelt about it were composed of three peoples; these, namely, were known as Panchaeans, Oceanites, and Doians, who were expelled at a later time by Ammon. For Ammon, men say, not only drove this nation into exile but also totally destroyed their cities, razing to the ground both Doia and Asterusia. And once a year, we are told, the priests hold a sacrifice in this mountain with great solemnity.

**45.** Beyond this mountain and throughout the rest of the land of Panchaeitis, the account continues, there is found a multitude of beasts of every description; for the land possesses many elephants and lions and leopards and gazelles and an unusual number of other wild animals which differ in their aspect and are of marvellous ferocity. This island also contains three notable cities, Hyracia, Dalis, and Oceanis. The whole country, moreover, is fruitful and possesses in particular a multitude of vines of every variety. The men are warlike and use chariots in battle after the ancient manner.

The entire body politic of the Panchaeans is divided into three castes: The first caste among them is that of the priests, to whom are assigned the artisans, the second consists of the farmers, and the third is that of the soldiers, to whom are added the herdsmen. The priests served as the leaders in all things, rendering the decisions in legal disputes and possessing the final authority in all other affairs which concerned the community; and the farmers, who are engaged in the tilling of the soil, bring the fruits into the common store, and the man among them who is thought to have practised the best farming receives a special reward when the fruits are portioned out, the priests deciding who has been first, who second, and so in order to the tenth, this being done in order to spur on the rest. In the same manner the herdsmen also turn both the sacrificial animals and all others into the treasury of the state with all precision, some by number and some by weight. For, speaking generally, there is not a thing except a home and a garden which a man may possess for his own, but all the products and the revenues are taken over by the priests, who portion out with justice to each man his share, and to the priests alone is given two-fold.

The clothing of the Panchaeans is soft, because the wool of the sheep of the land is distinguished above all other for its softness; and they wear ornaments of gold, not only the women but the men as well, with collars of twisted gold about their necks, bracelets on their wrists, and rings hanging from their ears after the manner of the Persians. The same kind of shoes are worn by both sexes, and they are worked in more varied colours than is usual.

**46.** The soldiers receive a pay which is apportioned to them and in return protect the land by means of forts and posts fixed at intervals; for there is one section of the country which is infested with robber bands, composed of bold and lawless men who lie in wait for the farmers and war upon them. As for the priests, they far excel the rest in luxury and in every other refinement and elegance of their manner of life; so, for instance, their robes are of linen and exceptionally sheer and soft, and at times they wear garments woven of the softest wool; furthermore, their headdress is interwoven with gold, their footgear consists of sandals which are of varied colours and ingeniously worked, and they wear the same gold ornaments as do the women, with the exception of the earrings. The first duties of the priests are concerned with the services paid to the gods and with the hymns and praises which are accorded them, and in them they recite in song the achievements of the gods one after another and the benefactions they have bestowed upon mankind. According to the myth which the priests give, the gods had their origin in Crete, and were led by Zeus to Panchaea at the time when he sojourned among men and was king of the inhabited earth. In proof of this they cite their language, pointing out that most of the things they have about them still retain their Cretan names; and they add that the kinship which they have with the Cretans and the kindly regard they feel toward them are traditions they received from their ancestors, since this report is ever handed down from one generation to another. And it has been their practice, in corroboration of these claims, to point to inscriptions which, they said, were made by Zeus during the time he still sojourned among men and founded the temple.

The land possesses rich mines of gold, silver, copper, tin, and iron, but none of these metals is allowed to be taken from the island; nor may the priests for any reason whatsoever set foot outside of the hallowed land, and if one of them does so, whoever meets him is authorised to slay him. There are many great dedications of gold and of silver which have been made to the gods, since time has amassed the multitude of such offerings. The doorways of the temple are objects of wonder in their construction, being worked in silver and gold and ivory and citrus-wood. And there is the couch of the god, which is six cubits long and four wide and is entirely of gold and skilfully constructed in every detail of its workmanship. Similar to it both in size and in costliness in general is the table of the god which stands near the couch. And on the centre of the couch stands a large gold stele which carries letters which the Egyptians call sacred, and the inscription recounts the deeds both of Uranus and of Zeus; and to them there were added by Hermes the deeds also of Artemis and of Apollo.

As regards the islands, then, which lie in the ocean opposite Arabia, we shall rest content with what has been said.

### On Samothrace and the mysteries celebrated on the island (47-49).

**47.** We shall now give an account of the islands which lie in the neighbourhood of Greece and in the Aegean Sea, beginning with Samothrace. This island, according to some, was called Samos in ancient times, but when the island now known as Samos came to be settled, because the names were the same, the ancient Samos came to be called Samothrace from the land of Thrace which lies opposite it. It was settled by men who were sprung from the soil itself; consequently no tradition has been handed down regarding who were the first men and leaders on the island. But some say that in ancient days it was called Saonnesus [Saon] and that it received the name of Samothrace because of the settlers who emigrated to it from both Samos and Thrace. The first and original inhabitants used an ancient language which was peculiar to them and of which many words are preserved to this day in the ritual of their sacrifices. The Samothracians have a story that, before the floods which befell other peoples, a great one took place among them, in the course of which the outlet at the Cyanean Rocks was first rent asunder and then the Hellespont. For the Pontus, which had at the time the form of a lake, was so swollen by the rivers which flow into it, that, because of the great flood which had poured into it, its waters burst forth violently into the Hellespont and flooded a large part of the coast of Asia and made no small amount of the level part of the land of Samothrace into a sea; and this is the reason, we are told, why in later times fishermen have now and then brought up in their nets the stone capitals of columns, since even cities were covered by the inundation. The inhabitants who had been caught by the flood, the account continues, ran up to the higher regions of the island; and when the sea kept rising higher and higher, they prayed to the native gods, and since their lives were spared, to commemorate their rescue they set up boundary stones about the entire circuit of the island and dedicated altars upon which they offer sacrifices even to the present day. For these reasons it is patent that they inhabited Samothrace before the flood.

**48.** After the events we have described one of the inhabitants of the island, a certain Saon, who was a son, as some say, of Zeus and Nymphê, but, according to others, of Hermes and Rhenê, gathered into one body the peoples who were dwelling in scattered habitations and established laws for them; and he was given the name Saon after the island, but the multitude of the people he distributed among five tribes which he named after his sons. And while the Samothracians were living under a government of this kind, they say that there were born in that land to Zeus and Electra, who was one of the Atlantids, Dardanus and Iasion and Harmonia. Of these children Dardanus, who was a man who entertained great designs and was the first to make his way across to Asia in a make-shift boat, founded at the outset a city called Dardanus, organised the kingdom which lay about the city which was called Troy at a later time, and called the peoples Dardanians after himself. They say also that he ruled over many nations throughout Asia and that the Dardani who dwell beyond Thrace were colonists sent forth by him, but Zeus desired that the other of his two sons might also attain to honour, and so he instructed him in the initiatory rite of the mysteries, which had existed on the island since ancient times but was at that time, so to speak, put in his hands; it is not lawful, however, for any but the initiated to hear about the mysteries. Iasion is reputed to have been the first to initiate strangers into them and by this means to bring the initiatory rite to high esteem. After this Cadmus, the son of Agenor, came in the course of his quest for Europe to the Samothracians, and after participating in the initiation he married Harmonia, who was the sister of Iasion and not, as the Greeks recount in their mythologies, the daughter of Ares.

**49.** This wedding of Cadmus and Harmonia was the first, we are told, for which the gods provided the marriage-feast, and Demeter, becoming enamoured of Iasion, presented him with the fruit of the corn, Hermes gave a lyre, Athena the renowned necklace and a robe and a flute, and Electra the sacred rites of the Great Mother of the Gods, as she is called, together with cymbals and kettledrums and the instruments of her ritual; and Apollo played upon the lyre and the Muses upon their flutes, and the rest of the gods spoke them fair and gave the pair their aid in the celebration of the wedding. After this Cadmus, they say, in accordance with the oracle he had received, founded Thebes in Boeotia, while Iasion married Cybelê and begat Corybas. And after Iasion had been removed into the circle of the gods, Dardanus and Cybelê and Corybas conveyed to Asia the sacred rites of the Mother of the Gods and removed with them to Phrygia. Thereupon Cybelê, joining herself to the first Olympus, begat Alcê and called the goddess Cybelê after herself; and Corybas gave the name of Corybantes to all who, in celebrating the rites of his mother, acted like men possessed, and married Thebê, the daughter of Cilix. In like manner he also transferred the flute from Samothrace to Phrygia and to Lyrnessus the lyre which Hermes gave and which at a later time Achilles took for himself when he sacked that city. To Iasion and Demeter, according to the story the myths relate, was born Plutus or Wealth, but the reference is, as a matter of fact, to the wealth of the corn, which was presented to Iasion because of Demeter's association with him at the time of the wedding of Harmonia. Now the details of the initiatory rite are guarded among the matters not to be divulged and are communicated to the initiates alone; but the fame has travelled wide of how these gods [the Cabeiri] appear to mankind and bring unexpected aid to those initiates of theirs who call upon them in the midst of perils. The claim is also made that men who have taken part in the mysteries become both more pious and more just and better in every respect than they were before. And this is the reason, we are told, why the most famous both of the ancient heroes and of the demi-gods were eagerly desirous of taking part in the initiatory rite; and in fact Jason and the Dioscori, and Heracles and Orpheus as well, after their initiation attained success in all the campaigns they undertook, because these gods appeared to them.

### *On Naxos and Symê and Calydna (50-54).*

**50.** Since we have set forth the facts concerning Samothrace, we shall now, in accordance with our plan, discuss Naxos. This island was first called Strongylê and its first settlers were men from Thrace, the reasons for their coming being somewhat as follows. The myth relates that two sons, Butes and Lycurgus, were born to Boreas, but not by the same mother; and Butes, who was the younger, formed a plot against his brother, and on being discovered he received no punishment from Lycurgus beyond that he was ordered by Lycurgus to gather ships and, together with his accomplices in the plot, to seek out another land in which to make his home. Consequently Butes, together with the Thracians who were implicated with him, set forth, and making his way through the islands of the Cyclades he seized the island of Strongylê, where he made his home and proceeded to plunder many of those who sailed past the island. Since they had no women they sailed here and there and seized them from the land. Now some of the islands of the Cyclades had no inhabitants whatsoever and others were sparsely settled; consequently they sailed further, and having been repulsed once from Euboea, they sailed to Thessaly, where Butes and his companions, upon landing, came upon the female devotees of Dionysus as they were celebrating the orgies of the god near Drius, as it is called, in Achaea Phthiotis. As Butes and his companions rushed at the women, these threw away the sacred objects, and some of them fled for safety to the sea, and others to the mountain called Drius; but

Coronis, the myth continues, was seized by Butes and forced to lie with him. She, in anger at the seizure and at the insolent treatment she had received, called upon Dionysus to lend her his aid, and the god struck Butes with madness, because of which he lost his mind and, throwing himself into a well, met his death. The rest of the Thracians seized some of the other women, the most renowned of whom were Iphimedeia, the wife of Aloeus, and Pancratis, her daughter, and taking these women along with them, they sailed off to Strongylê. And in place of Butes the Thracians made Agassamenus king of the island, and to him they united in marriage Pancratis, the daughter of Aloeus, who was a woman of surpassing beauty; for, before their choice fell on Agassamenus, the most renowned among their leaders, Sicelus and Hecetorus, had quarrelled over Pancratis and had slain each other. Agassamenus appointed one of his friends his lieutenant and united Iphimedeia to him in marriage.

**51.** Aloeus dispatched his sons Otus and Ephialtes in search of his wife and daughter, and they, sailing to Strongylê, defeated the Thracians in battle and reduced the city. Some time afterward Pancratis died, and Otus and Ephialtes essayed to take the island for their dwelling and to rule over the Thracians, and they changed the name of the island to Dia. At a later time they quarrelled among themselves, and joining battle they slew many of the other combatants and then destroyed one another, and from that time on these two men have received at the hands of the natives the honours accorded to heroes. The Thracians dwelt on the island for more than two hundred years and then were driven out of it by a succession of droughts. And after that Carians removed to the island from Latmia, as it is now called, and made it their home; their king was Naxos, the son of Polemon, and he called the island Naxos after himself, in place of Dia. Naxos was an upright and famous man and left behind him a son Leucippus, whose son Smerdius became king of the island, and it was during the reign of Smerdius that Theseus, on his voyage back from Crete together with Ariadne, was entertained as a guest by the inhabitants of the island; and Theseus, seeing in a dream Dionysus threatening him if he would not forsake Ariadne in favour of the god, left her behind him there in his fear and sailed away. Dionysus led Ariadne away by night to the mountain which is known as Drius; and first of all the god disappeared, and later Ariadne also was never seen again.

**52.** The myth which the Naxians have to relate about Dionysus is like this: He was reared, they say, in their country, and for this reason the island has been most dear to him and is called by some Dionysias. For according to the myth which has been handed down to us, Zeus, on the occasion when Semelê had been slain by his lightning before the time for bearing the child, took the babe and sewed it up within his thigh, and when the appointed time came for its birth, wishing to keep the matter concealed from Hera, he took the babe from his thigh in what is now Naxos and gave it to the Nymphs of the island, Philia, Coronis, and Cleidê, to be reared. The reason Zeus slew Semelê with his lightning before she could give birth to her child was his desire that the babe should be born, not of a mortal woman but of two immortals, and thus should be immortal from its very birth. Because of the kindness which the inhabitants of Naxos had shown to Dionysus in connection with his rearing they received marks of his gratitude; for the island increased in prosperity and fitted out notable naval forces, and the

Book V

Naxians were the first to withdraw from the naval forces of Xerxes and to aid in the defeat at sea which the barbarian suffered, and they participated with distinction in the battle of Plataeae. Also the wine of the island possesses an excellence which is peculiarly its own and offers proof of the friendship which the god entertains for the island.

53. As for the island which is called Symê and was uninhabited in ancient times, its first settlers were men who came together with Triops, under the leadership of Chthonius, the son of Poseidon and Symê, from whom the island received the name it bears. At a later time its king was Nireus, the son of Charops and Aglaia, an unusually handsome man who also took part with Agamemnon in the war against Troy both as ruler of the island and as lord of a part of Cnidia. After the period of the Trojan War Carians seized the island, during the time when they were rulers of the sea. At a later time, however, when droughts came, the Carians fled the island and made their home in Uranium, as it is called. Thereupon Symê continued to be uninhabited, until the expedition which the Lacedaemonians and the Argives made came to these parts, and at that time the island became settled again in the following manner. One of the companions of Hippotes, a certain Nausus by name, was a member of the colony, and taking those who had come too late to share in the allotment of the land he settled Symê, which was uninhabited at that time, and later, when certain other men, under the leadership of Xuthus, put in at the island, he gave them a share in the citizenship and in the land, and all of them in common settled the island. And we are told that both Cnidians and Rhodians were members of this colony.

54. Calydna and Nisyros were settled in ancient times by Carians, and after that Thettalus, the son of Heracles, took possession of both islands. This explains why both Antiphus and Pheidippus, who were kings of the Coans, in the expedition against Troy led those who sailed from the two islands just mentioned. On the return from Troy four of Agamemnon's ships were wrecked off Calydna, and the survivors mingled with the natives of the island and made their home there. The ancient inhabitants of Nisyros were destroyed by earthquakes, and at a later time the Coans settled the island, as they had done in the case of Calydna; and after that, when an epidemic had carried away the population of the island, the Rhodians dispatched colonists to it.

As for Carpathos, its first inhabitants were certain men who joined with Minos in his campaigns at the time when he was the first of the Greeks to be master of the sea; and many generations later Iolcus, the son of Demoleon, an Argive by ancestry, in obedience to a certain oracle dispatched a colony to Carpathos.

### *On Rhodes and the myths which are recounted concerning it (55-59)*

55. The island which is called Rhodes was first inhabited by the people who were known as Telchines; these were children of Thalatta [the Sea], as the mythical tradition tells us, and the myth relates that they, together with Capheira, the daughter of Oceanus, nurtured Poseidon, whom Rhea committed as a babe to their care. We are told that they were also the discoverers of certain arts and that they introduced other things which are useful for the life of mankind. They were also the first, men say, to fashion statues of gods, and some of the ancient images of gods have been named after them; so, for example, among the Lindians there

is an "Apollo Telchinius," as it is called, among the Ialysians a Hera and Nymphae, both called "Telchinian," and among the Cameirans a "Hera Telchinia." And men say that the Telchines were also wizards and could summon clouds and rain and hail at their will and likewise could even bring snow; these things, the accounts tell us, they could do even as could the Magi of Persia; and they could also change their natural shapes and were jealous of teaching their arts to others.

Poseidon, the myth continues, when he had grown to manhood, became enamoured of Halia, the sister of the Telchines, and lying with her he begat six male children and one daughter, called Rhodos, after whom the island was named. At this period in the eastern parts of the island there sprung up the Giants, as they were called; and at the time when Zeus is said to have subdued the Titans, he became enamoured of one of the nymphs, Himalia by name, and begat by her three sons, Spartaeus, Cronius, and Cytus, and while these were still young men, Aphrodite, they say, as she was journeying from Cytherae to Cyprus and dropped anchor near Rhodes, was prevented from stopping there by the sons of Poseidon, who were arrogant and insolent men; whereupon the goddess, in her wrath, brought a madness upon them, and they lay with their mother against her will and committed many acts of violence upon the natives. When Poseidon learned of what had happened he buried his sons beneath the earth, because of their shameful deed, and men called them the "Eastern Demons"; and Halia cast herself into the sea, and she was afterwards given the name of Leucothea and attained to immortal honour in the eyes of the natives.

**56.** At a later time, the myth continues, the Telchines, perceiving in advance the flood that was going to come, forsook the island and were scattered. Of their number Lycus went to Lycia and dedicated there beside the Xanthus river a temple of Apollo Lycius. When the flood came the rest of the inhabitants perished, and since the waters, because of the abundant rains, overflowed the island, its level parts were turned into stagnant pools, but a few fled for refuge to the upper regions of the island and were saved, the sons of Zeus being among their number. Helius [the Sun], the myth tells us, becoming enamoured of Rhodos, named the island Rhodes after her and caused the water which had overflowed it to disappear. But the true explanation is that, while in the first forming of the world the island was still like mud and soft, the sun dried up the larger part of its wetness and filled the land with living creatures, and there came into being the Heliadae [children of the Sun], who were named after him, seven in number, and other peoples who were, like them, sprung from the land itself. In consequence of these events the island was considered to be sacred to Helius, and the Rhodians of later times made it their practice to honour Helius above all the other gods, as the ancestor and founder from whom they were descended. His seven sons were Ochimus, Cercaphus, Macar, Actis, Tenages, Triopas, and Candalus, and there was one daughter, Electryone, who quit this life while still a maiden and attained at the hands of the Rhodians to honours like those accorded to the heroes. When the Heliadae attained to manhood they were told by Helius that the first people to offer sacrifices to Athena would ever enjoy the presence of the goddess; and the same thing, we are told, was disclosed by him to the inhabitants of Attica. Consequently, men say, the Heliadae, forgetting in their haste to put fire beneath the victims, nevertheless laid them on the altars at the time, whereas Cecrops, who was king at that time of the Athenians, performed the sacrifice over fire, but later than the Heliadae. This is the reason, men say, why the peculiar practice as regards the manner of sacrificing persists in Rhodes to this day, and why the goddess has her seat on the island.

Such, then, is the account which certain writers of myths give about the antiquities of the Rhodians, one of them being Zenon, who has composed a history of the island.

57. The Heliadae, besides having shown themselves superior to all other men, likewise surpassed them in learning and especially in astrology; and they introduced many new practices in seamanship and established the division of the day into hours. The most highly endowed of them by nature was Tenages, who was slain by his brothers because of their envy of him; but when their treacherous act became known, all who had had a hand in the murder took to flight. Of their number Macar came to Lesbos, and Candalus to Cos; and Actis, sailing off to Egypt, founded there the city men call Heliopolis, naming it after his father; and it was from him that the Egyptians learned the laws of astrology. When at a later time there came a flood among the Greeks and the majority of mankind perished by reason of the abundance of rain, it came to pass that all written monuments were also destroyed in the same manner as mankind; and this is the reason why the Egyptians, seizing the favourable occasion, appropriated to themselves the knowledge of astrology, and why, since the Greeks, because of their ignorance, no longer laid any claim to writing, the belief prevailed that the Egyptians were the first men to effect the discovery of the stars. Likewise the Athenians, although they were the founders of the city in Egypt men call Saïs, suffered from the same ignorance because of the flood. It was because of reasons such as these that many generations later men supposed that Cadmus, the son of Agenor, had been the first to bring the letters from Phoenicia to Greece; and after the time of Cadmus onwards the Greeks were believed to have kept making new discoveries in the science of writing, since a sort of general ignorance of the facts possessed the Greeks.

Triopas sailed to Caria and seized a promontory which was called Triopium after him. But the rest of the sons of Helius, since they had had no hand in the murder, remained behind in Rhodes and made their homes in the territory of Ialysus, where they founded the city of Achaea. Ochimus, who was the oldest of them and their king, married Hegetoria, one of the Nymphs of that region, and begat by her a daughter Cydippê, whose name was afterwards changed to Cyrbia; and Cercaphus, another of the brothers, married Cyrbia and succeeded to the throne. Upon the death of Cercaphus his three sons, Lindus, Ialysus, and Cameirus, succeeded to the supreme power; and during their lifetime there came a great deluge and Cyrbe was buried beneath the flood and laid waste, whereupon the three divided the land among themselves, and each of them founded a city which bore his name.

58. About this time Danaüs together with his daughters fled from Egypt, and when he put ashore at Lindus in Rhodes and received the kindly welcome of the inhabitants, he established there a temple of Athena and dedicated in it a statue of the goddess. Of the daughters of Danaüs three died during their stay in Lindus,

but the rest sailed on to Argos together with their father Danaüs, and a little after this time Cadmus, the son of Agenor, having been dispatched by the king to seek out Europe, put ashore at Rhodes. He had been severely buffeted by tempests during the voyage and had taken a vow to found a temple to Poseidon, and so, since he had come through with his life, he founded in the island a sacred precinct to this god and left there certain of the Phoenicians to serve as its overseers. These men mingled with the Ialysians and continued to live as fellow-citizens with them, and from them, we are told, the priests were drawn who succeeded to the priestly office by heredity. Now Cadmus honoured likewise the Lindian Athena with votive offerings, one of which was a striking bronze cauldron worked after the ancient manner, and this carried an inscription in Phoenician letters, which, men say, were first brought from Phoenicia to Greece.

Subsequent to these happenings, when the land of Rhodes brought forth huge serpents, it came to pass that the serpents caused the death of many of the natives; consequently the survivors dispatched men to Delos to inquire of the god how they might rid themselves of the evil. Apollo commanded them to receive Phorbas and his companions and to colonise together with them the island of Rhodes; Phorbas was a son of Lapithes and was tarrying in Thessaly together with a considerable number of men, seeking a land in which he might make his home, and the Rhodians summoned him as the oracle had commanded and gave him a share in the land. Phorbas destroyed the serpents, and after he had freed the island of its fear he made his home in Rhodes; furthermore, since in other respects he proved himself a great and good man, after his death he was accorded honours like those offered to heroes.

59. At a later time than the events we have described Althaemenes, the son of Catreus the king of Crete, while inquiring of the oracle regarding certain other matters, received the reply that it was fated that he should slay his father by his own hand. So wishing to avoid such an abominable act, he fled of his free will from Crete together with such as desired to sail away with him, these being a considerable company. Althaemenes, then, put ashore on Rhodes at Cameirus, and on Mount Atabyrus he founded a temple of Zeus who is called Zeus Atabyrius; and for this reason the temple is held in special honour even to this day, situated as it is upon a lofty peak from which one can descry Crete. So Althaemenes with his companions made his home in Cameirus, being held in honour by the natives; but his father Catreus, having no male children at home and dearly loving Althaemenes, sailed to Rhodes, being resolved upon finding his son and bringing him back to Crete. Now the fated destiny prevailed: Catreus disembarked by night upon the land of Rhodes with a few followers, and when there arose a hand-to-hand conflict between them and the natives, Althaemenes, rushing out to aid them, hurled his spear, and struck in ignorance his father and killed him. When he realised what he had done, Althaemenes, being unable to bear his great affliction, shunned all meetings and association with mankind, and betook himself to unfrequented places and wandered about alone, until the grief put an end to his life; and at a later time he received at the hands of the Rhodians, as a certain oracle had commanded, the honours which are accorded to heroes. Shortly before the Trojan War Tlepolemus, the son of Heracles, who was a fugitive because of the death of Licymnius, whom he had unwittingly slain, fled

BOOK V

of his free will from Argos; and upon receiving an oracular response regarding where he should go to found a settlement, he put ashore at Rhodes together with a few people, and being kindly received by the inhabitants he made his home there, and becoming king of the whole island he portioned out the land in equal allotments and continued in other respects as well to rule equitably. In the end, when he was on the point of taking part with Agamemnon in the war against Ilium, he put the rule of Rhodes in the hands of Butas, who had accompanied him in his flight from Argos, and he gained great fame for himself in the war and met his death in the Troad.

### On the Cherronesus which lies over against the territory of Rhodes (60-63).

**60.** Since the affairs of Rhodes, as it happened, became interwoven with certain events occurring in the Cherronesus which lies opposite the island, I think it will not be foreign to my purpose to discuss the latter. The Cherronesus, as some men say, received in ancient times the name it bears from the fact that the natural shape of the region is that of an isthmus, but others have written that the name Cherronesus is given it from the man who once ruled over those parts. The account runs like this: Not long after Cherronesus had ruled, five Curetes passed over to it from Crete, and these were descendants of those who had received Zeus from his mother Rhea and had nurtured him in the mountains of Ide in Crete, and sailing to the Cherronesus with a notable expedition they expelled the Carians who dwelt there, and settling down in the land themselves they divided it into five parts, each of them founding a city which he named after himself. Not long after this Inachus, the king of the Argives, since his daughter Io had disappeared, sent forth Cyrnus, one of his men in high command, fitting him out with a considerable fleet, and ordered him to hunt for Io in every region and not to return unless he had got possession of her. Cyrnus, after having wandered over many parts of the inhabited world without being able to find her, put ashore in Caria on the Cherronesus we are discussing; and despairing of ever returning to his house, he made his home in the Cherronesus, where, partly by persuasive means and partly by the use of force, he became king of a part of the land and founded a city which bore his name Cyrnus. By administering affairs in a popular fashion he enjoyed great favour among his fellow-citizens.

**61.** After this, the account continues, Triopas, one of the sons of Helius and Rhodos, who was a fugitive because of the murder of his brother Tenages, came to the Cherronesus, and after he had been purified there of the murder by Melisseus the king, he sailed to Thessaly to give assistance as an ally to the sons of Deucalion, and with their aid he expelled from Thessaly the Pelasgians and took for his portion the plain which is called Dotium. There he cut down the sacred grove of Demeter and used the wood to build a palace; and for this reason he incurred the hatred of the natives, whereupon he fled from Thessaly and put ashore, together with the peoples who sailed with him, in the territory of Cnidus, where he founded Triopium, as it was called after him. Setting out from this place as his base he won for himself both the Cherronesus and a large part of neighbouring Caria. As regards the ancestry of Triopas there is disagreement among many of the historians and poets; for some have recorded that he was the son of Canache, the daughter of Aeolus, and Poseidon, but others that he was born of Lapithes, the son of Apollo, and Stilbê, the daughter of Peneius.

**62.** In Castabus, on the Cherronesus, there is a temple which is sacred to Hemithea, and there is no reason why we should omit to mention the strange occurrence which befell this goddess. Now many and various accounts have been handed down regarding her, but we shall recount that which has prevailed and is in accord with what the natives relate.

To Staphylus and Chrysothemis were born three daughters, Molpadia, Rhoeo, and Parthenos by name. Apollo lay with Rhoeo and brought her with child; and her father, believing that her seduction was due to a man, was angered, and in his anger he shut up his daughter in a chest and cast her into the sea, but the chest was washed up upon Delos, where she gave birth to a male child and called the babe Anius. Rhoeo, who had been saved from death in this unexpected manner, laid the babe upon the altar of Apollo and prayed to the god to save its life if it was his child. Thereupon Apollo, the myth relates, concealed the child for the time, but afterwards he gave thought to its rearing, instructed it in divination, and conferred upon it certain great honours. The other sisters of the maiden who had been seduced, namely, Molpadia and Parthenos, while watching their father's wine, a drink which had only recently been discovered among men, fell asleep; and while they were asleep some swine which they were keeping entered in and broke the jar which contained the wine and so destroyed the wine. The maidens, when they learned what had happened, in fear of their father's severity fled to the edge of the sea and hurled themselves down from some lofty rocks. Apollo, because of his affection for their sister, rescued the maidens and established them in the cities of the Cherronesus. The one named Parthenos, as the god brought it to pass, enjoyed honours and a sacred precinct in Bubastus of the Cherronesus, while Molpadia, who came to Castabus, was given the name Hemithea [half-godess], because the god had appeared to men, and she was honoured by all who dwelt in the Cherronesus. In the sacrifices which are held in her honour a mixture of honey and milk is used in the libations, because of the experience which she had had in connection with the wine, while anyone who has touched a hog or eaten of its flesh is not permitted to draw near to the sacred precinct.

**63.** In later times the temple of Hemithea enjoyed so great a development that not only was it held in special honour by the inhabitants of the place and of neighbouring regions, but even peoples from afar came to it in their devotion and honoured it with costly sacrifices and notable dedications. Most important of all, when the Persians were the dominant power in Asia and were plundering all the temples of the Greeks, the precinct of Hemithea was the sole shrine on which they did not lay hands, and the robbers who were pillaging everything they met left this shrine alone entirely un-plundered, and this they did despite the fact that it was unwalled and the pillaging of it would have entailed no danger. The reason which men advance for its continued development is the benefactions which the goddess confers upon all mankind alike; for she appears in visible shape in their sleep to those who are in suffering and gives them healing, and many who are in the grip of diseases for which no remedy is known are restored to health; furthermore, to women who are suffering in childbirth the goddess gives relief from the agony and perils of travail. Consequently, since many have been saved

## Book V

in these ways from most ancient times, the sacred precinct is filled with votive offerings, nor are these protected by guards or by a strong wall, but by the habitual reverence of the people.

### On Crete and the myths which are recounted about it, down to comparatively recent times (64-80).

**64.** Now as regards Rhodes and the Cherronesus we shall rest content with what has been said, and we shall at this point discuss Crete. The inhabitants of Crete claim that the oldest people of the island were those who are known as Eteocretans [genuine Cretans], who were sprung from the soil itself, and that their king, who was called Cres, was responsible for the greatest number of the most important discoveries made in the island which contributed to the improvement of the social life of mankind. Also the greater number of the gods who, because of their benefactions to all men alike, have been accorded immortal honours, had their origin, so their myths relate, in their land; and of the tradition regarding these gods we shall now give a summary account, following the most reputable writers who have recorded the affairs of Crete.

The first of these gods of whom tradition has left a record made their home in Crete about Mt. Ide and were called Idaean Dactyli. These, according to one tradition, were one hundred in number, but others say that there were only ten to receive this name, corresponding in number to the fingers (*dactyli*) of the hands, but some historians, and Ephorus is one of them, record that the Idaean Dactyli were in fact born on the Mt. Ide which is in Phrygia and passed over to Europe together with Mygdon; and since they were wizards, they practised charms and initiatory rites and mysteries, and in the course of a sojourn in Samothrace they amazed the natives of that island not a little by their skill in such matters. It was at this time, we are further told, that Orpheus, who was endowed with an exceptional gift of poesy and song, also became a pupil of theirs, and he was subsequently the first to introduce initiatory rites and mysteries to the Greeks.

However this may be, the Idaean Dactyli of Crete, so tradition tells us, discovered both the use of fire and what the metals copper and iron are, as well as the means of working them, this being done in the territory of the city of Aptera at Berecynthus, as it is called; and since they were looked upon as the originators of great blessings for the race of men, they were accorded immortal honours. And writers tell us that one of them was named Heracles, and excelling as he did in fame, he established the Olympic Games, and that the men of a later period thought, because the name was the same, that it was the son of Alcmenê who had founded the institution of the Olympic Games. Evidences of this, they tell us, are found in the fact that many women even to this day take their incantations from this god and make amulets in his name, on the ground that he was a wizard and practised the arts of initiatory rites; but they add that these things were indeed very far removed from the habits of the Heracles who was born of Alcmenê.

**65.** After the Idaean Dactyli, according to accounts we have, there were nine Curetes. Some writers of myths relate that these gods were born of the earth, but according to others, they were descended from the Idaean Dactyli. Their home they made in mountainous places which were thickly wooded and full of ravines, and which, in a word, provided a natural shelter and coverage, since it had not yet been discovered how to build houses. Since these Curetes excelled in wisdom they discovered many things which are of use to men generally; so, for instance, they were the first to gather sheep into flocks, to domesticate the several other kinds of animals which men fatten, and to discover the making of honey. In the same manner they introduced the art of shooting with the bow and the ways of hunting animals, and they showed mankind how to live and associate together in a common life, and they were the originators of concord and, so to speak, of orderly behaviour. The Curetes also invented swords and helmets and the war-dance, by means of which they raised a great alarum and deceived Cronus. We are told that, when Rhea, the mother of Zeus, entrusted him to them unbeknown to Cronus his father, they took him under their care and saw to his nurture; but since we purpose to set forth this affair in detail, we must take up the account at a little earlier point.

**66.** The myth the Cretans relate runs like this: When the Curetes were young men, the Titans, as they are called, were still living. These Titans had their dwelling in the land about Cnosus, at the place where even to this day men point out foundations of a house of Rhea and a cypress grove which has been consecrated to her from ancient times. The Titans numbered six men and five women, being born, as certain writers of myths relate, of Uranus and Ge, but according to others, of one of the Curetes and Titaea, from whom as their mother they derive the name they have. The males were Cronus, Hyperion, Coeus, Iapetus, Crius, and Oceanus, and their sisters were Rhea, Themis, Mnemosyne, Phoebe, and Tethys. Each one of them was the discoverer of things of benefit to mankind, and because of the benefaction they conferred upon all men they were accorded honours and everlasting fame.

Cronus, since he was the eldest of the Titans, became king and caused all men who were his subjects to change from a rude way of living to civilised life, and for this reason he received great approbation and visited many regions of the inhabited earth. Among all he met he introduced justice and sincerity of soul, and this is why the tradition has come down to later generations that the men of Cronus' time were good-hearted, altogether guileless, and blest with felicity. His kingdom was strongest in the western regions, where indeed he enjoyed his greatest honour; consequently, down even to comparatively recent times, among the Romans and the Carthaginians, while their city still stood, and other neighbouring peoples, notable festivals and sacrifices were celebrated in honour of this god and many places bore his name. Because of the exceptional obedience to laws no injustice was committed by any one at any time and all the subjects of the rule of Cronus lived a life of blessedness, in the unhindered enjoyment of every pleasure. To this the poet Hesiod also bears witness in the following words:

> And they who were of Cronus' day, what time
> He reigned in heav'n, lived like the gods, no care
> In heart, remote and free from ills and toils
> Severe, from grievous sicknesses and cares;
> Old age lay not upon their limbs, but they,
> Equal in strength of leg and arm, enjoyed
> Endless delight of feasting far from ills,
> And when death came, they sank in it as in

## Book V

> A sleep. And many other things were theirs:
> Grain-giving earth, unploughed, bore for them fruit
> Abundantly and without stint; and glad
> Of heart they dwelt upon their tilth throughout
> The earth, in midst of blessings manifold,
> Rich in their flocks, loved by the blessed gods.

This, then, is what the myths have to say about Cronus.

**67.** Of Hyperion we are told that he was the first to understand, by diligent attention and observation, the movement of both the sun and the moon and the other stars, and the seasons as well, in that they are caused by these bodies, and to make these facts known to others; and that for this reason he was called the father of these bodies, since he had begotten, so to speak, the speculation about them and their nature. To Coeus and Phoebê was born Leto, and to Iapetus was born Prometheus, of whom tradition tells us, as some writers of myths record, that he stole fire from the gods and gave it to mankind, though the truth is that he was the discoverer of those things which give forth fire and from which it may be kindled. Of the female Titans they say that Mnemosyne discovered the uses of the power of reason, and that she gave a designation to every object about us by means of the names which we use to express whatever we would and to hold conversation one with another; though there are those who attribute these discoveries to Hermes. To this goddess is also attributed the power to call things to memory and to remembrance (*mnemê*) which men possess, and it is this power which gave her the name she received. Themis, the myths tell us, was the first to introduce divinations and sacrifices and the ordinances which concern the gods, and to instruct men in the ways of obedience to laws and of peace. Consequently men who preserve what is holy with respect to the gods and the laws of men are called "law-guardians" (*thesmophulakes*) and "law-givers" (*thesmothetai*), and we say that Apollo, at the moment when he is to return the oracular responses, is "issuing laws and ordinances" (*themisteuein*), in view of the fact that Themis was the discoverer of oracular responses. So these gods, by reason of the many benefactions which they conferred upon the life of man, were not only accorded immortal honours, but it was also believed that they were the first to make their home on Mount Olympus after they had been translated from among men.

**68.** To Cronus and Rhea, we are told, were born Hestia, Demeter, and Hera, and Zeus, Poseidon, and Hades. Of these, they say, Hestia discovered how to build houses, and because of this benefaction of hers practically all men have established her shrine in every home, according her honours and sacrifices. Demeter, since the corn still grew wild together with the other plants and was still unknown to men, was the first to gather it in, to devise how to prepare and preserve it, and to instruct mankind how to sow it. Now she had discovered the corn before she gave birth to her daughter Persephonê, but after the birth of her daughter and the rape of her by Pluton, she burned all the fruit of the corn, both because of her anger at Zeus and because of her grief over her daughter. After she had found Persephonê, however, she became reconciled with Zeus and gave Triptolemus the corn to sow, instructing him both to share the gift with men everywhere and to teach them everything concerned with the labour of sowing. Some men say that it was she also who introduced laws, by obedience to which men have become accustomed to deal justly one with another, and that mankind has called this goddess Thesmophoros after the laws which she gave them. Since Demeter has been responsible for the greatest blessings to mankind, she has been accorded the most notable honours and sacrifices, and magnificent feasts and festivals as well, not only by the Greeks, but also by almost all barbarians who have partaken of this kind of food.

**69.** There is dispute about the discovery of the fruit of the corn on the part of many peoples, who claim that they were the first among whom the goddess was seen and to whom she made known both the nature and use of the corn. The Egyptians, for example, say that Demeter and Isis are the same, and that she was first to bring the seed to Egypt, since the river Nile waters the fields at the proper time and that land enjoys the most temperate seasons. Also the Athenians, though they assert that the discovery of this fruit took place in their country, are nevertheless witnesses to its having been brought to Attica from some other region; for the place which originally received this gift they call Eleusis [place of Advent], from the fact that the seed of the corn came from others and was conveyed to them, but the inhabitants of Sicily, dwelling as they do on an island which is sacred to Demeter and Core, say that it is reasonable to believe that the gift of which we are speaking was made to them first, since the land they cultivate is the one the goddess holds most dear; for it would be strange indeed, they maintain, for the goddess to take for her own, so to speak, a land which is the most fertile known and yet to give it, the last of all, a share in her benefaction, as though it were nothing to her, especially since she has her dwelling there, all men agreeing that the Rape of Core took place on this island. Moreover, this land is the best adapted for these fruits, even as the poet also says:

> But all these things grow there for them unsown
> And e'en untilled, both wheat and barley.

This, then, is what the myths have to say about Demeter.

As for the rest of the gods who were born to Cronus and Rhea, the Cretans say that Poseidon was the first to concern himself with sea-faring and to fit out fleets, Cronus having given him the lordship in such matters; and this is why the tradition has been passed along to succeeding generations that he controls whatever is done on the sea, and why mariners honour him by means of sacrifices. Men further bestow upon Poseidon the distinction of having been the first to tame horses and to introduce the knowledge of horsemanship (*hippikê*), because of which he is called "Hippius." Of Hades it is said that he laid down the rules which are concerned with burials and funerals and the honours which are paid to the dead, no concern having been given to the dead before this time; and this is why tradition tells us that Hades is lord of the dead, since there were assigned to him in ancient times the first offices in such matters and the concern for them.

**70.** Regarding the birth of Zeus and the manner in which he came to be king, there is no agreement. Some say that he succeeded to the kingship after Cronus passed from among men into the company of the gods, not by overcoming his father with violence, but in the manner prescribed by custom and justly, having been judged worthy of that honour, but others recount a myth, which runs as follows: There was delivered to Cronus an oracle regarding the birth of Zeus which stated that the son who would be born to him would wrest the kingship from him by force. Consequently Cronus time and again did away with the children whom he begot; but Rhea, grieved as she was, and yet lacking the power to change her husband's purpose, when she had given birth to Zeus, concealed him in Idê, as it is called, and, without the knowledge of Cronus, entrusted the rearing of him to the Curetes who dwelt in the neighbourhood of Mount Idê. The Curetes bore him off to a certain cave where they gave him over to the Nymphs, with the command that they should minister to his every need. The Nymphs nurtured the child on a mixture of honey and milk and gave him upbringing at the udder of the goat which was named Amaltheia. And many evidences of the birth and upbringing of this god remain to this day on the island. For instance, when he was being carried away, while still an infant, by the Curetes, they say that the umbilical cord (*omphalos*) fell from him near the river known as Triton, and that this spot has been made sacred and has been called Omphalus after that incident, while in like manner the plain about it is known as Omphaleium. On Mount Idê, where the god was nurtured, both the cave in which he spent his days has been made sacred to him, and the meadows round about it, which lie upon the ridges of the mountain, have in like manner been consecrated to him. But the most astonishing of all that which the myth relates has to do with the bees, and we should not omit to mention it: The god, they say, wishing to preserve an immortal memorial of his close association with the bees, changed the colour of them, making it like copper with the gleam of gold, and since the region lay at a very great altitude, where fierce winds blew about it and heavy snows fell, he made the bees insensible to such things and unaffected by them, since they must range over the most wintry stretches. To the goat (*aeg-*) which suckled him Zeus also accorded certain honours, and in particular took from it a surname, being called Aegiochus [Aegis-bearing]. When he had attained to manhood he founded first a city in Dicta, where indeed the myth states that he was born; in later times this city was abandoned, but some stone blocks of its foundations are still preserved.

**71.** Now Zeus, the myth goes on to say, surpassed all others in manly spirit and wisdom and justice and in the other virtues one and all, and, as a consequence, when he took over the kingly power from Cronus, he conferred benefactions of the greatest number and importance upon the life of mankind. He was the first of all, for instance, to lay down rules regarding acts of injustice and to teach men to deal justly one with another, to refrain from deeds of violence, and to settle their differences by appeals to men and to courts of justice. In short, he contributed in abundance to the practices which are concerned with obedience to law and with peace, prevailing upon good men by persuasion and intimidating evil men by threat of punishment and by their fear. He also visited practically the entire inhabited earth, putting to death robbers and impious men and introducing equality and democracy; and it was in this connection, they say, that he slew the Giants and their followers, Mylinus in Crete and Typhon in Phrygia. Before the battle against the Giants in Crete, we are told, Zeus sacrificed a bull to Helius and to Uranus and to Gê; and in connection with each of the rites there was revealed to him what was the will of the gods in the affair, the omens indicating the victory of the gods and a defection to them of the enemy. The outcome of the war accorded with the omens; for Musaeus deserted to him from the enemy, for which he was accorded peculiar honours, and all who opposed them were cut down by the gods.

Zeus also had other wars against the Giants, we are told, in Macedonia near Pallene and in Italy on the plain which of old was named Phlegraean ("fiery") after the region about it which had been burned, but which in later times men called Cumaean. Now the Giants were punished by Zeus because they had treated the rest of mankind in a lawless fashion and, confiding in their bodily superiority and strength, had enslaved their neighbours, and because they were also disobeying the rules of justice which he was laying down and were raising up war against those whom all mankind considered to be gods because of the benefactions they were conferring upon men generally. Zeus, then, we are told, not only totally eradicated the impious and evil-doers from among mankind, but he also distributed honours as they were merited among the noblest of the gods and heroes and men, and because of the magnitude of his benefactions and his superior power all men accorded to him as with one voice both the everlasting kingship which he possesses and his dwelling upon Mount Olympus.

72. And it was ordained, the myth continues, that sacrifices should be offered to Zeus surpassing those offered to all the other gods, and that, after he passed from earth into the heavens, a just belief should spring up in the souls of all who had received his benefactions that he is lord of all the phenomena of heaven, that is, both of rain and of thunder and of lightning and of everything else of that nature. It is for this reason also that names have been given him: Zen, because in the opinion of mankind he is the cause of life (*zên*), bringing as he does the fruits to maturity by tempering the atmosphere; Father, because of the concern and goodwill he manifests toward all mankind, as well as because he is considered to be the first cause of the race of men; Most High and King, because of the preeminence of his rule; Good Counsellor and All-wise, because of the sagacity he manifests in the giving of wise counsel.

Athena, the myths relate, was likewise begotten of Zeus in Crete, at the sources of the river Triton, this being the reason why she has been given the name Tritogeneia. And there stands, even to this day, at these sources a temple which is sacred to this goddess, at the spot where the myth relates that her birth took place. Men say also that the marriage of Zeus and Hera was held in the territory of the Cnosians, at a place near the river Theren, where now a temple stands in which the natives of the place annually offer holy sacrifices and imitate the ceremony of the marriage, in the manner in which tradition tells it was originally performed.

To Zeus also were born, they say, the goddesses Aphroditê and the Graces, Eileithyia and her helper Artemis, the Hours, as they are called, Eunomia and Dikê and Eirenê, and Athena and the Muses, and the gods Hephaestus and Ares and Apollo, and Hermes and Dionysus and Heracles.

73. To each one of the deities we have named, the myth goes on to relate, Zeus imparted the knowledge of the things which he had discovered and was perfecting, and likewise assigned to them the honour of their discovery, wishing in this way to endow them with immortal fame among all mankind. To Aphroditê was entrusted the youth of maidens, the years in which they are expected to marry, and the supervision of such matters as are observed even yet in

## Book V

connection with weddings, together with the sacrifices and drink-offerings which men perform to this goddess. Nevertheless, all men make their first sacrifices to Zeus the Perfecter and Hera the Perfectress, because they are the originators and discoverers of all things, as we have stated above. To the Graces was given the adornment of personal appearance and the beautifying of each part of the body with an eye to making it more comely and pleasing to the gaze, and the further privilege of being the first to bestow benefactions and, on the other hand, of requiting with appropriate favours such men as have performed good acts. Eileithyia received the care of expectant mothers and the alleviation of the travail of childbirth; and for this reason women when they are in perils of this nature call first of all upon this goddess. Artemis, we are told, discovered how to effect the healing of young children and the foods which are suitable to the nature of babes, this being the reason why she is also called Kourotrophos [child-rearer]. As for the Hours, as they are called, to each of them, according as her name indicates, was given the ordering and adornment of life, so as to serve to the greatest advantage of mankind; for there is nothing which is better able to build a life of felicity than obedience to law (Eunomia) and justice (Dikê) and peace (Eirenê).

To Athena men ascribe the gift to mankind of the domestication and cultivation of the olive-tree, as well as the preparation of its fruit; for before the birth of this goddess this kind of tree was found only along with the other wild woody growths, and this goddess is the source of the care and the experience which men even to this day devote to these trees. Furthermore, Athena introduced among mankind the making of clothing and carpentry and many of the devices which are used in the other arts; and she also was the discoverer of the making of the pipes and of the music which they produce and, in a word, of many works of cunning device, from which she derives her name of Worker.

**74.** To the Muses, we are further told, it was given by their father Zeus to discover the letters and to combine words in the way which is designated poetry. In reply to those who say that the Syrians are the discoverers of the letters, the Phoenicians having learned them from the Syrians and then passed them on to the Greeks, and that these Phoenicians are those who sailed to Europe together with Cadmus and this is the reason why the Greeks call the letters "Phoenician," men tell us, on the other hand, that the Phoenicians were not the first to make this discovery, but that they did no more than to change the forms of the letters, whereupon the majority of mankind made use of the way of writing them as the Phoenicians devised it, and so the letters received the designation we have mentioned above.

Hephaestus, we are told, was the discoverer of every manner of working iron and copper and gold and silver and everything else which requires fire for working, and he also discovered all the other uses to be made of fire and turned them over both to the workers in the crafts and to all other men as well. Consequently the workmen who are skilled in these crafts offer up prayers and sacrifices to this god before all others, and both they and all mankind as well call the fire "Hephaestus," handing down in this way to eternal remembrance and honour the benefaction which was bestowed in the beginning upon man's social life. Ares, the myths record, was the first to make a suit of armour, to fit out soldiers with arms, and to introduce the battle's fury of contest, slaying himself those who were disobedient to the gods. Of Apollo men recount that he was the discoverer of the lyre and of the music which is got from it; that he introduced the knowledge of healing, which is brought about through the faculty of prophecy, whereby it was the practice in ancient times that the sick were healed; and as the discoverer of the bow he taught the people of the land all about the use of the bow, this being the reason why the art of archery is especially cultivated by the Cretans and the bow is called "Cretan." To Apollo and Coronis was born Asclepius, who learned from his father many matters which pertain to the healing art, and then went on to discover the art of surgery and the preparations of drugs and the strength to be found in roots, and, speaking generally, he introduced such advances into the healing art that he is honoured as if he were its source and founder.

**75.** To Hermes men ascribe the introduction of the sending of embassies to sue for peace, as they are used in wars, and negotiations and truces and also the herald's wand, as a token of such matters, which is customarily borne by those who are carrying on conversations touching affairs of this kind and who, by means of it, are accorded safe conduct by the enemy; and this is the reason why he has been given the name "Hermes Koinos" because the benefit is common (*koinê*) to both the parties when they exchange peace in time of war. They also say that he was the first to devise measures and weights and the profits to be gained through merchandising, and how also to appropriate the property of others all unknown to them. Tradition also says that he is the herald of the gods and their most trusted messenger, because of his ability to express clearly (*hermêneuein*) each command that has been given him; and this is the reason why he has received the name he bears, not because he was the discoverer of words and of speech, as some men say, but because he has perfected, to a higher degree than all others, the art of the precise and clear statement of a message. He also introduced wrestling-schools and invented the lyre out of a tortoise-shell after the contest in skill between Apollo and Marsyas, in which, we are told, Apollo was victorious and thereupon exacted an excessive punishment of his defeated adversary, but he afterwards repented of this and, tearing the strings from the lyre, for a time had nothing to do with its music.

As for Dionysus, the myths state that he discovered the vine and its cultivation, and also how to make wine and to store away many of the autumn fruits and thus to provide mankind with the use of them as food over a long time. This god was born in Crete, men say, of Zeus and Persephone, and Orpheus has handed down the tradition in the initiatory rites that he was torn in pieces by the Titans. The fact is that there have been several who bore the name Dionysus, regarding whom we have given a detailed account at greater length in connection with the more appropriate period of time. The Cretans, however, undertake to advance evidences that the god was born in their country, stating that he formed two islands near Crete in the Twin Gulfs, as they are called, and called them after himself Dionysiadae, a thing which he has done, they say, nowhere else in the inhabited earth.

**76.** Of Heracles the myths relate that he was sprung from Zeus many years before that Heracles who was born of Alcmenê. As for this son of Zeus, tradition has not given us the name of his mother, but only states that he far excelled all others in vigour of body, and that he visited the inhabited earth, inflicting punishment upon the unjust and destroying the wild beasts which were making the land uninhabitable; for men everywhere he won their freedom, while remaining himself unconquered and unwounded, and because of his good deeds he attained to immortal honour at the hands of mankind. The Heracles who was born of Alcmenê was very much later, and, since he emulated the plan of life of the ancient Heracles, for the same reasons he attained to immortality, and, as time went on, he was thought by men to be the same as the other Heracles because both bore the same name, and the deeds of the earlier Heracles were transferred to the later one, the majority of men being ignorant of the actual facts, and it is generally agreed that the most renowned deeds and honours which belong to the older god were concerned with Egypt, and that these, together with a city which he founded, are still known in that country.

Britomartis, who is also called Dictynna, the myths relate, was born at Caeno in Crete of Zeus and Carme, the daughter of Eubulus who was the son of Demeter; she invented the nets (*dictya*) which are used in hunting, whence she has been called Dictynna, and she passed her time in the company of Artemis, this being the reason why some men think Dictynna and Artemis are one and the same goddess; and the Cretans have instituted sacrifices and built temples in honour of this goddess, but those men who tell the tale that she has been named Dictynna because she fled into some fishermen's nets when she was pursued by Minos, who would have ravished her, have missed the truth; for it is not a probable story that the goddess should ever have got into so helpless a state that she would have required the aid that men can give, being as she is the daughter of the greatest one of the gods, nor is it right to ascribe such an impious deed to Minos, who tradition unanimously declares avowed just principles and strove to attain a manner of life which was approved by men.

77. Plutus, we are told, was born in Cretan Tripolus to Demeter and Iasion, and there is a double account of his origin. For some men say that the earth, when it was sowed once by Iasion and given proper cultivation, brought forth such an abundance of fruits that those who saw this bestowed a special name upon the abundance of fruits when they appear and called it *plutus* (wealth); consequently it has become traditional among later generations to say that men who have acquired more than they actually need have *plutus*. There are some who recount the myth that a son was born to Demeter and Iasion whom they named Plutus, and that he was the first to introduce diligence into the life of man and the acquisition and safeguarding of property, all men up to that time having been neglectful of amassing and guarding diligently any store of property.

Such, then, are the myths which the Cretans recount of the gods who they claim were born in their land. They also assert that the honours accorded to the gods and their sacrifices and the initiatory rites observed in connection with the mysteries were handed down from Crete to the rest of men, and to support this they advance the following most weighty argument, as they conceive it: The initiatory rite which is celebrated by the Athenians in Eleusis, the most famous, one may venture, of them all, and that of Samothrace, and the one practised in Thrace among the Cicones, whence Orpheus came who introduced them, these are all handed down in the form of a mystery, whereas at Cnosus in Crete it has been the custom from ancient times that these initiatory rites should be handed down to all openly, and what is handed down among other peoples as not to be divulged, this the Cretans conceal from no one who may wish to inform himself upon such matters. Indeed, the majority of the gods, the Cretans say, had their beginning in Crete and set out from there to visit many regions of the inhabited world, conferring benefactions upon the races of men and distributing among each of them the advantage which resulted from the discoveries they had made. Demeter, for example, crossed over into Attica and then removed from there to Sicily and afterwards to Egypt; and in these lands her choicest gift was that of the fruit of the corn and instructions in the sowing of it, whereupon she received great honours at the hands of those whom she had benefited. Likewise Aphroditê made her seat in Sicily in the region of Eryx, among the islands near Cythera and in Paphos in Cyprus, and in Asia in Syria; and because of the manifestation of the goddess in their country and her extended sojourn among them the inhabitants of the lands appropriated her to themselves, calling her, as the case might be, Erycinian Aphrodite, and Cytherian, and Paphian, and Syrian. In the same manner Apollo revealed himself for the longest time in Delos and Lycia [Didyma] and Delphi, and Artemis in Ephesus and the Pontus and Persis and Crete; and the consequence has been that, either from the names of these regions or as a result of the deeds which they performed in each of them, Apollo has been called Delian and Lycian and Pythian, and Aphrodite has been called Ephesian and Cretan and Tauropolian and Persian, although both of them were born in Crete. And this goddess is held in special honour among the Persians, and the barbarians hold mysteries which are performed among other peoples even down to this day in honour of the Persian Artemis. Similar myths are also recounted by the Cretans regarding the other gods, but to draw up an account of them would be a long task for us, and it would not be easily grasped by our readers.

**78.** Many generations after the birth of the gods, the Cretans go on to say, not a few heroes were to be found in Crete, the most renowned of whom were Minos and Rhadamanthys and Sarpedon. These men, their myth states, were born of Zeus and Europe, the daughter of Agenor, who, men say, was brought across to Crete upon the back of a bull by the design of the gods. Now Minos, by virtue of his being the eldest, became king of the island, and he founded on it not a few cities, the most renowned of which were the three, Cnosus in those parts of the island which look toward Asia, Phaestus on the seashore to the south, and Cydonia in the regions to the west facing the Peloponnesus. And Minos established not a few laws for the Cretans, claiming that he had received them from his father Zeus when conversing with him in a certain cave. Furthermore, he came to possess a great naval power, and he subdued the majority of the islands and was the first man among the Greeks to be master of the sea. After he had gained great renown for his manly spirit and justice, he ended his life in Sicily in the course of his campaign against Cocalus, the details of which we have recounted in connection with our account of Daedalus, because of whom the campaign was made.

## Book V

**79.** Of Rhadamanthys the Cretans say that of all men he rendered the most just decisions and inflicted inexorable punishment upon robbers and impious men and all other malefactors. He came also to possess no small number of islands and a large part of the sea coast of Asia, all men delivering themselves into his hands of their free will because of his justice. Upon Erythrus, one of his sons, Rhadamanthys bestowed the kingship over the city which was named after him Erythrae, and to Oenopion, the son of Minos' daughter Ariadnê, he gave Chios, we are told, although some writers of myths state that Oenopion was a son of Dionysus and learned from his father the art of making wine. To each one of his other generals, the Cretans say, he made a present of an island or a city Lemnos to Thoas, Cyrnus to Enyeus, Peparethos to Staphylus, Maroneia to Euanthes, Paros to Alcaeus, Delos to Anion, and to Andreus the island which was named after him Andros. Moreover, because of his very great justice, the myth has sprung up that he was appointed to be judge in Hades, where his decisions separate the good from the wicked. The same honour has also been attained by Minos, because he ruled wholly in accordance with law and paid the greatest heed to justice.

The third brother, Sarpedon, we are told, crossed over into Asia with an army and subdued the regions about Lycia. Euandrus, his son, succeeded him in the kingship in Lycia, and marrying Deidameia, the daughter of Bellerophon, he begat that Sarpedon who took part in the expedition against Troy, although some writers have called him a son of Zeus. Minos' sons, they say, were Deucalion and Molus, and to Deucalion was born Idomeneus and to Molus was born Meriones. These two joined with Agamemnon in the expedition against Ilium with ninety ships, and when they had returned in safety to their fatherland they died and were accorded a notable burial and immortal honours, and the Cretans point out their tomb at Cnosus, which bears the following inscription:

> Behold Idomeneus the Cnosian's tomb,
> And by his side am I, Meriones,
> The son of Molus.

These two the Cretans hold in special honour as heroes of renown, offering up sacrifices to them and calling upon them to come to their aid in the perils which arise in war.

**80.** But now that we have examined these matters it remains for us to discuss the peoples who have become intermixed with the Cretans. That the first inhabitants of the island were known as Eteo-Cretans and that they are considered to have sprung from the soil itself, we have stated before; and many generations after them Pelasgians, who were in movement by reason of their continuous expeditions and migrations, arrived at Crete and made their home in a part of the island. The third people to cross over to the island, we are told, were Dorians, under the leadership of Tectamus the son of Dorus; and the account states that the larger number of these Dorians was gathered from the regions about Olympus, but that a part of them consisted of Achaeans from Laconia, since Dorus had fixed the base of his expedition in the region about Cape Malea. And a fourth people to come to Crete and to become intermixed with the Cretans, we are told, was a heterogeneous collection of barbarians who in the course of time adopted the language of the native Greeks. After these events

Minos and Rhadamanthys, when they had attained to power, gathered the peoples on the island into one union, and last of all, after the Return of the Heracleidae, Argives and Lacedaemonians sent forth colonies which they established on certain other islands and likewise took possession of Crete, and on these islands they colonised certain cities; with regard to these cities, however, we shall give a detailed account in connection with the period of time to which they belong. Since the greatest number of writers who have written about Crete disagree among themselves, there should be no occasion for surprise if what we report should not agree with every one of them; we have, indeed, followed as our authorities those who give the more probable account and are the most trustworthy, in some matters depending upon Epimenides who has written about the gods, in others upon Dosiades, Sosicrates, and Laosthenidas.

## On Lesbos and the colonies which were led by Macareus to Chios, Samos, and Cos (81-82).

**81.** Now that we have discussed the subject of Crete at sufficient length, we shall undertake at this point to speak about Lesbos. This island has been inhabited in ancient times by many peoples, since it has been the scene of many migrations. The first people to seize it, while it was still uninhabited, was the Pelasgians, and in the following manner: Xanthus, the son of Triopas, who was king of the Pelasgians of Argos, seized a portion of Lycia, and, making his home there, at the outset he became king over the Pelasgians who had accompanied him; but later he crossed over to Lesbos, which was uninhabited, and divided the land among the folk, and he named the island, which had formerly been called Issa, Pelasgia after the people who had settled it. Seven generations later, after the flood of Deucalion had taken place and much of mankind had perished, it came to pass that Lesbos was also laid desolate by the deluge of waters, and after these events Macareus came to the island, and, recognising the beauty of the land, he made his home in it. This Macareus was the son of Crinacus, the son of Zeus, as Hesiod and certain other poets state, and was a native of Olenus in what was then called Ias, but is now called Achaia. The folk with him had been gathered from here and there, some being Ionians and the rest those who had streamed to him from every sort of people. Now at first Macareus made his home in Lesbos, but later, as his power kept steadily increasing because of the fertility of the island and also of his own fairness and sense of justice, he won for himself the neighbouring islands and portioned out the land, which was uninhabited, and it was during this time that Lesbos, the son of Lapithes, the son of Aeolus, the son of Hippotes, in obedience to an oracle of Pytho, sailed with colonists to the island we are discussing, and, marrying Methyma, the daughter of Macareus, he made his home there with her; and when he became a man of renown, he named the island Lesbos after himself and called the folk Lesbians. There was born to Macareus, in addition to other daughters, Mytilene and Methymna, from whom the cities in the island got their names. Moreover, Macareus, essaying to bring under his control the neighbouring islands, dispatched a colony to Chios first of all, entrusting the leadership of the colony to one of his own sons; and after this he dispatched another son, Cydrolaiis by name, to Samos, where he settled, and after portioning out the island in allotments to the colonists he became king over it. The third island he settled was Cos, and he appointed Neandrus to be its king;

and then he dispatched Leucippus, together with a large body of colonists, to Rhodes, and the inhabitants of Rhodes received them gladly, because there was a lack of men among them, and they dwelt together as one people on the island.

**82.** The mainland opposite the islands, we find, had suffered great and terrible misfortunes, in those times, because of the floods. Thus, since the fruits were destroyed over a long period by reason of the deluge, there was a dearth of the necessities of life and a pestilence prevailed among the cities because of the corruption of the air. The islands, on the other hand, since they were exposed to the breezes and supplied the inhabitants with wholesome air, and since they also enjoyed good crops, were filled with greater and greater abundance, and they quickly made the inhabitants objects of envy. Consequently they have been given the name Islands of the Blessed, the abundance they enjoy of good things constituting the reason for the epithet. But there are some who say that they were given the name Islands of the Blessed (*macarioi*) after Macareus, since his sons were the rulers over them. Speaking generally, the islands we have mentioned have enjoyed a felicity far surpassing that of their neighbours, not only in ancient times but also in our own age; for being as they are the finest of all in richness of soil, excellence of location, and mildness of climate, it is with good reason that they are called, what in truth they are, "blessed." As for Macareus himself, while he was king of Lesbos he issued a law which contributed much to the common good, and he called the law the "Lion," giving it this name after the strength and courage of that beast.

### On Tenedos, the colonisation of the island, and the fabulous tales told by the Tenedians about Tennes (83).

**83.** When a considerable time had elapsed after the settlement of Lesbos, the island known as Tenedos came to be inhabited in somewhat the following manner. Tennes was a son of Cycnus, who had been king of Colone in the Troad, and was a man who had gained renown because of his high achievements. Gathering together colonists and using as his base the mainland opposite to it, he seized an uninhabited island called Leucophrys; this island he portioned out in allotments among his followers, and he founded a city on it which he named Tenedos after himself. Since he governed uprightly and conferred many benefactions upon the inhabitants, during his lifetime he was in high favour, and upon his death he was granted immortal honours; for they built for him a sacred precinct and honoured him with sacrifices as though he were a god, and these sacrifices they have continued to perform down to modern times.

We must not omit to mention what the myths of the Tenedians have to tell about Tennes, the founder of the city. Cycnus his father, they say, giving credence to the unjust slanders of his wife, put his son Tennes in a chest and cast it into the sea; this chest was borne along by the waves and brought to shore on Tenedos, and since Tennes had been saved alive in this astonishing fashion by the providence of some one of the gods, he became king of the island, and becoming distinguished by reason of the justice he displayed and his other virtues, he was granted immortal honours; but it had happened, when his stepmother was slandering him, that a certain flute player had borne false witness against him, and so the Tenedians passed a law that no flute player should ever enter his sacred precinct. When Tennes was slain by Achilles in the course of the

Trojan War, on the occasion when the Greeks sacked Tenedos, the Tenedians passed a law that no man should ever pronounce the name of Achilles in the sacred precinct of the founder of their city. Such, then, is the account which the myths give regarding Tenedos and its ancient inhabitants.

## On the colonisation by Minos of the islands of the smaller Cyclades (84).

**84.** Since we have set forth the facts concerning the most notable islands, we shall now give an account of the smaller ones. While in ancient times the Cyclades were still uninhabited, Minos, the son of Zeus and Europe, who was king of Crete and possessed great forces both land and naval, was master of the sea and sent forth from Crete many colonies, and he settled the greater number of the Cyclades, portioning the islands out in allotments among the folk, and he seized no small part of the coast of Asia. This circumstance explains why harbours on the islands as well as on the coast of Asia have the same designation as those of Crete, being called "Minoan". The power of Minos advanced to great heights; and having his brother Rhadamanthys as co-ruler, he envied him because of his fame for righteousness, and wishing to get Rhadamanthys out of the way he sent him off to the farthest parts of his dominion. Rhadamanthys went to the islands which lie off Ionia and Caria, spending his time upon them, and caused Erythrus to found the city which bears his name [Erythrae] in Asia, while he established Oenopion, the son of Minos' daughter Ariadne, as lord of Chios. Now these events took place before the Trojan War; and after Troy was taken the Carians steadily increased their power and became masters of the sea; and taking possession of the Cyclades, some of the islands they appropriated to themselves, expelling the Cretans who had their homes on them, but in some islands they settled jointly with the Cretans who had been the first to dwell there. At a later time, when the power of the Greeks increased, the major number of the Cyclades came to be inhabited by them, and the Carians, who were non-Greeks, were driven out of them. But of these matters we shall give a detailed account in connection with the appropriate period of time.

# BOOK VI FRAGMENTS

[Our first six books embrace the events and legends prior to the Trojan War, the first three setting forth the antiquities of the barbarians, and the next three almost exclusively those of the Greeks.]

**1.** The foregoing is told by Diodorus in the Third Book of his history, and the same writer, in the sixth Book as well, confirms the same view regarding the gods, drawing from the writing of Euhemerus of Messenê, and using the following words:

"As regards the gods, then, men of ancient times have handed down to later generations two different conceptions: Certain of the gods, they say, are eternal and imperishable, such as the sun and the moon and the other stars of the heavens, and the winds as well and whatever else possesses a nature similar to theirs; for of each of these the genesis and duration are from everlasting to everlasting; but the other gods, we are told, were terrestrial beings who attained to immortal honour and fame because of their benefactions to mankind, such as Heracles, Dionysus, Aristaeus, and the others who were like them. Regarding these terrestrial gods many and varying accounts have been handed down by the writers of history and of mythology; of the historians, Euhemerus, who composed the *Sacred History,* has written a special treatise about them, while, of the writers of myths, Homer and Hesiod and Orpheus and the others of their kind have invented rather monstrous stories about the gods. For our part, we shall endeavour to run over briefly the accounts which both groups of writers have given, aiming at due proportion in our exposition.

"Now Euhemerus, who was a friend of King Cassander and was required by him to perform certain affairs of state and to make great journeys abroad, says that he travelled southward as far as the ocean; for setting sail from Arabia the Blest he voyaged through the ocean for a considerable number of days and was carried to the shore of some islands in the sea, one of which bore the name of Panchaea. On this island he saw the Panchaeans who dwell there, who excel in piety and honour the gods with the most magnificent sacrifices and with remarkable votive offerings of silver and of gold. The island is sacred to the gods, and there are a number of other objects on it which are admired both for their antiquity and for the great skill of their workmanship, regarding which severally we have written in the preceding Books. There is also on the island, situated upon an exceedingly high hill, a sanctuary of Zeus Triphylius, which was established by him during the time when he was king of all the inhabited world and was still in the company of men. And in this temple there is a stele of gold on which is inscribed in summary, in the writing employed by the Panchaeans, the deeds of Uranus and Cronus and Zeus.

"Euhemerus goes on to say that Uranus was the first to be king, that he was an honourable man and beneficent, who was versed in the movement of the stars, and that he was also the first to honour the gods of the heavens with sacrifices, whence he was called Uranus or "Heaven." There were born to him by his wife

Hestia two sons, Titan and Cronus, and two daughters, Rhea and Demeter. Cronus became king after Uranus, and marrying Rhea he begat Zeus and Hera and Poseidon. And Zeus, on succeeding to the kingship, married Hera and Demeter and Themis, and by them he had children, the Curetes by the first named, Persephone by the second, and Athena by the third. And going to Babylon he was entertained by Belus, and after that he went to the island of Panchaea, which lies in the ocean, and here he set up an altar to Uranus, the founder of his family. From there he passed through Syria and came to Casius, who was ruler of Syria at that time, and who gave his name to Mt. Casius [Jebel el-Akra], and coming to Cilicia he conquered in battle Cilix, the governor of the region, and he visited very many other nations, all of which paid honour to him and publicly proclaimed him a god."

After recounting what I have given and more to the same effect about the gods, as if about mortal men, Diodorus goes on to say: "Now regarding Euhemerus, who composed the *Sacred History,* we shall rest content with what has been said, and shall endeavour to run over briefly the myths which the Greeks recount concerning the gods, as they are given by Hesiod and Homer and Orpheus." Thereupon Diodorus goes on to add the myths as the poets give them.

**2.** Regarding the gods, the most learned Diodorus also says in his writings that those gods whom men were wont to address as immortal, considering them to be so because of their beneficences, had indeed been born human beings; but that certain of them had acquired the appellations they have after the lands they conquered.

**3.** Diodorus says, following the account preserved in the myths, that Xanthus and Balius were formerly Titans and had come to the aid of Zeus, Xanthus as a companion of Poseidon and Balius of Zeus; and in the battle they asked that their shape might be changed, since they were ashamed to be seen by their brethren the Titans, and their request was granted; and it was these horses which were given to Peleus. This explains, Diodorus says, why Xanthus is able to prophesy his death to Achilleus.

**4.** Pherecydes records that Saturnus was the first, before all others, to wear a crown, and Diodorus relates that, after he had defeated the Titans, Jupiter was rewarded by the rest with this same distinction; the same writer gives even to Priapus fillets and to Ariadne a wreath made of gold and precious stones from India, this wreath becoming also a distinction of Vulcan, and then of Liber, and later a constellation [Ariadne's Crown].

**5.** Ninus' brother, Picus, who was also called Zeus, became king of Italy, holding sway over the west for one hundred and twenty years. And he had many sons and daughters by the most comely women; for he assumed in some cases mysterious aspects when seducing them, and these women, when they were being debauched by him, looked upon him as a god. This same Picus, who was also called Zeus, had a son named Faunus, whom he also called Hermes for the name of the wandering star Mercury]. When Zeus was on the point of death he gave orders that his remains be laid away on the island of Crete; and his sons built him a temple there in which they laid him. This monument exists even to the present day, and it bears the inscription, "Here lies Picus whom men also call

Zeus." Diodorus, the most learned chronographer, has composed an account of this Picus.

According to tradition, Castor and Polydeuces, who were also known as the Dioscori, far surpassed all other men in valour and gained the greatest distinction in the campaign in which they took part with the Argonauts; and they have come to the aid of many who have stood in need of succour. Speaking generally, their manly spirit and skill as generals, and their justice and piety as well, have won them fame among practically all men, since they make their appearance as helpers of those who fall into unexpected perils. Moreover, because of their exceptional valour they have been judged to be sons of Zeus, and when they departed from among mankind they attained to immortal honours.

Epopeus, the king of Sicyon, challenged the gods to battle and violated their sanctuaries and altars.

Sisyphus, we are told, excelled all other men in knavery and ingenuity, and by means of his skill in divination by inspection of victims he discovered everything that was to happen and foretold it to mankind.

Salmoneus was impious and arrogant and made it his practice to ridicule the divinity, and he declared that his achievements excelled those of Zeus. Consequently he used to make a tremendous noise by means of a machine he contrived and to imitate in this way peals of thunder, and he would celebrate neither sacrifices nor festivals.

The same Salmoneus had a daughter named Tyro [cheese], who received this name by reason of the whiteness and softness of her body.

For Salmoneus, being impious and arrogant, made it his practice to ridicule the divinity and to declare that his achievements excelled those of Zeus; consequently he used to make a tremendous noise by means of a machine he contrived, and by imitating claps of thunder he would declare that he had thundered more loudly than Zeus. Speaking generally, in his mockery of the gods he would celebrate neither sacrifices nor festivals in their honour, <as the other rulers were accustomed to do>. There was born to him an only daughter, Tyro, to whom he thought this name was appropriate by reason of the softness of her body and the whiteness of her skin. Poseidon became enamoured of this maiden because of her beauty, and lying with her he begat Pelias and Neleus, and Salmoneus, not believing that it was Poseidon who had taken her virginity, would not leave off ill-treating Tyro; but in the end he paid the penalty to the deity for his impiety, ending his life when struck by lightning from the hand of Zeus. Of the sons born of Poseidon and Tyro, Pelias, when very young, was banished from his native land by Mimas, and going into exile together with his friends, he seized, with their aid, two islands, Sciathos and Peparethos; but at a later time, since Cheiron conferred benefactions upon him and shared his own country with him he departed from the islands we have mentioned, and became king of the city of Iolci [Iolcus], and there were born to him a number of daughters who took their name from their father, being called the Peliades, regarding whom we shall rest content with what has been said.

**8.** Admetus was very dear to the gods because of his unusual righteousness and piety. His uprightness brought him such honour that once, when Apollo had offended Zeus, the command was given him that he should serve as a menial at the court of Admetus. We are told that Alcestis, the daughter of Pelias, who was the only one of his daughters who had no part in the impiety practised upon their father, was given as wife to Admetus because of her piety.

Melampus was a man of exceptional piety and became a friend of Apollo.

**9.** Bellerophon, who was in exile because of a murder he had unwittingly committed, came to Proetus who exchanged hospitality with his father; and the wife of Proetus became enamoured of Bellerophon because of his beauty, and since she was unable to win him by persuasion she accused him to her husband of having offered violence to her. Now Proetus was unwilling to slay his guest, and so instead he sent him to Lycia, having a written message to Iobates the king, who was his father-in-law. Iobates received the letter and discovered that in it was written that he should slay Bellerophon with all speed; but, being unwilling to put him to death, he commanded him instead to go join combat with the fire-breathing Chimaera.

# BOOK VII FRAGMENTS

[In the following eleven Books we have written a universal history of events from the Trojan War to the death of Alexander.]

[In the preceding six Books we have set down a record of events from the Trojan War to the war which the Athenians decreed against the Syracusans.]

[In the preceding Books we have set down a record of events from the capture of Troy to the end of the Peloponnesian War and of the Athenian Empire, covering a period of seven hundred and seventy-nine years .]

**1.** Orpheus was contemporary with Heracles, both of them living one hundred years before the period of the Trojan War; and as I read in the work of Orpheus *On Stones,* where he speaks about himself, he says that he lived just a little after Helenus, and that Homer was one generation after Helenus. Homer, according to Dionysius the writer of cycles, is said to have lived at the time of two expeditions, that against Thebes and the one which the Greeks undertook on behalf of Helen. And Diodorus agrees with Dionysius, as do countless others.

**2.** Diodorus states that Homer died before the Return of the Heracleidae.

**3.** Aegialeia, the wife of Diomedes, fell altogether from favour with her husband, and in her hatred she acted unjustly toward her husband and called upon her kinsmen to take vengeance upon him. They, taking as their helper Aegisthus, who had lately possessed himself of the throne of Mycenae, passed judgment of death upon Diomedes, alleging that, although his father had been a foreigner, he was planning to banish the nobles from the state and to settle in their place some of his kinsmen from Aetolia. And since this false charge was generally believed, Diomedes became afraid and fled from Argos, together with any who wished to accompany him.

**4.** When Troy was taken, Aeneas, together with some other Trojans, seized a part of the city and held off the attackers, and when the Greeks let them depart under a truce and agreed with them that each man might take with him as many of his possessions as he could, all the rest took silver or gold or some other costly article, whereas Aeneas lifted upon his shoulders his father, who was now grown quite old, and bore him away. For this deed he won the admiration of the Greeks and was again given permission to choose out what he would of his household possessions. When he bore off the household gods, all the more was his virtue approved, receiving the plaudits even of his enemies; for the man showed that in the midst of the greatest perils his first concern was piety toward parents and reverence for the gods, and this was the reason, we are told, why he, together with the Trojans who still survived, was allowed to leave the Troad in complete safety and to go to whatever land he wished.

## *From Eusebius, Chronicle*

Let us now turn to another witness to the same affairs, namely, to Diodorus, who gathered in summary form all libraries into one and the same clearinghouse of knowledge. For he writes of the history of the Romans in his seventh Book, in the following words:

5. Certain historians have assumed, though in error, that the Romulus who was born of the daughter of Aeneas was the founder of Rome, but the truth is otherwise, since there were many kings in the period between Aeneas and Romulus, and the city was founded in the second year of the Seventh Olympiad, and the date of this founding falls after the Trojan War by four hundred and thirty-three years [751]. For three years elapsed after the taking of Troy before Aeneas received the kingship over the Latins; this kingship he held for three years, and then he disappeared from among men and received immortal honours. His son Ascanius succeeded him on the throne and founded Alba Longa, as it is now called, naming it after the river which was then called Alba and now bears the name Tiber. As for the name of the city, however, Fabius, who wrote a history of the Romans, presents a different story. This is what he says: An oracle was given to Aeneas, stating that a four-footed animal would lead him to the place where he should found a city, and once, when he was in the act of sacrificing a sow, white in colour, which was pregnant, it escaped from his hands and was pursued to a certain hill, where it dropped a farrow of thirty pigs. Aeneas was astounded at this strange happening, and then, calling to mind the oracle, he made preparations to found a city on the spot. In his sleep he saw a vision which strictly forbade him to do so and counselled him to found the city thirty years hence, corresponding to the number of the farrow of pigs, and so he gave up his design.

Upon the death of Aeneas his son Ascanius ascended the throne, and after thirty years he founded a settlement on the hill and gave the city the name of Alba after the colour of the sow; for the Latins call what is white *alba*. Ascanius also added another name, Longa, which translated means "the long," since the city was narrow in width and of great length.

He (Diodorus) goes on to say, "Ascanius made Alba the capital of his kingdom and subdued no small number of the settlements round about; and he became a famous man and died after a reign of thirty-eight years."

At the end of this period there arose a division among the people, because of two men who were contending with each other for the throne. For Iulius, since he was the son of Ascanius, maintained, "The rule which my father had belongs to me," and Silvius, the brother of Ascanius and, furthermore, a son of Aeneas by Lavinia, the daughter of Latinus, whereas Ascanius was a son of Aeneas by his first wife, who had been a woman of Ilium, maintained, "The rule belongs to me." Indeed, after Aeneas' death Ascanius had plotted against the life of Silvius; and it was while the latter as a child was being reared, because of this plot, by certain herdsmen on a mountain that he came to be called Silvius, after the name of the mountain, which the Latins called Silva. In this struggle of the two groups Silvius finally received the vote of the people and gained the throne. Iulius, however, though he lost the supreme power, was made *pontifex maximus* and became a kind of second king; and from him we are told, was sprung the Julian gens which exists in Rome even to this day.

Silvius accomplished nothing of note during his reign and died after a rule of forty-nine years. He was followed in the kingship by his son Aeneas, who was given the surname of Silvius and reigned over thirty years. After him Latinus, who was also called Silvius, reigned for fifty years. He was a vigorous ruler both in internal administration and in war, laying waste the neighbouring territory and founding the eighteen ancient cities which were formerly known as the "Latin cities": Tibur, Praeneste, Gabii, Tusculum, Cora, Pometia, Lanuvium, Labici, Scaptia, Satricum, Aricia, Tellenae, Crustumerium, Caenina, Fregellae, Cameria, Medullia, and Boilum, which some men also write Bola.

After Latinus died, his son Alba Silvius was chosen king, and he reigned for thirty-eight years; and after him Epitus Silva ruled for twenty-six years. At his death Capys replaced him in the kingship and reigned twenty-eight years. After him his son Calpetus reigned for thirteen years, and then Tiberius Silvius for eight years. The latter undertook a campaign against the Etruscans, but while leading his army across the Alba river he fell into the flood and met his death, whence the name of the river was made Tiber. And after his death Agrippa reigned over the Latins for forty-one years, and after him Aramulius Silvius for nineteen years.

Of Aramulius the story is told that he carried himself haughtily during his entire life and opposed the might of Jupiter in obstinate strife. Indeed, when at harvest time there would come incessant peals of heavy thunder, he used to order his soldiers, at the word of command, with one accord to strike their shields with the swords; and he would claim that the noise made in this fashion surpassed that of thunder. He paid the penalty of his arrogance toward the gods, since he was slain by a stroke of lightning and his entire house was submerged in the Alban lake, and to this day the Romans who dwell near the lake point to evidences of this event in the form of columns which stand up in the lake from the ruins of the royal palace lying in its depths.

After Aramulius the next king to be chosen was Aventius, who ruled thirty-seven years. Once, when pressed back in a war with some neighbours, he withdrew for protection to the Aventine hill, and for this reason the hill received the name Aventine. Upon his death he was succeeded in the kingship by his son Proca Silvius, who reigned twenty-three years. At his death his younger son Amulius seized the kingship by violence, since Numitor, who as his elder brother and his full-brother as well, was away in a distant region. Amulius reigned a little more than forty-three years and was slain by Remus and Romulus, who were the founders of Rome.

**6.** After the death of Aeneas a plot was formed by Ascanius against Silvius, who was still a child. He had been reared in the mountains by certain herdsmen and was given the name Silvius, because the Latins called the mountain Silva.

**7.** Romulus Silvius was an arrogant man throughout his entire life and dared to contend with God. For example, when God would thunder he used to order his soldiers at a single signal to strike their shields with their blades, and he would then say that the noise they raised was greater than the thunder. It was for this reason that he was struck by lightning.

[The third city he seized was Meschela, which was a very large place and had been settled in ancient times by Greek refugees from Troy, about whom we have already spoken in the third Book.]

[Thessalus, they say, after this removed to Iolcus; and finding on his arrival that Acastus, the son of Pelias, had recently died, he took over the throne which had belonged to him by inheritance and called the people who were subject to him Thessalians after his own name. I am not unaware that this is not the only explanation given of the name the Thessalians bear, but the fact is that the other accounts which have been handed down to us are likewise at variance with one another, and concerning these we shall speak on a more appropriate occasion.]

[The Heracleidae gave up, as they had promised, their effort to return and made their way back to Tricorythus. Some time later Licymnius and his sons and Tlepolemus, the son of Heracles, made their home in Argos, the Argives admitting them to citizenship of their own accord; but all the rest who had made their homes in Tricorythus, when the fifty-year period had expired, returned to the Peloponnesus. Their deeds we shall record when we have come to those times.]

## From Eusebius, Chronicle

Kings of Lacedaemon from the Books of Diodorus

8. Since it so happens that the interval is difficult to determine from the time of the events which gather around Troy to the first Olympiad, since there were no annual magistrates in this period either in Athens or in any other city, we shall use for our purpose the kings of Lacedaemon. From the Destruction of Troy to the First Olympiad, as Apollodorus of Athens says, is a period of four hundred and eight years. It was eighty years to the Return of the Heracleidae, and the remaining years were included in the reigns of the Lacedaemonian kings, Procles and Eurystheus, and their descendants; we shall now enumerate the individual kings by the two houses down to the First Olympiad.

Eurystheus began to reign in the eightieth year after the events which gather around Troy, and he ruled forty-two years; after him Agis ruled one year; Echestratus thirty-one; Labotas thirty-seven; Doristhus twenty-nine; Agesilaüs, his successor, forty-four; Arehelaus sixty; Teleclus forty; and Alcamenes thirty-eight. In the tenth year of the last reign fell the beginning of the First Olympiad, that in which Curibus of Elea won the "stadion."

Of the other house Procles was the first ruler and reigned forty-nine years; after him Pritanis reigned forty-nine years; Eunomius forty-five; after him Chariclus sixty; after him Nicandrus thirty-eight; and Theopompus forty-seven. In the tenth year also of the last reign begins the First Olympiad. And the total length of time from the taking of Troy to the Return of the Heracleidae is eighty years.

9. Now that we have examined into these matters, it remains for us to speak of Corinth and of Sicyon, and of the manner in which the territories of these cities were settled by the Dorians. For it came to pass that practically all the peoples throughout the Peloponnesus, except the Arcadians, were driven out on the occasion of the Return of the Heracleidae. Now when the Heracleidae divided up the land they made an exception of the territory of Corinth and the country lying about it, and sending word to Aletes they handed this territory over to him. Aletes, becoming a notable man, increased the city of Corinth in power and reigned as king over it thirty-eight years. After his death the kingship was

assumed from time to time by the eldest son of his descendants, until the tyranny of Cypselus, which falls four hundred and forty-seven years after the Return of the Heracleidae. [657] The first of the Heracleidae to succeed to the kingship was Ixion, who reigned thirty-eight years; after him Agelas ruled for thirty-seven years, and then Prymnis for thirty-five. Bacchis, who ruled for an equal number of years, became a more famous man than any of his predecessors, and this was the reason why the kings who followed him came to be called no longer Heracleidae, but Bacchidae. Agelas followed Bacchis and reigned for thirty years, Eudemus for twenty-five, and Aristomedes for thirty-five. At his death Aristomedes left a son Telestes, who was still a child in years, and Telestes was deprived of the kingship he had inherited by Agemon, his father's brother and his own guardian, who reigned sixteen years. After him Alexander held the royal power for twenty-five years. Alexander was slain by that Telestes who had been deprived of the ancestral rule, and he then reigned for twelve years; and Telestes was slain by his kinsmen and Automenes reigned for a year. The Bacchidae, who were descendants of Heracles, were two hundred in number when they seized the rule, and they all maintained control over the state as a body; out of their own number they annually chose one man to be chief magistrate, who held the position of the king, this form of government continuing for ninety years until it was destroyed by the tyranny which Cypselus established.

**10.** In the city of Cymê there was a tyrant by the name of Malacus. He established his domination by ingratiating himself with the masses and by constantly calumniating the most influential citizens, and he continually put to the sword the wealthiest citizens, seized their possessions and thus maintained mercenaries, and was a terror to the Cymêans.

[And last of all, after the Return of the Heracleidae, Argives and Lacedaemonians sent forth colonies which they established on certain other islands and likewise took possession of Crete, and on these islands they took certain cities for their homes; but with regard to these cities we shall give a detailed account in connection with the period of time to which they belong.]

[After Troy was taken the Carians steadily increased their power and became masters of the sea; and taking possession of the Cyclades, some of the islands they appropriated to themselves, expelling the Cretans who inhabited them, but in some islands they settled jointly with the Cretans, who had been the first to dwell there. At a later time, when the power of the Greeks increased, the major number of the Cyclades came to be inhabited by them, and the Carians, who were non-Greeks, were driven out by them, but of these matters we shall give a detailed account in connection with the appropriate period of time.]

### From 11. Eusebius, Chronicle

The Periods when Certain Peoples were Masters of the Sea, Excerpted from the Writings of Diodorus.

After the Trojan War the mastery of the sea was held by:

|   |   | years |
|---|---|---|
| 1 | Lydians and Maeonians | 92 |
| 2 | Pelasgians | 85 |

| 3 | Thracians | 79 |
| 4 | Rhodians | 23 |
| 5 | Phrygians | 25 |
| 6 | Cyprians | 33 |
| 7 | Phoenicians | 45 |
| 8 | Egyptians | ? |
| 9 | Milesians | ? |
| 10 | Carians? Megarians? | ? |
| 11 | Lesbians | ? |
| 12 | Phocians | 44 |
| 13 | Samians | ? |
| 14 | Lacedaemonians | 2 |
| 15 | Naxians | 10 |
| 16 | Eretrians | 15 |
| 17 | Aeginetans | 10 |

down to the time when Xerxes crossed over to the other side.

**12.** Such was the magnitude of the qualities of virtue possessed by Lycurgus that once, when he went to Delphi, the Pythian priestess delivered to him this utterance:

> Lycurgus, loved of Zeus and all whose homes
> Are on Olympus, thou art come unto
> My wealthy shrine. I wonder how I shall
> Reveal myself to thee, as god or man;
> Yet more a god, Lycurgus, hold I thee.
> Thou com'st in search of goodly laws; and such
> A system of fair laws shall I now give
> To thee as never city upon earth
> Shall e'er possess.

The same Lycurgus inquired of the Pythian priestess what sort of customs he should establish for the Lacedaemonians whereby they might receive the greatest advantage. When she replied that he should legislate in such fashion that the one group should govern fairly and the other group should obey those in authority, he inquired of her again, what should be done by those who were to govern fairly and by those who were to be obedient to men in authority. Whereupon the priestess delivered the following oracle:

> Two paths there be which farthest parted are,
> One leading on to freedom's honoured halls,
> The other to the house of slavery which
> All mortals shun. The former path is trod
> By those of manly soul and concord sweet;
> And on this way I charge you lead the folk;
> The latter is the path of loathsome strife
> And weak delusion: This the way which thou
> Must guard against most carefully.

The sum and substance of the oracle was that the greatest attention should be devoted to concord and manly spirit, since it is by these alone that freedom can be maintained, and unless a man possesses freedom nothing he has is of use to him, nor indeed any goods which the majority of mankind consider of value, seeing that he is the subject of other men. For all such things belong to those who hold authority, not to subjects; and so, if any man wishes to lay up the good things of life for himself, and not for others, to use, he must first of all win freedom. The oracle commanded that both possessions [good things & freedom] should be the concern of men, since neither one of them, without the other, can be of advantage to him who has won it; for there is no advantage to men to be brave, if they are at odds among themselves, or to be wholly of one mind, if they are cowards.

The same Lycurgus received from Delphi an oracle with regard to covetousness, which is handed down to memory in the form of a proverb:

> Covetousness, and it alone, will work
> The ruin of Sparta.

The Pythian priestess delivered to Lycurgus an oracle regarding a political constitution in these words:

> Thus Lord Apollo, he of silver bow,
> Far-darter, golden haired, has made response
> From out his wealthy shrine: Let kings, to whom
> Is honour 'mongst the gods, and in whose hearts
> Is care for Sparta's lovely city, hold
> In Council the first place; and let old men,
> Of ancient worth, and after them from out
> The folk the warriors, all in turn yielding
> Obedience to straight *rhetrae,* speak fair and hold
> To justice in their ev'ry deed; nor let
> Them profer crooked counsel to this state;
> And in the body of the folk let there
> Reside decision and the power. Tis thus
> That Phoebus hath appointed for the city.

They who do not cherish piety toward the divinity show all the less concern to observe justice toward men.

The Lacedaemonians, by observing the laws of Lycurgus, from a lowly people grew to be the most powerful among the Greeks and maintained the leadership among the Greek states for over four hundred years, but after that time, as they little by little began to relax each one of the institutions and to turn to luxury and indifference, and as they grew so corrupted as to use coined money and to amass wealth, they lost the leadership.

**13.** Temenus, who obtained the territory of Argos as his portion, together with his army invaded the land of his enemies. And in the course of the war, which was a long one, he did not advance his sons to positions of command, but he assigned to Deïphontes, his daughter's husband whom he especially favoured, the undertakings which carried with them the most renown. For this reason his sons, Cissus and Phalces and Cerynes, became wroth with him and formed a plot against their father by the hands of certain villains; and the latter, at the instigation of the sons, lay in wait for Temenus beside a certain river. But they did not succeed in slaying him, and took to flight after only wounding him.

The Argives, since they had suffered serious reverses in the war which they together with their king had undertaken against the Lacedaemonians, and had been forced to hand over their ancestral homes to the Arcadians, laid the blame for this upon their king, on the ground that he had given over their land to the exiles and had not divided it in lots among them. The mass of citizens rose up against him and in their despair laid violent hands upon him, whereupon he fled to Tegea, where he spent his days in the enjoyment of honours at the hands of those who had received his favours.

**14.** The kingship among the Argives lasted for five hundred and forty-nine years, as the most learned Diodorus has stated in his history.

### From 15. Eusebius, Chronicle

After the rule of the Assyrians came to an end [612] with the death of their last king, Sardanapallus, there followed the period of the Macedonians.

Caranus, who was covetous of possessions, before the First Olympiad gathered forces from the Argives and from the rest of the Peloponnesus, and with this army he advanced against the territory of the Macedonians. It happened that at the same time the king of the Orestae was at war with his neighbours, who were known as Eordaei. He asked Caranus to come to his assistance and promised to give him half of his land, when he had established peace among the Orestae. The king was as good as his word, and Caranus received the land and ruled as king over it for thirty years. He died in his old age and was succeeded on the throne by his son who was known as Coenus, who reigned twenty-eight years. After him Tirimmus reigned for forty-three years, and Perdicas for forty-eight years. Perdicas wished to enlarge his kingdom and so made inquiry of Delphi.

And a little further on he writes on the same matters:

Perdicas reigned forty-eight years and left the kingship to Argaeus. And after a reign of thirty-one years Argaeus was succeeded on the throne by Philip, who reigned thirty-three years and left the rule to Aeeropas. He ruled for twenty years, and then Alcetas succeeded to the throne and reigned eighteen years, leaving the kingship to Amintas. After his rule of forty-nine years Alexander followed on the throne, which he held for forty-four years. After him Perdicas reigned for twenty-two years, then Archelaüs for seventeen, and Aeorpus for six. After him Pausanias for one year, Ptolemaeus for three, then Perdicas for five, and Philip for twenty-four. And Alexander spent over twelve years warring with the Persians.

By such a genealogy trustworthy historians trace the line of the kings of Macedonia back to Heracles. From Caranus, who was the first to unite the power of Macedon and to hold it, to Alexander, who subdued the land of Asia, there are reckoned twenty-four kings and four hundred and eighty years.

**16.** Perdiccas, wishing to increase the strength of his kingdom, sent to Delphi to consult the oracle. And the Pythian priestess replied to him:

> Stands o'er a wealthy land a might of kings
> Of Temenus' right noble line,

> Of Aegis-bearing Zeus. But swiftly go
> To Bottiaïs, rich in flocks; and then
> Where thou shalt see white-horned goats, with fleece
> Like snow, resting at dawn, make sacrifice
> Unto the blessed gods upon that spot
> And raise the chief city of a state.

**17.** The genealogy of Caranus is given in this wise, as Diodorus reports, as well as the majority of historians, one of whom is also Theopompus. Caranus was the son of Pheidon, the son of Aristodamis, the son of Merops, the son of Thestius, the son of Cissius, the son of Temenus, the son of Aristomachus, the son of Cleodaeus, the son of Hyllus, the son of Heracles. But there are some, he says, who adduce a different genealogy, saying that Caranus was the son of Poeas, the son of Croesus, the son of Cleodaeus the son of Eurybiades, the son of Deballus, the son of Lachares, the son of Temenus, who likewise returned into the Peloponnesus.

BOOK VIII

# BOOK VIII FRAGMENTS

**1.** Since the Eleans were becoming a numerous people and were governing themselves in accordance with law, the Lacedaemonians viewed their growing power with suspicion and assisted them in establishing a settled mode of life for the community, in order that they might enjoy the benefits of peace and never experience the activities of war. They made the Eleans sacred to the god, with the concurrence of practically the whole Greek world. As a consequence the Eleans took no part in the campaign against Xerxes, but they were relieved of service because of their responsibility for the honour due to the god, and further, in local struggles, when the Greeks were warring among themselves, no state caused them any annoyance, since all Greek states were zealous to preserve the sanctity and inviolability of the land and city. Many generations later, however, the Eleans also began to join in campaigns and to enter upon wars of their own choosing.

The Eleans took no part in the wars in which all the rest of the Greeks shared. In fact, when Xerxes advanced against the Greeks with so many myriads of soldiers, the allies relieved them of service in the field, the leaders instructing them that they would be returning a greater service if they should undertake responsibility for the honour due to the gods.

**2.** Nor was she [Vestal Rhea Silvia] allowed the embraces of a man, even in secret; for no one (Aemulius though) would ever be so foolish as to exchange the felicities of an entire life for the pleasure of a moment.

**3.** Numitor had been deprived of the kingship by his own brother, whose name was Amulius and who was king of the Albans, but when, contrary to his hopes, Numitor recognised his own grandsons, Remus and Romulus, he laid a plot against this same brother to work his death, and the plot worked out: Summoning the herdsmen they marched against the palace, forced their way inside the entrance and slew all who opposed them, and later also Amulius himself.

**4.** When these children, Romulus and Remus, who had been exposed in infancy, had attained in the course of time to manhood, they far surpassed all the rest in beauty of body and in strength. Consequently they provided protection for all the herds and flocks, easily repelling those who practised robbery, slaying many of them in their raids and even taking some alive. In addition to the zeal they displayed in these matters, they were friendly towards all the herdsmen of the region, joining in their gatherings and proving their character, to any who needed their aid, to be modest and sociable. Consequently, since the safety of all hung upon Remus and Romulus, the majority of the people subjected themselves to them and carried out their commands, assembling in whatever place they ordered.

**5.** When Remus and Romulus were observing the flight of birds for divination with a view to founding a city, there appeared (to Romulus), as we are told, a favourable omen, and Remus, amazed, said to his brother, "In this city it will happen many a time that clumsy counsels will be followed by a favourable turn of fortune." The fact was that, although Romulus had been too hasty in dispatching the messenger and, on his own part, had been altogether wrong, yet his ignorance had been made right by mere chance.

**6.** Romulus, in connection with his founding of Rome, was hastily throwing a ditch about it, to prevent any of his neighbours from attempting to hinder his undertaking. Remus, angered at his failure to gain the chief place and jealous of the good fortune of his brother, came up to the labourers and belittled their work; for he declared that the ditch was too narrow and that the city would easily fall, since enemies would have no difficulty in getting over it, but Romulus replied in anger, "I give orders to all citizens to exact vengeance of any man who attempts to get over the ditch." A second time Remus cast insults at the labourers, and said they were making the ditch too narrow. "Why, enemies will get over it with no trouble; see, I can do it myself, easily." And with these words he leaped over it. A certain Celer, one of the labourers, answered him, "I will exact vengeance of the man who jumps over the ditch, even as the king commanded;" and with these words he raised his spade, and striking Remus on the head, slew him.

**7.** Polychares, a Messenian of great wealth and conspicuous ancestry, agreed with Euaephnus, a Spartan, to share together the border land. And when Euaephnus took over the oversight and protection of the flocks and herdsmen, he tried to take advantage of Polychares, but he was found out. The way of it was this: He sold some of the cattle and herdsmen to merchants, on the understanding that they would be taken out of the country, and then alleged that the loss was due to the violent attack of robbers. The merchants, who were going by ship to Sicily, were making their way along the Peloponnesus; and when a storm arose they dropped anchor near the land, whereupon the herdsmen slipped off the boat at night and made their escape, feeling safe in their knowledge of the region. They then made their way to Messenê and revealed to their master all the facts; and Polychares concealed the slaves and then asked his partner to come to him from Sparta. When Euaephnus held to his story that some of the herdsmen had been carried off by the robbers and the rest had been killed by them, Polychares produced the men. When Euaephnus saw the men he was struck with consternation, and, since his refutation was patent, he turned to entreaties, promising that he would restore the cattle and leaving no word unsaid whereby he might be spared. Polychares, in reverence for the obligations of hospitality, made no mention of what the Spartan had done, and sent his son along with him, to receive his dues at his hands, but Euaephnus not only forgot the promises he had made but even slew the youth who had been along with him to Sparta. At this deed Polychares was so enraged at such acts of lawlessness that he demanded the person of the criminal. The Lacedaemonians, however, paid no attention to his demand, but sent the son of Euaephnus to Messenê with a reply, to the effect that Polychares should come to Sparta and prefer charges before the ephors and the kings for the wrongs he had suffered. Polychares, now that he had the opportunity to return like for like, slew the youth and in reprisal plundered the city.

**8.** While the dogs were howling and the Messenians were in despair, one of the elders advanced and urged the people to pay no heed to the off-hand pronouncements of the seers. For even in their private affairs, he said, they fall into many errors, by reason of their inability to foresee the future, and in this case, when matters were so involved as only the gods could be expected to know, they, being but men, could not understand them. He urged the people, therefore, to send a messenger to Delphi, and the Pythian priestess gave them the following answer: They should offer up in sacrifice a maiden from the house of the Aepytidae, any one at all; and if the one on whom the lot fell could not be devoted to the gods, they should sacrifice whatever maiden any father from the same family might freely offer. "If you will do this," the oracle continued, "you will gain the victory in the war and power." . . . For no honour, great as it might be, appeared in the eyes of the parents of equal weight with the life of their children, since compassion for one of his own blood stole into each man's heart as he pictured to his mind's eye the slaughter, while at the same time he was filled with misgivings that he should, like a traitor, deliver up his child to certain death.

9. He [Archias?] rushed headlong into errors unworthy of his fame; for the power of love is mighty to trip up youth, especially such youth as are proud of the strength of their bodies. And this is the reason why the ancient writers of myths have represented Heracles, him who was unconquerable by any others, as being conquered by the might of love.

10. Archias the Corinthian, being seized with love for Actaeon, first of all dispatched a messenger to the youth, making him marvellous promises; and when he was unable to win him over to act contrary to the honourable principles of his father and to the modesty of the youth himself, he gathered together the greater number of his associates, with the intention of using force on the youth who would not yield to favour or entreaty. Finally once, when Archias had become drunken in the company of the men he had called together, his passion drove him to such madness that he broke into the house of Melissus and began to carry off the boy by force, but the father and the other inmates of the house held fast to him, and in the violent struggle which ensued between the two groups the boy was found, without any knowing it, to have given up the ghost while in the arms of his defenders. Consequently, when we reflect upon the strange turn of the affair, we are forced both to pity the fate of the victim and to wonder at the unexpected reversal of fortune. For the boy came to the same manner of death as did he [Actaeon] whose very name he bore, since they both lost their lives in similar manner at the hands of those who had aided them most.

11. Agathocles was chosen to be superintendent of the building of the temple of Athena, and picking out the finest blocks of the hewn stone, he paid for them out of his own means, but making an improper use of the stones he built with them a costly house. At this act of his, we are told, the deity made itself manifest to men; for Agathocles was struck by lightning and he together with his house was consumed in flames. The Geomori [land-owners] ruled that his property should be confiscated to the state, although his heirs offered evidence that he had taken no money which belonged to either the sanctuary or the state. The house they consecrated to the goddess and forbade that anyone should enter it, and to this day it is called the House Struck by Lightning.

**12.** After this the king [Euphaës of Messenê], when he had recovered from his wounds, proposed that they hold a trial for the meed of valour. Two men entered the contest, Cleonnis and Aristomenes, each of whom possessed his own peculiar claim to fame. For Cleonnis had covered the king with his shield when he had fallen and had accounted for the death of eight Spartans who charged against him, two of them were distinguished chieftains, and he had stripped the complete armour from all whom he had slain and given it to his shield-bearers, in order that he might have it as evidence of his valour for the trial. Though he had received many wounds, he had got them all in front, thus providing the fullest proof that he had given way before no one of his foes. As for Aristomenes, he had slain five Lacedaemonians in the struggle over the body of the king and had stripped their complete armour from the foemen who had set upon him. He had also kept his body free from any wound, and on his way back to the city from the battle he had performed a deed which was deserving of praise. For Cleonnis lay so weakened by his wounds that he could neither walk without support nor be led by the hand; and Aristomenes, raising him on his shoulders, brought him back to the city, notwithstanding that he was also carrying his own complete armour and that Cleonnis surpassed all other men in size and strength of body. Such were their resources as they came to the trial for the meed of valour, and the king together with his chief captains took his seat as the law prescribed. Thereupon Cleonnis spoke first and addressed them with the following words:

"Only a brief speech is necessary regarding the meed of valour, since the judges are men who themselves have witnessed the exploits of each of us; and I need only to remind you that, as we both fought against the same foemen on this single occasion and in this single place, it was I who killed the greater number. It is obvious, therefore, that he who, under identical circumstances, was first in the number of foemen he slew is also first in his just claim to the meed of valour. Furthermore, the bodies of the two of us supply the most manifest proofs where is the superiority, for the one came out of the battle covered with wounds which are in front, while the other, returning as from a festive gathering and not from so fierce a pitched battle as that was, did not experience the might of an enemy's sword. More fortunate Aristomenes may well be, but he may not justly be judged to be the braver of us two. For it is manifest that the man who endured such lacerations of his body offered himself unsparingly for his fatherland; whereas the man who, in close grips with the enemy and amidst such perils, kept himself unwounded was able to do that only because he shunned hurt to his person, and so it would be absurd if, before judges who have themselves witnessed the battle, that man shall have the preference who slew a smaller number of the foe and exposed his own body to less danger, before the man who holds first place on both these counts. Furthermore, his carrying a body all worn out by its wounds, and when no further peril threatens, is no indication of bravery, though it does perhaps betoken strength of body. What I have said to you is sufficient; for the contest which you are to decide is one, not of words, but of deeds."

It was now the turn of Aristomenes to speak, and he addressed the judges as follows: "I am astonished that the man who has been saved thinks to strive with his saviour for the meed of valour; for the necessary conclusion is, either that he charges the judges with folly, or that he thinks that the decision will be rendered on the basis of the words spoken now, not of the deeds done then. It will be shown that Cleonnis is not only inferior to me in bravery, but wholly ungrateful as well. For, omitting to recount his own brave achievements, he set about disparaging my deeds, thus showing himself to be more grasping for honour than is just; for from the man to whom he owed the greatest gratitude for saving his life, from him he in his envy has taken away the praise earned by his own noble deeds. I am ready to concede that in the perils encountered in the battle I was fortunate, but I maintain that I showed myself his superior in bravery. If, indeed, I had come off unwounded because I avoided the onslaught of the foe, it would have been more fitting for me to call myself, not fortunate, but cowardly, and not even to plead for the meed of valour, but to have suffered the punishments prescribed by the law. However, since it was while fighting in the front of battle and slaying those who opposed me that I did not suffer what I inflicted on others, the necessary conclusion is that I was not only fortunate but also brave. For if the enemy, in terror, did not dare to face my valour, then am I, whom they feared, deserving of great praise; or else, if they fought with spirit, and yet I slaughtered them as they came on, taking thought at the same time for my body, then am I both courageous and cunning. For the man who, while fighting desperately, meets the threatening danger with calm mind, has a double claim to bravery, that of body and that of soul. Yet these just claims of mine I should plead against other men who are better than my opponent. For when I carried the disabled Cleonnis from the scene of battle to the city, keeping my arms the while, he himself, in my judgment, had acknowledged the justice of my claim. Yet quite possibly, if I had paid no attention to him at that time, he would not now be striving with me for the meed of valour, nor would he be disparaging that great kindness I showed him, by claiming that the great deed I performed was nothing, because by that time the enemy had withdrawn from the field. Who, indeed, does not know that many times armies which have left the battle-field have made it their practice to wheel about and renew the attack, and to win the victory by the use of strategy of this kind? But I have said enough; for I cannot think you have need of further words."

After these speeches the judges with one accord gave their votes for Aristomenes.

13. The Lacedaemonians recovered their zeal; for if men have practised manly virtue and bravery from their youth, even though some turn of fortune has humbled them, yet a brief speech will recall them to their sense of duty. On the other hand the Messenians were not second to them in their zeal; nay rather, confiding in their own valour. . . .

Since the Lacedaemonians were being worsted by the Messenians, they sent to inquire of Delphi. And the priestess made answer to them:

> 'Tis not alone the deeds of battle thou
> Should ply at Phoebus' order. Guile it is
> Whereby the folk doth hold Messenê's land,
> And by the same device as it was gained
> Shall it be won.

The thought is that it is not alone by deeds of strength but by those of craft as well. . . .

**14.** Pompilius, the Roman king, lived at peace for his entire life. And certain writers state that he was a pupil of Pythagoras, and that he received from him the ordinances he laid down regarding the worship of the gods and was instructed in many other matters; and it was because of this that he became a man of renown and was summoned by the Romans to be their king.

**15.** It is not within our power, much as we may wish it, to honour the deity in a worthy manner. Consequently, if we were not ready, according to our ability, to show ourselves grateful, what hope should we have of the life to come, seeing that we transgress against those whom evil-doers may neither elude nor escape? For, to sum up all, it is evident that, with respect to those in whose power are both unending reward and unending punishment, we should see to it that their anger is not aroused and that their favour is everlasting. For so great is the difference between the life of the impious and the life of the pious, that though both expect of the deity the fulfilment of their prayers, the former expect the fulfilment of their own, the latter those of their enemies. . . . In fine, if we give aid to enemies when they flee for refuge to altars, and if we pledge with oaths to hostile foes that we will do them no wrong, what sort of zeal should we show towards the gods themselves, who show kindnesses to the pious not only in this life, but also after death, and who, if we place confidence in the Mysteries, also have ready for them a happy existence and good fame for all eternity? Consequently there is nothing in this life about which we should be so in earnest as concerning the honour due to the gods.

Our conclusion is that bravery and justice and all the other virtues of mankind the other animals also have acquired, but that reverence for the deity in so far transcends all the other virtues as the gods themselves are in all respects superior to mortals.

While reverence for the deity is a desirable thing for men in private life, far more is it appropriate to states; for states, by reason of their nearer approach to immortality, enjoy a nature akin to that of the gods and, in the considerable length of time they endure, they may expect the reward they merit, sovereignty as the reward for reverence, punishment for slighting the divinity.

**16.** Deïoces, the king of the Medes, despite the great lawlessness which prevailed, practised justice and the other virtues.

**17.** Myscellus, an Achaean by birth, went from Rhypê [in Achaea] to Delphi and inquired of the god concerning the begetting of children. And the Pythian priestess gave him the following answer:

> Myscellus, too short of back [hunchback], beloved art thou
> Of him, even Apollo, who works afar,
> And he will give thee children; yet this first
> Is his command, Croton the great to found
> Amidst fair fields.

And since he did not understand the reference to Croton, the Pythian priestess gave answer a second time:

> To thee the Far-darter in person now doth speak,
> And give thou heed. Here lieth the Taphian land,
> Untouched by plough, and Chalcis there, and there
> The home of the Curetes, sacred soil,

> And there the isles of the Echinades:
> And on the islands' left a mighty sea.
> This way thou cans't not miss the Lacinian Head,
> Nor sacred Crimise, nor Aesarus' stream.

Although the oracle thus commanded Myscellus to found Croton, he, because of his admiration of the territory of Sybaris, wished to found a city there; whereupon the following oracle was delivered to him:

> Myscellus, too short of back, in searching things
> Other than god commands, thou seekest naught
> But tears. Approve the gift the god doth give.

**18.** The Sybarites are slaves to their belly and lovers of luxury. And so great was their devotion to luxury that of the peoples elsewhere their preference was above all for the Ionians and the Tyrrhenians, because they found that the former surpassed the other Greeks, and the latter the other barbarians, in the extravagance of their manner of life.

We are told that a wealthy Sybarite, on hearing some persons say that a man had suffered a rupture at the sight of some men working, begged the speaker not to be astounded at that. "For I," he said, "at the mere hearing of it, have suffered a stitch in my side." Of another Sybarite it is told that he remarked after a visit to Sparta that he used to wonder at the bravery of the Spartans, but that now, after witnessing what a frugal and utterly miserable life they led, he could only conclude that they were no better than the lowest of men. "For the most cowardly Sybarite," he said, "would choose to die thrice rather than to endure a life like theirs." The man among them who, we are told, indulged in the greatest luxury was known as Mindyrides.

**19.** Mindyrides, men say, surpassed the other Sybarites in luxury. For when Cleisthenes, the tyrant of Sicyon, after winning the chariot-race made proclamation that any who purposed to marry his daughter, who was considered a girl of surpassing beauty, should gather at his home, Mindyrides, we are told, set sail from Sybaris in a ship of fifty oars, the rowers being slaves of his own household, some of them fishermen and others fowlers. Upon his arrival in Sicyon he surpassed, in the equipage his fortune afforded him, not only the rival suitors but also the tyrant himself, although the whole city was participating eagerly in the occasion. At the dinner which was held after his arrival, when a certain man approached Mindyrides to recline beside him at the table, the latter remarked that he was here in accordance with the proclamation and intended to recline either with the lady or by himself.

**20.** The Milesians lived in luxury, and we are told that a Sybarite who had paid them a visit, after he returned to his native city remarked, among other things which he recounted to his fellow-citizens, that in his absence from home he had seen but one free city and that was the city of the Milesians.

**21.** The Epeunactae [Spartan helots] had agreed with Phalanthus that they would rise in revolt in the market-place, as soon as Phalanthus, in full armour, should pull his helmet over his forehead; but a certain man disclosed to the ephors what was going to take place. The majority of the ephors believed that they should put Phalanthus to death, but Agathiadas, who had become a lover of his, stated that if they did this they would plunge Sparta into the greatest civil strife, in which, if they were victorious, they would win a profitless victory, and, if they lost, they would utterly destroy their fatherland. He gave as his advice, therefore, that the herald should publicly proclaim that Phalanthus should let his helmet rest as it was. This was done, and the Partheniae gave up the undertaking and began to seek a reconciliation.

The Epeunactae sent envoys to Delphi and inquired of the god if he would give them the territory of Sicyon; the priestess replied:

> Fair is the plain 'twixt Corinth and Sicyon;
> But not a home for thee, though thou wert clad
> Throughout in bronze. Mark thou Satyrion
> And Taras' gleaming flood, the harbour on
> The left, and where the goat catches with joy
> The salt smell of the sea, wetting the tip
> Of his gray beard. There build thou Taras firm
> Within Satyrion's land.

When they heard this reply they could not understand it; whereupon the priestess spoke more plainly:

> Satyrion is my gift to thee wherein
> To dwell, and the fat land of Taras too,
> A bane to be to the Iapygian folk.

**22.** Hippomenes, the Athenian archon, exacted of his daughter, who had been violated by an unknown person, a punishment which was cruel and extraordinary. He shut her up together with a horse in a small stall, and by keeping the beast without food for some days he forced it, through hunger, to eat the body of the girl who had been thrown to it.

**23.** Antiphemus and Entimus, who founded Gela, made inquiry of the Pythian priestess, who gave them the following answer:

> Entimus and thou, illustrious Craton's son
> Sagacious, fare ye two forth to Sicele,
> On her fair soil to dwell, where ye shall build
> A city, home for men of Crete and Rhodes,
> E'en Gela, at that sacred river's mouth
> Whose name it too shall bear.

The Chalcidians, a tenth of whom had been dedicated to Apollo, came to the god to inquire about sending forth a colony, and they received the reply:

> Where Apsia, most sacred river, falls
> Into the sea, and as one enters it
> The female weds the male, a city found
> Thou there, the land of Auson is thy gift.

They, finding on the banks of the river Apsia a grape-vine entwined about a wild fig-tree, founded there a city.

As he passed by he cried with a loud voice, "Is there anyone who is ready to win immortal glory in exchange for a mortal life? Who will be the first to say, 'I give my life for the safety of the commonwealth?'"

Once a worthless fellow, meeting a man on his way to the countryside, asked him whether there was anything unusual taking place in the city. And the fellow was fined by the Locrian magistrates, so intent were they upon the maintenance of justice.

**24.** The inhabitants of Sicyon received from the Pythian priestess the oracle that they would be "governed by the scourge" for one hundred years. And when they inquired further who would ply the scourge, she answered the second time that it would be the first man to whom they should hear, after they put ashore, a son had been born. Now it so happened that a cook by the name of Andreas [father of Myron, tyrant of Sicyon] had accompanied the envoys, to have charge of the sacrifices. He was a hired servant of the magistrates, charged with bearing the scourges.

**25.** While Tullus Hostilius was king of the Romans, the Albans, viewing with suspicion the rising power of the Romans and wishing to humble them, claimed that the Romans had robbed their territory and sent ambassadors to Rome to demand justice, and, in case the Romans should give them no heed, to declare war. Hostilius, the Roman king, learning that the Albans were only seeking a pretext for war, gave orders that his friends should receive the ambassadors and invite them to be their guests; while as for himself, avoiding any meeting with the ambassadors, he sent men to the Albans to make similar demands of them. This he did in pursuance of an ancient custom, because men of ancient times were concerned about nothing else so much as that the wars they waged should be just ones; for he was cautious lest, if he were unable to discover the men responsible for the robbery and to hand them over to those who demanded them, it should be thought that he was entering upon an unjust war. By good fortune his ambassadors to Alba were the first to be refused justice, and they therefore declared war for the thirtieth day following, and the ambassadors of the Albans, therefore, when they presented their demands, received the answer that, since the Albans had been the first to refuse justice, the Romans had declared war upon them. Such, then, was the reason why these two peoples, who enjoyed mutual rights of marriage and of friendship, got at variance with each other.

**26.** In former times the Romans, who were by origin Latins, never waged war upon a people without formal announcement; but they would first hurl a spear, as a signal, into the territory of the opposing people, the spear denoting the beginning of hostilities. After doing this they commenced war upon the people. This is what Diodorus says, as well as every other writer on Latin affairs.

**27.** The Spartans, having suffered defeat at the hands of the Messenians, sent to Delphi and asked the god for advice concerning the war. They were told to get a commander from the Athenians.

The Lacedaemonians, under the inspiration of Tyrtaeus, became so eager for battle that, when about to enter the conflict, they wrote their names on little sticks which they fastened to their arms, in order that, if they died, they would not be unidentified by their kinsmen. So ready were they in spirit to accept gladly an honourable death, if victory were beyond their grasp.

**28.** Terpander, who sang to the cithara, was a native of Methymna; once, when the Lacedaemonians were embroiled in civil strife, an oracle came to them, that they would again be reconciled among themselves if Terpander of Methymna should sing to them to the accompaniment of the cithara, and Terpander did in fact so sing a song to them with an artist's skill, and by his harmonious lay, as Diodorus writes, brought harmony again into their midst. In fact they were entirely changed, and fell to embracing and tearfully kissing one another.

**29.** Aristotle, who was also called Battus [stutterer], wishing to found the city of Cyrene, received an oracle to the following effect:

> O Battus, thou did'st come about a voice;
> But Phoebus, even Lord Apollo, sends
> Thee forth to fair-crowned Libya, there to rule
> O'er broad Cyrene and enjoy the place
> Reserved to kings. Barbarian warriors there,
> Clad in the skins of beasts, will rush against
> Thee, when thou settest foot on Libyan soil.
> But pray to Cronus' son, to Pallas who
> Stirs up the fight, of flashing eye, withal
> To Phoebus, ever-young, the son of Zeus,
> And in thy hand shall lie the victory.
> And over fair-crowned Libya shalt thou rule
> Blessed, thou and thy house: Thy guide thereto
> Is Phoebus Apollo.

For envy by its nature lies in wait for success, and therefore works the destruction of those who are pre-eminent in fame.

**30.** Arcesilaus, the king of the Cyrenians, bitterly complaining of his misfortunes, made inquiry of Delphi, and received this reply: The gods were wroth; for the later kings were not ruling after the manner of Battus, the first king. For Battus had contented himself with the appellation alone of king, and had been an equitable ruler, friendly to the people, maintaining the while, the most important thing, the honours due to the gods. The rule of the later kings had taken on more and more the character of tyranny, and they had appropriated to themselves the public revenues and had neglected reverence toward the deity.

For the civil strife which arose among the Cyrenians an arbitrator appeared in the person of Demonax of Mantinea, who was considered to be a man of unusual sagacity and justice. Accordingly he sailed to Cyrene, and receiving from all the stewardship of public affairs, he reconciled the cities on the following conditions.

**31.** Lucius Tarquinius, the king of the Romans, received a careful rearing, and since he proved to be an eager seeker after knowledge, his virtue made him the object of no little admiration. For when he had attained to manhood, he became associated with the Roman king Ancus Marcius, grew to be a most intimate friend of his, and aided the king in the administration of many affairs of the kingdom. And growing very wealthy, he aided by gifts of money many who were in need, and mingling as he did in friendly fashion with all men, he lived without reproach and was famed for his wisdom.

**32.** The [Epizephyrian] Locrians sent to Sparta asking her aid in war. The Lacedaemonians, however, hearing of the great military strength of the inhabitants of Croton, replied, as if responding in a perfunctory manner, and as though the Locrians could be saved only in the way they suggested, that they were giving the Locrians for allies the sons of Tyndareüs, and the ambassadors, whether under the guidance of the providence of God or because they took the reply as an omen, accepted the aid they proffered, and after they had received favourable signs in a sacrifice, they prepared a couch on their ship for the Dioscori and sailed back to their native land.

How (he asked) will the fathers who have accompanied them feel when they, seeing their sons suffering unspeakable torment at the hands of the barbarians, can bring them no aid, and all they can do is to tear their grey hair and make lament to the deaf ears of Fate?

# BOOK IX FRAGMENTS

1. Solon was the son of Execestides and his family was of Salamis in Attica; and in wisdom and learning he surpassed all the men of his time. Being by nature far superior as regards virtue to the rest of men, he cultivated assiduously a virtue that wins applause; for he devoted much time to every branch of knowledge and became practised in every kind of virtue. While still a youth, for instance, he availed himself of the best teachers, and when he attained to manhood he spent his time in the company of the men who enjoyed the greatest influence for their pursuit of wisdom. As a consequence, by reason of his companionship and association with men of this kind, he came to be called one of the Seven Wise Men and won for himself the highest rank in sagacity, not only among the men just mentioned, but also among all who were regarded with admiration.

The same Solon, who had acquired great fame by his legislation, also in his conversations and answers to questions as a private citizen became an object of wonder by reason of his attainments in learning.

The same Solon, although the city [Athens] followed the whole Ionian manner of life and luxury and a carefree existence had made the inhabitants effeminate, worked a change in them by accustoming them to practise virtue and to emulate the deeds of virile folk. It was because of this that Harmodius and Aristogeiton, their spirits equipped with the panoply of his legislation, made the attempt to destroy the rule of the Peisistratidae.

2. Croesus, the king of the Lydians, who was possessed of great military forces and had purposely amassed a large amount of silver and gold, used to call to his court the wisest men from among the Greeks, spend some time in their company, and then send them away with many presents, he himself having been greatly aided thereby toward a life of virtue. On one occasion he summoned Solon, and showing him his military forces and his wealth he asked him whether he thought there was any other man more blest than he. Solon replied, with the freedom of speech customary among lovers of wisdom, that no man while yet living was blest; for the man who waxes haughty over his prosperity and thinks that he has Fortune as his helpmeet does not know whether she will remain with him to the last. Consequently, he continued, we must look to the end of life, and only of the man who has continued until then to be fortunate may we properly say that he is blest. At a later time, when Croesus had been taken prisoner by Cyrus and was about to be burned upon a great pyre [546], he recalled the answer Solon had given him, and so, while the fire was already blazing about him, he kept continually calling the name of Solon. Cyrus sent men to find out the reason for his continual calling of the name of Solon; and on learning the cause Cyrus changed his purpose, and since he believed that Solon's reply was the truth, he ceased regarding Croesus with contempt, put out the burning pyre, saved the life of Croesus, and counted him henceforth as one of his friends.

Solon believed that the boxers and short-distance runners and all other athletes contributed nothing worth mentioning to the safety of states, but that only men who excel in prudence and virtue are able to protect their native lands in times of danger.

**3.** When there was a dispute about the golden tripod, the Pythian priestess delivered the following oracle:

> Miletus' son, dost ask Apollo's will
> About the tripod? Who is first of all
> In wisdom, his the tripod is, I say.

But some writers have a different account, as follows: War had broken out among the Ionians, and when the tripod was brought up in their seine by some fishermen, they inquired of the god how they might end the war. And the priestess replied:

> Never shall cease the war twixt Meropes
> And Iones, until that golden stand
> Hephaestus worked with skill ye send away;
> And it shall come to that man's dwelling-place
> Who in his wisdom hath foreseen the things
> That are and likewise things that are to be.

The Milesians, wishing to follow the injunction of the oracle, desired to award the prize to Thales of Miletus, but Thales said that he was not the wisest of all and advised them to send it to another and wiser man. In this manner the other six of the Seven Wise Men likewise rejected the tripod, and it was given to Solon, who was thought to have surpassed all men in both wisdom and understanding. Solon advised that it be dedicated to Apollo, since he was wiser than all of them.

**4.** Solon, seeing toward the end of his life how Peisistratus, to please the masses, was playing the demagogue and was on the road to tyranny, tried at first by arguments to turn him from his intention; and when Peisistratus paid no attention to him, he once appeared in the market-place arrayed in full armour, although he was already a very old man. When the people, the sight being so incongruous, flocked to him, he called upon the citizens to seize their arms and at once make an end of the tyrant, but no man paid any attention to him, all of them concluding that he was mad and some declaring that he was in his dotage. Peisistratus, who had already gathered a guard of a few spearmen, came up to Solon and asked him, "Upon what resources do you rely that you wish to destroy my tyranny?" Solon replied, "Upon my old age," Peisistratus, in admiration of his common sense, did him no harm.

**5.** The man who puts his hands to lawless and unjust deeds may never properly be considered wise.

**6.** We are told that the Scythian Anacharsis, who took great pride in his wisdom, once came to Pytho and inquired of the oracle who of the Greeks was wiser than he: the oracle replied:

> A man of Oeta, Myson, they report,
> Is more endowed than thou with prudent brains.

Myson was a Malian and had his home on Mt. Oeta in a village called Chenae.

**7.** Myson was a man of Malis who dwelt in a village called Chenae, and he spent his entire time in the country and was unknown to most men. He was

# BOOK IX

included among the Seven Wise Men in the place of Periander of Corinth, who was rejected because he had turned into a harsh tyrant.

**8.** Solon was curious to see the place where Myson spent his days, and found him at the threshing-floor fitting a handle to a plough. To make trial of the man Solon said, "Now is not the season for the plough, Myson." "Not to use it," he replied, "but to make it ready."

**9.** In the case of Chilon his life agreed with his teaching, a thing one rarely finds. As for the philosophers of our time, for instance, most of them are to be seen uttering the noblest sentiments, but following the basest practices, and the solemnity and sagacity expressed in their pronouncements are refuted when the speakers are put to the proof, but as for Chilon, not to mention the virtue which he displayed in every deed throughout his life, he thought out and expressed many precepts which are worthy of record.

**10.** When Chilon came to Delphi he thought to dedicate to the god the firstlings, as it were, of his own wisdom, and engraved upon a column these three maxims: "Know thyself"; "Nothing overmuch"; and the third, "A pledge, and ruin is nigh." Each of these maxims, though short and laconic, displays deep reflection. For the maxim "Know thyself" exhorts us to become educated and to get prudence, it being only by these means that a man may come to know himself, either because it is chiefly those who are uneducated and thoughtless that think themselves to be very sagacious, and that, according to Plato, is of all kinds of ignorance the worst, or because such people consider wicked men to be virtuous, and honest men, on the contrary, to be of no account; for only in this one way may a man know himself and his neighbour: by getting an education and a sagacity that are superior.

Likewise, the maxim "Nothing overmuch" exhorts us to observe due measure in all things and not to make an irrevocable decision about any human affairs, as the Epidamnians once did. This people, who dwelt on the shores of the Adriatic, once quarrelled among themselves, and casting red-hot masses of iron right into the sea they swore an oath that they would never make up their mutual enmity until the masses of iron should be brought up hot out of the sea. Although they had sworn so severe an oath and had taken no thought of the admonition "Nothing overmuch," later under the compulsion of circumstances they put an end to their enmity, leaving the masses of iron to lie cold in the depths of the sea.

As for the maxim "A pledge, and ruin is nigh," some have assumed that by it Chilon was advising against marriage; for among most Greek peoples the agreement to marry is also called a "pledge," and this is confirmed by the common experience of men in that the worst and most numerous ills of life are due to wives, but some writers say that such an interpretation is unworthy of Chilon, because if marriage were destroyed life could not continue, and that he declares that "ruin" is nigh to such pledges as those made in connection with contracts and with agreements on other matters, all of which are concerned with money. As Euripides says:

> No pledge I give, observing well the loss
> Which those incur who of the pledge are fond;
> And writings there at Pytho say me nay.

Some also say that it is not the meaning of Chilon nor is it the act of a good citizen, not to come to the aid of a friend when he needs help of this kind; but rather that he advises against strong asseverations, against eagerness in giving pledges, and against irrevocable decisions in human affairs, such as the Greeks once made in connection with their victory over Xerxes. For they took oath at Plataea [479] that they would hand down enmity to the Persians as an inheritance even to their children's children, so long as the rivers run into the sea, as the race of men endures, and as the earth brings forth fruit; and yet, despite the binding pledge they had taken against fickle fortune, after a time they were sending ambassadors to Artaxerxes, Xerxes' son, to negotiate a treaty of friendship and alliance.

Chilon's precepts, though brief, embrace the entire counsel necessary for the best life, since these pithy sayings of his are worth more than all the votive offerings set up in Delphi. The golden ingots of Croesus and other handiwork like them have vanished and were but great incentives to men who chose to lift impious hands against the temple; but Chilon's maxims are kept alive for all time, stored up as they are in the souls of educated men and constituting the fairest treasure, on which neither Phocians nor Gauls would be quick to lay their hands.

**11.** Pittacus of Mitylenê was not only admired of men for his wisdom, but he was also such a citizen as the island never produced again, nor, in my opinion, could produce in time to come, not until it bears wine both more abundant and more delicious. For he was an excellent law-giver, in his dealings with individual citizens affable and kindly, and he freed his native land from the three greatest evils, from tyranny, civil strife, and war.

Pittacus was a man of consequence, gentle and inclined to self-disparagement. Consequently he was regarded by all as a man who, beyond dispute, was perfect in respect of every virtue: for as to his legislation, he showed himself statesmanlike and prudent, as to keeping his plighted faith strictly just, as to his distinction in armed combat, courageous, and as to his greatness of soul in the matter of lucre, having no trace of avarice.

**12.** When the inhabitants of Mitylenê offered to Pittacus the half of the land for which he had fought in single combat, he would not accept it, but arranged to assign to every man by lot an equal part, uttering the maxim, "The equal share is more than the greater." For in measuring "the greater" in terms of fair dealing, not of profit, he judged wisely; since he reasoned that equality would be followed by fame and security, but greediness by opprobrium and fear, which would speedily have taken away from him the people's gift.

Pittacus acted consistently with these principles toward Croesus also, when the latter offered him as much money from his treasury as Pittacus might desire to take. For on that occasion, we are told, in refusing the gift he said that he already had twice as much as he wished, and when Croesus expressed his surprise at the man's freedom from avarice and inquired of him the meaning of his reply, Pittacus said, "My brother died childless and I inherited his estate, which was the equal of my own, and I have experienced no pleasure in having received the extra amount."

The poet Alcaeus, who had been a most confirmed enemy of Pittacus and had reviled him most bitterly in his poems, once fell into his hands, but Pittacus let him go free, uttering the maxim: "Forgiveness is preferable to punishment."

**13.** The inhabitants of Prienê recount that Bias ransomed from robbers some maidens of distinguished families of Messenia and reared them in honour, as if they were his own daughters. After some time, when their kinsfolk came in search of them, he gave the maidens over to them, asking for neither the cost of their rearing nor the price of their ransom, but on the contrary giving them many presents from his own possessions. The maidens, therefore, loved him as a father, both because they had lived in his home and because he had done so much for them, so that, even when they had departed together with their own families to their native land, they did not forget the kindness they had received in a foreign country.

Some Messenian fishermen, when casting their net, brought up nothing at all except a brazen tripod, which bore the inscription, "To the wisest." And they took the tripod out of the sea and gave it to Bias.

Bias was a most able speaker, and surpassed in this respect all his contemporaries. He used his great eloquence far otherwise than do many men; for he employed it, not to gain fees or income, but to give aid to those who were being wronged. Rarely indeed is a thing like this to be found.

**14.** It is no great thing to possess strength, what ever kind it is, but to use it as one should. For of what advantage to Milo of Croton was his enormous strength of body?

The death of Polydamas, the Thessalian, when he was crushed by the rocks, made clear to all men how precarious it is to have great strength but little sense.

**15.** This Polydamas was of the city of Scotusa, and he used to slay lions with his bare hands as if they were sheep and easily outstrip swift-running chariots with winged feet. He also endeavoured to support with his hand the crumbling roof of a cave, as Diodorus the Sicilian recounts the story.

**16.** After the people of Cirrha had been besieged for a long time because they had attempted to plunder the oracle, some of the Greeks returned to their native cities, but others of them inquired of the Pythian priestess and received the following response:

> Ye shall not seize and lay in ruins the tower
> Of yonder city, before the plashing wave
> Of dark-eyed Amphitrite inundates
> My sacred precinct, here on these holy cliffs.

**17.** It should be known that Solon lived in Athens in the period of the tyrants before the Persian wars, and that Draco lived forty-seven years before him, as Diodorus says.

**18.** The sculptor Perilaüs made a brazen bull for Phalaris the tyrant to use in punishing his own people, but he was himself the first to make trial of that terrible form of punishment; in general, those who plan an evil thing aimed at others are usually snared in their own devices.

**19.** This Phalaris burned to death Perilaüs, the well-known Attic worker in bronze, in the brazen bull. Perilaüs had fashioned in bronze the contrivance of the bull, making small sounding pipes in the nostrils and fitting a door for an opening in the bull's side and this bull he brings as a present to Phalaris, and Phalaris welcomes the man with presents and gives orders that the contrivance be dedicated to the gods. Then that worker in bronze opens the side, the evil device of treachery, and says with inhuman savagery, "If you ever wish to punish some man, O Phalaris, shut him up within the bull and lay a fire beneath it; by his groaning the bull will be thought to bellow and his cries of pain will give you pleasure as they come through the pipes in the nostrils." When Phalaris learned of this scheme, he was filled with loathing of the man and says, "Come then, Perilaüs, do you be the first to illustrate this; imitate those who will play the pipes and make clear to me the working of your device." As soon as Perilaüs had crept in, to give an example, so he thought, of the sound of the pipes, Phalaris closes up the bull and heaps fire under it, but in order that the man's death might not pollute the work of bronze, he took him out, when half-dead, and hurled him down the cliffs. This tale about the bull is recounted by Lucian of Syria, by Diodorus, by Pindar, and countless others beside them.

**20.** Solon the law-giver once entered the assembly and urged the Athenians to overthrow the tyranny before it became all-powerful. When no man paid attention to him, he put on his full armour and appeared in the market-place, although an old man, and calling upon the gods as witnesses he declared that by word and deed, so far as in him lay, he had brought aid to the fatherland when it was in peril. Since the populace did not perceive the design of Peisistratus, it turned out that Solon, though he spoke the truth, was disregarded. It is said that Solon also predicted the approaching tyranny to the Athenians in elegiac verse:

> From cloud is born the might of snow and hail
> And from bright lightning's flash the thunder comes.
> And from great men a city finds its doom;
> The people in their ignorance have bowed
> In slavery to a monarch's single rule.
> For him who puts too far from shore 'tis hard
> The harbour later on to make; but now
> At once one needs must think of everything.

And later, when the tyranny was already established, he said:

> If now you suffer grievous things because
> Of your own cowardice, charge not this fate
> Unto the gods' account; for you yourselves
> Exalted these men's power by giving them
> A guard, and on this count have you put on
> The yoke of evil slavery. Each by each
> With fox's steps you move, but meeting all
> Together trifling judgement do you show.
> For to man's tongue and shifty word you look,
> But to the deed he does you ne'er give heed.

Peisistratus urged Solon to hold his peace and to share with him in the advantages arising from the tyranny. And when he could find no means to change Solon's purpose, but saw in fact that he was ever more and more aroused and steadfastly threatening to bring him to punishment, he asked him upon what resources he relied in his opposition to his designs. We are told that Solon replied, "Upon my old age."

[Herodotus, who lived in the time of Xerxes, gives this account: After the Assyrians had ruled Asia for five hundred years they were conquered by the Medes, and thereafter no king arose for many generations to lay claim to supreme power, but the city-states, enjoying a regimen of their own, were administered in a democratic fashion; finally, how ever, after many years a man distinguished for his justice, named Cyaxares, was chosen king among the Medes. He was the first to try to attach to himself the neighbouring peoples and became for the Medes the founder of their universal empire; and after him each of his successive descendants extended the kingdom by adding a great deal of the adjoining country, until the reign of Astyages, who was conquered by Cyrus and the Persians [549]. We have for the present given only the most important of these events in summary and shall later give a detailed account of them one by one when we come to the periods in which they fall; for it was in the second year of the Seventeenth Olympiad [711-10], according to Herodotus, that Cyaxares was chosen king of the Medes.]

[When Astibaras, the king of the Medes, died of old age in Ecbatana, his son Aspandas, whom the Greeks call Astyages, succeeded to the throne. When he had been defeated by Cyrus the Persian, the kingdom passed to the Persians. Of them we shall give a detailed and exact account at the proper time.]

**21.** Cyrus became king of the Persians in the opening year of the Fifty-fifth Olympiad [560-59], as may be found in the *Library* of Diodorus and in the histories of Thallus and Castor and Polybius and Phlegon and all others who have used the reckoning by Olympiads. For all these writers agree as to the date.

**22.** Cyrus, the son of Cambyses and Mandane, the daughter of Astyages who was king of the Medes, was pre-eminent among the men of his time in bravery and sagacity and the other virtues; for his father had reared him after the manner of kings and had made him zealous to emulate the highest achievements. It was clear that he would take hold of great affairs, since he revealed an excellence beyond his years.

**23.** When Astyages, the king of the Medes, had been defeated and was in disgraceful flight, he vented his wrath upon his soldiers; and he displaced all who had been assigned positions of command, appointing others in their stead, and he picked out all who were responsible for the flight and put them to the sword, thinking that by punishing them in that way he could force the rest to show themselves brave fighters in times of danger, since he was a cruel man and, by nature, hard. Nevertheless, the people were not dismayed at the harsh treatment he meted out; on the contrary, every man, hating his violent and lawless manner, yearned for a change of affairs. Consequently there were gatherings of small groups and seditious conversations, the larger number exhorting one another to take vengeance on him.

**24.** Cyrus, we are told, was not only a courageous man in war, but he was also considerate and humane in his treatment of his subjects. And it was for this reason that the Persians called him Father.

**25.** Croesus was once building ships of war, we are told, with the intention of making a campaign against the islands, and Bias, or Pittacus, who happened to be visiting Lydia at the time and was observing the building of the ships, was asked by the king whether he had heard of any news among the Greeks. When he was given the reply that all the islanders were collecting horses and were planning a campaign against the Lydians, Croesus is said to have exclaimed, "Would that some one could persuade the islanders to fight against the Lydians on horseback!" For the Lydians are skilled horsemen and Croesus believed that they would come off victorious on land. Whereupon Pittacus, or Bias, answered him, "Well, you say that the Lydians, who live on the mainland, would be eager to catch islanders on the land; but do you not suppose that those who live on the islands have prayed the gods that they may catch Lydians on the sea, in order that, in return for the evils which have befallen the Greeks on the mainland, they may avenge themselves at sea on the man who has enslaved their kinsmen?" Croesus, in admiration of this reply, changed his purpose at once and stopped building the ships.

**26.** Croesus used to send for the most distinguished wise men from Greece, to display to them the magnitude of his felicity, and would honour with rich gifts those who lauded his good fortune. He also sent for Solon as well as for such others as enjoyed the greatest fame for their love of wisdom, wishing to have the witness of these men set the seal of approval upon his own felicity, and there came to him Anacharsis the Scythian and Bias and Solon and Pittacus, to whom he showed the highest honour at banquets and at his council, and he displayed his wealth before them and the magnitude of his own power. Now in those days men of learning sought brevity of speech, and Croesus, after he had displayed to the men the felicity of his kingdom and the multitude of the peoples subject to him, asked Anacharsis, who was older than the other men of wisdom, "Whom do you consider to be the bravest of living beings?" He replied, "The wildest animals; for they alone willingly die in order to maintain their freedom." Croesus, believing that he had erred in his reply, and that a second time he would give an answer to please him, asked him, "Whom do you judge to be the most just of living beings?" Anacharsis again answered, "The wildest animals; for they alone live in accordance with nature, not in accordance with laws; since nature is a work of god, while law is an ordinance of man, and it is more just to follow the institutions of gods than those of men." Then Croesus, wishing to make Anacharsis appear ridiculous, inquired of him, "Are the beasts, then, also the wisest?" Anacharsis agreed that they were, adding this explanation: "The peculiar characteristic of wisdom consists in showing a greater respect to the truth which nature imparts than to the ordinance of the law." Croesus laughed at him and the answers he had given, as those of one coming from Scythia and from a bestial manner of living.

**27.** Croesus asked Solon who of all living beings he had seen enjoyed the most felicitous life, thinking that Solon would by all means concede this distinction to him; but Solon replied, "I cannot justly apply this term to anyone, since I have not seen the end of life of anyone still living; for until that time no one may properly be considered to be blest. For it often happens that those who have been regarded before then as blest of Fortune all their lives have at the very close of their lives fallen upon the greatest misfortunes." The king then said, "Do you not judge me to be the wealthiest?" Solon made the same reply, explaining that not those who have the greatest possessions, but those who consider wisdom to be the most valuable of all possessions, are to be regarded as the wealthiest; and that wisdom, seeing that there is nothing which can be balanced against it, confers upon those who value it highly, and upon them alone, a wealth which is the greatest and most secure.

Croesus then asked Bias whether, in his opinion, Solon had answered correctly or had erred, and he replied, "Correctly; for he wishes to make his decision after he has seen the possessions you have in yourself, whereas up to now he has seen only the possessions which lie about you; and it is through the former, not the latter, that men have felicity." The king said, "But even if you do not give first honour to wealth in gold, at least you see my friends, so great a multitude as no other man possesses." Bias answered, "Even the number of friends is uncertain because of your good fortune."

And Croesus, we are told, asked Pittacus, "What is the best form of government you have seen?" And he replied, "That of the painted wood," referring to the laws.

28. Aesop flourished in the same period of time as the Seven Wise Men, and he remarked once, "These men do not know how to act in the company of a ruler; for a man should associate with rulers either as little as possible, or with the best grace possible."

29. Adrastus, a man of Phrygia, while out hunting with Atys, as he was called, the son of the Lydian king, Croesus, unwittingly struck and killed the boy while hurling his spear at a boar. Although he had slain the boy unwittingly, he declared that he did not deserve to live; consequently he urged the king not to spare his life, but to slay him at once upon the tomb of the dead youth. Croesus at first was enraged at Adrastus for the murder, as he considered it, of his son, and threatened to burn him alive; but when he saw that Adrastus was ready and willing to give his life in punishment for the dead boy, he thereupon abandoned his anger and gave up his thought of punishing the slayer, laying the blame upon his own fortune and not upon the intent of Adrastus. Nevertheless Adrastus, on his own initiative, went to the tomb of Atys and slew himself upon it.

30. Phalaris, seeing a multitude of doves being pursued by a single hawk, remarked, "Do you observe, sirs, how fear will make so great a multitude flee before a single pursuer? If they should summon the courage to turn about, they would easily overcome their pursuer." (But it was Phalaris himself who was falsifying; for the victory was won by courage and not by superiority of numbers.) As a result of this speech Phalaris lost his dominion, as it is recorded in the section "On the Succession of Kings."

31. When Croesus was taking the field [547] against Cyrus the Persian, he made inquiry of the oracle. And the answer ran:

> If Croesus crosses Halys, a mighty realm
> Will he destroy.

He received and interpreted the ambiguous answer of the oracle in the light of his own purpose and so came to grief.

Croesus inquired a second time whether he was to enjoy a rule of long duration. And the oracle spoke the following verses:

> The day a mule becomes the king of Medes,
> Then, tender-footed Lydian, do thou flee
> Along the pebbly bed of Hermus, nor
> Abide, nor be ashamed a coward to be.

By a "mule" Cyrus was meant, because his mother was a Mede and his father a Persian.

Cyrus, the king of the Persians, appeared with all his host at the passes of Cappadocia and sent messengers to Croesus both to spy out his power and to declare to him that Cyrus would forgive his previous misdeeds and appoint him satrap of Lydia, provided he presented himself at Cyrus' court and acknowledged, as others did, that he was his slave; but Croesus answered the messengers that it would be more fitting if Cyrus and the Persians should submit to be the slaves of Croesus, reminding them that theretofore they had been slaves of the Medes and that he had never yet taken orders from another.

**32.** Croesus, the king of the Lydians, under the guise of sending to Delphi, dispatched Eurybatus of Ephesus to the Peloponnesus, having given him money with which to recruit as many mercenaries as he could from among the Greeks. This agent of Croesus went over to Cyrus the Persian and revealed everything to him. Consequently the wickedness of Eurybatus became a by-word among the Greeks, and to this day whenever a man wishes to cast another's knavery in his teeth he calls him a Eurybatus.

**33.** Although evil men may avoid for the moment punishment at the hands of those whom they have wronged, yet the evil report of them is preserved for all time and punishes them so far as possible even after death.

We are told that Croesus, on the eve of his war with Cyrus, dispatched ambassadors to Delphi to inquire by what means it would be possible for his son [born dumb] to speak; and that the Pythian priestess replied:

> O thou of Lydian stock, o'er many king,
> Thou great fool Croesus, never wish to hear
> Within thy halls the much-desired sound
> Of thy son speaking. Better far for thee
> That he remain apart; for the first words
> He speaks shall be upon a luckless day.

A man should bear good fortune with moderation and not put his trust in the successes such as fall to human beings, since they can take a great shift with a slight turn of the scale.

After Croesus had been taken prisoner and the pyre had been quenched, when he observed that the city was being plundered and that much silver and gold, besides everything else, were being carried off, he asked Cyrus, "What are the soldiers doing?" Cyrus laughingly replied, "They are making plunder of your wealth"; whereupon Croesus said, "Not so, by Zeus, but of yours; for Croesus has no longer a thing of his own." And Cyrus, impressed by his words, at once changed his purpose, and putting a stop to the plundering of the soldiers he took the possessions of the inhabitants of Sardis for the Royal Treasury.

**34.** Cyrus, believing Croesus to be a pious man because a rainstorm had burst forth and quenched the flame, and calling to mind the reply of Solon, kept Croesus at his side in a position of honour. He gave him a place also in his council, believing him to be a person of sagacity by reason of his having associated with many men of learning and wisdom.

**35.** Harpagus had been appointed commander on the sea by Cyrus the Persian, and when the Greeks of Asia sent an embassy to Cyrus [545] for the purpose of making a treaty of friendship with him, Harpagus remarked to them that what they were doing was very much like a former experience of his own. Once when he wished to marry he had asked a girl's father for the hand of his daughter. At first, however, her father decided that he was not worthy to marry his daughter and betrothed her to a man of higher position, but later, observing that Harpagus was being honoured by the king, he offered him his daughter; but he replied that he would no longer have her as his wife, but would consent to take her as a concubine. By such words he pointed out to the Greeks that formerly, when Cyrus had urged them to become friends of the Persians, they had been unwilling, but now, after matters had taken a different turn and they were anxious to agree upon relations of friendship, Cyrus would make no terms with them as with allies, but he would receive them as slaves if they would throw themselves upon the good-faith of the Persians.

**36.** When the Lacedaemonians learned that the Greeks of Asia were in peril, they sent a message to Cyrus [545] stating that the Lacedaemonians, being kinsmen of the Greeks of Asia, forbade him to enslave the Greek cities. Cyrus, marvelling at such words, remarked that he would judge of their valour when he should send one of his own slaves to subdue Greece.

When the Lacedaemonians were setting out to conquer Arcadia [560], they received the following oracle:

> Arcadia dost thou demand of me?
> A high demand, nor will I give it thee.
> For many warriors, acorn-eaters all,
> Dwell in Arcadia, and they will ward
> Thee off. Yet for my part I grudge thee not.
> Tegea's land, smitten with tripping feet,
> I'll give to thee, wherein to dance and plot
> The fertile plain with measuring-line for tilth.

The Lacedaemonians sent to Delphi to inquire in what place the bones of Orestes, the son of Agamemnon, were buried, and the oracle replied in this wise:

> A certain Tegea there is of Arcady
> In a smooth and level plain, where two winds blow
> Before a stern necessity, to stroke
> Comes answering stroke, and bane is heaped on bane.
> There the life-giving earth holds fast the son
> Of Agamemnon; bring thou him thence and then
> The overlord of Tegea thou shalt be.

It was a smithy that was referred to, and the oracle means by the two winds the bellows, signifying by "stroke" the anvil and the hammers, and by "bane heaped on bane," the iron upon iron; for iron is called a "bane" because the discovery of it has worked to the hurt of mankind.

It is better to die, than to live and witness yourself and your kinsmen meeting misfortune as bad as death.

**37.** Once when the daughter of Peisistratus was carrying the sacred basket in procession and she was thought to excel all others in beauty, a young man stepped up and with a superior air kissed the maiden. The girl's brothers, on learning what had been done, were incensed at the youth's insolence, and leading him to their father they demanded that he be punished. Peisistratus laughingly said, "What shall we do then to those who hate us, if we heap punishments on those who love us?"

Once when Peisistratus was journeying through the country he saw a man on the slopes of Hymettus working in a field where the soil was exceedingly thin and stony, and wondering at the man's zeal for the work, he sent some of his company to inquire of him what return he got from working ground like that. When the men had carried out the command, the farmer replied that he got from the field only grievous pains; but he did not care, since he gave the tenth part of them to Peisistratus. The ruler, on hearing the reply, laughed, and made the field exempt from taxation, whence arose the proverb, Even spasms give tax-exemption.

# BOOK X FRAGMENTS

**1.** Servius Tullius, on the occasion of the uprising of Tarquinius [Superbus], came into the Senate, and when he saw the extent of the intrigue against him, he did no more than to say, "What presumption, O Tarquinius, is this?" Tarquinius replied, "Nay, what presumption is yours, who, though slave and son of a slave, have presumed to rule as king over the Romans, and who, although the leadership my father had belongs to me, have illegally taken from me the rule to which you in no single respect have a claim?" With these words he rushed at Tullius, and seizing him by the arm he hurled him down the steps. Tullius picked himself up and, limping from the fall, endeavoured to flee, but was put to death.

**2.** Servius Tullius, the king of the Romans, enjoyed a rule of forty-four years [578-535], successfully establishing not a few institutions in the commonwealth by virtue of his own high character.

**3.** When Thericles was archon in Athens in the Sixty-first Olympiad,[536] Pythagoras, the philosopher was generally recognised, having already far advanced in learning; for if there is any man of those who have cultivated learning deserving of a place in history, it is he. By birth he was a Samian, though some men say that he was a Tyrrhenian [Etruscan]. There was such persuasion and charm in his words that every day almost the entire city turned to him, as to a god present among them, and all men ran in crowds to hear him. Not only in eloquence of speech did he show himself great, but he also displayed a character of soul which was temperate and constituted a marvellous model of a life of modesty for the youth to emulate. Whoever associated with him he converted from their ways of extravagance and luxury, whereas all men, because of their wealth, were giving themselves over without restraint to indulgence and an ignoble dissipation of body and soul.

Pythagoras, learning that his old teacher Pherecydes lay ill in Delos and was at the point of death, set sail from Italy to Delos. There he took care of the old man for a considerable time and made every effort to bring the aged man safely through his malady. When Pherecydes was overcome by his advanced years and the severity of the disease, Pythagoras made every provision for his burial, and after performing the accustomed rites for him, as a son would for his father, he returned to Italy.

Whenever any of the companions of Pythagoras lost their fortune, the rest would divide their own possessions with them as with brothers. Such a disposition of their property they made, not only with their acquaintances who passed their daily lives with them, but also, speaking generally, with all who shared in their projects.

**4.** Cleinias of Tarentum, who was a member of the order of which we have spoken, learning that Prorus of Cyrene had lost his fortune because of a political upheaval and was completely impoverished, went over from Italy to Cyrene with sufficient funds and restored to Prorus his fortune, although he had never seen the man before and knew no more of him than that he was a Pythagorean. Of many others also it is recorded that they have done something of this kind. It was not only in the giving away of money that they showed themselves so devoted to their friends, but they also shared each other's dangers on occasions of greatest peril. So, for example, while Dionysius was tyrant and a certain Phintias, a Pythagorean, who had formed a plot against the tyrant, was about to suffer the penalty for it, he asked Dionysius for time in which to make such disposition as he wished of his private affairs; and he said that he would give one of his friends as surety for his death. When the ruler expressed his wonder whether such a friend was to be found as would take his place in prison, Phintias called upon one of his acquaintances, a Pythagorean philosopher named Damon, who without hesitation came forward at once as surety for his death.

Now there were some who expressed approval of so great a love for one's friends, whereas some charged the surety with rashness and folly, and at the appointed hour all the people ran together, anxious to learn whether the man who had provided a surety for himself would keep faith. When the hour drew close and all were giving up hope, Phintias unexpectedly arrived on the run at the last moment, just as Damon was being led off to his fate. Such a friendship was in the eyes of all men a thing of wonder, and Dionysius remitted the punishment of the condemned man, urging the two men to include himself as a third in their friendship.

5. The Pythagoreans also insisted upon a very great exercise of the memory, setting up the following way of giving it practice. They would not arise from their beds until they had frankly disclosed to one another everything they had done the day before, beginning with early dawn and closing with the evening. If they had the time and more leisure than usual, they would add to their account what they had done on the third day past, the fourth, and even earlier days. This practice they followed to gain knowledge and judgement in all matters and experience in the ability to call many things to mind.

The Pythagoreans trained themselves in the exercise of self-control in the following manner. They would have prepared for them everything which is served up at the most brilliant banquets, and would gaze upon it for a considerable time; then, after through mere gazing they had aroused their natural desires with a view to their gratification, they would command the slaves to clear away the tables and would at once depart without having tasted of what had been served.

6. Pythagoras believed in the transmigration of souls and considered the eating of flesh as an abominable thing, saying that the souls of all living creatures pass after death into other living creatures. As for himself, he used to declare that he remembered having been in Trojan times Euphorbus, the son of Panthus, who was slain by Menelaüs.

We are told that once, when Pythagoras was sojourning in Argos, he saw a shield from the spoils of Troy fastened by nails to the wall and wept. When the Argives inquired of him the cause of his grief, he replied that he himself had carried this shield in the land of Troy when he was Euphorbus, and when all were incredulous and judged him to be mad, he replied that he would give them convincing evidence that what he had said was so; for on the inner side of the shield there had been inscribed in ancient characters "of Euphorbus." At this surprising answer all said to take down the shield, and on the inner side in fact was found the inscription.

Callimachus once said about Pythagoras that of the problems of geometry some he discovered and certain others he was the first to introduce from Egypt to the Greeks, in the passage where he writes:

> This Phrygian Euphorbus first for men
> Found out, who taught about triangle shapes
> And scalenes, aye and a circle in seven lengths,
> And taught full abstinence from tasting flesh
> Of living things; but all would not to this Give heed.

**7.** Pythagoras urged his followers to cultivate the simple life, since extravagance, he maintained, ruins not only the fortunes of men but their bodies as well. For most diseases, he held, come from indigestion, and indigestion, in turn, from extravagance. Many men were also persuaded by him to eat uncooked food and to drink only water all their life long, in order to pursue what is in truth the good. Yet, as for the men of our day, were one to suggest that they refrain for but a few days from one or two of the things which men consider to be pleasant, they would renounce philosophy, asserting that it would be silly, while seeking for the good which is unseen, to let go that which is seen. Whenever it becomes necessary to court the mob or to meddle in affairs which are none of their business, they have the time for it and will let nothing stand in their way; whereas, whenever it becomes necessary to bestir themselves about education and the repairing of character, they reply that the matter is not opportune for them, the result of it all being that they busy themselves when they have no business and show no concern when they are concerned.

We are told that Archytas of Tarentum, who was a follower of Pythagoras, once became angry with his slaves because of some serious offences; but when he recovered from his rage, he said to them, "You would not have got off without punishment after such misconduct, had I not lost my temper."

**8.** The Pythagoreans laid the greatest store upon constancy toward one's friends, believing as they did that the loyalty of friends is the greatest good to be found in life.

A man may consider that the greatest and most marvellous thing about the Pythagoreans was the cause of their loyalty to their friends. What indeed were the habits, what the manner of their practices, or the powerful arguments which enabled them to inculcate such a disposition in all who joined their common manner of life? Many outsiders, being eager to know the cause, expended great effort on the endeavour, but no man of them was ever able to learn it. The reason why their system of instruction for this purpose was kept inviolate was that the Pythagoreans made it a fundamental tenet to put nothing on this subject in writing, but to carry their precepts only in their memory.

**9.** Pythagoras, in addition to his other injunctions, commanded his pupils rarely to take an oath, and, when they did swear an oath, to abide by it under any circumstances and to bring to fulfilment whatever they have sworn to do; and that they should never reply as did Lysander the Laconian and Demades the Athenian, the former of whom once declared that boys should be cheated with dice and men with oaths, and Demades affirmed that in the case of oaths, as in all other affairs, the most profitable course is the one to choose, and that it was his observation that the perjurer forthwith continued to possess the things regarding which he had taken the oath, whereas the man who had kept his oath had manifestly lost what had been his own. For neither of these men looked upon the oath, as did Pythagoras, as a firm pledge of faith, but as a bait to use for ill-gotten gain and deception.

Pythagoras commanded his pupils rarely to take an oath, and when they did swear an oath, to abide by it under every circumstance.

The same Pythagoras, in his reflections upon the pleasures of love, taught that it was better to approach women in the summer not at all, and in the winter only sparingly. For in general he considered every kind of pleasure of love to be harmful, and believed that the uninterrupted indulgence in them is altogether weakening and destructive.

It is told of Pythagoras that once, when he was asked by someone when he should indulge in the pleasures of love, he replied, "When you wish not to be master of yourself."

The Pythagoreans divided the life of mankind into four ages, that of a child, a lad, a young man, and an old man; and they said that each one of these had its parallel in the changes which take place in the seasons in the year's course, assigning the spring to the child, the autumn to the man, the winter to the old man, and the summer to the lad.

The same Pythagoras taught that when men approach the gods to sacrifice, the garments they wear should be not costly, but only white and clean, and that likewise they should appear before the gods with not only a body clean of every unjust deed but also a soul that is undefiled.

Pythagoras declared that prudent men should pray to the gods for good things on behalf of imprudent men; for the foolish are ignorant of what in life is in very truth the good.

Pythagoras used to assert that in their supplications men should pray simply for "all good things," and not name them singly, as, for example, power, strength, beauty, wealth, and the like; for it frequently happens that any one of these works to the utter ruin of those who receive them in reply to their desire; this may be recognised by any man who has reflected upon the lines in *The Phoenician Maidens* of Euripides which give the prayer of Polyneices to the gods, beginning:

> Then, gazing Argos-ward,

and ending

> Yea, from this arm, may smite my brother's breast.

For Polyneices and Eteocles thought that they were praying for the best things for themselves, whereas in truth they were calling down curses upon their own heads.

During the time that Pythagoras was delivering many other discourses designed to inculcate the emulation of a sober life and manliness and perseverance and the other virtues, he received at the hands of the inhabitants of Croton honours the equal of those accorded to the gods [c.530].

**10.** Pythagoras called the principles he taught *philosophia* or love of wisdom, but not *sophia* or wisdom. For he criticised the Seven Wise Men, as they were called, who lived before his time, saying that no man is wise, being human, and many a time, by reason of the weakness of his nature, has not the strength to bring all matters to a successful issue, but that he who emulates both the ways and the manner of life of a wise man may more fittingly be called a "lover of wisdom."

Although both Pythagoras himself and the Pythagoreans after his time made such advancement and were cause of so great blessings to the states of Greece, yet they did not escape the envy which besmirches all noble things. Indeed there is no noble thing among men, I suppose, which is of such a nature that the long passage of time works it no damage or destruction.

**11.** A certain inhabitant of Croton, Cylon by name, the foremost citizen in wealth and repute, was eager to become a Pythagorean, but since he was a harsh man and violent in his ways, and both seditious and tyrannical as well, he was rejected by them. Consequently, being irritated at the order of the Pythagoreans, he formed a large party and never ceased working against them in every way possible both by word and by deed.

Lysis, the Pythagorean, came to Thebes in Boeotia and became the teacher of Epaminondas; and he developed him, with respect to virtue, into a perfect man and became his father by adoption because of the affection he had for him. Epaminondas, because of the incitements toward perseverance and simplicity and every other virtue which he received from the Pythagorean philosophy, became the foremost man, not only of Thebes, but of all who lived in his time.

**12.** To recount the lives of men of the past is a task which presents difficulties to writers and yet is of no little advantage to society as a whole. For such an account which clearly portrays in all frankness their evil as well as their noble deeds renders honour to the good and abases the wicked by means of the censures as well as the praises which appropriately come to each group respectively. The praise constitutes, one may say, a reward of virtue which entails no cost, and the censure is a punishment of depravity which entails no physical chastisement, and it is an excellent thing for later generations to bear in mind, that whatever is the manner of life a man chooses to live while on this earth, such is the remembrance which he will be thought worthy of after his death; this principle should be followed, in order that later generations may not set their hearts upon the erection of memorials in stone which are limited to a single spot and subject to quick decay, but upon reason and the virtues in general which range everywhere upon the lips of fame. Time, which withers all else, preserves for these virtues an immortality, and the further it may itself advance in age, the fresher the youth it imparts to them. What we have said is clearly exemplified in the case of these men who have been mentioned; for though they were of the distant past, all mankind speaks of them as if they were alive to-day.

**13.** Cyrus, the king of the Persians, after he had reduced the land of the Babylonians and the Medes [550], was encompassing in his hopes all the inhabited world. For now that he had subdued these powerful and great nations he thought that there was no king or people which could withstand his might;

since of those who are possessed of irresponsible power, some are wont not to bear their good fortune as human beings should.

**14.** Cambyses was by nature half-mad and his powers of reasoning perverted, and the greatness of his kingdom rendered him much the more cruel and arrogant.

Cambyses the Persian, after he had taken Memphis and Pelusium [525], since he could not bear his good fortune as men should, dug up the tomb of Amasis, the former king of Egypt, and finding his mummified corpse in the coffin, he outraged the body of the dead man, and after showing every despite to the senseless corpse, he finally ordered it to be burned. Since it was not the practice of the natives to consign the bodies of their dead to fire, he supposed that in this fashion also he would be giving offence to him who had been long dead.

When Cambyses was on the point of setting out upon his campaign against Ethiopia, he dispatched a part of his army against the inhabitants of Ammonium, giving orders to its commanders to plunder and burn the oracle and to make slaves of all who dwelt near the shrine.

**15.** After Cambyses, the king of the Persians, had made himself lord of all Egypt, the Libyans and Cyrenaeans, who had been allies of the Egyptians, sent presents to him and declared their willingness to obey his every command.

**16.** Polycrates the tyrant of the Samians [540-523], used to dispatch triremes to the most suitable places and plunder all who were on the seas, and he would return the booty which he had taken only to those who were allies of his, and to those of his companions who criticised this practice he used to say that all his friends would feel more grateful to him by getting back what they had lost than by having lost nothing in the first place.

Unjust deeds, as a general thing, carry in their train a retribution which exacts appropriate punishments of the wrongdoers.

Every act of kindness, since attended by no regret, bears goodly fruit in the praise of those who benefit therefrom; for even if not all the recipients repay the kindness, at least some one of them, it sometimes happens, makes payment on behalf of all.

Certain Lydians, who were fleeing from the domineering rule of the satrap Oroetes, took ship to Samos, bringing with them many possessions, and became suppliants of Polycrates. At first he received them kindly, but after a little time he put them all to the sword and confiscated their possessions.

**17.** Thettalus, the son of Peisistratus, was wise enough to renounce the tyranny, and since he strove after equality, he enjoyed great favour among the citizens of Athens; but the other sons, Hipparchus and Hippias, being violent and harsh men, maintained a tyranny over the city. They committed many other acts of lawlessness against the Athenians, and Hipparchus, becoming enamoured of a youth [Harmodius] of extraordinary beauty, because of that got into a dangerous situation. . . . Now the attack upon the tyrants and the earnest desire to achieve the freedom of the fatherland were shared in by all the men mentioned above; but the unyielding steadfastness of soul amid the tortures and the stout courage to endure cruel pains were shown by Aristogeiton alone, who, in the most fearful moments, maintained two supreme virtues, fidelity to his friends and vengeance on his enemies.

Aristogeiton made it clear to all men that nobility of soul is able to prevail over the greatest agonies of the body.

**18.** When Zeno [of Elea] the philosopher was suffering the agonies of the torture because of the conspiracy he had entered into against the tyrant Nearchus and was being asked by Nearchus who his fellow conspirators were, he replied, "Would that I were as much the master of my body as I am of my tongue!"

When Zeno's native city was being ground down by the tyranny of Nearchus, Zeno formed a conspiracy against the tyrant, but he was found out, and when he was asked by Nearchus, while suffering the agonies of the torture, who his fellow conspirators were, he replied, "Would that I were as much the master of my body as I am of my tongue!" When the tyrant made the torture more and more severe, Zeno still withstood it for a while; and then, being eager to be rid at last of the agony and at the same time to be revenged upon Nearchus, he devised the following plan. During the greatest intensity of the torture, pretending that his spirit was yielding to his bodily pains, he cried out, "Relax it! I will tell the whole truth," and when they did so, he asked Nearchus to come near and listen to him privately, asserting that many matters he was about to disclose would best be kept secret. When the tyrant came up to him readily and placed his ear close to Zeno's lips, Zeno took the tyrant's ear into his mouth and sank his teeth into it. When the attendants quickly approached and applied every torment to make Zeno relax his hold, he held on all the tighter. Finally, being unable to shake the fortitude of the man, they stabbed him to death that they might in this way break the hold of his teeth. By this device Zeno got release from the agonies he was suffering and exacted of the tyrant the only punishment within his grasp.

[Many generations later Dorieus [c.510] the Lacedaemonian came to Sicily, and taking back the land founded the city of Heracleia. Since the city grew rapidly, the Carthaginians, being jealous of it and also afraid that it would grow stronger than Carthage and take from the Phoenicians their sovereignty, came up against it with a great army, took it by storm, and razed it to the ground. This affair we shall discuss in detail in connection with the period in which it falls.]

**19.** When men make definite pronouncements on certain matters, saying that they can never possibly be brought to pass, their words usually are followed by a kind of retribution which exposes the weakness which is the lot of mankind.

When Megabyzus, who was also called Zopyrus and was a friend of King Darius, had scourged himself and mutilated his countenance, because he had resolved to become a deserter and betray Babylon to the Persians, we are told that Darius was deeply moved and declared that he would rather have Megabyzus whole again, if it were possible, than bring ten Babylons under his power, although his wish could not be achieved.

The Babylonians chose Megabyzus to be their general, being unaware that the benefaction he would render them would be a kind of bait to entice them to the destruction which was soon to follow.

The successful turn of events constitutes a sufficient proof of what has been predicted.

After Darius had made himself master of practically the whole of Asia, he desired to subdue Europe [519]. For since the desires he entertained for further possessions were boundless and he had confidence in the greatness of the power of Persia, he was set upon embracing in his power the inhabited world, thinking it to be a disgraceful thing that the kings before his time, though possessing inferior resources, had reduced in war the greatest nations, whereas he, who had forces greater than any man before him had ever acquired, had accomplished no deed worthy of mention.

When the Tyrrhenians were leaving Lemnos [c.520], because of their fear of the Persians, they claimed that they were doing so because of certain oracles, and they gave the island over to Miltiades. The leader of the Tyrrhenians in this affair was Hermon, and as a result presents of this kind have from that time been called "gifts of Hermon."

**20.** Sextus, the son of Lucius Tarquinius (Superbus), the king of the Romans [535-510], left and came to the city of Collatia, as it was called, and stopped at the home of Lucius Tarquinius [Collatinus], a cousin of the king, whose wife was Lucretia, a woman of great beauty and virtuous in character. Lucretia's husband being with the army in camp, the guest, awakening, left his bed-room during the night and set out to the wife who was sleeping in a certain chamber, and suddenly taking his stand at the door and drawing his sword, he announced that he had a slave all ready for slaughter, and that he would slay her together with the slave, as having been taken in adultery and having received at the hand of her husband's nearest of kin the punishment she deserved. Therefore, he continued, it would be the wiser thing for her to submit to his desires without calling out, and as a reward for her favour she would receive great gifts and be his wife and become queen, exchanging the hearth of a private citizen for the first place in the state. Lucretia, panic-stricken at so unexpected a thing and fearing that men would in truth believe that she had been slain because of adultery, made no outcry at the time, but when the day came and Sextus departed, she summoned her kinsmen and asked them not to allow the man to go unpunished who had sinned against the laws both of hospitality and of kinship. As for herself, she said, it was not proper for the victim of a deed of such wanton insolence to look upon the sun, and plunging a dagger into her breast she slew herself.

**21.** In connection with the violation of Lucretia by Sextus and her suicide because of the wrong done her, we do not believe it would be right to leave no record of the nobility of her choice. For the woman who renounced life of her own will in order that later generations might emulate her deed we should judge to be fittingly worthy of immortal praise, in order that women who choose to maintain the purity of their persons altogether free from censure may compare themselves with an authentic example. Other women, indeed, even when such an act as this on their part is known, conceal what has been done, as a means of avoiding the punishment which is meted out for guilty acts; but she made known to the world what had been done in secret and then slew herself, leaving in the end of her life her fairest defence. Whereas other women advance a claim for pardon in matters done against their will, she fixed the penalty of death for the outrage done to her by force, in order that, even if one should wish to defame her, he should not have it in his power to condemn her choice as having been made of her own free will. For since men by nature prefer slander to praise, she cut the ground from under the accusation men who love to find fault might raise; for she considered it to be shameful that anyone could say that while her husband, to whom she was wedded, in accordance with the laws, was still living, she had had relations with another man, contrary to the laws, and shameful also that she who had been involved in an act for which the laws decree the penalty of death upon the guilty should cling to life any longer. So she chose by a brief anticipation of death, a debt that in any case she owed to nature, to exchange disgrace for the highest approval. Consequently, not only did she win immortal glory in exchange for mortal life through her own act of virtue, but she also impelled her kinsmen and all the people to exact implacable punishment from those who had committed this lawless act against her.

**22.** King Lucius Tarquinius ruled in a tyrannical and violent fashion and made it his practice to slay the wealthy citizens among the Romans, advancing false charges against them in order to appropriate their possessions. Consequently Lucius Junius (Brutus), since he was an orphan and the wealthiest of all the Romans, for both these reasons viewed with mistrust Tarquin's grasping ambition; and because he was the king's nephew and therefore close to him on every occasion, he acted the part of a stupid person, his purpose being both to avoid arousing envy because of any ability of his, and at the same time to observe, without rousing suspicion, whatever was taking place and to watch for the favourable moment to strike at the royal power.

**23.** The people of Sybaris who took the field with three hundred thousand men against the inhabitants of Croton and had entered upon an unjust war, were completely unsuccessful [510]; and since they were not shrewd enough to bear their prosperity, they left their own destruction as a sufficient warning example that men should be on their guard far more in times of their own good fortunes than of their afflictions.

**24.** Diodorus says with respect to Herodotus, "We have made this digression, not so much out of any desire to criticise Herodotus, as to show by examples that tales of wonder are wont to prevail over tales of truth."

It is fitting that bravery be honoured, even when it is shown by women.

The Athenians made a clever use of their victory [of 506], and after defeating the Boeotians and Chalcidians, they at once after the battle made themselves masters of the city of Chalcis, and as a tenth part of the booty won from the Boeotians they dedicated a bronze chariot on the Acropolis, inscribing upon it the following elegiac lines:

> Having conquered the tribes of Boeotia and those of Chalcis
> Midst the labours of war, sons of Athenians quenched
> Insolence high in dark bonds of iron; and taking the ransom's
> Tithe set up here these mares, vowed unto Pallas their god.

**25.** The Persians learned from the Greeks the burning of temples, repaying those who had been the first to offend justice with the same wanton act.

When the Carians were becoming exhausted in their struggles with the Persians, they made inquiry respecting an alliance, whether they should take the Milesians to be their allies, and the oracle replied:

Of old Miletus' sons were mighty men.

But the terror which lay close at hand caused them to forget their former rivalry with one another and compelled them to man the triremes with all speed.

Hecataeus, the Milesian, whom the Ionians dispatched as an ambassador, asked what cause Artaphernes had to put no faith in them, and when Artaphernes replied that he was afraid that they would harbour resentment because of the injuries they had received during their defeat [Ladê, 494], Hecataeus said, "Well then, if suffering ill treatment has the effect of creating bad faith, receiving kind treatment will surely cause our cities to be well disposed toward the Persians" Artaphernes, approving the statement, restored to the cities their laws and laid upon them fixed tributes according to their ability to pay.

26. The hatred which those who possessed citizenship held for the commons, though it had been concealed up to this time, now burst forth in full force, when it found the occasion, and because of their jealous rivalry they freed the slaves, preferring rather to share freedom with their servants than citizenship with the free.

27. Datis, the general of the Persians and a Mede by descent, having received from his ancestors the tradition that the Athenians were descendants of Medus, who had established the kingdom of Media, sent a message to the Athenians declaring that he was come with an army to demand the return of the sovereignty which had belonged to his ancestors; for Medus, he said, who was the oldest of his own ancestors, had been deprived of the kingship by the Athenians, and removing to Asia had founded the kingdom of Media. Consequently, he went on to say, if they would return the kingdom to him, he would forgive them for this guilty act and for the campaign they had made against Sardis; but if they opposed his demand, they would suffer a worse fate than had the Eretrians. Miltiades, voicing the decision reached by the ten generals, replied that according to the statement of the envoys it was more appropriate for the Athenians to hold the mastery over the empire of the Medes than for Datis to hold it over the state of the Athenians; for it was a man of Athens who had established the kingdom of the Medes, whereas no man of Median race had ever controlled Athens. Datis, on hearing this reply, made ready for battle.

28. Hippocrates, the tyrant of Gela, after his victory over the Syracusans [Helorus, c.491], pitched his camp in the temple area of Zeus, and he seized the person of the priest of the temple and certain Syracusans who were in the act of taking down the golden dedications and removing in particular the robe of the statue of Zeus in the making of which a large amount of gold had been used. After sternly rebuking them as despoilers of the temple, he ordered them to return to the city, but he himself did not touch the dedications, since he was intent upon gaining a good name and he thought not only that one who had commenced a war of such magnitude should commit no sin against the deity, but also that he would set the commons at variance with the administrators of the affairs of Syracuse, because men would think the latter were ruling the state to their own advantage and not to that of all the people nor on the principle of equality.

# Book X

Theron of Acragas in birth and wealth, as well as in the humanity he displayed towards the commons, far surpassed not only his fellow citizens but also the other Sicilian Greeks.

**29.** Gelon of Syracuse cried out in his sleep, for he was dreaming that he had been struck by lightning, and his dog, when he noticed that he was crying out immoderately, did not stop barking until he awakened him. Gelon was also once saved from death by a wolf. As a boy he was seated in a school and a wolf came and snatched away the tablet he was using. While he was chasing after the wolf itself and his tablet too, the school was shaken by an earthquake and crashed down from its very foundations, killing every one of the boys together with the teacher. Historians, like Timaeus, Dionysius, Diodorus, and also Dio, celebrate the number of the boys, which amounted to more than one hundred. The precise number I do not know.

**30.** Cimon, the son of Miltiades, when his father had died in the state prison because he was unable to pay in full the fine, in order that he might receive his father's body for burial, delivered himself up to prison and assumed the debt.

Cimon, who was ambitious to take part in the conduct of the state, at a later time became an able general and performed glorious deeds by virtue of his personal bravery.

**31.** Cimon, as certain writers say, was the son of Miltiades, but according to others his father was known as Stesagoras [Miltiades' brother]. He had a son Callias by Isodicê, and this Cimon was married to his own sister Elpinice as Ptolemy was at a later time to Berenice, and Zeus to Hera before them, and as the Persians do at the present time. Callias pays a fine of fifty talents, in order that his father Cimon may not suffer punishment because of his disgraceful marriage, that, namely, of brother with sister. The number of those who write about this it would be a long task for me to recount; for the multitude of those who have written about it is boundless, such as the comic poets and orators and Diodorus and others.

**32.** Themistocles, the son of Neoeles, when a certain wealthy person approached him to find out where he could find a wealthy son-in-law, advised him not to seek for money which lacked a man, but rather a man who was lacking in money, and when the inquirer agreed with this advice, Themistocles counselled him to marry his daughter to Cimon. This was the reason, therefore, for Cimon becoming a wealthy man, and he was released from prison, and calling to account the magistrates who had shut him up he secured their condemnation.

[The preceding Book, which is the tenth of our narrative, closed with the events of the year [481] just before the crossing of Xerxes into Europe and the formal deliberations which the general assembly of the Greeks held in Corinth on the alliance between Gelon and the Greeks.]

**33.** When all the Greeks, at the time Xerxes was about to cross over into Europe [480], dispatched an embassy to Gelon to discuss an alliance, and when he answered that he would ally himself with them and supply them with grain, provided that they would grant him the supreme command either on the land or on the sea, the tyrant's ambition for glory in his demanding the supreme command thwarted the alliance; and yet the magnitude of the aid he could supply and the fear of the enemy were impelling them to share the glory with Gelon.

**34.** For though the supremacy which the Persians enjoy entails, for the satisfaction of cupidity, the gifts they require, yet a tyrant's greed does not overlook even any small gain.

The surest guardian of safety is mistrust.

Now children, when they are being ill treated, turn for aid to their parents, but states turn to the peoples who once founded them.

A tyrant's greed does not rest satisfied with what he possesses, but it yearns after the property of others and is never sated.

As for those whose character will oppose his domination, he will not, when the opportunity offers, allow them to become powerful.

For you are descendants of those men who have bequeathed to glory their own virtues, deathless after their death.

For as the reward for the alliance it is not money he requires, which one can often see despised by even the lowest man in private life when he has once gained wealth, but praise and glory, to gain which noble men do not hesitate to die; for the reward which glory offers is to be preferred above silver.

For the inheritance which the Spartans receive from their fathers is not wealth, as is the case with all other men, but an eagerness to die for the sake of liberty, so that they set all the good things which life can offer second to glory.

Let us not in our eagerness for mercenary troops throw away our own citizen forces, and, in reaching for what is unseen, lose our mastery of that which is in sight.

I deny that I am dismayed at the magnitude of the Persians' armaments; for valour decides the issue of war, not numbers.

For the inheritance they have received from their fathers is to live their own lives, and to die in response to their country's need.

Why should we fear the gold with which they deck themselves out as they go into battle, as women deck themselves for marriage, since as a result victory will bring us the prize not only of glory, but of wealth? For valour fears not gold, which cold steel has ever taken captive, but the military skill of the leaders.

For every army which exceeds the proper proportion carries in itself its undoing in almost every case. For before the serried ranks have heard the command we shall have anticipated them in obtaining our objectives.

BOOK X

# FRAGMENTS OF UNCERTAIN PROVENIENCE

[Last of all, many generations later, the people of the Siceli crossed over in a body from Italy into Sicily and made their home in the land which had been abandoned by the Sicani. Since the Siceli steadily grew more avaricious and kept ravaging the land which bordered on theirs, frequent wars arose between them and the Sicani, until at last they struck covenants and set up boundaries of their territory, upon which they had agreed. With regard to these matters we shall give a detailed account in connection with the appropriate period of time.]

1. Diodorus, however, recognises a distinction between them, when he speaks of Sicani and Siceli.

Diodorus, when he speaks somewhere in the first ten Books about both Siceli and Sicani, recognises a distinction, as I have already said, between Sicelus and Sicanus.

2. Diodorus of Sicily and Oppian state that this city of Neapolis was founded by Heracles.

3. The Palladium of Athena was like this we have mentioned, three cubits tall, made of wood, having fallen from heaven, men say, in Pesinous [*pes* = to fall] in Phrygia, and Diodorus and Dio say that the region received its name from this event.

4. And Diodorus records that a certain peak of the Alps, which has the appearance of being the highest part of the entire range, is called by the natives the "Ridge of Heaven."

# BOOK XI

## *On the crossing of Xerxes into Europe (1-4).*

**1.** The preceding Book, which is the tenth of our narrative, closed with the events of the year just before the crossing of Xerxes into Europe and the formal deliberations which the general assembly of the Greeks held in Corinth on the alliance between Gelon and the Greeks; and in this Book we shall supply the further course of the history, beginning with the campaign of Xerxes against the Greeks, and we shall stop with the year which precedes the campaign of the Athenians against Cyprus under the leadership of Cimon.

Calliades was archon in Athens, [480] and the Romans made Spurius Cassius and Proculus Verginius Tricostus consuls, and the Eleians celebrated the Seventy-fifth Olympiad, that in which Astylus of Syracuse won the stadion. It was in this year that king Xerxes made his campaign against Greece, for the following reason. Mardonius the Persian was a cousin of Xerxes and related to him by marriage, and he was also greatly admired by the Persians because of his sagacity and courage. This man, being elated by pride and at the height of his physical vigour, was eager to be the leader of great armaments; consequently he persuaded Xerxes to enslave the Greeks, who had ever been enemies of the Persians. Xerxes, being won over by him and desiring to drive all the Greeks from their homes, sent an embassy to the Carthaginians to urge them to join him in the undertaking and closed an agreement with them, to the effect that he would wage war upon the Greeks who lived in Greece, while the Carthaginians should at the same time gather great armaments and subdue those Greeks who lived in Sicily and Italy. In accordance, then, with their agreements, the Carthaginians, collecting a great amount of money, gathered mercenaries from both Italy and Liguria and also from Galatia and Iberia; and in addition to these troops they enrolled men of their own race from the whole of Libya and of Carthage; and in the end, after spending three years in constant preparation, they assembled more than three hundred thousand foot-soldiers and two hundred war vessels.

**2.** Xerxes, vying with the zeal displayed by the Carthaginians, surpassed them in all his preparations to the degree that he excelled the Carthaginians in the multitude of peoples at his command. He began to have ships built throughout all the territory along the sea that was subject to him, both Egypt and Phoenicia and Cyprus, Cilicia and Pamphylia and Pisidia, and also Lycia, Caria, Mysia, the Troad, and the cities on the Hellespont, and Bithynia, and Pontus. Spending a period of three years, as did the Carthaginians, on his preparations, he made ready more than twelve hundred warships. He was aided in this by his father Darius, who before his death had made preparations of great armaments; for Darius, after Datis, his general, had been defeated by the Athenians at

Marathon, had continued to be angry with the Athenians for having won that battle. Darius, when already about to cross over against the Greeks, was stopped in his plans by death, whereupon Xerxes, induced both by the design of his father and by the counsel of Mardonius, as we have stated, made up his mind to wage war upon the Greeks.

Now when all preparations for the campaign had been completed, Xerxes commanded his admirals to assemble the ships at Cymê and Phocaea, and he himself collected the foot and cavalry forces from all the satrapies and advanced from Susa. When he had arrived at Sardis, he dispatched heralds to Greece, commanding them to go to all the states and to demand of the Greeks water and earth. Then, dividing his army, he sent in advance a sufficient number of men both to bridge the Hellespont and to dig a canal through Athos at the neck of the Cherronesus, in this way not only making the passage safe and short for his forces but also hoping by the magnitude of his exploits to strike the Greeks with terror before his arrival. Now the men who had been sent to make ready these works completed them with dispatch, because so many labourers co-operated in the task, and the Greeks, when they learned of the great size of the Persian armaments, dispatched ten thousand hoplites into Thessaly to seize the passes of Tempe; Synetus commanded the Lacedaemonians and Themistocles the Athenians. These commanders dispatched ambassadors to the states and asked them to send soldiers to join in the common defence of the passes; for they eagerly desired that all the Greek states should each have a share in the defence and make common cause in the war against the Persians. Since the larger number of the Thessalians and other Greeks who dwelt near the passes had given the water and earth to the envoys of Xerxes when they arrived, the two generals despaired of the defence at Tempe and returned to their own soil.

3. And now it will be useful to distinguish those Greeks who chose the side of the barbarians, in order that, incurring our censure here, their example may, by the obloquy visited upon them, deter for the future any who may become traitors to the common freedom. The Aenianians, Dolopians, Melians [Malis], Perrhaebians, and Magnetans took the side of the barbarians even while the defending force was still at Tempe, and after its departure the Achaeans of Phthia, Locrians, Thessalians, and the majority of the Boeotians went over to the barbarians. The Greeks who were meeting in congress at the Isthmus voted to make the Greeks who voluntarily chose the cause of the Persians pay a tithe to the gods, when they should be successful in the war, and to send ambassadors to those Greeks who were neutral to urge them to join in the struggle for the common freedom. Of the latter, some joined the alliance without reservation, while others postponed any decision for a considerable time, clinging to their own safety alone and anxiously waiting for the outcome of the war; the Argives, however, sending ambassadors to the common congress, promised to join the alliance if the congress would give them a share in the command. To them the representatives declared plainly that, if they thought it a more terrible thing to

have a Greek as general than a barbarian as master, they would do well to remain neutral, but if they were ambitious to secure the leadership of the Greeks, they should, it was stated, first have accomplished deeds deserving of this leadership and then strive for such an honour. After these events, when the ambassadors sent by Xerxes came to Greece and demanded both earth and water, all the states manifested in their replies the zeal they felt for the common freedom.

When Xerxes learned that the Hellespont had been bridged and the canal had been dug through Athos, he left Sardis and made his way toward the Hellespont; and when he had arrived at Abydus, he led his army over the bridge into Europe. As he advanced through Thrace, he added to his forces many soldiers from both the Thracians and neighbouring Greeks. When he arrived at the city called Doriscus, he ordered his fleet to come there, and so both arms of his forces were gathered into one place, and he held there also the enumeration of the entire army, and the number of his land forces was over eight hundred thousand men, while the sum total of his ships of war exceeded twelve hundred, of which three hundred and twenty were Greek, the Greeks providing the complement of men and the king supplying the vessels. All the remaining ships were listed as barbarian; and of these the Egyptians supplied two hundred, the Phoenicians three hundred, the Cilicians eighty, the Pamphylians forty, the Lycians the same number, also the Carians eighty, and the Cyprians one hundred and fifty. Of the Greeks the Dorians who dwelt off Caria, together with the Rhodians and Coans, sent forty ships, the Ionians, together with the Chians and Samians, one hundred, the Aeolians, together with the Lesbians and Tenedans, forty, the peoples of the region of the Hellespont, together with those who dwelt along the shores of the Pontus, eighty, and the inhabitants of the islands fifty; for the king had won over to his side the islands lying within the Cyanean Rocks and Triopium and Sunium. Triremes made up the multitude we have listed, and the transports for the cavalry numbered eight hundred and fifty, and the triaconters three thousand. Xerxes, then, was busied with the enumeration of the armaments at Doriscus.

**4.** The Greeks who were in assembly, when word came to them that the Persian forces were near, took action to dispatch the ships of war with all speed to Artemisium in Euboea, recognising that this place was well situated for meeting the enemy, and a considerable body of hoplites to Thermopylae to forestall them in occupying the passes at the narrowest part of the defile and to prevent the barbarians from advancing against Greece; for they were eager to throw their protection inside of Thermopylae about those who had chosen the cause of the Greeks and to do everything in their power to save the allies. The leader of the entire expedition was Eurybiades the Lacedaemonian, and of the troops sent to Thermopylae the commander was Leonidas the king of the Spartans, a man who set great store by his courage and generalship. Leonidas, when he received the appointment, announced that only one thousand men should follow him on the campaign. When the ephors said that he was leading altogether too few soldiers against a great force and ordered him to take along a larger number, he replied to them in secret, "For preventing the barbarians from getting through the passes they are few, but for the task to which they are now bound they are many." Since this reply proved riddle-like and obscure, he was asked again whether he believed he was leading the soldiers to some paltry task. Whereupon he replied, "Ostensibly I am leading them to the defence of the passes, but in fact to die for the freedom of all; and so, if a thousand set forth, Sparta will be the more renowned when they have died, but if the whole body of the Lacedaemonians take the field, Lacedaemon will be utterly destroyed, for not a man of them, in order to save his life, will dare to turn in flight." There were, then, of the Lacedaemonians one thousand, and with them three hundred Spartiates, while the rest of the Greeks who were dispatched with them to Thermopylae were three thousand.

Leonidas, then, with four thousand soldiers advanced to Thermopylae. The Locrians, however, who dwelt in the neighbourhood of the passes had already given earth and water to the Persians, and had promised that they would seize the passes in advance; but when they learned that Leonidas had arrived at Thermopylae, they changed their minds and went over to the Greeks, and there gathered at Thermopylae also a thousand Locrians, an equal number of Melians [Melis], and almost a thousand Phocians, as well as some four hundred Thebans of the other party; for the inhabitants of Thebes were divided against each other with respect to the alliance with the Persians. Now the Greeks who were drawn up with Leonidas for battle, being as many in number as we have set forth, tarried in Thermopylae, awaiting the arrival of the Persians.

### On the battle of Thermopylae (5-11).

**5.** Xerxes, after having enumerated his armaments, pushed on with the entire army, and the whole fleet accompanied the land forces in their advance as far as the city of Acanthus, and from there the ships passed through the place where the canal had been dug into the other sea expeditiously and without loss. When Xerxes arrived at the Gulf of Melis, he learned that the enemy had already seized the passes. Consequently, having joined to his forces the armament there, he summoned his allies from Europe, a little less than two hundred thousand men; so that he now possessed in all not less than one million soldiers exclusive of the naval contingent, and the sum total of the masses who served on the ships of war and who transported the food and general equipment was not less than that of those we have mentioned, so that the account usually given of the multitude of the men gathered together by Xerxes need cause no amazement; for men say that the unfailing rivers ran dry because of the unending stream of the multitude, and that the seas were hidden by the sails of the ships. However this may be, the greatest forces of which any historical record has been left were those which accompanied Xerxes.

After the Persians had encamped on the Spercheius River, Xerxes dispatched envoys to Thermopylae to discover, among other things, how the Greeks felt about the war with him; and he commanded them to make this proclamation:

"King Xerxes orders all to give up their arms, to depart unharmed to their native lands, and to be allies of the Persians; and to all Greeks who do this he will give more and better lands than they now possess." When Leonidas heard the commands of the envoys, he replied to them: "If we should be allies of the king we should be more useful if we kept our arms, and if we should have to wage war against him, we should fight the better for our freedom if we kept them; and as for the lands which he promises to give, the Greeks have learned from their fathers to gain lands, not by cowardice, but by valour."

**6.** The king, on hearing from his envoys the replies of the Greeks, sent for Demaratus, a Spartan who had been exiled from his native land and taken refuge with him, and with a scoff at the replies he asked the Laconian, "Will the Greeks flee more swiftly than my horses can run, or will they dare to face such armaments in battle?" Demaratus, we are told, replied, "You yourself are not unacquainted with the courage of the Greeks, since you use Greek forces to quell such barbarians as revolt. So do not think that those who fight better than the Persians to maintain your sovereignty, will risk their lives less bravely against the Persians to maintain their own freedom." But Xerxes with a scoff at him ordered Demaratus to stay by his side in order that he might witness the Lacedaemonians in flight.

Xerxes with his army came against the Greeks at Thermopylae, and he put the Medes in front of all the other peoples, either because he preferred them by reason of their courage or because he wished to destroy them in a body; for the Medes still retained a proud spirit, the supremacy which their ancestors had exercised having only recently been overthrown. He also designated together with the Medes the brothers and sons of those who had fallen at Marathon, believing that they would wreak vengeance upon the Greeks with the greatest fury. The Medes, then, having been drawn up for battle in the manner we have described, attacked the defenders of Thermopylae; but Leonidas had made careful preparation and massed the Greeks in the narrowest part of the pass.

**7.** The fight which followed was a fierce one, and since the barbarians had the king as a witness of their valour and the Greeks kept in mind their liberty and were exhorted to the fray by Leonidas, it followed that the struggle was amazing. For since the men stood shoulder to shoulder in the fighting and the blows were struck in close combat, and the lines were densely packed, for a considerable time the battle was equally balanced. Since the Greeks were superior in valour and in the great size of their shields, the Medes gradually gave way; for many of them were slain and not a few wounded. The place of the Medes in the battle was taken by Cissians and Sacae, selected for their valour, who had been stationed to support them; and joining the struggle fresh as they were against men who were worn out they withstood the hazard of combat for a short while, but as they were slain and pressed upon by the soldiers of Leonidas, they gave way. For the barbarians used small round or irregularly shaped shields, by which they enjoyed an advantage in open fields, since they were thus enabled to move more easily,

## Book XI

but in narrow places they could not easily inflict wounds upon an enemy who were formed in close ranks and had their entire bodies protected by large shields, whereas they, being at a disadvantage by reason of the lightness of their protective armour, received repeated wounds.

At last Xerxes, seeing that the entire area about the passes was strewn with dead bodies and that the barbarians were not holding out against the valour of the Greeks, sent forward the picked Persians known as the "Immortals," who were reputed to be pre-eminent among the entire host for their deeds of courage, but when these also fled after only a brief resistance, then at last, as night fell, they ceased from battle, the barbarians having lost many dead and the Greeks a small number.

**8.** On the following day Xerxes, now that the battle had turned out contrary to his expectation, choosing from all the peoples of his army such men as were reputed to be of outstanding bravery and daring, after an earnest exhortation announced before the battle that if they should storm the approach he would give them notable gifts, but if they fled the punishment would be death. These men hurled themselves upon the Greeks as one mighty mass and with great violence, but the soldiers of Leonidas closed their ranks at this time, and making their formation like a wall took up the struggle with ardour, and so far did they go in their eagerness that the lines which were wont to join in the battle by turns would not withdraw, but by their unrelenting endurance of the hardship they got the better and slew many of the picked barbarians. The day long they spent in conflict, vying with one another; for the older soldiers challenged the fresh vigour of the youth, and the younger matched themselves against the experience and fame of their elders. When finally even the picked barbarians turned in flight, the barbarians who were stationed in reserve blocked the way and would not permit the picked soldiers to flee; consequently they were compelled to turn back and renew the battle.

While the king was in a state of dismay, believing that no man would have the courage to go into battle again, there came to him a certain Trachinian, a native of the region, who was familiar with the mountainous area. This man was brought into the presence of Xerxes and undertook to conduct the Persians by way of a narrow and precipitous path, so that the men who accompanied him would get behind the forces of Leonidas, which, being surrounded in this manner, would be easily annihilated. The king was delighted, and heaping presents upon the Trachinian he dispatched twenty thousand soldiers with him under cover of night, but a certain man among the Persians named Tyrrhastiadas, a Cymaean by birth, who was honourable and upright in his ways, deserting from the camp of the Persians in the night came to Leonidas, who knew nothing of the act of the Trachinian, and informed him.

**9.** The Greeks, on hearing of this, gathered together about the middle of the night and conferred about the perils which were bearing down on them. Although some declared that they should relinquish the pass at once and make their way in safety to the allies, stating that any who remained in the place could not possibly come off with their lives, Leonidas, the king of the Lacedaemonians, being eagerly desirous to win both for himself and for the Spartans a garland of great glory, gave orders that the rest of the Greeks should all depart and win safety for themselves, in order that they might fight together with the Greeks in the battles which still remained; but as for the Lacedaemonians, he said, they must remain and not abandon the defence of the pass, for it was fitting that those who were the leaders of Hellas should gladly die striving for the meed of honour. Immediately, then, all the rest departed, but Leonidas together with his fellow citizens performed heroic and astounding deeds; and although the Lacedaemonians were but few (he detained only the Thespiaeans) and he had all told not more than five hundred men, he was ready to meet death on behalf of Hellas.

After this the Persians who were led by the Trachinian, after making their way around the difficult terrain, suddenly caught Leonidas between their forces, and the Greeks, giving up any thought of their own safety and choosing renown instead, with one voice asked their commander to lead them against the enemy before the Persians should learn that their men had made their way around them, and Leonidas, welcoming the eagerness of his soldiers, ordered them to prepare their breakfast quickly, since they would dine in Hades, and he himself, in accordance with the order he had given, took food, believing that by so doing he could keep his strength for a long time and endure the strain of contest. When they had hastily refreshed themselves and all were ready, he ordered the soldiers to attack the camp, slaying any who came in their way, and to strike for the very pavilion of the king.

**10.** The soldiers, then, in accordance with the orders given them, forming in a compact body fell by night upon the encampment of the Persians, Leonidas leading the attack; and the barbarians, because of the unexpectedness of the attack and their ignorance of the reason for it, ran together from their tents with great tumult and in disorder, and thinking that the soldiers who had set out with the Trachinian had perished and that the entire force of the Greeks was upon them, they were struck with terror. Consequently many of them were slain by the troops of Leonidas, and even more perished at the hands of their comrades, who in their ignorance took them for enemies. For the night prevented any understanding of the true state of affairs, and the confusion, extending as it did throughout the entire encampment, occasioned, we may well believe, great slaughter; since they kept killing one another, the conditions not allowing of a close scrutiny, because there was no order from a general nor any demanding of a password nor, in general, any recovery of reason. Indeed, if the king had remained at the royal pavilion, he also could easily have been slain by the Greeks and the whole war would have reached a speedy conclusion; but as it was, Xerxes had rushed out to the tumult, and the Greeks broke into the pavilion and slew almost to a man all whom they caught there. So long as it was night they

## Book XI

wandered throughout the entire camp seeking Xerxes, a reasonable action; but when the day dawned and the entire state of affairs was made manifest, the Persians, observing that the Greeks were few in number, viewed them with contempt; the Persians did not, however, join battle with them face to face, fearing their valour, but they formed on their flanks and rear, and shooting arrows and hurling javelins at them from every direction they slew them to a man. Now as for the soldiers of Leonidas who guarded the passes of Thermopylae, such was the end of life they met.

**11.** The merits of these men, who would not regard them with wonder? They with one accord did not desert the post to which Greece had assigned them, but gladly offered up their own lives for the common salvation of all Greeks, and preferred to die bravely rather than to live shamefully. The consternation of the Persians also, no one could doubt that they felt it. For what man among the barbarians could have conceived of that which had taken place? Who could have expected that a band of only five hundred ever had the daring to charge against the hundred myriads? Consequently what man of later times might not emulate the valour of those warriors who, finding themselves in the grip of an overwhelming situation, though their bodies were subdued, were not conquered in spirit? These men, therefore, alone of all of whom history records, have in defeat been accorded a greater fame than all others who have won the fairest victories. For judgement must be passed upon brave men, not by the outcome of their actions, but by their purpose; in the one case Fortune is mistress, in the other it is the purpose which wins approval. What man would judge any to be braver than were those Spartans who, though not equal in number to even the thousandth part of the enemy, dared to match their valour against the unbelievable multitudes? Nor had they any hope of overcoming so many myriads, but they believed that in bravery they would surpass all men of former times, and they decided that, although the battle they had to fight was against the barbarians, yet the real contest and the award of valour they were seeking was in competition with all who had ever won admiration for their courage. Indeed they alone of those of whom we have knowledge from time immemorial chose rather to preserve the laws of their state than their own lives, not feeling aggrieved that the greatest perils threatened them, but concluding that the greatest boon for which those who practise valour should pray is the opportunity to play a part in contests of this kind, and one would be justified in believing that it was these men who were more responsible for the common freedom of the Greeks than those who were victorious at a later time in the battles against Xerxes; for when the deeds of these men were called to mind, the Persians were dismayed whereas the Greeks were incited to perform similar courageous exploits.

Speaking in general terms, these men alone of the Greeks down to their time passed into immortality because of their exceptional valour. Consequently not only the writers of history but also many of our poets have celebrated their brave exploits; and one of them is Simonides, the lyric poet, who composed the following encomium in their praise, worthy of their valour:

> Of those who perished at Thermopylae
> All glorious is the fortune, fair the doom;
> Their grave's an altar, ceaseless memory's theirs
> Instead of lamentation, and their fate
> Is chant of praise. Such winding-sheet as this
> Nor mould nor all-consuming time shall waste.
> This sepulchre of valiant men has taken
> The fair renown of Hellas for its inmate.
> And witness is Leonidas, once king
> Of Sparta, who hath left behind a crown
> Of valour mighty and uncying fame.

### On the naval battle which Xerxes fought against the Greeks (12-13).

**12.** Now that we have spoken at sufficient length of the valour of these men we shall resume the course of our narrative. Xerxes, now that he had gained the passes in the manner we have described and had won, as the proverb runs, a "Cadmeian victory," had destroyed only a few of the enemy, while he had lost great numbers of his own troops. After he had become master of the passes by means of his land forces, he resolved to make trial of contest at sea. At once, therefore, summoning the commander of the fleet, Megabates, he ordered him to sail against the naval force of the Greeks and to make trial, with all his fleet, of a sea-battle against them. And Megabates, in accordance with the king's orders, set out from Pydne in Macedonia with all the fleet and put in at a promontory of Magnesia which bears the name of Sepias. At this place a great wind arose and he lost more than three hundred warships and great numbers of cavalry transports and other vessels. When the wind ceased, he weighed anchor and put in at Aphetae in Magnesia. From here he dispatched two hundred triremes, ordering the commanders to take a roundabout course and, by keeping Euboea on the right, to encircle the enemy.

The Greeks were stationed at Artemisium in Euboea and had in all two hundred and eighty triremes; of these ships one hundred and forty were Athenian and the remainder were furnished by the rest of the Greeks. Their admiral was Eurybiades the Spartan, and Themistocles the Athenian supervised the affairs of the fleet; for the latter, by reason of his sagacity and skill as a general, enjoyed great favour not only with the Greeks throughout the fleet but also with Eurybiades himself, and all men looked to him and harkened to him eagerly. When a meeting of the commanders of the ships was held to discuss the engagement, the rest of them all favoured waiting to receive the advance of the enemy; but Themistocles alone expressed the opposite opinion, showing them that it was to their advantage to sail against the enemy with the whole fleet in one array; for in this way, he declared, they would have the upper hand, attacking as they would with their ships in a single body an enemy whose formation was broken by disorder, as it must be, for they would be issuing out of many harbours at some distance apart. In the end the Greeks followed the opinion of Themistocles and sailed against the enemy with the entire fleet, and since the barbarians put out from many harbours, at the outset Themistocles, engaging with the scattered Persians, sank many ships and not a few he forced to turn in flight and pursued as far as the land; but later, when the whole fleet had gathered and a fierce battle ensued, each side gained the superiority in one part of the line but neither won a complete victory, and at nightfall the engagement was broken off.

**13.** After the battle a great storm arose and destroyed many ships which were anchored outside the harbour, so that it appeared as if Providence were taking the part of the Greeks in order that, the multitude of the barbarians' ships having been lessened, the Greek force might become a match for them and strong enough to offer battle. As a result the Greeks grew ever more bold, whereas the barbarians became ever more timorous before the conflicts which faced them. Nevertheless, recovering themselves after the shipwreck, they put out with all their ships against the enemy, and the Greeks, with fifty Attic triremes added to their number, took position opposed to the barbarians. The sea-battle which followed was much like the fighting at Thermopylae; for the Persians were resolved to overwhelm the Greeks and force their way through the Euripus [strait], while the Greeks, blocking the narrows, were fighting to preserve their allies in Euboea. A fierce battle ensued and many ships were lost on both sides, and nightfall compelled them to return to their respective harbours. The prize of valour, we are told, in both battles was accorded to the Athenians for the Greeks and to the Sidonians for the barbarians.

After this the Greeks, on hearing of the course events had taken at Thermopylae and discovering that the Persians were advancing by land against Athens, became dispirited; consequently they sailed off to Salamis and awaited events there. The Athenians, surveying the dangers threatening each and every inhabitant of Athens, put on boats their children and wives and every useful article they could and brought them to Salamis. And the Persian admiral, on learning that the enemy had withdrawn, set sail for Euboea with his entire fleet, and taking the city of the Histiaeans by storm he plundered and ravaged their territory.

### *How Themistocles outgeneralled Xerxes and the Greeks conquered the barbarians in the naval battle of Salamis (14-18).*

**14.** While these events were taking place, Xerxes set out from Thermopylae and advanced through the territory of the Phocians, sacking the cities and destroying all property in the countryside. Now the Phocians had chosen the cause of the Greeks, but seeing that they were unable to offer resistance, the whole populace deserted all their cities and fled for safety to the rugged regions about Mount Parnassus. Then the king passed through the territory of the Dorians, doing it no harm since they were allies of the Persians. Here he left behind a portion of his army and ordered it to proceed to Delphi, to burn the precinct of Apollo and to carry off the votive offerings, while he advanced into Boeotia with the rest of the barbarians and encamped there. The force that had been dispatched to sack the oracle had proceeded as far as the shrine of Athena Pronaea, but at that spot a great thunderstorm, accompanied by incessant lightning, suddenly burst from the heavens, and more than that, the storm wrenched loose huge rocks and hurled them into the host of the barbarians; the result was that large numbers of the Persians were killed and the whole force, dismayed at the intervention of the gods, fled from the region. So the oracle of Delphi, with the aid of some divine Providence, escaped pillage. The Delphians, desiring to leave to succeeding generations a deathless memorial of the appearance of the gods among men, set up beside the temple of Athena Pronaea a trophy on which they inscribed the following elegiac lines:

> To serve as a memorial to war,
> The warder-off of men, and as a witness
> To victory the Delphians set me up,
> Rendering thanks to Zeus and Phoebus who
> Thrust back the city-sacking ranks of Medes
> And threw their guard about the bronze-crowned shrine.

Meanwhile Xerxes, as he passed through Boeotia, laid waste the territory of the Thespiaeans and burned Plataea which was without habitants; for the residents of these two cities had fled in a body into the Peloponnesus. After this he entered Attica and ravaged the countryside, and then he razed Athens to the ground and sent up in flames the temples of the gods. And while the king was concerned with these affairs, his fleet sailed from Euboea to Attica, having sacked on the way both Euboea and the coast of Attica.

**15.** During this time the Cercyraeans, who had fitted out sixty triremes, were waiting off the Peloponnesus, being unable, as they themselves allege, to round the promontory at Malea, but, as certain historians tell us, anxiously awaiting the turn of the war, in order that, if the Persians prevailed, they might then give them water and earth, while if the Greeks were victorious, they would get the credit of having come to their aid. The Athenians who were waiting in Salamis, when they saw Attica being laid waste with fire and heard that the sacred precinct of Athena had been razed, were exceedingly disheartened. Likewise great fear gripped the other Greeks who, driven from every quarter, were now contained in the Peloponnesus alone. Consequently they thought it desirable that all who had been charged with command should meet in council and deliberate regarding the kind of place that would best serve their purpose in fighting a naval battle. Many ideas of various kinds were expressed. The Peloponnesians, thinking only of their own safety, declared that the contest should be held at the Isthmus; for it had been strongly fortified with a wall, and so, if they should suffer any reverse in the battle, the defeated would be able to withdraw for refuge into the most suitable place of safety available, the Peloponnesus, whereas, if they exposed themselves on the little island of Salamis, perils would beset them from which it would be difficult for them to be rescued. Themistocles counselled that the

# Book XI

contest of the ships be held at Salamis, for he believed that those who had few ships to fight with would have many advantages, in the narrows of Salamis, against a vastly superior number of vessels, and speaking generally, he showed that the region about the Isthmus would be altogether unsuitable for the sea-battle; for the contest would take place on the open sea, and the Persians because of the room for manoeuvring would easily subdue the small force of ships by their vastly superior numbers. By presenting in like fashion many other facts pertinent to the occasion he persuaded all present to cast their votes with him for the plan he recommended.

**16.** When at last a decision was reached by all to fight the sea-battle at Salamis, the Greeks set about making the preparations necessary to meet the Persians and the peril of battle. Accordingly Eurybiades, accompanied by Themistocles, undertook to encourage the crews and incite them to face the impending struggle. However, the crews would not heed them, but since they were one and all dismayed at the magnitude of the Persian forces, not a man of them paid any attention to his commander, every one being intent upon sailing from Salamis to the Peloponnesus. The army of the Greeks on land was no whit less terrified by the armament of the enemy, and not only the loss at Thermopylae of their most illustrious warriors caused them dismay, but also the disasters which were taking place in Attica before their very eyes were filling the Greeks with utter despair. Meanwhile the members of the congress of the Greeks, observing the unrest of the masses and the dismay prevailing everywhere, voted to build a wall across the Isthmus. The works were completed speedily because of the enthusiasm and the multitude of those engaged in the task; but while the Peloponnesians were strengthening the wall, which extended a distance of forty stades, from Lechaeum to Cenchreae, the forces which were inactive at Salamis, together with the entire fleet, were so terror-stricken that they no longer obeyed the orders of their commanders.

**17.** Themistocles, perceiving that the admiral, Eurybiades, was unable to overcome the mood of his forces, and yet recognising that the narrow quarters at Salamis could be a great aid in achieving the victory, contrived the following ruse: He induced a certain man to desert to Xerxes and to assure him that the ships at Salamis were going to slip away from that region and assemble at the Isthmus. Accordingly the king, believing the man because what he reported was in itself plausible, made haste to prevent the naval forces of the Greeks from making contact with their armies on land. Therefore he at once dispatched the Egyptian fleet with orders to block the strait which separates Salamis from the territory of Megaris. The main body of his ships he dispatched to Salamis, ordering it to establish contact with the enemy and by fighting there decide the issue. The triremes were drawn up by peoples one after another, in order that, speaking the same language and knowing one another, the several contingents might assist each other with alacrity. When the fleet had been drawn up in this manner, the right wing was held by the Phoenicians and the left by the Greeks who were associated with the Persians.

The commanders of the Ionian contingents of the Persian fleet sent a man of Samos to the Greeks to inform them of what the king had decided to do and of the disposition of his forces for battle, and to say that in the course of the battle they were going to desert from the barbarians. When the Samian had swum across without being observed and had informed Eurybiades about this plan, Themistocles, realising that his stratagem had worked out as he had planned, was beside himself with joy and exhorted the crews to the fight; and as for the Greeks, they were emboldened by the promise of the Ionians, and although the circumstances were compelling them to fight against their own preference, they came down eagerly in a body from Salamis to the shore in preparation for the sea-battle.

**18.** When at last Eurybiades and Themistocles had completed the disposition of their forces, the left wing was held by the Athenians and Lacedaemonians, who in this way would be opposed to the ships of the Phoenicians; for the Phoenicians possessed a distinct superiority by reason both of their great number and of the experience in seamanship which they inherited from their ancestors. The Aeginetans and Megarians formed the right wing, since they were generally considered to be the best seamen after the Athenians and it was believed that they would show the best spirit, seeing that they alone of the Greeks would have no place of refuge in case any reverse should occur in the course of the battle. The centre was held by the rest of the Greek forces.

This, then, was the battle-order in which the Greeks sailed out, and they occupied the strait between Salamis and the Heracleium; and the king gave order to his admiral to advance against the enemy, while he himself moved down the coast to a spot directly opposite Salamis from which he could watch the course of the battle. The Persians, as they advanced, could at the outset maintain their line, since they had plenty of space; but when they came to the narrow passage, they were compelled to withdraw some ships from the line, creating in this way much disorder. The admiral, who was leading the way before the line and was the first to begin the fighting, was slain after having acquitted himself valiantly. When his ship went down, disorder seized the barbarian fleet, for there were many now to give orders, but each man did not issue the same commands. Consequently they halted the advance, and holding back their ships, they began to withdraw to where there was plenty of room. The Athenians, observing the disorder among the barbarians, now advanced upon the enemy, and some of their ships they struck with their rams, while from others they sheared off the rows of oars; and when the men at the oars could no longer do their work, many Persian triremes, getting sidewise to the enemy, were time and again severely damaged by the beaks of the ships. Consequently they ceased merely backing water, but turned about and fled precipitately.

BOOK XI

## *How Xerxes, leaving Mardonius behind as commander, withdrew with a portion of his army to Asia (19).*

19. While the Phoenician and Cyprian ships were being mastered by the Athenians, the vessels of the Cilicians and Pamphylians, and also of the Lycians, which followed them in line, at first were holding out stoutly, but when they saw the strongest ships taking to flight they likewise abandoned the fight. On the other wing the battle was stubbornly fought and for some time the struggle was evenly balanced; but when the Athenians had pursued the Phoenicians and Cyprians to the shore and then turned back, the barbarians, being forced out of line by the returning Athenians, turned about and lost many of their ships. In this manner, then, the Greeks gained the upper hand and won a most renowned naval victory over the barbarians; and in the struggle forty ships were lost by the Greeks, but more than two hundred by the Persians, not including those which were captured together with their crews.

The king, for whom the defeat was unexpected, put to death those Phoenicians who were chiefly responsible for beginning the flight, and threatened to visit upon the rest the punishment they deserved. The Phoenicians, frightened by his threats, first put into port on the coast of Attica, and then, when night fell, set sail for Asia. Themistocles, who was credited for having brought about the victory, devised another stratagem no less clever than the one we have described. For, since the Greeks were afraid to battle on land against so many myriads of Persians, he greatly reduced the number of the Persian troops in the following manner: he sent to Xerxes the attendant of his own sons to inform him that the Greeks were about to sail to the bridge of boats and to destroy it. Accordingly the king, believing the report because it was plausible, became fearful lest he should be cut off from the route whereby he could get back to Asia, now that the Greeks controlled the sea, and decided to cross over in all possible haste from Europe into Asia, leaving Mardonius behind in Greece with picked cavalry and infantry, the total number of whom was not less than four hundred thousand. Thus Themistocles by the use of two stratagems brought about signal advantages for the Greeks.

These were the events that took place in Greece at this time.

## *How the Carthaginians with great armaments made war upon Sicily (20-21)*

20. Now that we have described at sufficient length the events in Europe, we shall shift our narrative to the affairs of another people. The Carthaginians, we recall, had agreed with the Persians to subdue the Greeks of Sicily at the same time and had made preparations on a large scale of such materials as would be useful in carrying on a war, and when they had made everything ready, they chose for general Hamilcar, having selected him as the man who was held by them in the highest esteem. He assumed command of huge forces, both land and naval, and sailed forth from Carthage with an army of not less than three hundred thousand men and a fleet of over two hundred ships of war, not to mention many-cargo ships for carrying supplies, numbering more than three thousand.

Now as he was crossing the Libyan sea he encountered a storm and lost the vessels which were carrying the horses and chariots. When he came to port in Sicily in the harbour of Panormus [Palermo] he remarked that he had finished the war; for he had been afraid that the sea would rescue the Siceliotes from the perils of the conflict. He took three days to rest his soldiers and to repair the damage which the storm had inflicted on his ships, and then advanced together with his host against Himera, the fleet skirting the coast with him. When he had arrived near the city we have just mentioned, he pitched two camps, the one for the army and the other for the naval force. All the warships he hauled up on land and threw about them a deep ditch and a wooden palisade, and he strengthened the camp of the army, which he placed so that it fronted the city, and prolonged so that it took in the area from the wall extending along the naval camp as far as the hills which overhung the city. Speaking generally, he took control of the entire west side, after which he unloaded all the supplies from the cargo vessels and at once sent off all these boats, ordering them to bring grain and the other supplies from Libya and Sardinia. Then, taking his best troops, he advanced to the city, and routing the Himerans who came out against him and slaying many of them, he struck the inhabitants of the city with terror. Consequently Theron, the ruler of the Acragantini, who with a considerable force was standing by to guard Himera, in fear hastily sent word to Syracuse, asking Gelon to come to his aid as rapidly as possible.

**21.** Gelon, who had likewise held his army in readiness, on learning that the Himerans were in despair set out from Syracuse with all speed, accompanied by not less than fifty thousand foot-soldiers and over five thousand cavalry. He covered the distance swiftly, and as he drew near the city of the Himerans he inspired boldness in the hearts of those who before had been dismayed at the forces of the Carthaginians. For after pitching a camp which was appropriate to the terrain about the city, he not only fortified it with a deep ditch and a palisade but also dispatched his entire body of cavalry against such forces of the enemy as were ranging over the countryside in search of booty. The cavalry, unexpectedly appearing to men who were scattered without military order over the countryside, took prisoner as many as each man could drive before him, and when prisoners to the number of more than ten thousand had been brought into the city, not only was Gelon accorded great approbation but the Himerans also came to hold the enemy in contempt. Following up what he had already accomplished, all the gates which Theron through fear had formerly blocked up were now, on the contrary, opened up by Gelon through his contempt of the enemy, and he even constructed additional ones which might prove serviceable to him in case of urgent need.

In a word Gelon, excelling as he did in skill as a general and in shrewdness, set about at once to discover how he might without any risk to his army outgeneral the barbarians and utterly destroy their power. His own ingenuity was greatly aided by accident, because of the following circumstance. He had decided to set fire to the ships of the enemy; and while Hamilcar was occupied in the naval camp with the preparation of a magnificent sacrifice to Poseidon, cavalrymen came from the countryside bringing to Gelon a letter-carrier who was conveying dispatches from the people of Selinus, in which was written that they would send the cavalry for that day for which Hamilcar had written to dispatch them. The day was that on which Hamilcar planned to celebrate the sacrifice, and on that day Gelon dispatched cavalry of his own, who were under orders to skirt the immediate neighbourhood and to ride up at daybreak to the naval camp, as if they were the allies from Selinus, and when they had once got inside the wooden palisade, to slay Hamilcar and set fire to the ships. He also sent scouts to the hills which overlook the city, ordering them to raise the signal as soon as they saw that the horsemen were inside the wall. For his part, at daybreak he drew up his army and awaited the sign which was to come from the scouts.

**How Gelon, after outgeneralling the barbarians, slew some of them and took others captive (22-23).**

22. At sunrise the cavalrymen rode up to the naval camp of the Carthaginians, and when the guards admitted them, thinking them to be allies, they at once galloped to where Hamilcar was busied with the sacrifice, slew him, and then set fire to the ships; thereupon the scouts raised the signal and Gelon advanced with his entire army in battle order against the Carthaginian camp. The commanders of the Phoenicians in the camp at the outset led out their troops to meet the Siceliotes and as the lines closed they put up a vigorous fight; at the same time in both camps they sounded with the trumpets the signal for battle and a shout arose from the two armies one after the other, each eagerly striving to outdo their adversaries in the volume of their cheering. The slaughter was great, and the battle was swaying back and forth, when suddenly the flames from the ships began to rise on high and sundry persons reported that the general had been slain; then the Greeks were emboldened and with spirits elated at the rumours and by the hope of victory they pressed with greater boldness upon the barbarians, while the Carthaginians, dismayed and despairing of victory, turned in flight.

Since Gelon had given orders to take no prisoners, there followed a great slaughter of the enemy in their flight, and in the end no less than one hundred and fifty thousand of them were slain. All who escaped the battle and fled to a strong position at first warded off the attackers, but the position they had seized had no water, and thirst compelled them to surrender to the victors. Gelon, who had won a victory in a most remarkable battle and had gained his success primarily by reason of his own skill as a general, acquired a fame that was noised abroad, not only among the Siceliotes, but among all other men as well; for memory recalls no man before him who had used a stratagem like this, nor one who had slain more barbarians in one engagement or had taken so great a multitude of prisoners.

**23.** Because of this achievement many historians compare this battle with the one which the Greeks fought at Plataea and the stratagem of Gelon with the ingenious schemes of Themistocles, and the first place they assign, since such exceptional merit was shown by both men, some to the one and some to the other. The reason is that, when the people of Greece on the one hand and those of Sicily on the other were struck with dismay before the conflict at the multitude of the barbarian armies, it was the prior victory of the Sicilian Greeks which gave courage to the people of Greece when they learned of Gelon's victory; and as for the men in both affairs who held the supreme command, we know that in the case of the Persians the king escaped with his life and many myriads together with him, whereas in the case of the Carthaginians not only did the general perish but also everyone who participated in the war was slain, and, as the saying is, not even a man to bear the news got back alive to Carthage. Furthermore, of the most distinguished of the leaders of the Greeks, Pausanias and Themistocles, the former was put to death by his fellow citizens because of his overweening greed of power and treason, and the latter was driven from every corner of Greece and fled for refuge to Xerxes, his bitterest enemy, on whose hospitality he lived to the end of his life; whereas Gelon after the battle received greater approbation every year at the hands of the Syracusans, grew old in the kingship, and died in the esteem of his people, and so strong was the goodwill which the citizens felt for him that the kingship was maintained for three members of this house.

However, now that these men, who enjoy a well deserved fame, have received from us also the eulogies they merit, we shall pass on to the continuation of the preceding narrative.

### *How Gelon, when the Carthaginians sued for peace, exacted money of them and then concluded the peace (24-26).*

**24.** Now it so happened that Gelon won his victory on the same day that Leonidas and his soldiers were contesting against Xerxes at Thermopylae, as if the deity intentionally so arranged that both the fairest victory and the most honourable defeat should take place at the same time. After the battle at the city of the Himerans twenty warships made their escape from the fight, being those which Hamilcar, to serve his routine requirements, had not hauled up on shore. Consequently, although practically all the rest of the combatants were either slain or taken prisoner, these vessels managed to set sail before they were noticed. They picked up many fugitives, and while heavily laden on this account, they encountered a storm and were all lost. A handful only of survivors got safely to Carthage in a small boat to give their fellow citizens a statement which was brief: "All who crossed over to Sicily have perished."

The Carthaginians, who had suffered a great disaster so contrary to their hopes, were so terror-stricken that every night they kept vigil guarding the city, in the belief that Gelon with his entire force must have decided to sail forthwith against Carthage, and because of the multitude of the lost the city went into public mourning, while privately the homes of citizens were filled with wailing and lamentation. For some kept inquiring after sons, others after brothers, while a very large number of children who had lost their fathers, alone now in the world, grieved at the death of those who had begotten them and at their own desolation through the loss of those who could succour them. And the Carthaginians, fearing lest Gelon should forestall them in crossing over to Libya, at once dispatched to him as ambassadors plenipotentiary their ablest orators and counsellors.

**25.** As for Gelon, after his victory he not only honoured with gifts the horsemen who had slain Hamilcar but also decorated with rewards for prowess all others who had played the part of men. The fairest part of the booty he put to one side, since he wished to embellish the temples of Syracuse with the spoils; as for the rest of the booty, much of it he nailed to the most notable of the temples in Himera, and the rest of it, together with the captives, he divided among the allies, apportioning it in accordance with the number who had served with him. The cities put the captives allotted to them in chains and used them for building their public works. A very great number was received by the Acragantini, who embellished their city and countryside; for so great was the multitude of prisoners at their disposal that many private citizens had five hundred captives in their homes. A contributing reason for the vast number of the captives among them was not only that they had sent many soldiers into the battle, but also that, when the flight took place, many of the fugitives turned into the interior, especially into the territory of the Acragantini, and since every man of them was taken captive by the Acragantini, the city was crammed full of the captured. Most of these were handed over to the state, and it was these men who quarried the stones of which not only the largest temples of the gods were constructed but also the underground conduits were built to lead off the waters from the city; these are so large that their construction is well worth seeing, although it is little thought of since they were built at slight expense. The builder in charge of these works, who bore the name of Phaeax, brought it about that, because of the fame of the construction, the underground conduits got the name "Phaeaces" from him. The Acragantini also built an expensive kolumbethra [swiming bath], seven stades in circumference and twenty cubits deep. Into it the waters from rivers and springs were conducted and it became a fish-pond, which supplied fish in great abundance to be used for food and to please the palate; and since swans also in the greatest numbers settled down upon it, the pool came to be a delight to look upon. In later years, however, the pool became choked up through neglect and was destroyed by the long passage of time; but the entire site, which was fertile, the inhabitants planted in vines and in trees of every description placed close together, so that they derived from it great revenues. Gelon, after dismissing the allies, led the citizens of Syracuse back home, and because of the magnitude of his success he was enthusiastically received not only among his fellow citizens but also throughout the whole of Sicily; for he brought with him such a multitude of captives that it looked as if the island had made the whole of Libya captive.

**26.** And at once there came to him ambassadors from both the cities and rulers which had formerly opposed him, asking forgiveness for their past mistakes and promising for the future to carry out his every command. With all of them he dealt equitably and concluded alliances, bearing his good fortune as men should, not toward them alone but even toward the Carthaginians, his bitterest foes. For when the ambassadors who had been dispatched from Carthage came to him and begged him with tears to treat them humanely, he granted them peace, exacting of them the expense he had incurred for the war, two thousand talents of silver, and requiring them further to build two temples in which they should place copies of the treaty. The Carthaginians, having unexpectedly gained their deliverance, not only agreed to all this but also promised to give in addition a gold crown to Damarete, the wife of Gelon. For Damarete at their request had contributed the greatest aid toward the conclusion of the peace, and when she had received the crown of one hundred gold talents from them, she struck a coin which was called from her a *Damareteion*. This was worth ten Attic drachmas and was called by the Sicilian Greeks, according to its weight, a *pentekontalitron*.

Gelon treated all men fairly, primarily because that was his disposition, but not the least motive was that he was eager to make all men his own by acts of goodwill. For instance, he was making ready to sail to Greece with a large force and to join the Greeks in their war against the Persians. He was already on the point of setting out to sea, when certain men from Corinth put in at Syracuse and brought the news that the Greeks had won the sea-battle at Salamis and that Xerxes and a part of his armament had retreated from Europe. Consequently he stopped his preparations for departure, while welcoming the enthusiasm of the soldiers; and then he called them to an assembly, issuing orders for each man to appear fully armed. As for himself, he came to the assembly not only with no arms but not even wearing a tunic and clad only in a cloak, and stepping forward he rendered an account of his whole life and of all he had done for the Syracusans; and when the throng shouted its approval at each action he mentioned and showed especially its amazement that he had given himself unarmed into the hands of any who might wish to slay him, so far was he from being a victim of vengeance as a tyrant that they united in acclaiming him with one voice Benefactor and Saviour and King. After this incident Gelon built noteworthy temples to Demeter and Corê out of the spoils, and making a golden tripod of sixteen talents value he set it up in the sacred precinct at Delphi as a thank-offering to Apollo. At a later time he purposed to build a temple to Demeter at Aetna, since she had none in that place; but he did not complete it, his life having been cut short by fate.

Of the lyric poets Pindar was in his prime in this period. Now these are in general the most notable events which took place in this year.

## BOOK XI

***Judgement passed on the Greeks who distinguished themselves in the war (27). The battle of the Greeks against Mardonius and the Persians about Plataea and the victory of the Greeks (27-39).***

**27.** While Xantliippus was archon in Athens, [479] the Romans elected as consuls Quintus Fabius Silvanus and Servius Cornelius Tricostus. At this time the Persian fleet, with the exception of the Phoenician contingent, after its defeat in the sea-battle of Salamis lay at Cymê. Here it passed the winter, and at the coming of summer it sailed down the coast to Samos to keep watch on Ionia; and the total number of the ships in Samos exceeded four hundred. Now they were keeping watch upon the cities of the Ionians who were suspected of hostile sentiments.

Throughout Greece, after the battle of Salamis, since the Athenians were generally believed to have been responsible for the victory, and on this account were themselves exultant, it became manifest to all that they were intending to dispute with the Lacedaemonians for the leadership on the sea; consequently the Lacedaemonians, foreseeing what was going to happen, did all they could to humble the pride of the Athenians. When, therefore, a judgement was proposed to determine the prizes to be awarded for valour, through the superior favour they enjoyed they caused the decision to be that of states Aegina had won the prize, and of men Ameinias of Athens, the brother of Aeschylus the poet; for Ameinias, while commanding a trireme, had been the first to ram the flagship of the Persians, sinking it and killing the admiral. When the Athenians showed their anger at this undeserved humiliation, the Lacedaemonians, fearful lest Themistocles should be displeased at the outcome and should devise some great evil against them and the Greeks, honoured him with double the number of gifts awarded to those who had received the prize of valour, and when Themistocles accepted the gifts, the Athenians in assembly removed him from the generalship and bestowed the office upon Xanthippus the son of Ariphron.

**28.** When the estrangement which had arisen between the Athenians and the other Greeks became noised abroad, there came to Athens ambassadors from the Persians and from the Greeks. Now those who had been dispatched by the Persians bore word that Mardonius the general assured the Athenians that, if they should choose the cause of the Persians, he would give them their choice of any land in Greece, rebuild their walls and temples, and allow the city to live under its own laws; but those who had been sent from the Lacedaemonians begged the Athenians not to yield to the persuasions of the barbarians but to maintain their loyalty toward the Greeks, who were men of their own blood and of the same speech. The Athenians replied to the barbarians that the Persians possessed no land rich enough nor gold in sufficient abundance which the Athenians would accept in return for abandoning the Greeks; while to the Lacedaemonians they said that as for themselves the concern which they had formerly held for the welfare of Greece they would endeavour to maintain hereafter also, and of the Lacedaemonians they only asked that they should come with all speed to Attica together with all their allies. For it was evident, they added, that Mardonius, now that the Athenians had declared against him, would advance with his army against Athens. This is what actually took place. For Mardonius, who was stationed in Boeotia with all his forces, at first attempted to cause certain cities in the Peloponnesus to come over to him, distributing money among their leading men, but afterwards, when he learned of the reply the Athenians had given, in his rage he led his entire force into Attica. Apart from the army Xerxes had given him he had himself gathered many other soldiers from Thrace and Macedonia and the other allied states, more than two hundred thousand men. With the advance into Attica of so large a force as this, the Athenians dispatched couriers bearing letters to the Lacedaemonians, asking their aid; and since the Lacedaemonians still loitered and the barbarians had already crossed the border of Attica, they were dismayed, and again, taking their children and wives and whatever else they were able to carry off in their haste, they left their native land and a second time fled for refuge to Salamis. Mardonius was so angry with them that he ravaged the entire countryside, razed the city to the ground, and utterly destroyed the temples that were still standing.

**29.** When Mardonius and his army had returned to Thebes, the Greeks gathered in congress decreed to make common cause with the Athenians and advancing to Plataea in a body, to fight to a finish for liberty, and also to make a vow to the gods that, if they were victorious, the Greeks would unite in celebrating the Festival of Liberty on that day and would hold the games of the Festival in Plataea. When the Greek forces were assembled at the Isthmus, all of them agreed that they should swear an oath about the war, one that would make staunch the concord among them and would compel them nobly to endure the perils of the battle. The oath ran as follows: "I will not hold life dearer than liberty, nor will I desert the leaders, whether they be living or dead, but I will bury all the allies who have perished in the battle; and if I overcome the barbarians in the war, I will not destroy any one of the cities which have participated in the struggle; nor will I rebuild any one of the sanctuaries which have been burnt or demolished, but I will let them be and leave them as a reminder to coming generations of the impiety of the barbarians." After they had sworn the oath, they marched to Boeotia through the pass of Cithaeron, and when they had descended as far as the foothills near Erythrae, they pitched camp there. The command over the Athenians was held by Aristeides, and the supreme command by Pausanias, who was the guardian of the son of Leonidas.

**30.** When Mardonius learned that the enemy's army was advancing in the direction of Boeotia, he marched forth from Thebes, and when he arrived at the Asopus River he pitched a camp, which he strengthened by means of a deep ditch and surrounded with a wooden palisade. The total number of the Greeks approached one hundred thousand men, that of the barbarians some five hundred thousand. The first to open the battle were the barbarians, who poured out upon the Greeks by night and charged with all their cavalry upon the camp. The

Athenians observed them in time and with their army in battle formation boldly advanced to meet them, and a mighty battle ensued. In the end all the rest of the Greeks put to flight the barbarians who were arrayed against them; but the Megarians alone, who faced the commander of the cavalry and the best horsemen the Persians had, being hard pressed in the fighting, though they did not leave their position, sent some of their men as messengers to the Athenians and Lacedaemonians asking them to come to their aid with all speed. Aristeides quickly dispatched the picked Athenians who constituted his body-guard, and these, forming themselves into a compact body and falling on the barbarians, rescued the Megarians from the perils which threatened them, slew of the Persians both the commander of the cavalry and many others, and put the remainder to flight.

The Greeks, now that they had shown their superiority so brilliantly in a kind of prelude or rehearsal, were encouraged to hope for a decisive victory; and after this encounter they moved their camp from the foothills to a place which was better suited to a complete victory. For on the right was a high hill, on the left the Asopus River, and the space between was held by the camp, which was fortified by the natural impregnability of the general terrain. Thus for the Greeks, who had laid their plans wisely, the limited space was a great aid to their victory, since the Persian battle-line could not be extended to a great length, and the result was, as the event was to show, that no use could be made of the many myriads of the barbarians. Consequently Pausanias and Aristeides, placing their confidence in the position they held, led the army out to battle, and when they had taken positions in a manner suitable to the terrain they advanced against the enemy.

**31.** Mardonius, having been forced to increase the depth of his line, arranged his troops in the way that he thought would be to his advantage, and raising the battle-cry, advanced to meet the Greeks. The best soldiers were about him and with these he led the way, striking at the Lacedaemonians who faced him; he fought gallantly and slew many of the Greeks. The Lacedaemonians, however, opposed him stoutly and endured every peril of battle willingly, and so there was a great slaughter of the barbarians. Now so long as Mardonius and his picked soldiers continued to bear the brunt of the fighting, the barbarians sustained the shock of battle with good spirit; but when Mardonius fell, fighting bravely, and of the picked troops some were slain and others wounded, their spirits were dashed and they began to flee. When the Greeks pressed hard upon them, the larger part of the barbarians fled for safety within the palisade, but as for the rest of the army, the Greeks serving with Mardonius withdrew to Thebes, and the remainder, over four hundred thousand in number, were taken in hand by Artabazus, a man of repute among the Persians, who fled in the opposite direction, and withdrew by forced marches toward Phocis.

**32.** Since the barbarians were thus separated in their flight, so the body of the Greeks was similarly divided; for the Athenians and Plataeans and Thespiaeans pursued after those who had set out for Thebes, and the Corinthians and Sicyonians and the Phliasians and certain others followed after the forces which were retreating with Artabazus; and the Lacedaemonians together with the rest pursued the soldiers who had taken refuge within the palisade and trounced them spiritedly. The Thebans received the fugitives, added them to their forces, and then set upon the pursuing Athenians; a sharp battle took place before the walls, the Thebans fighting brilliantly, and not a few fell on both sides, but at last this body was overcome by the Athenians and took refuge again within Thebes.

After this the Athenians withdrew to the aid of the Lacedaemonians and joined with them in assaulting the walls against those Persians who had taken refuge within the camp; both sides put up a vigorous contest, the barbarians fighting bravely from the fortified positions they held and the Greeks storming the wooden walls, and many were wounded as they fought desperately, while not a few were also slain by the multitude of missiles and met death with stout hearts. Nevertheless the powerful onset of the Greeks could be withstood neither by the wall the barbarians had erected nor by their great numbers, but resistance of every kind was forced to give way; for it was a case of rivalry between the foremost peoples of Greece, the Lacedaemonians and the Athenians, who were buoyed up by reason of their former victories and supported by confidence in their valour. In the end the barbarians were overpowered, and they found no mercy even though they pled to be taken prisoner. For the Greek general, Pausanias, observing how superior the barbarians were in number, took pains to prevent anything due to miscalculation from happening, the barbarians being many times more numerous than the Greeks; consequently he had issued orders to take no man prisoner, and soon there was an incredible number of dead. In the end, when the Greeks had slaughtered more than one hundred thousand of the barbarians, they reluctantly ceased slaying the enemy.

**33.** After the battle had ended in the way we have described, the Greeks buried their dead, of which there were more than ten thousand, and after dividing up the booty according to the number of the soldiers, they made their decision as to the award for valour, and in response to the urging of Aristeides they bestowed the prize for cities upon Sparta and for men upon Pausanias the Lacedaemonian. Meanwhile Artabazus with as many as four hundred thousand of the fleeing Persians made his way through Phocis into Macedonia, availing himself of the quickest routes, and got back safely together with the soldiers into Asia.

The Greeks, taking a tenth part of the spoils, made a gold tripod and set it up in Delphi as a thanks offering to the God, inscribing on it the following couplet:

> This is the gift the saviours of far-flung Hellas upraised here,
> Having delivered their states from loathsome slavery's bonds.

Inscriptions were also set up for the Lacedaemonians who died at Thermopylae; for the whole body of them as follows:

> Here on a time there strove with two hundred myriads of foemen
> Soldiers in number but four thousand from Pelops' fair Isle;

and for the Spartans alone as follows:
> To Lacedaemon's folk, O stranger, carry the message,
> How we lie here in this place, faithful and true to their laws.

In like manner the citizen-body of the Athenians embellished the tombs of those who had perished in the Persian War, held the Funeral Games then for the first time, and passed a law that laudatory addresses upon men who were buried at the public expense should be delivered by speakers selected for each occasion.

After the events we have described Pausanias the general advanced with the army against Thebes and demanded for punishment the men who had been responsible for the alliance of Thebes with the Persians. The Thebans were so overawed by the multitude of their enemy and by their prowess in battle, that the men most responsible for their desertion from the Greeks agreed of their own accord to being handed over, and they all received at the hands of Pausanias the punishment of death.

**34.** Also in Ionia the Greeks fought a great battle with the Persians on the same day as that which took place in Plataea, and since we propose to describe it, we shall take up the account of it from the beginning. Leotychides the Lacedaemonian and Xanthippus [Pericles' father] the Athenian, the commanders of the naval force, after the battle of Salamis collected the fleet in Aegina, and after spending some days there they sailed to Delos with two hundred and fifty triremes. While they lay at anchor there, ambassadors came to them from Samos asking them to liberate the Greeks of Asia. Leotychides took counsel with the commanders, and after they had heard all the Samians had to say, they decided to undertake to liberate the cities and speedily sailed forth from Delos. When the Persian admirals, who were then at Samos, learned that the Greeks were sailing against them, they withdrew from Samos with all their ships, and putting into port at Mycale in Ionia they hauled up their ships, since they saw that the vessels were unequal to offering battle, and threw about them a wooden palisade and a deep ditch; despite these defences they also summoned land forces from Sardis and the neighbouring cities and gathered in all about one hundred thousand men. Furthermore, they made ready all the other equipment that is useful in war, believing that the Ionians also would go over to the enemy. Leotychides advanced with all the fleet ready for action against the barbarians at Mycale, dispatching in advance a ship carrying a herald who had the strongest voice of anyone in the fleet. This man had been ordered to sail up to the enemy and to announce in a loud voice, "The Greeks, having conquered the Persians, are now come to liberate the Greek cities of Asia." This Leotychides did in the belief that the Greeks in the army of the barbarians would revolt from the Persians and that great confusion would arise in the camp of the barbarians; and that is what actually happened, for as soon as the herald approached the ships which had been hauled up on the shore, and made the announcement as he had been ordered, it came about that the Persians lost confidence in the Greeks and that the Greeks began to agree among themselves about revolting.

**35.** After the Greeks under Leotychides had found out how the Greeks in the Persians' camp felt, they disembarked their forces, and on the following day, while they were making preparation for battle, the rumour came to them of the victory which the Greeks had won over the Persians at Plataea. At this news Leotychides, after calling an assembly, exhorted his troops to the battle, and among the other considerations which he presented to them he announced in histrionic manner the victory of Plataea, in the belief that he would make more confident those who were about to fight. Marvellous indeed was the outcome, for it has become known that it was on the same day that the two battles took place, the one which was fought at Mycale and the other which occurred at Plataea. It would seem, therefore, that Leotychides had not yet learned of the victory, but that he was deliberately inventing the military success and did so as a stratagem; the great distance separating the places proved that the transmission of the message was impossible. The leaders of the Persians, placing no confidence in the Greeks of their own forces, took away their arms and gave them to men who were friendly to them; and then they called all the soldiers together and told them that Xerxes was coming in person to their aid with a great armament, inspiring them thereby with courage to face the peril of the battle.

**36.** When both sides had drawn out their troops in battle-order and were advancing against each other, the Persians, observing how few the enemy were, disdained them and bore down on them with great shouting. Now the Samians and Milesians had decided unanimously beforehand to support the Greek cause and were pushing forward all together at the double; and as their advance brought them in sight of the Greek army, although the Ionians thought that the Greeks would be encouraged, the result was the very opposite. For the troops of Leotychides, thinking that Xerxes was come from Sardis with his army and advancing upon them, were filled with fear, and confusion and division among themselves arose in the army, some saying that they should take to their ships with all speed and depart and others that they should remain and boldly hold their lines. While they were still in disorder, the Persians came in sight, equipped in a manner to inspire terror and bearing down on them with shouting. The Greeks, having no respite for deliberation, were compelled to withstand the attack of the barbarians.

At the outset both sides fought stoutly and the battle was indecisive, great numbers falling in both armies; but when the Samians and Milesians put in their appearance, the Greeks plucked up courage, whereas the barbarians were filled with terror and broke in flight. A great slaughter followed, as the troops of Leotychides and Xanthippus pressed upon the beaten barbarians and pursued them as far as the camp; and Aeolians participated in the battle, after the issue had already been decided, as well as many other peoples of Asia, since an overwhelming desire for their liberty entered the hearts of the inhabitants of the cities of Asia. Therefore practically all of them gave no thought either to hostages or to oaths, but they joined with the other Greeks in slaying the

BOOK XI

barbarians in their flight. This was the manner in which the Persians suffered defeat, and there were slain of them more than forty thousand, while of the survivors some found refuge in the camp and others withdrew to Sardis. When Xerxes learned of both the defeat in Plataea and the rout of his own troops in Mycale, he left a portion of his armament in Sardis to carry on the war against the Greeks, while he himself, in bewilderment, set out with the rest of his army on the way to Ecbatana.

37. Leotychides and Xanthippus now sailed back to Samos and made allies of the Ionians and Aeolians, and then they endeavoured to induce them to abandon Asia and to move their homes to Europe. They promised to expel the peoples who had espoused the cause of the Medes and to give their lands to them; for as a general thing, they explained, if they remained in Asia, they would always have the enemy on their borders, an enemy far superior in military strength, while their allies, who lived across the sea, would be unable to render them any timely assistance. When the Aeolians and Ionians had heard these promises, they resolved to take the advice of the Greeks and set about preparing to sail with them to Europe; but the Athenians changed to the opposite opinion and advised them to stay where they were, saying that even if no other Greeks should come to their aid, the Athenians, as their kinsmen, would do so independently. They reasoned that, if the Ionians were given new homes by the Greeks acting in common they would no longer look upon Athens as their mother-city. It was for this reason that the Ionians changed their minds and decided to remain in Asia.

After these events it came to pass that the armament of the Greeks was divided, the Lacedaemonians sailing back to Laconia and the Athenians together with the Ionians and the islanders weighing anchor for Sestus, and Xanthippus the general, as soon as he reached that port, launched assaults upon Sestus and took the city, and after establishing a garrison in it he dismissed the allies and himself with his fellow citizens returned to Athens.

Now the Median War, as it has been called, after lasting two years, came to the end which we have described, and of the historians, Herodotus, beginning with the period prior to the Trojan War, has written in nine books a general history of practically all the events which occurred in the inhabited world, and brings his narrative to an end with the battle of the Greeks against the Persians at Mycale and the siege of Sestus.

In Italy the Romans waged a war against the Volscians, and conquering them in battle slew many of them. Spurius Cassius, who had been consul the preceding year, [480] because he was believed to be aiming at a tyranny and was found guilty, was put to death.

These, then, were the events of this year.

38. When Timosthenes was archon at Athens, in 478, [478] in Rome Caeso Fabius and Lucius Aemilius Mamercus succeeded to the consulship. During this year throughout Sicily an almost complete peace pervaded the island, the Carthaginians having finally been humbled, and Gelon had established a

beneficent rule over the Sicilian Greeks and was providing their cities with a high degree of orderly government and an abundance of every necessity of life. Since the Syracusans had by law put an end to costly funerals and done away with the expense which customarily had been incurred for the dead, and there had been specified in the law even the altogether inexpensive obsequies, King Gelon, desiring to foster and maintain the people's interest in all matters, kept the law regarding burials intact in his own case; for when he fell ill and had given up hope of life, he handed over the kingship to Hieron, his eldest brother, and respecting his own burial he gave orders that the prescriptions of the law should be strictly observed. Consequently at his death his funeral was held by his successor to the throne just as he had ordered it. His body was buried on the estate of his wife in the Nine Towers, as it is called, which is a marvel to men by reason of its strong construction. And the entire populace accompanied his body from the city, although the place was two hundred stades distant. Here he was buried, and the people erected a noteworthy tomb and accorded Gelon the honours which belong to heroes; but at a later time the monument was destroyed by the Carthaginians in the course of a campaign against Syracuse, while the towers were thrown down by Agathocles out of envy. Nevertheless, neither the Carthaginians out of enmity nor Agathocles out of his native baseness, nor any other man has ever been able to deprive Gelon of his glory; for the just witness of history has guarded his fair fame, heralding it abroad with piercing voice for evermore. It is indeed both just and beneficial to society that history should heap imprecations upon base men who have held positions of authority, but should accord immortal remembrance to those who have been beneficent rulers; for in this way especially, it will be found, many men of later generations will be impelled to work for the general good of mankind.

Gelon reigned for seven years [485-478], and Hieron his brother succeeded him in the rule and reigned over the Syracusans eleven years and eight months 478-467].

**39.** In Greece the Athenians after the victory at Plataea brought their children and wives back to Athens from Troezen and Salamis, and at once set to work fortifying the city and were giving their attention to every other means which made for its safety. The Lacedaemonians, observing that the Athenians had gained for themselves great glory by the actions in which their navy had been engaged, looked with suspicion upon their growing power and decided to prevent the Athenians from rebuilding their walls. They at once, therefore, dispatched ambassadors to Athens who would ostensibly advise them not at present to fortify the city, as not being of advantage to the general interests of the Greeks; for, they pointed out, if Xerxes should return with larger armaments than before he would have walled cities ready to hand outside the Peloponnesus which he would use as bases and thus easily subjugate the Greeks. When no attention was paid to their advice, the ambassadors approached the men who were building the wall and ordered them to stop work immediately.

While the Athenians were at a loss what they should do, Themistocles, who enjoyed at that time the highest favour among them, advised them to take no action; for he warned them that if they had recourse to force, the Lacedaemonians could easily march up against them together with the Peloponnesians and prevent them from fortifying the city. He told the Council in confidence that he and certain others would go as ambassadors to Lacedaemon to explain the matter of the wall to the Lacedaemonians; and he instructed the magistrates, when ambassadors should come from Lacedaemon to Athens, to detain them until he himself should return from Lacedaemon, and in the meantime to put the whole population to work fortifying the city. In this manner, he declared to them, they would achieve their purpose.

### The war which the Romans waged against the Aequi and the inhabitants of Tusculum (40).

40. After the Athenians had accepted the plan of Themistocles, he and the ambassadors set out for Sparta, and the Athenians began with great enthusiasm to build the walls, sparing neither houses nor tombs. Everyone joined in the task, both children and women and, in a word, every alien and slave, no one of them showing any lack of zeal, and when the work was being accomplished with amazing speed both because of the many workmen and the enthusiasm of them all, Themistocles was summoned by the chief magistrates and upbraided for the building of the walls; but he denied that there was any construction, and urged the magistrates not to believe empty rumours but to dispatch to Athens trustworthy ambassadors, from whom, he assured them, they would learn the truth; and as surety for them he offered himself and the ambassadors who had accompanied him. The Lacedaemonians, following the advice of Themistocles, put him and his companions under guard and dispatched to Athens their most important men who were to spy out whatever matter should arouse their curiosity. Time had passed, and the Athenians had already got so far along with the construction that, when the Lacedaemonian ambassadors arrived in Athens and with denunciations and threats of violence upbraided them, the Athenians took them into custody, saying that they would release them only when the Lacedaemonians in turn should release the ambassadors who accompanied Themistocles. In this manner the Laconians were outgeneralled and compelled to release the Athenian ambassadors in order to get back their own, a Themistocles, having by means of so clever a stratagem fortified his native land speedily and without danger, enjoyed high favour among his fellow citizens.

While the events we have described were taking place, a war broke out between the Romans and the Aequi and the inhabitants of Tusculum, and meeting the Aequi in battle the Romans overcame them and slew many of the enemy, and then they took Tusculum after a siege and occupied the city of the Aequi.

## On the construction of the Peiraeus by Themistocles (41-50).

**41.** At the close of the year the archon in Athens was Adeimantus, [477] and in Rome the consuls elected were Marcus Fabius Vibulanus and Lucius Valerius Publius. At this time Themistocles, because of his skill as a general and his sagacity, was held in esteem not only by his fellow citizens but by all Greeks. He was, therefore, elated over his fame and had recourse to many other far more ambitious undertakings which would serve to increase the dominant position of his native state. Thus the Peiraeus, as it is called, was not at that time a harbour, but the Athenians were using as their ship-yard the bay called Phaleric, which was quite small; and so Themistocles conceived the plan of making the Peiraeus into a harbour, since it would require only a small amount of construction and could be made into a harbour, the best and largest in Greece. He also hoped that when this improvement had been added to what the Athenians possessed, the city would be able to compete for the hegemony at sea; for the Athenians possessed at that time the largest number of triremes and through an unbroken succession of battles at sea which the city had waged had gained experience and renown in naval conflicts. Furthermore, he reasoned that they would have the Ionians on their side because they were kinsmen, and that with their aid the Athenians would liberate the other Greeks of Asia, who would then turn in goodwill to the Athenians because of this benefaction, and that all the Greeks of the islands, being immensely impressed by the magnitude of their naval strength, would readily align themselves with the people which had the power both to inflict the greatest injury and to bestow the greatest advantages. For he saw that the Lacedaemonians, though excellently equipped so far as their land forces were concerned, had no natural talent for fighting on ships.

**42.** Now as Themistocles pondered these matters, he decided that he should not make public announcement of his plan, knowing with certainty that the Lacedaemonians would endeavour to stop it; and so he announced to the citizens in Assembly that he wished both to advise upon and to introduce important matters which were also to the advantage of the city. What these matters were, he added, it was not in the public interest to state openly, but it was fitting that a few men should be charged with putting them into effect; and he therefore asked the people to select two men in whom they had the greatest confidence and to entrust to them to pass upon the matter in question. The people acceded to his advice, and the Assembly chose two men, Aristeides and Xanthippus, selecting them not only because of their upright character, but also because they saw that these men were in active rivalry with Themistocles for glory and leadership and were therefore opposed to him. These men heard privately from Themistocles about his plan and then declared to the Assembly that what Themistocles had disclosed to them was of great importance, was to the advantage of the state, and was feasible.

The people admired the man and at the same time harboured suspicions of him, lest it should be with the purpose of preparing some sort of tyranny for

BOOK XI

himself that he was embarking upon plans of such magnitude and importance, and they urged him to declare openly what he had decided upon, but he made the same reply, that it was not to the interests of the state that there should be a public disclosure of his intentions. Thereupon the people were far the more amazed at the man's shrewdness and greatness of mind, and they urged him to disclose his ideas secretly to the Council, assuring him that, if that body decided that what he said was feasible and advantageous, then they would advise it to carry his plan to completion. Consequently, when the Council learned all the details and decided that what he said was for the advantage of the state and was feasible, the people, without more ado, agreed with the Council, and Themistocles received authority to do whatever he wished, and every man departed from the Assembly in admiration of the high character of the man, being also elated in spirit and expectant of the outcome of the plan.

43. Themistocles, having received authority to proceed and enjoying every assistance ready at hand for his undertakings, again conceived a way to deceive the Lacedaemonians by a stratagem; for he was fully assured that just as the Lacedaemonians had interfered with the building of the wall about the city, they would in the same manner endeavour to obstruct the plans of the Athenians in the case of the making of the harbour. Accordingly he decided to dispatch ambassadors to the Lacedaemonians to show them how it was to the advantage of the common interests of Greece that it should possess a first-rate harbour in view of the expedition which was to be expected on the part of the Persians. When he had in this way somewhat dulled the impulse of the Spartans to interfere, he devoted himself to that work, and since everybody enthusiastically co-operated it was speedily done and the harbour was finished before anyone expected. Themistocles persuaded the people each year to construct and add twenty triremes to the fleet they already possessed, and also to remove the tax upon metics and artisans, in order that great crowds of people might stream into the city from every quarter and that the Athenians might easily procure labour for a greater number of crafts. Both these policies he considered to be most useful in building up the city's naval forces. The Athenians, therefore, were busy over the matters we have described.

44. The Lacedaemonians, having appointed Pausanias, who had held the command at Plataea, admiral of their fleet, instructed him to liberate the Greek cities which were still held by barbarian garrisons. Taking fifty triremes from the Peloponnesus and summoning from the Athenians thirty commanded by Aristeides, he first of all sailed to Cyprus and liberated those cities which still had Persian garrisons; and after this he sailed to the Hellespont and took Byzantium, which was held by the Persians, and of the other barbarians some he slew and others he expelled, and thus liberated the city, but many important Persians whom he captured in the city he turned over to Gongylus of Eretria to guard. Ostensibly Gongylus was to keep these men for punishment, but actually he was to get them off safe to Xerxes; for Pausanias had secretly made a pact of

361

friendship with the king and was about to marry the daughter of Xerxes, his purpose being to betray the Greeks. The man who was acting as negotiator in this affair was the general Artabazus, and he was quietly supplying Pausanias with large sums of money to be used in corrupting such Greeks as could serve their ends.

The plan of Pausanias, however, was brought to light and he got his punishment in the following manner. Pausanias emulated the luxurious life of the Persians and dealt with his subordinates in the manner of a tyrant, so that they were all angry with him, and especially those Greeks who had been assigned to some command. Consequently, while many, as they mingled together in the army both by peoples and by cities, were railing at the harshness of Pausanias, some Peloponnesians deserted him and sailed back to the Peloponnesus, and dispatching ambassadors to Sparta they lodged an accusation against Pausanias; and Aristeides the Athenian, making wise use of the opportunity, in the course of his public conferences with the states won them over and by his personal intimacy with them made them adherents of the Athenians, but even more did matters play by mere chance into the hands of the Athenians by reason of the following facts.

**45.** Pausanias had stipulated that the men who carried the messages from him to the king should not return and thus become betrayers of their secret communications; consequently, since they were being put to death by the receivers of the letters, no one of them was ever returning alive. So one of the couriers, reasoning from this fact, opened his letters, and discovering that his inference was correct as to the killing of all who carried the messages, he turned the letters over to the ephors. When the ephors were loath to believe this, because the letters had been turned over to them already opened, and demanded further and more substantial proof, the man offered to produce Pausanias acknowledging the facts in person. Consequently he went to Taenarum, and seating himself as a suppliant at the shrine of Poseidon he set up a tent with two rooms and concealed the ephors and certain other Spartans; and when Pausanias came to him and asked why he was a suppliant, the man upbraided him for directing in the letter that he should be put to death. Pausanias said that he was sorry and went on to ask the man to forgive the mistake; he even implored him to help keep the matter secret, promising him great gifts, and the two then parted. As for the ephors and the others with them, although they had learned the precise truth, at that time they held their peace, but on a later occasion, when the Lacedaemonians were taking up the matter together with the ephors, Pausanias learned of it in advance, acted first, and fled for safety into the temple, of Athena of the Brazen House, and while the Lacedaemonians were hesitating whether to punish him now that he was a suppliant, we are told that the mother of Pausanias, coming to the temple, neither said nor did anything else than to pick up a brick and lay it against the entrance of the temple, and after she had done this she returned to her home. The Lacedaemonians, falling in with the mother's decision, walled up the entrance and in this manner forced Pausanias to meet his end through starvation. Now the body of the dead man was turned over to his relatives for burial; but the divinity showed its displeasure at the violation of the sanctity of suppliants, for once when the Lacedaemonians were consulting the oracle at Delphi about some other matters, the god replied by commanding them to restore her suppliant to the goddess. Consequently the Spartans, thinking the oracle's command to be impracticable, were at a loss for a considerable time, being unable to carry out the injunction of the god. Concluding, however, to do as much as was within their power, they made two bronze statues of Pausanias and set them up in the temple of Athena.

**46.** As for us, since throughout our entire history we have made it our practice in the case of good men to enhance their glory by means of the words of praise we pronounce over them, and in the case of bad men, when they die, to utter the appropriate obloquies, we shall not leave the turpitude and treachery of Pausanias to go un-condemned. For who would not be amazed at the folly of this man who, though he had been a benefactor of Greece, had won the battle of Plataea, and had performed many other deeds which won applause, not only failed to safeguard the esteem he enjoyed but by his love of the wealth and luxury of the Persians brought dishonour upon the good name he already possessed? Indeed, elated by his successes he came to abhor the Laconian manner of life and to imitate the licentiousness and luxury of the Persians, he who least of all had reason to emulate the customs of the barbarians; for he had not learned of them from others, but in person by actual contact he had made trial of them and was aware how greatly superior with respect to virtue his ancestors' way of life was to the luxury of the Persians.

In truth because of his own baseness Pausanias not only himself received the punishment he deserved, but he also brought it about that his countrymen lost the supremacy at sea. In comparison, for instance, take the fine tact of Aristeides in dealing with the allies: when they took note of it, both because of his affability toward his subordinates and his uprightness in general, it caused them all as with one impulse to incline toward the Athenian cause. Consequently the allies no longer paid any heed to the commanders who were sent from Sparta, but in their admiration of Aristeides they eagerly submitted to him in every matter and thus brought it about that he received the supreme command by sea without having to fight for it.

**47.** At once, then, Aristeides advised all the allies as they were holding a general assembly to designate the island of Delos as their common treasury and to deposit there all the money they collected, and towards the war which they suspected would come from the Persians to impose a levy upon all the cities according to their means, so that the entire sum collected would amount to five hundred and sixty talents, and when he was appointed to allocate the levy, he distributed the sum so accurately and justly that all the cities consented to it. Consequently, since he was considered to have accomplished an impossible thing, he won for himself a very high reputation for justice, and because he excelled in that virtue he was given the epithet of "the Just." Thus at one and the same time the baseness of Pausanias deprived his countrymen of the supremacy on the sea, and the all-round virtue of Aristeides caused Athens to gain the leadership which she had not possessed before.

These, then, were the events of this year.

**48.** When Phaedon was archon in Athens, [476] the Seventy-sixth Olympiad was celebrated, that in which Scamandrius of Mytilene won the "stadion," and in Rome the consuls were Caeso Fabius and Spurius Furius Menellaeus. In the course of this year Leotychides, the king of the Lacedaemonians, died after a reign of twenty-two years, and he was succeeded on the throne by Archidamus, who ruled for forty-two years. There died also Anaxilas, the tyrant of Rhegium and Zanclê, after a rule of eighteen years, and he was succeeded in the tyranny by Micythus, who was entrusted with the position on the understanding that he would restore it to the sons of Anaxilas, who were not yet of age. Hieron, who became king of the Syracusans after the death of Gelon, observing how popular his brother Polyzelus was among the Syracusans and believing that he was waiting to seize the kingship, was eager to put him out of the way, and so, enlisting foreign soldiers and gathering about his person an organised body of mercenaries, he thought that by these means he could hold the kingship securely. So, when the Sybarites were being besieged by the Crotoniates and called on Hieron for help, he enrolled many soldiers in the army, which he then put under the command of his brother Polyzelus in the belief that he would be slain by the Crotoniates. When Polyzelus, suspecting what we have mentioned, refused to undertake the campaign, Hieron was enraged at his brother, and when Polyzelus took refuge with Theron, the tyrant of Acragas, he began making preparation for war upon Theron.

Subsequently to these events, Thrasydaeus the son of Theron was governing the city of Himera more harshly than was proper, and the result was that the Himerans became altogether alienated from him. Now they rejected the idea of going to his father and entering an accusation with him, since they did not believe they would have in him a fair listener; but they dispatched to Hieron ambassadors, who presented their complaints against Thrasydaeus and offered to hand Himera over to Hieron and join him in his attack upon Theron. Hieron, however, having decided to be at peace with Theron, betrayed the Himerans and disclosed to him their secret plans. Consequently Theron, after examining into the reported plan and finding the information to be true, composed his differences with Hieron and restored Polyzelus to the favour he had previously enjoyed, and then he arrested his opponents, who were many, among the Himerans and put them to death.

**49.** Hieron removed the people of Naxos and Catana from their cities and sent there settlers of his own choosing, having gathered five thousand from the Peloponnesus and added an equal number of others from Syracuse; and the name of Catana he changed to Aetna, and not only the territory of Catana but also much neighbouring land which he added to it he portioned out in allotments, up to the full sum of ten thousand settlers. This he did out of a desire, not only that he might have a substantial help ready at hand for any need that might arise, but also that from the recently founded state of ten thousand men he might receive the honours accorded to heroes. The Naxians and Catanians whom he had removed from their native states he transferred to Leontini and commanded them to make their homes in that city along with the native population. Theron, seeing that after the slaughter of the Himerans the city was in need of settlers, made a mixed multitude there, enrolling as its citizens both Dorians and any others who so wished. These citizens lived together on good terms in the state for fifty-eight years; but at the expiration of this period the city was conquered and razed to the ground by the Carthaginians [408] and has remained without inhabitants to this day.

**50.** When Dromocleides was archon in Athens, [475] the Romans elected as consuls Marcus Fabius and Gnaeus Manlius. In this year the Lacedaemonians, now that for no good reason they had lost the command of the sea, were resentful; consequently they were incensed at the Greeks who had fallen away from them and continued to threaten them with the appropriate punishment. When a meeting of the Gerousia was convened, they considered making war upon the Athenians for the sake of regaining the command of the sea. Likewise, when the general Assembly was convened, the younger men and the majority of the others were eager to recover the leadership, believing that, if they could secure it, they would enjoy great wealth, Sparta in general would be made greater and more powerful, and the estates of its private citizens would receive a great increase of prosperity. They kept calling to mind also the ancient oracle in which the god commanded them to beware lest their leadership should be a "lame" one, and the oracle, they insisted, meant nothing other than the present; for "lame" indeed their rule would be if, having two leaderships, they should lose one of them.

Since practically all the citizens had been eager for this course of action and the Gerousia was in session to consider these matters, no one entertained the hope that any man would have the temerity to suggest any other course; but a member of the Gerousia, Hetomaridas by name, who was a direct descendant of Heracles and enjoyed favour among the citizens by reason of his character, undertook to advise that they leave the Athenians with their leadership, since it was not to Sparta's interest, he declared, to lay claim to the sea. He was able to bring pertinent arguments in support of his surprising proposal, so that, against the expectation of all, he won over both the Gerousia and the people. In the end the Lacedaemonians decided that the opinion of Hetoemaridas was to their advantage and abandoned their zest for the war against the Athenians. As for the Athenians, at first they expected to have a great war with the Lacedaemonians for the command of the sea, and for this reason were building additional triremes, raising a large sum of money, and dealing honourably with their allies; but when they learned of the decision of the Lacedaemonians, they were relieved of their fear of war and set about increasing the power of their city.

### On the aid which king Hiero dispatched to the Cymaeans (51).

51. When Acestorides was archon in Athens, [474] in Rome Caeso Fabius and Titus Verginius succeeded to the consulship, and in this year Hieron, the king of the Syracusans, when ambassadors came to him from Cumae in Italy and asked his aid in the war which the Tyrrhenians, who were at that time masters of the sea, were waging against them, he dispatched to their aid a considerable number of triremes. After the commanders of this fleet had put in at Cumae, joining with the men of that region they fought a naval battle with the Tyrrhenians, and destroying many of their ships and conquering them in a great sea-fight, they humbled the Tyrrhenians and delivered the Cumaeans from their fears, after which they sailed back to Syracuse.

### On the war which arose between the Tarantini and the Iapyges (52).

52. When Menon was archon in Athens, [473] the Romans chose as consuls Lucius Aemilius Mamercus and Gaius Cornelius Lentulus, and in Italy a war broke out between the Tarantini and the Iapygians. For these peoples, disputing with each other over some land on their borders, had been engaging for some years in skirmishing and in raiding each other's territory, and since the difference between them kept constantly increasing and frequently resulted in deaths, they finally went headlong into out-and-out contention. Now the Iapygians not only made ready the army of their own men but they also joined with them an auxiliary force of their neighbours, collecting in this way a total body of more than twenty thousand soldiers; and the Tarantini, on learning of the great size of the army gathered against them, both mustered the soldiers of their state and added to them many more of the Rhegians, who were their allies. A fierce battle took place and many fell on both sides, but in the end the Iapygians were victorious. When the defeated army split in the flight into two bodies, the one retreating to Tarentum and the other fleeing to Rhegium, the Iapygians, following their example, also divided. Those who pursued the Tarantini, the distance being short, slew many of the enemy, but those who were pressing after the Rhegians were so eager that they broke into Rhegium together with the fugitives and took possession of the city.

### How Thrasydaeus, the son of Theron and tyrant of the Acragantini, was defeated by the Syracusans and lost his overlordship (53).

53. The next year Chares was archon in Athens, [472] and in Rome the consuls elected were Titus Menenius and Gaius Horatius Pulvillus, and the Eleians celebrated the Seventy-seventh Olympiad, that in which Dandes of Argos won the stadion. In this year in Sicily Theron, the despot of Acragas, died after a reign of sixteen years, and his son Thrasydaeus succeeded to the throne. Now Theron, since he had administered his office equitably, not only enjoyed great

favour among his countrymen during his lifetime, but also upon his death he was accorded the honours which are paid to heroes; but his son, even while his father was still living, was violent and murderous, and after his father's death ruled over his native city without respect for the laws and like a tyrant. Consequently he quickly lost the confidence of his subjects and was the constant object of plots, living a life of execration; and so he soon came to an end befitting his own lawlessness. For Thrasydaeus after the death of his father Theron gathered many mercenary soldiers and enrolled also citizens of Acragas and Himera, and thus got together in all more than twenty thousand cavalry and infantry. Since he was preparing to make war with these troops upon the Syracusans, Hieron the king made ready a formidable army and marched upon Acragas. A fierce battle took place, and a very large number fell, since Greeks were marshalled against Greeks. Now the fight was won by the Syracusans, who lost some two thousand men against more than four thousand for their opponents. Thereupon Thrasydaeus, having been humbled, was expelled from his position, and fleeing to Nisaean Megara, as it is called, he was there condemned to death and met his end; and the Acragantini, having now recovered their democratic form of government, sent ambassadors to Hieron and secured peace.

In Italy war broke out between the Romans and the Veiians and a great battle was fought at the site called Cremera. The Romans were defeated and many of them perished, among their number, according to some historians, being the three hundred Fabii, who were of the same gens and hence were included under the single name.

These, then, were the events of this year.

### *How Themistocles, who had fled for safety to Xerxes and was put on trial for his life, was set at liberty (54-59).*

**54.** When Praxiergus was archon in Athens, [471] the Romans elected as consuls Aulus Verginius Tricostus and Gaius Servilius Structus. At this time the Eleians, who dwelt in many small cities, united to form one state which is known as Elis. The Lacedaemonians, seeing that Sparta was in a humbled state by reason of the treason of their general Pausanias, whereas the Athenians were in good repute because no one of their citizens had been found guilty of treason, were eager to involve Athens in similar discreditable charges. Consequently, since Themistocles was greatly esteemed by the Athenians and enjoyed great fame for his high character, they accused him of treason, maintaining that he had been a close friend of Pausanias and had agreed with him that together they would betray Greece to Xerxes. They also carried on conversations with the enemies of Themistocles, inciting them to lodge an accusation against him, and gave them money; and they explained that, when Pausanias decided to betray the Greeks, he disclosed the plan he had to Themistocles and urged him to participate in the project, and that Themistocles neither agreed to the request nor decided that it was his duty to accuse a man who was his friend. At any rate a charge was brought against Themistocles, but at the time he was not found guilty of treason. Hence at first after he was absolved he stood high in the opinion of the Athenians; for his fellow citizens were exceedingly fond of him on account of his achievements. But afterwards those who feared the eminence he enjoyed, and others who were envious of his glory forgot his services to the state, and began to exert themselves to diminish his power and to lower his presumption.

55. First of all they removed Themistocles from Athens, employing against him what is called ostracism, an institution which was adopted in Athens after the overthrow of the tyranny of Peisistratus and his sons; and the law was as follows. Each citizen wrote on a piece of pottery (*ostracon*) the name of the man who in his opinion had the greatest power to destroy the democracy; and the man who got the largest number of ostraca was obliged by the law to go into exile from his native land for a period of five years. The Athenians, it appears, passed such a law, not for the purpose of punishing wrongdoing, but in order to lower through exile the presumption of men who had risen too high. Now Themistocles, having been ostracised in the manner we have described, fled as an exile from his native city to Argos. The Lacedaemonians, learning of this and considering that Fortune had given them a favourable moment to attack Themistocles, again dispatched ambassadors to Athens. These accused Themistocles of complicity in the treason of Pausanias, and asserted that his trial, since their crimes affected all Greece, should not be held privately among the Athenians alone but rather before the General Congress of the Greeks which, according to custom, was to meet at that time.

Themistocles, seeing that the Lacedaemonians were bent upon defaming and humbling the Athenian state, and that the Athenians were anxious to clear themselves of the charge against them, assumed that he would be turned over to the General Congress. This body, he knew, made its decisions, not on the basis of justice, but out of favour to the Lacedaemonians, inferring this not only from its other actions but also from what it had done in making the awards for valour. For in that instance those who controlled the voting showed such jealousy of the Athenians that, although these had contributed more triremes than all the others who took part in the battle, they made them out to be no whit better than the rest of the Greeks. These, then, were the reasons why Themistocles distrusted the members of the Congress. Furthermore, it was from the speech in his own defence which Themistocles had made in Athens on the former occasion that the Lacedaemonians had got the basis for the accusation they afterwards made. For in that defence Themistocles had acknowledged that Pausanias had sent letters to him, urging him to share in the act of treason, and using this as the strongest piece of evidence in his behalf, he had established that Pausanias would not have urged him, unless he had opposed his first request.

56. It was for these reasons, as we have stated above, that Themistocles fled from Argos to Admetus, the king of the Molossians; and taking refuge at Admetus' hearth he became his suppliant. The king at first received him kindly, urged him to be of good courage, and, in general, assured him that he would

provide for his safety; but when the Lacedaemonians dispatched some of the most distinguished Spartans as ambassadors to Admetus and demanded the person of Themistocles for punishment, stigmatising him as the betrayer and destroyer of the whole Greek world, and when they went further and declared that, if Admetus would not turn him over to them, they together with all the Greeks would make war on him, then indeed the king, fearing on the one hand the threats and yet pitying the suppliant and seeking to avoid the disgrace of handing him over, persuaded Themistocles to make his escape with all speed without the knowledge of the Lacedaemonians and gave him a large sum of gold to meet his expenses on the flight. Themistocles, being persecuted as he was on every side, accepted the gold and fled by night out of the territory of the Molossians, the king furthering his flight in every way; and finding two young men, Lyncestians by birth, who were traders and therefore familiar with the roads, he made his escape in their company. By travelling only at night he eluded the Lacedaemonians, and by virtue of the goodwill of the young men and the hardship they endured for him he made his way to Asia. Here Themistocles had a personal friend, Lysitheides by name, who was highly regarded for his fame and wealth, and to him he fled for refuge.

Now it so happened that Lysitheides was a friend of Xerxes the king and on the occasion of his passage through Asia Minor had entertained the entire Persian host. Consequently, since he enjoyed an intimate acquaintance with the king and yet wished out of mercy to save Themistocles, he promised to co-operate with him in every way, but when Themistocles asked that he lead him to Xerxes, at first he demurred, explaining that Themistocles would be punished because of his past activities against the Persians; later, however, when he realised that it was for the best, he acceded, and unexpectedly and without harm he got him through safe to Persia. For it was a custom among the Persians that when one conducted a concubine to the king one brought her in a closed wagon, and no man who met it interfered or came face to face with the passenger; and it came about that Lysitheides availed himself of this means of carrying out his undertaking. After preparing the wagon and embellishing it with costly hangings he put Themistocles in it; and when he had got him through in entire safety, he came into the presence of the king, and after he had conversed with him cautiously he received pledges from the king that he would do Themistocles no wrong. Then Lysitheides introduced him to the presence of the king, who, when he had allowed Themistocles to speak and learned that he had done the king no wrong, absolved him from punishment.

**57.** But when it seemed that the life of Themistocles had unexpectedly been saved by an enemy, he fell again into even greater dangers for the following reasons. Mandane was the daughter of the Darius who had slain the Magi and the full sister of Xerxes, and she enjoyed high esteem among the Persians. She had lost her sons at the time Themistocles had defeated the Persian fleet in the sea-battle at Salamis and sorely grieved over the death of her children, and because of her great affliction she was the object of the pity of the people. When she learned of the presence of Themistocles, she went to the palace clad in raiment of mourning and with tears entreated her brother to wreak vengeance upon Themistocles. And when the king paid no heed to her, she visited in turn the noblest Persians with her request and, speaking generally, spurred on the people to vengeance upon Themistocles. When the mob rushed to the palace and with loud shouts demanded the person of Themistocles for punishment, the king replied that he would form a jury of the noblest Persians and that its verdict would be carried out. This decision was approved by all, and since a considerable time was given to make the preparations for the trial, Themistocles meanwhile learned the Persian language, and using it in his defence he was acquitted of the charges. The king was overjoyed that Themistocles had been saved and honoured him with great gifts; so, for example, he gave him in marriage a Persian woman, who was of outstanding birth and beauty and, besides, praised for her virtue, and [she brought as her dower] not only a multitude of household slaves for their service but also of drinking-cups of every kind and such other furnishings as comport with a life of pleasure and luxury. Furthermore, the king made him a present also of three cities which were well suited for his support and enjoyment, Magnesia upon the Maeander River, which had more grain than any city of Asia, for bread, Myus for meat, since the sea there abounded in fish, and Lampsacus, whose territory contained extensive vineyards, for wine.

**58.** Themistocles, being now relieved of the fear which he had felt when among Greeks, the man who had unexpectedly, on the one hand, been driven into exile by those who had profited most by the benefits he had bestowed and, on the other, had received benefits from those who had suffered the most grievously at his hands, spent his life in the cities we have mentioned, being well supplied with all the good things that conduce to pleasure, and at his death he was given a notable funeral in Magnesia and a monument that stands even to this day. Some historians say that Xerxes, desiring to lead a second expedition against Greece, invited Themistocles to take command of the war, and that he agreed to do so and received from the king guaranties under oath that he would not march against the Greeks without Themistocles. When a bull had been sacrificed and the oaths taken, Themistocles, filling a cup with its blood, drank it down and immediately died. They add that Xerxes thereupon relinquished that plan of his, and that Themistocles by his voluntary death left the best possible defence that he had played the part of a good citizen in all matters affecting the interests of Greece.

We have come to the death of one of the greatest of the Greeks, about whom many dispute whether it was because he had wronged his native city and the other Greeks that he fled to the Persians, or whether, on the contrary, his city and all the Greeks, after enjoying great benefits at his hands, forgot to be grateful for them but unjustly plunged him, their benefactor, into the uttermost perils, but if any man, putting envy aside, will estimate closely not only the man's natural gifts but also his achievements, he will find that on both counts Themistocles holds first place among all of whom we have record. Therefore one may well be amazed that the Athenians were willing to rid themselves of a man of such genius.

**59.** What other man, while Sparta still had the superior strength and the Spartan Eurybiades held the supreme command of the fleet, could by his singlehanded efforts have deprived Sparta of that glory? Of what other man have we learned from history that by a single act he caused himself to surpass all the commanders, his city all the other Greek states, and the Greeks the barbarians? In whose term as general have the resources been more inferior and the dangers they faced greater? Who, facing the united might of all Asia, has found himself at the side of his city when its inhabitants had been driven from their homes, and still won the victory? Who in time of peace has made his fatherland powerful by deeds comparable to his? Who, when a gigantic war enveloped his state, brought it safely through and by the one single ruse of the bridge reduced the land armament of the enemy by half, so that it could be easily vanquished by the Greeks? Consequently, when we survey the magnitude of his deeds and, examining them one by one, find that such a man suffered disgrace at the hands of his city, whereas it was by his deeds that the city rose to greatness, we have good reason to conclude that the city which is reputed to rank highest among all cities in wisdom and fair-dealing acted towards him with great cruelty.

Now on the subject of the high merits of Themistocles, even if we have dwelt over-long on the subject in this digression, we believed it not seemly that we should leave his great ability unrecorded.

While these events were taking place, in Italy Micythus, who was ruler of Rhegium and Zancle, founded the city of Pyxus.

### How the Athenians freed the Greek cities throughout Asia (60-62).

**60.** When Demotion was archon in Athens, [470] the Romans elected as consuls Publius Valerius Publicola and Gaius Nautius Rufus. In this year the Athenians, electing as general Cimon the son of Miltiades and giving him a strong force, sent him to the coast of Asia to give aid to the cities which were allied with them and to liberate those which were still held by Persian garrisons. Cimon, taking along the fleet which was at Byzantium and putting in at the city which is called Eïon, took it from the Persians who were holding it and captured by siege Scyros, which was inhabited by Pelasgians and Dolopes; and setting up an Athenian as the founder of a colony he portioned out the land in allotments. After this, with a mind to begin greater enterprises, he put in at the Peiraeus, and after adding more triremes to his fleet and arranging for general supplies on a notable scale, he at that time put to sea with two hundred triremes; but later, when he had called for additional ships from the Ionians and everyone else, he had in all three hundred. So sailing with the entire fleet to Caria he at once succeeded in persuading the cities on the coast which had been settled from

Greece to revolt from the Persians, but as for the cities whose inhabitants spoke two languages and still had Persian garrisons, he had recourse to force and laid siege to them; then, after he had brought over to his side the cities of Caria, he likewise won over by persuasion those of Lycia. Also, by taking additional ships from the allies, who were continually being added, he still further increased the size of his fleet.

Now the Persians had composed their land forces from their own peoples, but their navy they had gathered from both Phoenicia and Cyprus and Cilicia, and the commander of the Persian armaments was Tithraustes, who was an illegitimate son of Xerxes. And when Cimon learned that the Persian fleet was lying off Cyprus, sailing against the barbarians he engaged them in battle, pitting two hundred and fifty ships against three hundred and forty. A sharp struggle took place and both fleets fought brilliantly, but in the end the Athenians were victorious, having destroyed many of the enemy ships and captured more than one hundred together with their crews. The rest of the ships escaped to Cyprus, where their crews left them and took to the land, and the ships, being bare of defenders, fell into the hands of the enemy.

**61.** Thereupon Cimon, not satisfied with a victory of such magnitude, set sail at once with his entire fleet against the Persian land army, which was then encamped on the bank of the Eurymedon River [Pisidia], and wishing to overcome the barbarians by a stratagem, he manned the captured Persian ships with his own best men, giving them tiaras for their heads and clothing them in the Persian fashion generally. The barbarians, so soon as the fleet approached them, were deceived by the Persian ships and garb and supposed the triremes to be their own. Consequently they received the Athenians as if they were friends, and Cimon, night having fallen, disembarked his soldiers, and being received by the Persians as a friend, he fell upon their encampment. A great tumult arose among the Persians, and the soldiers of Cimon cut down all who came in their way, and seizing in his tent Pherendates, one of the two generals of the barbarians and a nephew of the king, they slew him; and as for the rest of the Persians, some they cut down and others they wounded, and all of them, because of the unexpectedness of the attack, they forced to take flight. In a word, such consternation as well as bewilderment prevailed among the Persians that most of them did not even know who it was that was attacking them. For they had no idea that the Greeks had come against them in force, being persuaded that they had no land army at all; and they assumed that it was the Pisidians, who dwelt in neighbouring territory and were hostile to them, who had come to attack them. Consequently, thinking that the attack of the enemy was coming from the mainland, they fled to their ships in the belief they were in friendly hands. Since it was a dark night without a moon, their bewilderment was increased all the more and not a man was able to discern the true state of affairs. Consequently, after a great slaughter had occurred on account of the disorder among the barbarians, Cimon, who had previously given orders to the soldiers to come

# BOOK XI

running to the torch which would be raised, had the signal raised beside the ships, being anxious lest, if the soldiers should scatter and turn to plundering, some miscarriage of his plans might occur. When the soldiers had all been gathered at the torch and had stopped plundering, for the time being they withdrew to the ships, and on the following day they set up a trophy and then sailed back to Cyprus, having won two glorious victories, the one on land and the other on the sea; for not to this day has history recorded the occurrence of so unusual and so important actions on the same day by a host that fought both afloat and on land.

62. After Cimon had won these great successes by means of his own skill as general and his valour, his fame was noised abroad not only among his fellow citizens but among all other Greeks as well. For he had captured three hundred and forty ships, more than twenty thousand men, and a considerable sum of money. The Persians, having met with so great reverses, built other triremes in greater number, since they feared the growing might of the Athenians. For from this time the Athenian state kept receiving significant enhancement of its power, supplied as it was with an abundance of funds and having attained to great renown for courage and for able leadership in war, and the Athenian people, taking a tenth part of the booty, dedicated it to the god, and the inscription which they wrote upon the dedication they made ran as follows:

> E'en from the day when the sea divided Europe from Asia,
> And the impetuous god, Ares, the cities of men
> Took for his own, no deed such as this among earth-dwelling mortals
> Ever was wrought at one time both upon land and at sea.
> These men indeed upon Cyprus sent many a Mede to destruction,
> Capturing out on the sea warships a hundred in sum
> Filled with Phoenician men; and deeply all Asia grieved o'er them,
> Smitten thus with both hands, vanquished by war's mighty power.

**On the earthquake that occurred in Laconia (63). On the revolt of the Messenians and Helots against the Lacedaemonians (63-64).**

63. Such, then, were the events of this year.

When Phaeon was archon in Athens, [469] in Rome the consulship was taken over by Lucius Furius Mediolanus and Marcus Manilius Vaso. During this year a great and incredible catastrophe befell the Lacedaemonians; for great earthquakes occurred in Sparta, and as a result the houses collapsed from their foundations and more than twenty thousand Lacedaemonians perished. Since the tumbling down of the city and the falling in of the houses continued uninterruptedly over a long period, many persons were caught and crushed in the collapse of the walls and no little household property was ruined by the quake. Although they suffered this disaster because some god, as it were, was wreaking his anger upon them, it so happened that other dangers befell them at the hands of men for the following reasons. The Helots and Messenians, although enemies of the Lacedaemonians, had remained quiet up to this time, since they stood in fear of the eminent position and power of Sparta; but when they observed that the larger part of them had perished because of the earthquake, they held in contempt the survivors, who were few. Consequently they came to an agreement with each other and joined together in the war against the Lacedaemonians. The king of the Lacedaemonians, Archidamus, by his personal foresight not only was the saviour of his fellow citizens even during the earthquake, but in the course of the war also he bravely fought the aggressors. For instance, when the terrible earthquake struck Sparta, he was the first Spartan to seize his armour and hasten from the city into the country, calling upon the other citizens to follow his example. The Spartans obeyed him and thus those who survived the shock were saved and these men King Archidamus organised into an army and prepared to make war upon the revolters.

**64.** The Messenians together with the Helots at first advanced against the city of Sparta, assuming that they would take it because there would be no one to defend it; but when they heard that the survivors were drawn up in a body with Archidamus the king and were ready for the struggle on behalf of their native land, they gave up this plan, and seizing a stronghold in Messenia they made it their base of operations and from there continued to overrun Laconia. The Spartans, turning for help to the Athenians, received from them an army; and they gathered troops as well from the rest of their allies and thus became able to meet their enemy on equal terms. At the outset they were much superior to the enemy, but at a later time, when a suspicion arose that the Athenians were about to go over to the Messenians, they broke the alliance with them, stating as their reason that in the other allies they had sufficient men to meet the impending battle. The Athenians, although they believed that they had suffered an affront, at the time did no more than withdraw; later, however, their relations to the Lacedaemonians being unfriendly, they were more and more inclined to fan the flames of hatred. Consequently the Athenians took this incident as the first cause of the estrangement of the two states, and later on they quarrelled and, embarking upon great wars, filled all Greece with vast calamities. We shall give an account of these matters severally in connection with the appropriate periods of time. At the time in question the Lacedaemonians together with their allies marched forth against Ithomê and laid siege to it, and the Helots, revolting in a body from the Lacedaemonians, joined as allies with the Messenians, and at one time they were winning and at another losing. Since for ten years no decision could be reached in the war, for that length of time they never ceased injuring each other.

### How the Argives razed Mycenae to the ground and made the city desolate (65)

**65.** The following year Theageneides was archon in Athens, [468] and in Rome the consuls elected were Lucius Aemilius Mamercus and Lucius Julius Iulus, and the Seventy-eighth Olympiad was celebrated, that in which Parmenides of Posidonia won the stadion. In this year a war broke out between the Argives and Mycenaeans for the following reasons. The Mycenaeans, because of the ancient prestige of their country, would not be subservient to the Argives as the other cities of Argolis were, but they maintained an independent position and would take no orders from the Argives; and they kept disputing with them also over the shrine of Hera and claiming that they had the right to administer the Nemean Games by themselves. Furthermore, when the Argives voted not to join with the Lacedaemonians in the battle at Thermopylae unless they were given a share in the supreme command, the Mycenaeans were the only people of Argolis who fought at the side of the Lacedaemonians. In a word, the Argives were suspicious of the Mycenaeans, fearing lest, if they got any stronger, they might, on the strength of the ancient prestige of Mycenae, dispute the right of Argos to the leadership. Such, then, were the reasons for the bad blood between them; and from of old the Argives had ever been eager to exalt their city, and now they thought they had a favourable opportunity, seeing that the Lacedaemonians had been weakened and were unable to come to the aid of the Mycenaeans. Therefore the Argives, gathering a strong army from both Argos and the cities of their allies, marched against the Mycenaeans, and after defeating them in battle and shutting them within their walls, they laid siege to the city. The Mycenaeans for a time resisted the besiegers with vigour, but afterwards, since they were being worsted in the fighting and the Lacedaemonians could bring them no aid because of their own wars and the disaster that had overtaken them in the earthquakes, and since there were no other allies, they were taken by storm through lack of support from outside. The Argives sold the Mycenaeans into slavery, dedicated a tenth part of them to the god, and razed Mycenae. So this city, which in ancient times had enjoyed such felicity, possessing great men and having to its credit memorable achievements, met with such an end, and has remained uninhabited down to our own times.

These, then, were the events of this year.

**66.** When Lysistratus was archon in Athens, [467] the Romans elected as consuls Lucius Pinarius Mamertinus and Publius Furius Fifron. In this year Hieron, the king of the Syracusans, summoning to Syracuse the sons of Anaxilas, the former tyrant of Zanclê, and giving them great gifts, reminded them of the benefactions Gelon had rendered their father, and advised them, now that they had come of age, to require an accounting of Micythus, their guardian, and themselves to take over the government of Zanclê. And when they had returned to Rhegium and required of their guardian an accounting of his administration, Micythus, who was an upright man, gathered together the old family friends of the children and rendered so honest an accounting that all present were filled with admiration of both his justice and good faith; and the children, regretting the steps they had taken, begged Micythus to take back the administration and to conduct the affairs of the state with a father's power and position. Micythus, however, did not accede to the request, but after turning everything over to them punctiliously and putting his own goods aboard a boat he set sail from Rhegium, accompanied by the goodwill of the populace; and reaching Greece he spent the rest of his life in Tegea in Arcadia, enjoying the approval of men. Hieron, the king of the Syracusans, died in Catana and received the honours which are accorded to heroes, as having been the founder of the city. He had ruled eleven years, and he left the kingdom to his brother Thrasybulus, who ruled over the Syracusans for one year.

### How the Syracusans overthrew the royal line of Gelon (67-68).

67. When Lysanias was archon in Athens, [466] the Romans elected as consuls Appius Claudius and Titus Quinctius Capitolinus. During this year Thrasybulus, the king of the Syracusans, was driven from his throne, and since we are writing a detailed account of this event, we must go back a few years and set forth clearly the whole story from the beginning.

Gelon, the son of Deinomenes, who far excelled all other men in valour and strategy and out- generalled the Carthaginians, defeated these barbarians in a great battle, as has been told; and since he treated the peoples whom he had subdued with fairness and, in general, conducted himself humanely toward all his immediate neighbours, he enjoyed high favour among the Sicilian Greeks. Thus Gelon, being beloved by all because of his mild rule, lived in uninterrupted peace until his death; but Hieron, the next oldest among the brothers, who succeeded to the throne, did not rule over his subjects in the same manner; for he was avaricious and violent and, speaking generally, an utter stranger to sincerity and nobility of character. Consequently there were a good many who wished to revolt, but they restrained their inclinations because of Gelon's reputation and the goodwill he had shown towards all the Sicilian Greeks. After the death of Hieron, however, his brother Thrasybulus, who succeeded to the throne, surpassed in wickedness his predecessor in the kingship. For being a violent man and murderous by nature, he put to death many citizens unjustly and drove not a few into exile on false charges, confiscating their possessions into the royal treasury; and since, speaking generally, he hated those he had wronged and was hated by them, he enlisted a large body of mercenaries, preparing in this way a legion with which to oppose the citizen soldiery. Since he kept incurring more and more the hatred of the citizens by outraging many and executing others, he compelled the victims to revolt. Consequently the Syracusans, choosing men who would take the lead, set about as one man to destroy the tyranny, and once they had been organised by their leaders they clung stubbornly to their freedom. When Thrasybulus saw that the whole city was in arms against him, he at first attempted to stop the revolt by persuasion; but after he observed that the movement of the Syracusans could not be halted, he gathered together both the colonists whom Hieron had settled in Catana and his other allies, as well as a multitude of mercenaries, so that his army numbered all told almost fifteen thousand men. Then, seizing Achradine, as it is called, and the Island, which was fortified, and using them as bases, he began a war upon the revolting citizens.

**68.** The Syracusans at the outset seized a part of the city which is called Tyche, and operating from there they dispatched ambassadors to Gela, Acragas, and Selinus, and also to Himera and the cities of the Siceli in the interior of the island, asking them to come together with all speed and join with them in liberating Syracuse. Since all these cities acceded to this request eagerly and hurriedly dispatched aid, some of them infantry and cavalry and others warships fully equipped for action, in a brief time there was collected a considerable armament with which to aid the Syracusans. Consequently the Syracusans, having made ready their ships and drawn up their army for battle, demonstrated that they were ready to fight to a finish both on land and on sea. Now Thrasybulus, abandoned as he was by his allies and basing his hopes only upon the mercenaries, was master only of Achradine and the Island, whereas the rest of the city was in the hands of the Syracusans. After this Thrasybulus sailed forth with his ships against the enemy, and after suffering defeat in the battle with the loss of numerous triremes, he withdrew with the remaining ships to the Island. Similarly he led forth his army also from Achradine and drew them up for battle in the suburbs, but he suffered defeat and was forced to retire with heavy losses back to Achradine. In the end, giving up hope of maintaining the tyranny, he opened negotiations with the Syracusans, came to an understanding with them, and retired under a truce to [Epizephyrian] Locri. The Syracusans, having liberated their native city in this manner, gave permission to the mercenaries to withdraw from Syracuse, and they liberated the other cities, which were either in the hands of tyrants or had garrisons, and re-established democracies in them. From this time the city enjoyed peace and increased greatly in prosperity, and it maintained its democracy for almost sixty years, until the tyranny which was established by Dionysius [406]. But Thrasybulus, who had taken over a kingship which had been established on so fair a foundation, disgracefully lost his kingdom through his own wickedness, and fleeing to Locri he spent the rest of his life there in private station.

While these events were taking place, in Rome this year for the first time four tribunes were elected to office, Gaius Sicinius, Lucius Numitorius, Marcus Duillius, and Spurius Acilius.

### *How Xerxes was slain by treachery and Artaxerxes became king (69).*

**69.** With the passing of this year, in Athens Lysitheüs was archon, [465] and in Rome the consuls elected were Lucius Valerius Publicola and Titus Aemilius Mamercus. During this year, in Asia Artabanus, an Hyrcanian by birth, who enjoyed the greatest influence at the court of King Xerxes and was captain of the royal body-guard, decided to slay Xerxes and transfer the kingship to himself. He communicated the plot to Mithridates the eunuch, who was the king's chamberlain and enjoyed his supreme confidence, and he, since he was also a relative of Artabanus as well as his friend, agreed to the plot. Artabanus, being led at night by Mithridates into the king's bed-chamber, slew Xerxes and then set out after the king's sons. These were three in number, Darius the eldest and

Artaxerxes, who were both living in the palace, and the third, Hystaspes, who happened to be away from home at the time, since he was administering the satrapy of Bactria. Now Artabanus, coming while it was yet night to Artaxerxes, told him that his brother Darius had murdered his father and was shifting the kingship to himself. He counselled him, therefore, before Darius should seize the throne, to see to it that he should not become a slave through sheer indifference but that he should ascend the throne after punishing the murderer of his father; and he promised to get the body-guard of the king to support him in the undertaking. Artaxerxes fell in with the advice and at once, with the help of the body-guard, slew his brother Darius. And when Artabanus saw how his plan was prospering, he called his own sons to his side and crying out that now was his time to win the kingship he strikes Artaxerxes with his sword. Artaxerxes, being wounded merely and not seriously hurt by the blow, held off Artabanus and dealing him a fatal blow killed him. Thus Artaxerxes, after being saved in this unexpected fashion and having taken vengeance upon the slayer of his father, took over the kingship of the Persians. So Xerxes died in the manner we have described, after having been king of the Persians for more than twenty years, and Artaxerxes succeeded to the kingship and ruled for forty years.

**70.** When Archedemides was archon in Athens, [464] the Romans elected as consuls Aulus Verginius and Titus Minucius, and the Seventy-ninth Olympiad was celebrated, that in which Xenophon of Corinth won the stadion. In this year the Thasians revolted from the Athenians because of a quarrel over mines [Mt. Pangaeus]; but they were forced to capitulate by the Athenians and compelled to subject themselves again to their rule. Similarly also, when the Aeginetans revolted, the Athenians, intending to reduce them to subjection, undertook the siege of Aegina; for this state, being often successful in its engagements at sea, was puffed up with pride and was also well provided with both money and triremes, and, in a word, was constantly at odds with the Athenians. Consequently they sent an army against it and laid waste its territory, and then, laying siege to Aegina, they bent every effort on taking it by storm. For, speaking generally, the Athenians, now that they were making great advances in power, no longer treated their allies fairly, as they had formerly done, but were ruling them harshly and arrogantly. Consequently most of the allies, unable longer to endure their severity, were discussing rebellion with each other, and some of them, scorning the authority of the [Delian] General Congress, were acting as independent states.

While these events were taking place, the Athenians, who were now masters of the sea, dispatched ten thousand colonists to Amphipolis, recruiting a part of them from their own citizens and a part from the allies. They portioned out the territory in allotments, and for a time held the upper hand over the Thracians, but at a later time, as a result of their further advance into Thrace, all who entered the country of the Thracians were slain [at Drabescus] by a people known as the Edones.

BOOK XI

## *On the revolt of the Egyptians against the Persians (71).*

**71.** When Tlepomemus was archon in Athens, [463] the Romans elected as consuls Titus Quinctius and Quintus Servilius Structus. This year Artaxerxes, the king of the Persians, who had just recovered the throne, first of all punished those who had had a part in the murder of his father and then organised the affairs of the kingdom to suit his own personal advantage. Thus with respect to the satraps then in office, those who were hostile to him he dismissed and from his friends he chose such as were competent and gave the satrapies to them. He also concerned himself with both the revenues and the preparation of armaments, and since in general his administration of the entire kingdom was mild, he enjoyed the favour of the Persians to a high degree.

But when the inhabitants of Egypt learned of the death of Xerxes and of the general attempt upon the throne and the disorder in the Persian kingdom, they decided to strike for their liberty. At once, then, mustering an army, they revolted from the Persians, and after expelling the Persians whose duty it was to collect the tribute from Egypt, they set up as king a man named Inaros. He at first recruited soldiers from the native Egyptians, but afterwards he gathered also mercenaries from the other nations and amassed a considerable army. He dispatched ambassadors also to the Athenians to effect an alliance, promising them that, if they should liberate the Egyptians, he would give them a share in the kingdom and grant them favours many times greater than the good service they had rendered. The Athenians, having decided that it was to their advantage to humble the Persians as far as they could and to attach the Egyptians closely to themselves against the unpredictable shiftings of Fortune, voted to send three hundred triremes to the aid of the Egyptians. The Athenians, therefore, with great enthusiasm set about the preparation of the expedition. As for Artaxerxes, when he learned of the revolt of the Egyptians and their preparations for war, he concluded that he must surpass the Egyptians in the size of his armaments. So he at once began to enrol soldiers from all the satrapies, build ships, and give his attention to every other kind of preparation.

These were the events of this year in Asia and Egypt.

## *On the civil discords which took place among the Syracusans (72-73).*

**72.** In Sicily, as soon as the tyranny of Syracuse had been overthrown and all the cities of the island had been liberated, the whole of Sicily was making great strides toward prosperity. For the Sicilian Greeks were at peace, and the land they cultivated was fertile, so that the abundance of their harvests enabled them soon to increase their estates and to fill the land with slaves and domestic animals and every other accompaniment of prosperity, taking in great revenues on the one hand and spending nothing upon the wars to which they had been accustomed. Later on they were again plunged into wars and civil strife for the following reasons. After the Syracusans had overthrown the tyranny of Thrasybulus, they held a meeting of the Assembly, and after deliberating on forming a democracy of their own they all voted unanimously to make a colossal statue of Zeus the Liberator and each year to celebrate with sacrifices the Festival of Liberation and hold games of distinction on the day on which they had overthrown the tyrant and liberated their native city; and they also voted to sacrifice to the gods, in connection with the games, four hundred and fifty bulls and to use them for the citizens' feast. As for all the magistracies, they proposed to assign them to the original citizens, but the aliens who had been admitted to citizenship under Gelon they did not see fit to allow to share in this dignity, either because they judged them to be unworthy or because they were suspicious lest men who had been brought up in the way of tyranny and had served in war under a monarch might attempt a revolution, and that is what actually happened. For Gelon had enrolled as citizens more than ten thousand foreign mercenaries, and of these there were left at the time in question more than seven thousand.

**73.** These aliens resented their being excluded from the dignity attending magistracies and with one accord revolted from the Syracusans, and they seized in the city both Achradine and the Island, both these places having their own well-built fortifications. The Syracusans, who were again plunged into disorder, held possession of the rest of the city; and that part of it which faced Epipolae they blocked off by a wall and made their own position very secure; for they at once easily cut off the rebels from access to the countryside and soon caused them to be in want of provisions. Though in number the mercenaries were inferior to the Syracusans, yet in experience of warfare they were far superior; consequently, when attacks took place here and there throughout the city and isolated encounters, the mercenaries regularly had the upper hand in the combats, but since they were shut off from the countryside, they were in want of equipment and short of food.

Such were the events in Sicily of this year.

**74.** When Conon was archon in Athens, [462] in Rome the consulship was held by Quintus Fabius Vibulanus and Tiberius Aemilius Mamercus. This year Artaxerxes, the king of the Persians, appointed Achaemenes, who was a son of Darius and his own uncle, to be commander in the war against the Egyptians; and turning over to him more than three hundred thousand soldiers, counting both cavalry and infantry, he commanded him to subdue the Egyptians. Now Achaemenes, when he had entered Egypt, pitched his camp near the Nile, and when he had rested his army after the march, he made ready for battle; but the Egyptians, having gathered their army from Libya and Egypt, were awaiting the auxiliary force of the Athenians. After the Athenians had arrived in Egypt with two hundred ships and had been drawn up with the Egyptians in battle order against the Persians, a mighty struggle took place. For a time the Persians with their superior numbers maintained the advantage, but later, when the Athenians seized the offensive, put to flight the forces opposing them, and slew many of them, the remainder of the barbarians turned to flight *en masse.* There was much slaughter in the course of the flight, and finally the Persians, after losing the larger part of their army, found refuge in the White Fortress, as it is called, while the Athenians, who had won the victory by their own deeds of valour, pursued the barbarians as far as the aforesaid stronghold and did not hesitate to besiege it.

Artaxerxes, on learning of the defeat of his troops, at first sent some of his friends with a large sum of money to Lacedaemon and asked the Lacedaemonians to make war upon the Athenians, thinking that if they complied the Athenian troops who had won the victory in Egypt would sail back to Athens in order to defend their native city. When the Lacedaemonians, however, neither accepted money nor paid any attention whatever to the requests of the Persians, Artaxerxes despaired of getting any aid from the Lacedaemonians and set about preparing other armaments. In command of them he placed Artabazus and Megabyzus, men of outstanding merit, and dispatched them to make war upon the Egyptians.

75. When Euthippus was archon in Athens, [461] the Romans chose as consuls Quintus Servilius and Spurius Postumius Albinus. During this year, in Asia Artabazus and Megabyzus, who had been dispatched to the war against the Egyptians, set out from Persia with more than three hundred thousand soldiers, counting both cavalry and infantry. When they arrived in Cilicia and Phoenicia, they rested their land forces after the journey and commanded the Cyprians and Phoenicians and Cilicians to supply ships. When three hundred triremes had been made ready, they fitted them out with the ablest marines and arms and missiles and everything else that is useful in naval warfare. So these leaders were busy with their preparations and with giving their soldiers training and accustoming every man to the practice of warfare, and they spent almost this entire year in this way. Meanwhile the Athenians in Egypt were besieging the troops which had taken refuge near Memphis in the White Fortress; but since the Persians were putting up a stout defence, they were unable to take the stronghold and so spent the, year in the siege.

76. In Sicily the Syracusans, in their war upon the mercenaries who had revolted, kept launching attack after attack upon both Achradine and the Island, and they defeated the rebels in a sea-battle, but on land they were unable to expel them from the city because of the strength of these two places. Later, however, after an open battle had been fought on land, the soldiers engaged on both sides fighting spiritedly, finally, although both armies suffered not a few casualties, victory lay with the Syracusans. After the battle the Syracusans honoured with the prize of valour the elite troops, six hundred in number, who were responsible for the victory, giving them each a mina of silver.

While these events were taking place, Ducetius, the leader of the Siceli, harbouring a grudge against the inhabitants of Catana because they had robbed the Siceli of their land, led an army against them. Since the Syracusans had likewise sent an army against Catana, they and the Siceli joined in portioning out the land in allotments among themselves and made war upon the settlers who had been sent by Hieron when he was ruler of Syracuse. The Catanians opposed them with arms, but were defeated in a number of engagements and were expelled from Catana, and they took possession of what is now Aetna, which was formerly called Inessa; and the original inhabitants of Catana, after a long period, got back their native city.

After these events the peoples who had been expelled from their own cities while Hieron was king, now that they had assistance in the struggle, returned to their fatherlands and expelled from their cities the men who had wrongfully seized for themselves the habitations of others; among these were inhabitants of Gela, Acragas, and Himera. In like manner Rhegians along with Zanclians expelled the sons of Anaxilas, who were ruling over them, and liberated their fatherlands. Later on Geloans, who had been the original settlers of Camarina, portioned that land out in allotments, and practically all the cities, being eager to make an end of the wars, came to a common decision, whereby they made terms with the mercenaries in their midst; they then received back the exiles and restored the cities to the original citizens, but to the mercenaries who because of the former tyrannical governments were in possession of the cities belonging to others, they gave permission to take with them their own goods and to settle one and all in Messenia. In this manner, then, an end was put to the civil wars and disorders which had prevailed throughout the cities of Sicily, and the cities, after driving out the forms of government which aliens had introduced, with almost no exceptions portioned out their lands in allotments among all their citizens.

77. When Phrasicleides was archon in Athens, [460] the Eightieth Olympiad was celebrated, that in which Toryllas the Thessalian won the stadion; and the Romans elected as consuls Quintus Fabius and Titus Quinctius Capitolinus. During this year, in Asia the Persian generals who had passed over to Cilicia made ready three hundred ships, which they fitted out fully for warfare, and then with their land force they advanced overland through Syria and Phoenicia; and with the fleet accompanying the army along the coast, they arrived at Memphis in Egypt. At the outset they broke the siege of the White Fortress, having struck the Egyptians and the Athenians with terror; but later on, adopting a prudent course, they avoided any frontal encounters and strove to bring the war to an end by the use of stratagems. Accordingly, since the Attic ships lay moored at the island known as Prosopitis, they diverted by means of canals the river which flowed around the island, and thus made the island a part of the mainland. When the ships thus all of a sudden came to rest on dry land, the Egyptians in alarm left the Athenians in the lurch and came to terms with the Persians. The Athenians, being now without allies and seeing that their ships had become useless, set fire to them to prevent their falling into the hands of the enemy, and then themselves, undismayed at the alarming plight they were in, fell to exhorting one another to do nothing unworthy of the fights they had won in the past. Consequently, with a display of deeds of valour surpassing in heroism the men who perished in Thermopylae in defence of Greece, they stood ready to fight it out with the enemy. The Persian generals, Artabazus and Megabyzus, taking note of the exceptional courage of their foes and reasoning that they would be unable to

annihilate such men without sacrificing many myriads of their own, made a truce with the Athenians whereby they should with impunity depart from Egypt. So the Athenians, having saved their lives by their courage, departed from Egypt, and making their way through Libya to Cyrene got safely back, as by a miracle, to their native land.

While these events were taking place, in Athens Ephialtes the son of Sophonides, who, being a popular leader, had provoked the masses to anger against the Areopagites, persuaded the Assembly to vote to curtail the power of the Council of the Areopagus and to destroy the renowned customs which their fathers had followed. Nevertheless, he did not escape the punishment for attempting such lawlessness, but he was done to death by night and none ever knew how he lost his life.

### How the Athenians defeated in war the Aeginetans and Corinthians (78-79).

78. At the conclusion of this year [459] Philocles was archon in Athens, and in Rome Aulus Postumius Regulus and Spurius Furius Mediolanus succeeded to the consulship. During this year a war arose between the Corinthians and Epidaurians on the one hand and the Athenians on the other, and the Athenians took the field against them and after a sharp battle were victorious. With a large fleet they put in at a place called Halieis, landed on the Peloponnesus, and slew not a few of the enemy. The Peloponnesians rallied and gathered a strong force, and it came to a battle with the Athenians near the place called Cecryphaleia [island off Epidaurus] in which the Athenians were again victorious. After such successes the Athenians, seeing that the Aeginetans were not only puffed up over their former achievements but also hostile to Athens, decided to reduce them by war. Therefore the Athenians dispatched a strong fleet against them. The inhabitants of Aegina, however, who had great experience in fighting at sea and enjoyed a great reputation therefor, were not dismayed at the superiority of the Athenians, but since they had a considerable number of triremes and had built some new ones, they engaged the Athenians in battle, but were defeated with the loss of seventy ships; and, their spirits crushed by so great a disaster, they were forced to join the league which paid tribute to Athens. This was accomplished for the Athenians by their general Leocrates, who was engaged in the war with the Aeginetans nine months in all.

While these events were taking place, in Sicily the king of the Siceli, Ducetius, a man of famous family and influential at this time, founded the city of Menaenum and distributed the neighbouring territory among the settlers, and making a campaign against the strong city of Morgantina and reducing it, he won fame among his own people.

### How the Phocians made war on the Dorians (79).

79. At the close of the year Bion was archon in Athens, [458] and in Rome Publius Servilius Structus and Lucius Aebutius Albas succeeded to the consulship. During this year a quarrel arose between the Corinthians and

Megarians over land on their borders and the cities went to war. At first they kept making raids on each other's territory and engaging in clashes of small parties; but as the quarrel increased, the Megarians, who were increasingly getting the worse of it and stood in fear of the Corinthians, made allies of the Athenians. As a result the cities were again equal in military strength, and when the Corinthians together with Peloponnesians advanced into Megaris with a strong army, the Athenians sent troops to the aid of the Megarians under the command of Myronides, a man who was admired for his valour. A fierce engagement took place which lasted a long time and each side matched the other in deeds of courage, but at last victory lay with the Athenians, who slew many of the enemy. And after a few days there was another fierce battle at Cimolia, as it is called, and again the Athenians were victorious and slew many of the enemy.

The Phocians went to war with the Dorians, who are the original stock of the Lacedaemonians and dwell in the three cities, Cytinium, Boeum and Erineüs, which lie at the base of Mt. Parnassus. Now at first they subdued the Dorians by force of arms and occupied their cities; but after this the Lacedaemonians, because of their kinship, dispatched Nicomedes, the son of Cleomenes, to the aid of the Dorians. He had fifteen hundred Lacedaemonians and ten thousand men from the rest of the Peloponnesians. So Nicomedes, who was the guardian of Pleistonax the king, who was still a child, came to the aid of the Dorians with this large army, and after inflicting a defeat upon the Phocians and recovering the cities they had seized, he made peace between the Phocians and the Dorians.

**80.** When the Athenians learned that the Lacedaemonians had concluded the war against the Phocians and were about to make their return home, they decided to attack the Lacedaemonians while on the march. Accordingly they dispatched an army against them, including in it Argives and Thessalians; and with the intention of falling upon them with fifty ships and fourteen thousand men, they occupied the passes about Mt. Geraneia. The Lacedaemonians, having information of the plans of the Athenians, took the route to Tanagra in Boeotia. The Athenians advanced into Boeotia and formed in line of battle, and a fierce struggle took place; and although in the fighting the Thessalians deserted to the Lacedaemonians, nonetheless the Athenians and the Argives fought the battle through and not a few fell in both armies before night put an end to the struggle. After this, when a large supply-train was on its way from Attica for the Athenians, the Thessalians decided to attack it, and taking their evening meal at once, they intercepted by night the supply-train. The Athenians who were guarding the train were unaware that the Thessalians had changed sides and received them as friends, so that many conflicts of various kinds broke out around the convoy. For at first the Thessalians, who had been welcomed by the enemy in their ignorance, kept cutting down all whom they met, and being an organised band engaging with men who had fallen into confusion they slew many of the guards, but the Athenians in the camp, when they learned of the attack of the Thessalians, came up with all speed, and routing the Thessalians at

BOOK XI

the first charge, they were making a great slaughter of them. The Lacedaemonians, however, now came to the rescue of the Thessalians with their army in battle order, and a pitched battle between the two armies ensued, and such was their rivalry that many were slain on both sides. Finally, since the battle [Tanagra] ended in a tie, both the Lacedaemonians and the Athenians laid claim to the victory. However, since night intervened and the victory was still a matter of dispute, each sent envoys to the other and they concluded a truce of four months.

**How Myronides the Athenian with a few soldiers defeated the Boeotians who far outnumbered them (81-82).**

**81.** When the year ended, in Athens Mnesitheides was archon, [457] and in Rome the consuls elected were Lucius Lucretius and Titus Veturius Cicurinus. During this year the Thebans, who had been humbled because of their alliance with Xerxes, sought a way by which they might recover both their ancient influence and reputation. Consequently, since all the Boeotians held the Thebans in disdain and no longer paid any attention to them, the Thebans asked the Lacedaemonians to aid them in winning for their city the hegemony over all Boeotia; and they promised that in return for this favour they would make war by themselves upon the Athenians, so that it would no longer be necessary for the Spartans to lead troops beyond the border of the Peloponnesus. The Lacedaemonians [assented], judging the proposal to be to their advantage and believing that, if Thebes should grow in strength, she would be a kind of counterweight to the increasing power of the Athenians; consequently, since they had at the time a large army in readiness at Tanagra, they increased the extent of the circuit wall of Thebes and compelled the cities of Boeotia to subject themselves to the Thebans. The Athenians, however, being eager to break up the plan of the Lacedaemonians, made ready a large army and elected as general Myronides the son of Callias. He enrolled the required number of citizens and gave them orders, announcing a day on which he planned to march forth from the city. When the appointed time arrived and some of the soldiers had not put in appearance at the specified rendezvous, he took those who had reported and advanced into Boeotia, and when certain of his officers and friends said that he should wait for the tardy men, Myronides, who was not only a sagacious general but energetic as well, replied that he would not do so; for, he declared, men who of their own choice are late for the departure will in battle also play an ignoble and cowardly part, and will therefore not withstand the perils of war in defence of their country either, whereas the men who presented themselves ready for service on the appointed day gave clear evidence that they would not desert their posts in the war, and this is what actually took place; for leading forth soldiers who were few in number but the bravest in courage, he drew them up in Boeotia against a vastly superior force and utterly defeated his opponents.

**82.** In my opinion this action was in no way inferior to any of the battles fought by the Athenians in former times; for neither the victory at Marathon nor the success over the Persians at Plataea nor the other renowned exploits of the Athenians seem in any way to surpass the victory which Myronides won over the Boeotians. For of those other battles, some were fought against barbarians and others were gained with the aid of allies, but this struggle was won by the Athenians single-handed in pitched battle, and they were pitted against the bravest warriors to be found among the Greeks. For in staunchness in the face of perils and in the fierce contests of war the Boeotians are generally believed to be surpassed by no other people; at any rate, sometime after this the Thebans at Leuctra [371] and Mantineia [362], when they unaided confronted all the Lacedaemonians and their allies, won for themselves the highest reputation for courage, and contrary to expectation became the leading nation of all Greece. Yet, although this battle of Myronides has become famous, none of our historians has described either the way it was fought or the disposition of the troops engaged in it. Myronides, then, after defeating the Boeotians in a remarkable battle, came to rival the reputations of the most renowned commanders before his time, namely, Themistocles, Miltiades, and Cimon. Myronides after this victory took Tanagra by siege, leveled its walls, and then he passed through all Boeotia, breaking it up and destroying it, and dividing the booty among his soldiers he loaded them all down with spoil in abundance.

83. The Boeotians, exasperated by the wasting of their land, sprang to arms as a nation and when they had taken the field constituted a great army. A battle took place at Oenophyta in Boeotia, and since both sides withstood the stress of the conflict with stout hearts, they spent the day in fighting; but after a severe struggle the Athenians put the Boeotians to flight and Myronides became master of all the cities of Boeotia with the exception of Thebes. After this he marched out of Boeotia and led his army against the Locrians who are known as Opuntian. These he overpowered at the first attack, and taking hostages from them he then entered Parnasia. In like manner as he had done with the Locrians, he also subdued the Phocians, and after taking hostages he marched into Thessaly, finding fault with the Thessalians for their act of treachery and ordering them to receive back their exiles; and when the Pharsalians would not open their gates to him, he laid siege to the city. Since he could not master the city by force and the Pharsalians held out for a long time against the siege, for the present he gave up his designs regarding Thessaly and returned to Athens. Thus Myronides, who had performed great deeds in a short space of time, won among his fellow citizens the renown which was so widely acclaimed.

These, then, were the events of this year.

### On the campaign of Tolmides against Cephallenia (84).

84. While Callias was archon in Athens, [456] in Elis the Eighty-first Olympiad was celebrated, that in which Polymnastus of Cyrene won the "stadion," and in Rome the consuls were Servius Sulpicius and Publius Volumnius Amentinus. During this year Tolmides, who was commander of the naval forces and vied with both the valour and fame of Myronides, was eager to

accomplish a memorable deed. Consequently, since in those times no one had ever yet laid waste Laconia, he urged the Athenian people to ravage the territory of the Spartans, and he promised that by taking one thousand hoplites aboard the triremes he would with them lay waste Laconia and dim the fame of the Spartans. When the Athenians acceded to his request, he then, wishing to take with him secretly a larger number of hoplites, had recourse to the following cunning subterfuge. The citizens thought that he would enrol for the force the young men in the prime of youth and most vigorous in body; but Tolmides, determined to take with him in the campaign not merely the stipulated one thousand, approached every young man of exceptional hardihood and told him that he was going to enrol him; it would be better, however, he added, for him to go as a volunteer than be thought to have been compelled to serve under compulsion by enrolment. When by this scheme he had persuaded more than three thousand to enrol voluntarily and saw that the rest of the youth showed no further interest, he then enrolled the thousand he had been promised from all who were left.

When all the other preparations for his expedition had been made, Tolmides set out to sea with fifty triremes and four thousand hoplites, and putting in at Methone in Laconia, he took the place; and when the Lacedaemonians came to defend it, he withdrew, and cruising along the coast to Gytheium, which was a seaport of the Lacedaemonians, he seized it, burned the city and also the dockyards of the Lacedaemonians, and ravaged its territory. From here he set out to sea and sailed to Zacynthos which belonged to Cephallenia; he took the island and won over all the cities on Cephallenia, and then sailed across to the opposite mainland and put in at Naupactus. This city he likewise seized at the first assault and in it he settled the prominent Messenians whom the Lacedaemonians had allowed to go free under a truce. At this time, it may be explained, the Lacedaemonians had finally overcome both the Helots and Messenians, with whom they had been at war over a long period, and the Messenians they had allowed to depart from Ithome under a truce, as we have said, but of the Helots they had punished those who were responsible for the revolt and had enslaved the rest.

**85.** When Sosistratus was archon in Athens, [455] the Romans elected as consuls Publius Valerius Publicola and Gaius Clodius Regillus. In this year Tolmides was occupied in Boeotia and the Athenians elected as general a man of the aristocracy, Pericles the son of Xanthippus, and giving him fifty triremes and a thousand hoplites, sent him against the Peloponnesus. He ravaged a large part of the Peloponnesus, and then sailed across to Acarnania and won over to Athens all the cities with the exception of Oeniadae. So the Athenians during this year controlled a very large number of cities and won great fame for valour and generalship.

## On the war in Sicily between the Egestaeans and Lilybaeans (86).

**86.** When Ariston was archon in Athens, [454] the Romans elected as consuls Quintus Fabius Vibulanus and Lucius Cornelius Curitinus. This year the Athenians and Peloponnesians agreed to a truce of five years, Cimon the Athenian having conducted the negotiations.

In Sicily a war arose between the peoples of Egesta and Lilybaeum over the land on the Mazarus River, and in a sharp battle which ensued both cities lost heavily but did not slacken their rivalry. After the enrolment of citizens which had taken place in the cities and the redistribution of the lands, since many had been added to the roll of citizens without plan and in a haphazard fashion, the cities were in an unhealthy state and falling back again into civil strife and disorders; and it was especially in Syracuse that this malady prevailed. For a man by the name of Tyndarides, a rash fellow full of effrontery, began by gathering about him many of the poor, and organising them into an armed unit he proceeded to make of them a personal bodyguard ready for an attempt to set up a tyranny. After this, when it was evident that he was grasping after supreme power, he was brought to trial and condemned to death, but while he was being led off to prison, the men upon whom he had lavished his favours rushed together and laid hands upon those who were arresting him, and in the confusion which arose throughout the city the most respectable citizens, who had organised themselves, seized the revolutionists and put them to death along with Tyndarides. Since this sort of thing kept happening time and again and there were men whose hearts were set on a tyranny, the people were led to imitate the Athenians and to establish a law very similar to the one they had passed on ostracism.

## On the framing of the law of petalism by the Syracusans (87).

**87.** Now among the Athenians each citizen was required to write on a potsherd (*ostracon*) the name of the man who, in his opinion, was most able through his influence to tyrannise over his fellow citizens; but among the Syracusans the name of the most influential citizen had to be written on an olive leaf, and when the leaves were counted, the man who received the largest number of leaves had to go into exile for five years. For by this means they thought that they would humble the arrogance of the most powerful men in these two cities; for, speaking generally, they were not exacting from violators of the law a punishment for a crime committed, but were effecting a diminution of the influence and growing power of the men in question. Now while the Athenians called this kind of legislation ostracism, from the way it was done, the Syracusans used the name petalism [*petalon* = leaf]. This law remained in force among the Athenians for a long time, but among the Syracusans it was soon repealed for the following reasons. Since the most influential men were being sent into exile, the most respectable citizens and such as had it in their power, by reason of their personal high character, to effect many reforms in the affairs of the commonwealth were taking no part in public affairs, but consistently remained in private life because of their fear of the law, attending to their personal fortunes and leaning towards a life of luxury; whereas it was the basest citizens and such as excelled in effrontery who were giving their attention to public affairs and inciting the masses to disorder and revolution. Consequently, since factional quarrels were again arising and the masses were turning to wrangling, the city fell back into continuous and serious disorders. For a multitude of demagogues and sycophants was arising, the youth were cultivating cleverness in oratory, and, in a word, many were exchanging the ancient and sober way of life for the ignoble pursuits; wealth was increasing because of the peace, but there was little if any concern for concord and honest conduct. As a result the Syracusans changed their minds and repealed the law of petalism, having used it only a short while.

Such, then, was the state of affairs in Sicily.

### *The campaign of Pericles against the Peloponnesus (88).*
### *The campaign of the Syracusans against Tyrrhenia (88).*

**88.** When Lysicrates was archon in Athens, [453] in Rome the consuls elected were Gaius Nautius Rutilus and Lucius Minucius Carutianus. During this year Pericles, the general of the Athenians, landed in the Peloponnesus and ravaged the territory of the Sicyonians, and when the Sicyonians came out against him in full force and a battle was fought, Pericles was victorious, slew many as they fled, and shut them up in their city, to which he laid siege. When he was unable by making assaults upon the walls to take the city, and when, besides, the Lacedaemonians sent aid to the besieged, he withdrew from Sicyon; then he sailed to Acarnania, where he overran the territory of Oeniadae, amassed much booty, and then sailed away from Acarnania. After this he arrived at the [Thracian] Cherronesus and portioned out the land in allotments to one thousand citizens. While these events were taking place, Tolmides, the other general, passed over into Euboea and divided it and the land of the Naxians among another thousand citizens.

As for the events in Sicily, since the Tyrrhenians were practising piracy at sea, the Syracusans chose Phayllus as admiral and sent him to Tyrrhenia. He sailed at first to the island known as Aethaleia [Elba] and ravaged it, but he secretly accepted a bribe of money from the Tyrrhenians and sailed back to Sicily without having accomplished anything worthy of mention. The Syracusans found him guilty of treachery and exiled him, and choosing another general, Apelles, they dispatched him with sixty triremes against the Tyrrhenians. He overran the coast of Tyrrhenia and then passed over to Cyrnus [Corsica], which was held at those times by the Tyrrhenians, and after sacking many places in this island and subduing Aethaleia, he returned to Syracuse accompanied by a multitude of captives and not a little other spoil. After this Ducetius, the leader of the Siceli, gathered all the cities which were of the same race, with the exception of Hybla, into one and a common federation; and being an energetic man, he was always grasping after innovations, and so he gathered a large army from the Sicilian

League and removed the city of Menae, which was his native state, and planted it in the plain. Also near the sacred precinct of the Palici, as they are called, he founded an important city, which he named Palice after the gods just mentioned.

## On the Palici, as they are called, in Sicily (89).

**89.** Since we have spoken of these gods, we should not omit to mention both the antiquity and the incredible nature of the shrine, and, in a word, the peculiar phenomenon of The Craters [mixing bowls], as they are called. The myth relates that this sacred area surpasses all others in antiquity and the reverence paid to it, and many marvels there are reported by tradition. For first of all there are craters which are not at all large in size, but they throw up extraordinary streams of water from a depth beyond telling and have very much the nature of cauldrons which are heated by a strong fire and throw up boiling water. Now the water that is thrown up gives the impression of being boiling hot, but this is not known for certain because of the fact that no man dares touch it; for the amazement caused by the spout of water is so great that men believe the phenomenon to be due to some divine power. For not only does the water give out a strongly sulphurous smell but the yawning mouth emits a mighty and terrifying roar; and what is still more astonishing than this, the water neither pours over nor recedes, but has a motion and force in its current that lifts it to a marvellous height. Since so divine a majesty pervades the sacred area, the most sacred oaths are taken there and men who swear falsely are immediately overtaken by the punishment of heaven; thus certain men have lost their sight when they depart from the sacred precinct. So great is the awe of the deities of this shrine, that men who are pressing claims, when, for instance, they are being overborne by a person of superior dignity, have their claims adjudicated on the strength of the preliminary examination of the witnesses supported by oaths taken in the name of these deities. This sacred area has also been recognised for some time as a place of sanctuary and has been a source of great aid to luckless slaves who have fallen into the hands of brutal masters; for if they have fled there for refuge, their masters have no power to remove them by force, and they remain there protected from harm until their masters, having gained their consent upon conditions of humane treatment and having given pledges, supported by such oaths, to fulfil their agreements, lead them away.

History records no case, out of all who have given slaves such a pledge as this, of a violation; so faithful to their slaves does the awe in which these gods are held make those who have taken the oath, and the sacred area, which lies on a plain meet for a god, has been appropriately embellished with colonnades and every other kind of lounging-place. Let what we have said suffice for this subject, and we shall return to the narrative at the point where our history broke off.

**90.** Ducetius, after founding Palice and enclosing it with strong walls, portioned out the neighbouring countryside in allotments, and it came to pass that this city, on account of the fertility of the soil and the multitude of colonists, enjoyed a rapid growth. It did not, however, prosper for long, but was razed to the ground and has remained without habitation until our own day; regarding this we shall give a detailed account in connection with the appropriate period of time.

Such, then, was the state of affairs in Sicily. In Italy, fifty-eight years after the Crotoniates had destroyed Sybaris, a Thessalian gathered together the Sybarites who remained and founded Sybaris anew; it lay between two rivers, the Sybaris and the Crathis, and since the settlers possessed a fertile land they quickly advanced in wealth. They had possessed the city only a few years when they were again driven out of Sybaris, regarding which event we shall undertake to give a detailed account in the following Book.

(The year 452 is lacking.)

## On the defeat of Ducetius and his astounding escape from death (91-92).

**91.** When Antidotus was archon in Athens, [451] the Romans elected as consuls Lucius Postumius and Marcus Horatius. During this year Ducetius, who held the leadership of the Siceli, seized the city of Aetna, having treacherously slain its leader, and then he moved with an army into the territory of the Acragantini and laid siege to Motyum, which was held by a garrison of Acragantini; and when the Acragantini and the Syracusans came to the aid of the city, he joined battle with them, was successful, and drove them both out of their camps. Since at the time winter was setting in, they separated and returned to their homes; and the Syracusans found their general Bolcon, who was responsible for the defeat and was thought to have had secret dealings with Ducetius, guilty of treason and put him to death. With the beginning of summer they appointed a new general, to whom they assigned a strong army with orders to subdue Ducetius. This general, setting out with his army, came upon Ducetius while he was encamped near Nomae; a fierce struggle ensued and many fell on both sides, but with difficulty the Syracusans overpowered and routed the Siceli, slaying many of them as they fled. Of those who survived the battle the larger number found safety in the strongholds of the Siceli, but a few chose to share the hopes of Ducetius. While these things were taking place, the Acragantini forced the capitulation of the stronghold of Motyum, which was held by the Siceli who stayed with Ducetius, and then, uniting their troops with the Syracusans who had already won the victory, they now camped together. As for Ducetius, now that he had been completely crushed by his defeat and that some of his soldiers were deserting and others plotting against him, he had come to the depths of despair.

**92.** Finally, when Ducetius saw that his remaining friends were about to lay hands upon him, he anticipated them by slipping away at night and riding off to Syracuse. While it was still night he entered the market-place of the Syracusans, and seating himself at the altars he became a suppliant of the city, placing both his person and the land which he controlled at the disposition of the Syracusans. When the multitude poured into the market-place in amazement at the unexpected event, the magistrates called a meeting of the Assembly and laid before it the question of what should be done with Ducetius. Some of those who were accustomed to curry favour with the people advised that they should punish him as an enemy and inflict on him for his misdeeds the appropriate penalty; but the more fair minded of the elder citizens came forward and declared it as their opinion that they should spare the suppliant and show due regard for Fortune and the wrath of the gods. The people should consider, they continued, not what punishment Ducetius deserved, but what action was proper for the Syracusans; for to slay the victim of Fortune was not fitting, but to maintain reverence for the gods as well as to spare the suppliant was an act worthy of the magnanimity of the people. The people thereupon cried out as with one voice from every side to spare the suppliant. The Syracusans, accordingly, released Ducetius from punishment and sent him off to Corinth, ordering him to spend his life in that city and also giving him sufficient means for his support.

Since we are now at the year preceding the campaign of the Athenians against Cyprus under the leadership of Cimon, pursuant to the plan announced at the beginning of this Book we herewith bring it to an end.

# BOOK XII

## *On the campaign of the Athenians against Cyprus (1-4).*

**1.** A man may justly feel perplexed when he stops to consider the inconsistency that is to be found in the life of mankind; for no thing which we consider to be good is ever found to have been given to human beings unadulterated, nor is there any evil in an absolute form without some admixture of advantage. Proofs of this will be obtained if we give thought to the events of the past, especially to those of outstanding importance. For instance, the campaign of Xerxes, the king of the Persians, against Greece aroused the greatest fear among the Greeks by reason of the immensity of his armaments, since the war they were entering might well decide their slavery, and since the Greek cities of Asia had already been enslaved, all men assumed that those of Greece would also suffer a similar fate, but the war, contrary to expectation, came to an amazing end, and not only were the peoples of Greece freed of the dangers threatening them, but they also won for themselves great glory, and every city of Hellas enjoyed such an abundant prosperity that all men were filled with wonder at the complete reversal of their fortune. For from this time over the next fifty years Greece made great advance in prosperity. In these years, for example, plenty brought increase to the arts, and the greatest artists of whom we have record, including the sculptor Pheidias, flourished at that time; and there was likewise great advance in education, and philosophy and oratory had a high place of honour among all Greeks, and especially the Athenians. For the philosophers were Socrates and Plato and Aristotle, and the orators were Pericles and Isocrates and his pupils; and there were likewise men who have become renowned for generalship, Miltiades, Themistocles, Aristeides, Cimon, Myronides, and others more than these, regarding whom it would be a long task to write.

**2.** First place belonged to the Athenians, who had advanced so far in both fame and prowess that their name was known throughout practically the entire inhabited world; for they increased their leadership to such a degree that, by their own resources and without the aid of Lacedaemonians or Peloponnesians, they overcame great Persian armaments both on land and on sea, and humbled the famed leadership of the Persians to such an extent that they forced them by the terms of a treaty to liberate all the cities of Asia. Of these matters we have given a detailed and fairly precise account in two Books, this and the preceding, and we shall turn now to the events next in order, after we have first set the time-limits of this section. Now in the preceding Book we began with the campaign of Xerxes and presented a universal history down to the year before the campaign of the Athenians against Cyprus under the command of Cimon [450-451]; and in this Book we shall commence with the campaign of the Athenians against Cyprus and continue as far as the war which the Athenians voted to undertake against the Syracusans.

**3.** When Euthydemus was archon at Athens, [450] the Romans elected as consuls Lucius Quinctius Cincinnatus and Marcus Fabius Vibulanus. In this year the Athenians, who had been at war with the Persians on behalf of the Egyptians and had lost all their ships at the island which is known as Prosopitis, after a short time resolved to make war again upon the Persians on behalf of the Greeks in Asia Minor, and fitting out a fleet of two hundred triremes, they chose Cimon, the son of Miltiades, to be general and commanded him to sail to Cyprus to make war on the Persians. Cimon, taking the fleet which had been furnished with excellent crews and abundant supplies, sailed to Cyprus. At that time the generals of the Persian armaments were Artabazus and Megabyzus. Artabazus held the supreme command and was tarrying in Cyprus with three hundred triremes, and Megabyzus was encamped in Cilicia with the land forces, which numbered three hundred thousand men. Cimon, when he arrived in Cyprus and was master of the sea, reduced by siege Citium and Marium, treating the conquered in humane fashion. After this, when triremes from Cilicia and Phoenicia bore down upon the island, Cimon, putting out to sea against them and forcing battle upon them, sank many of the ships, captured one hundred together with their crews, and pursued the remainder as far as Phoenicia. Now the Persians with the ships that were left sought refuge on the land in the region where Megabyzus lay encamped with the land force, and the Athenians, sailing up and disembarking the soldiers, joined battle, in the course of which Anaxicrates, the other general, who had fought brilliantly, ended his life heroically; but the rest were victorious in the battle and after slaying many returned to the ships. After this the Athenians sailed back again to Cyprus.

Such, then, were the events of the first year of the war.

**4.** When Pedieus was archon in Athens, [449] the Romans elected as consuls Marcus Valerius Lactuca and Spurius Verginius Tricostus. In this year Cimon, the general of the Athenians, being master of the sea, subdued the cities of Cyprus. Since a large Persian garrison was there in Salamis and the city was filled with missiles and arms of every description, and of grain and supplies of every other kind, he decided that it would be to his advantage to reduce it by siege. For Cimon reasoned that this would be the easiest way for him not only to become master of all Cyprus but also to confound the Persians, since their being unable to come to the aid of the Salaminians, because the Athenians were masters of the sea, and their having left their allies in the lurch would cause them to be despised, and that, in a word, the entire war would be decided if all Cyprus were reduced by arms. That is what actually happened. The Athenians began the siege of Salamis and were making daily assaults, but the soldiers in the city, supplied as they were with missiles and materiel, were with ease warding off the besiegers from the walls. Artaxerxes the king, however, when he learned of the reverses his forces had suffered at Cyprus, took counsel on the war with his friends and decided that it was to his advantage to conclude a peace with the Greeks. Accordingly he dispatched to the generals in Cyprus and to the satraps the written terms on which they were permitted to come to a settlement with the Greeks. Consequently Artabazus and Megabyzus sent ambassadors to Athens to discuss a settlement. The Athenians were favourable and dispatched ambassadors plenipotentiary, the leader of whom was Callias the son of Hipponicus; and so the Athenians and their allies concluded with the Persians a treaty of peace, the principal terms of which run as follows: All the Greeks cities of Asia are to live

BOOK XII

under laws of their own making; the satraps of the Persians are not to come nearer to the sea than a three days' journey and no Persian warship is to sail inside of Phaselis or the Cyanean Rocks; and if these terms are observed by the king and his generals, the Athenians are not to send troops into the territory over which the king is ruler. After the treaty had been solemnly concluded, the Athenians withdrew their armaments from Cyprus, having won a brilliant victory and concluded most noteworthy terms of peace, and it so happened that Cimon died of an illness during his stay in Cyprus.

### On the revolt of the Megarians from the Athenians (5).

5. When Philiscus was archon in Athens, [448] the Romans elected as consuls Titus Romilius Vaticanus and Gaius Veturius Cichorius; and the Eleians celebrated the Eighty-third Olympiad, that in which Crison of Himera won the stadion. In this year the Megarians revolted from the Athenians, and dispatching ambassadors to the Lacedaemonians they concluded an alliance with them. Irritated at this the Athenians sent soldiers into the territory of the Megarians, plundering their properties and seizing much booty. When the Megarians issued from their city to defend their territory, a battle ensued in which the Athenians were victorious and chased them back within their walls.

### On the battle at Coroneia between the Athenians and Boeotians (6).

6. When Timarchides was archon in Athens, [447] the Romans elected as consuls Spurius Tarpeius and . Aulus Asterius Fontinius. In this year the Lacedaemonians invaded Attica and ravaged a large part of the countryside, and after laying siege to some of the Athenian fortresses they withdrew to the Peloponnesus; and Tolmides, the Athenian general, seized Chaeroneia. When the Boeotians gathered their forces and caught Tolmides' troops in an ambush, a violent battle took place at Coroneia, in the course of which Tolmides fell fighting and of the remaining Athenians some were massacred and others were taken alive. The result of a disaster of such magnitude was that the Athenians were compelled to allow all the cities throughout Boeotia to live under laws of their own making, in order to get back their captured citizens.

### On the campaign of the Athenians against Euboea (7).

7. When Callimachus was archon in Athens, [446] the Romans elected as consuls Sextus Quinctius . . . Trigeminus. In this year, since the Athenians had been weakened in Greece because of their defeat in Boeotia at Coroneia, many cities revolted from them. Since the inhabitants of Euboea were taking the lead in the revolution, Pericles, who had been chosen general, made a campaign against Euboea with a strong force, and taking the city of Hestiaea by storm he removed the inhabitants from their native city; and the other cities he terrified and forced back into obedience to the Athenians.

A truce was made for thirty years, Callias and Chares negotiating and confirming the peace.

### The war in Sicily between the Syracusans and the Acragantini (8)

8. In Sicily a war broke out between the Syracusans and Acragantini for the following reasons. The Syracusans had overcome Ducetius, the ruler of the Siceli, cleared him of all charges when he became a suppliant, and specified that

he should make his home in the city of the Corinthians. After Ducetius had spent a short time in Corinth he broke the agreement, and on the plea that the gods had given him an oracular reply that he should found a city on the Fair [Northern] Shore (*Cale Acte*) of Sicily, he sailed to the island with a number of colonists; some Siceli were also included, among whom was Archonides, the ruler of Herbita. He, then, was busied with the colonisation of *Cale Acte*. The Acragantini, partly because they were envious of the Syracusans and partly because they were accusing them of letting Ducetius, who was their common enemy, go free without consulting them, declared war upon the Syracusans. The cities of Sicily were divided, some of them taking the field with the Acragantini and others with the Syracusans, and so large armaments were mustered on both sides. Great emulation was shown by the cities as they pitched opposing camps at the Himera River, and in the conflict which followed the Syracusans were victorious and slew more than a thousand Acragantini. After the battle the Acragantini sent ambassadors to discuss terms and the Syracusans concluded a peace.

### *The founding in Italy of Thurii and its civil strife (9-11).*

**9.** These, then, were the events in Sicily. And in Italy the city of Thurii came to be founded [444?], for the following reasons. When in former times the Greeks had founded Sybaris in Italy, the city had enjoyed a rapid growth because of the fertility of the land. For lying as the city did between two rivers, the Crathis and the Sybaris, from which it derived its name, its inhabitants, who tilled an extensive and fruitful countryside, came to possess great riches. Since they kept granting citizenship to many aliens, they increased to such an extent that they were considered to be far the first among the inhabitants of Italy; indeed they so excelled in population that the city possessed three hundred thousand citizens.

Now there arose among the Sybarites a leader of the people named Telys, who brought charges against the most influential men and persuaded the Sybarites to exile the five hundred wealthiest citizens and confiscate their estates. When these exiles went to Croton and took refuge at the altars in the marketplace, Telys dispatched ambassadors to the Crotoniates, commanding them either to deliver up the exiles or to expect war. An assembly of the people was convened and deliberation proposed on the question whether they should surrender the suppliants to the Sybarites or face a war with a superior foe, and the Council and people were at a loss what to do. At first the sentiments of the masses, from fear of the war, leaned toward handing over the suppliants, but after this, when Pythagoras the philosopher advised that they grant safety to the suppliants, they changed their opinions and accepted the war on behalf of the safety of the suppliants. When the Sybarites advanced against them with three hundred thousand men, the Crotoniates opposed them with one hundred thousand under the command of Milo the athlete, who by reason of his great physical strength was the first to put to flight his adversaries. For we are told that this man, who had won the prize in Olympia six times and whose courage was of the measure of his physical body, came to battle wearing his Olympic crowns and equipped with the gear of Heracles, lion's skin and club; and he won the admiration of his fellow citizens as responsible for their victory.

**10.** Since the Crotoniates in their anger would take no prisoners but slew all who fell into their hands in the flight, the larger number of the Sybarites perished; and they plundered the city of Sybaris and laid it entirely waste. Fifty-eight years later [453] Thessalians joined in settling the city, but after a little while they were driven out by the Crotoniates, in the period we are now discussing, and shortly thereafter the city was moved to another site and received another name, its founders being Lampon and Xenocritus; the circumstances of its re-founding were as follows.

The Sybarites who were driven a second time from their native city dispatched ambassadors to Greece, to the Lacedaemonians and Athenians, requesting that they assist their repatriation and take part in the settlement. Now the Lacedaemonians paid no attention to them, but the Athenians promised to join in the enterprise, and they manned ten ships and sent them to the Sybarites under the leadership of Lampon and Xenocritus; they further sent word to the several cities of the Peloponnesus, offering a share in the colony to anyone who wished to take part in it. Many accepted the offer and received an oracular response from Apollo that they should found a city in the place where there would be:

Water to drink in due measure, but bread to eat without measure.

They put in at Italy and arriving at Sybaris they set about hunting the place which the god had ordered them to colonise. Having found not far from Sybaris a spring called Thuria, which had a bronze pipe which the natives of the region called *medimnos* [a measure of grain], and believing this to be the place which the god had pointed out, they threw a wall about it, and founding a city there they named it Thurium after the spring. They divided the city lengthwise by four streets, the first of which they named Heracleia, the second Aphrodisia, the third Olympias, and the fourth Dionysias, and breadthwise they divided it by three streets, of which the first was named Heroa, the second Thuria, and the last Thurina. And since the quarters formed by these streets were filled with dwellings, the construction of the city appeared to be good.

**11.** For a short time only did the Thurians live together in peace, and then they fell into serious civil strife, not without reason. The former Sybarites, it appears, were assigning the most important offices to themselves and the lower ones to the citizens who had been enrolled later; their wives they also thought should enjoy precedence among the citizens in the offering of sacrifices to the gods, and the wives of the later citizens should take second place to them; furthermore, the land lying near the city they were portioning out in allotments among themselves, and the more distant land to the newcomers. When a division arose for the causes we have mentioned, the citizens who had been added to the rolls after the others, being more numerous and more powerful, put to death practically all of the original Sybarites and took upon themselves the colonisation of the city. Since the countryside was extensive and rich, they sent for colonists in large numbers from Greece, and to these they assigned parts of the city and gave them equal shares of the land. Those who continued to live in the city quickly came to possess great wealth, and concluding friendship with the Crotoniates they administered their state in admirable fashion. Establishing a democratic form of government, they divided the citizens into ten tribes, to each of which they assigned a name based on the nationality of those who constituted it: three tribes composed of peoples gathered from the Peloponnesus they named the Arcadian, the Achaean, and the Eleian; the same number, gathered from related peoples living outside the Peloponnesus, they named the Boeotian, Amphictyonian, and Dorian; and the remaining four, constituted from other peoples, the Ionian, the Athenian, the Euboean, and the Islander. They also chose for their lawgiver the best man among such of their citizens as were admired for their learning, this being Charondas. He, after examining the legislations of all peoples, singled out the best principles and incorporated them in his laws; and he also worked out many principles which were his own discovery, and these it is not foreign to our purpose to mention for the edification of our readers.

### How Charondas, who was chosen lawgiver of Thurii, was responsible for many benefits to his native city (12-19).

**12.** First of all, in the case of men who brought home a stepmother over their children he ordained as their punishment that they should have no part in counselling their fatherland, since he believed that men who planned so badly with respect to their own children would likewise be bad counsellors for their fatherland. For, he said, whoever had been fortunate in their first marriages should rest satisfied with their good lot, whereas whoever had been unfortunate in marriage and then made the same mistake a second time should be regarded as men without sense. Men who had been found guilty of false accusation should, he decreed, wear wherever they went a wreath of tamarisk, in order that they might show to all their fellow citizens that they had won the highest prize for wickedness. As a consequence certain men who had been judged guilty of this charge, being unable to bear their great disgrace, voluntarily removed themselves from life. When this took place, every man who had made a practice of false accusation was banished from the city, and the government enjoyed a blessed life of freedom from this evil.

Charondas also wrote a unique law on evil association, which had been overlooked by all other lawgivers. He took it for granted that the characters of good men are in some cases perverted to evil by reason of their friendship and intimacy with bad persons, and that badness, like a pestilent disease, sweeps over the life of mankind and infects the souls of the most upright; for the road to the worse slopes downward and so provides an easier way to take; and this is the reason why many men of fairly good character, ensnared by deceptive pleasures, get stranded upon very bad habits. Wishing, therefore, to remove this source of corruption, the lawgiver forbade the indulgence in friendship and intimacy with unprincipled persons, provided actions at law against evil association, and by means of severe penalties diverted from their course those who were about to err in this manner.

Charondas also wrote another law which is far superior to the one just mentioned and had also been overlooked by lawgivers before his time. He framed the law that all the sons of citizens should learn to read and write, the city providing the salaries of the teachers; for he assumed that men of no means and unable to provide the fees from their own resources would be cut off from the noblest pursuits.

**13.** In fact the lawgiver rated reading and writing above every other kind of learning, and with right good reason; for it is by means of them that most of the affairs of life and such as are most useful are concluded, like votes, letters, covenants, laws, and all other things which make the greatest contribution to orderly life. What man, indeed, could compose a worthy laudation of the knowledge of letters? For it is by such knowledge alone that the dead are carried in the memory of the living and that men widely separated in space hold converse through written communication with those who are at the furthest distance from them, as if they were at their side; and in the case of covenants in time of war between states or kings the firmest guarantee that such agreements will abide is provided by the unmistakable character of writing. Indeed, speaking generally, it is writing alone which preserves the cleverest sayings of men of wisdom and the oracles of the gods, as well as philosophy and all knowledge, and is constantly handing them down to succeeding generations for the ages to come. Consequently, while it is true that nature is the cause of life, the cause of the good life is the education which is based upon reading and writing. And so Charondas, believing as he did that the illiterate were being deprived of certain great advantages, by his legislation corrected this wrong and judged them to be deserving of concern and expense on the part of the state; and he so far excelled former lawgivers who had required that private citizens when ill should enjoy the service of physicians at state expense that, whereas those legislators judged men's bodies to be worthy of healing, he gave healing to the souls which were in distress through want of education, and whereas it is our prayer that we may never have need of those physicians, it is our heart's desire that all our time may be spent in the company of teachers of knowledge.

**14.** To both the matters we have mentioned above many poets have borne witness in verse; to the law on evil association as follows:

> The man who takes delight in converse with
> The base, I never ask his kind, aware
> He's just like those with whom he likes to be;

to the law he proclaimed on a stepmother as follows:

> Charondas, giver of laws, so men relate,
> In legal code says many things, but this
> Above all else: Let him who on his offspring
> A second mother foists be held without
> Esteem nor count among his countrymen
> For aught, since it's a bane that he hath brought
> From alien source upon his own affairs.
> For if, he says to him, you fortunate were
> When wedded first, forbear when you're well off,
> And if your luck was bad, a madman's act
> It surely is to try a second wife.

For in truth the man who errs twice in the same matter may justly be considered a fool, and Philemon, the writer of comedy, when introducing men who repeatedly sail the seas, after commending the law, says:

> Amazement holds me, no longer if a man
> Has gone to sea, but if he's done it twice.

Similarly one may say that one is not amazed if a man has married, but if he has married a second time; for it is better to expose oneself twice to the sea than to a woman. Indeed the greatest and most grievous quarrels in homes between children and fathers are caused by stepmothers, and this fact is the cause of many lawless acts which are portrayed in tragic scenes upon the stage.

**15.** Charondas also wrote another law which merits approbation, that which deals with the protection of orphans. On the surface this law appears to contain nothing unusual or worthy of approbation, but when it is scrutinised more closely and examined with care, it indicates not only earnest study but also a high claim to regard. For his law provided that the property of orphans should be managed by the next of kin on the father's side, but that the orphans should be reared by their relatives on the mother's side. Now at first glance a man sees nothing wise or outstanding in this law, but when it is explored deeply it is found to be justly worthy of praise. For if the reason is sought out why he entrusted the property of orphans to one group and the rearing of them to another, the lawgiver is seen to have shown an unusual kind of ingenuity. That is, the relatives on the mother's side will not plot to take the lives of the orphans, since they have no share in their inheritance, and the kin on the father's side do not have the opportunity to plot against their lives, since they are not entrusted with the care of their persons; furthermore, since they inherit the property if the orphans die of disease or some other circumstance, they will administer the estate with greater care, believing that they hold as their own what are hopes based upon an act of Fortune.

**16.** Charondas also wrote a law against men who had left their post in war or had refused to take up arms at all in defence of their fatherland. Other lawmakers had made death the punishment of such men, but Charondas ordered that they should sit for three days in the market-place dressed in women's clothes. This law is not only more humane than those of other peoples but it also imperceptibly, by the severity of the disgrace it inflicts, diverts others of like mind from cowardice; for it is better to die than to experience such a gross indignity in one's fatherland. Moreover, he did not do away with the guilty men but preserved them for the state against the needs of wartime, believing that they would make amends, by reason of the punishment caused by that disgrace, and would be eager to wipe out their former shame by bolder deeds of bravery.

The lawgiver also preserved the laws he made by means of their severity. That is, he commanded that under every circumstance obedience should be rendered to the law even if it had been altogether wrongly conceived; but he allowed any law to be corrected, if it needed correction. For he took the position that although it was right enough that a man should be overruled by a lawgiver, to be overruled by one in private station was quite preposterous, even if that serves the general interest. It was especially by this means that he prevented men who present in jury-courts the pretences and cunning devices of those who have violated the laws in place of the literal terms of the laws from destroying by inventive sophistries their supremacy. As a consequence, we are told, to certain men who had offered such arguments before the jurors who were passing on the punishment of men who had violated the law, he said, "You must save either the law or the man."

**17.** But the most amazing legislation of Charondas, we are told, was that which related to the revision of the laws. Observing that in most states the multitude of men who kept endeavouring to revise the laws led continually to the vitiation of the previously existing body of the laws and incited the masses to civil strife, he wrote a law which was peculiar and altogether unique. He commanded, namely, that the man who proposed to revise any law should put his neck in a noose at the time he made his proposal of a revision, and remain in that position until the people had reached a decision on the revision of the law, and if the Assembly approved the revised law, the introducer was to be freed of the noose, but if the proposal of revision did not carry, the noose was to be drawn and the man die on the spot. Such being the legislation relating to revision, fear restrained subsequent lawmakers and not a man dared to utter a word about revising laws; and in all subsequent time history records but three men who proposed revision among the Thurians, and these appeared because circumstances arose which rendered proposals of revision imperative.

Thus, there was a law that if a man put out the eye of another, he should have his own eye put out, and a man with but one eye, having had that eye put out and thus lost his entire sight, claimed that the offender, by the loss in requital of but one eye, had paid a less penalty; for, he maintained, if a man who had blinded a fellow citizen paid only the penalty fixed by the law, he would not have suffered the same loss; it would be just, therefore, that the man who had destroyed the entire sight of a man with but one eye should have both his eyes put out, if he were to receive a like punishment. Consequently the man with one eye, taking the matter strongly to heart, made bold to raise in the Assembly the case of the loss he had suffered, at the same time both lamenting bitterly over his personal misfortune to his fellow citizens and suggesting to the commons that they revise the law; and in the end, putting his neck in a noose, he won his proposal, set at naught the existing law, and had the revision approved, and he escaped the death by the noose as well.

**18.** A second law, which gave a wife the right to divorce her husband and marry whomever she chose, was also revised. A certain man, who was well advanced in years and had a wife who was younger than he and had left him, proposed to the Thurians that they revise the law by the added provision that the wife who leaves a husband may marry whomever she chooses, provided the man is not younger than her former husband; and that likewise, if a man sends his wife away he may not marry a woman younger than the wife whom he had sent away. The elderly man won his proposal and set at naught the former law, also escaping the peril of the noose which threatened him; and his wife, who had thus been prevented from living with a younger husband, married again the man she had left.

A third law to be revised had to do with heiresses and is also found in the legislation of Solon. Charondas ordered that the next of kin be assigned in marriage to an heiress and that likewise an heiress be assigned in marriage to her nearest relative, who was required to marry her or, if she were poor, to contribute five hundred drachmas as a dowry of the penniless heiress. A certain orphan who was an heiress, of good birth but altogether without means of support and so unable by reason of her poverty to find a husband, turned to the people for aid, explaining to them with tears how helpless and scorned she was; and she went on to outline the revision of the law whereby, in place of the payment of five hundred drachmas, it should specify that the next of kin be required to marry the heiress who had been assigned to him. The people took pity on her and voted for the revision of the law, and thus the orphan escaped the peril which threatened her from the noose, while the nearest of kin, who was wealthy, was compelled to take to wife a penniless heiress without a dowry.

**19.** It remains for us to speak of the death of Charondas, in connection with which a peculiar and unexpected thing happened to him. He had set out to the country carrying a dagger because of the robbers, and on his return the Assembly was in session and the commons in an uproar, whereupon he approached it because he was curious about the matter in dispute, but he had made a law that no man should enter the Assembly carrying a weapon, and since he had forgotten he was carrying the dagger at his side, he provided certain of his enemies with an occasion to bring an accusation against him. When one of them said, "You have annulled your own law," he replied, "Not so, by Zeus, I will uphold it," and drawing the dagger he slew himself. Some historians, however, attribute this act to Diocles, the lawgiver of the Syracusans.

But now that we have discoursed at sufficient length upon Charondas the lawmaker, we wish to speak briefly also of the lawmaker Zaleucus, since the two men not only followed similar principles of life but were also natives of neighbouring cities.

### *How Zaleucus, the lawgiver in Locri, won for himself great fame (20-21).*

**20.** Now Zaleucus was by birth a Locrian of Italy, a man of noble family, admired for his education, and a pupil of the philosopher Pythagoras. Having been accorded high favour in his native city, he was chosen lawmaker and committed to writing a thoroughly novel system of law, making his beginning, first of all, with the gods of the heavens. For at the outset in the introduction to his legislation as a whole he declared it to be necessary that the inhabitants of the city should first of all assume as an article of their creed that gods exist, and that, as their minds survey the heavens and its orderly scheme and arrangement, they should judge that these creations are not the result of Chance or the work of men's hands; that they should revere the gods as the cause of all that is noble and good in the life of mankind; and that they should keep the soul pure from every kind of evil, in the belief that the gods take no pleasure in either the sacrifices or costly gifts of the wicked but in the just and honourable practices of good men. After inviting the citizens in this introduction to reverence and justice, he appended the further command that they should consider no one of their fellow citizens as an enemy with whom there can be no reconciliation, but that the quarrel be entered into with the thought that they will again come to agreement and friendship; and that the one who acts otherwise should be considered by his fellow citizens to be savage and untamed of soul. Also the magistrates were urged by him not to be wilful or arrogant, and not to render judgement out of enmity or friendship. And among his several ordinances a number were added of his own devising, which showed exceptionally great wisdom.

**21.** To cite examples, whereas everywhere else wayward wives were required to pay fines, Zaleucus stopped their licentious behaviour by a cunningly devised punishment. That is, he made the following laws: a free-born woman may not be accompanied by more than one female slave, unless she is drunk; she may not leave the city during the night, unless she is planning to commit adultery; she may not wear gold jewellery or a garment with a purple border, unless she is a courtesan; and a husband may not wear a gold-studded ring or a cloak of Milesian fashion unless he is bent upon prostitution or adultery. Consequently, by the elimination, with its shameful implications, of the penalties he easily turned men aside from harmful luxury and wanton living; for no man wished to incur the sneers of his fellow citizens by acknowledging the disgraceful licentiousness. He wrote many other excellent laws, such as those on contracts and other relations of life which are the cause of strife, but it would be a long task for us to recount them and foreign to the plan of our history, and so we shall resume our account at the point where we digressed from the course of our narrative.

### How the Athenians expelled the Hestiaeans and sent there their own colonists (22).

22. When Lysimachides was archon in Athens, [445] the Romans elected as consuls Titus Menenius and Publius Sestius Capitolinus. In this year the Sybarites who were fleeing from the danger threatening them in the civil strife made their home on the Traïs River. Here they remained for a time, but later they were driven out by the Brettii and destroyed. And in Greece the Athenians, regaining control of Euboea and driving the Hestiaeans from their city, dispatched, under Pericles as commander, a colony of their own citizens to it and sending forth a thousand colonists they portioned out both the city and countryside in allotments.

### On the war between the Thurians and the Tarantini (23).

23. When Praxiteles was archon in Athens, [444] the Eighty-fourth Olympiad was celebrated, that in which Crison of Himera won the "stadion," and in Rome the following ten men [Decemvirate] were elected to draft laws: Publius Clodius Regillanus, Titus Minucius, Spurius Veturius, Gaius Julius, Gaius Sulpicius, Publius Sestius, Romulus (Romilius), Spurius Postumius Calvinius. These men drew up the laws. This year the Thurians and the Tarantini kept up continuous warfare and ravaged each other's territory both by land and by sea. They engaged in many light battles and skirmishes, but accomplished no deed worthy of mention.

### On the civil strife in Rome (24-26).

24. When Lysanias was archon in Athens, [443] the Romans again chose ten men as lawmakers: Appius Clodius, Marcus Cornelius, Lucius Minucius, Gaius Sergius, Quintus Publius, Manius Rabuleius, and Spurius Veturius. These men, however, were not able to complete the codification of the laws. One [Appius Claudius] of them had conceived a passion for a maiden who was penniless but of good family, and at first he tried to seduce the girl [Verginia] by means of money; and when she would have nothing to do with him, he sent an agent to her home with orders to lead her into slavery. The agent, claiming that she was his own slave, brought her, serving in that capacity, before the magistrate, in whose court Appius charged her with being his slave, and when the magistrates had

listened to the charge and handed the girl over to him, the agent led her oft as his own slave.

The maiden's father, who had been present at the scene and had complained bitterly of the injustice he had suffered, since no attention had been paid to him, passed, as it happened, a butcher's shop, and snatching up the cleaver lying on the block, he struck his daughter with it and killed her, to prevent her experiencing the violation which awaited her; then he rushed out of the city and made his way to the army which was encamped at the time on Mount Algidus, as it is called. There he laid his case before the common soldiers, denounced with tears the misfortune that had befallen him, and won their complete pity and great sympathy. The entire body sallied forth to bring help to the unfortunates and burst into Rome during the night fully armed. There they seized the hill known as the Aventine.

**25.** When with the day the hatred of the soldiers toward the evil which had been done became known, the ten lawmakers, rallying to the aid of their fellow magistrate, collected a body of young men, with the intention of settling the issue by a test of arms. Since a great spirit of contention now threatened the state, the most respectable citizens, foreseeing the greatness of the danger, acted as ambassadors between both parties to reach an agreement and begged them with great earnestness to cease from the civil discord and not plunge their fatherland into such serious distress. In the end all were won over and a mutual agreement was reached as follows: that ten tribunes should be elected who should wield the highest authority among the magistrates of the state and should act as guardians of the freedom of the citizens; and that of the annual consuls one should be chosen from the patricians and one, without exception, should be taken from the plebeians, the people having the power to choose even both consuls from the plebeians. This they did in their desire to weaken the supremacy of the patricians; for the patricians, by reason both of their noble birth and of the great fame that came down to them from their ancestors, were lords, one might say, of the state. It was furthermore stipulated in the agreement that when tribunes had served their year of office they should see that an equal number of tribunes were appointed in their place, and that if they failed to do this they should be burned alive; also, in case the tribunes could not *agree* among themselves, the will of the interceding tribune must not be prevented. Such then, we find, was the conclusion of the civil discord in Rome.

**26.** When Diphilus was archon in Athens, [442] the Romans elected as consuls Marcus Horatius and Lucius Valerius Turpinus. In Rome during this year, since the legislation remained unfinished because of the civil discord, the consuls brought it to conclusion; that is, of the Twelve Tables, as they are called, ten had been drawn up, and the consuls wrote into law the two remaining. After the legislation they had undertaken had been concluded, the consuls engraved the laws on twelve bronze tablets and affixed them to the Rostra before the Senate-house. And the legislation as it was drawn up, since it is couched in such brief and pithy language, has continued to be admired by men down to our own day.

While the events we have described were taking place, the greater number of the nations of the inhabited world were quiet, practically all of them being at peace. For the Persians had two treaties with the Greeks, one with the Athenians and their allies according to which the Greek cities of Asia were to live under laws of their own making, and they also concluded one later with the Lacedaemonians, in which exactly the opposite terms had been incorporated, whereby the Greek cities of Asia were to be subject to the Persians. Likewise, the Greeks were at peace with one another, the Athenians and Lacedaemonians having concluded a truce of thirty years. Affairs likewise in Sicily also were in a peaceful state, since the Carthaginians had made a treaty with Gelon, the Greek cities of Sicily had voluntarily conceded the hegemony to the Syracusans, and the Acragantini, after their defeat at the river Himera, had come to terms with the Syracusans. There was quiet also among the peoples of Italy and Celtice, as well as over Iberia and almost all the rest of the inhabited world. Consequently no deed of arms worthy of mention was accomplished in this period, a single peace prevailed, and festive gatherings, games, sacrificial festivals of the gods, and everything else which accompanies a life of felicity prevailed among all mankind.

### On the war between the Samians and the Milesians (27-28).

**27.** When Timocles was archon in Athens, [441] the Romans elected as consuls Lar Herminius and Titus Stertinius Structor. In this year the Samians went to war with the Milesians because of a quarrel over Priene, and when they saw that the Athenians were favouring the Milesians, they revolted from the Athenians, who thereupon chose Pericles as general and dispatched him with forty ships against the Samians. And sailing forth against Samos, Pericles got into the city and mastered it, and then established a democracy in it. He exacted of the Samians eighty talents and took an equal number of their young men as hostages, whom he put in the keeping of the Lemnians; then, after having finished everything in a few days, he returned to Athens.

But civil discord arose in Samos, one party preferring the democracy and the Other wanting an aristocracy, and the city was in utter tumult. The opponents of the democracy crossed over to Asia, and went on to Sardis to get aid from Pissuthnes, the Persian satrap. Pissuthnes gave them seven hundred soldiers, hoping that in this way he would get the mastery of the island, and the Samians, sailing to Samos by night with the soldiers which had been given them, slipped unnoticed into the city with the aid of the citizens, seized the island without difficulty, and expelled from the city those who opposed them. Then, after they had stolen and carried off the hostages from Lemnos and had made everything secure in Samos, they publicly declared themselves to be enemies of the Athenians. The Athenians again chose Pericles as general and dispatched him against the Samians with sixty ships. Thereupon Pericles fought a naval battle against seventy triremes of the Samians and defeated them; and then, summoning twenty-five ships from the Chians and Mytilenaeans, together with them he laid siege to the city of Samos. But a few days later Pericles left a part of his force to continue the siege and set out to sea to meet the Phoenician ships which the Persians had dispatched to the aid of the Samians.

**28.** The Samians, believing that because of the departure of Pericles they had a suitable opportunity to attack the ships that had been left behind, sailed against them, and having won the battle they were puffed up with pride. When Pericles received word of the defeat of his forces, he at once turned back and gathered an imposing fleet, since he desired to destroy once and for all the fleet of the enemy. The Athenians rapidly dispatched sixty triremes and the Chians and Mytilenaeans thirty, and with this great armament Pericles renewed the siege both by land and by sea, making continuous assaults. He built also siege machines, being the first of all men to do so, such as those called "rams" and "tortoises," Artemon of Clazomenae having built them; and by pushing the siege with energy and throwing down the walls by means of the siege machines he gained the mastery of Samos. After punishing the ringleaders of the revolt he exacted of the Samians the expenses incurred in the siege of the city, fixing the penalty at two hundred talents. He also took from them their ships and razed their walls; then he restored the democracy and returned to his country.

As for the Athenians and Lacedaemonians, the thirty-year truce between them remained unshaken to this time.

These, then, were the events of this year.

### How the Syracusans campaigned against the Picenians and razed their city (29).

**29.** When Myrichides was archon in Athens, [440] the Romans elected as consuls Lucius Julius and Marcus Geganius, and the Eleians celebrated the Eighty-fifth Olympiad, that in which Crison of Himera won the stadion for the second time. In Sicily, in this year, Ducetius, the former leader of the cities of the Siceli, founded the native city of the Calactians, and when he had established many colonists there, he laid claim to the leadership of the Siceli, but his attempt was cut short by illness and his life was ended. The Syracusans had made subject to them all the cities of the Siceli with the exception of Trinacie, as it is called, and against it they decided to send an army; for they were deeply apprehensive lest the Trinacians should make a bid for the leadership of the Siceli, who were their kinsmen. There were many great men in this city, since it had always occupied the chief position among the cities of the Siceli; for it was full of military leaders who took an immense pride in their own manly spirit. Consequently the Syracusans marched against it after having mustered all their own armaments and those of their allied states. The Trinacians were without allies, since all the other cities were subject to the Syracusans, but they none the less offered a strong resistance. They held out valiantly against the perils they encountered and slew great numbers, and they all ended their lives fighting heroically. In like manner even the majority of the older men removed themselves from life, being unwilling to endure the despite they would suffer at the capture of their city. The Syracusans, after conquering in brilliant fashion men who had never before been subdued, sold the inhabitants into slavery and utterly destroyed the city, and the choicest of the booty they sent to Delphi as a thank-offering to the god.

### How the Corinthian War, as it is called, broke out in Greece (30).

**30.** When Glaucides was archon in Athens, [439] the Romans elected as consuls Titus Quinctius and Agrippa Furius. During this year the Syracusans, because of the successes we have described, built one hundred triremes and doubled the number of their cavalry; they also developed their infantry forces and made financial preparations by laying heavier tributes upon the Siceli who were now subject to them. This they were doing with the intention of subduing all Sicily little by little.

While these events were taking place it came about in Greece that the Corinthian War [435], as it is called, began for the following causes. Civil strife broke out among the Epidamnians who dwell upon the Adriatic Sea and are colonists of the Cercyraeans and Corinthians. The successful group sent into exile large numbers of their opponents, but the exiles gathered into one body, associated the Illyrians with themselves, and sailed together with them against Epidamnus. Since the [Illyriana] barbarians had taken the field with a large army, had seized the countryside, and were investing the city, the Epidamnians, who of themselves were not equal to them in battle, dispatched ambassadors to Cercyra, asking the Cercyraeans on the grounds of kinship to come to their aid. When the Cercyraeans paid no attention to the request, they sent ambassadors to seek an alliance with the Corinthians and declared Corinth to be their single mother-city; at the same time they asked for colonists, and the Corinthians, partly out of pity for the Epidamnians and partly out of hatred for the Cercyraeans, since they alone of the colonists who had gone from Corinth would not send the customary sacrificial animals to the mother-city, decided to go to the aid of the Epidamnians. Consequently they sent to Epidamnus both colonists and soldiers in sufficient numbers to garrison the city. At this the Cercyraeans became irritated and sent out a squadron of fifty triremes under the command of a general. He, sailing up to the city, issued orders to receive back the exiles, while they dispatched ambassadors to the guards from Corinth demanding that the question of the origin of the colony be decided by a court of arbiters, not by war. When the Corinthians made no answer to this proposal, both sides decided upon war, and they set about fitting out great naval armaments and gathering allies, and so the Corinthian War, as it has been called, broke out for the reasons we have narrated.

The Romans were at war with the Volscians and at first they engaged only in skirmishes and unimportant engagements, but later they conquered them in a great pitched battle and slew the larger number of the enemy.

### How the nation of the Campani was formed in Italy (31).
### The naval battle between the Corinthians and the Cercyraeans (31-33).

31. When Theodoras was archon in Athens, [438] the Romans elected as consuls Marcus Genucius and Agrippa Curtius Chilo. In Italy, during this year, the nation of the Campani was formed, deriving their name from the fertility of the plain about them.

In Asia the dynasty of the Cimmerian Bosporus, whose kings were known as the Archaeanactidae, ruled for forty-two years; and the successor to the kingship was Spartacus, who reigned seven years.

In Greece the Corinthians were at war with the Cercyraeans, and after preparing naval armaments they made ready for a battle at sea. Now the Corinthians with seventy excellently equipped ships sailed against their enemy; but the Cercyraeans opposed them with eighty triremes and won the battle, and then they forced the surrender of Epidamnus and put to death all the captives except the Corinthians, whom they cast in chains and imprisoned. After the sea battle the Corinthians withdrew in dismay to the Peloponnesus, and the Cercyraeans, who were now masters of the sea in those regions, made frequent descents upon the allies of the Corinthians, ravaging their lands.

**32.** At the end of the year the archon in Athens [437] was Euthymenes, and in Rome instead of consuls three military tribunes were elected, Aulus Sempronius, Lucius Atilius, and Titus Quinclius. During this year the Corinthians, who had suffered defeat in the sea-battle, decided to build a more imposing fleet. Consequently, having procured a great amount of timber and hiring shipbuilders from other cities, they set about with great eagerness building triremes and fabricating arms and missiles of every description; and, speaking generally, they were making ready all the equipment needed for the war and, in particular, triremes, of which they were building some from their keels, repairing others which had been damaged, and requisitioning still others from their allies. Since the Cercyraeans were doing the same thing and were not being outdone in eagerness, it was clear that the war was going to increase greatly in intensity.

While these events were taking place the Athenians founded the colony of Amphipolis, selecting the colonists in part from their own citizens and in part from garrisons in the neighbourhood.

**33.** When Lysimachus was archon in Athens, [436] the Romans elected as consuls Titus Quinctius and Marcus Geganius Macerinus, and the Eleians celebrated the Eighty-sixth Olympiad, that in which Theopompus the Thessalian won the stadion. In this year the Cercyraeans, learning of the great scale of the armaments which were being prepared against them, dispatched ambassadors to the Athenians asking their aid. Since the Corinthians did the same thing, an Assembly was convened, and the Athenian people after listening to the ambassadors voted to form an alliance with the Cercyraeans. Consequently they dispatched at once ten fully equipped triremes and promised that they would send more later if necessary. The Corinthians, after their failure to conclude an alliance with the Athenians, manned by themselves ninety triremes and received in addition sixty from their allies. With, therefore, one hundred and fifty fully equipped triremes and after selecting their most accomplished generals, they put to sea against Cercyra, having decided to join battle at once. When the Cercyraeans learned that the enemy's fleet was not far off, they put out to sea against them with one hundred and twenty triremes including the Athenian. A sharp battle took place, and at the outset the Corinthians had the upper hand; but later, when the Athenians came on the scene with twenty additional ships which they had sent in accordance with the second alliance, it turned out that the Cercyraeans were victorious, and on the next day, when the Cercyraeans sailed against them in full force for battle, the Corinthians did not put out.

### The revolt of Potidaea and the Chalcidians from the Athenians, and on the campaign of the Athenians against the Potidaeans (34).

**34.** When Antiochides was archon in Athens, [435] the Romans elected as consuls Marcus Fabius and Postumus Aebutius Ulecus. In this year, since the Athenians had fought at the side of the Cercyraeans and been responsible for their victory in the sea-battle, the Corinthians were incensed at them. Being eager, therefore, to retaliate upon the Athenians, they incited the city of Potidaea, which was one of their own colonies, to revolt from the Athenians, and in like manner Peridiccas, the king of the Macedonians, who was also at odds with the Athenians, persuaded the Chalcidians, who had revolted from the Athenians, to abandon their cities on the sea and unite in forming a single city known as Olynthus. When the Athenians heard of the revolt of the Potidaeans, they dispatched thirty ships with orders to ravage the territory of the rebels and to sack their city; and the expedition landed in Macedonia, as the Athenian people had ordered them to do, and undertook the siege of Potidaea. Thereupon the Corinthians came to the help of the besieged with two thousand soldiers and the Athenian people also sent two thousand. In the battle which took place on the isthmus near Pallene the Athenians were victorious and slew over three hundred of the enemy, and the Potidaeans were entirely beleaguered. While these events were taking place, the Athenians founded in the Propontis a city which was given the name of Astacus.

In Italy the Romans sent colonists to Ardea and portioned out the land in allotments.

### On the civil strife which arose in Thurii (35).

**35.** When Crates was archon in Athens, [434] the Romans elected as consuls Quint us Furius Fusus and Manius Papirius Crassus. This year in Italy the inhabitants of Thurii, who had been gathered together from many cities, divided into factions over the question from what city the Thurians should say they came as colonists and what man should justly be called the founder of the city. The situation was that the Athenians were laying claim to this colony on the grounds, as they alleged, that the majority of its colonists had come from Athens; and, besides, the cities of the Peloponnesus, which had provided from their people not a few to the founding of Thurii, maintained that the colonisation of the city should be ascribed to them. Likewise, since many able men had shared in the founding of the colony and had rendered many services, there was much discussion on the matter, since each one of them was eager to have this honour fall to him. In the end the Thurians sent a delegation to Delphi to inquire what man they should call the founder of their city, and the god replied that he himself should be considered to be its founder. After the dispute had been settled in this manner, they declared Apollo to have been the founder of Thurii, and the people, being now freed from the civil discord, returned to the state of harmony which they had previously enjoyed.

In Greece Archidamus [d.426], the king of the Lacedaemonians, died after a reign of forty-two years, and Agis succeeded to the throne and was king for twenty-five years.

### How Meton of Athens was the first to expound the nineteen-year cycle (36).

### How the Tarantini founded the city of Heracleia in Italy (36).

**36.** When Apseudes was archon in Athens, [433] the Romans elected as consuls Titus Menenius and Proculus Geganius Macerinus. During this year Spartacus, the king of the Bosporus, died after a reign of seven years, and Seleucus succeeded to the throne and was king for forty years.

In Athens Meton, the son of Pausanias, who had won fame for his study of the stars, revealed to the public his nineteen-year cycle, as it is called, the beginning of which he fixed on the thirteenth day of the Athenian month of Scirophorion. In this number of years the stars accomplish their return to the same place in the heavens and conclude, as it were, the circuit of what may be called a Great Year; consequently it is called by some the Year of Meton. We find that this man was astonishingly fortunate in this prediction which he published; for the stars complete both their movement and the effects they produce in accordance with his reckoning. Consequently, even down to our own day, the larger number of the Greeks use the nineteen-year cycle and are not cheated of the truth.

In Italy the Tarantini removed the inhabitants of Siris, as it is called, from their native city, and adding to them colonists from their own citizens, they founded a city which they named Heracleia.

### How in Rome Spurius Maelius attempted to seize the supreme power and was put to death (37).

37. When Pythodorus was archon in Athens, [432] the Romans elected as consuls Titus Quinctius and Nittus Menenius, and the Eleians celebrated the Eighty-seventh Olympiad, that in which Sophron of Ambracia won the stadion. In Rome in this year Spurius Maelius was put to death while striving for despotic power, and the Athenians, who had won a striking victory around Potidaea, dispatched a second general, Phormion, in the place of their general Callias who had fallen on the field. After taking over the command of the army Phormion settled down to the siege of the city of the Potidaeans, making continuous assaults upon it; but the defenders resisted with vigour and the siege became a long affair.

Thucydides, the Athenian, commenced his history with this year, giving an account of the war between the Athenians and the Lacedaemonians, the war which has been called the Peloponnesian. This war lasted twenty-seven years, but Thucydides described twenty-two years in eight Books or, as others divide it, in nine.

### On the Peloponnesian War, as it is called (38-41).

38. When Euthydemus was archon in Athens, [431] the Romans elected in place of consuls three military tribunes, Manius Aemilianus Mamercus, Gaius Julius, and Lucius Quinctius. In this year there began the Peloponnesian War, as it has been called, between the Athenians and the Peloponnesians, the longest of all the wars which history records; and it is necessary and appropriate to the plan of our history to set forth at the outset the causes of the war.

While the Athenians were still striving for the mastery of the sea, the funds which had been collected as a common undertaking and placed at Delos, amounting to some eight thousand talents, they had transferred to Athens [454] and given over to Pericles to guard. This man stood far above his fellow citizens in birth, renown, and ability as an orator, but after some time he had spent a very considerable amount of this money for his own purposes, and when he was called upon for an accounting he fell ill, since he was unable to render the statement of the monies with which he had been entrusted. While he was worried over the matter, Alcibiades, his nephew, who was an orphan and was being reared at the home of Pericles, though still a lad showed him a way out of making an explanation of the use of the money. Seeing how his uncle was troubled he asked him the cause of his worry. When Pericles said, "I am asked for the explanation of the use of the money and I am seeking some means whereby I may be able to render an accounting of it to the citizens," Alcibiades replied, "You should be seeking some means not how to render but how not to render an accounting." Consequently Pericles, accepting the reply of the boy, kept pondering in what way he could embroil the Athenians in a great war; for that would be the best way, he thought, because of the disturbance and distractions and fears which would beset the city, for him to escape giving an exact accounting of the money. Bearing upon this expedient an incident happened to him by mere chance for the following causes.

**39.** The [Parthenon] statue of Athena was a work of Pheidias, and Pericles, the son of Xanthippus, had been appointed overseer of the undertaking. Some of the assistants of Pheidias, who had been prevailed upon by Pericles' enemies, took seats as suppliants at the altars of the gods; and when they were called upon to explain their surprising action, they claimed that they would show that Pheidias had possession of a large amount of the sacred funds, with the connivance and assistance of Pericles the overseer. Consequently, when the Assembly convened to consider the affair, the enemies of Pericles persuaded the people to arrest Pheidias and lodged a charge against Pericles himself of stealing sacred property. Furthermore, they falsely accused the sophist Anaxagoras, who was Pericles' teacher, of impiety against the gods; and they involved Pericles in their accusations and malicious charges, since jealousy made them eager to discredit the eminence as well as the fame of the man.

But Pericles, knowing that during the operations of war the populace has respect for noble men because of their urgent need of them, whereas in times of peace they keep bringing false accusations against the very same men because they have nothing to do and are envious, came to the conclusion that it would be to his own advantage to embroil the state in a great war, in order that the city, in its need of the ability and skill in generalship of Pericles, should pay no attention to the accusations being lodged against him and would have neither leisure nor time to scrutinise carefully the accounting he would render of the funds.

Now when the Athenians voted to exclude the Megarians from both their market and harbours, the Megarians turned to the Spartans for aid, and the Lacedaemonians, being won over by the Megarians, in the most open manner dispatched ambassadors in accordance with the decision of the Council of the [Peloponnesian] League, ordering the Athenians to rescind the action against the Megarians and threatening, if they did not accede, to wage war upon them together with the forces of their allies. When the Assembly convened to consider the matter, Pericles, who far excelled all his fellow citizens in skill of oratory, persuaded the Athenians not to rescind the action, saying that for them to accede to the demands of the Lacedaemonians, contrary to their own interests, would be the first step toward slavery. Accordingly he advised that they bring their possessions from the countryside into the city and fight it out with the Spartans by means of their command of the sea.

**40.** Speaking of the war, Pericles, after defending his course in well-considered words, enumerated first the multitude of allies Athens possessed and the superiority of its naval strength, and then the large sum of money which had been removed from Delos to Athens and which had in fact been gathered from the tribute into one fund for the common use of the cities; from the ten thousand talents in the common fund four thousand had been expended on the building of the Propylaea and the siege of Potidaea; and each year there was an income from the tribute paid by the allies of four hundred and sixty talents. Beside this he declared that the vessels employed in solemn processions and the booty taken from the Medes were worth five hundred talents, and he pointed to the multitude of votive offerings in the various sanctuaries and to the fact that the fifty talents of gold on the statue of Athena for its embellishment was so constructed as to be removable: and he showed that all these, if dire need befell them, they could borrow from the gods and return to them again when peace came, and that also by reason of the long peace the manner of life of the citizens had made great strides toward prosperity.

In addition to these financial resources Pericles pointed out that, omitting the allies and garrisons, the city had available twelve thousand hoplites, the garrisons and metics amounted to more than seventeen thousand, and the triremes available to three hundred. He also pointed out that the Lacedaemonians were both lacking in money and far behind the Athenians in naval armaments. After he had recounted these facts and incited the citizens to war, he persuaded the people to pay no attention to the Lacedaemonians. This he accomplished readily by reason of his great ability as an orator, which is the reason he has been called "The Olympian." Mention has been made of this even by Aristophanes, the poet of the Old Comedy, who lived in the period of Pericles, in the following tetrameters:

> O ye farmers, wretched creatures,
> listen now and understand,
> If you fain would learn the reason
> why it was Peace left the land.
> Pheidias began the mischief,
> having come to grief and shame,
> Pericles was next in order,
> fearing he might share the blame,
> By his Megara-enactment
> lighting first a little flame,
> Such a bitter smoke ascended
> while the flames of war he blew,
> That from every eye in Hellas
> everywhere the tears it drew.

And again in another place:

> The Olympian Pericles
> Thundered and lightened and confounded Hellas.

And Eupolis the poet wrote:

> One might say Persuasion rested
> On his lips; such charm he'd bring,
> And alone of all the speakers
> In his list'ners left his sting.

**41.** Now the causes of the Peloponnesian War [431] were in general what I have described, as Ephorus has recorded them. And when the leading states had become embroiled in war in this fashion, the Lacedaemonians, sitting in council with the Peloponnesians, voted to make war upon the Athenians, and dispatching ambassadors to the king of the Persians, urged him to ally himself with them, while they also treated by means of ambassadors with their allies in Sicily and Italy and persuaded them to come to their aid with two hundred triremes; and for their own part they, together with the Peloponnesians, got ready their land forces, made all other preparations for the war, and were the first to commence the conflict. For in Boeotia the city of the Plataeans was an independent state and had an alliance with the Athenians, but certain of its citizens, wishing to destroy its independence, had engaged in parleys with the Boeotians, promising that they would range that state under the [Boeotian] confederacy [431] organised by the Thebans and hand Plataea over to them if they would send soldiers to aid in the undertaking. Consequently, when the Boeotians dispatched by night three hundred picked soldiers, the traitors got them inside the walls and made them masters of the city. The Plataeans, wishing to maintain their alliance with the Athenians, since at first they assumed that the Thebans were present in full force, began negotiations with the captors of the city and urged them to agree to a truce; but as the night wore on and they perceived that the Thebans were few in number, they rallied *en masse* and began putting up a vigorous struggle for their freedom. The fighting took place in the streets, and at first the Thebans held the upper hand because of their valour and were slaying many of their opponents; but when the slaves and children began pelting the Thebans with tiles from the houses and wounding them, they turned in flight; and some of them escaped from the city to safety, but some who found refuge in a house were forced to give themselves up. When the Thebans learned the outcome of the attempt from the survivors of the battle, they at once marched forth in all haste in full force. Since the Plataeans who dwelt in the rural districts were unprepared because they were not expecting the attack, many of them were slain and not a small number were taken captive alive, and the whole land was filled with tumult and plundering.

### On the battle between the Boeotians and the Plataeans (42).

**42.** The Plataeans dispatched ambassadors to the Thebans demanding that they leave Plataean territory and receive their own captives back, and so, when this had been agreed upon, [431] the Thebans received their captives back, restored the booty they had taken, and returned to Thebes. The Plataeans dispatched ambassadors to the Athenians asking for aid, while they themselves gathered the larger part of their possessions into the city. The Athenians, when they learned of what had taken place in Plataea, at once sent a considerable body of soldiers; these arrived in haste, although not before the Thebans, and gathered the rest of the property from the countryside into the city, and then, collecting both the children and women and the rabble, sent them off to Athens.

The Lacedaemonians, deciding that the Athenians had broken the truce, mustered a strong army from both Lacedaemon and the rest of the Peloponnesians. The allies of the Lacedaemonians at this time were all the inhabitants of the Peloponnesus with the exception of the Argives, who remained neutral; and of the peoples outside of the Peloponnesus the Megarians,

Ambraciotes, Leucadians, Phocians, Boeotians, and of the Locrians, the majority of those facing Euboea, and the Amphissians of the rest. The Athenians had as allies the peoples of the coast of Asia, namely, the Carians, Dorians, Ionians, and Hellespontines, also all the islanders except the inhabitants of Melos and Thera, likewise the dwellers in Thrace except the Chalcidians and Potidaeans, furthermore the Messenians who dwelt in Naupactus and the Cercyraeans. Of these, the Chians, Lesbians, and Cercyraeans furnished ships, and all the rest supplied infantry. The allies, then, on both sides were as we have listed them.

After the Lacedaemonians had prepared for service a strong army, they placed the command in the hands of Archidamus their king. He invaded Attica with his army, made repeated assaults upon its fortified places, and ravaged a large part of the countryside. When the Athenians, being incensed because of the raiding of their countryside, wished to offer battle to the enemy, Pericles, who was a general and held in his hands the entire leadership of the state, urged the young men to make no move, promising that he would expel the Lacedaemonians from Attica without the peril of battle. Whereupon, fitting out one hundred triremes and putting on them a strong force of men, he appointed Carcinus general over them together with certain others and sent them against the Peloponnesus. This force, by ravaging a large extent of the Peloponnesian territory along the sea and capturing some fortresses, struck terror into the Lacedaemonians; consequently they speedily recalled their army from Attica and thus provided a large measure of safety to the Peloponnesians. In this manner Athens was delivered from the enemy, and Pericles received approbation among his fellow citizens as having the ability to perform the duties of a general and to fight it out with the Lacedaemonians

### How, when Methone was being besieged by the Athenians, Brasidas the Spartan won distinction and fame (43).

**43.** When Apollodorus was archon in Athens, [430] the Romans elected as consuls Marcus Geganius and Lucius Sergius. During this year the general of the Athenians never ceased plundering and harrying the territory of the Peloponnesians and laying siege to their fortresses; and when there were added to his command fifty triremes from Cercyra, he ravaged all the more the territory of the Peloponnesians, and in particular he laid waste the part of the coast which is called Acte and sent up the farm-buildings in flames. After this, sailing to Methone in Laconia, he both ravaged the countryside and made repeated assaults upon the city. There Brasidas the Spartan, who was still a youth in years but already distinguished for his strength and courage, seeing that Methone was in danger of capture by assault, took some Spartans, and boldly breaking through the hostile forces, which were scattered, he slew many of them and got into the stronghold. In the siege which followed Brasidas fought so brilliantly that the Athenians found themselves unable to take the stronghold and withdrew to their ships, and Brasidas, who had saved Methone by his individual bravery and valour, received the approbation of the Spartans. Because of this hardihood of his, Brasidas, having become inordinately proud, on many subsequent occasions fought recklessly and won for himself a great reputation for valour. The Athenians, sailing around to Elis, ravaged the countryside and laid siege to Pheia, a stronghold of the Eleians. The Eleians who came out to its defence they defeated in battle, slaying many of their opponents, and took Pheia by storm, but after this, when the Eleians *en masse* offered them battle, the Athenians were driven back to their ships, whereupon they sailed off to Cephallenia, where they brought the inhabitants of that island into their alliance, and then voyaged back to Athens.

**How the Athenians campaigned against the Locrians and pillaged the city of Thronium (44).**

**How the Aeginetans, who had been expelled by the Athenians, colonised Thyreae, as it is called (44).**

44. After these events the Athenians chose Cleopompus general and sent him to sea with thirty ships under orders both to keep careful guard over Euboea and to make war upon the Locrians. He, sailing forth, ravaged the coast of Locris and reduced by siege the city of Thronium, and the Locrians who opposed him he met in battle and defeated near the city of Alope. Following this he made the island known as Atalante, which lies off Locris, into a fortress on the border of Locris for his operations against the inhabitants of that country. Also the Athenians, accusing the Aeginetans of having collaborated with the Lacedaemonians, expelled them from their state, and sending colonists there from their own citizens they portioned out to them in allotments both the city of Aegina and its territory. To the Aeginetan refugees the Lacedaemonians gave Thyreae, as it is called, to dwell in, because the Athenians had also once given Xaupactus as a home for the people whom they had driven out of Messenê. The Athenians also dispatched Pericles with an army to make war upon the Megarians. He plundered their territory, laid waste their possessions, and returned to Athens with much booty.

**How the Lacedaemonians sent an army into Attica and destroyed the properties (45).**

45. The Lacedaemonians together with the Peloponnesians and their other allies invaded Attica for a second time. In their advance through the country they chopped down orchards and burned the farm-buildings, and they laid waste almost the entire land with the exception of the region known as the Tetrapolis. This area they spared because their ancestors had once dwelt there and had gone forth from it as their base on the occasion when they had defeated Eurystheus; for they considered it only fair that the benefactors of their ancestors should in turn receive from their descendants the corresponding benefactions. As for the Athenians, they could not venture to meet them in a pitched battle, and being confined as they were within the walls, found themselves involved in an emergency caused by a plague; for since a vast multitude of people of every description had streamed together into the city, there was good reason for their falling victim to diseases as they did, because of the cramped quarters, breathing air which had become polluted. Consequently, since they were unable to expel the enemy from their territory, they again dispatched many ships against the Peloponnesus, appointing Pericles general. He ravaged a large part of the territory bordering on the sea, plundered some cities, and brought it about that the Lacedaemonians withdrew from Attica. After this the Athenians, now that the trees of their countryside had been cut down and the plague was carrying off

great numbers, were plunged into despondency and became angry with Pericles, considering him to have been responsible for their being at war. Consequently they removed him from the generalship, and on the strength of some petty grounds for accusation they imposed a fine upon him of eighty talents. After this they dispatched embassies to the Lacedaemonians and asked that the war be brought to an end; but when not a man paid any attention to them, they were forced to elect Pericles general again.

These, then, were the events of this year.

### The second campaign of the Athenians against the Potidaeans (46).

**46.** When Epameinon was archon in Athens, [429] the Romans elected as consuls Lucius Papirius and Aulus Cornelius Macerinus. This year in Athens Pericles the general died, a man who not only in birth and wealth, but also in eloquence and skill as a general, far surpassed his fellow citizens.

Since the people of Athens desired for the glory of it to take Potidaea by storm, they sent Hagnon there as general with the army which Pericles had formerly commanded. He put in at Potidaea with the whole expedition and made all his preparations for the siege; for he had made ready every kind of engine used in sieges, a multitude of arms and missiles, and an abundance of grain, sufficient for the entire army. Hagnon spent much time making continuous assaults every day, but without the power to take the city. For on the one side the besieged, spurred on by their fear of capture, were putting up a sturdy resistance and, confiding in the superior height of the walls, held the advantage over the Athenians attacking from the harbour, whereas the besiegers were dying in large numbers from the plague and despondency prevailed throughout the army. Hagnon, knowing that the Athenians had spent more than a thousand talents on the siege and were angry with the Potidaeans because they were the first to go over to the Lacedaemonians, was afraid to raise the siege; consequently he felt compelled to continue it and to compel the soldiers, beyond their strength, to force the issue against the city. Since many Athenian citizens were being slain in the assaults and by the ravages of the plague, he left a part of his army to maintain the siege and sailed back to Athens, having lost more than a thousand of his soldiers. After Hagnon had withdrawn, the Potidaeans, since their grain supply was entirely exhausted and the people in the city were disheartened, sent heralds to the besiegers to discuss terms of capitulation. These were received eagerly and an agreement to cessation of hostilities was reached on the following terms: All the Potidaeans should depart from the city, taking nothing with them, with the exception that men could have one garment and women two. When this truce had been agreed upon, all the Potidaeans Together with their wives and children left their native land in accordance with the terms of the compact and went to the Chalcidians in Thrace among whom they made their home; and the Athenians sent out as many as a thousand of their citizens to Potidaea as colonists and portioned out to them in allotments both the city and its territory.

### The campaign of the Lacedaemonians against Acarnania and the naval battle with the Athenians (47-48).

**47.** The Athenians elected Phormio general and sent him to sea with twenty triremes. He sailed around the Peloponnesus and put in at Naupactus, and by gaining the mastery of the Crisaean Gulf prevented the Lacedaemonians from sailing in those parts, and the Lacedaemonians sent out a strong army under Archidamus their king, who marched into Boeotia and took up positions before Plataea. Under the threat of ravaging the territory of the Plataeans he called upon them to revolt from the Athenians, and when they paid no attention to him, he plundered their territory and laid waste their possessions everywhere. After this he threw a wall about the city, in the hope that he could force the Plataeans to capitulate because of lack of the necessities of life; at the same time the Lacedaemonians continued bringing up engines with which they kept shattering the walls and making assaults without interruption, but when they found themselves unable to take the city through their assaults, they left an adequate guard before it and returned to the Peloponnesus.

The Athenians appointed Xenophon and Phanomachus generals and sent them to Thrace with a thousand soldiers. When this force arrived at Spartolus in the territory of Bottice, it laid waste the land and cut the grain in the first growth. The Olynthians came to the aid of the Bottiaeans and defeated them in battle; and there were slain of the Athenians both the generals and the larger part of the soldiers. While this was taking place, the Lacedaemonians, yielding to the request of the Ambraciotes, made a campaign against Acarnania. Their leader was Cnemus and he had a thousand foot-soldiers and a few ships. To these he added a considerable number of soldiers from their allies and entered Acarnania, pitching his camp near the city known as Stratus, but the Acarnanians gathered their forces and, laying an ambush, slew many of the enemy, and they forced Cnemus to withdraw his army to the city called Oeniadae.

**48.** During the same time Phormio, the Athenian general, with twenty triremes fell in with forty-seven Lacedaemonian warships, and engaging them in battle he sank the flagship of the enemy and put many of the rest of the ships out of action, capturing twelve together with their crews and pursuing the remaining as far as the land. The Lacedaemonians, after having suffered defeat contrary to their expectations, fled for safety with the ships which were left them to Patrae in Achaea. This sea battle took place off Rhium, as it is called. The Athenians set up a Trophy, dedicated a ship to Poseidon at the strait, and then sailed off to the city of Naupactus, which was in their alliance. The Lacedaemonians sent other ships to Patrae. These ships joined to themselves the triremes which had survived the battle and assembled at Rhium, and also the land force of the Peloponnesians met them at the same place and pitched camp near the fleet. Phormio, having become puffed up with pride over the victory he had just won, had the daring to attack the ships of the enemy, although they far outnumbered his; and some of them he sank, though losing ships of his own, so that the victory he won was equivocal. After this, when the Athenians had dispatched twenty triremes, the Lacedaemonians sailed off in fear to Corinth, not daring to offer battle.

These, then, were the events of this year.

**49.** When Diotimus was archon in Athens, [428] the Romans elected as consuls Gaius Julius and Proculus Verginius Tricostus, and the Eleians celebrated the Eighty-eighth Olympiad, that in which Symmachus of Messenê in Sicily won the stadion. In this year Cnemus, the Lacedaemonian admiral, who was inactive in Corinth, decided to seize the Peiraeus. He had received information that no ships in the harbour had been put into the water for duty and no soldiers had been detailed to guard the port; for the Athenians, as he learned, had become negligent about guarding it because they by no means expected any enemy would have the audacity to seize the place. Consequently Cnemus, launching forty triremes which had been hauled up on the beach at Megara, sailed by night to Salamis, and falling unexpectedly on the fortress on Salamis called Boudorium, he towed away three ships and overran the entire island. When the Salaminians signalled by beacon-fires to the inhabitants of Attica, the Athenians, thinking that the Peiraeus had been seized, quickly rushed forth in great confusion to its succour; but when they learned what had taken place, they quickly manned a considerable number of warships and sailed to Salamis. The Peloponnesians, having been disappointed in their main design, sailed away from Salamis and returned home, and the Athenians, after the retreat of the enemy, in the case of Salamis gave it a more vigilant guard and left on it a considerable garrison, and the Peiraeus they strengthened here and there with booms and adequate guards.

### The campaign of Sitalces against Macedonia, and of the Lacedaemonians against Attica (50-51).

**50.** In the same period Sitalces, the king of the Thracians, had succeeded to the kingship of a small land indeed but nonetheless by his personal courage and wisdom he greatly increased his dominion, equitably governing his subjects, playing the part of a brave soldier in battle and of a skilful general, and furthermore giving close attention to his revenues. In the end he attained to such power that he ruled over more extensive territory than had any who had preceded him on the throne of Thrace. For the coastline of his kingdom began at the territory of the Abderites and stretched as far as the Ister River, and for a man going from the sea to the interior the distance was so great that a man on foot travelling light required thirteen days for the journey. Ruling as he did over a territory so extensive he enjoyed annual revenues of more than a thousand talents; and when he was waging war in the period we are discussing he mustered from Thrace more than one hundred and twenty thousand infantry and fifty thousand cavalry. But with respect to this war we must set forth its causes, in order that the discussion of it may be clear to our readers.

Now Sitalces, since he had entered into a treaty of friendship with the Athenians [431], agreed to support them in their war in Thrace; and consequently, since he desired, with the help of the Athenians, to subdue the Chalcidians, he made ready a very considerable army. Since he was at the same time on bad terms with Perdiccas, the king of the Macedonians, he decided to bring back Amyntas, the son of Philip, and place him upon the Macedonian throne. It was for these two reasons, therefore, as we have described them, that he was forced to raise an imposing army. When all his preparations for the campaign had been made, he led forth the whole army, marched through Thrace, and invaded Macedonia. The Macedonians, dismayed at the great size of the army, did not dare face him in battle, but they removed both the grain and all the property they could into their most powerful strongholds, in which they remained inactive. The Thracians, after placing Amyntas upon the throne, at the outset made an effort to win over the cities by means of parleys and embassies, but when no one paid any attention to them, they forthwith made an assault on the first stronghold and took it by storm. After this some of the cities and strongholds submitted to them of their own accord through fear. And after plundering all Macedonia and appropriating much booty the Thracians turned against the Greek cities in Chalcidicê.

51. While Sitalces was engaged in these operations, the Thessalians, Achaeans, Magnesians, and all the other Greeks dwelling between Macedonia and Thermopylae took counsel together and united in raising a considerable army; for they were apprehensive lest the Thracians with all their myriads of soldiers should invade their territory and they themselves should be in peril of losing their native lands. Since the Chalcidians made the same preparations, Sitalces, having learned that the Greeks had mustered strong armies and realising that his soldiers were suffering from the hardships of the winter, came to terms with Perdiccas, concluded a connection by marriage with him, and then led his forces back to Thrace.

52. While these events were taking place, the Lacedaemonians, accompanied by their allies of the Peloponnesus, invaded Attica under the command of Archidamus their king, destroyed the grain, which was in its first growth, ravaged the countryside, and then returned home. The Athenians, since they did not dare meet the invaders in the field and were distressed because of the plague and the lack of provisions, had only bleak hopes for the future.

These, then, were the events of this year.

### On the embassy from Leontini to Athens and the powerful oratory of Gorgias their ambassador (53).

53. When Eucleides was archon in Athens,[427] the Romans elected in place of consuls three military tribunes, Marcus Manius, Quintus Sulpicius Praetextatus, and Servius Cornelius Cossus. This year in Sicily the Leontines, who were colonists from Chalcis but also kinsmen of the Athenians, were attacked, as it happened, by the Syracusans, and being hard-pressed in the war and in danger of having their city taken by storm because of the superior power of the Syracusans, they dispatched ambassadors to Athens asking the Athenian people to send them immediate aid and save their city from the perils threatening it. The leader of the embassy was Gorgias the rhetorician, who in eloquence far surpassed all his contemporaries. He was the first man to devise rules of rhetoric and so far excelled all other men in the instruction offered by the sophists that he received from his pupils a fee of one hundred minas. Now when Gorgias had arrived in Athens and been introduced to the people in assembly, he discoursed to them upon the subject of the alliance, and by the novelty of his speech he filled the Athenians, who are by nature clever and fond of dialectic, with wonder. For he was the first to use the rather unusual and carefully devised structures of speech, such as antithesis, sentences with equal members or balanced clauses or similar endings, and the like, all of which at that time was enthusiastically received because the device was exotic, but is now looked upon as laboured and to be ridiculed when employed too frequently and tediously. In the end he won the Athenians over to an alliance with the Leontines, and after having been admired in Athens for his rhetorical skill he made his return to Leontini.

## On the war between the Leontines and the Syracusans (54).

**54.** For some time past the Athenians had been covetous of Sicily because of the fertility of its land, and so at the moment, gladly accepting the proposals of Gorgias, they voted to send an allied force to the Leontines, offering as their excuse the need and request of their kinsmen, whereas in fact they were eager to get possession of the island. Indeed not many years previously, when the Corinthians and Cercyraeans were at war with one another and both were bent upon getting the Athenians as allies, the popular Assembly chose the alliance with the Cercyraeans for the reason that Cercyra was advantageously situated on the sea route to Sicily. For, speaking generally, the Athenians, having won the supremacy of the sea and accomplished great deeds, not only enjoyed the aid of many allies and possessed powerful armaments, but also had taken over a great sum of ready money, since they had transferred from Delos to Athens the funds of the confederacy of the Greeks, which amounted to more than ten thousand talents; they also enjoyed the services of great commanders who had stood the test of actual leadership; and by means of all these assets it was their hope not only to defeat the Lacedaemonians but also, after they had won the supremacy over all Greece, to lay hands on Sicily.

These, then, were the reasons why the Athenians voted to give aid to the Leontines, and they sent twenty ships to Sicily and as generals Laches and Charoeades. These sailed to Rhegium, where they added to their force twenty ships from the Rhegians and the other Chalcidian colonists. Making Rhegium their base they first of all overran the islands of the Liparaeans because they were allies of the Syracusans, and after this they sailed to [Italian] Locri, where they captured five ships of the Locrians, and then laid siege to the stronghold of Mylae. When the neighbouring Sicilian Greeks came to the aid of the Mylaeans, a battle developed in which the Athenians were victorious, slaying more than a thousand men and taking prisoner not less than six hundred; and at once they captured and occupied the stronghold.

While these events were taking place there arrived forty ships which the Athenian people had sent, deciding to push the war more vigorously; the commanders were Eurymedon and Sophocles. When all the triremes were gathered into one place, a fleet of considerable strength had been fitted out, consisting as it did of eighty triremes. Since the war was dragging on, the Leontines entered into negotiations with the Syracusans and came to terms with them. Consequently the Athenian triremes sailed back home, and the Syracusans, granting the Leontines the right of citizenship, made them all Syracusans and their city a stronghold of the Syracusans.

Such were the affairs in Sicily at this time.

## The revolt of the Lesbians from the Athenians and the seizure and destruction of Plataea by the Lacedaemonians (55-56).

**55.** In Greece the Lesbians revolted from the Athenians; for they harboured against them the complaint that, when they wished to merge all the cities of Lesbos with the city of the Mytilenaeans, the Athenians had prevented it. Consequently, after dispatching ambassadors to the Peloponnesians and concluding an alliance with them, they advised the Spartans to make an attempt to seize the supremacy at sea, and toward this design they promised to supply many triremes for the war. The Lacedaemonians were glad to accept this offer, but while they were busied with the building of the triremes, the Athenians forestalled their completion by sending forthwith a force against Lesbos, having manned forty ships and chosen Cleinippides as their commander, He gathered reinforcements from the allies and put in at Mytilene. In a naval battle which followed the Mytilenaeans were defeated and enclosed within a siege of their city. Meanwhile the Lacedaemonians had voted to send aid to the Mytilenaeans and were making ready a strong fleet, but the Athenians forestalled them by sending to Lesbos additional ships along with a thousand hoplites. Their commander, Paches the son of Epiclerus, upon arriving at Mytilene, took over the force already there, threw a wall about the city, and kept launching continuous assaults upon it not only by land but by sea as well.

The Lacedaemonians sent forty-five triremes to Mytilene under the command of Alcidas, and they also invaded Attica together with their allies; here they visited the districts of Attica which they had passed by before, ravaged the countryside, and then returned home. The Mytilenaeans, who were distressed by lack of food and the war and were also quarrelling among themselves, formally surrendered the city to the besiegers. While in Athens the people were deliberating on what action they should take against the Mytilenaeans, Cleon, the leader of the populace and a man of cruel and violent nature, spurred on the people, declaring that they should slay all the male Mytilenaeans from the youth upward and sell into slavery the children and women. In the end the Athenians were won over and voted as Cleon had proposed, and messengers were dispatched to Mytilene to make known to the general the measures decreed by the popular assembly. Even as Paches had finished reading the decree a second decree arrived, the opposite of the first. Paches was glad when he learned that the Athenians had changed their minds, and gathering the Mytilenaeans in assembly he declared them free of the charges as well as of the greatest fears. The Athenians pulled down the walls of Mytilene and portioned out in allotments the entire island of Lesbos with the exception of the territory of the Methymnaeans.

Such, then, was the end of the revolt of the Lesbians from the Athenians.

**56.** About the same time the Lacedaemonians who were besieging Plataea threw a wall about the city and kept a guard over it of many soldiers. As the siege dragged on and the Athenians still sent them no help, the besieged not only were suffering from lack of food but had also lost many of their fellow citizens in the assaults. While they were thus at a loss and were conferring together how they could be saved, the majority were of the opinion that they should make no move, but the rest, some two hundred in number, decided to force a passage through the guards by night and make their way to Athens, and so, on a moonless night for which they had waited, they persuaded the rest of the Plataeans to make an assault upon one side of the encircling wall; they themselves then made ready ladders, and when the enemy rushed to defend the opposite parts of the walls, they managed by means of the ladders to get up on the wall, and after slaying the guards they made their escape to Athens. The next day the Lacedaemonians, provoked at the flight of the men who had got away from the city, made an assault upon the city of the Plataeans and strained every nerve to subdue the besieged by storm; and the Plataeans in dismay sent envoys to the enemy and surrendered to them both themselves and the city. The commanders of the Lacedaemonians, summoning the Plataeans one by one, asked what good deed he had ever performed for the Lacedaemonians, and when each confessed that he had done them no good turn, they asked further if he had ever done the Spartans any harm; and when not a man could deny that he had, they condemned all of them to death. Consequently they slew all who still remained, razed the city to the ground, and farmed out its territory. So the Plataeans, who had maintained with the greatest constancy their alliance with the Athenians, fell unjust victims to the most tragic fate.

### *The civil strife among the Cercyraeans (57).*

57. While these events were taking place, in Cercyra bitter civil strife and contentiousness arose for the following reasons. In the fighting about Epidamnus many Cercyraeans had been taken prisoner and cast into the state prison, and these men promised the Corinthians that, if the Corinthians set them free, they would hand Cercyra over to them. The Corinthians gladly agreed to the proposals, and the Cercyraeans, after going through the pretence of paying a ransom, were released on bail of a considerable sum of talents furnished by the proxeni. Faithful to their promises the Cercyraeans, as soon as they had returned to their native land, arrested and put to death the men who had always been popular leaders and had acted as champions of the people. They also put an end to the democracy; but when, a little after this time, the Athenians came to the help of the popular party, the Cercyraeans, who had now recovered their liberty, undertook to mete out punishment to the men responsible for the revolt against the established government. These, in fear of the usual punishment, fled for refuge to the altars of the gods and became suppliants of the people and of the gods, and the Cercyraeans, out of reverence for the gods, absolved them from that punishment but expelled them from the city. But these exiles, undertaking a second revolution, fortified a strong position on the island, and continued to harass the Cercyraeans.

These, then, were the events of this year.

### **How the Athenians were seized by a pestilential disease and lost many of their citizens (58).**

58. When Euthynes was archon in Athens, [426] the Romans elected in place of consuls three military tribunes, Marcus Fabius, Marcus Falinius, and Lucius Servilius. In this year the Athenians, who had enjoyed a period of relief from the plague, became involved again in the same misfortunes; for they were so seriously attacked by the disease that of their soldiers they lost more than four thousand infantry and four hundred cavalry, and of the rest of the population, both free and slave, more than ten thousand. Since history seeks to ascertain the cause of the malignancy of this disease, it is our duty to explain these matters.

As a result of heavy rains in the previous winter the ground had become soaked with water, and many low-lying regions, having received a vast amount of water, turned into shallow pools and held stagnant water, very much as marshy regions do; and when these waters became warm in the summer and grew putrid, thick foul vapours were formed, which, rising up in fumes, corrupted the surrounding air, the very thing which may be seen taking place in marshy grounds which are by nature pestilential. Contributing also to the disease was the bad character of the food available; for the crops which were raised that year were altogether watery and their natural quality was corrupted. And a third cause of the disease proved to be the failure of the etesian winds to blow, by which normally most of the heat in summer is cooled; and when the heat intensified and the air grew fiery, the bodies of the inhabitants, being without anything to cool them, wasted away. Consequently all the illnesses which prevailed at that time were found to be accompanied by fever, the cause of which was the excessive heat. This was the reason why most of the sick threw themselves into the cisterns and springs in their craving to cool their bodies. The Athenians, however, because the disease was so severe, ascribed the causes of their misfortune to the deity. Consequently, acting upon the command of a certain oracle, they purified the island of Delos, which was sacred to Apollo and had been defiled, as men thought, by the burial there of the dead. Digging up, therefore, all the graves on Delos, they transferred the remains to the island of Rheneia, as it is called, which lies near Delos. They also passed a law that neither birth nor burial should be allowed on Delos. And they also celebrated the [Amphictyony] festival assembly, the Delia, which had been held in former days but had not been observed for a long time.

### *How the Lacedaemonians founded Heracleia, a city in Trachis (59).*

**59.** While the Athenians were busied with these matters, the Lacedaemonians, taking with them the Peloponnesians, pitched camp at the Isthmus with the intention of invading Attica again; but when great earthquakes took place, they were filled with superstitious fear and returned to their native lands. So severe in fact were the shocks in many parts of Greece that the sea actually swept away and destroyed some cities lying on the coast, while in Locris the strip of land forming a peninsula was torn through and the island known as Atalante was formed.

While these events were taking place, the Lacedaemonians colonised Trachis, as it was called, and renamed it Heracleia, for the following reasons. The Trachinians had been at war with the neighbouring Oetaeans for many years and had lost the larger number of their citizens. Since the city was deserted, they thought it proper that the Lacedaemonians, who were colonists from Trachis, should assume the care of it, and the Lacedaemonians, both because of their kinship and because Heracles, their ancestor, in ancient times had made his home in Trachis, decided to make it a great city. Consequently the Lacedaemonians and the Peloponnesians sent forth four thousand colonists and accepted any other Greeks who wished to have a part in the colony; the latter numbered not less than six thousand. The result was that they made Trachis a city of ten thousand inhabitants, and after portioning out the territory in allotments they named the city Heracleia.

### *How the Athenians slew many of the Ambraciotes and laid waste their city (60).*

**60.** When Stratocles was archon in Athens, [425] in Rome in place of consuls three military tribunes were elected, Lucius Furius, Spurius Pinarius, and Gaius

Metellus. This year the Athenians chose Demosthenes general and sent him forth with thirty ships and an adequate body of soldiers. He added to his force fifteen ships from the Cercyraeans and soldiers from the Cephallenians, Acarnanians, and the Messenians in Naupactus, and then sailed to Leucas. After ravaging the territory of the Leucadians he sailed to Aetolia and plundered many of its villages. The Aetolians rallied to oppose him and there was a battle in which the Athenians were defeated, whereupon they withdrew to Naupactus. The Aetolians, elated by their victory, after adding to their army Three thousand Lacedaemonian soldiers, marched upon Naupactus, which was inhabited at the time by Messenians, but were beaten off. After this they marched upon the city called Molycria and captured it. The Athenian general, Demosthenes, being concerned lest the Aetolians should reduce by siege Naupactus also, summoned a thousand hoplites from Acarnania and sent them to Naupactus, and Demosthenes, while tarrying in Acarnania, fell in with a thousand Ambraciotes, who were encamped there, and joining battle with them he destroyed nearly the entire force. When the men of Ambracia came out against him *en masse,* again Demosthenes slew the larger number of them, so that their city became almost uninhabited. Demosthenes then believed that he should take Ambracia by storm, hoping that he would have an easy conquest because the city had no one to defend it, but the Acarnanians, fearing lest, if the Athenians became masters of the city, they should be harder neighbours to deal with than the Ambraciotes, refused to follow him. Since they were thus in disagreement, the Acarnanians came to terms with the Ambraciotes and concluded with them a peace of one hundred years, while Demosthenes, being left in the lurch by the Acarnanians, sailed back with his twenty ships to Athens. The Ambraciotes, who had experienced a great disaster, sent for a garrison of Lacedaemonians, since they stood in fear of the Athenians.

### On the Lacedaemonians who were made prisoners on the island of Sphacteria (61-63).

**61.** Demosthenes now led an expedition against Pylos, intending to fortify this stronghold as a threat to the Peloponnesus; for it is an exceptionally strong place, situated in Messenia and four hundred stades distant from Sparta. Since he had at the time both many ships and an adequate number of soldiers, in twenty days he threw a wall about Pylos. The Lacedaemonians, when they learned that Pylos had been fortified, gathered together a large force, both infantry and ships. Consequently, when they set sail for Pylos, they not only had a fleet of forty-five fully equipped triremes but also marched with an army of twelve thousand soldiers; for they considered it to be a disgraceful thing that men who were not brave enough to defend Attica while it was being ravaged should fortify and hold a fortress in the Peloponnesus. Now these forces under the command of Thrasymedes pitched their camp in the neighbourhood of Pylos. Since the troops were seized by an eager desire to undergo any and every danger and to take Pylos by storm, the Lacedaemonians stationed the ships with their prows facing the entrance to the harbour in order that they might use them for blocking the enemy's attempt to enter, and assaulting the walls with the infantry in successive waves and displaying all possible rivalry, they put up contests of amazing valour. Also to the island called Sphacteria, which extends lengthwise to the harbour and protects it from the winds, they transported the best troops of the Lacedaemonians and their allies. This they did in their desire to forestall the Athenians in getting control of the island before them, since its situation was especially advantageous to the prosecution of the siege. Though they were engaged every day in the fighting before the fortifications and were suffering wounds because of the superior height of the wall, they did not relax the violence of their fighting; as a consequence, many of them were slain and not a few were wounded as they pressed upon a position which had been fortified. The Athenians, who had secured beforehand a place which was also a natural stronghold and possessed large supplies of missiles and a great abundance of everything else they might need, kept defending their position with spirit; for they hoped that, if they were successful in their design, they could carry the whole war to the Peloponnesus and ravage, bit by bit, the territory of the enemy.

### On the punishment inflicted by Postumius on his son because he left his place in the ranks (64).

62. Both sides displayed unsurpassable energy in the siege, and as for the Spartans in their assaults upon the walls, while many others were objects of wonder for their deeds of valour, the greatest acclaim was won by Brasidas. For when the captains of the triremes lacked the courage to bring the ships to land because of the rugged nature of the shore, he, being himself the commander of a trireme, called out in a loud voice to the pilot, ordering him not to spare the vessel but to drive the trireme at full speed to the land; for it would be disgraceful, he cried, for Spartans to be unsparing of their lives as they fought for victory, and yet to spare their vessels and to endure the sight of Athenians holding the soil of Laconia. Finally he succeeded in forcing the pilot to drive the ship forward and, when the trireme struck the shore, Brasidas, taking his stand on the gangway, fought off from there the multitude of Athenians who converged upon him; at the outset he slew many as they came at him, but after a while, as numerous missiles assailed him, he suffered many wounds on the front of his body. In the end he suffered much loss of blood from the wounds, and as he lost consciousness his arm extended over the side of the ship and his shield, slipping off and falling into the sea, came into the hands of the enemy. After this Brasidas, who had built up a heap of many corpses of the enemy, was himself carried off half-dead from the ship by his men, having surpassed to such a degree all other men in bravery that, whereas in the case of all other men those who lose their shields are punished with death, he for that very reason won for himself glory.

Now the Lacedaemonians, although they kept making continuous assaults upon Pylos and had lost many soldiers, remained steadfast in the fierce struggles, and one may well be amazed at the strange perversity of Fortune and at the singular character of her ordering of what happened at Pylos. For the Athenians, defending themselves from a base on Laconian soil, were gaining the mastery over the Spartans, whereas the Lacedaemonians, regarding their own soil as the enemy's, were assaulting the enemy from the sea as their base; and, as it happened, those who were masters of the land in this case controlled the sea, and those who held first place on the sea were beating off an attack on land which they held.

**63.** Since the siege dragged on and the Athenians, after their victory with their ships, were preventing the conveyance of food to the land, the soldiers caught on the island were in danger of death from starvation. Consequently the Lacedaemonians, fearing for the men left on the island, sent an embassy to Athens to discuss the ending of the war. When no agreement was being reached, they asked for an exchange of men, the Athenians to get back an equal number of their soldiers now held prisoner; but not even to this would the Athenians agree. Whereupon the ambassadors spoke out frankly in Athens, that by their unwillingness to effect an exchange of prisoners the Athenians acknowledged that Lacedaemonians were better men than they. Meanwhile the Athenians wore down the bodily strength of the Spartans on Sphacteria through their lack of provisions and accepted their formal surrender. Of the men who gave themselves up one hundred and twenty were Spartans and one hundred and eighty were of their allies. These, then, were brought by Cleon the leader of the populace, since he held the office of general when this took place, in chains to Athens; and the people voted to keep them in custody in case the Lacedaemonians should be willing to end the war, but to slay all the captives if they should decide to continue it. After this they sent for select troops from the Messenians who had been settled in Naupactus, joined to them an adequate force from their other allies, and turned over to them the garrisoning of Pylos; for they believed that the Messenians, by reason of their hatred of the Spartans, would show the greatest zeal in harrying Laconia by forays, once they were operating from a strong position as their base.

Such were the events about Pylos in this year.

**64.** Artaxerxes, the king of the Persians, died [425] after a reign of forty years, and Xerxes succeeded to the throne and ruled for a year.

In Italy, when the Aequi revolted from the Romans, in the war which followed Aulus Postumius was made Dictator and Lucius Julius was named Master of the Horse. The Romans, having marched against the territory of the rebels with a large and strong army, first of all plundered their possessions, and when the Aequi later drew up against them, a battle ensued in which the Romans were victorious, slaying many of the enemy, taking not a few captive, and capturing great quantities of booty. After the battle the revolters, being broken in spirit because of the defeat, submitted themselves to the Romans, and Postumius, because he had conducted the war brilliantly, as the Romans thought, celebrated the customary triumph. Postumius, we are told, did a peculiar thing and altogether unbelievable; for in the battle his own son in his eagerness leaped forward from the station assigned him by his father, and his father, preserving the ancient discipline, had his son executed as one who had left his station.

**65.** At the close of this year, [424] in Athens the archon was Isarchus and in Rome the consuls elected were Titus Quinctius and Gaius Julius, and among the Eleians the Eighty-ninth Olympiad was celebrated, that in which Symmachus won the stadion for the second time. This year the Athenians chose as general Nicias, the son of Niceratus, and assigning to him sixty triremes and three thousand hoplites, they ordered him to plunder the allies of the Lacedaemonians. He sailed to Melos as the first place, where he ravaged their territory and for a number of days laid siege to the city; for it was the only island of the Cyclades which was maintaining its alliance with the Lacedaemonians, being a Spartan colony. Nicias was unable to take the city, however, since the Melians defended themselves gallantly, and he then sailed to Oropus in Boeotia. Leaving his ships there, he advanced with his hoplites into the territory of the Tanagraeans, where he fell in with another Athenian force which was commanded by Hipponicus, the son of Callias. When the two armies had united, the generals pressed forward, plundering the land; and when the Thebans sallied forth to the rescue, the Athenians offered them battle, in which they inflicted heavy casualties and were victorious.

After the battle the soldiers with Hipponicus made their way back to Athens, but Nicias, returning to his ships, sailed along the coast to Locris, and when he had laid waste the country on the coast, he added to his fleet forty triremes from the allies, so that he possessed in all one hundred ships. He also enrolled no small number of soldiers and gathered together a strong armament, whereupon he sailed against Corinth. There he disembarked the soldiers, and when the Corinthians drew up their forces against them, the Athenians gained the victory in two battles, slew many of the enemy, and set up a trophy. There perished in the fighting eight Athenians and more than three hundred Corinthians. Nicias then sailed to [Megaris] Crommyon, ravaged its territory, and seized its stronghold. Then he immediately removed from there and built a stronghold near Methone, in which he left a garrison for the twofold purpose of protecting the place and ravaging the neighbouring countryside; then Nicias plundered the coast and returned to Athens.

After these events the Athenians sent sixty ships and two thousand hoplites to Cythera, the expedition being under the command of Nicias and certain other generals. Nicias attacked the island, hurled assaults upon the city, and received its formal surrender, and leaving a garrison behind on the island he sailed off to the Peloponnesus and ravaged the territory along the coast. Thyreae, which lies on the border between Laconia and Argolis, he took by siege, making slaves of its inhabitants, and razed it to the ground; and the Aeginetans, who inhabited the city, together with the commander of the garrison, Tantalus the Spartan, he took captive and carried off to Athens. And the Athenians fettered Tantalus and kept him under guard together with the other prisoners, as well as the Aeginetans.

### On the war between the Lacedaemonians and Athenians over the Megarians (66).

**66.** While these events were taking place the Megarians were finding themselves in distress because of their war with the Athenians on the one hand and with their exiles on the other hand. While representatives were exchanging opinions regarding the exiles, certain citizens who were hostile to the exiles approached the Athenian generals with the offer to deliver the city to them. The generals. Hippocrates and Demosthenes, agreeing to this betrayal, sent by night six hundred soldiers to the city, and the conspirators admitted the Athenians within the walls. When the betrayal became known throughout the city and while the multitude were divided according to party, some being in favour of fighting on the side of the Athenians and others of aiding the Lacedaemonians, a certain man, acting on his own initiative, made the proclamation that any who so wished could take up arms on the side of the Athenians and Megarians. Consequently, when the Lacedaemonians were on the point of being left in the lurch by the Megarians, it so happened that the Lacedaemonian garrison of the long walls abandoned them and sought safety in Nisaea, as it is called, which is the sea-port of the Megarians. The Athenians thereupon dug a ditch about Nisaea and put it under siege, and then, bringing skilled workmen from Athens, they threw a wall about it; the Peloponnesians, fearing lest they should be taken by storm and put to death, surrendered Nisaea to the Athenians.

Such, then, were the affairs of the Megarians at this time.

### The war between the Lacedaemonians and Athenians over the Chalcidians (67-68).

**67.** Brasidas, taking an adequate force from Lacedaemon and the other Peloponnesian states, advanced against Megara. And striking terror into the Athenians he expelled them from Nisaea, and then he set free the city of the Megarians and brought it back into the alliance of the Lacedaemonians. After this he made his way with his army through Thessaly and came to Dium in Macedonia. From there he advanced against Acanthus and associated himself with the cause of the Chalcidians. The city of the Acanthians was the first which he brought, partly through fear and partly through kindly and persuasive arguments, to revolt from the Athenians; and afterwards he induced many also of the other peoples of Thrace to join the alliance of the Lacedaemonians. After this Brasidas, wishing to prosecute the war more vigorously, proceeded to summon soldiers from Lacedaemon, since he was eager to gather a strong army. The Spartans, wishing to destroy the most influential among the Helots, sent him a thousand of the most high-spirited Helots, thinking that the larger number of them would perish in the fighting. They also committed another violent and savage act whereby they thought to humble the pride of the Helots: They made public proclamation that any Helots who had rendered some good service to Sparta should submit their names, and promised that after passing upon their claims they would set them free; and when two thousand had tendered their names, they then commanded the most influential citizens to slay these Helots, each in his own home. For they were deeply concerned lest the Helots should seize an opportune moment to line up with the enemy and bring Sparta into peril. Nevertheless, since Brasidas had been joined by a thousand Helots and troops had been levied among the allies, a satisfactory force was assembled.

**68.** Brasidas, confiding in the multitude of his soldiers, now advanced with his army against the city known as Amphipolis. This city Aristagoras of Miletus at an earlier time had undertaken to found as a colony [497], when he was fleeing from Darius, the king of the Persians; after his death the colonists were driven out by the Thracians who are called Edones, and thirty-two years after this event the Athenians dispatched ten thousand colonists to the place. In like manner these colonists also were utterly destroyed by Thracians at Drabescus, and two years later the Athenians again recovered the city, under the leadership of Hagnon. Since the city had been the object of many a battle, Brasidas was eager to master it. Consequently he set out against it with a strong force, and pitching his camp near the bridge, he first of all seized the suburb of the city and then on the next day, having struck terror into the Amphipolitans, he received the

BOOK XII

formal surrender of the city on the condition that anyone who so wished could take his property and leave the city.

Immediately after this Brasidas brought over to his side a number of the neighbouring cities, the most, important of which were Oesyme and Galepsus, both colonies of the Thasians, and also Myrcinus, a small Edonian city. He also set about building a number of triremes on the Strymon River and summoned soldiers from both Lacedaemon and the rest of the allies. Also he had many complete suits of armour made, which he distributed among the young men who possessed no arms, and he gathered supplies of missiles and grain and everything else. When all his preparations had been made, he set out from Amphipolis with his army and came to Acte [Mt. Athos], as it is called, where he pitched his camp. In this area there were five cities, of which some were Greek, being colonies from Andros, and the others had a populace of barbarians of Bisaltic origin, which were bilingual. After mastering these cities Brasidas led his army against the city of Torone, which was a colony of the Chalcidians but was held by Athenians. Since certain men were ready to betray the city, Brasidas was by night admitted by them and got Torone in his power without a fight.

To such a height did the fortunes of Brasidas attain in the course of this year.

### *The battle in Boeotia between the Athenians and the Boeotians (69-70).*

**69.** While these events were happening, at Delium in Boeotia a pitched battle took place between the Athenians and the Boeotians for the following reasons. Certain Boeotians, who were restive under the form of government which obtained at the time and were eager to establish democracies in the cities, discussed their policy with the Athenian generals, Hippocrates and Demosthenes, and promised to deliver the cities of Boeotia into their hands. The Athenians gladly accepted this offer and, having in view the arrangements for the attack, the generals divided their forces: Demosthenes, taking the larger part of the army, invaded Boeotia, but finding the Boeotians already informed of the betrayal he withdrew without accomplishing anything; Hippocrates led the popular levy of the Athenians against Delium, seized the place, and threw a wall about it before the approach of the Boeotians. The town lies near the territory of Oropus and the boundary of Boeotia. Pagondas, who commanded the Boeotians, having summoned soldiers from all the cities of Boeotia, came to Delium with a great army, since he had little less than twenty thousand infantry and about a thousand cavalry. The Athenians, although superior to the Boeotians in number, were not so well equipped as the enemy; for they had left the city hurriedly and on short notice, and in such haste they were unprepared.

**70.** Both armies advanced to the fray in high spirits and the forces were disposed in the following manner. On the Boeotian side, the Thebans were drawn up on the right wing, the Orchomenians on the left, and the centre of the line was made up of the other Boeotians; the first line of the whole army was formed of what they called "charioteers and footmen," a select group of three hundred. The Athenians were forced to engage the enemy while still marshalling their army. A fierce conflict ensued and at first the Athenian cavalry, fighting brilliantly, compelled the opposing cavalry to flee; but later, after the infantry had become engaged, the Athenians who were opposed to the Thebans were overpowered and put to flight, although the remaining Athenians overcame the other Boeotians, slew great numbers of them, and pursued them for some distance, but the Thebans, whose bodily strength was superior, turned back from the pursuit, and falling on the pursuing Athenians forced them to flee; and since they had won a conspicuous victory [Delium], they gained for themselves great fame for valour. Of the Athenians some fled for refuge to Oropus and others to Delium; certain of them made for the sea and the Athenian ships; still others scattered this way and that, as chance dictated. When night fell, the Boeotian dead were not in excess of five hundred, the Athenian many times that number. However, if night had not intervened, most of the Athenians would have perished, for it broke the drive of the pursuers and brought safety to those in flight. Even so the multitude of the slain was so great that from the proceeds of the booty the Thebans not only constructed the great colonnade in their market-place but also embellished it with bronze statues, and their temples and the colonnades in the market-place they covered with bronze by the armour from the booty which they nailed to them; furthermore, it was with this money that they instituted the festival called Delia.

After the battle the Boeotians launched assaults upon Delium and took the place by storm; of the garrison of Delium the larger number died fighting gallantly and two hundred were taken prisoner; the rest fled for safety to the ships and were transported with the other refugees to Attica. Thus the Athenians, who devised a plot against the Boeotians, were involved in the disaster we have described.

71. In Asia King Xerxes died after a reign of one year, or, as some record, two months; and his brother Sogdianus succeeded to the throne and ruled for seven months. He was slain by Darius, who reigned nineteen years.

Of the historians Antiochus of Syracuse concluded with this year [424] his history of Sicily, which began with Cocalus, the king of the Sicani, and embraced nine Books.

### *The campaign of the Athenians against the Lesbian exiles (72).*

72. When Ameinias was archon in Athens, [423] the Romans elected as consuls Gaius Papirius and Lucius Junius. In this year the people of Scione, holding the Athenians in contempt because of their defeat at Delium, revolted to the Lacedaemonians and delivered their city into the hands of Brasidas, who was in command of the Lacedaemonian forces in Thrace.

In Lesbos, after the Athenian seizure of Mytilene, the exiles, who had escaped the capture in large numbers, had for some time been trying to return to Lesbos, and they succeeded at this time in rallying and seizing Antandrus, from which as their base they then carried on war with the Athenians who were in possession of Mytilene. Exasperated by this state of affairs the Athenian people sent against them as generals Aristeides and Symmachus with an army. They put in at Lesbos and by means of sustained assaults took possession of Antandrus, and of the exiles some they put to death and others they expelled from the city; then they left a garrison to guard the place and sailed away from Lesbos. After this Lamachus the general sailed with ten triremes into the Pontus and anchored at Heracleia, on the river Cales, as it is called, but he lost all his ships; for when heavy rains fell, the river brought down so violent a current that his vessels were driven on certain rocky places and broken to pieces on the bank.

The Athenians concluded a truce with the Lacedaemonians for a year, on the terms that both of them should remain in possession of the places of which they were masters at the time. They held many discussions and were of the opinion that they should stop the war and put an end to their mutual rivalry; and the Lacedaemonians were eager to recover their citizens who had been taken captive at Sphacteria. When the truce had been concluded on the terms here mentioned, they were in entire agreement on all other matters, but both of them laid claim to Scione. And so bitter a controversy followed that they renounced the truce and continued their war against each other over the issue of Scione.

At this time the city of Mende also revolted to the Lacedaemonians and made the quarrel over Scione:he more bitter. Consequently Brasidas removed the children and women and all the most valuable property from Mende and Scione and safeguarded the cities with strong garrisons, whereupon the Athenians, being incensed at what had taken place, voted to put to the sword all the Scionaeans from:he youth upward, when they should take the city, and sent a naval force of fifty triremes against them, the command of which was held by Nicias and Nicostratus. They sailed to Mende first and conquered it with the aid of certain men who betrayed it; then they threw a wall about Scione, settled down to a siege, and launched unceasing assaults upon it. The garrison of Scione, which was strong in numbers and abundantly provided with missiles and food and all other supplies, had no difficulty in repulsing the Athenians and, because they held a higher position, in wounding many of their men.

Such, then, were the events of this year.

### *The expulsion of the Delians by the Athenians (73).*
### *The capture and destruction of Toronê by the Athenians (73).*

**73.** The next year Alcaeus was archon in Athens [422] and in Rome the consuls were Opiter Lucretius and Lucius Sergius Fideniates. During this year the Athenians, accusing the Delians of secretly concluding an alliance with the Lacedaemonians, expelled them from the island and took their city for their own. To the Delians who had been expelled the satrap Pharniaces gave the city of Adramytium to dwell in.

The Athenians elected as general Cleon, the leader of the popular party, and supplying him with a strong body of infantry sent him to the regions lying off Thrace. He sailed to Scione, where he added to his force soldiers from the besiegers of the city, and then sailed away and put in at Torone; for he knew that Brasidas had gone from these parts and that the soldiers who were left in Torone were not strong enough to offer battle. After encamping near Torone and besieging the city both by land and by sea, he took it by storm, and the children and women he sold into slavery, but the men who garrisoned the city he took captive, fettered them, and sent them to Athens. Then, leaving an adequate garrison for the city, he sailed away with his army and put in at the Strymon River in Thrace. Pitching camp near the city of Eïon, which is about thirty stades distant from Amphipolis, he launched successive assaults upon the town.

***How, after the Athenians and Lacedaemonians had concluded an alliance between them, the rest of the cities were alienated from them (74-76).***

**74.** Cleon, learning that Brasidas and his army were tarrying at the city of Amphipolis, broke camp and marched against him, and when Brasidas heard of the approach of the enemy, he formed his army in battle-order and went out to meet the Athenians. A fierce battle ensued, in which both armies engaged brilliantly, and at first the fight was evenly balanced, but later, as the leaders on both sides strove to decide the battle through their own efforts, it was the lot of many important men to be slain, the generals injecting themselves into the battle and bringing into it a rivalry for victory that could not be surpassed. Brasidas, after fighting with the greatest distinction and slaying a very large number, ended his life heroically; and when Cleon also, after displaying like valour, fell in the battle, both armies were thrown into confusion because they had no leaders, but in the end the Lacedaemonians were victorious and set up a trophy. The Athenians got back their dead under a truce, gave them burial, and sailed away to Athens. And when certain men from the scene of the battle arrived at Lacedaemon and brought the news of Brasidas' victory as well as of his death, the mother of Brasidas, on learning of the course of the battle, inquired what sort of a man Brasidas had shown himself to be in the conflict; when she was told that of all the Lacedaemonians he was the best, the mother of the dead man said, "My son Brasidas was a brave man, and yet he was inferior to many others." When this reply passed throughout the city, the ephors accorded the woman public honours, because she placed the fair name of her country above the fame of her son.

After the battle we have described the Athenians decided to make a truce of fifty years with the Lacedaemonians, upon the following terms: The prisoners with both sides were to be released and each side should give back the cities which had been taken in the course of the war. Thus the Peloponnesian War, which had continued up to that time for ten years, came to an end in the manner we have described.

**75.** When Ariston was archon in Athens, [421] the Romans elected as consuls Titus Quinctius and Aulus Cornelius Cossus. During this year, although the Peloponnesian War had just come to an end, again tumults and military movements occurred throughout Greece, for the following reasons. Although the Athenians and Lacedaemonians had concluded a truce and cessation of hostilities in company with their allies, they had formed an alliance without consultation with the allied cities. By this act they fell under suspicion of having formed an alliance for their private ends, with the purpose of enslaving the rest of the Greeks. As a consequence the most important of the cities maintained a mutual exchange of embassies and conversations regarding a union of policy and an alliance against the Athenians and Lacedaemonians. The leading states in this undertaking were the four most powerful ones, Argos, Thebes, Corinth, and Elis.

There was good reason to suspect that Athens and Lacedaemon had common designs against the rest of Greece, since a clause had been added to the compact which the two had made, namely, that the Athenians and Lacedaemonians had the right, according as these states may deem it best, to add to or subtract from the agreements. Moreover, the Athenians by decree had lodged in ten men the power to take counsel regarding what would be of advantage to the city; and since much the same thing had also been done by the Lacedaemonians, the selfish ambitions of the two states were open for all to see. Many cities answered to the call of their common freedom, and since the Athenians were disdained by reason of the defeat they had suffered at Delium and the Lacedaemonians had had their fame reduced because of the capture of their citizens on the island of Sphacteria, a large number of cities joined together and selected the city of the Argives to hold the position of leader. For this city enjoyed a high position by reason of its achievements in the past, since until the return of the Heracleidae practically all the most important kings had come from the Argolis, and furthermore, since the city had enjoyed peace for a long time, it had received revenues of the greatest size and had a great store not only of money but also of men. The Argives, believing that the entire leadership was to be conceded to them, picked out one thousand of their younger citizens who were at the same time the most vigorous in body and the most wealthy, and freeing them also from every other service to the state and supplying them with sustenance at public expense, they had them undergo continuous training and exercise. These young men, therefore, by reason of the expense incurred for them and their continuous training, quickly formed a body of athletes trained to deeds of war.

**76.** The Lacedaemonians, seeing the Peloponnesus uniting against them and foreseeing the magnitude of the impending war, began exerting every possible effort to make sure their position of leadership. First of all the Helots who had served with Brasidas in Thrace, a thousand in all, were given their freedom; then the Spartans, who had been taken prisoner on the island of Sphacteria and had been disgraced on the ground that they had diminished the glory of Sparta, were freed from their state of disgrace. Also, in pursuance of the same policy, by means of the commendations and honours accorded in the course of the war they were incited to surpass in the struggles which lay before them the deeds of valour they had already performed; and toward their allies they conducted themselves more equitably and conciliated the most unfavourably disposed of them with kindly treatment. The Athenians, on the contrary, desiring to strike with fear those whom they suspected of planning secession, displayed an example for all to see in the punishment they inflicted on the inhabitants of Scione; for after reducing them by siege, they put to the sword all of them from the youth upwards, sold into slavery the children and women, and gave the island to the Plataeans to dwell in, since they had been expelled from their native land on account of the Athenians.

In the course of this year in Italy the Campanians advanced against Cymê with a strong army, defeated the Cymaeans in battle, and destroyed the larger part of the opposing forces, and settling down to a siege, they launched a number of assaults upon the city and took it by storm. They then plundered the city, sold into slavery the captured prisoners, and selected an adequate number of their own citizens to settle there.

*How the Delians were restored by the Athenians to their native state (77).*

**77.** When Astyphilus was archon in Athens, [420] the Romans elected as consuls Lucius Quinctius and Aulus Sempronius, and the Eleians celebrated the Ninetieth Olympiad, that in which Hyperbius of Syracuse won the stadion. This year the Athenians, in obedience to a certain oracle, returned their island to the Delians, and the Delians who were dwelling in Adramytium a returned to their native land. And since the Athenians had not returned the city of Pylos to the Lacedaemonians, these cities were again at odds with each other and hostile. When this was known to the Assembly of the Argives, that body persuaded the Athenians to close a treaty of friendship with the Argives, and since the quarrel kept growing, the Lacedaemonians persuaded the Corinthians to desert the league of states and ally themselves with the Lacedaemonians. Such being the confusion that had arisen together with a lack of leadership, the situation throughout the Peloponnesus was as has been described.

In the regions outside, the Aenianians, Dolopians, and Melians, having come to an understanding, advanced with strong armaments against Heracleia in Trachis. The Heracleians drew up to oppose them and a great battle took place, in which the people of Heracleia were defeated. Since they had lost many soldiers and had sought refuge within their walls, they sent for aid from the Boeotians. The Thebans dispatched to their help a thousand picked hoplites, with whose aid they held off their adversaries.

While these events were taking place, the Olynthians dispatched an army against the city of Mecyberna which had an Athenian garrison, drove out the garrison, and themselves took possession of the city.

### How the Lacedaemonians waged war upon the Mantineans and Argives (78-79).

**78.** When Archias was archon in Athens, [419] the Romans elected as consuls Lucius Papirius Mugilanus and Gaius Servilius Structus. In this year the Argives, charging the Lacedaemonians with not paying the sacrifices to Apollo Pythaeus, declared war on them; and it was at this very time that Alcibiades, the Athenian general, entered Argolis with an army. Adding these troops to their forces, the Argives advanced against Troezen, a city which was an ally of the Lacedaemonians, and after plundering its territory and burning its farm-buildings they returned home. The Lacedaemonians, being incensed at the lawless acts committed against the Troezenians, resolved to go to war against the Argives; consequently they mustered an army and out their king Agis in command. With this force Agis advanced against the Argives and ravaged their territory, and leading his army to the vicinity of the city he challenged the enemy to battle. The Argives, adding to their army three thousand soldiers from the Eleians and almost as many from the Mantineians, led out their forces from the city. When a pitched battle was imminent, the generals conducted negotiations with each other and agreed upon a cessation of hostilities for four months, but when the armies returned to their homes without accomplishing anything, both cities were angry with the generals who had agreed upon the truce. Consequently the Argives hurled stones at their commanders and began to menace them with death; only reluctantly and after much supplication their lives were spared, but their property was confiscated and their homes razed to the ground. The Lacedaemonians took steps to punish Agis, but when he promised to atone for his error by worthy deeds, they reluctantly let him off, and for the future they chose ten of their wisest men, whom they appointed his advisers, and they ordered him to do nothing without learning their opinion.

**79.** After this the Athenians dispatched to Argos by sea a thousand picked hoplites and two hundred cavalry, under the command of Laches and Nicostratus; and Alcibiades also accompanied them, although in a private capacity, because of the friendly relations he enjoyed with the Eleians and Mantineians; and when they were all gathered in council, they decided to pay no attention to the truce but to set about making war. Consequently each general urged on his own troops to the conflict, and when they all responded eagerly, they pitched camp outside the city. Now they agreed that they should march first of all against Orchomenus in Arcadia; and so, advancing into Arcadia, they settled down to the siege of the city and made daily assaults upon its walls. After they had taken the city, they encamped near Tegea, having decided to besiege it also, but when the Tegeatans called upon the Lacedaemonians for immediate aid, the Spartans gathered all their own soldiers and those of their allies and moved on Mantineia, believing that, once Mantineia was attacked in the war, the enemy would raise the siege of Tegea. The Mantineians gathered their allies, and marching forth themselves *en masse,* formed their lines opposite the Lacedaemonians. A sharp battle followed, and the picked troops of the Argives, one thousand in number, who had received excellent training in warfare, were the first to put to flight their opponents and made great slaughter of them in their pursuit. The Lacedaemonians, after putting to flight the other parts of the army and slaying many, wheeled about to oppose the Argives and by their superior numbers surrounded them, hoping to destroy them to a man. Now although the picked troops of the Argives, though in numbers far inferior, were superior in feats of courage, the king of the Lacedaemonians led the fight and held out firmly against the perils he encountered; and he would have slain all the Argives, for he was resolved to fulfil the promises he had made to his fellow citizens and wipe out, by a great deed, his former ill repute, but he was not allowed to consummate that purpose. For Pharax the Spartan, who was one of the advisers of Agis and enjoyed the highest reputation in Sparta, directed him to leave a way of escape for the picked men and not, by hazarding the issue against men who had given up all hope of life, to learn what valour is when abandoned by Fortune. So the king was compelled, in obedience to the command recently given him, to leave a way of escape even as Pharax advised. So the Thousand, having been allowed to pass through in the manner described, made their way to safety, and the Lacedaemonians, having won the victory in a great battle, erected a trophy and returned home.

**80.** When this year had come to an end, in Athens [418] the archon was Antiphon, and in Rome in place of consuls four military tribunes were elected, Gaius Furius, Titus Quinctius, Marcus Postumius, and Aulus Cornelius. During this year the Argives and Lacedaemonians, after negotiations with each other, concluded a peace and formed an alliance. Consequently the Mantineians, now that they had lost the help of the Argives, were compelled to subject themselves to the Lacedaemonians. About the same time in the city of the Argives the Thousand who had been selected out of the total muster of citizens came to an agreement among themselves and decided to dissolve the democracy and establish an aristocracy from their own number. Having as they did many to aid them, because of the prominent position their wealth and brave exploits gave them, they first of all seized the men who had been accustomed to be the leaders of the people and put them to death, and then, by terrorising the rest of the citizens, they abolished the laws and were proceeding to take the management of the state into their own hands. They maintained this government for eight months and then were overthrown, the people having united against them; and so these men were put to death and the people got back the democracy.

Another movement also took place in Greece. The Phocians also, having quarrelled with the Locrians, settled the issue in pitched battle by virtue of their own valour. For the victory lay with the Phocians, who slew more than one thousand Locrians.

The Athenians under the command of Nicias seized two cities, Cythera and Nisaea; and they reduced Melos by siege, slew all the males from the youth upward, and sold into slavery the children and women.

Such were the affairs of the Greeks in this year. In Italy the Fidenates, when ambassadors came to their city from Rome, put them to death for trifling reasons. Incensed at such an act, the Romans voted to go to war, and mobilising a strong army they appointed Anius Aemilius Dictator and with him, following their custom, Aulus Cornelius Master of Horse. Aemilius, after making all the preparations for the war, marched with his army against the Fidenates. When the Fidenates drew up their forces to oppose the Romans, a fierce battle ensued which continued a long time; heavy losses were incurred on both sides and the conflict was indecisive.

**81.** When Euphemus was archon in Athens, [417] in Rome in place of consuls military tribunes were elected, Lucius Furius, Lucius Quinctius, and Aulus Sempronius. In this year the Lacedaemonians and their allies took the field against Argolis and captured the stronghold of Hysiae, and slaying the inhabitants they razed the fortress to the ground; and when they learned that the Argives had completed the construction of the long walls clear to the sea, they advanced there, razed the walls that had been finished, and then made their way back home.

The Athenians chose Alcibiades general, and giving him twenty ships commanded him to assist the Argives in establishing the affairs of their government; for conditions were still unsettled among them because many still remained of those who preferred the aristocracy. So when Alcibiades had arrived at the city of the Argives and had consulted with the supporters of the democracy, he selected those Argives who were considered to be the strongest adherents of the Lacedaemonian cause; these he removed from the city, and when he had assisted in establishing the democracy on a firm basis, he sailed back to Athens.

Toward the end of the year the Lacedaemonians invaded Argolis with a strong force, and after ravaging a large part of the country they settled the exiles from Argos in Orneae; this place they fortified as a stronghold against Argolis, and leaving in it a strong garrison, they ordered it to harass the Argives. But when the Lacedaemonians had withdrawn from Argolis, the Athenians dispatched to the Argives a supporting force of forty triremes and twelve hundred hoplites. The Argives then advanced against Orneae together with the Athenians and took the city by storm, and of the garrison and exiles some they put to death and others they expelled from Orneae.

These, then, were the events of the fifteenth year of the Peloponnesian War.

## *The campaign of the Byzantians and Calchedonians against Bithynia (82).*

**82.** In the sixteenth year of the War [416] Arimnestus was archon among the Athenians, and in Rome in place of consuls four military tribunes were elected, Titus Claudius, Spurius Nautius, Lucius Sentius, and Sextus Julius. And in this year among the Eleians the Ninety-first Olympiad was celebrated, that in which Exaenetus of Acragas won the stadion. The Byzantines and Chalcedonians, accompanied by Thracians, made war in great force against Bithynia, plundered the land, reduced by siege many of the small settlements, and performed deeds of exceeding cruelty; for of the many prisoners they took, both men and women and children, they put all to the sword.

About the same time in Sicily war broke out between the Egestaeans and the Selinuntians from a difference over territory, where a river divided the lands of the quarrelling cities. The Selinuntians, crossing the stream, at first seized by force the land along the river, but later they cut off for their own a large piece of the adjoining territory, utterly disregarding the rights of the injured parties. The people of Egesta, aroused to anger, at first endeavoured to persuade them by verbal arguments not to trespass on the territory of another city; however, when no one paid any attention to them, they advanced with an army against those who held the territory, expelled them all from their fields, and themselves seized the land. Since the quarrel between the two cities had become serious, the two parties, having mustered soldiers, sought to bring-about the decision by recourse to arms. Consequently, when both forces were drawn up in battle-order, a fierce battle took place in which the Selinuntians were the victors, having slain not a few Egestaeans. Since the Egestaeans had been humbled and were not strong enough of themselves to offer battle, they at first tried to induce the Acragantini and the Syracusans to enter into an alliance with them. Failing in this, they sent ambassadors to Carthage to beseech its aid. And when the Carthaginians would not listen to them, they looked about for some alliance overseas; and in this, chance came to their aid.

## *On the reasons why the Athenians launched a campaign against Syracuse (83-84).*

**83.** For since the Leontines had been forced by the Syracusans to leave their city for another place and had thus lost their city and their territory, those of them who were living in exile got together and decided once more to take the Athenians, who were their kinsmen, as allies. When they had conferred with the Egestaeans on the matter and come to an agreement, the two cities jointly dispatched ambassadors to Athens, asking the Athenians to come to the aid of their cities, which were victims of ill treatment, and promising to assist the Athenians in establishing order in the affairs of Sicily. When, now, the ambassadors had arrived in Athens, and the Leontines stressed their kinship and the former alliance and the Egestaeans promised to contribute a large sum of money for the war and also to fight as an ally against the Syracusans, the Athenians voted to send some of their foremost men and to investigate the situation on the island and among the Egestaeans. When these men arrived at

Egesta, the Egestaeans showed them a great sum of money which they had borrowed partly from their own citizens and partly from neighbouring peoples for the sake of making a good show. When the envoys had returned and reported on the wealth of the Egestaeans, a meeting of the people was convened to consider the matter. When the proposal was introduced to dispatch an expedition to Sicily, Nicias the son of Niceratus, a man who enjoyed the respect of his fellow citizens for his uprightness, counselled against the expedition to Sicily. They were in no position, he declared, at the same time both to carry on a war against the Lacedaemonians and to send great armaments overseas; and so long as they were unable to secure their supremacy over the Greeks, how could they hope to subdue the greatest island in the inhabited world? Even the Carthaginians, he added, who possessed a most extensive empire and had waged war many times to gain Sicily, had not been able to subdue the island, and the Athenians, whose military power was far less than that of the Carthaginians, could not possibly win by the spear and acquire the most powerful of the islands.

**84.** After Nicias had set forth these and many other considerations appropriate to the proposal before the people, Alcibiades, who was the principal advocate of the opposite view and a most prominent Athenian, persuaded the people to enter upon the war; for this man was the ablest orator among the citizens and was widely known for his high birth, wealth, and skill as a general. At once, then, the people got ready a strong fleet, taking thirty triremes from their allies and equipping one hundred of their own. When they had fitted these ships out with every kind of equipment that is useful in war, they enrolled some five thousand hoplites and elected three generals, Alcibiades, Nicias, and Lamachus, to be in charge of the campaign.

Such were the matters with which the Athenians were occupied, and as for us, since we are now at the beginning of the war between the Athenians and the Syracusans, pursuant to the plan we announced at the beginning of this Book we shall assign to the next Book the events which follow.

# BOOK XIII

### *The campaign of the Athenians against the Syracusans, with great armaments both land and naval (1-3).*

1. If we were composing a history after the manner of the other historians, we should, I suppose, discourse upon certain topics at appropriate length in the introduction to each Book and by this means turn our discussion to the events which follow; surely, if we were picking out a brief period of history for our treatise, we should have the time to enjoy the fruit such introductions yield, but since we engaged ourselves in a few Books not only to set forth, to the best of our ability, the events but also to embrace a period of more than eleven hundred years, we must forgo the long discussion which such introductions would involve and come to the events themselves, with only this word by way of preface, namely, that in the preceding six Books we have set down a record of events from the Trojan War to the war which the Athenians by decree of the people declared against the Syracusans, the period to this war from the capture of Troy embracing seven hundred and sixty-eight years; and in this Book, as we add to our narrative the period next succeeding, we shall commence with the expedition against the Syracusans and stop with the beginning of the second war between the Carthaginians and Dionysius the tyrant of the Syracusans [415-404].

2. When Chabrias was archon in Athens, [415] the Romans elected in place of consuls three military tribunes, Lucius Sergius, Marcus Papirius, and Marcus Servilius. This year the Athenians, pursuant to their vote of the war against the Syracusans, got ready the ships, collected the money, and proceeded with great zeal to make every preparation for the campaign. They elected three generals, Alcibiades, Nicias, and Lamachus, and gave them full powers over all matters pertaining to the war. Of the private citizens those who had the means, wishing to indulge the enthusiasm of the populace, in some instances fitted out triremes at their own expense and in others engaged to donate money for the maintenance of the forces; and many, not only from among the citizens and aliens of Athens who favoured the democracy but also from among the allies, voluntarily went to the generals and urged that they be enrolled among the soldiers. To such a degree were they all buoyed up in their hopes and looking forward forthwith to portioning out Sicily in allotments.

And the expedition was already fully prepared when it came to pass that in a single night the statues of Hermes which stood everywhere throughout the city were mutilated. At this the people, believing that the deed had not been done by ordinary persons but by men who stood in high repute and were bent upon the overthrow of the democracy, were incensed at the sacrilege and undertook a search for the perpetrators, offering large rewards to anyone who would furnish information against them. A certain private citizen [Diocleides?], appearing before the Council, stated that he had seen certain men enter the house of an alien about the middle of the night on the first day of the new moon and that one of them was Alcibiades. When he was questioned by the Council and asked how he could recognise the faces at night, he replied that he had seen them by the light of the moon. Since, then, the man had convicted himself of lying, no credence was given to his story, and of other investigators not a man was able to discover a single clue to the deed.

One hundred and forty triremes were equipped, and of transports and ships to carry horses as well as ships to convey food and all other equipment there was a huge number; and there were also hoplites and slingers as well as cavalry, and in addition more than seven thousand men from the allies, not including the crews. At this time the generals, sitting in secret session with the Council, discussed what disposition they should make of Sicilian affairs, if they should get control of the island, and it was agreed by them that they would enslave the Selinuntians and Syracusans, but upon the other peoples they would merely lay a tribute severally which they would pay annually to the Athenians.

3. On the next day the generals together with the soldiers went down to the Peiraeus, and the entire populace of the city, citizens and aliens thronging together, accompanied them, everyone bidding godspeed to his own kinsmen and friends. The triremes lay at anchor over the whole harbour, embellished with their insignia on the bows and the gleam of their armour; and the whole circumference of the harbour was filled with censers and silver mixing-bowls, from which the people poured libations with gold cups, paying honour to the gods and beseeching them to grant success to the expedition. Now after leaving the Peiraeus they sailed around the Peloponnesus and put in at Corcyra, since they were under orders to wait at that place and add to their forces the allies in that region. When they had all been assembled, they sailed across the Ionian Strait and came to land on the tip of Iapygia, from where they skirted along the coast of Italy. They were not received by the Tarantini, and they also sailed on past the Metapontines and Heracleians; but when they put in at Thurii they were accorded every kind of courtesy. From there they sailed on to Croton, from whose inhabitants they got a market, and then they sailed on past the temple of Hera Lacinia and doubled the promontory known as Dioscurias. After this they passed by Scylletium, as it is called, and Locri, and dropping anchor near Rhegium they endeavoured to persuade the Rhegians to become their allies; but the Rhegians replied that they would consult with the other Greek cities of Italy.

### *The arrival of the Athenians in Sicily (4).*

4. When the Syracusans heard that the Athenian armaments were at the Strait, they appointed three generals with supreme power, Hermocrates, Sicanus, and Heracleides, who enrolled soldiers and dispatched ambassadors to the cities of Sicily, urging them to do their share in the cause of their common liberty; for the Athenians, they pointed out, while beginning the war, as they alleged, upon the Syracusans, were in fact intent upon subduing the entire island. Now the Acragantini and Naxians declared that they would ally themselves with the Athenians; the Camarinaeans and Messenians gave assurances that they would maintain the peace, while postponing a reply to the request for an alliance; but the Himeraeans, Selinuntians, Geloans, and Catanaeans promised that they would fight at the side of the Syracusans. The cities of the Siceli, while tending to be favourably inclined toward the Syracusans, nevertheless remained neutral, awaiting the outcome.

# Book XIII

After the Aegestaeans had refused to give more than thirty talents, the Athenian generals, having remonstrated with them, put out to sea from Rhegium with their force and sailed to Naxos in Sicily. They were kindly received by the inhabitants of this city and sailed on from there to Catane. Although the Catanaeans would not receive the soldiers into the city, they allowed the generals to enter and summoned an assembly of the citizens, and the Athenian generals presented their proposal for an alliance. While Alcibiades was addressing the assembly, some of the soldiers burst open a postern-gate and broke into the city. It was by this cause that the Catanaeans were forced to join in the war against the Syracusans.

### *The recall of Alcibiades the general and his flight to Lacedaemon (5).*

5. While these events were taking place, those in Athens who hated Alcibiades with a personal enmity, possessing now an excuse in the mutilation of the statues, accused him in speeches before the Assembly of having formed a conspiracy against the democracy. Their charges gained colour from an incident that had taken place among the Argives; for private friends of his in that city had agreed together to destroy the democracy in Argos, but they had all been put to death by the citizens. Accordingly the people, having given credence to the accusations and having had their feelings deeply aroused by their demagogues, dispatched their ship, the Salaminia, to Sicily with orders for Alcibiades to return with all speed to face trial. When the ship arrived at Catane and Alcibiades learned of the decision of the people from the ambassadors, he took the others who had been accused together with him aboard his own trireme and sailed away in company with the Salaminia, but when he had put in at Thurii, Alcibiades, either because he was privy to the deed of impiety or because he was alarmed at the seriousness of the danger which threatened him, made his escape together with the other accused men and got away. The ambassadors who had come on the Salaminia at first set up a hunt for Alcibiades, but when they could not find him, they sailed back to Athens and reported to the people what had taken place. Accordingly the Athenians brought the names of Alcibiades and the other fugitives with him before a court of justice and condemned them in default to death. Alcibiades made his way across from Italy to the Peloponnesus, where he took refuge in Sparta and spurred on the Lacedaemonians to attack the Athenians.

### *How the Athenians sailed through into the Great Harbour of the Syracusans and seized the regions about the Olympieum (6).*

6. The generals in Sicily sailed on with the armament of the Athenians to Aegesta and captured Hyccara, a small town of the Siceli, from the booty of which they realised one hundred talents; and after receiving thirty talents in addition from the Aegestaeans they continued their voyage to Catane. And wishing to seize, without risk to themselves, the position on the Great Harbour of the Syracusans, they sent a man of Catane, who was loyal to themselves and was also trusted by the Syracusan generals, with instructions to say to the Syracusan commanders that a group of Catanaeans had banded together and were ready to seize unawares a large number of Athenians, who made it their practice to pass the night in the city away from their arms, and set fire to the ships in the harbour; and he was to ask the generals that, in order to effect this, they should appear at

the place with troops so that they might not fail in their design. When the Catanaean went to the commanders of the Syracusans and told them what we have stated, the generals, believing his story, decided on the night on which they would lead out their troops and sent the man back to Catane.

Now on the appointed night the Syracusans brought the army to Catane, whereupon the Athenians, sailing down into the Great Harbour of the Syracusans in dead silence, not only became masters of the Olympieum but also, after seizing the entire area about it, constructed a camp. The generals of the Syracusans, however, when they learned of the deceit which had been practised on them, returned speedily and assaulted the Athenian camp. When the enemy came out to meet them, there ensued a battle, in which the Athenians slew four hundred of their opponents and compelled the Syracusans to take to flight. The Athenian generals, seeing that the enemy were superior in cavalry and wishing to improve their equipment for the siege of the city, sailed back to Catane, and they dispatched men to Athens and addressed letters to the people in which they asked them to send cavalry and funds; for they believed that the siege would be a long affair; and the Athenians voted to send three hundred talents and a contingent of cavalry to Sicily.

While these events were taking place, Diagoras, who was dubbed "the Atheist," was accused of impiety and, fearing the people, fled from Attica; and the Athenians announced a reward of a talent of silver to the man who should slay Diagoras.

In Italy the Romans went to war with the Aequi and reduced Labici by siege.

These, then, were the events of this year.

### How the Athenians seized Epipolae and, after victories in battle in both areas, laid siege to Syracuse (7).

7. When Tisandrus was archon in Athens, [414] the Romans elected in place of consuls four military tribunes, Publius Lucretius, Gaius Servilius, Agrippa Menenius, and Spurius Veturius. In this year the Syracusans, dispatching ambassadors to both Corinth and Lacedaemon, urged these cities to come to their aid and not to stand idly by when total ruin threatened the Syracusans. Since Alcibiades supported their request, the Lacedaemonians voted to send aid to the Syracusans and chose Gylippus to be general, and the Corinthians made preparations to send a number of triremes, but at the moment they sent in advance to Sicily, accompanying Gylippus, Pythes with two triremes. In Catane Nicias and Lamachus, the Athenian generals, after two hundred and fifty cavalry and three hundred talents of silver had come to them from Athens, took their army aboard and sailed to Syracuse. They arrived at the city by night and unobserved by the Syracusans took possession of Epipolae. When the Syracusans learned of this, they speedily came to its defence, but were chased back into the city with the loss of three hundred soldiers. After this, with the arrival for the Athenians of three hundred horsemen from Aegesta and two hundred and fifty from the Siceli, they mustered in all eight hundred cavalry. Then, having built a fort at Labdalum, they began constructing a wall about the city of the Syracusans and aroused great fear among the populace. Therefore they advanced out of the city and endeavoured to hinder the builders of the wall;

but a cavalry battle followed in which they suffered heavy losses and were forced to flee. The Athenians with a part of their troops now seized the region lying above the harbour and by fortifying Polichne, as it is called, they not only enclosed the temple of Zeus [Olympieum] but were also besieging Syracuse from both sides. Now that such reverses as these had befallen the Syracusans, the inhabitants of the city were disheartened; but when they learned that Gylippus had put in at Himera and was gathering soldiers, they again took heart, for Gylippus, having put in at Himera with four triremes, had hauled his ships up on shore, persuaded the Himeraeans to ally themselves with the Syracusans, and was gathering soldiers from them and the Geloans, as well as from the Selinuntians and the Sicani. And after he had assembled three thousand infantry in all and two hundred cavalry, he led them through the interior of the island to Syracuse.

**How, after the Lacedaemonians and Corinthians had sent them aid, the Syracusans took courage (8).**

**How the Syracusans, having gained control of Epipolae, compelled the Athenians to withdraw to the single camp before the Olympieum (8).**

**How the Athenians, after the death of their general Lamachus and the recall of Alcibiades, dispatched in their place as generals Eurymedon and Demosthenes with reinforcements and money (8).**

**The termination of the truce by the Lacedaemonians, and the Peloponnesian War, as it is called, against the Athenians (8).**

**The great battle about Epipolae and the victory of the Syracusans (8).**

8. After a few days Gylippus led forth his troops together with the Syracusans against the Athenians. A fierce battle took place and Lamachus, the Athenian general, died in the fighting; and although many were slain on both sides, victory lay with the Athenians. After the battle, when thirteen triremes had arrived from Corinth, Gylippus, after taking the crews of the ships, with them and the Syracusans attacked the camp of the enemy and sought to storm Epipolae. When the Athenians came out, they joined battle and the Syracusans, after slaying many Athenians, were victorious and they razed the wall throughout the length of Epipole; at this the Athenians abandoned the area of Epipolae and withdrew their entire force to the other camp.

After these events the Syracusans dispatched ambassadors to Corinth and Lacedaemon to get help; and the Corinthians together with the Boeotians and Sicyonians sent them one thousand men and the Spartans six hundred. And Gylippus went about the cities of Sicily and persuaded many peoples to join the alliance, and after gathering three thousand soldiers from the Himeraeans and Sicani he led them through the interior of the island. When the Athenians learned that these troops were near at hand, they attacked and slew half of them; the survivors, however, got safely to Syracuse.

Upon the arrival of the allies the Syracusans, wishing to try their hand also in battles at sea, launched the ships they already possessed and fitted out additional ones, giving them their trials in the small harbour. Nicias, the Athenian general, dispatched letters to Athens in which he made known that many allies were now with the Syracusans and that they had fitted out no small number of ships and had resolved upon offering battle at sea; he therefore asked them to send speedily both triremes and money and generals to assist him in the conduct of the war, explaining that with the flight of Alcibiades and the death of Lamachus he was the only general left and at that was not in good health. The Athenians dispatched to Sicily ten ships with Eurymedon the general and one hundred and forty talents of silver, at the time of the winter solstice; meantime they busied themselves with preparations to dispatch a great fleet in the spring. Consequently they were enrolling soldiers everywhere from their allies and gathering together money.

In the Peloponnesus the Lacedaemonians, being spurred on by Alcibiades, broke the truce with the Athenians, and the war which followed continued for twelve years [413-404].

### The battle between the Athenians and the Syracusans and the great victory of the Athenians (9).

### The sea-battle between the Syracusans and the Athenians and the victory of the Athenians; the capture of the fortresses by the Syracusans and their victory on land (9).

**9.** At the close of this year [413] Cleocritus was archon of the Athenians, and in Rome in place of consuls there were four military tribunes, Aulus Sempronius, Marcus Papirius, Quintus Fabius, and Spurius Nautius. This year the Lacedaemonians together with their allies invaded Attica, under the leadership of Agis and Alcibiades the Athenian, and seizing the stronghold of Deceleia they made it into a fortress for attacks upon Attica, and this, as it turned out, was why this war came to be called the Deceleian War. The Athenians dispatched thirty triremes to lie off Laconia under Charicles as general and voted to send eighty triremes and five thousand hoplites to Sicily. And the Syracusans, having made up their minds to join battle at sea, fitted out eighty triremes and sailed against the enemy. The Athenians put out against them with sixty ships, and when the battle was at its height, all the Athenians in the fortresses went down to the sea; for some were desirous of watching the battle, while others hoped that, in case of some reverse in the sea-battle, they could be of help to those in flight. But the Syracusan generals, foreseeing what really happened, had dispatched the troops in the city against the strongholds of the Athenians, which were filled with money and naval supplies as well as every other kind of equipment; when the Syracusans found the strongholds guarded by a totally inadequate number, they seized them, and slew many of those who came up from the sea to their defence. Since a great uproar arose about the forts and the camp, the Athenians who were engaged in the sea-battle turned about in dismay and fled toward the last remaining fort. The Syracusans pursued them without order, but the Athenians, when they saw themselves unable to find safety on land because the Syracusans controlled two forts, were forced to turn about and renew the sea-battle. Since the Syracusans had broken their battle order and had become scattered in the pursuit, the Athenians, attacking with their ships in a body, sank eleven triremes and pursued the rest as far as the island. When the fight was ended, each side set up a trophy, the Athenians for the sea-battle and the Syracusans for their successes on land.

# Book XIII

## *The battle between the same opponents and the victory of the Syracusans (10).*

**10.** After the sea-battle had ended in the manner we have described, the Athenians, learning that the fleet under Demosthenes would arrive within a few days, decided to run no more risks before that force should join them, whereas the Syracusans, on the contrary, wishing to reach a final decision before the arrival of Demosthenes and his army, kept sailing out every day against the ships of the Athenians and continuing the fight. When Ariston the Corinthian pilot advised them to make the prows of their ships shorter and lower, the Syracusans followed his advice and for that reason enjoyed great advantage in the fighting which followed. For the Attic triremes were built with weaker and high prows, and for this reason it followed that, when they rammed, they damaged only the parts of a ship that extended above the water, so that the enemy suffered no great damage; whereas the ships of the Syracusans, built as they were with the structure about the prow strong and low, would often, as they delivered their ramming blows, sink with one shock the triremes of the Athenians.

Now day after day the Syracusans attacked the camp of the enemy both by land and by sea, but to no effect, since the Athenians made no move; but when some of the captains of triremes, being no longer able to endure the scorn of the Syracusans, put out against the enemy in the Great Harbour, a sea-battle commenced in which all the triremes joined. Now though the Athenians had fast-sailing triremes and enjoyed the advantage from their long experience at sea as well as from the skill of their pilots, yet their superiority in these respects brought them no return since the sea-battle was in a narrow area; and the Syracusans, engaging at close quarters and giving the enemy no opportunity to turn about to ram, not only cast spears at the soldiers on the decks, but also, by hurling stones, forced them to leave the prows, and in many cases simply by ramming a ship that met them and then boarding the enemy vessel they made it a land-battle on the ship's deck. The Athenians, being pressed upon from every quarter, turned to flight; and the Syracusans, pressing in pursuit, not only sank seven triremes but made a large number unfit for use.

## *How the Syracusans, having gained control of Epipolae, compelled the Athenians to withdraw to the single camp before the Olympieum (11-12).*

## *The sea-battle of all the ships in the Great Harbour and the victory of the Syracusans (11-17).*

## *The arrival from Athens of Demosthenes and Eurymedon with a strong force (11).*

**11.** At the moment when the hopes of the Syracusans had raised their spirits high because of their victory over the enemy both by land and by sea, Eurymedon and Demosthenes arrived, having sailed there from Athens with a great force and gathered on the way allied troops from the Thurians and Messapians. They brought more than eighty triremes and five thousand soldiers, excluding the crews; and they also conveyed on merchant vessels arms and money as well as siege machines and every other kind of equipment. As a result the hopes of the Syracusans were dashed again, since they believed that they could not now readily find the means to bring themselves up to equality with the enemy.

Demosthenes persuaded his fellow commanders to assault Epipolae, for it was impossible by any other means to wall off the city, and taking ten thousand hoplites and as many more light-armed troops, he attacked the Syracusans by night. Since the assault had not been expected, they overpowered some forts, and breaking into the fortifications of Epipole threw down a part of the wall, but when the Syracusans ran together to the scene from every quarter and Hermocrates also came to the aid with the picked troops, the Athenians were forced out and, it being night, because of their unfamiliarity with the region were scattered some to one place and others to another. The Syracusans and their allies, pursuing after them, slew two thousand five hundred of the enemy, wounded not a few, and captured much armour. After the battle the Syracusans dispatched Sicanus, one of their generals, with twelve triremes to the other cities, both to announce the victory to the allies and to ask them for aid.

12. The Athenians, now that their affairs had taken a turn for the worse and a wave of pestilence had struck the camp because the region round about it was marshy, counselled together how they should deal with the situation. Demosthenes thought that they should sail back to Athens with all speed, stating that to risk their lives against the Lacedaemonians in defence of their fatherland was preferable to settling down on Sicily and accomplishing nothing worth while; but Nicias said that they ought not to abandon the siege in so disgraceful a fashion, while they were well supplied with triremes, soldiers, and funds; furthermore, he added, if they should make peace with the Syracusans without the approval of the Athenian people and sail back to their country, peril would attend them from the men who make it their practice to bring false charges against their generals. Of the participants in the council some agreed with Demosthenes on putting to sea, but others expressed the same opinion as Nicias; and so they came to no clear decision and took no action. Since help came to the Syracusans from the Siceli, Selinuntians, and Geloans, as well as from the Himeraeans and Camarinaeans, the Syracusans were the more emboldened, but the Athenians became apprehensive. When the epidemic greatly increased, many of the soldiers were dying and all regretted that they had not set out upon their return voyage long since. Consequently, since the multitude was in an uproar and all the others were eager to take to the ships, Nicias found himself compelled to yield on the matter of their returning home, and when the generals were agreed, the soldiers began gathering together their equipment, loading the triremes, and raising the yard-arms; and the generals issued orders to the multitude that at the signal not a man in the camp should be late, for he who lagged would be left behind. When they were about to sail on the following day, on the night of the day before, the moon was eclipsed. Consequently Nicias, who was not only by nature a superstitiously devout man but also cautious because of the epidemic in the camp, summoned the soothsayers, and when they declared that the departure must be postponed for the customary three days, Demosthenes and the others were also compelled, out of respect for the deity, to accede.

## Book XIII

### *How the Syracusans prepared a naval force and decided to offer battle at sea (13).*

**13.** When the Syracusans learned from some deserters why the departure had been deferred, they manned all their triremes, seventy-four in number, and leading out their ground forces attacked the enemy both by land and by sea. The Athenians, having manned eighty-six triremes, assigned to Eurymedon, the general, the command of the right wing, opposite to which was stationed the general of the Syracusans, Agatharchus; on the other wing Euthydemus had been stationed and opposite to him was Sicanus commanding the Syracusans; and in command of the centre of the line were Menander for the Athenians and Pythes the Corinthian for the Syracusans. Although the Athenian line was the longer since they were engaging with a superior number of triremes, yet the very factor which they thought would work to their advantage was not the least in their undoing. For Eurymedon endeavoured to outflank the opposing wing; but when he had become detached from his line, the Syracusans turned to face him and he was cut off and forced into a bay called Dascon which was held by the Syracusans. Being hemmed in as he was into a narrow place, he was forced to run ashore, where some man gave him a mortal wound and he lost his life, and seven of his ships were destroyed in this place. The battle had now spread throughout both fleets, and when the word was passed along that the general had been slain and some ships lost, at first only those ships gave way which were nearest to those which had been destroyed, but later, as the Syracusans pressed forward and pushed the fight boldly because of the success they had won, the whole Athenian force was overpowered and compelled to turn in flight, and since the pursuit turned toward the shallow part of the harbour, not a few triremes ran aground in the shoals. When this took place, Sicanus, the Syracusan general, straightway filling a merchant ship with faggots and pine-wood and pitch, set fire to the ships which were wallowing in the shoals. Although they were put on fire, the Athenians not only quickly extinguished the flames but, finding no other means of safety, also vigorously fought off from their ships the men who were rushing against them; and the land forces ran to their aid along the beach on which the ships had run ashore. Since they all withstood the attack with vigour, on land the Syracusans were turned back, but at sea they won the decision and sailed back to the city. The losses of the Syracusans were few, but of the Athenians not less than two thousand men and eighteen triremes.

**14.** The Syracusans, believing that the danger no longer was the losing of their city but that, far more, the contest had become one for the capture of the camp together with the enemy, blocked off the entrance to the harbour by the construction of a barrier. For they moored at anchor both small vessels and triremes as well as merchant-ships, with iron chains between them, and to the vessels they built bridges of boards, completing the undertaking in three days. The Athenians, seeing their hope of deliverance shut off in every direction, decided to man all their triremes and put on them their best land troops, and thus, by means both of the multitude of their ships and of the desperation of the men who would be fighting for their lives, eventually to strike terror into the Syracusans. Consequently they put on board the officers and choicest troops from the whole army, manning in this way one hundred and fifteen triremes, and the other soldiers they stationed on land along the beach. The Syracusans drew up their infantry before the city, and fully manned seventy-four triremes; and the triremes were attended by free boys on small boats, who were in years below manhood and were fighting at the side of their fathers. And the walls about the harbour and every high place in the city were crowded with people; for wives and maidens and all who, because of age, could not render the service war demands, since the whole war was coming to its decision, were eyeing the battle with the greatest anguish of spirit.

**15.** At this time Nicias, the general of the Athenians, as he surveyed the ships and measured the magnitude of the struggle, could not remain at his station on shore, but leaving the land troops he boarded a boat and passed along the line of the Athenian triremes. Calling each captain by name and stretching forth his hands, he implored them all, now if ever before, to grasp the only hope left to them, for on the valour of those who were about to join battle at sea depended the preservation both of themselves, every man of them, and of their fatherland. Those who were fathers of children he reminded of their sons; those who were sons of distinguished fathers he exhorted not to bring disgrace upon the valorous deeds of their ancestors; those who had been honoured by their fellow citizens he urged to show themselves worthy of their crowns; and all of them he reminded of the trophies erected at Salamis and begged them not to bring to disrepute the far-famed glory of their fatherland nor surrender themselves like slaves to the Syracusans.

After Nicias had spoken to this effect, he returned to his station, and the men of the fleet advanced singing the paean and broke through the barrier of boats before the enemy could prevent them, but the Syracusans, putting quickly out to sea, formed their triremes in battle order and coming to grips with the enemy forced them to withdraw from the barrier of boats and fight a pitched battle. As the ships backed water, some toward the beach, others toward the middle of the harbour, and still others in the direction of the walls, all the triremes were quickly separated from each other, and after they had got clear of the boom across its entrance the harbour was full of ships fighting in small groups. Thereupon both sides fought with abandon for the victory. The Athenians, cheered by the multitude of their ships and seeing no other hope of safety, carried on the fight boldly and faced gallantly their death in battle, and the Syracusans, with their parents and children as spectators of the struggle, vied with one another, each man wishing the victory to come to his country through his own efforts.

**16.** Consequently many leaped on the prows of the hostile ships, when their own had been damaged by another, and were isolated in the midst of their enemies. In some cases they dropped grappling-irons and forced their adversaries to fight a land-battle on their ships. Often men whose own ships had been shattered leaped on their opponents' vessels, and by slaying the defenders or pushing them into the sea became masters of their triremes. In a word, over the entire harbour came the crash of ship striking ship and the cry of desperately struggling men slaying and being slain. For when a ship had been intercepted by several triremes and struck by their beaks from every direction, the water would pour in and it would be swallowed together with the entire crew beneath the sea.

Some who would be swimming away after their ship had been sunk would be wounded by arrows or slain by the blows of spears. The pilots, as they saw the confusion of the battle, every spot full of uproar, and often a number of ships converging upon a single one, did not know what signal to give, since the same orders were not suitable to all situations, nor was it possible, because of the multitude of missiles, for the oarsmen to keep their eyes upon the men who gave them their orders. In short, not a man could hear any of the commands amid the shattering of boats and the sweeping off of oars, as well as amid the uproar of the men in combat on the ships and of their zealous comrades on land. For of the entire beach a part was held by the Athenian infantry and a part by the Syracusans, so that at times the men fighting the sea-battle had as helpers, when along the shore, the soldiers lined up on the land. The spectators on the walls, whenever they saw their own fighters winning, would sing songs of victory, but when they saw them being vanquished, they would groan and with tears offer prayers to the gods. For now and then it happened that some Syracusan triremes would be destroyed along the walls and their crews slain before the eyes of their kinsmen, and parents would witness the destruction of their children, sisters and wives the pitiable end of husbands and brothers.

**17.** For a long time, despite the many who were dying, the battle would not come to an end, since not even the men who were in desperate straits would dare flee to the land. For the Athenians would ask those who were breaking off the battle and turning to the land, "Do you think to sail to Athens by land?" and the Syracusan infantry would inquire of any who were bringing their ships towards them, "Why, when we wanted to go aboard the triremes, did you prevent us from engaging in the battle, if now you are betraying the fatherland?" "Was the reason you blocked the mouth of the harbour that, after preventing the enemy from getting out, you might yourselves flee to the beach?" "Since it is the lot of all men to die, what fairer death do you seek than dying for the fatherland, which you are disgracefully abandoning though you have it as a witness of your fighting!" When the soldiers on the land hurled such up-braidings at the sailors who drew near, those who were fleeing for refuge to the beach would turn back again, even though their ships were shattered and they themselves were weighed down by their wounds. When the Athenians who were engaged near the city had been thrust back and began to flee, the Athenians next in line gave way from time to time and gradually the whole host took to flight. Thereupon the Syracusans with great shouting pursued the ships to the land; and those Athenians who had not been slain out at sea, now that they had come to shallow water, leaped from the ships and fled to the land troops, and the harbour was full of arms and wreckage of boats, since of the Attic ships sixty were lost and of the Syracusan eight were completely destroyed and sixteen badly damaged. The Syracusans drew up on the shore as many of their triremes as they could, and taking up the bodies of their citizens and allies who had died, honoured them with a public funeral.

*The flight of the Athenians and the capture of the entire host (18-19).*

**18.** The Athenians thronged to the tents of their commanders and begged the generals to take thought, not for the ships, but for the safety of themselves. Demosthenes, accordingly, declared that, since the barrier of boats had been broken, they should straightway man the triremes, and he expressed the belief that, if they delivered an unexpected attack, they would easily succeed in their design. But Nicias advised that they leave the ships behind and withdraw through the interior to the cities which were their allies. This plan was agreed to by all, and they burned some of the ships and made preparations for the retreat.

When it was evident that the Athenians were going to withdraw during the night, Hermocrates advised the Syracusans to lead forth their entire army in the night and seize all the roads beforehand. And when the generals would not agree to this, both because many of the soldiers were wounded and because all of them were worn-out in body from the fighting, he sent some of the horsemen to the camp of the Athenians to tell them that the Syracusans had already dispatched men to seize in advance the roads and the most important positions. It was already night when the horsemen carried out these orders, and the Athenians, believing that it was men from Leontini who out of goodwill had brought them the word, were not a little disturbed and postponed the departure. If they had not been deceived by this trick, they would have got safely away. The Syracusans at daybreak dispatched the soldiers who were to seize in advance the narrow passes in the roads, and the Athenian generals, dividing the soldiers into two bodies, put the pack-animals and the sick and injured in the centre and stationed those who were in condition to fight in the van and the rear, and then set out for Catane, Demosthenes commanding one group and Nicias the other.

**How the Syracusans gathered in assembly and considered the question what disposition should be made of the captives (19).**

**19.** The Syracusans took in tow the fifty ships left behind and brought them to the city, and then, taking off all the crews of their triremes and providing them with arms, they followed after the Athenians with their entire armament, harassing them and hindering their forward progress. For three days following close on their heels and encompassing them on all sides they prevented them from taking a direct road toward Catane, their ally; instead they compelled them to retrace their steps through the plain of Elorium, and surrounding them at the Asinarus River, slew eighteen thousand and took captive seven thousand, among whom were also the generals Demosthenes and Nicias. The remainder were seized as their plunder by the soldiers; for the Athenians, since their escape was blocked in every direction, were obliged to surrender their weapons and their persons to the enemy. After this had taken place, the Syracusans set up two trophies, nailing to each of them the arms of a general, and turned back to the city.

Now at that time the whole city of Syracuse offered sacrifices to the gods, and on the next day, after the Assembly had gathered, they considered what disposition they should make of the captives. A man named Diocles, who was a most notable leader of the populace, declared his opinion that the Athenian generals should be put to death under torture and the other prisoners should for the present all be thrown into the quarries; but that later the allies of the Athenians should be sold as booty and the Athenians should labour as prisoners under guard, receiving two cotyls of barley meal. When this motion had been read, Hermocrates took the floor and endeavoured to show that a fairer thing than victory is to bear the victory with moderation [Better than victory is a noble use of victory]. When the people shouted their disapproval and would not allow him to continue, a man named Nicolaüs, who had lost two sons in the war, made his way, supported by his slaves because of his age, to the platform. When the people saw him, they stopped shouting, believing that he would denounce the prisoners. As soon, then, as there was silence, the old man began to speak.

### The speeches which were delivered on both sides of the proposal (20-32).

**20.** "Of the misfortunes of the war, men of Syracuse, I have shared in a part, and not the least; for being the father of two sons, I sent them into the struggle on behalf of the fatherland, and I received back, in place of them, a message which announced their death. Therefore, as I miss their companionship each day and call to mind once more that they are dead, I deem them happy, but pity my own lot, believing myself to be the most unfortunate of men. For they, having expended for the salvation of their fatherland the death which mankind owes to Nature, have left behind them deathless renown for themselves, whereas I, bereft at the end of my days of those who were to minister to my old age, bear a twofold sorrow, in that it is both the children of my own body and their valour that I miss. For the more gallant their death, the more poignant the memory of themselves they have left behind. I have good reason, then, for hating the Athenians, since it is because of them that I am being guided here, not by my own sons, but, as you can see, by slaves. Now if I perceived, men of Syracuse, that the matter under discussion was merely a decision affecting the Athenians, I with good reason, both because of the misfortunes of our country, shared by all, and because of my personal afflictions, should have dealt bitterly with them; but since, along with consideration of the pity which is shown to unfortunates, the question at issue concerns both the good of the State and the fame of the people of the Syracusans which will be spread abroad to all mankind, I shall direct my proposal solely to the question of expediency.

**21.** "The people of the Athenians have received a punishment their own folly deserved, first of all from the hands of the gods and then from us whom they had wronged. Good it is indeed that the deity involves in unexpected disasters those who begin an unjust war and do not bear their own superiority as men should. For who could have expected that the Athenians, who had removed ten thousand talents from Delos to Athens and had dispatched to Sicily two hundred triremes and more than forty thousand men to fight, would ever suffer disasters of such magnitude? for from the preparations they made on such a scale not a ship, not a man has returned home, so that not even a survivor is left to carry to them word of the disaster. Knowing, therefore, men of Syracuse, that the arrogant are hated among gods and men, do you, humbling yourselves before Fortune, commit no act that is beyond man's powers. What nobility is there in slaying the man who lies at your feet? What glory is there in wreaking vengeance on him? He who maintains his savagery unalterable amid human misfortunes also fails to take proper account of the common weakness of mankind. For no man is so wise that his strength can prevail over Fortune, which of its nature finds delight in the sufferings of men and works swift changes in prosperity.

"Some, perhaps, will say, 'They have committed a wrong, and we have the power to punish them.' But have you, then, not inflicted a many times greater punishment on the Athenian people, and are you not satisfied with your chastisement of the prisoners? For they have surrendered themselves together with their arms, trusting in the reasonableness of their conquerors; it is, therefore, not seemly that they should be cheated of our expected humaneness. For those who maintained unalterable their enmity toward us have died fighting, but these who delivered themselves into our hands have become suppliants, no longer enemies. For those who in battle deliver their persons into the hands of their opponents do so in the hope of saving their lives; and should the men who have shown this trust receive so severe a punishment, though the victims will accept their misfortune, yet the punishers would be called hard-hearted, but those who lay claim to leadership, men of Syracuse, should not strive to make themselves strong in arms so much as they should show themselves reasonable in their character.

**22.** "The fact is that subject peoples bide their time against those who dominate them by fear and, because of their hatred, retaliate upon them, but they steadfastly cherish those who exercise their leadership humanely and thereby always aid them in strengthening their supremacy. What destroyed the kingdom of the Medes? Their brutality toward the weaker. For after the Persians revolted from them, their kingdom was attacked by most of the nations also. Else how did Cyrus rise from private citizen to the kingship over all of Asia? By his considerate treatment of the conquered. When, for example, he took King Croesus captive, far from doing him any injustice he actually became his benefactor; and in much the same way did he also deal with all the other kings as well as peoples. As a consequence, when the fame of his clemency had been spread abroad to every region, all the inhabitants of Asia vied with one another in entering into alliance with the king.

"But why do I speak of things distant in both place and time? In this our city, not long since, Gelon rose from private citizen to be lord of the whole of Sicily, the cities willingly putting themselves under his authority; for the fairness of the man, combined with his sympathy for the unfortunate, drew all men to him. Since from those times our city has laid claim to the leadership in Sicily, let us not bring into disrepute the fair name our ancestors won nor show ourselves brutal and implacable toward human misfortune. Indeed it is not fitting to give envy an occasion to criticise us by saying that we make an unworthy use of our good fortune; for it is a fine thing to have those who will grieve with us when Fortune is adverse and rejoice in turn at our successes. The advantages which are won in arms are often determined by Fortune and opportunity, but clemency amid constant success is a distinctive mark of the virtue of men whose affairs prosper. Do not, therefore, begrudge our country the opportunity of being acclaimed by all mankind, because it has surpassed the Athenians not only in feats of arms but also in humanity. For it will be manifest that the people who vaunt their superiority to all others in civilisation have received by our kindness all consideration, and they who were the first to raise an altar to Mercy will find that mercy in the city of the Syracusans. From this it will be clear to all that they suffered a just defeat and we enjoyed a deserved success, if it so be that, although they sought to wrong men who had treated with kindness even their foes, we, on the contrary, defeated men who ventured treacherously to attack a people which shows mercy even to its bitterest enemies, so the Athenians would not only stand accused by all the world, but even they themselves would condemn themselves, that they had undertaken to wrong such men.

**23.** "A fine thing it is, men of Syracuse, to take the lead in establishing a friendship and, by showing mercy to the unfortunate, to make up the quarrel. For goodwill toward our friends should be kept imperishable, but hatred toward our enemies perishable, since by this practice it will come about that one's allies increase in number and one's enemies decrease, but for us to maintain the quarrel forever and to pass it on to children's children is neither kindly nor safe; since it sometimes happens that those who appear to be more powerful turn out to be weaker by the decision of a moment than their former subjects. A witness to this is the war which has just now ceased: The men who came here to lay siege to the city and, by means of their superior power, threw a wall about it have by a change in fortune become captives, as you can see. It is a fine thing, therefore, by showing ourselves lenient amid the misfortunes of other men, to have reserved for us the hope of mercy from all men, in case some ill befall us of such as come to mortal men. For many are the unexpected things life holds: civic strifes, robberies, wars, amid which one may not easily avoid the peril, being but human. Consequently, if we shall exclude the thought of mercy for the defeated, we shall be setting up, for all time to come, a harsh law against ourselves. For it is impossible that men who have shown no compassion for others should themselves ever receive humane treatment at the hands of another and that men who have outraged others should be treated indulgently, or that we, after murdering so many men contrary to the traditions of the Greeks, should in the reversals which attend life appeal to the usages common to all mankind. For what Greek has ever judged that those who have surrendered themselves and put their trust in the kindness of their conquerors are deserving of implacable punishment? or who has ever held mercy less potent than cruelty, precaution than rashness?

**24.** "All men sturdily oppose the enemy which is lined up for battle but fall back when he has surrendered, wearing down the hardihood of the former and showing pity for the misfortune of the latter. For our ardour is broken whenever the former enemy, having by a change of fortune become a suppliant, submits to suffer whatever suits the pleasure of his conquerors, and the spirits of civilised men are gripped, I believe, most perhaps by mercy, because of the sympathy which nature has planted in all. The Athenians, for example, although in the Peloponnesian War they had blockaded many Lacedaemonians on the island of Sphacteria and taken them captive, released them to the Spartans on payment of ransom. On another occasion the Lacedaemonians, when they had taken prisoner many of the Athenians and their allies, disposed of them in the same manner. In so doing they both acted nobly. For hatred should exist between Greeks only until victory has been won and punishment only until the enemy has been overcome. Whoever goes farther and wreaks vengeance upon the vanquished who flees for refuge to the leniency of his conqueror is no longer punishing his enemy but, far more, is guilty of an offence against human weakness. For against harshness such as this one may mention the adages of the wise men of old: 'O man, be not high-spirited'; 'Know thyself'; 'Observe how Fortune is lord of all.' For what reason did the ancestors of all the Greeks ordain that the trophies set up in celebrating victories in war should be made, not of stone, but of any wood at hand? Was it not in order that the memorials of the enmity, lasting as they would for a brief time, should quickly disappear? Speaking generally, if you wish to establish the quarrel for all time, know that in doing so you are treating with disdain human weakness; for a single moment, a slight turn of Fortune, often brings low the arrogant.

**25.** "If, as is likely, you will make an end of the war, what better time will you find than the present, in which you will make your humane treatment of the prostrate the occasion for friendship? For do not assume that the Athenian people have become completely exhausted by their disaster in Sicily, seeing that they hold sway over practically all the islands of Greece and retain the supremacy over the coasts of both Europe and Asia. Indeed once before, after losing three hundred triremes together with their crews in Egypt, they compelled the King, who seemed to hold the upper hand, to accept ignominious terms of peace, and again, when their city had been razed to the ground by Xerxes, after a short time they defeated him also and won for themselves the leadership of Greece. For that city has a clever way, in the midst of the greatest misfortunes, of making the greatest growth in power and of never adopting a policy that is mean-spirited. It would be a fine thing, therefore, instead of increasing their enmity, to have the Athenians as allies after sparing the prisoners. For if we put them to death we shall merely be indulging our anger, sating a fruitless passion, whereas if we put them under guard, we shall have the gratitude of the men we succoured and the approbation of all other peoples.

**26.** "Yes, some will answer, but there are Greeks who have executed their prisoners. What of it? If praise accrues to them from that deed, let us nevertheless imitate those who have paid heed to their reputation; but if we are the first by whom they are accused, let us not ourselves commit the same crimes as those who by their own admission have sinned. So long as the men who entrusted their lives to our good faith have suffered no irremediable punishment, all men will justly censure the Athenian people; but if they hear that, contrary to the generally accepted customs of mankind, faith has been broken with the captives, they will shift their accusation against us. For in truth, if it can be said of any other people, the prestige of the city of the Athenians deserves our reverence, and we may well return to them our gratitude for the benefactions they have bestowed upon man. For it is they who first gave to the Greeks a share in a food gained by cultivation of the soil, which, though they had received it from the gods for their exclusive use, they made available to all. They it was who discovered laws, by the application of which the manner of men's living has advanced from the savage and unjust existence to a civilised and just society. It was they who first, by sparing the lives of any who sought refuge with them, contrived to cause the laws on suppliants to prevail among all men, and since they were the authors of these laws, we should not deprive them of their protection. So much to all of you; but some among you I shall remind of the claims of human kindness.

**27.** "All you who in that city have participated in its eloquence and learning, show mercy to men who offer their country as a school for the common use of mankind; and do all you, who have taken part in the most holy Mysteries, save the lives of those who initiated you, some by way of showing gratitude for kindly services already received and others, who look forward to partaking of them, not in anger depriving yourselves of that hope. For what place is there to which foreigners may resort for a liberal education once the city of the Athenians has been destroyed? Brief is the hatred aroused by the wrong they have committed, but important and many are their accomplishments which claim goodwill.

"But apart from consideration for the city, one might, in examining the prisoners individually, find those who would justly receive mercy. For the allies of Athens, being under constraint because of the superior power of their rulers, were compelled to join the expedition. It follows, then, that if it is just to take vengeance upon those who have done wrong from design, it would be fitting to treat as worthy of leniency those who sin against their will. What shall I say of Nicias, who from the first, after initiating his policy in the interest of the Syracusans, was the only man to oppose the expedition against Sicily, and who has continually looked after the interests of Syracusans resident in Athens and served as their proxenus a It would be extraordinary indeed that Nicias, who had sponsored our cause as a politician in Athens, should be punished, and that he should not be accorded humane treatment because of the goodwill he has shown toward us but because of his service in business of his country should meet with implacable punishment, and that Alcibiades, the man who brought on the war against the Syracusans, should escape his deserved punishment both from us and from the Athenians, whereas he who has proved himself by common consent the most humane among Athenians should not even meet with the mercy accorded to all men. Therefore for my part, when I consider the change in his circumstances, I pity his lot. For formerly, as one of the most distinguished of all Greeks and applauded for his knightly character, he was one to be deemed happy and was admired in every city; but now, with hands bound behind his back in a tunic squalid in appearance, he has experienced the piteous state of captivity, as if Fortune wished to give, in the life of this man, an example of her power. The prosperity which Fortune gives it behooves us to bear as human beings should and not show barbarous savagery toward men of our own race."

**28.** Such were the arguments used by Nicolaüs in addressing the people of Syracuse and before he ceased he had won the sympathy of his hearers, but the Laconian Gylippus, who still maintained implacable his hatred of Athenians, mounting the rostrum began his argument with that topic. "I am greatly surprised, men of Syracuse, to see that you so quickly, on a matter in which you have suffered grievously by deeds, are moved to change your minds by words. For if you who, in order to save your city from desolation, faced peril against men who came to destroy your country, have become relaxed in temper, why, then, should we who have suffered no wrong exert ourselves? Do you in heaven's name, men of Syracuse, grant me pardon as I set forth my counsel with all frankness; for, being a Spartan, I have also a Spartan's manner of speech. And first of all one might inquire how Nicolaüs can say, 'Show mercy to the Athenians,' who have rendered his old age piteous because childless, and how, coming before the Assembly in mourner's dress, he can weep and say that you should show pity to the murderers of his own children. For that man is no longer equitable who ceases to think of his nearest of kin after their death but elects to save the lives of his bitterest foes. Why how many of you who are assembled here have mourned sons who have been slain in the war?" (Many of the audience at least raised a great outcry.) And Gylippus interrupting it said, "Do you see, Nicolaüs, those who by their outcry proclaim their misfortune? And how many of you look in vain for brothers or relatives or friends whom you have lost?" (A far greater number shouted agreement.) Gylippus then continued: "Do you observe, Nicolaüs, the multitude of those who have suffered because of Athenians? All these, though guilty of no wrong done to Athenians, have been robbed of their nearest kinsmen, and they are bound to hate the Athenians in as great a measure as they have loved their own.

**29.** "Will it not be strange, men of Syracuse, if those who have perished chose death on your behalf of their own accord, but that you on their behalf shall not exact punishment from even your bitterest enemies? and that, though you praise those who gave their very lives to preserve their country's freedom, you shall make it a matter of greater moment to preserve the lives of the murderers than to safeguard the honour of these men? You have voted to embellish at public expense the tombs of the departed; yet what fairer embellishment will you find than the punishing of their slayers? Unless, by Zeus, it would be by enrolling them among your citizens, you should wish to leave living trophies of the departed. It may be said, they have renounced the name of enemies and have become suppliants. On what grounds, pray, would this humane treatment have been accorded them? For those who first established our ordinances regarding these matters prescribed mercy for the unfortunates, but punishment for those who from sheer depravity practise iniquity. In which category, now, are we to place the prisoners? In that of unfortunates? Why, what Fortune compelled them, who had suffered no wrong, to make war on Syracusans, to abandon peace, which all men praise, and to come here with the purpose of destroying your city? Consequently let those who of their free will chose an unjust war bear its hard consequences with courage, and let not those who, if they had conquered, would have kept implacable their cruelty toward you, now that they have been thwarted in their purpose, beg off from punishment by appealing to the human kindness which is due to the prayer of a suppliant. And if they stand convicted of having suffered their serious defeats because of wickedness and greed, let them not blame Fortune for them nor summon to their aid the name of 'supplication.' For that term is reserved among men for those who are pure in heart but have found Fortune unkind. These men, however, whose lives have been crammed with every malefaction, have left for themselves no place in the world which will admit them to mercy and refuge.

**30.** "For what utterly shameful deed have they not planned, what deed most shocking have they not perpetrated? It is a distinctive mark of greed that a man, not being content with his own gifts of Fortune, covets those which are distant and belong to someone else; and this these men have done. For though the Athenians were the most prosperous of all the Greeks, dissatisfied with their felicity as if it were a heavy burden, they longed to portion out to colonists Sicily, separated as it was from them by so great an expanse of sea, after they had sold the inhabitants into slavery. It is a terrible thing to begin a war, when one has not first been wronged; yet that is what they did. For though they were your

Book XIII

friends until then, on a sudden, without warning, with an armament of such strength they laid siege to Syracusans. It is characteristic of arrogant men, anticipating the decision of Fortune, to decree the punishment of peoples not yet conquered; and this also they have not left undone. For before the Athenians ever set foot on Sicily they approved a resolution to sell into slavery the citizens of Syracuse and Selinus and to compel the remaining Sicilians to pay tribute. When there is to be found in the same men greediness, treachery, arrogance, what person in his right mind would show them mercy? How then, mark you, did the Athenians treat the Mitylenaeans? Why after conquering them, although the Mitylenaeans had no intention of doing them any wrong but only desired their freedom, they voted to put to the sword all the inhabitants of the city [this decree was not executed]. A cruel and barbarous deed. And that crime too they committed against Greeks, against allies, against men who had often been their benefactors. Let them not now complain if, after having done such things to the rest of mankind, they themselves shall receive like punishment; for it is altogether just that a man should accept his lot without complaint when he is himself affected by the law he has laid down for others. What shall I say also of the Melians, whom they reduced by siege and slew from the youth upward? and of the Scionaeans, who, although their kinsmen, shared the same fate as the Melians? Consequently two peoples who had fallen foul of Attic fury had left not even any of their number to perform the rites over the bodies of their dead. It is not Scythians who committed such deeds, but the people who claim to excel in love of mankind have by their decrees utterly destroyed these cities. Consider now what they would have done if they had sacked the city of the Syracusans; for men who dealt with their kinsmen with such savagery would have devised a harsher punishment for a people with whom they had no ties of blood.

**31.** "There is, therefore, no just measure of mercy in store for them to call upon, since as for the use of it on the occasion of their own mishaps they themselves have destroyed it. Where is it worth their while to flee for safety? To gods, whom they have chosen to rob of their traditional honours? To men, whom they have visited only to enslave? Do they call upon Demeter and Core and their Mysteries now that they have laid waste the sacred island [Sicily] of these goddesses? Yes, some will say, but not the whole people of the Athenians are to blame, but only Alcibiades who advised this expedition. We shall find, however, that in most cases their advisers pay every attention to the wishes of their audience, so that the voter suggests to the speaker words that suit his own purpose. For the speaker is not the master of the multitude, but the people, by adopting measures that are honest, train the orator to propose what is best. If we shall pardon men guilty of irrevocable injustices when they lay the responsibility upon their advisers, we shall indeed be providing the wicked with an easy defence! It is clear that nothing in the world could be more unjust than that, while in the case of benefactions it is not the advisers but the people who receive the thanks of the recipients, in the matter of injustices the punishment is passed on to the speakers.

"Yet some have lost their reasoning powers to such a degree as to assert that it is Alcibiades, over whom we have no power, who should be punished, but that we should release the prisoners, who are being led to their deserved punishment, and thus make it known to the world that the people of the Syracusans have no righteous indignation against base men. If the advocates of the war have in truth been the cause of it, let the people blame the speakers for the consequences of their deception, but you will with justice punish the people for the wrongs which you have suffered, and, speaking generally, if they committed the wrongs with full knowledge that they were so doing, because of their very intention they deserve punishment, but if they entered the war without a considered plan, even so they should not be let off, in order that they may not grow accustomed to act offhand in matters which affect the lives of other men. For it is not just that the ignorance of the Athenians should bring destruction to Syracusans or that in a case where the crime is irremediable, the criminals should retain a vestige of defence.

**32.** "Yet, by Zeus, someone will say, Nicias took the part of the Syracusans in the debate and was the only one who advised against making war. As for what he said there we know it by hearsay, but what has been done here we have witnessed with our own eyes. For the man who there opposed the expedition was here commander of the armament; he who takes the part of Syracusans in debate walled off your city; and he who is humanely disposed toward you, when Demosthenes and all the others wished to break off the siege, alone compelled them to remain and continue the war. Therefore for my part I do not believe that his words should have greater weight with you than his deeds, report than experience, things unseen than things that have been witnessed by all.

"Yet, by Zeus, someone will say, it is a good thing not to make our enmity eternal. Very well, then, after the punishment of the malefactors you will, if you so agree, put an end to your enmity in a suitable manner. For it is not just that men who treat their captives like slaves when they are the victors, should, when they in turn are the vanquished, be objects of pity as if they had done no wrong, and though they will have been freed of paying the penalty for their deeds, by specious pleas they will remember the friendship only so long as it is to their advantage. For I omit to mention the fact that, if you take this course, you will be wronging not only many others but also the Lacedaemonians, who for your sake both entered upon the war over there and also sent you aid here; for they might have been well content to maintain peace and look on while Sicily was being laid waste. Consequently, if you free the prisoners and thus enter into friendly relations with Athens, you will be looked upon as traitors to your allies and, when it is in your power to weaken the common enemy, by releasing so great a number of soldiers you will make our enemy again formidable. For I could never bring myself to believe that Athenians, after getting themselves involved in so bitter an enmity, will keep the friendly relation unbroken; on the contrary, while they are weak they will feign goodwill, but when they have recovered their strength, they will carry their original purpose to completion. I therefore adjure you all, in the name of Zeus and all the gods, not to save the lives of your enemies, not to leave your allies in the lurch, not again for a second time to bring peril upon your country. You yourselves, men of Syracuse, if you let these men go and then some ill befalls you, will leave for yourselves not even a respectable defence."

# Book XIII

### *The decrees which the Syracusans passed regarding the captives (33).*

33. After the Laconian had spoken to this effect, the multitude suddenly changed its mind and approved the proposal of Diocles. Consequently the generals and the allies were forthwith put to death, and the Athenians were consigned to the quarries; and at a later time such of them as possessed a better education were rescued from there by the younger men and thus got away safe, but practically all the rest ended their lives pitiably amid the hardships of this place of confinement.

After the termination of the war Diocles set up the laws for the Syracusans, and it came to pass that this man experienced a strange reversal of fortune. For having become implacable in fixing penalties and severe in punishing offenders, he wrote in the laws that, if any man should appear in the market-place carrying a weapon, the punishment should be death, and he made no allowance for either ignorance or any other circumstance. When word had been received that enemies were in the land, he set forth carrying a sword; but since sudden civil strife had arisen and there was uproar in the market-place, he thoughtlessly entered the market-place with the sword, and when one of the ordinary citizens, noticing this, said that he himself was annulling his own laws, he cried out, "Not so, by Zeus, I will even uphold them," and drawing the sword he slew himself.

These, then, were the events of this year.

### *How, after the failure of the Athenians in Sicily, many of their allies revolted (34).*

### *How the citizen-body of the Athenians, having lost heart, turned their back upon the democracy and put the government into the hands of four hundred men chaps. (34, 36).*

### *How the Lacedaemonians defeated the Athenians in sea-battles (34).*

### *How the Syracusans honoured with notable gifts the men who had played a brave part in the war (34).*

### *How Diocles was chosen law-giver and wrote their laws for the Syracusans (34-35).*

### *How the Syracusans sent a notable force to the aid of the Lacedaemonians (34).*

34. When Callias was archon in Athens, [412] the Romans elected in place of consuls four military tribunes, Publius Cornelius . . . Gaius Fabius, and among the Eleians the Ninety-second Olympiad was celebrated, that in which Exaenetus of Acragas won the stadion. In this year it came to pass that, after the Athenians had collapsed in Sicily, their supremacy was held in contempt; for immediately the peoples of Chios, Samos, Byzantium, and many of the allies revolted to the Lacedaemonians. Consequently the Athenian people, being disheartened, of their own accord renounced the democracy, and choosing four hundred men they turned over to them the administration of the state. The leaders of the oligarchy, after building a number of triremes, sent out forty of them together with generals. Although these were at odds with one another, they sailed off to Oropus, for the enemy's triremes lay at anchor there. In the battle which followed the Lacedaemonians were victorious and captured twenty-two vessels.

After the Syracusans had brought to an end the war with the Athenians, they honoured with the booty taken in the war the Lacedaemonians who had fought with them under the command of Gylippus, and they sent back with them to Lacedaemon, to aid them in the war against the Athenians, an allied force of thirty-five triremes under the command of Hermocrates, their foremost citizen. As for themselves, after gathering the spoil that accrued from the war, they embellished their temples with dedications and with arms taken from the enemy and honoured with the appropriate gifts those soldiers who had fought with distinction. After this Diocles, who was the most influential among them of the leaders of the populace, persuaded the citizens to change their form of government so that the administration would be conducted by magistrates chosen by lot and that lawgivers also should be elected for organising the polity and drafting new laws privately.

**35.** Consequently the Syracusans elected lawgivers from such of their citizens as excelled in judgement, the most distinguished of them being Diocles. For he so far excelled the rest in understanding and renown that, although the writing of the code was a task of all in common, they were called "The Laws of Diocles," and not only did the Syracusans admire this man during his lifetime, but also, when he died, they rendered him the honours accorded to heroes and built a temple in his honour at public expense; the one which was torn down by Dionysius at a later time when the walls of the city were being constructed [402]. This man was held in high esteem among the other Sicilian Greeks as well; indeed many cities of the island continued to use his laws down to the time when the Sicilian Greeks as a body were granted Roman citizenship. Accordingly, when in later times laws were framed for the Syracusans by Cephalus [339] in the time of Timoleon and by Polydorus in the time of King Hiero, they called neither one of these men a "lawgiver," but rather an "interpreter of the lawgiver," since men found the laws of Diocles, written as they were in an ancient style, difficult to understand. Profound reflection is displayed in his legislation, the lawmaker showing himself to be a hater of evil, since he sets heavier penalties against all wrongdoers than any other legislator, just, in that more precisely than by any predecessor the punishment of each man is fixed according to his deserts, and both practical and widely experienced, in that he judges every complaint and every dispute, whether it concerns the state or the individual, to be deserving of a fixed penalty. He is also concise in his style and leaves much for the readers to reflect upon. And the dramatic manner of his death bore witness to the uprightness and austerity of his soul.

Now these qualities of Diocles I have been moved to set forth in considerable detail by reason of the fact that most historians have rather slighted him in their treatises.

**36.** When the Athenians learned of the total destruction of their forces in Sicily, they were deeply distressed at the magnitude of the disaster. Yet they would not at all on that account abate their ardent aspiration for the supremacy, but set about both constructing more ships and providing themselves with funds wherewith they might contend to the last hope for the primacy. Choosing four hundred men they put in their hands the supreme authority to direct the conduct of the war; for they assumed that an oligarchy was more suitable than a democracy in critical circumstances like these. The events, however, did not turn out according to the judgement of those who held that opinion, but the Four Hundred conducted the war far less competently. For, although they dispatched forty ships, they sent along to command them two generals who were at odds with each other. Although, with the affairs of the Athenians at such low ebb, the emergency called for complete concord, the generals kept quarrelling with each other. And finally they sailed to Oropus without preparation and met the Peloponnesians in a sea-battle; but since they made a wretched beginning of the battle and stood up to the fighting like churls, they lost twenty-two ships and barely got the rest safe over to Eretria.

After these events had taken place, the allies of the Athenians, because of the defeats they had suffered in Sicily as well as the estranged relations of the commanders, revolted to the Lacedaemonians, and since Darius, the king of the Persians, was an ally of the Lacedaemonians, Pharnabazus, who had the military command of the regions bordering on the sea, supplied money to the Lacedaemonians; and he also summoned the three hundred triremes supplied by Phoenicia, having in mind to dispatch them to the aid of the Lacedaemonians.

37. Inasmuch as the Athenians had experienced setbacks so serious at one and the same time, everyone had assumed that the war was at an end; for no one expected that the Athenians could possibly endure such reverses any longer, even for a moment. However, events did not come to an end that tallied with the assumption of the majority, but on the contrary it came to pass, such was the superiority of the combatants, that the whole situation changed for the following reasons.

Alcibiades, who was in exile from Athens, had for a time fought on the side of the Lacedaemonians and had rendered them great assistance in the war; for he was a most able orator and far the outstanding citizen in daring, and, besides, he was in high birth and wealth first among the Athenians. Now since Alcibiades was eager to be allowed to return to his native city, he contrived every device whereby he could do the Athenians some good turn, and in particular at the crucial moments when the Athenians seemed doomed to utter defeat. Accordingly, since he was on friendly terms with Pharnabazus, the satrap of Darius, and saw that he was on the point of sending three hundred ships to the support of the Lacedaemonians, he persuaded him to give up the undertaking; for he showed him that it would not be to the advantage of the King to make the Lacedaemonians too powerful. That would not, he said, help the Persians, and so a better policy would be to maintain a neutral attitude toward the combatants so long as they were equally matched, in order that they might continue their quarrel as long as possible. Thereupon Pharnabazus, believing that Alcibiades was giving him good advice, sent the fleet back to Phoenicia. Now on that occasion Alcibiades deprived the Lacedaemonians of so great an allied force; and some time later, when he had been allowed to return to Athens and been given command of a military force, he defeated the Lacedaemonians in many battles and completely restored again the sunken fortunes of the Athenians; we shall discuss these matters in more detail in connection with the appropriate period of time, in order that our account may not by anticipation violate the natural order of events.

## The sea-battle between the Athenians and Lacedaemonians off Sigeium and the victory of the Athenians (38-40).

**38.** After the close of the year Theopompus was archon in Athens [411] and the Romans elected in place of consuls four military tribunes, Tiberius Postumius, Gaius Cornelius, Gaius Valerius, and Caeso Fabius. At this time the Athenians dissolved the oligarchy of the Four Hundred and formed the constitution of the government from the citizens at large. The author of all these changes was Theramenes, a man who was orderly in his manner of life and was reputed to surpass all others in judgement; for he was the only person to advise the recall from exile of Alcibiades, through whom the Athenians recovered themselves, and since he was the author of many other measures for the benefit of his country, he was the recipient of no small approbation.

But these events took place at a little later time, and for the war the Athenians appointed Thrasyllus and Thrasybulus generals, who collected the fleet at Samos and trained the soldiers for battle at sea, giving them daily exercises. Mindarus, the Lacedaemonian admiral, was inactive for some time at Miletus, expecting the aid promised by Pharnabazus; and when he heard that three hundred triremes had arrived from Phoenicia, he was buoyed up in his hopes, believing that with so great a fleet he could destroy the empire of the Athenians, but when a little later he learned from sundry persons that Pharnabazus had been won over by Alcibiades and had sent the fleet back to Phoenicia, he gave up the hopes he had placed in Pharnabazus, and by himself, after equipping both the ships brought from the Peloponnesus and those supplied by his allies from abroad, he dispatched Dorieus with thirteen ships to Rhodes, since he had learned that certain Rhodians were banding together for a revolution. (The ships we have mentioned had recently been sent to the Lacedaemonians as an allied force by certain Greeks of Italy.) Mindarus himself took all the other ships, numbering eighty-three, and set out for the Hellespont, since he had learned that the Athenian fleet was tarrying at Samos. The moment the generals of the Athenians saw them sailing by, they put out to sea against them with sixty ships. But when the Lacedaemonians put in at Chios, the Athenian generals decided to sail on to Lesbos and there to gather triremes from their allies, in order that it should not turn out that the enemy surpassed them in number of ships.

## How the Athenians overcame the Lacedaemonian admiral in a sea-fight and captured Cyzicus (39-40).

**39.** Now the Athenians were engaged in gathering ships. But Mindarus, the Lacedaemonian admiral, setting out by night with his entire fleet, made in haste for the Hellespont and arrived on the second day at Sigeium. When the Athenians learned that the fleet had sailed by them, they did not wait for all the triremes of their allies, but after only three had been added to their number they set out in pursuit of the Lacedaemonians. When they arrived at Sigeium, they found the fleet already departed, but three ships left behind they at once captured; after this they put in at Eleüs and made preparations for the sea-battle. The Lacedaemonians, seeing the enemy rehearsing for the battle, did likewise, spending five days in proving their ships and exercising their rowers; then they drew up the fleet for the battle, its strength being eighty-eight ships. Now the Lacedaemonians stationed their ships on the Asian side of the channel, while the

Athenians lined up against them on the European side, being fewer in number but of superior training. The Lacedaemonians put on their right wing the Syracusans, whose leader was Hermocrates, and the Peloponnesians themselves formed the whole left wing with Mindarus in command. For the Athenians Thrasyllus was stationed on the right wing and Thrasybulus on the left. At the outset both sides strove stubbornly for position in order that they might not have the current against them. Consequently they kept sailing around each other for a long time, endeavouring to block off the straits and struggling for an advantageous position; for the battle took place between Abydus and Sestus and it so happened that the current was of no little hindrance where the strait was narrow. However, the pilots of the Athenian fleet, being far superior in experience, contributed greatly to the victory.

**40.** For although the Peloponnesians had the advantage in the number of their ships and the valour of their marines, the skill of the Athenian pilots rendered the superiority of their opponents of no effect. For whenever the Peloponnesians, with their ships in a body, would charge swiftly forward to ram, the pilots would manoeuvre their own ships so skilfully that their opponents were unable to strike them at any other spot but could only meet them bows on, ram against ram. Consequently Mindarus, seeing that the force of the rams was proving ineffective, gave orders for his ships to come to grips in small groups, or one at a time, but not by this manoeuvre either, as it turned out, was the skill of the Athenian pilots rendered ineffective; on the contrary, cleverly avoiding the oncoming rams of the ships, they struck them on the side and damaged many. Such a spirit of rivalry pervaded both forces that they would not confine the struggle to ramming tactics, but tangling ship with ship fought it out with the marines. Although they were hindered by the strength of the current from achieving great success, they continued the struggle for a considerable time, neither side being able to gain the victory. While the fighting was thus equally balanced, there appeared beyond a cape twenty-five ships which had been dispatched to the Athenians from their allies. The Peloponnesians thereupon in alarm turned in flight toward Abydus, the Athenians clinging to them and pursuing them the more vigorously.

Such was the end of the battle; and the Athenians captured eight ships of the Chians, five of the Corinthians, two of the Ambraciotes, and one each of the Syracusans, Pellenians, and Leucadians, while they themselves lost five ships, all of them, as it happened, having been sunk. After this Thrasybulus set up a trophy on the cape where stands the memorial of Hecabe and sent messengers to Athens to carry word of the victory, and himself made his way to Cyzicus with the entire fleet. For before the sea-battle this city had revolted to Pharnabazus, the general of Darius, and to Clearchus, the Lacedaemonian commander. Finding the city unfortified the Athenians easily achieved their end, and after exacting money of the Cyziceni they sailed off to Sestus.

*How, when the Lacedaemonians dispatched fifty ships from Euboea to the aid of the defeated, they together with their crews were all lost in a storm off Athos (41).*

*The return of Alcibiades and his election as a general (41-42).*

**41.** Mindarus, the Lacedaemonian admiral, after his flight to Abydus from the scene of his defeat repaired the ships that had been damaged and also sent the Spartan Epicles to the triremes at Euboea with orders to bring them with all speed. When Epicles arrived at Euboea, he gathered the ships, which amounted to fifty, and hurriedly put out to sea; but when the triremes were off Mt. Athos there arose a storm of such fury that all the ships were lost and of their crews twelve men alone survived. These facts are set forth by a dedication, as Ephorus states, which stands in the temple at Coroneia and bears the following inscription:

> These from the crews of fifty ships, escaping destruction,
> Brought their bodies to land hard by Athos' sharp crags;
> Only twelve, all the rest the yawning depth of the waters
> Took to their death with their ships, meeting with terrible winds.

At about the same time Alcibiades with thirteen triremes came by sea to the Athenians who were lying at Samos and had already heard that he had persuaded Pharnabazus not to come, as he had intended, with his three hundred ships to reinforce the Lacedaemonians. Since the troops at Samos gave him a friendly welcome, he discussed with them the matter of his return from exile, offering promises to render many services to the fatherland; and in like manner he defended his own conduct and shed many tears over his own fortune, because he had been compelled by his enemies to give proof of his own valour at the expense of his native land.

**42.** And since the soldiers heartily welcomed the offers of Alcibiades and sent messages to Athens regarding them, the people voted to dismiss the charges against Alcibiades and to give him a share in the command; for as they observed the efficiency of his daring and the fame he enjoyed among the Greeks, they assumed, and with good reason, that his adherence to them would add no little weight to their cause. Moreover, Theramenes, who at the time enjoyed the leadership in the government and who, if anyone, had a reputation of sagacity, advised the people to recall Alcibiades. When word of this action was reported to Samos, Alcibiades added nine ships to the thirteen he already had, and sailing with them to Halicarnassus he exacted money from that city. After this he sacked Meropis [on Cos] and returned to Samos with much plunder, and since a great amount of booty had been amassed, he divided the spoils among the soldiers at Samos and his own troops, thereby soon causing the recipients of his benefactions to be well disposed toward himself.

About the same time the Antandrians, who were held by a [Persian] garrison, sent to the Lacedaemonians for soldiers, with whose aid they expelled the garrison and thus made their country a free place to live in; for the Lacedaemonians, finding fault with Pharnabazus for the sending of the three hundred ships back to Phoenicia, gave their aid to the inhabitants of Antandrus.

Of the historians, Thucydides ended his history, having included a period of twenty-two years in eight Books, although some divide it into nine; and

Xenophon and Theopompus have begun at the point where Thucydides left off. Xenophon embraced a period of forty-eight years, and Theopompus set forth the facts of Greek history for seventeen years and brings his account to an end with the sea-battle of Cnidus in twelve Books.

Such was the state of affairs in Greece and Asia. The Romans were waging war with the Aequi and invaded their territory with a strong army; and investing the city named Bolae they took it by siege.

### The war between the Aegestaeans and the Seli-nuntians over the land in dispute (43-44).

**43.** When the events of this year had come to an end, in Athens [410] Glaucippus was archon and in Rome the consuls elected were Marcus Cornelius and Lucius Furius. At this time in Sicily the Aegestaeans, who had allied themselves with the Athenians against the Syracusans, had fallen into great fear at the conclusion of the war; for they expected, and with good reason, to pay the penalty to the Sicilian Greeks for the wrongs they had inflicted upon them. When the Selinuntians went to war with them over the land in dispute, they withdrew from it of their free will, being concerned lest the Syracusans should use this excuse to join the Selinuntians in the war and they should thereby run the risk of destroying their country, but when the Selinuntians proposed, quite apart from the territory in dispute, to carve off for themselves a large portion of the neighbouring territory, the inhabitants of Aegesta thereupon dispatched ambassadors to Carthage, asking for aid and putting their city in the hands of the Carthaginians. When the envoys arrived and laid before the Senate the instructions the people had given them, the Carthaginians found themselves in no little quandary; for while they were eager to acquire a city so strategically situated, at the same time they stood in fear of the Syracusans, having just witnessed their defeat of the armaments of the Athenians. When Hannibal, their foremost citizen, also advised them to acquire the city, they replied to the ambassadors that they would come to their aid, and to supervise the undertaking, in case it should lead to war, they selected as general Hannibal, who at the time lawfully exercised sovereign powers. He was the grandson of Hamilcar, who fought in the war against Gelon and died at Himera, and the son of Gescon, who had been exiled because of his father's defeat and had ended his life in Selinus.

Now Hannibal, who by nature was a hater of the Greeks and at the same time desired to wipe out the disgraces which had befallen his ancestors, was eager by his own efforts to achieve some advantage for his country. Hence, seeing that the Selinuntians were not satisfied with the cession of the territory in dispute, he dispatched ambassadors together with the Aegestaeans to the Syracusans, referring to them the decision of the dispute; and though ostensibly he pretended to be seeking that justice be done, in fact he believed that, after the Selinuntians refused to agree to arbitration, the Syracusans would not join them as allies. Since the Selinuntians also dispatched ambassadors, refusing the arbitration and answering at length the ambassadors of the Carthaginians and Aegestaeans, in the end the Syracusans decided to vote to maintain their alliance with the Selinuntians and their state of peace with the Carthaginians.

**44.** After the return of their ambassadors the Carthaginians dispatched to the Aegestaeans five thousand Libyans and eight hundred Campanians. These troops had been hired by the Chalcidians [of Sicily] to aid the Athenians in the war against the Syracusans, and on their return after its disastrous conclusion they found no one to hire their services; but the Carthaginians purchased horses for them all, gave them high pay, and sent them to Aegesta.

The Selinuntians, who were prosperous in those days and whose city was heavily populated, held the Aegestaeans in contempt, and at first, deploying in battle order, they laid waste the land which touched their border, since their armies were far superior, but after this, despising their foe, they scattered everywhere over the countryside. The generals of the Aegestaeans, watching their opportunity, attacked them with the aid of the Carthaginians and Campanians. Since the attack was not expected, they easily put the Selinuntians to flight, killing about a thousand of the soldiers and capturing all their loot. After the battle both sides straightway dispatched ambassadors, the Selinuntians to the Syracusans and the Aegestaeans to the Carthaginians, asking for help. Both parties promised their assistance and the Carthaginian War thus had its beginning. The Carthaginians, foreseeing the magnitude of the war, entrusted the responsibility for the size of their armament to Hannibal as their general and enthusiastically rendered him every assistance. And Hannibal during the summer and the following winter enlisted many mercenaries from Iberia and also enrolled not a few from among the citizens; he also visited Libya, choosing the stoutest men from every city, and he made ready ships, planning to convey the armies across with the opening of spring.

Such, then, was the state of affairs in Sicily.

**45.** In Greece Dorieus the Rhodian, the admiral of the triremes from Italy, after he had quelled the tumult in Rhodes, set sail for the Hellespont, being eager to join Mindarus; for the latter was lying at Abydus and collecting from every quarter the ships of the Peloponnesian alliance. When Dorieus was already in the neighbourhood of Sigeium in the Troad, the Athenians who were at Sestus, learning that he was sailing along the coast, put out against him with their ships, seventy-four in all. Dorieus held to his course for a time in ignorance of what was happening; but when he observed the great strength of the fleet he was alarmed, and seeing no other way to save his force he put in at Dardanus. Here he disembarked his soldiers and took over the troops who were guarding the city, and then he speedily got in a vast supply of missiles and stationed his soldiers both on the fore-parts of the ships and in advantageous positions on the land. The Athenians, sailing in at full speed, set to work hauling the ships away from the shore, and they were wearing down the enemy, having crowded them on every side by their superior numbers. When Mindarus, the Peloponnesian admiral, learned of the situation, he speedily put out from Abydus with his entire fleet and sailed to the Dardanian Promontory with eighty-four ships to the aid of the fleet of Dorieus; and the land army of Pharnabazus was also there, supporting the Lacedaemonians.

When the fleets came near one another, both sides drew up the triremes for battle; Mindarus, who had ninety-seven ships, stationed the Syracusans on his left wing, while he himself took command of the right; as for the Athenians, Thrasybulus led the right wing and Thrasyllus the other. After the forces had made ready in this fashion, their commanders raised the signal for battle and the trumpeters at a single word of command began to sound the attack: and since the rowers showed no lack of eagerness and the pilots managed their helms with skill, the contest which ensued was an amazing spectacle. For whenever the triremes would drive forward to ram, at that moment the pilots, at just the critical instant, would turn their ships so effectively that the blows were made ram on. As for the marines, whenever they would see their own ships borne along with their sides to the triremes of the enemy, they would be terror-stricken, despairing of their lives; but whenever the pilots, employing the skill of practice, would frustrate the attack, they would in turn be overjoyed and elated in their hopes.

**46.** Nor did the men whose position was on the decks fail to maintain the zeal which brooked no failure; but some, while still at a considerable distance from the enemy, kept up a stream of arrows and soon the space was full of missiles, while others, each time that they drew near, would hurl their javelins, some doing their best to strike the defending marines and others the enemy pilots themselves; and whenever the ships would come close together, they would not only fight with their spears but at the moment of contact would also leap over on the enemy's triremes and carry on the contest with their swords. And since at each reverse the victors would raise the war-cry and the others would rush to aid with shouting, a mingled din prevailed over the entire area of the battle.

For a long time the battle was equally balanced because of the very high rivalry with which both sides were inspired; but later on Alcibiades unexpectedly appeared from Samos with twenty ships, sailing by mere chance to the Hellespont. While these ships were still at a distance, each side, hoping that reinforcement had come for themselves, was elated in its hopes and fought on with far greater courage; but when the fleet was now near and for the Lacedaemonians no signal was to be seen, but for the Athenians Alcibiades ran up a purple flag from his own ship, which was the signal they had agreed upon, the Lacedaemonians in dismay turned in flight and the Athenians, elated by the advantage they now possessed, pressed eagerly upon the ships trying to escape. They speedily captured ten ships, but then a storm and violent winds arose, as a result of which they were greatly hindered in the pursuit; for because of the high waves the boats would not respond to the tillers, and the attempts at ramming proved fruitless, since the ships were receding when struck. In the end the Lacedaemonians, gaining the shore, fled to the land army of Pharnabazus, and the Athenians at first essayed to drag the ships from the shore and put up a desperate battle, but when they were checked in their attempts by the Persian forces they sailed off to Sestus. For Pharnabazus, wishing to build a defence for himself before the Lacedaemonians against the charges they were bringing against him, put up all the more vigorous fight against the Athenians; while at the same time, with respect to his sending the three hundred triremes to Phoenicia, he explained to them that he had done so on receiving information that the king of the Arabians and the king of the Egyptians had designs upon Phoenicia.

### *How the Lacedaemonians filled up Euripus with earth and made Euboea a part of the mainland (47).*

**47.** When the sea-battle had ended as we have related, the Athenians sailed off at the time to Sestus, since it was already night, but when day came they collected their ships which had been damaged and set up another trophy near the former one. Mindarus about the first watch of the night set out to Abydus, where he repaired his ships that had been damaged and sent word to the Lacedaemonians for reinforcements of both soldiers and ships; for he had in mind, while the fleet was being made ready, to lay siege with the army together with Pharnabazus to the cities in Asia which were allied with the Athenians.

The people of Chalcis and almost all the rest of the inhabitants of Euboea had revolted from the Athenians and were therefore highly apprehensive lest, living as they did on an island, they should be forced to surrender to the Athenians, who were masters of the sea; and they therefore asked the Boeotians to join with them in building a causeway across the Euripus and thereby joining Euboea to Boeotia. The Boeotians agreed to this, since it was to their special advantage that Euboea should be an island to everybody else but a part of the mainland to themselves. Consequently all the cities threw themselves vigorously into the building of the causeway and vied with one another; for orders were issued not only to the citizens to report *en masse* but to the foreigners dwelling among them as well, so that by reason of the great number that came forward to the work the proposed task was speedily completed. On Euboea the causeway was built at Chalcis, and in Boeotia in the neighbourhood of Aulis, since at that place the channel was narrowest. Now it so happened that in former times also there had always been a current in that place and that the sea frequently reversed its course, and at the time in question the force of the current was far greater because the sea had been confined into a very narrow channel; for passage was left for only a single ship. High towers were also built on both ends and wooden bridges were thrown over the channel.

Theramenes, who had been dispatched by the Athenians with thirty ships, at first attempted to stop the workers, but since a strong body of soldiers was at the side of the builders of the causeway, he abandoned this design and directed his voyage toward the islands. Since he wished to relieve both the citizens and the allies from their contributions, he laid waste the territory of the enemy and collected great quantities of booty. He visited also the allied cities and exacted money of such inhabitants as were advocating a change in government. And when he put in at Paros and found an oligarchy in the city, he restored their freedom to the people and exacted a great sum of money of the men who had participated in the oligarchy.

### *On the civil discord and massacre in Corcyra (48).*

**48.** It happened at this time that a serious civil strife occurred in Corcyra accompanied by massacre, which is said to have been due to various causes but most of all to the mutual hatred that existed between its own inhabitants. For never in any state have there taken place such murdering of citizens nor have there been greater quarrelling and contentiousness which culminated in bloodshed. For it would seem that the number of those who were slain by their fellow citizens before the present civil strife was some fifteen hundred, and all of these were leading citizens. And although these misfortunes had already befallen them, Fortune brought upon them a second disaster, in that she increased once more the disaffection which prevailed among them. For the foremost Corcyraeans, who desired the oligarchy, favoured the cause of the Lacedaemonians, whereas the masses which favoured the democracy were eager

BOOK XIII

to ally themselves with the Athenians. For the peoples who were struggling for leadership in Greece were devoted to opposing principles; the Lacedaemonians, for example, made it their policy to put the control of the government in the hands of the leading citizens of their allied states, whereas the Athenians regularly established democracies in their cities. Accordingly the Corcyraeans, seeing that their most influential citizens were planning to hand the city over to the Lacedaemonians, sent to the Athenians for an army to protect their city, and Conon, the general of the Athenians, sailed to Corcyra and left in the city six hundred men from the Messenians in Naupactus, while he himself sailed on with his ships and cast anchor off the sacred precinct of Hera. The six hundred, setting out unexpectedly with the partisans of the people's party at the time of full market against the supporters of the Lacedaemonians, arrested some of them, slew others, and drove more than a thousand from the state; they also set the slaves free and gave citizenship to the foreigners living among them as a precaution against the great number and influence of the exiles. Now the men who had been exiled from their country fled to the opposite mainland; but a few days later some people still in the city who favoured the cause of the exiles seized the market-place, called back the exiles, and essayed a final decision of the struggle. When night brought an end to the fighting they came to an agreement with each other, stopped their quarrelling, and resumed living together as one people in their fatherland.

Such, then, was the end of the massacre in Corcyra.

### *How Alcibiades and Theramenes won most notable victories over the Lacedaemonians on both land and sea (49-51).*

**49.** Archelaüs, the king of the Macedonians [413-399], since the people of Pydna would not obey his orders, laid siege to the city with a great army. He received reinforcement also from Theramenes, who brought a fleet; but he, as the siege dragged on, sailed to Thrace, where he joined Thrasybulus who was commander of the entire fleet. Archelaüs now pressed the siege of Pydna more vigorously, and after reducing it he removed the city some twenty stades distant from the sea.

Mindarus, when the winter had come to an end, collected his triremes from all quarters, for many had come to him from the Peloponnesus as well as from the other allies. The Athenian generals in Sestus, when they learned of the great size of the fleet that was being assembled by the enemy, were greatly alarmed lest the enemy, attacking with all their triremes, should capture their ships. Consequently the generals on their side hauled down the ships they had at Sestus, sailed around the Chersonesus, and moored them at Cardia; and they sent triremes to Thrasybulus and Theramenes in Thrace, urging them to come with their fleet as soon as possible, and they summoned Alcibiades also from Lesbos with what ships he had, and the whole fleet was gathered into one place, the generals being eager for a decisive battle. Mindarus, the Lacedaemonian admiral, sailing to Cyzicus, disembarked his whole force and invested the city. Pharnabazus was also there with a large army and with his aid Mindarus laid siege to Cyzicus and took it by storm.

The Athenian generals, having decided to sail to Cyzicus, put out to sea with all their ships and sailed around the Chersonesus. They arrived first at Eleüs; and after that they made a special point of sailing past the city of Abydus at night, in order that the great number of their vessels might not be known to the enemy. When they had arrived at Proconnesus [Marmora], they spent the night there and the next day they disembarked the soldiers who had shipped with them on the territory of the Cyzicenes and gave orders to Chaereas, their commander, to lead the army against the city.

50. As for the generals themselves, they divided the naval force into three squadrons, Alcibiades commanding one, Theramenes another, and Thrasybulus the third. Now Alcibiades with his own squadron advanced far ahead of the others, wishing to draw the Lacedaemonians out to a battle, whereas Theramenes and Thrasybulus planned the manoeuvre of encircling the enemy and, if they sailed out, of blocking their retreat to the city. Mindarus, seeing only the ships of Alcibiades approaching, twenty in number, and having no knowledge of the others, held them in contempt and boldly set sail from the city with eighty ships to attack him. Then, when he had come near the ships of Alcibiades, the Athenians, as they had been commanded, pretended to flee, and the Peloponnesians, in high spirits, pursued after them vigorously in the belief they were winning the victory, but after Alcibiades had drawn them a considerable distance from the city, he raised the signal; and when this was given, the ships of Alcibiades suddenly at the same time turned about to face the enemy, and Theramenes and Thrasybulus sailed toward the city and cut off the retreat of the Lacedaemonians. The troops of Mindarus, when they now observed the multitude of the enemy ships and realised that they had been outgeneralled, were rilled with great fear. Finally, since the Athenians were appearing from every direction and had shut off the Peloponnesians from their line of approach to the city, Mindarus was forced to seek safety on land near Cleri, as it is called, where also Pharnabazus had his army. Alcibiades, pursuing him vigorously, sank some ships, damaged and captured others, and the largest number, which were moored on the land itself, he seized and threw grappling-irons on, endeavouring by this means to drag them from the land. When the infantry of Pharnabazus rushed to the aid of the Lacedaemonians, there was great bloodshed, inasmuch as the Athenians because of the advantage they had won were fighting with greater boldness than expediency, while the Peloponnesians were in number far superior; for the army of Pharnabazus was supporting the Lacedaemonians and fighting as it was from the land the position it had was more secure. When Thrasybulus saw the infantry aiding the enemy, he put the rest of his marines on the land with intent to assist Alcibiades and his men, and he also urged Theramenes to join up with the land troops of Chaereas and come with all speed, in order to wage a battle on land.

51. While the Athenians were busying themselves with these matters, Mindarus, the Lacedaemonian commander, was himself fighting with Alcibiades for the ships that were being dragged off, and he dispatched Clearchus the Spartan with a part of the Peloponnesians against the troops with Thrasybulus; and with him he also sent the mercenaries in the army of Pharnabazus. Thrasybulus with the marines and archers at first stoutly withstood the enemy, and though he slew many of them, he also saw not a few of his own men falling; but when the mercenaries of Pharnabazus were surrounding the Athenians and

## Book XIII

were crowding about them in great numbers from every direction, Theramenes appeared, leading both his own troops and the infantry with Chaereas. Although the troops of Thrasybulus were exhausted and had given up hope of rescue, their spirits were suddenly revived again when reinforcements so strong were at hand. An obstinate battle which lasted a long time ensued; but at first the mercenaries of Pharnabazus began to withdraw and the continuity of their battle line was broken; and finally the Peloponnesians who had been left behind with Clearchus, after having both inflicted and suffered much punishment, were expelled.

Now that the Peloponnesians had been defeated, the troops of Theramenes rushed to give aid to the soldiers who had been fighting under Alcibiades. Although the forces had rapidly assembled at one point, Mindarus was not dismayed at the attack of Theramenes, but, after dividing the Peloponnesians, with half of them he met the advancing enemy, while with the other half which he himself commanded, first calling upon each soldier not to disgrace the fair name of Sparta, and that too in a fight on land, he formed a line against the troops of Alcibiades. He put up a heroic battle about the ships, fighting in person before all his troops, but though he slew many of the opponents, in the end he was killed by the troops of Alcibiades as he battled nobly for his fatherland. When he had fallen, both the Peloponnesians and all the allies banded together and broke into terror-stricken flight. The Athenians pursued the enemy for a distance, but when they learned that Pharnabazus was hurrying up at full speed with a strong force of cavalry, they returned to the ships, and after they had taken the city [Cyzicus] they set up two trophies for the two victories, one for the sea-battle at the island of Polydorus, as it is called, and one for the land-battle where they forced the first flight of the enemy. Now the Peloponnesians in the city and all the fugitives from the battle fled to the camp of Pharnabazus; and the Athenian generals not only captured all the ships but they also took many prisoners and an immeasurable quantity of booty, since they had won the victory at the same time over two armaments of such size.

**52.** When the news of the victory came to Athens, the people, contemplating the unexpected good fortune which had come to the city after their former disasters, were elated over their successes and the populace in a body offered sacrifices to the gods and gathered in festive assemblies; and for the war they selected from their most stalwart men one thousand hoplites and one hundred horsemen, and in addition to these they dispatched thirty triremes to Alcibiades, in order that, now that they dominated the sea, they might lay waste with impunity the cities which favoured the Lacedaemonians. The Lacedaemonians, on the other hand, when they heard of the disaster they had suffered at Cyzicus, sent ambassadors to Athens to treat for peace, the chief of whom was Endius. When permission was given him, he took the floor and spoke succinctly and in the terse fashion of Laconians, and for this reason I have decided not to omit the speech as he delivered it.

"We want to be at peace with you, men of Athens, and that each party should keep the cities which it now possesses and cease to maintain its garrisons in the other's territory, and that our captives be ransomed, one Laconian for one Athenian. We are not unmindful that the war is hurtful to both of us, but far more to you. Never mind the words I use but learn from the facts. As for us, we till the entire Peloponnesus, but you only a small part of Attica. While to the Laconians the war has brought many allies, from the Athenians it has taken away as many as it has given to their enemies. For us the richest king to be found in the inhabited world defrays the cost of the war, for you the most poverty-stricken folk of the inhabited world. Consequently our troops, in view of their generous pay, make war with spirit, while your soldiers, because they pay the war-taxes out of their own pockets, shrink from both the hardships and the costs of war. In the second place, when we make war at sea, we risk losing only hulls among resources of the state, while you have on board crews most of whom are citizens, and, what is the most important, even if we meet defeat in our actions at sea, we still maintain without dispute the mastery on land, for a Spartan foot-soldier does not even know what flight means, but you, if you are driven from the sea, contend, not for the supremacy on land, but for survival.

"It remains for me to show you why, despite so many and great advantages we possess in the fighting, we urge you to make peace. I do not affirm that Sparta is profiting from the war, but only that she is suffering less than the Athenians. Only fools find satisfaction in sharing the misfortunes of their enemies, when it is in their power to make no trial whatsoever of misfortune. For the destruction of the enemy brings no joy that can balance the grief caused by the distress of one's own people. Not for these reasons alone are we eager to come to terms, but because we hold fast to the custom of our fathers; for when we consider the many terrible sufferings which are caused by the rivalries which accompany war, we believe we should make it clear in the sight of all gods and men that we are least responsible of all men for such things."

**53.** After the Laconian had made these and similar representations, the sentiments of the most reasonable men among the Athenians inclined toward the peace, but those who made it their practice to foment war and to turn disturbances in the state to their personal profit chose the war. A supporter of this sentiment was, among others, Cleophon, who was the most influential leader of the populace at this time. He, taking the floor and arguing at length on the question in his own fashion, buoyed up the people, citing the magnitude of their military successes, as if indeed it is not the practice of Fortune to adjudge the advantages in war now to one side and now to the other. Consequently the Athenians, after taking unwise counsel, repented of it when it could do them no good, and, deceived as they were by words spoken in flattery, they made a blunder so vital that never again at any time were they able truly to recover. These events, which took place at a later date, will be described in connection with the period of time to which they belong; at the time we are discussing the Athenians, being elated by their successes and entertaining many great hopes because they had Alcibiades as the leader of their armed forces, thought that they had quickly won back their supremacy.

*How the Carthaginians transported great armaments to Sicily and took by storm Selinus and Himera (54-62).*

**54.** When the events of this year had come to an end, in Athens [409] Diocles took over the chief office, and in Rome Quintus Fabius and Gaius Furius held the consulship. At this time Hannibal, the general of the Carthaginians, gathered together both the mercenaries he had collected from Iberia and the soldiers he had enrolled from Libya, manned sixty ships of war, and made ready some fifteen hundred transports. On these he loaded the troops, the siege-engines, missiles, and all the other accessories. After crossing with the fleet the Libyan Sea he came to land in Sicily on the promontory which lies opposite Libya and is called Lilybaeum; and at that very time some Selinuntian cavalry were tarrying in those regions, and having seen the great size of the fleet as it came to land, they speedily informed their fellow citizens of the presence of the enemy. The Selinuntians at once dispatched their letter-carriers to the Syracusans, asking their aid; and Hannibal disembarked his troops and pitched a camp, beginning at the well which in those times had the name Lilybaeum, and many years after these events, when a city was founded near it [396], the presence of the well occasioned the giving of the name to the city [Lilybaeum]. Hannibal had all told, as Ephorus has recorded, two hundred thousand infantry and four thousand cavalry, but as Timaeus says, not many more than one hundred thousand men. His ships he hauled up on land in the bay about Motyê, every one of them, wishing to give the Syracusans the impression that he had not come to make war upon them or to sail along the coast with his naval force against Syracuse. After adding to his army the soldiers supplied by the Aegestaeans and by the other allies he broke camp and made his way from Lilybaeum towards Selinus. When he came to the Mazarus River, he took at the first assault the trading-station situated by it, and when he arrived before the city, he divided his army into two parts; then, after he had invested the city and put his siege-engines in position, he began the assaults with all speed. He set up six towers of exceptional size and advanced an equal number of battering-rams plated with iron against the walls; furthermore, by employing his archers and slingers in great numbers he beat back the fighters on the battlements.

**55.** The Selinuntians, who had for a long time been without experience in sieges and had been the only Sicilian Greeks to fight on the side of the Carthaginians in the war against Gelon, had never conceived that they would be brought to such a state of fear by the people whom they had befriended. When they saw the great size of the engines of war and the hosts of the enemy, they were filled with dread and dismayed at the magnitude of the danger threatening them. However, they did not totally despair of their deliverance, but in the expectation that the Syracusans and their other allies would soon arrive, the whole populace fought off the enemy from the walls. Indeed all the men in the prime of life were armed and battled desperately, while the older men busied themselves with the supplies and, as they made the rounds of the wall, begged the young men not to allow them to fall under subjection to the enemy; and women and girls supplied the food and missiles to the defenders of the fatherland, counting as naught the modesty and the sense of shame which they cherished in time of peace. Such consternation prevailed that the magnitude of the emergency called for even the aid of their women.

Hannibal, who had promised the soldiers that he would give them the city to pillage, pushed the siege-engines forward and assaulted the walls in waves with his best soldiers. All together the trumpets sounded the signal for attack and at one command the army of the Carthaginians as a body raised the war-cry, and by the power of the rams the walls were shaken, while by reason of the height of the towers the fighters on them slew many of the Selinuntians. For in the long period of peace they had enjoyed they had given no attention whatever even to their walls and so they were easily subdued, since the wooden towers far exceeded the walls in height. When the wall fell the Campanians, being eager to accomplish some outstanding feat, broke swiftly into the city. Now at the outset they struck terror into their opponents, who were few in number; but after that, when many gathered to the aid of the defenders, they were thrust out with heavy losses among their own soldiers; for since they had forced a passage when the wall had not yet been completely cleared and in their attack had fallen foul of difficult terrain, they were easily overcome. At nightfall the Carthaginians broke off the assault.

**56.** The Selinuntians, picking out their best horsemen, dispatched them at once by night, some to Acragas, and others to Gela and Syracuse, asking them to come to their aid with all speed, since their city could not withstand the strength of the enemy for any great time. Now the Acragantini and Geloans waited for the Syracusans, since they wished to lead their troops as one body against the Carthaginians; and the Syracusans, on learning the facts about the siege, first stopped the war they were engaged in with the Chalcidians and then spent some time in gathering the troops from the countryside and making great preparations, thinking that the city might be forced by siege to surrender but would not be taken by storm.

Hannibal, when the night had passed, at daybreak launched assaults from every side, and the part of the city's wall which had already fallen and the portion of the wall next the breach he broke down with the siege-engines. He then cleared the area of the fallen part of the wall and, attacking in relays of his best troops, gradually forced out the Selinuntians; it was not possible, however, to overpower by force men who were fighting for their very existence. Both sides suffered heavy losses, but for the Carthaginians fresh troops kept taking over the fighting, while for the Selinuntians there was no reserve to come to their support. The siege continued for nine days with unsurpassed stubbornness, and in the event the Carthaginians suffered and inflicted many terrible injuries. When the Iberians mounted where the wall had fallen, the women who were on the housetops raised a great cry, whereupon the Selinuntians, thinking that the city was being taken, were struck with terror, and leaving the walls they gathered in bands at the entrances of the narrow alleys, endeavoured to barricade the streets, and held off the enemy for a long time. As the Carthaginians pressed the attack, the multitudes of women and children took refuge on the housetops whence they threw both stones and tiles on the enemy. For a long time the Carthaginians came off badly, being unable either, because of the walls of the houses, to surround the men in the alleys or, because of those hurling at them from the roofs, to fight it out on equal terms. However, as the struggle went on until the afternoon, the missiles of the fighters from the houses were exhausted, whereas the troops of the Carthaginians, which constantly relieved those which were suffering heavily, continued the fighting in fresh condition. Finally, since the troops within the walls were being steadily reduced in number and the enemy entered the city in ever-increasing strength, the Selinuntians were forced out of the alleys.

**57.** And so, while the city was being taken, there was to be observed among the Greeks lamentation and weeping, and among the barbarians there was cheering and commingled outcries; for the former, as their eyes looked upon the great disaster which surrounded them, were filled with terror, while the latter, elated by their successes, urged on their comrades to slaughter. The Selinuntians gathered into the market-place and all who reached it died fighting there; and the barbarians, scattering throughout the entire city, plundered whatever of value was to be found in the dwellings, while of the inhabitants they found in them some they burned together with their homes and when others struggled into the streets, without distinction of sex or age but whether infant children or women or old men, they put them to the sword, showing no sign of compassion. They mutilated even the dead according to the practice of their people, some carrying bunches of hands about their bodies and others heads which they had spitted upon their javelins and spears. Such women as they found to have taken refuge together with their children in the temples they called upon their comrades not to kill, and to these alone did they give assurance of their lives. This they did, however, not out of pity for the unfortunate people, but because they feared lest the women, despairing of their lives, would burn down the temples, and thus they would not be able to make booty of the great wealth which was stored up in them as dedications. To such a degree did the barbarians surpass all other men in cruelty, that whereas the rest of mankind spare those who seek refuge in the sanctuaries from the desire not to commit sacrilege against the deity, the Carthaginians, on the contrary, would refrain from laying hands on the enemy in order that they might plunder the temples of their gods. By nightfall the city had been sacked, and of the dwellings some had been burned and others razed to the ground, while the whole area was filled with blood and corpses. Sixteen thousand was the sum of the inhabitants who were found to have fallen, not counting the more than five thousand who had been taken captive.

**58.** The Greeks serving as allies of the Carthaginians, as they contemplated the reversal in the lives of the hapless Selinuntians, felt pity at their lot. The women, deprived now of the pampered life they had enjoyed, spent the nights in the very midst of the enemies' lasciviousness, enduring terrible indignities, and some were obliged to see their daughters of marriageable age suffering treatment improper for their years. For the savagery of the barbarians spared neither free-born youths nor maidens, but exposed these unfortunates to dreadful disasters. Consequently, as the women reflected upon the slavery that would be their lot in Libya, as they saw themselves together with their children in a condition in which they possessed no legal rights and were subject to insolent treatment and thus compelled to obey masters, and as they noted that these masters used an unintelligible speech and had a bestial character, they mourned for their living children as dead, and receiving into their souls as a piercing wound each and every outrage committed against them, they became frantic with suffering and vehemently deplored their own fate; while as for their fathers and brothers who had died fighting for their country, them they counted blessed, since they had not witnessed any sight unworthy of their own valour. The Selinuntians who had escaped capture, twenty-six hundred in number, made their way in safety to Acragas and there received all possible kindness; for the Acragantini, after portioning out food to them at public expense, divided them for billeting among their homes, urging the private citizens, who were indeed eager enough, to supply them with every necessity of life.

**59.** While these events were taking place there arrived at Acragas three thousand picked soldiers from the Syracusans, who had been dispatched in advance with all speed to bring aid. On learning of the fall of Selinus, they sent ambassadors to Hannibal urging him both to release the captives on payment of ransom and to spare the temples of the gods. Hannibal replied that the Selinuntians, having proved incapable of defending their freedom, would now undergo the experience of slavery, and that the gods had departed from Selinus, having become offended with its inhabitants. However, since the fugitives had sent Empedion as an ambassador, to him Hannibal restored his possessions; for Empedion had always favoured the cause of the Carthaginians and before the siege had counselled the citizens not to go to war against the Carthaginians. Hannibal also graciously delivered up to him his kinsmen who were among the captives and to the Selinuntians who had escaped he gave permission to dwell in the city and to cultivate its fields upon payment of tribute to the Carthaginians. Now this city was taken after it had been inhabited from its founding for a period of two hundred and forty-two years. Hannibal, after destroying the walls of Selinus, departed with his whole army to Himera, being especially bent upon razing this city to the ground, for it was this city which had caused his father to be exiled and before its walls his grandfather Hamilcar had been outgeneralled by Gelon and then met his end, and with him one hundred and fifty thousand soldiers had perished and no fewer than these had been taken captive. These were the reasons why Hannibal was eager to exact punishment, and with forty thousand men he pitched camp upon some hills not far from the city, while with the rest of his entire army he invested the city, twenty thousand additional soldiers from both Siceli and Sicani having joined him. Setting up his siege-engines he shook the walls at a number of points, and since he pressed the battle with waves of troops in great strength, he wore down the defenders, especially since his soldiers were elated by their successes. He also set about undermining the walls, which he then shored up with wooden supports, and when these were set on fire, a large section of the wall soon fell. Thereupon there ensued a most bitter battle, one side struggling to force its way inside the wall and the other fearing lest they should suffer the same fate as the Selinuntians. Consequently, since the defenders put up a struggle to the death on behalf of children and parents and the fatherland which all men fight to defend, the barbarians were thrust out and the section of the wall quickly restored. To their aid came also the Syracusans from Acragas and troops from their other allies, some four thousand in all, who were under the command of Diodes the Syracusan.

**60.** At that juncture, when night brought an end to all further striving for victory, the Carthaginians abandoned the attack. And when day came, the Himeraeans decided not to allow themselves to be shut in and surrounded in this ignominious manner, as were the Selinuntians, and so they stationed guards on the walls and led out of the city the rest of their soldiers together with the allies who had arrived, some ten thousand men, and by engaging the enemy thus unexpectedly, they threw the barbarians into consternation, thinking as they did that allied forces had arrived to aid those who were penned in by the siege.

Because the Himeraeans were far superior in deeds of daring and of skill, and especially because their single hope of safety lay in their prevailing in the battle, at the outset they slew the first opponents, and since the multitude of the barbarians thronged together in great disorder because they never would have expected that the besieged would dare such a move, they were under no little disadvantage; for when eighty thousand men streamed together without order into one place, the result was that the barbarians clashed with each other and suffered more heavily from themselves than from the enemy. The Himeraeans, having as spectators on the walls parents and children as well as all their relatives, spent their own lives unsparingly for the salvation of them all, and since they fought brilliantly, the barbarians, dismayed by their deeds of daring and unexpected resistance, turned in flight. They fled in disorder to the troops encamped on the hills, and the Himeraeans pressed hard upon them, crying out to each other to take no man captive, and they slew more than six thousand of them, according to Timaeus, or, as Ephorus states, more than twenty thousand. Hannibal, seeing that his men were becoming exhausted, brought down his troops who were encamped on the hills, and reinforcing his beaten soldiers caught the Himeraeans in disorder as they were pushing the pursuit. In the fierce battle which ensued the main body of the Himeraeans turned in flight, but three thousand of them who tried to oppose the Carthaginian army, though they accomplished great deeds, were slain to a man.

**61.** This battle had already come to an end when there arrived at Himera from the Sicilian Greeks the twenty-five triremes which had previously been sent to aid the Lacedaemonians but at this time had returned from the campaign, and a report also spread through the city that the Syracusans *en masse* together with their allies were on the march to the aid of the Himeraeans and that Hannibal was preparing to man his triremes in Motyê with his choicest troops and, sailing to Syracuse, seize that city while it was stripped of its defenders. Consequently Diocles, who commanded the forces in Himera, advised the admirals of the fleet to set sail with all speed for Syracuse, in order that it might not happen that the city should be taken by storm while its best troops were fighting a war abroad. They decided, therefore, that their best course was to abandon the city, and that they should embark half the populace on the triremes (for these would convey them until they had got beyond Himeraean territory) and with the other half keep guard until the triremes should return. Although the Himeraeans complained indignantly at this conclusion, since there was no other course they could take, the triremes were hastily loaded by night with a mixed throng of women and children and of other inhabitants also, who sailed on them as far as Messenê; and Diocles, taking his own soldiers and leaving behind the bodies of those who had fallen in the fighting, set forth upon the journey home. And many Himeraeans with children and wives set out with Diocles, since the triremes could not carry the whole populace.

**62.** Those who had been left behind in Himera spent the night under arms on the walls; and when with the coming of day the Carthaginians surrounded the city and launched repeated attacks, the remaining Himeraeans fought with no thought for their lives, expecting the arrival of the ships. For that day, therefore, they continued to hold out, but on the next, even when the triremes were already in sight, it so happened that the wall began to fall before the blows of the siege-engines and the Iberians to pour in a body into the city. Some of the barbarians thereupon would hold off the Himeraeans who rushed up to bring aid, while others, gaining command of the walls, would help their comrades get in. Now that the city had been taken by storm, for a long time the barbarians continued, with no sign of compassion, to slaughter everyone they seized. When Hannibal issued orders to take prisoners, although the slaughter stopped, the wealth of the dwellings now became the objects of plunder. Hannibal, after sacking the temples and dragging out the suppliants who had fled to them for safety, set them afire, and the city he razed to the ground, two hundred and forty years after its founding. Of the captives the women and children he distributed among the army and kept them under guard, but the men whom he took captive, some three thousand, he led to the spot where once his grandfather Hamilcar had been slain by Gelon and after torturing them put them all to death. After this, breaking up his army, he sent the Sicilian allies back to their countries, and accompanying them also were the Campanians, who bitterly complained to the Carthaginians that, though they had been the ones chiefly responsible for the Carthaginian successes, the rewards they had received were not a fair return for their accomplishments. Then Hannibal embarked his army on the warships and merchant vessels, and leaving behind sufficient troops for the needs of his allies he set sail from Sicily. When he arrived at Carthage with much booty, the whole city came out to meet him, paying him homage and honour as one who in a brief time had performed greater deeds than any general before him.

**63.** Hermocrates the Syracusan arrived in Sicily. This man, who had served as general in the war against the Athenians and had been of great service to his country, had acquired the greatest influence among the Syracusans, but afterwards, when he had been sent as admiral in command of thirty-five triremes to support the Lacedaemonians, he was overpowered by his political opponents and, upon being condemned to exile, he handed over the fleet in the Peloponnesus to the men who had been dispatched to succeed him. Since he had struck up a friendship with

Pharnabazus, the satrap of the Persians, as a result of the campaign, he accepted from him a great sum of money with which, after he had arrived at Messenê, he had five triremes built and hired a thousand soldiers. Then, after adding to this force also about a thousand of the Himeraeans who had been driven from their home, he endeavoured with the aid of his friends to make good his return to Syracuse; but when he failed in this design, he set out through the middle of the island and seizing Selinus he built a wall about a part of the city and called to him from all quarters the Selinuntians who were still alive. He also received many others into the place and thus gathered a force of six thousand picked warriors. Making Selinus his base he first laid waste the territory of the inhabitants of Motyê and defeating in battle those who came out from the city against him he slew many and pursued the rest within the wall of the city. After this he ravaged the territory of the people of Panormus [Palermo] and acquired countless booty, and when the inhabitants offered battle *en masse* before the city he slew about five hundred of them and shut up the rest within their walls. Since he also laid waste in like fashion all the rest of the territory in the hands of the

Carthaginians, he won the commendation of the Sicilian Greeks, and at once the majority of the Syraeusans also repented of their treatment of him, realising that Hermocrates had been banished contrary to the merits of his valour. Consequently, after much discussion of him in meetings of the assembly, it was evident that the people desired to receive the man back from exile, and Hermocrates, on hearing of the talk about himself that was current in Syracuse, laid careful plans regarding his return from exile, knowing that his political opponents would work against it.

Such was the course of events in Sicily.

**64.** In Greece Thrasybulus, who had been sent out by the Athenians with thirty ships and a strong force of hoplites as well as a hundred horsemen, put in at Ephesus; and after disembarking his troops at two points he launched assaults upon the city. The inhabitants came out of the city against them and a fierce battle ensued; and since the entire populace of the Ephesians joined in the fighting, four hundred Athenians were slain and the remainder Thrasybulus took aboard his ships and sailed off to Lesbos. The Athenian generals who were in the neighbourhood of Cyzicus, sailing to Chalcedon, established there the fortress of Chrysopolis and left an adequate force behind; and the officers in charge they ordered to collect a tenth from all merchants sailing out of the Pontus. After this they divided their forces and Theramenes was left behind with fifty ships with which to lay siege to Chalcedon and Byzantium, and Thrasybulus was sent to Thrace, where he brought the cities in those regions over to the Athenians. Alcibiades, after giving Thrasybulus a separate command with the thirty ships, sailed to the territory held by Pharnabazus, and when they had conjointly laid waste a great amount of that territory, they not only sated the soldiers with plunder but also themselves realised money from the booty, since they wished to relieve the Athenian people of the property-taxes imposed for the prosecution of the war.

When the Lacedaemonians learned that all the armaments of the Athenians were in the region of the Hellespont, they undertook a campaign against Pylos, which the Messenians held with a garrison; on the sea they had eleven ships, of which five were from Sicily and six were manned by their own citizens, while on land they had gathered an adequate army, and after investing the fortress they began to wreak havoc both by land and by sea. As soon as the Athenian people learned of this they dispatched to the aid of the besieged thirty ships and as general Anytus [Socrates' accuser] the son of Anthemion. Now Anytus sailed out on his mission, but when he was unable to round Cape Malea because of storms he returned to Athens. The people were so incensed at this that they accused him of treason and brought him to trial; but Anytus, being in great danger, saved his own life by the use of money, and he is reputed to have been the first Athenian to have bribed a jury. Meanwhile the Messenians in Pylos held out for some time, awaiting aid from the Athenians; but since the enemy kept launching successive assaults and of their own number some were dying of wounds and others were reduced to sad straits for lack of food, they abandoned the place under a truce, and so the Lacedaemonians became masters of Pylos, after the Athenians had held it fifteen years from the time Demosthenes had fortified it.

**65.** While these events were taking place, the Megarians seized Nisaea, which was in the hands of Athenians, and the Athenians dispatched against them Leotrophides and Timarchus with a thousand infantry and four hundred cavalry. The Megarians went out to meet them *en masse* under arms, and after adding to their number some of the troops from Sicily they drew up for battle near the hills called "The Cerata." [the horns] Since the Athenians fought brilliantly and put to flight the enemy, who greatly outnumbered them, many of the Megarians were slain but only twenty Lacedaemonians; for the Athenians, made angry by the seizure of Nisaea, did not pursue the Lacedaemonians but slew great numbers of the Megarians with whom they were indignant.

The Lacedaemonians, having chosen Cratesippidas as admiral and manned twenty-five of their own ships with troops furnished by their allies, ordered them to go to the aid of their allies. Cratesippidas spent some time near Ionia without accomplishing anything worthy of mention; but later, after receiving money from the exiles of Chios, he restored them to their homes and seized the acropolis of the Chians, and the returned exiles of the Chians banished the men who were their political opponents and had been responsible for their exile to the number of approximately six hundred. These men then seized a place called Atarneus on the opposite mainland, which was by nature extremely rugged, and henceforth, from that as their base, continued to make war on their opponents who held Chios.

**66.** While these events were taking place Alcibiades and Thrasybulus, after fortifying Lampsacus, left a strong garrison in that place and themselves sailed with their force to Theramenes, who was laying waste Chalcedon with seventy ships and five thousand soldiers. When the armaments had been brought together into one place they threw a wooden stockade about the city from sea to sea. Hippocrates, who had been stationed by the Lacedaemonians in the city as commander (the Laconians call such a man a "harmost"), led against them both his own soldiers and all the Chalcedonians. A fierce battle ensued, and since the troops of Alcibiades fought stoutly, not only Hippocrates fell but of the rest of the soldiers some were slain, and the others, disabled by wounds, took refuge in a body in the city. After this Alcibiades sailed out into the Hellespont and to Chersonesus, wishing to collect money, and

Theramenes concluded an agreement with the Chalcedonians whereby the Athenians received from them as much tribute as before. Then leading his troops from there to Byzantium he laid siege to the city and with great alacrity set about walling it off. Alcibiades, after collecting money, persuaded many of the Thracians to join his army and he also took into it the inhabitants of Chersonesus *en masse;* then, setting forth with his entire force, he first took Selybria [Silivri] by betrayal, in which, after exacting from it much money, he left a garrison, and then himself came speedily to Theramenes at Byzantium. When the armaments had been united, the commanders began making the preparations for a siege; for they were setting out to conquer a city of great wealth which was crowded with defenders, since, not counting the Byzantines, who were many, Clearchus, the Lacedaemonian harmost, had in the city many Peloponnesians and mercenaries. Consequently, though they kept launching assaults for some time, they continued to inflict no notable damage on the defenders; but when the governor [Clearchus] left the city to visit Pharnabazus in order to get money, thereupon certain Byzantines, hating the severity of his administration (for Clearchus was a harsh man), agreed to deliver up the city to Alcibiades and his colleagues.

**67.** The Athenian generals, giving the impression that they intended to raise the siege and take their armaments to Ionia, sailed out in the afternoon with all their ships and withdrew the land army some distance; but when night came, they turned back again and about the middle of the night drew near the city, and they dispatched the triremes with orders to drag off the boats and to raise a clamour as if the entire force were at that point, while they themselves, holding the land army before the walls, watched for the signal which had been agreed upon with those who were yielding the city. When the crews of the triremes set about carrying out their orders, shattering some of the boats with their rams, trying to haul off others with their grappling irons, and all the while raising a tremendous outcry, the Peloponnesians in the city and everyone who was unaware of the trickery rushed out to the harbours to bring aid. Consequently the betrayers of the city raised the signal from the wall and admitted Alcibiades' troops by means of ladders in complete safety, since the multitude had thronged down to the harbour. When the Peloponnesians learned what had happened, at first they left half their troops at the harbour and with the rest speedily rushed back to attack the walls which had been seized. Although practically the entire force of the Athenians had already effected an entrance, they nonetheless were not panic-stricken but resisted stoutly for a long while and battled the Athenians with the help of the Byzantines, and in the end the Athenians would not have conquered the city by fighting, had not Alcibiades, perceiving his opportunity, had the announcement made that no wrong should be done to the Byzantines; for at this word the citizens changed sides and turned upon the Peloponnesians. Thereupon the most of them were slain fighting gallantly, and the survivors, about five hundred, fled for refuge to the altars of the temples. The Athenians returned the city to the Byzantines, having first made them allies, and then came to terms with the suppliants at the altars: the Athenians would take away their arms and carrying their persons to Athens turn them over to the decision of the Athenian people.

### *How Alcibiades sailed into the Peiraeus with much booty and was the object of great acclaim (68-69).*

**68.** At the end of the year the Athenians bestowed the office of archon upon Euctemon [408] and the Romans elected as consuls Marcus Papirius and Spurius Nautius, and the Ninety-third Olympiad was celebrated, that in which Eubatus of Cyrene won the stadion. About this time the Athenian generals, now that they had taken possession of Byzantium proceeded against the Hellespont and took every one of the cities of that region with the exception of Abydus. Then they left Diodorus and Mantitheüs in charge with an adequate force and themselves sailed to Athens with the ships and the spoils, having performed many great deeds for the fatherland. When they drew near the city, the populace in a body, overjoyed at their successes, came out to meet them, and great numbers of the aliens, as well as children and women, flocked to the Peiraeus. For the return of the generals gave great cause for amazement, in that they brought no less than two hundred captured vessels, a multitude of captive soldiers, and a great store of spoils; and their own triremes they had gone to great care to embellish with gilded arms and garlands and, besides, with spoils and all such decorations. Most men thronged to the harbours to catch sight of Alcibiades, so that the city was entirely deserted, the slaves vying with the free. For at that time it had come to pass that this man was such an object of admiration that the leading Athenians thought that they had at long last found a strong man capable of opposing the people openly and boldly, while the poor had assumed that they would have in him an excellent supporter who would recklessly throw the city into confusion and relieve their destitute condition. For in boldness he far excelled all other men, he was a most eloquent speaker, in generalship he was unsurpassed, and in daring he was most successful; furthermore, in appearance he was exceedingly handsome and in spirit brilliant and intent upon great enterprises. In a word, practically all men had conceived such assumptions regarding him that they believed that along with his return from exile good fortune in their undertakings had also come again to the city. Furthermore, just as the Lacedaemonians enjoyed success while he was fighting on their side, so they expected that they in turn would again prosper when they had this man as an ally.

**69.** So when the fleet came to land the multitude turned to the ship of Alcibiades, and as he stepped from it all gave their welcome to the man, congratulating him on both his successes and his return from exile. He in turn, after greeting the crowds kindly, called a meeting of the Assembly, and offering a long defence of his conduct he brought the masses into such a state of goodwill to him that all agreed that the city had been to blame for the decrees issued against him. Consequently they not only returned to him his property, which they had confiscated, but went farther and cast into the sea the stelae on which were written his sentence and all the other acts passed against him; and they also voted that the Eumolpidae should revoke the curse they had pronounced against him at the time when men believed he had profaned the Mysteries, and to cap all they appointed him general with supreme power both on land and on sea and put in his hands all their armaments. They also chose as generals others whom he wished, namely, Adeimantus and Thrasybulus.

Alcibiades manned one hundred ships and sailed to Andros, and seizing Gaurium, a stronghold, he strengthened it with a wall, and when the Andrians, together with the Peloponnesians who were guarding the city, came out against him *en masse,* a battle ensued in which the Athenians were the victors; and of the inhabitants of the city many were slain, and of those who escaped some were scattered throughout the countryside and the rest found safety within the walls. As for Alcibiades, after having launched assaults upon the city he left an adequate garrison in the fort he had occupied, appointing Thrasybulus commander, and himself sailed away with his force and ravaged both Cos and Rhodes, collecting abundant booty to support his soldiers.

**70.** Although the Lacedaemonians had entirely lost not only their sea force but Mindarus, the commander, together with it, nevertheless they did not let their spirits sink, but they chose as admiral Lysander, a man who was believed to excel all others in skill as a general and who possessed a daring that was ready to meet every situation. As soon as Lysander assumed the command he enrolled an adequate number of soldiers from the Peloponnesus and also manned as many ships as he was able. Sailing to Rhodes he added to his force the ships which the cities of Rhodes possessed, and then sailed to Ephesus and Miletus. After equipping the triremes in these cities he summoned those which were supplied by Chios and thus fitted out at Ephesus a fleet of approximately seventy ships. And hearing that Cyrus [the Younger], the son of King Darius, had been dispatched by his father to aid the Lacedaemonians in the war, he went to him at Sardis, and stirring up the youth's [age 17] enthusiasm for the war against the Athenians he received on the spot ten thousand darics for the pay of his soldiers; and for the future Cyrus told him to make requests without reserve, since, as he stated, he carried orders from his father to supply the Lacedaemonians with whatever they should want. Then Lysander, returning to Ephesus, called to him the most influential men of the cities, and arranging with them to form cabals he promised that if his undertakings were successful he would put each group in control of its city. It came to pass for this reason that these men, vying with one another, gave greater aid than was required of them and that Lysander was quickly supplied in startling fashion with all the equipment that is useful in war.

**71.** When Alcibiades learned that Lysander was fitting out his fleet in Ephesus, he set sail for there with all his ships. He sailed up to the harbours, but when no one came out against him, he had most of his ships cast anchor at Notium, entrusting the command of them to Antiochus, his personal pilot, with orders not to accept battle until he should be present, while he took the troop-ships and sailed in haste to Clazomenae; for this city, which was an ally of the Athenians, was suffering from forays by some of its exiles. But Antiochus, who was by nature an impetuous man and was eager to accomplish some brilliant deed on his own account, paid no attention to the orders of Alcibiades, but manning ten of the best ships and ordering the captains to keep the others ready in case they should need to accept battle, he sailed up to the enemy in order to challenge them to battle. Lysander, who had learned from certain deserters of the departure of Alcibiades and his best soldiers, decided that the favourable time had come for him to strike a blow worthy of Sparta. Accordingly, putting out to sea for the attack with all his ships, he encountered the leading one of the ten ships, the one on which Antiochus had taken his place for the attack, and sank it, and then, putting the rest to flight, he chased them until the Athenian captains manned the rest of their vessels and came to the rescue, but in no battle order at all. In the sea-battle which followed between the two entire fleets not far from the land the Athenians, because of their disorder, were defeated and lost twenty-two ships, but of their crews only a few were taken captive and the rest swam to safety ashore. When Alcibiades learned what had taken place, he returned in haste to Notium and manning all the triremes sailed to the harbours which were held by the enemy; but since Lysander would not venture to come out against him, he directed his course to Samos.

### How King Agis with a great army undertook to lay siege to Athens and was unsuccessful (72-73).

**72.** While these events were taking place Thrasybulus, the Athenian general, sailing to Thasos with fifteen ships defeated in battle the troops who came out from the city and slew about two hundred of them; then, having bottled them up in a siege of the city, he forced them to receive back their exiles, that is the men who favoured the Athenians, to accept a garrison, and to be allies of the Athenians. After this, sailing to Abdera, he brought that city, which at that time was among the most powerful in Thrace, over to the side of the Athenians.

Now the foregoing is what the Athenian generals had accomplished since they sailed from Athens. Agis, the king of the Lacedaemonians, as it happened, was at the time in Deceleia with his army, and when he learned that the best Athenian troops were engaged in an expedition with Alcibiades, he led his army on a moonless night to Athens. He had twenty-eight thousand infantry, one-half of whom were picked hoplites and the other half light-armed troops; there were also attached to his army some twelve hundred cavalry, of whom the Boeotians furnished nine hundred and the rest had been sent with him by Peloponnesians. As he drew near the city, he came upon the outposts before they were aware of him, and easily dispersing them because they were taken by surprise he slew a few and pursued the rest within the walls. When the Athenians learned what had happened, they issued orders for all the older men and the sturdiest of the youth to present themselves under arms. Since these promptly responded to the call, the circuit of the wall was manned with those who had rushed together to meet the common peril; and the Athenian generals, when in the morning they surveyed the army of the enemy extended in a line four men deep and eight stades in length, at the moment were at first dismayed, seeing as they did that approximately two-thirds of the wall was surrounded by the enemy. After this, however, they sent out their cavalry, who were about equal in number to the opposing cavalry, and when the two bodies met in a cavalry-battle before the city, sharp fighting ensued which lasted for some time. For the line of the infantry was some five stades from the wall, but the cavalry which had engaged each other were fighting at the very walls. Now the Boeotians, who by themselves alone had formerly defeated the Athenians at Delium, thought it would be a terrible thing if they should prove to be inferior to the men they had once conquered, while the Athenians, since they had as spectators of their valour the populace standing upon the walls and were known every one to them, were ready to endure everything for the sake of victory. Finally, overpowering their opponents they slew great numbers of them and pursued the remainder as far as the line of the infantry. After this when the infantry advanced against them, they withdrew within the city.

**73.** Agis, deciding for the time not to lay siege to the city, pitched camp in the Academy, but on the next day, after the Athenians had set up a trophy, he drew up his army in battle order and challenged the troops in the city to fight it out for the possession of the trophy. The Athenians led forth their soldiers and drew them up along the wall, and at first the Lacedaemonians advanced to offer battle, but since a great multitude of missiles was hurled at them from the walls, they led their army away from the city. After this they ravaged the rest of Attica and then departed to the Peloponnesus.

Alcibiades, having sailed with all his ships from Samos to Cymê, hurled false charges against the Cymaeans, since he wished to have an excuse for plundering their territory, and at the outset he gained possession of many captives and was taking them to his ships; but when the men of the city came out *en masse* to the rescue and fell unexpectedly on Alcibiades' troops, for a time they stood off the attack, but as later many from the city and countryside reinforced the Cymaeans, they were forced to abandon their prisoners and flee for safety to their ships. Alcibiades, being greatly distressed by his reverses, summoned his hoplites from Mitylenê, and drawing up his army before the city he challenged the Cymaeans to battle; but when no one came out of the city, he ravaged its territory and sailed off to Mitylenê. The Cymaeans dispatched an embassy to Athens and denounced Alcibiades for having laid waste an allied city which had done no wrong; and there were also many other charges brought against him; for some of the soldiers at Samos, who were at odds with him, sailed to Athens and accused Alcibiades in the Assembly of favouring the Lacedaemonian cause and of forming ties of friendship with Pharnabazus whereby he hoped that at the conclusion of the war he should lord it over his fellow citizens.

## The banishment of Alcibiades and the founding of Thermae in Sicily (74, 79).

**74.** Since the multitude soon began to believe these accusations, not only was the fame of Alcibiades damaged because of his defeat in the sea-battle and the wrongs he had committed against Cymê, but the Athenian people, viewing with suspicion the boldness of the man, chose as the ten generals Conon, Lysias, Diomedon, and Pericles, and in addition Erasinides, Aristocrates, Archestratus, Protomachus, Thrasybulus, and Aristogenes. Of these they gave first place to Conon and dispatched him at once to take over the fleet from Alcibiades. After Alcibiades had relinquished his command to Conon and handed over his armaments, he gave up any thought of returning to Athens, but with one trireme withdrew to Pactye in Thrace, since, apart from the anger of the multitude, he was afraid of the law-suits which had been brought against him. For there were many who, on seeing how he was hated, had filed numerous complaints against him, the most important of which was the one about the horses, involving the sum of eight talents. Diomedes, it appears, one of his friends, had sent in his care a four-horse team to Olympia; and Alcibiades, when entering it in the usual way, listed the horses as his own; and when he was the victor in the four-horse race, Alcibiades took for himself the glory of the victory and did not return the horses to the man who had entrusted them to his care. As he thought about all these things he was afraid lest the Athenians, seizing a suitable occasion, would inflict punishment upon him for all the wrongs he had committed against them. Consequently he himself condemned himself to exile.

**75.** The two-horse chariot race was added in this same Olympic Festival [93rd.]; and among the Lacedaemonians Pleistonax, their king, died after a reign of fifty years, and Pausanias succeeded to the throne and reigned for fourteen years. Also the inhabitants of the island of Rhodes left the cities of Ielysus, Lindus, and Cameirus and settled in one city, that which is now called Rhodes.

Hermocrates, the Syracusan, taking his soldiers set out from Selinus, and on arriving at Himera he pitched camp in the suburbs of the city, which lay in ruins. Finding out the place where the Syracusans had made their stand, he collected the bones of the dead and putting them upon wagons which he had constructed and embellished at great cost he conveyed them to Syracuse. Now Hermocrates himself stopped at the border of Syracusan territory, since the exiles were forbidden by the laws from accompanying the bones farther, but he sent on some of his troops who brought the wagons to Syracuse. Hermocrates acted in this way in order that Diodes, who opposed his return and was generally believed to be responsible for the lack of concern over the failure to bury the dead, should fall out with the masses, whereas he, by his humane consideration for the dead, would win the multitude back to the feeling of goodwill in which they had formerly held him. Now when the bones had been brought into the city, civil discord arose among the masses. Diocles objecting to their burial and the majority favouring it. Finally the Syracusans not only buried the remains of the dead but also by turning out *en masse* paid honour to the burial procession. Diodes was exiled; but even so they did not receive Hermocrates back, since they were wary of the daring of the man and feared lest, once he had gained a position of leadership, he should proclaim himself tyrant. Accordingly Hermocrates, seeing that the time was not opportune for resorting to force, withdrew again to Selinus. Some time later, when his friends sent for him, he set out with three thousand soldiers, and making his way through the territory of Gela he arrived at night at the place agreed upon. Although not all his soldiers had been able to accompany him, Hermocrates with a small number of them came to the gate on Achradine, and when he found that some of his friends had already occupied the region, he waited to pick up the latecomers. When the Syracusans heard what had happened, they gathered in the market-place under arms, and here, since they appeared accompanied by a great multitude, they slew both Hermocrates and most of his supporters. Those who had not been killed in the fighting were brought to trial and sentenced to exile; consequently some of them who had been severely wounded were reported by their relatives as having died, in order that they might not be given over to the wrath of the multitude. Among their number was also Dionysius, who later became tyrant of the Syracusans [405-367].

**76.** When the events of this year came to an end, in Athens [407] Antigenes took over the office of archon and the Romans elected as consuls Gaius Manius Aemilius and Gaius Valerius. About this time Conon, the Athenian general, now that he had taken over the armaments in Samos, fitted out the ships which were in that place and also collected those of the allies, since he was intent upon making his fleet a match for the ships of the enemy. The Spartans, when Lysander's period of command as admiral had expired, dispatched Callicratidas to succeed him. Callicratidas was a very young man, without guile and straightforward in character, since he had had as yet no experience of the ways of foreign peoples, and was the most just man among the Spartans; and it is agreed by all that also during his period of command he committed no wrong against either a city or a private citizen but dealt summarily with those who tried to corrupt him with money and had them punished. He put in at Ephesus and took over the fleet, and since he had already sent for the ships of the allies, the sum total he took over, including those of Lysander, was one hundred and forty. Since the Athenians held Delphinium in the territory of the Chians, he sailed against them with all his ships and undertook to lay siege to it. The Athenians, who numbered some five hundred, were dismayed at the great size of his force and abandoned the place, passing through the enemy under a truce. Callicratidas took over the fortress and levelled it to the ground, and then, sailing against the Teïans, he stole inside the walls of the city by night and plundered it. After this he sailed to Lesbos and with his force attacked Methymne, which held a garrison of Athenians. Although he launched repeated assaults, at first he accomplished nothing, but soon afterward, with the help of certain men who betrayed the city to him, he broke inside its walls, and although he plundered its wealth, he spared the lives of the inhabitants and returned the city to the Methymnaeans. After these exploits he made for Mitylenê; and assigning the hoplites to Thorax, the Lacedaemonian, he ordered him to advance by land with all speed and himself sailed on past Thorax with his fleet.

77. Conon, the Athenian general, had seventy ships which he had fitted out with everything necessary for making war at sea more carefully than any other general had ever done by way of preparation. Now it so happened that he had put out to sea with all his ships when he went to the aid of Methymne; but on discovering that it had already fallen, at the time he had bivouacked at one of the Hundred Isles, as they are called, and at daybreak, when he observed that the enemy's ships were bearing down on him, he decided that it would be dangerous for him to join battle in that place with triremes double his in number, but he planned to avoid battle by sailing outside the Isles and, drawing some of the enemy's triremes after him, to engage them off Mitylenê. For by such tactics, he assumed, in case of victory he could turn about and pursue and in case of defeat he could withdraw for safety to the harbour. Consequently, having put his soldiers on board ship, he set out with the oars at a leisurely stroke in order that the ships of the Peloponnesians might draw near him. The Lacedaemonians, as they approached, kept driving their ships faster and faster in the hope of seizing the hindmost ships of the enemy. As Conon withdrew, the commanders of the best ships of the Peloponnesians pushed the pursuit hotly, and they wore out the rowers by their continued exertion at the oars and were themselves separated a long distance from the others. Conon, noticing this, when his ships were already near Mitylenê, raised from his flagship a red banner, for this was a signal for the captains of the triremes. At this his ships, even as the enemy was overhauling them, suddenly turned about at the same moment, and the crews raised the battle-song and the trumpeters sounded the attack. The Peloponnesians, dismayed at the turn of events, hastily endeavoured to draw up their ships to repel the attack, but as there was not time for them to turn about they had fallen into great confusion because the ships coming up after them had left their accustomed position.

78. Conon, making clever use of the opportunity, at once pressed upon them, and prevented their establishing any order, damaging some ships and shearing off the rows of oars of others. Of the ships opposing Conon not one turned to flight, but they continued to back water while waiting for the ships which tarried behind; but the Athenians who held the left wing, putting to flight their opponents, pressed upon them with increasing eagerness and pursued them for a long time. When the Peloponnesians had brought all their ships together, Conon, fearing the superior numbers of the enemy, stopped the pursuit and sailed off to Mitylenê with forty ships. As for the Athenians who had set out in pursuit, all the Peloponnesian ships, swarming around them, struck terror into them, and cutting them off from return to the city compelled them to turn in flight to the land, and since the Peloponnesians pressed upon them with all their ships, the Athenians, seeing no other means of deliverance, fled for safety to the land and deserting their vessels found refuge in Mitylenê.

Callicratidas, by the capture of thirty ships, was aware that the naval power of the enemy had been destroyed, but he anticipated that the fighting on land remained. Consequently he sailed on to the city, and Conon, who was expecting a siege when he arrived, began upon preparations about the entrance to the harbour; for in the shallow places of the harbour he sank small boats filled with rocks and in the deep waters he anchored merchantmen armed with stones. Now the Athenians and a great throng of the Mitylenaeans who had gathered from the fields into the city because of the war speedily completed the preparations for the siege. Callicratidas, disembarking his soldiers on the beach near the city, pitched a camp, and then he set up a trophy for the sea-battle. On the next day, after choosing out his best ships and commanding them not to get far from his own ship, he put out to sea, being eager to sail into the harbour and break the barrier constructed by the enemy. Conon put some of his soldiers on the triremes, which he placed with their prows facing the open passage, and some he assigned to the large vessels, while others he sent to the breakwaters of the harbour in order that the harbour might be fenced in on every side, both by land and by sea. Then Conon himself with his triremes joined the battle, filling with his ships the space lying between the barriers; and the soldiers stationed on the large ships hurled the stones from the yard-arms upon the ships of the enemy, while those drawn up on the breakwaters of the harbour held off those who might have ventured to disembark on the land.

79. The Peloponnesians were not a whit outdone by the emulation displayed by the Athenians. Advancing with their ships in mass formation and with their best soldiers lined up on the decks they made the sea-battle also a fight between infantry; for as they pressed upon their opponents' ships they boldly boarded their prows, in the belief that men who had once been defeated would not stand up to the terror of battle. The Athenians and Mitylenaeans, seeing that the single hope of safety left to them lay in their victory, were resolved to die nobly rather than leave their station, and so, since an unsurpassable emulation pervaded both forces, a great slaughter ensued, all the participants exposing their bodies, without regard of risk, to the perils of battle. The soldiers on the decks were wounded by the multitude of missiles which flew at them, and some of them, who were mortally struck, fell into the sea, while some, so long as their wounds were fresh, fought on without feeling them; but very many fell victims to the stones that were hurled by the stone-carrying yardarms, since the Athenians kept up a shower of huge stones from these commanding positions. The fighting had continued, none the less, for a long while and many had met death on both sides, when Callicratidas, wishing to give his soldiers a breathing-spell, sounded the recall. After some time he again manned his ships and continued the struggle over a long period, and with great effort, by means of the superior number of his ships and the strength of the marines, he thrust out the Athenians. When the Athenians fled for refuge to the harbour within the city, he sailed through the barriers and brought his ships to anchor near the city of the Mitylenaeans. It may be explained that the entrance for whose control they had fought had a good harbour, which, however, lies outside the city. For the ancient city is a small island, and the later city, which was founded near it, is opposite it on the island of Lesbos; and between the two cities is a narrow strait which also adds strength

to the city. Callicratidas now, disembarking his troops, invested the city and launched assaults upon it from every side.

Such was the state of affairs at Mitylenê.

In Sicily the Syracusans, sending ambassadors to Carthage, not only censured them for the war but required that for the future they cease from hostilities. To them the Carthaginians gave ambiguous answers and set about assembling great armaments in Libya, since their desire was fixed on enslaving all the cities of the island; but before sending their forces across to Sicily they picked out volunteers from their citizens and the other inhabitants of Libya and founded in Sicily right at the warm (*therma*) springs a city which they named Therma.

### The sea-battle between the Syracusans and the Carthaginians and the victory of the Syracusans (80).

**80.** When the events of this year came to an end, in Athens [406] Callias succeeded to the office of archon and in Rome the consuls elected were Lucius Furius and Gnaeus Pompeius. At this time the Carthaginians, being elated over their successes in Sicily and eager to become lords of the whole island, voted to prepare great armaments; and electing as general Hannibal, who had razed to the ground both the city of the Selinuntians and that of the Himeraeans, they committed to him full authority over the conduct of the war. When he begged to be excused because of his age, they appointed besides him another general, Himilcon, the son of Hanno and of the same family. These two, after full consultation, dispatched certain citizens who were held in high esteem among the Carthaginians with large sums of money, some to Iberia and others to the Baliarides Islands, with orders to recruit as many mercenaries as possible. And they themselves canvassed Libya, enrolling as soldiers Libyans and Phoenicians and the stoutest from among their own citizens. Moreover they summoned soldiers also from the nations and kings who were their allies, Maurusians and Nomads and certain peoples who dwell in the regions toward Cyrene. Also from Italy they hired Campanians and brought them over to Libya; for they knew that their aid would be of great assistance to them and that the Campanians who had been left behind in Sicily, because they had fallen out with the Carthaginians, would fight on the side of the Sicilian Greeks. When the armaments were finally assembled at Carthage, the sum total of the troops collected together with the cavalry was a little over one hundred and twenty thousand, according to Timaeus, but three hundred thousand, according to Ephorus.

The Carthaginians, in preparation for their crossing over to Sicily, made ready and equipped all their triremes and also assembled more than a thousand cargo ships, and when they dispatched in advance forty triremes to Sicily, the Syracusans speedily appeared with about the same number of warships in the region of Eryx. In the long sea-battle which ensued fifteen of the Phoenician ships were destroyed and the rest, when night fell, fled for safety to the open sea. When word of the defeat was brought to the Carthaginians, Hannibal the general set out to sea with fifty ships, since he was eager both to prevent the Syracusans from exploiting their advantage and to make the landing safe for his own armaments.

## On the felicity of life in Acragas and the city's buildings (81-84).

**81.** When news of the reinforcements which Hannibal was bringing was noised throughout Sicily, everyone expected that his armaments would also be brought over at once, and the cities, as they heard of the great scale of the preparations and came to the conclusion that the struggle was to be for their very existence, were distressed without measure. Accordingly the Syracusans set about negotiating alliances both with the Greeks of Italy and with the Lacedaemonians; and they also continued to dispatch emissaries to the cities of Sicily to arouse the masses to fight for the common freedom. The Acragantini, because they were the nearest to the empire of the Carthaginians, assumed what indeed took place, that the weight of the war would fall on them first. They decided, therefore, to gather not only their grain and other crops but also all their possessions from the countryside within their walls. At this time, it so happened, both the city and the territory of the Acragantini enjoyed great prosperity, which I think it would not be out of place for me to describe. Their vineyards excelled in their great extent and beauty and the greater part of their territory was planted in olive-trees from which they gathered an abundant harvest and sold to Carthage; for since Libya at that time was not yet planted in fruit-trees, the inhabitants of the territory belonging to Acragas took in exchange for their products the wealth of Libya and accumulated fortunes of unbelievable size. Of this wealth there remain among them many evidences, which it will not be foreign to our purpose to discuss briefly.

**82.** Now the sacred buildings which they constructed, and especially the temple of Zeus, bear witness to the grand manner of the men of that day. Of the other sacred buildings some have been burned and others completely destroyed because of the many times the city has been taken in war, but the completion of the temple of Zeus, which was ready to receive its roof, was prevented by the war; and after the war, since the city had been completely destroyed, never in the subsequent years did the Acragantini find themselves able to finish their buildings. The temple has a length of three hundred and forty feet, a width of sixty, and a height of one hundred and twenty not including the foundation, and being as it is the largest temple in Sicily, it may not unreasonably be compared, so far as the magnitude of its substructure is concerned, with the temples outside of Sicily; for even though, as it turned out, the design could not be carried out, the scale of the undertaking at any rate is clear. Though all other men build their temples either with walls forming the sides or with rows of columns, thus enclosing their sanctuaries, this temple combines both these plans; for the columns were built in with the walls, the part extending outside the temple being rounded and that within square; and the circumference of the outer part of the column which extends from the wall is twenty feet and the body of a man may be contained in the fluting, while that of the inner part is twelve feet. The porticoes were of enormous size and height, and in the east pediment they portrayed The Battle between the Gods and the Giants in sculptures which excelled in size and beauty, and in the west The Capture of Troy, in which each one of the heroes may be seen portrayed in a manner appropriate to his role. There was at that time also an artificial pool outside the city, seven stades in circumference and twenty cubits deep; into this they brought water and ingeniously contrived to produce a multitude of fish of every variety for their public feasting, and with the fish swans spent their time and a vast multitude of every other kind of bird, so that the pool was an object of great delight to gaze upon, and witness to the luxury of the inhabitants is also the extravagant cost of the monuments which they erected, some adorned with sculptured race-horses and others with the pet birds kept by girls and boys in their homes, monuments which Timaeus [d.250] says he had seen extant even in his own lifetime. In the Olympiad previous to the one we are discussing, namely, the Ninety-second, when Exaenetus of Acragas won the "stadion," he was conducted into the city in a chariot and in the procession there were, not to speak of the other things, three hundred chariots each drawn by two white horses, all the chariots belonging to citizens of Acragas. Speaking generally, they led from youth onward a manner of life which was luxurious, wearing as they did exceedingly delicate clothing and gold ornaments and, besides, using strigils and oil-flasks made of silver and even of gold.

**83.** Among the Acragantini of that time perhaps the richest man was Tellias, who had in his mansion a considerable number of guest-chambers and used to station servants before his gates with orders to invite every stranger to be his guest. There were also many other Acragantini who did something of this kind, mingling with others in an old-fashioned and friendly manner; consequently also Empedocles speaks of them as

> Havens of mercy for strangers, unacquainted with evil.

Indeed once when five hundred cavalry from Gela arrived there during a wintry storm, as Timaeus says in his Fifteenth Book, Tellias entertained all of them by himself and provided them all forthwith from his own stores with outer and under garments. And Polycleitus in his *Histories* describes the wine-cellar in the house as still existing and as he had himself seen it when in Acragas as a soldier; there were in it, he states, three hundred great casks hewn out of the very rock, each of them with a capacity of one hundred amphoras, and beside them was a wine-vat, plastered with stucco and with a capacity of one thousand amphoras, from which the wine flowed into the casks. And we are told that Tellias was quite plain in appearance but wonderful in character. So once when he had been dispatched on an embassy to the people of Centoripa and came forward to speak before the Assembly, the multitude broke into unseemly laughter as they saw how much he fell short of their expectation. But he, interrupting them, said, "Don't be surprised, for it is the practice of the Acragantini to send to famous cities their most handsome citizens, but to insignificant and most paltry cities men of their sort."

**84.** It was not in the case of Tellias only that such magnificence of wealth occurred, he says, but also of many other inhabitants of Acragas. Antisthenes at any rate, who was called Rhodus, when celebrating the marriage of his daughter, gave a party to all the citizens in the courtyards where they all lived and more than eight hundred chariots followed the bride in the procession; furthermore, not only the men on horseback from the city itself but also many from neighbouring cities who had been invited to the wedding joined to form the escort of the bride. Most extraordinary of all, we are told, was the provision for the lighting: the altars in all the temples and those in the courtyards throughout the city he had piled high with wood, and to the shopkeepers he gave firewood and brush with orders that when a fire was kindled on the acropolis they should all do the same; and when they did as they were ordered, at the time when the bride was brought to her home, since there were many torch-bearers in the procession, the city was filled with light, and the main streets through which the procession was to pass could not contain the accompanying throng, all the inhabitants zealously emulating the man's grand manner. For at that time the citizens of Acragas numbered more than twenty thousand, and when resident aliens were included, not less than two hundred thousand. Men say that once when Antisthenes saw his son quarrelling with a neighbouring farmer, a poor man, and pressing him to sell him his little plot of land, for a time he merely reproved his son; but when his son's cupidity grew more intense, he said to him that he should not be doing his best to make his neighbour poor but, on the contrary, to make him rich; for then the man would long for more land, and when he would be unable to buy additional land from his neighbour he would sell what he now had.

Because of the immense prosperity prevailing in the city the Acragantini came to live on such a scale of luxury that a little later, when the city was under siege, they passed a decree about the guards who spent the nights at their posts, that none of them should have more than one mattress, one cover, one sheepskin, and two pillows. When such was their most rigorous kind of bedding, one can get an idea of the luxury which prevailed in their living generally. Now it was our wish neither to pass these matters by nor yet to speak of them at greater length, in order that we may not fail to record the more important events.

### *How the Carthaginians made war upon Sicily with three hundred thousand soldiers and laid siege to Acragas (85-86).*

**85.** The Carthaginians, after transporting their armaments to Sicily, marched against the city of the Acragantini and made two encampments, one on certain hills where they stationed the Iberians and some Libyans to the number of about forty thousand, and the other they pitched not far from the city and surrounded it with a deep trench and a palisade. First they dispatched ambassadors to the Acragantini, asking them, preferably, to become their allies, but otherwise to stay neutral and be friends with the Carthaginians, thereby remaining in peace; and when the inhabitants of the city would not entertain these terms, the siege was begun at once. The Acragantini thereupon armed all those of military age, and forming them in battle order they stationed one group upon the walls and the other as a reserve to replace the soldiers as they became worn out. Fighting with them was also Dexippus the Lacedaemonian, who had lately arrived there from Gela with fifteen hundred mercenaries; for at that time, as Timaeus says, Dexippus was tarrying in Gela, enjoying high regard by reason of the city of his birth. Consequently the Acragantini invited him to recruit as many mercenaries as he could and come to Acragas; and together with them the Campanians who had formerly fought with Hannibal, some eight hundred, were also hired. These mercenaries held the height above the city which is called the Hill of Athena and is strategically situated overhanging the city. Himilcar and Hannibal, the Carthaginian generals, noting, after they had surveyed the walls, that in one place the city was easily assailable, advanced two enormous towers against the walls.

BOOK XIII

During the first day they pressed the siege from these towers, and after inflicting many casualties then sounded the recall for their soldiers; but when night had fallen the defenders of the city launched a counter-attack and burned the siege-engines.

**How the Syracusans gathered their allies and went to the aid of the people of Acragas with ten thousand soldiers (86).**

86. Hannibal, being eager to launch assaults in an increasing number of places, ordered the soldiers to tear down the monuments and tombs and to build mounds extending to the walls. When these works had been quickly completed because of the united labour of many hands, a deep superstitious fear fell upon the army. [406] For it happened that the tomb of Theron, which was exceedingly large, was shaken by a stroke of lightning; consequently, when it was being torn down, certain soothsayers, presaging what might happen, forbade it, and at once a plague broke out in the army, and many died of it while not a few suffered tortures and grievous distress. Among the dead was also Hannibal the general, and among the watch-guards who were sent out there were some who reported that in the night spirits of the dead were to be seen. Himilcar, on seeing how the throng was beset with superstitious fear, first of all put a stop to the destruction of the monuments, and then he supplicated the gods after the custom of his people by sacrificing a young boy to Cronus and a multitude of cattle to Poseidon by drowning them in the sea. He did not, however, neglect the siege works, but filling up the river which ran beside the city as far as the walls, he advanced all his siege-engines against them and launched daily assaults.

The Syracusans, seeing that Acragas was under siege and fearing lest the besieged might suffer the same fate as befell the Selinuntians and Himeraeans, had long been eager to send them their aid, and when at this juncture allied troops arrived from Italy and Messenê they elected Daphnaeus general. Collecting their forces they added along the way soldiers from Camarina and Gela, and summoning additional troops from the peoples of the interior they made their way towards Aeragas, while thirty of their ships sailed along beside them. The forces which they had numbered in all more than thirty thousand infantry and not less than five thousand cavalry.

**How, when forty thousand Carthaginians opposed them, the Syracusans gained the victory and slew more than six thousand of them (87).**

87. When Himilcon learned of the approach of the enemy, he dispatched to meet them both his Iberians and his Campanians and more than forty thousand other troops. The Syracusans had already crossed the Himera River when the barbarians met them, and in the long battle which ensued the Syracusans were victorious and slew more than six thousand men. They would have crushed the whole army completely and pursued it all the way to the city, but since the soldiers were pressing the pursuit without order, the general was concerned lest Himilcar should appear with the rest of his army and retrieve the defeat. For he remembered also how the Himeraeans had been utterly destroyed for the same reason. However, when the barbarians were in flight to their camp before Acragas, the soldiers in the city, seeing the defeat of the Carthaginians, begged their generals to lead them out, saying that the opportunity had come to destroy

493

the host of the enemy, but the generals, whether they had been bribed, as the report ran, or feared that Himilcon would seize the city if it were stripped of defenders, checked the ardour of their men. So the fleeing men quite safely made good their escape to the camp before the city. When Daphnaeus with his army arrived at the encampment which the barbarians had deserted, he took up his quarters there. At once both the soldiers from the city mingled with his troops and Dexippus accompanied his men, and the multitude gathered in a tumultuous throng in an assembly, everyone being vexed that the opportunity had been let slip and that although they had the barbarians in their power, they had not inflicted on them the punishment they deserved, but that the generals in the city, although able to lead them forth to attack and destroy the host of the enemy, had let so many myriads of men off scot-free. While great uproar and tumult prevailed in the assembly, Menes of Camarina, who had been put in command, came forward and lodged an accusation against the Acragantine generals and so incited all who were present that, when the accused tried to offer a defence, no one would let them speak and the multitude began to throw stones and killed four of them, but the fifth, Argeius by name, who was very much younger, they spared. Dexippus the Lacedaemonian, we are told, also was the object of abuse on the ground that, although he held a position of command and was reputed to be not inexperienced in warfare, he had acted as he did treacherously.

## How, when the Carthaginians cut off their supplies, the Acragantini were compelled, because of the lack of provisions, to leave their native city (88-89).

**88.** After the assembly Daphnaeus led forth his forces and undertook to lay siege to the camp of the Carthaginians, but when he saw that it had been fortified with great outlay, he gave up that design; however, by covering the roads with his cavalry he seized such as were foraging, and by cutting off the transport of supplies brought them into serious straits. The Carthaginians, not daring to wage a pitched battle and being hard pinched by lack of food, were enduring great misfortunes. [406] For many of the soldiers were dying of want, and the Campanians together with the other mercenaries, almost in a body, forced their way to the tent of Himilcar and demanded the rations which had been agreed upon; and if these were not given them, they threatened to go over to the enemy, but Himilcar had learned from some source that the Syracusans were conveying a great amount of grain to Acragas by sea. Consequently, since this was the only hope he had of salvation, he persuaded the soldiers to wait a few days, giving them as a pledge the goblets belonging to the troops from Carthage. He then summoned forty triremes from Panormus and Motyê and planned an attack upon the ships which were bringing the supplies; and the Syracusans, because up to this time the barbarians had retired from the sea and winter had already set in, held the Carthaginians in contempt, feeling assured that they would not again have the courage to man their triremes. Consequently, since they gave little concern to the convoying of the supplies, Himilcar, sailing forth unawares with forty triremes, sank eight of their warships and pursued the rest to the beach; and by capturing all the remaining vessels he effected such a reversal in the expectations of both sides that the Campanians who were in the service of the

Acragantini, considering the position of the Greeks to be hopeless, were bought off for fifteen talents and went over to the Carthaginians.

The Acragantini at first, when the Carthaginians were faring badly, had enjoyed their grain and other supplies without stint, expecting all the while that the siege would be quickly lifted; but when the hopes of the barbarians began to rise and so many myriads of human beings were gathered into one city, the grain was exhausted before they were aware of it. The story is told that also Dexippus the Lacedaemonian was corrupted by a bribe of fifteen talents; for without hesitation he replied to a question of the generals of the Italian Greeks, "Yes, it's better if the war is settled somewhere else, for our provisions have failed." Consequently the generals, offering as their excuse that the time agreed upon for the campaign had elapsed, led their troops off to the Strait. After the departure of these troops the generals met with the commanders and decided to make a survey of the supply of grain in the city, and when they discovered that it was quite low, they perceived that they were compelled to desert the city. At once, then, they issued orders that all should leave on the next night.

**89.** With such a throng of men, women, and children deserting the city, at once endless lamentation and tears pervaded all homes. For while they were panic-stricken from fear of the enemy, at the same time they were also under necessity, because of their haste, of leaving behind as booty for the barbarians the possessions on which they had based their happiness; for when Fortune was robbing them of the comforts they enjoyed in their homes, they thought that they should be content that at least they were preserving their lives, and one could see the abandonment not only of the opulence of so wealthy a city but also of a multitude of human beings. For the sick were neglected by their relatives, everyone taking thought for his own safety, and those who were already far advanced in years were abandoned because of the weakness of old age; and many, reckoning even separation from their native city to be the equivalent of death, laid hands upon themselves in order that they might breathe their last in the dwellings of their ancestors. However, the multitude which left the city was given armed escort by the soldiers to Gela; and the highway and all parts of the countryside which led away toward the territory of the Geloans were crowded with women and children intermingled with maidens, who, changing from the pampered life to which they had been accustomed to a strenuous journey by foot and extreme hardship, held out to the end, since fear nerved their souls. Now these got safely to Gela and at a later time made their home in Leontini, the Syracusans having given them this city for their dwelling-place.

**90.** Himilcar, leading his army at dawn within the walls, put to death practically all who had been left behind; yes, even those who had fled for safety to the temples the Carthaginians hauled out and slew, and we are told that Tellias, who was the foremost citizen in wealth and honourable character, shared in the misfortune of his country: He had decided to take refuge with certain others in the temple of Athena, thinking that the Carthaginians would refrain from acts of lawlessness against the gods, but when he saw their impiety, he set fire to the temple and burned himself together with the dedications in it. For by one deed, he thought, he would withhold from the gods impiety, from the enemy a vast store of plunder, and from himself, most important of all, certain physical indignity. Himilcar, after pillaging and industriously ransacking the temples and dwellings, collected as great a store of booty as a city could be expected to yield which had been inhabited by two hundred thousand people, had gone un-ravaged since the date of its founding, had been well-nigh the wealthiest of the Greek cities of that day, and whose citizens, furthermore, had shown their love of the beautiful in expensive collections of works of art of every description. Indeed a multitude of paintings executed with the greatest care was found and an extraordinary number of sculptures of every description and worked with great skill. The most valuable pieces, accordingly, Himilcar sent to Carthage, among which, as it turned out, was the bull of Phalaris, and the rest of the pillage he sold as booty. As regards this bull, although Timaeus in his *History* has maintained that it never existed at all, he has been refuted by Fortune herself; for some two hundred and sixty years after the capture of Acragas, when Scipio sacked Carthage [146], he returned to the Acragantini, together with their other possessions still in the hands of the Carthaginians, the bull, which was still in Acragas at the time this history was being written.

I have been led to speak of this matter rather copiously because Timaeus, who criticised most bitterly the historians before his time and left the writers of history bereft of all forgiveness, is himself caught improvising in the very province where he most proclaims his own accuracy. For historians should, in my opinion, be granted charity in errors that come of ignorance, since they are human beings and since the truth of ages past is hard to discover, but historians who deliberately do not give the exact facts should properly be open to censure, whenever in flattering one man or another or in attacking others from hatred too bitterly, they stray from the truth.

**91.** Since Hamilcar, after besieging the city for eight months, had taken it shortly before the winter solstice, he did not destroy it at once, in order that his forces might winter in the dwellings, but when the misfortune that had befallen Acragas was noised abroad, such fear took possession of the island that of the Sicilian Greeks some removed to Syracuse and others transferred their children and wives and all their possessions to Italy. The Acragantini who had escaped being taken captive, when they arrived in Syracuse, lodged accusations against their generals, asserting that it was due to their treachery that their country had perished, and it so happened that the Syracusans also came in for censure by the rest of the Sicilian Greeks, because, as they charged, they elected the kind of leaders through whose fault the whole of Sicily ran the risk of destruction. Nevertheless, even though an assembly of the people was held in Syracuse and great fears hung over them, not a man would venture to offer any counsel respecting the war. While everyone was at a loss what to do, Dionysius, the son of Hermocrates, taking the floor, accused the generals of betraying their cause to the Carthaginians and stirred up the assemblage to exact punishment of them, urging them not to await the futile procedure prescribed by the laws but to pass judgement upon them at once. When the archons, in accordance with the laws, laid a fine upon Dionysius on the charge of raising an uproar, Philistus, who later composed his *History,* a man of great wealth, paid the fine and urged Dionysius to speak out whatever he had had in his mind to say. When Philistus went on to say that if they wanted to fine Dionysius throughout the whole day he would provide the money for him, from then on Dionysius, full of confidence, kept stirring up the multitude, and throwing the assembly into confusion he accused the generals of taking bribes to put the security of the Acragantini in jeopardy. He also denounced the rest of the most renowned citizens, presenting them as friends of oligarchy. Consequently he advised them to choose as generals not the most influential citizens, but rather those who were the best disposed and most favourable to the people; for the former, he maintained, ruling the citizens as they do in a despotic manner, hold the many in contempt and consider the misfortunes of their country their own source of income, whereas the more humble will do none of such things, since they fear their own weakness.

## How Dionysius, after he was elected general, secured the tyranny over the Syracusans (92-96).

**92.** Dionysius, by suiting every word of his harangue to the people to the predilection of his hearers and his own personal design, stirred the anger of the assembly to no small degree; for the people, which for some time past had hated the generals for what they considered to be their bad conduct of the war and at the moment were spurred on by what was being said to them, immediately dismissed some of them from office and chose other generals, among whom was also Dionysius, who enjoyed the reputation of having shown unusual bravery in the battles against the Carthaginians and was admired of all the Syracusans. Having become elated, therefore, in his hopes, he tried every device to become tyrant of his country. For example, after assuming office he neither participated in the meetings of the generals nor associated with them in any way; and while acting in this manner he spread the report that they were carrying on negotiations with the enemy. For in this way he hoped that he could most effectively strip them of their power and clothe himself alone with the office of general.

While Dionysius was acting in this fashion, the most respectable citizens suspected what was taking place and in every gathering spoke disparagingly of him, but the common crowd, being ignorant of his scheme, gave him their approbation and declared that at long last the city had found a steadfast leader. However, when the assembly convened time and again to consider preparations for the war, Dionysius, observing that fear of the enemy had struck the Syracusans with terror, advised them to recall the exiles; for it was absurd, he said, to seek aid from peoples of other states in Italy and the Peloponnesus and to be unwilling to enlist the assistance of their fellow citizens in facing their own dangers, citizens who, although the enemy kept promising them great rewards for their military co-operation, chose rather to die as wanderers on foreign soil than plan some hostile act against their native land. In fact, he declared, men who were now in exile because of past civil strife in the city, if at this time they were the recipients of this benefaction, would fight with eagerness, showing in this way their appreciation to their benefactors. After reciting many arguments for this proposal that bore on the situation, he won the votes of the Syracusans to his view; for no one of his colleagues in office dared oppose him in the matter both because of the eagerness shown by the multitude and because each observed that he himself would gain only enmity, while Dionysius would reap a reward of gratitude from those who had received kindness from him. Dionysius took this course in the hope that he would win the exiles for himself, men who wished a change and would be favourably disposed toward the establishment of a tyranny; for they would be happy to witness the murder of their enemies, the confiscation of their property, and the restoration to themselves of their possessions. When finally the resolution regarding the exiles was passed, these returned at once to their native land.

**93.** When messages were brought from Gela requesting the dispatch of additional troops, Dionysius got a favourable means of accomplishing his own purpose. Having been dispatched with two thousand infantry and four hundred cavalry, he arrived speedily at the city of the Geloans, which at that time was under the eye of Dexippus, the Lacedaemonian, who had been put in charge by the Syracusans. When Dionysius on arrival found the wealthiest citizens engaged in strife with the people, he accused them in an assembly and secured their condemnation, whereupon he put them to death and confiscated their possessions. With the money thus gained he paid the guards of the city under the command of Dexippus the wages which were owing them, while to his own troops who had come with him from Syracuse he promised he would pay double the wages which the city had determined. In this manner he won over to himself the loyalty not only of the soldiers in Gela but also of those whom he had brought with him. He also gained the approval of the populace of the Geloans, who believed him to be responsible for their liberation; for in their envy of the most influential citizens they stigmatised the superiority these men possessed as a despotism over themselves. Consequently they dispatched ambassadors who sang his praises in Syracuse and reported decrees in which they honoured him with rich gifts. Dionysius also undertook to persuade Dexippus to associate himself with his design, and when Dexippus would not join with him, he was on the point of returning with his own troops to Syracuse. But the Geloans, on learning that the Carthaginians with their entire host were going to make Gela the first object of attack, besought Dionysius to remain and not to stand idly by while they suffered the same fate as the Acragantini. Dionysius replied to them that he would return speedily with a larger force and set forth from Gela with his own soldiers.

**94.** A play was being presented in Syracuse and Dionysius arrived in the city at the time when the people were leaving the theatre. When the populace rushed in throngs to him and were questioning him about the Carthaginians, they were unaware, he said, that they had more dangerous enemies than their foreign foes, the men within the city in charge of the public interests; these men the citizens trusted while they held public festivals, but these very men, while plundering the public funds, had let the soldiers go unpaid, and although the enemy was making their preparations for the war on a scale which could not be surpassed and were about to lead their forces upon Syracuse, the generals were giving these matters no concern whatsoever. The reason for such conduct, he continued, he had been aware of before, but now he had got fuller information. For Himilcon had sent a herald to him, ostensibly to treat about the captives, but in fact to urge him, now that Himilcon had induced a large number of Dionysius' colleagues not to bother themselves with what was taking place, at least to offer no opposition, since he, Dionysius, did not choose to co-operate with him. Consequently, Dionysius continued, he did not wish to serve longer as general, but was present in

# Book XIII

Syracuse to lay down his office; for it was intolerable for him, while the other generals were selling out their country, to be the only one to fight together with the citizens and yet be at the same time destined to be thought in after years to have shared in their betrayal.

Although the populace had been stirred by what Dionysius had said and his words spread through the whole army, at the time every man departed to his home full of anxiety. On the following day, when an assembly had been convened in which Dionysius won no small approval when he lodged many accusations against the magistrates and stirred up the populace against the generals, finally some of the members cried out to appoint him general with supreme power and not to wait until the enemy were storming their walls; for the magnitude of the war, they urged, made necessary such a general, through whose leadership their cause could prosper; as for the traitors, their case would be debated in another assembly, since it was foreign to the present situation; indeed at a former time three hundred thousand Carthaginians had been conquered at Himera when Gelon was general with supreme power.

**95.** Soon the multitude, as is their wont, swung to the worse decision and Dionysius was appointed general with supreme power. Now, since the situation corresponded to his desires, he proposed a decree that the pay of the mercenaries be doubled; for they would all, he said, if this were done, be more eager for the coming contest, and he urged them not to worry at all about the funds, since it would be an easy task to raise them.

After the assembly was adjourned no small number of the Syracusans condemned what had been done, as if they themselves had not had their way in the matter; for as their thoughts turned to their own state they could imagine the tyrannical power which was to follow. Now these men, in their desire to insure their freedom, had unwittingly established a despot over their country; Dionysius, on the other hand, wishing to forestall the change of mind on the part of the populace, kept seeking a means whereby he could ask for a guard for his person, for if this were granted him he would easily establish himself in the tyranny. At once, then, he issued orders that all men of military age up to forty years should provide themselves with rations for thirty days and report to him under arms at Leontini. This city was at that time an outpost of the Syracusans, being full of exiles and foreigners. For Dionysius hoped that he would have these men on his side, desiring as they did a change of government, and that the majority of the Syracusans would not even come to Leontini. However, while he was encamped at night in the countryside, he pretended that he was the object of a plot and had his personal servants raise a tumult and uproar; and after doing this he took refuge on the acropolis, where he passed the night, keeping fires burning and summoning to him his most trustworthy soldiers. At daybreak, when the common people were gathered into Leontini, he delivered a long plausible speech to further his design and persuaded the populace to give him a guard of six hundred soldiers whomsoever he should select. It is said that Dionysius did this in imitation of Peisistratus the Athenian; for he, we are told, after wounding himself, appeared before the assembly alleging that he had been the victim of a plot, and because of this he received a guard at the hands of the citizens, by means of which he established the tyranny. At this time Dionysius, having deceived the multitude by a similar device, put into effect the structure of his tyranny.

**96.** For instance Dionysius at once selected such citizens as were without property but bold in spirit, more than a thousand in number, provided them with costly arms, and buoyed them up with extravagant promises; the mercenaries also he won to himself by calling them to him and conversing with them in friendly fashion. He made changes also in the military posts, conferring their commands upon his most faithful followers; and Dexippus the Lacedaemonian he dismissed to Greece, for he was suspicious of this man lest he should seize a favourable opportunity and restore to the Syracusans their liberty. He also called to himself the mercenaries in Gela and gathered from all quarters the exiles and impious, hoping that in these men the tyranny would find its strongest support. While in Syracuse, however, he took up his quarters in the naval station, having openly proclaimed himself tyrant. Although the Syracusans were offended, they were compelled to keep quiet; for they were unable to effect anything now, since not only was the city thronged with mercenary soldiers but the people were filled with fear of the Carthaginians who possessed such powerful armaments. Now Dionysius straightway married the daughter of Hermocrates, the conqueror of the Athenians, and gave his sister in marriage to Polyxenus, the brother of Hermocrates' wife. This he did out of a desire to draw a distinguished house into relationship with him in order to make firm the tyranny. After this he summoned an assembly and had his most influential opponents, Daphnaeus and Demarchus, put to death.

Now Dionysius, from a scribe and ordinary private citizen, had become tyrant of the largest city of the Greek world; and he maintained his dominance until his death, having ruled as tyrant for thirty-eight years [405-367]. We shall give a detailed account of his deeds and of the expansion of his rule in connection with the appropriate periods of time; for it seems that this man, single-handed, established the strongest and longest tyranny of any recorded by history.

The Carthaginians, after their capture of the city [Acragas], transferred to Carthage both the votive offerings and statues and every other object of greatest value, and when they had burned down the temples and plundered the city, they spent the winter there. And in the springtime they made ready every kind of engine of war and of missile, planning to lay siege first to the city of the Geloans.

***How the Athenians, after winning a most famous sea-battle at Arginusae, unjustly condemned their generals to death (97-103).***

**97.** While these events were taking place, the Athenians, who had suffered a continued series of reverses, conferred citizenship upon the metics and any other aliens who were willing to fight with them; and when a great multitude was quickly enrolled among the citizens, the generals kept mustering for the campaign all who were in fit condition. They made ready sixty ships, and after fitting them out at great expense they sailed forth to Samos, where they found the other generals who had assembled eighty triremes from the rest of the islands. They also had asked the Samians to man and equip ten additional triremes, and with one hundred and fifty ships in all they set out to sea and put in at the

Arginusae Islands, being eager to raise the siege of Mitylenê. When Callicratidas, the admiral of the Lacedaemonians, learned of the approach of the ships, he left Eteohicus with the land troops in charge of the siege, while he himself manned one hundred and forty ships and hurriedly put out to sea on the other side of the Arginusae. These islands, which were inhabited at that time and contained a small settlement of Aeolians, lie between Mitylenê and Cymê and are but a very small distance from the mainland and the headland of Canis.

The Athenians learned at once of the approach of the enemy, since they lay at anchor no small distance away, but refused battle because of the strong winds and made ready for the conflict on the following day, the Lacedaemonians also doing likewise, although the seers on both sides forbade it. For in the case of the Lacedaemonians the head of the victim, which lay on the beach, was lost to sight when the waves broke on it, and the seer accordingly foretold that the admiral would die in the fight. At this prophecy Callicratidas, we are told, remarked, "If I die in the fight, I shall not have lessened the fame of Sparta." In the case of the Athenians Thrasybulus their general, who held the supreme command on that day, saw in the night the following vision. He dreamed that he was in Athens and the theatre was crowded, and that he and six of the other generals were playing the *Phoenician Women* of Euripides, while their competitors were performing the *Suppliants*; and that it resulted in a "Cadmean victory" for them and they all died, just as did those who waged the campaign against Thebes. When the seer heard this, he disclosed that seven of the generals would be slain. Since the omens revealed victory, the generals forbade any word going out to the others about their own death but they passed the news of the victory disclosed by the omens throughout the whole army.

**98.** The admiral Callicratidas, having assembled his whole force, encouraged them with the appropriate words and concluded his speech as follows. "So eager am I myself to enter battle for my country that, although the seer declares that the victims foretell victory for you but death for me, I am none the less ready to die. Accordingly, knowing that after the death of commanders forces are thrown into confusion, I designate at this time as admiral to succeed me, in case I meet with some mishap, Clearchus, a man who has proved himself in deeds of war." By these words Callicratidas led not a few to emulate his valour and to become more eager for the battle. The Lacedaemonians, exhorting one another, entered their ships, and the Athenians, after hearing the exhortations of their generals summoning them to the struggle, manned the triremes in haste and all took their positions. Thrasyllus commanded the right wing and also Pericles, the son of the Pericles who, by reason of his influence, had been dubbed "The Olympian"; and he associated with himself on the right wing also Theramenes, giving him a command. At the time Theramenes was on the campaign as a private citizen, although formerly he had often been in command of armaments. The rest of the generals he stationed along the entire line, and the Arginusae Islands, as they are called, he enclosed by his battle order, since he wished to extend his ships as far as possible. Callicratidas put out to sea holding himself the right flank, and the left he entrusted to the Boeotians, who were commanded by Thrasondas the Theban. Since he was unable to make his line equal to that of the enemy by reason of the large space occupied by the islands, he divided his force, and forming two fleets fought two battles separately, one on each wing. Consequently he aroused great amazement in the spectators on many sides, since there were four fleets engaged and the ships that had been gathered into one place did not lack many of being three hundred. For this is the greatest sea-battle on record of Greeks against Greeks.

**99.** At the very moment when the admirals gave orders to sound the trumpets the whole host on each side, raising the war-cry in turn, made a tremendous shout; and all, as they enthusiastically struck the waves, vied with one another, every man being anxious to be the first to begin the battle. For the majority were experienced in fighting, because the war had endured so long, and they displayed insuperable enthusiasm, since it was the choicest troops who had been gathered for the decisive contest; for all took it for granted that the conquerors in this battle would put an end to the war. Callicratidas especially, since he had heard from the seer of the end awaiting him, was eager to compass for himself a death that would be most renowned. Consequently he was the first to drive at the ship of Lysias the general, and shattering it at the first blow together with the triremes accompanying it, he sank it; and as for the other ships, some he rammed and made unseaworthy and from others he tore away the rows of oars and rendered them useless for the fighting. Last of all he rammed the trireme of Pericles with a rather heavy blow and broke a great hole in the trireme; then, since the beak of his ship stuck tight in the gap and they could not withdraw it, Pericles threw an iron hand on the ship of Callicratidas, and when it was fastened tight, the Athenians, surrounding the ship, sprang upon it, and pouring over its crew put them all to the sword. It was at this time, we are told, that Callicratidas, after fighting brilliantly and holding out for a long time, finally was worn down by numbers, as he was struck from all directions. As soon as the defeat of the admiral became evident, the result was that the Peloponnesians gave way in fear. Although the right wing of the Peloponnesians was in flight, the Boeotians, who held the left, continued to put up a stout fight for some time; for both they and the Euboeans who were fighting by their side as well as all the other Greeks who had revolted from the Athenians feared lest the Athenians, if they should once regain their sovereignty, would exact punishment of them for their revolt. When they saw that most of their ships had been damaged and that the main body of the victors was turning against them, they were compelled to take flight. Now of the Peloponnesians some found safety in Chios and some in Cymê.

**100.** The Athenians, while they pursued the defeated foe for a considerable distance, filled the whole area of the sea in the neighbourhood of the battle with corpses and the wreckage of ships. After this some of the generals thought that they should pick up the dead, since the Athenians are incensed at those who allow the dead to go unburied, but others of them said they should sail to Mitylenê and raise the siege with all speed. In the meantime a great storm arose, so that the ships were tossed about and the soldiers, by reason both of the hardships they had suffered in the battle and the heavy waves, opposed picking up the dead, and finally, since the storm increased in violence, they neither sailed to Mitylenê nor picked up the dead but were forced by the winds to put in at the Arginusae. The losses in the battle were twenty-five ships of the Athenians together with most of their crews and seventy-seven of the Peloponnesians; and as a result of the loss of so many ships and of the sailors who manned them the coastline of the territory of the Cymaeans and Phocaeans was strewn with corpses and wreckage.

When Eteonicus, who was besieging Mitylenê, learned from someone of the defeat of the Peloponnesians, he sent his ships to Chios and himself retreated with his land forces to the city of the Pyrrhaeans, which was an ally; for he feared lest, if the Athenians should sail against his troops with their fleet and the besieged make a sortie from the city, he should run the risk of losing his entire force. The generals of the Athenians, after sailing to Mitylenê and picking up Conon and his forty ships, put in at Samos, and from there as their base they set about laying waste the territory of the enemy. After this the inhabitants of Aeolis and Ionia and of the islands which were allies of the Lacedaemonians gathered in Ephesus, and as they counselled together they resolved to send to Sparta and to ask for Lysander as admiral; for during the time Lysander had been in command of the fleet he had enjoyed many successes and was believed to excel all others in skill as a general. The Lacedaemonians, however, having a law not to send the same man twice and being unwilling to break the custom of their fathers, chose Aracus as admiral but sent Lysander with him as an ordinary citizen, commanding Aracus to follow the advice of Lysander in every matter. These leaders, having been dispatched to assume the command, set about assembling the greatest possible number of triremes from both the Peloponnesus and their allies.

**101.** When the Athenians learned of their success at the Arginusae, they commended the generals for the victory but were incensed that they had allowed the men who had died to maintain their supremacy to go unburied. Since Theramenes and Thrasybulus had gone off to Athens in advance of the others, the generals, having assumed that it was they who had made accusations before the populace with respect to the dead, dispatched letters against them to the people stating that it was they whom the generals had ordered to pick up the dead, but this very thing turned out to be the principal cause of their undoing. For although they could have had the help of Theramenes and his associates in the trial, men who both were able orators and had many friends and, most important of all, had been participants in the events relative to the battle, they had them, on the contrary, as adversaries and bitter accusers. For when the letters were read before the people, the multitude was at once angered at Theramenes and his associates, but after these had presented their defence, it turned out that their anger was directed again on the generals. Consequently the people served notice on them of their trial and ordered them to turn over the command of the armaments to Conon, whom they freed of the responsibility, while they decreed that the should report to Athens with all speed. Of the generals Aristogenes and Protomachus, fearing the wrath of the populace, sought safety in flight, but Thrasyllus and Calliades and, besides, Lysias and Pericles and Aristocrates sailed home to Athens with most of their ships, hoping that they would have their crews, which were numerous, to aid them in the trial. When the populace gathered in the assembly, they gave attention to the accusation and to those who spoke to gratify them, but any who entered a defence they unitedly greeted with clamour and would not allow to speak. Not the least damaging to the generals were the relatives of the dead, who appeared in the assembly in mourning garments and begged the people to punish those who had allowed men who had gladly died on behalf of their country to go unburied. In the end the friends of these relatives and the partisans of Theramenes, being many, prevailed and the outcome was that the generals were condemned to death and their property confiscated.

**102.** After this action had been taken and while the generals were about to be led off by the public executioners to death, Diomedon, one of the generals, took the floor before the people, a man who was both vigorous in the conduct of war and thought by all to excel both in justice and in the other virtues. When all became still, he said: "Men of Athens, may the action which has been taken regarding us turn out well for the state; but as for the vows which we made for the victory, inasmuch as Fortune has prevented our paying them, since it is well that you give thought to them, do you pay them to Zeus the Saviour and Apollo and the Holy Goddesses [Erinyes]; for it was to these gods that we made vows before we overcame the enemy." Now after Diomedon had made this request he was led off to the appointed execution together with the other generals, though among the better citizens he had aroused great compassion and tears; for that the man who was about to meet an unjust death should make no mention whatsoever of his own fate but on behalf of the state which was wronging him should request it to pay his vows to the gods appeared to be an act of a man who was god-fearing and magnanimous and undeserving of the fate that was to befall him. These men, then, were put to death by the eleven magistrates who are designated by the laws, although far from having committed any crime against the state, they had won the greatest naval battle that had ever taken place of Greeks against Greeks and fought in splendid fashion in other battles and by reason of their individual deeds of valour had set up trophies of victories over their enemies. To such an extent were the people beside themselves at that time, and provoked unjustly as they were by their political leaders, they vented their rage upon men who were deserving, not of punishment, but of many praises and crowns.

**103.** Soon, however, both those who had urged this action and those whom they had persuaded repented, as if the deity had become wroth with them; for those who had been deceived got the wages of their error when not long afterwards they fell before the power of not one despot only but of thirty; and the deceiver, who had also proposed the measure, Callixenus, when once the populace had repented, was brought to trial on the charge of having deceived the people, and without being allowed to speak in his defence he was put in chains and thrown into the public prison; and secretly burrowing his way out of the prison with certain others he managed to make his way to the enemy at Deceleia, to the end that by escaping death he might have the finger of scorn pointed at his turpitude not only in Athens but also wherever else there were Greeks throughout his entire life.

Now these, we may say, were the events of this year. Of the historians Philistus ended his first History of Sicily with this year and the capture of Acragas, treating a period of more than eight hundred years in seven Books, and he began his second History where the first leaves off and wrote four Books.

At this same time Sophocles the son of Sophilus, the writer of tragedies, died at the age of ninety years, after he had won the prize eighteen times. We are told of this man that when he presented his last tragedy and won the prize, he was filled with insuperable jubilation which was also the cause of his death. Apollodorus, who composed his *Chronology,* states that Euripides also died in the same year; although others say that he was living at the court of Archelaus, the king of Macedonia, and that once when he went out in the countryside, he was set upon by dogs and torn to pieces a little before this time.

**How the Athenians, after suffering defeat in a great sea-battle, were forced to conclude peace on the best terms they could secure, and in this manner the Peloponnesian War came to an end (104-107).**

**104.** At the end of this year Alexias was archon in Athens [405] and in Home in the place of consuls three military tribunes were elected, Gaius Julius, Publius Cornelius, and Gaius Servilius. When these had entered office, the Athenians, after the execution of the generals, put Philocles in command, and turning over the fleet to him, they sent him to Conon with orders that they should share the leadership of the armaments in common. After he had joined Conon in Samos, he manned all the ships which numbered one hundred and seventy-three. Of these it was decided to leave twenty at Samos, and with all the rest they set out for the Hellespont under the command of Conon and Philocles.

Lysander, the admiral of the Lacedaemonians, having collected thirty-five ships from his neighbouring allies of the Peloponnesus, put in at Ephesus; and after summoning also the fleet from Chios he made it ready. He also went inland to Cyrus, the son of King Darius, and received from him a great sum of money with which to maintain his soldiers. And Cyrus, since his father was summoning him to Persia, turned over to Lysander the authority over the cities under his command and ordered them to pay the tribute to him. Lysander, then, after being thus supplied with every means for making war, returned to Ephesus.

At the same time certain men in Miletus, who were striving for an oligarchy, with the aid of the Lacedaemonians put an end to the government of the people. First of all, while the Dionysia was being celebrated, they seized in their homes and carried off their principal opponents and put some forty of them to the sword, and then, at the time when the market-place was full, they picked out three hundred of the wealthiest citizens and slew them. The most respectable citizens among those who favoured the people, not less than one thousand, fearing the situation they were in, fled to Pharnabazus the satrap, who received them kindly and giving each of them a gold stater settled them in Blauda, a fortress of Lydia.

Lysander, sailing with the larger part of his ships to Iasus in Caria, took the city, which was an ally of the Athenians, by storm, put to the sword the males of military age to the number of eight hundred, sold the children and women as booty, and razed the city to the ground. After this he sailed against Attica and many places, but accomplished nothing of importance or worthy of record; consequently we have not taken pains to recount these events. Finally, capturing Lampsacus, he let the Athenian garrison depart under a truce, but seized the property of the inhabitants and then returned the city to them.

105. The generals of the Athenians, on learning that the Lacedaemonians in full force were besieging Lampsacus, assembled their triremes from all quarters and put forth against them in haste with one hundred and eighty ships, but finding the city already taken, at the time they stationed their ships at Aegospotami [goat rivers] but afterward sailed out each day against the enemy and offered battle. When the Peloponnesians persisted in not coming out against them, the Athenians were at a loss what to do in the circumstances, since they were unable to find supplies for their armaments for any further length of time where they were. Alcibiades now came to them and said that Medocus and Seuthes, the kings of the Thracians, were friends of his and had agreed to give him a large army if he wished to make war to a finish on the Lacedaemonians; he therefore asked them to give him a share in the command, promising them one of two things, either to compel the enemy to accept battle or to contend with them on land with the aid of the Thracians. This offer Alcibiades made from a desire to achieve by his own efforts some great success for his country and through his benefactions to bring the people back to their old affection for him. But the generals of the Athenians, considering that in case of defeat the blame would attach to them and that in case of success all men would attribute it to Alcibiades, quickly bade him to be gone and not come near the camp ever again.

106. Since the enemy refused to accept battle at sea and famine gripped the army, Philocles, who held the command on that day, ordered the other captains to man their triremes and follow him, while he with thirty triremes which were ready set out in advance. Lysander, who had learned of this from some deserters, set out to sea with all his ships, and putting Philocles to flight, pursued him toward the other ships. The triremes of the Athenians had not yet been manned and confusion pervaded them all because of the unexpected appearance of the enemy, and when Lysander perceived the tumult among the enemy, he speedily put ashore Eteonicus and the troops who were practised in fighting on land. Eteonicus, quickly turning to his account the opportunity of the moment, seized a part of the camp, while Lysander himself, sailing up with all his triremes in trim for battle, after throwing iron hands on the ships which were moored along the shore began dragging them off. The Athenians, panic-stricken at the unexpected move, since they neither had respite for putting out to sea with their ships nor were able to fight it out by land, held out for a short while and then gave way, and at once, some deserting the ships, others the camp, they took to flight in whatever direction each man hoped to find safety. Of the triremes only ten escaped. Conon the general, who had one of them, gave up any thought of returning to Athens, fearing the wrath of the people, but sought safety with Evagoras, who was in control of Cyprus and with whom he had relations of friendship; and of the soldiers the majority fled by land to Sestus and found safety there. The rest of the ships Lysander captured, and taking prisoner Philocles the general, he took him to Lampsacus and had him executed.

After this Lysander dispatched messengers by the swiftest tireme to Lacedaemon to carry news of the victory, first decking the vessel out with the most costly arms and booty. After this, advancing against the Athenians who had found refuge in Sestus, he took the city but let the Athenians depart under a truce. Then he sailed at once to Samos with his troops and himself began the siege of the city, but Gylippus, who with a flotilla had fought in aid of the Syracusans in Sicily, he dispatched to Sparta to take there both the booty and with it fifteen hundred talents of silver. The money was in small bags, each of which contained a *skjtale* which carried the notation of the amount of the money. Gylippus, not knowing of the *skytale,* secretly undid the bags and took out three hundred talents, and when, by means of the notation, Gylippus was detected by the ephors, he fled the country and was condemned to death. Similarly it happens that Clearchus also, the father of Gylippus, fled the country at an earlier time, when he was believed to have accepted a bribe from Pericles not to make the planned raid into Attica, and was condemned to death, spending his life as an exile in Thurii in Italy. So these men, who in all other affairs were looked upon as individuals of ability, by such conduct brought shame upon the rest of their lives.

**107.** When the Athenians heard of the destruction of their armaments, they abandoned the policy of control of the sea, but busied themselves with putting the walls in order and with blocking the harbours, expecting, as well they might, that they would be besieged. For at once the kings of the Lacedaemonians, Agis and Pausanias, invaded Attica with a large army and pitched their camp before the walls, and Lysander with more than two hundred triremes put in at the Peiraeus. Although they were in the grip of such hard trials, the Athenians nevertheless held out and had no trouble defending their city for some time. The Peloponnesians decided, since the siege was offering difficulties, to withdraw their armies from Attica and to conduct a blockade at a distance with their ships, in order that no grain should come to the inhabitants. When this was done, the Athenians came into dire want of everything, but especially of food, because this had always come to them by sea. Since the suffering increased day by day, the city was filled with dead, and the survivors sent ambassadors and concluded peace with the Lacedaemonians on the terms that they should tear down the two long walls and those of the Peiraeus, keep no more than ten ships of war, withdraw from all the cities, and recognise the hegemony of the Lacedaemonians. And so the Peloponnesian War, the most protracted of any of which we have knowledge, having run for twenty-seven years, came to the end we have described.

**108.** Not long after the peace Darius, the King of Asia, died after a reign of nineteen years, and Artaxerxes, his eldest son, succeeded to the throne and reigned for forty-three years. During this period, as Apollodorus the Athenian says, the poet Antimachus flourished.

In Sicily at the beginning of summer Himilcon, the commander of the Carthaginians, razed to the ground the city of the Acragantini, and in the case of the temples which did not appear to have been sufficiently destroyed even by the fire he mutilated the sculptures and everything of rather exceptional workmanship; he then at once with his entire army invaded the territory of the Geloans. In his attack upon all this territory and that of Camarina he enriched his army with booty of every description. After this he advanced to Gela and pitched his camp along the river of the same name as the city. The Geloans had, outside the city, a bronze statue of Apollo of colossal size; this the Carthaginians seized as spoil and sent to Tyre. The Geloans had set up the statue in accordance with an oracular response of the god, and the Tyrians at a later time, when they were being besieged by Alexander of Macedon, treated the god disrespectfully on the ground that he was fighting on the side of the enemy, but when Alexander took the city, as Timaeus says, on the day with the same name and at the same hour on which the Carthaginians seized the Apollo at Gela, it came to pass that the god was honoured by the Greeks with the greatest sacrifices and processions as having been the cause of its capture. Although these events took place at different times, we have thought it not inappropriate to bring them together because of their astonishing nature.

Now the Carthaginians cut down the trees of the countryside and threw a trench about their encampment, since they were expecting Dionysius to come with a strong army to the aid of the imperilled inhabitants. The Geloans at first voted to remove their children and women out of danger to Syracuse because of the magnitude of the expected danger, but when the women fled to the altars about the market-place and begged to share the same fortune as the men, they yielded to them. After this, forming a very large number of detachments, they sent the soldiers in turn over the countryside; and they, because of their knowledge of the land, attacked wandering bands of the enemy, daily brought back many of them alive, and slew not a few. Although the Carthaginians kept launching assaults in relays upon the city and breaching the walls with their battering-rams, the Geloans defended themselves gallantly; for the portions of the walls which fell during the day they built up again at night, the women and children assisting. For those who were in the bloom of their physical strength were under arms and constantly in battle, and the rest of the multitude stood by to attend to the defences and the rest of the tasks with all eagerness. In a word, they met the attack of the Carthaginians so stoutly that, although their city lacked natural defences and they were without allies and they could, besides, see the walls falling in a number of places, they were not dismayed at the danger which threatened them.

**109.** Dionysius, the tyrant of the Syracusans, summoning aid from the Greeks of Italy and his other allies, led forth his army; and he also enlisted the larger part of the Syracusans of military age and enrolled the mercenaries in the army. He had in all, as some record, fifty thousand soldiers, but according to Timaeus, thirty thousand infantry, a thousand cavalry, and fifty decked vessels. With a force of such size he set out to the aid of the Geloans, and when he drew near the city, he pitched camp by the sea. For his intent was not to divide his army but to use the same base for the fighting by land as well as by sea; and with his light armed troops he engaged the enemy and did not allow them to forage over the countryside, while with his cavalry and ships he attempted to deprive the Carthaginians of the supplies which they got from the territory of which they were masters. Now for twenty days they were inactive, doing nothing worthy of mention, but after this Dionysius divided his infantry into three groups, and one division, which he formed of the Sicilian Greeks, he ordered to advance against the entrenched camp of their adversaries with the city on their left flank; the second division, which he formed of allies, he commanded to drive along the shore with the city on their right; and he himself with the contingent of mercenaries advanced through the city against the place where the Carthaginian engines of war were stationed. To the cavalry he gave orders that, as soon as they saw the infantry advancing, they should cross the river and overrun the plain, and if they should see their comrades winning, they should join in the fighting, but in case they were losing, they should receive any who were in distress; and to the troops on the ships his orders were, so soon as the Italian Greeks made their attack, to sail against the camp of the enemy.

**110.** When the fleet carried out their orders at the proper time, the Carthaginians rushed to the aid of that sector in an attempt to keep back the attackers disembarking from the ships; and in fact that portion of the camp which the Carthaginians occupied was unfortified, all the part which lay along the beach. At this very time the Italian Greeks, who had covered the entire distance along the sea, attacked the camp of the Carthaginians, having found that most of the defenders had gone to give aid against the ships, and putting to flight the troops which had been left behind at this place, they forced their way into the encampment. At this turn of affairs the Carthaginians, turning about with the greater part of their troops, after a sustained fight, thrust out with difficulty the men who had forced their way within the trench. The Italian Greeks, overcome by the multitude of the barbarians, encountered as they withdrew the acute angle of the palisade and no help came to them; for the Sicilian Greeks, advancing through the plain, came too late and the mercenaries with Dionysius encountered difficulties in making their way through the streets of the city and thus were unable to make such haste as they had planned. The Geloans, advancing for some distance from the city, gave aid to the Italian Greeks over only a short space of the area, since they were afraid to abandon the guarding of the walls, and as a result they were too late to be of any assistance. The Iberians and Campanians, who were serving in the army of the Carthaginians, pressing hard upon the Italian Greeks, slew more than a thousand of them, but since the crews of the ships held back the pursuers with showers of arrows, the rest of them got back in safety to the city. In the other part the Sicilian Greeks, who had engaged the Libyans who opposed them, slew great numbers of them and pursued the rest into the encampment; but when the Iberians and Campanians and, besides, the Carthaginians came up to the aid of the Libyans, they withdrew to the city, having lost some six hundred men. The cavalry, when they saw the defeat of their comrades, likewise withdrew to the city, since the enemy pressed hard upon them. Dionysius, having barely got through the city, found his army defeated and for the time being withdrew within the walls.

**111.** After this Dionysius called a meeting of his friends and took counsel regarding the war. When they all said that his position was unfavourable for a decisive battle with the enemy, he dispatched a herald toward evening to arrange for the taking up of the dead on the next day, and about the first watch of the night he sent out of the city the mass of the people, while he himself set out about the middle of the night, leaving behind some two thousand of his light-armed troops. These had been given orders to keep fires burning through the entire night and to make an uproar in order to cause the Carthaginians to believe that he was still in the city. Now these troops, as the day was beginning to break, set out to join Dionysius, and the Carthaginians, on learning what had taken place, moved their quarters into the city and plundered what had been left of the contents of the dwellings.

When Dionysius arrived at Camarina, he compelled the residents of that city also to depart with their children and wives to Syracuse. And since their fear admitted of no delay, some gathered together silver and gold and whatever could be easily carried, while others fled with only their parents and infant children, paying no attention to valuables; and some, who were aged or suffering from illness, were left behind because they had no relatives or friends, since the Carthaginians were expected to arrive almost immediately. For the fate that had befallen Selinus and Himera and Acragas as well terrified the populace, all of whom felt as if they had actually been eyewitnesses of the savagery of the Carthaginians. For among them there was no sparing their captives, but they were without compassion for the victims of Fortune of whom they would crucify some and upon others inflict unbearable outrages. Nevertheless, now that two cities had been driven into exile, the countryside teemed with women and children and the rabble in general. When the soldiers witnessed these conditions, they were not only enraged against Dionysius but also filled with pity at the lot of the unfortunate victims; for they saw free-born boys and maidens of marriageable years rushing pell-mell along the road in a manner improper for their age, since the stress of the moment had done away with the dignity and respect which are shown before strangers. Similarly they sympathised also with the elderly, as they watched them being forced to push onward beyond their strength while trying to keep up with those in the prime of life.

**112.** It was for these reasons that the hatred against Dionysius was flaring up, since men assumed that he had so acted from this definite plan: by using the dread of the Carthaginians to be lord of the remaining cities of Sicily without risk. For they reckoned up his delay in bringing aid; the fact that none of his mercenaries had fallen; that he had retreated without reason, since he had suffered no serious reverse; and, most important of all, that not a single one of the Carthaginians had pursued them. Consequently, for those who before this were eager to seize an opportunity to revolt, all things, as if by the foreknowledge of the gods, were working toward the overthrow of the tyrannical power.

Now the Italian Greeks, deserting Dionysius, made their way home through the interior of the island, and the Syracusan cavalry at first kept watch in the hope that they might be able to slay the tyrant along the road; but when they saw that the mercenaries were not deserting him, they rode off with one accord to Syracuse, and finding the guards of the dockyards knew nothing of the events at Gela, they entered these without hindrance, plundered the house of Dionysius which was filled with silver and gold and all other costly things, and seizing his wife left her so ill-used as to ensure the tyrant's keeping his anger fiercely alive, acting as they did in the belief that the vengeance they wreaked on Dionysius' wife would be the surest guarantee of their holding by each other in their attack upon him. Dionysius, guessing while on the way what had taken place, picked out the most trustworthy of his cavalry and infantry, with whom he pressed toward the city without checking speed; for he reasoned that he could overcome the cavalry by no other means than by speedy action, and he acted accordingly.

For if he should make his arrival even more of a surprise than theirs had been, he had hope that he would easily carry out his design; and that is what happened. For the cavalry assumed that Dionysius would now neither return to Syracuse nor remain with his army; consequently, in the belief that they had carried out their design, they said that he had pretended that in leaving Gela he was giving the slip to the Carthaginians whereas the truth in fact was that he had given the slip to the Syracusans.

**113.** Dionysius covered a distance of four hundred stades and arrived at the gates of Achradine about the middle of the night with a hundred cavalry and six hundred infantry, and finding the gate closed, he piled upon it reeds brought from the marshes such as the Syracusans are accustomed to use to bind their stucco. While the gates were being burned down, he gathered to his troops the laggards, and when the fire had consumed the gates, Dionysius with his followers made their way through Achradine, and the stoutest soldiers among the cavalry, when they heard what had happened, without waiting for the main body, and although they were very few in number, rushed forth at once to aid in the resistance. They were gathered in the market-place, and there they were surrounded by the mercenaries and shot down to a man. Then Dionysius, ranging through the city, slew any who came out here and there to resist him, and entering the houses of those who were hostile toward him, some of them he killed and others he banished from the city. The main body of the cavalry which was left fled from the city and occupied Aetne, as it is now called. At daybreak the main body of the mercenaries and the army of the Sicilian Greeks arrived at Syracuse, but the Geloans and Camarinaeans, who were at odds with Dionysius, left him and departed to Leontini.

*How the Carthaginians were struck by a pestilential disease and were compelled to conclude peace with Dionysius the tyrant (114).*

**114.** . . . Consequently Himilcar, acting under the stress of circumstances, dispatched a herald to Syracuse urging the vanquished to make up their differences. Dionysius was glad to comply and they concluded peace on the following terms: To the Carthaginians shall belong, together with their original colonists, the Elymi and Sicani; the inhabitants of Selinus, Acragas, and Himera as well as those of Gela and Camarina may dwell in their cities, which shall be unfortified, but shall pay tribute to the Carthaginians; the inhabitants of Leontini and Messenê and the Siceli shall all live under laws of their own making, and the Syracusans shall be subject to Dionysius; and whatever captives and ships are held shall be returned to those who lost them.

As soon as this treaty had been concluded, the Carthaginians sailed off to Libya, having lost more than half their soldiers from the plague; but the pestilence continued to rage no less in Libya also and great numbers both of the Carthaginians themselves and of their allies were struck down.

But for our part, now that we have arrived at the conclusion of the wars, in Greece the Peloponnesian and in Sicily the first between the Carthaginians and Dionysius, and our proposed task has been completed, we think that we should set down the events next in order in the following Book.

# BOOK XIV

**1.** All men, perhaps naturally, are disinclined to listen to obloquies that are uttered against them. Indeed even those whose evil-doing is in every respect so manifest that it cannot even be denied, none the less deeply resent it when they are the objects of censure and endeavour to make a reply to the accusation. Consequently all men should take every possible care not to commit any evil deed, and those especially who aspire to leadership or have been favoured by some striking gift of Fortune; for since the life of such men is in all things an open book because of their distinction, it cannot conceal its own unwisdom. Let no man, therefore, who has gained some kind of preeminence, cherish the hope that, if he commits great crimes, he will for all time escape notice and go uncensured. For even if during his own lifetime he eludes the sentence of rebuke, let him expect that at a later time Truth will find him out, frankly proclaiming abroad matters long hidden from mention. It is, therefore, a hard fate for wicked men that at their death they leave to posterity an undying image, so to speak, of their entire life; for even if those things that follow after death do not concern us, as certain philosophers keep chanting, nevertheless the life which has preceded death becomes far worse throughout all time for the evil memory that it enjoys. Manifest examples of this may be found by those who read the detailed story contained in this Book.

**2.** Among the Athenians, for example, thirty men who became tyrants from their own lust of gain, not only involved their native land in great misfortunes but themselves soon lost their power and have bequeathed a deathless memorial of their own disgrace. The Lacedaemonians, after winning for themselves the undisputed sovereignty of Greece, were shorn of it from the moment when they sought to carry out unjust projects at the expense of their allies. For the superiority of those who enjoy leadership is maintained by goodwill and justice, and is overthrown by acts of injustice and by the hatred of their subjects. Similarly Dionysius, the tyrant of the Syracusans, although he has been the most fortunate of such rulers, was incessantly plotted against while alive, was compelled by fear to wear an iron corselet under his tunic, and has bequeathed since his death his own life as an outstanding example unto all ages for the maledictions of men.

We shall record each one of these illustrations with more detail in connection with the appropriate period of time; for the present we shall take up the continuation of our account, pausing only to define our dates. In the preceding Books we have set down a record of events from the capture of Troy to the end of the Peloponnesian War and of the Athenian Empire, covering a period of seven hundred and seventy-nine years. [1184-405] In this Book, as we add to our narrative the events next succeeding, we shall commence with the establishment of the thirty tyrants and stop with the capture of Rome by the Gauls, embracing a period of eighteen years.

BOOK XIV

## *The overthrow of the democracy in Athens and the establishment of the thirty men (3-4).*

**3.** There was no archon in Athens [404] because of the overthrow of the government, it being the seven hundred and eightieth year from the capture of Troy, and in Rome four military tribunes succeeded to the consular magistracy, Gaius Fulvius, Gaius Servilius, Gaius Valerius, and Numerius Fabius; and in this year the Ninety-fourth Olympiad was celebrated, that in which Corcinas of Larisa was victor. At this time the Athenians, completely reduced by exhaustion, made a treaty with the Lacedaemonians whereby they were bound to demolish the walls of their city and to employ the polity of their fathers. They demolished the walls, but were unable to agree among themselves regarding the form of government. For those who were bent on oligarchy asserted that the ancient constitution should be revived, in which only a very few represented the state, whereas the greatest number, who were partisans of democracy, made the government of their fathers their platform and declared that this was by common consent a democracy.

After a controversy over this had continued for some days, the oligarchic party sent an embassy to Lysander the Spartan, who, at the end of the war, had been dispatched to administer the governments of the cities and had established oligarchies in the greater number of them, for they hoped that, as well he might, he would support them in their design. Accordingly they sailed across to Samos, for it happened that Lysander was tarrying there, having just seized the city. He gave his assent to their pleas for his co-operation, appointed Thorax the Spartan harmost of Samos, and put in himself at the Peiraeus with one hundred ships. Calling an assembly of the Athenians, he advised them to choose thirty men to head the government and to manage all the affairs of the state. When Theramenes opposed him and read to him the terms of the peace, which agreed that they should enjoy the government of their fathers, and declared that it would be a terrible thing if they should be robbed of their freedom contrary to the oaths, Lysander stated that the terms of peace had been broken by the Athenians, since, he asserted, they had destroyed the walls later than the days of grace agreed upon. He also invoked the direst threats against Theramenes, saying that he would have him put to death if he did not stop opposing the Lacedaemonians. Consequently Theramenes and the people, being struck with terror, were compelled to dissolve the democracy by a show of hands. Accordingly thirty men were elected with power to manage the affairs of the state, as directors ostensibly but tyrants in fact.

**4.** The people, observing the fair dealing of Theramenes and believing that his honourable principles would act to some extent to check the encroachments of the leaders, elected him also as one of the thirty officials. It was the duty of those selected to appoint both a Council and the other magistrates and to draw up laws in accordance with which they were to administer the state. Now they kept postponing the drawing up of laws, always putting forth fine-sounding excuses, but a Council and the other magistrates they appointed from their personal friends, so that these bore the name indeed of magistrates but actually were underlings of the Thirty. At first they brought to trial the lowest elements of the city and condemned them to death; and thus far the most honourable citizens approved of their actions, but after this, desiring to commit acts more violent and lawless, they asked the Lacedaemonians for a garrison, saying that they were going to establish a form of government that would serve the interests of the Lacedaemonians. For they realised that they would be unable to accomplish murders without foreign armed aid, since all men, they knew, would unite to support the common security. When the Lacedaemonians sent a garrison and Callibius to command it, the Thirty won the commander over by bribes and other accommodations.

Then, choosing out from the rich such men as suited their ends, they proceeded to arrest them as revolutionaries, put them to death, and confiscated their possessions. When Theramenes opposed his colleagues and threatened to join the ranks of those who claimed the right to be secure, the Thirty called a meeting of the Council. Critias was their spokesman, and in a long speech accused Theramenes of betraying this government of which he was a voluntary member; but Theramenes in his reply cleared himself of the several charges and gained the sympathy of the entire Council. Critias, fearing that Theramenes might overthrow the oligarchy, threw about him a band of soldiers with drawn swords. They were going to arrest him, but, forestalling them, Theramenes leaped up to the altar of Hestia of the Council Chamber, crying out, "I flee for refuge to the gods, not with the thought that I shall be saved, but to make sure that my slayers will involve themselves in an act of impiety against the gods."

### *The lawless conduct of the thirty men toward the citizens (5-6).*

**5.** When the attendants came forward and were dragging him off, Theramenes bore his bad fortune with a noble spirit, since indeed he had had no little acquaintance with philosophy in company with Socrates; the multitude, however, in general mourned the ill-fortune of Theramenes, but had not the courage to come to his aid since a strong armed guard stood around him. Now Socrates the philosopher and two of his intimates ran forward and endeavoured to hinder the attendants, but Theramenes entreated them to do nothing of the kind; he appreciated, he said, their friendship and bravery, but as for himself, it would be the greatest grief if he should be the cause of the death of those who were so intimately associated with him. Socrates and his helpers, since they had no aid from anyone else and saw the intransigence of those in authority increasing, made no move. Then those who had received their orders dragged Theramenes from the altar and hustled him through the centre of the market-place to his execution; and the populace, terror-stricken at the arms of the garrison, were filled with pity for the unfortunate man and shed tears, not only over his fate but also over their own slavery. For all the common sort, when they saw a man of such virtue as Theramenes treated with such contumely, had concluded that they in their weakness would be sacrificed without a thought.

After the death of Theramenes the Thirty drew up a list of the wealthy, lodged false charges against them, put them to death, and seized their estates. They slew even Niceratus, the son of Nicias who had commanded the campaign against the Syracusans, a man who had conducted himself toward all men with fairness and humanity, and who was perhaps first of all Athenians in wealth and reputation. It came about, therefore, that every house was filled with pity for the end of the man, as fond thoughts due to their memory of his honest ways provoked them to tears. Nevertheless, the tyrants did not cease from their lawless conduct; rather their madness became so much the more acute that of the metics they slaughtered sixty of the wealthiest in order to gain possession of their property, and as for the citizens, since they were being killed daily, the well-to-do among them fled from the city almost to a man. They also slew Autolycus, an outspoken man, and, in a word, selected the most respectable citizens. So far did their wasting of the city go that more than half of the Athenians took to flight.

**6.** The Lacedaemonians, seeing the city of the Athenians abased in power and having no desire that the Athenians should ever gain strength, were delighted and made their attitude clear; for they voted that the Athenian exiles should be delivered up to the Thirty from all over Greece and that anyone who attempted to prevent this should be liable to a fine of five talents. Though this decree was shocking, all the rest of the cities, dismayed at the power of the Spartans, obeyed it, with the exception of the Argives who, hating as they did the cruelty of the Lacedaemonians and pitying the hard lot of the unfortunate, were the first to receive the exiles in a spirit of humanity. Also the Thebans voted that anyone who witnessed an exile being led off and did not render him all aid within his power should be subject to a fine.

Such, then, was the state of the affairs of the Athenians.

### *How the tyrant Dionysius prepared a citadel and distributed the city and its territory among the masses (7).*

**7.** In Sicily, Dionysius, the tyrant of the Siceli, after concluding peace with the Carthaginians, planned to busy himself more with the strengthening of his tyranny; for he assumed that the Syracusans, now that they were relieved of the war, would have plenty of time to seek after the recovery of their liberty. Perceiving that the Island [Ortygia] was the strongest section of the city and could be easily defended, he divided it from the rest of the city by an expensive wall, and in this he set high towers at close intervals, while before it he built places of business and stoas capable of accommodating a multitude of the populace. He also constructed on the Island at great expense a fortified acropolis as a place of refuge in case of immediate need, and within its wall he enclosed the dockyards which are connected with the small harbour that is known as Laccium. The dockyards could accommodate sixty triremes and had an entrance that was closed off, through which only one ship could enter at a time. As for the territory of Syracuse, he picked out the best of it and distributed it in gifts to his friends as well as to higher officers, and divided the rest of it in equal portions both to aliens and to citizens, including under the name of citizens the manumitted slaves whom he designated as New Citizens. He also distributed the dwellings among the common people, except those on the island, which he gave to his friends and the mercenaries.

When Dionysius thought that he had now organised his tyranny properly, he led forth his army against the Siceli, being eager to bring all the independent peoples under his control, and the Siceli in particular, because of their previous alliance with the Carthaginians. Accordingly he advanced against the city of the Herbessini and made preparations for its siege, but the Syracusans who were in the army, now that they had arms in their hands, began to gather in groups and upbraid each other that they had not joined with the cavalry in overthrowing the tyrant. The man appointed by Dionysius to command the men at first warned one of those who were free spoken, and when the man retorted, stepped boldly up to him to give him a blow. The soldiers, in anger at this, slew the commander, whose name was Doricus, and, crying to the citizens to strike for their freedom, sent for the cavalry from Actne; for the cavalry, who had been banished at the beginning of the tyranny, occupied this outpost.

### How Dionysius, to the amazement of all, recovered his tyranny when it was collapsing (8-9).

**8.** Dionysius, terror-stricken at the revolt of the Syracusans, broke off the siege and hastened to Syracuse, being eager to secure the city. Upon his flight those who had revolted chose as generals the men who had slain the commander, and gathering to their number the cavalry from Aetne, they pitched a camp facing the tyrant on the height called Epipolae, and blocked his passage to the countryside. And they at once dispatched ambassadors to the Messenians and the Rhegians, urging these people to join in the bid for freedom by action at sea; for it had been the practice of these cities at this time to man no less than eighty triremes. These triremes the cities dispatched at that time to the Syracusans, being eager to support them in the cause of freedom. The revolters also proclaimed a large reward to any who would slay the tyrant and promised citizenship to any mercenaries who would come over to them. They also constructed engines of war with which to shatter and destroy the walls, launched daily assaults upon the Island, and kindly received any of the mercenaries who came over to them.

Dionysius, being shut off as he now was from access to the countryside and constantly being abandoned by the mercenaries, gathered together his friends to counsel with them on the situation; for he had so completely despaired of maintaining his tyrannical power that he no longer was studying how to defeat the Syracusans but rather how to meet death in such a way as to end his rule not altogether ingloriously. Now Heloris, one of his friends, or, as some say, his adopted father, declared to him, "Tyranny is a fair winding-sheet;" but Polyxenus, his brother-in-law, advised him to use his swiftest horse and ride off into the domain of the Carthaginians to the Campanians, whom Himilcon had left behind to guard the districts of Sicily. Philistus, however, who composed his history after these events, declared in opposition to Polyxenus that it was not fitting to dash from the tyranny on a galloping horse but to be cast out, dragged by the leg. Dionysius agreed with Philistus and decided to submit to anything rather than abandon the throne of his free will. Consequently he sent ambassadors to those in revolt and urged them to allow him and his companions to leave the city, while he secretly dispatched messengers to the Campanians and promised them any price they should ask for the duration of the siege.

**9.** After the events we have described the Syracusans, having given the tyrant permission to sail away with five ships, took matters with rather less concern; the cavalry, since they were of no use in the siege, they discharged, while as for the infantry, most of them roved off into the countryside, assuming that the tyranny was already at an end. The Campanians, being elated at the promises they had received, first of all came to Agyrium, and leaving their baggage there with Agyris, the ruler of the city, they set forth unencumbered for Syracuse, being in number twelve hundred cavalry. Completing the journey in quick time, they came upon the Syracusans unexpectedly and, slaying many of them, they forced their way through to Dionysius. At this same time three hundred mercenaries had also landed to aid the tyrant, so that his hopes revived. The Syracusans, as the despotic power again gathered strength, were at odds among themselves, some maintaining that they should remain and continue the siege and others that they should disband their forces and abandon the city.

As soon as Dionysius learned of this, he led his army out against them, and falling on them while they were disordered, he easily routed them near the New City, as it is called. Not many of them, however, were slain, since Dionysius, riding among his men, stopped them from killing the fugitives. The Syracusans were forthwith scattered over the countryside, but a little later more than seven thousand of them were gathered with the cavalry at Aetne. Dionysius, after burying the Syracusans who had fallen, dispatched ambassadors to Aetne, asking the exiles to accept terms and return to their native land, and giving his pledged word that he would not bear enmity against them. Now certain of them, who had left behind children and wives, felt compelled to accept the offer; but the rest replied, when the ambassadors cited the benefaction Dionysius had performed in the burial of the dead, that he deserved the same favour, and they prayed to the gods that they might, the sooner the better, see him obtain it. These men, accordingly, who would by no means put any trust in the tyrant, remained in Aetne, watching for an opportunity against him. Dionysius treated with humanity the exiles who returned, wishing to encourage the rest to return to their native land too. To the Campanians he awarded the gifts that were due and then dispatched them from the city, having regard to their fickleness. These made their way to Entella and persuaded the men of the city to receive them as fellow-inhabitants; then they fell upon them by night, slew the men of military age, married the wives of the men with whom they had broken faith, and possessed themselves of the city.

### *How the Lacedaemonians managed conditions in Greece (10).*

**10.** In Greece the Lacedaemonians, now that they had brought the Peloponnesian War to an end, held the supremacy by common acknowledgement both on land and on sea. Appointing Lysander admiral, they ordered him to visit the cities and set up in each the magistrates they call harmosts; for the Lacedaemonians, who had a dislike for the democracies, wished the cities to have oligarchic governments. They also levied tribute upon the peoples they had conquered, and although before this time they had not used coined money, they now collected yearly from the tribute more than a thousand talents.

When the Lacedaemonians had settled the affairs of Greece to their own taste, they dispatched Aristus, [Aretes?] one of their distinguished men, to Syracuse, ostensibly pretending that they would overthrow the government, but in truth with intent to increase the power of the tyranny; for they hoped that by helping to establish the rule of Dionysius they would obtain his ready service because of their benefactions to him. Aristus, after having put ashore at Syracuse and discussed secretly with the tyrant the matters we have mentioned, kept stirring up the Syracusans and promised to restore their liberty; then he slew Nicoteles the Corinthian, a leader of the Syracusans, made strong the tyrant by betraying those who put their faith in him, and by such conduct brought disgrace both upon himself and upon his native land. Dionysius, sending the Syracusans out to harvest their crops, entered their homes and carried off the arms of them all; after this he built a second wall about the acropolis, constructed war vessels, and also collected a great number of mercenaries; and he made every other provision to safeguard the tyranny, since he had learned by experience that the Syracusans would endure anything to escape slavery.

### The death of Alcibiades, and the tyranny of Clearchus the Lacedaemonian in Byzantium and its overthrow (11-12).

**11.** While these events were taking place, Pharnabazus, the satrap [of Phrygia and Bithynia] of King Darius, wishing to gratify the Lacedaemonians, seized Alcibiades the Athenian and put him to death, but since Ephorus recounts that his death was sought for other reasons, I think it not unprofitable to set forth the plot against Alcibiades as the historian has described it. He states in the Seventeenth Book that Cyrus and the Lacedaemonians were making secret plans for a joint war against Cyrus' brother Artaxerxes, and Alcibiades, learning of Cyrus' purpose from certain parties, went to Pharnabazus and told him of it in detail; and he asked him for someone to conduct him on a mission to Artaxerxes, since he wished to be the first to disclose the plot to the King, but Pharnabazus, on hearing the story, usurped the function of reporter and sent trusted men to disclose the matter to the King. When Pharnabazus did not provide escorts to the capital, Ephorus continues, Alcibiades set out to the satrap of Paphlagonia in order to make the trip with his assistance; but Pharnabazus, fearing lest the King should hear the truth of the affair, sent men after Alcibiades to slay him on the road. These came upon him where he had taken shelter in a village of Phrygia, and in the night enclosed the place with a mass of fuel. When a strong fire was kindled, Alcibiades endeavoured to save himself, but came to his death from the fire and the javelins of his attackers.

About the same time Democritus the philosopher died at the age of ninety. And Lasthenes the Theban, who was the victor in the Olympic Games of this year, won a race, we are told, against a race horse, the course being from Coroneia to the city of the Thebans. [30 miles]

In Italy the Roman garrison of Erruca, [Verrugo] a city of the Volsci, was attacked by the enemy, who captured the city and slew most of the defenders.

**12.** When the events of this year had come to an end, Eucleides was archon in Athens, [403] and in Rome four military tribunes succeeded to the consular magistracy, Publius Cornelius, Numerius Fabius, and Lucius Valerius. After these magistrates had taken office, the Byzantines were in serious difficulties both because of factional strife and of a war that they were waging with the neighbouring Thracians; and since they were unable to devise a settlement of their mutual differences, they asked the Lacedaemonians for a general. The Spartans, accordingly, sent them Clearchus to bring order to the affairs of the city; and he, after being entrusted with supreme authority, and having gathered a large body of mercenaries, was no longer their president but their tyrant. First of all, he invited their chief magistrates to attend a festival of some kind and put them to death, and after this, since there was no government in the city, he seized a group of thirty prominent Byzantines, put a cord about their necks, and strangled them to death. After appropriating for himself the property of those he had slain, he also picked out the wealthy among the rest of the citizens, and launching false charges against them, he put some to death and drove others into exile. Having thus acquired a large amount of money and assembled a great body of mercenaries, he made his tyrannical power secure.

When the cruelty and power of the tyrant became noised abroad, the Lacedaemonians first of all dispatched ambassadors to him to prevail upon him to lay down his tyrannical power, but when he paid no heed to their requests, they sent an army against him under the command of Panthoedas. Clearchus, on learning of his approach, transferred his army to Selymbria, being master also of this city, for he assumed that after the many crimes he had committed against the Byzantines, he would have as enemies not only the Lacedaemonians, but also the inhabitants of the city. Consequently, having decided that Selymbria would be a safer base for the war, he removed both his treasure and his army to that place. When he learned that the Lacedaemonians were close at hand, he advanced to meet them and joined battle with the troops of Panthoedas at the place called Porus. The struggle lasted a long while, but the Lacedaemonians fought splendidly and the forces of the tyrant were destroyed. Clearchus with a few companions was at first shut up in Selymbria and besieged there, but later he was fearful and slipped away by night, and crossed over to Ionia, where he became intimate with Cyrus, the brother of the Persian King, and won command of his troops. For Cyrus, who had been appointed supreme commander of the satrapies lying on the sea [Agean] and was afire with ambition, was planning to lead an army against his brother Artaxerxes. Observing, therefore, that Clearchus possessed daring and a prompt boldness, he supplied him with funds and instructed him to enrol as many mercenaries as he could, believing that he would have in Clearchus an apt partner for his bold undertakings.

***How Lysander the Lacedaemonian undertook to overthrow the descendants of Heracles and was unsuccessful (13).***

**13.** Lysander the Spartan, after he had introduced governments in all the cities under the Lacedaemonians in accordance with the will of the ephors, establishing a rule of ten men in some and oligarchies in others, was the cynosure of Sparta. For by bringing the Peloponnesian War to an end he had bestowed upon his native land the supreme power, acknowledged by all, both on land and on sea. Consequently, having become filled with pride on this account, he conceived the idea of putting an end to the kingship of the Heracleidae and making every Spartan eligible to election as king; for he hoped that the kingship would very soon come to him because of his achievements, which were very great and glorious. Knowing that the Lacedaemonians gave very great heed to the responses of oracles, he attempted to bribe the prophetess in Delphi, since he believed that, if he should receive an oracular response favourable to the designs he entertained, he should easily carry his project to a successful end, but when he could not win over the attendants of the oracle, despite the large sum he promised them, he opened negotiations on the same matter with the priestesses of the oracle of Dodone, through a certain Pherecrates, who was a native of Apollonia and intimate with the attendants of the shrine.

Meeting with no success, he made a journey to Cyrene, offering as his reason payment of vows to Ammon, but actually for the purpose of bribing the oracle; and he took with him a great sum of money with which he hoped to win over the attendants of the shrine. In fact Libys, the king of those regions, was a guest-friend of his father, and it so happened that Lysander's brother had been named Libys by reason of the friendship with the king. With the king's help, then, and the money he brought, he hoped to win them, but not only did he fail of his design, but the overseers of the oracle sent ambassadors to lay charges against Lysander for his effort to bribe the oracle. When Lysander arrived at Lacedaemon, a trial was proposed, but he presented a persuasive defence of his conduct. Now at that time the Lacedaemonians knew nothing of Lysander's purpose to abolish the kings in line of descent from Heracles; but some time later, after his death, when some documents were being searched for in his house, they found a speech, composed at great expense, which he had prepared to deliver to the people, to persuade them that the kings should be elected from all the citizens.

### How Dionysius sold into slavery Catane and Naxos and transplanted the inhabitants of Leontini to Syracuse (14-15).

**14.** Dionysius, the tyrant of the Syracusans, after he had made peace with the Carthaginians and had got free of the uprisings in the city, was eager to attach to himself the neighbouring cities of the Chalcidians, namely, Naxos, Catane, and Leontini. He was eager to be lord of them because they lay on the borders of Syracuse and possessed many advantages for further increase of his tyrannical power. First of all, then, he encamped near Aetne and won the fortress, the exiles there being no match for an army of such size; and after this he advanced to Leontini and pitched his camp near the city along the river Teria. Then he at first led out his army in battle-order and dispatched a herald to the Leon-tines, commanding them to surrender the city and believing that he had struck terror into the inhabitants. When the Leontines paid no attention to him and had made every preparation to withstand a siege, Dionysius, having no engines of war, gave up the siege for the time being, but plundered their entire territory. From there he set out against the Siceli, pretending that he was engaging in war against them in order that the Catanians and the Naxians might become slacker in the defence of their cities. While he was tarrying in the neighbourhood of Enna, he persuaded Aeimnestus, a native of the city, to make a bid for tyranny, promising to aid him in the undertaking, but when Aeimnestus had succeeded in his design and then did not admit Dionysius into the city, Dionysius in anger changed sides and urged the Ennaeans to overthrow the tyrant. These streamed into the market-place with their arms, contending for their freedom, and the city was filled with tumult. Dionysius, on learning of the strife, took his light-armed troops, speedily broke through an unoccupied place into the city, seized Aeimnestus, and handed him over to the Ennaeans to be punished. He himself, refraining from all injustice, departed from the city. This he did, not so much because he had regard for right as because he wanted to encourage the other cities to put faith in him.

**15.** From Enna Dionysius set out to the city of the Herbitaeans and attempted to ravage it, but accomplishing nothing, he made peace with them and led his army to Catane, for Arcesilaüs, the general of the Catanians, had offered to betray the city to him. Consequently, being admitted by Arcesilaüs about midnight, he became master of Catane. After taking their arms from the citizens, he placed an adequate garrison in the city. After this Procles, the commander of the Naxians, on being won over by great promises, delivered over his native city to Dionysius, who, after paying the promised gifts to the traitor and granting him his kinsmen, sold the inhabitants into slavery, turned their property over to the soldiers to plunder, and razed the walls and the dwellings. He also meted out a similar treatment to the Catanians, selling the captives he took as booty in Syracuse. Now the territory of the Naxians he gave as a present to the neighbouring Siceli and granted to the Campanians the city of the Catanians as their dwelling-place. After this he advanced to Leontini with his entire armed strength and laid siege to the city, and sending ambassadors to the inhabitants, he ordered them to hand over their city and enjoy citizenship in Syracuse. The Leontines, expecting that they would receive no help and reflecting on the fate of the Naxians and Catanians, were struck with terror in fear that they would suffer the same misfortune. Consequently, yielding to the exigency of the moment, they assented to the proposal, left their city, and removed to Syracuse.

### The founding of Halaesa in Sicily (16).

**16.** Archonides, the leader of Herbite, after the citizen-body of the Herbitaeans had concluded peace with Dionysius, determined to found a city. For he had not only many mercenaries but also a mixed throng who had streamed into the city in connection with the war against Dionysius; and many of the destitute among the Herbitaeans had promised him to join in the colony. Consequently, taking the multitude of refugees, he occupied a hill lying eight stades from the sea, on which he founded the city of Halaesa; and since there were other cities of Sicily with the same name, he called it Halaesa Archonidion after himself. When, in later times, the city grew greatly both because of the trade by sea and because the Romans exempted it from tribute, the Halaesians denied their kinship with the Herbitaeans, holding it a disgrace to be deemed colonists of an inferior city. Nevertheless, up to the present time numerous ties of relationships are to be found among both peoples, and they administer their sacrifices at the Temple of Apollo with the same routine. But there are those who state that Halaesa was founded by the Carthaginians at the time when Himilcon concluded his peace with Dionysius.

In Italy a war arose between the Romans and the people of Veii for the following reasons. [lacuna] In this campaign the Romans voted for the first time to give annual pay to the soldiers for their service. They also reduced by siege the city of the Volsci which was called at that time Anxor [Anxur] but now has the name Tarracine.

### The war between the Lacedaemonians and the Eleians (17).

**17.** At the close of the year Micion was archon in Athens, [402] and in Rome three military tribunes took over the consular magistracy, Titus Quinctius, Gaius Julius, and Aulus Mamilus. After these magistrates had entered office, the inhabitants of Oropus fell into civil strife and exiled some of their citizens. For a time the exiles undertook to effect their return by their own resources, but finding themselves unable to carry through their purpose, they persuaded the

Thebans to send an army to assist them. The Thebans took the field against the Oropians, and becoming masters of the city, resettled the inhabitants some seven stades from the sea; and for some time they allowed them to have their own government, but after this they gave them Theban citizenship and attached their territory to Boeotia.

While these events were taking place, the Lacedaemonians brought a number of charges against the Eleians, the most serious being that they had prevented Agis, their king, from offering sacrifices to the god and that they had not allowed the Lacedaemonians to compete in the Olympic Games. Consequently, having decided to wage war on the Eleians, they dispatched ten ambassadors to them, ordering them, in the first place, to allow their subject cities to be independent, and after that they demanded of them their quota of the cost of the war against the Athenians. This they did in quest of specious pretexts for themselves and of plausible openings for war. When the Eleians not only paid no heed to them but even accused them besides of enslaving the Greeks, they dispatched Pausanias, the other of their two kings, against them with four thousand soldiers. He was accompanied by many soldiers also from practically all the allies except the Boeotians and Corinthians. They, being offended by the proceedings of the Lacedaemonians, took no part in the campaign against Elis.

Pausanias, then, entered Elis by way of Arcadia and straightway took the outpost of Lasion at the first assault; then, leading his army through Acroreia, he won to his side the four cities of Thraestus, Halium, Epitalium, and Opus. Moving thence, he straightway encamped near Pylus and took this place, which was about seventy stades from Elis. After this, advancing to Elis proper, he pitched his camp on the hills across the river. [Peneus] A short time before this the Eleians had got from the Aetolians a thousand elite troops to help them, to whom they had given the region about the *gymnasion* to guard. When Pausanias first of all started to lay siege to this place, and in a careless manner, not supposing that the Eleians would ever dare to make a sortie against him, suddenly both the Aetolians and many of the citizens, pouring forth from the city, struck terror into the Lacedaemonians and slew some thirty of them. At the time Pausanias raised the siege, but after this, since he saw that the city would be hard to take, he traversed its territory, laying it waste and plundering it, even though it was sacred soil, and gathered great stores of booty. Since the winter was already at hand, he built walled outposts in Elis and left adequate forces in them, and himself passed the winter with the rest of the army in Dyme.

### How Dionysius constructed the wall at the Hexapyli (18).

18. In Sicily Dionysius, the tyrant of the Siceli, [401] since his government was making satisfactory progress, determined to make war upon the Carthaginians; but being not yet sufficiently prepared, he concealed this purpose of his while making the necessary preparations for the coming encounters. And realising that in the war with Athens the city had been blocked off by a wall that ran from the sea to the sea, he took care that he should never, where caught at a similar disadvantage, be cut off from contact with the countryside; for he saw that the site of Epipolae, as it is called, naturally commanded the city of the Syracusans. Sending, therefore, for his master-builders, in accord with their advice he decided that he must fortify Epipolae at the point where there stands

now the Wall with the Six Gates. For this place, which faces north, is precipitous in its entirety, and so steep that access is hardly to be won from the outside. Wishing to complete the building of the walls rapidly, he gathered the peasants from the countryside, from whom he selected some sixty thousand capable men and parcelled out to them the space to be walled. For each stade he appointed a master-builder and for each plethron a mason, and the labourers from the common people assigned to the task numbered two hundred for each plethron. Besides these, other workers, a multitude in number, quarried out the rough stone, and six thousand yoke of oxen brought it to the appointed place. The united labour of so many workers struck the watchers with great amazement, since all were zealous to complete the task assigned them. For Dionysius, in order to excite the enthusiasm of the multitude, offered valuable gifts to such as finished first, special ones for the master-builders, and still others for the masons and in turn for the common labourers; and he in person, together with his friends, oversaw the work through all the days required, visiting every section and ever lending a hand to the toilers. Speaking generally, he laid aside the dignity of his office and reduced himself to the ranks. Putting his hands to the hardest tasks, he endured the same toil as the other workers, so that great rivalry was engendered and some added even a part of the night to the day's labour, such eagerness had infected the multitude for the task. As a result, contrary to expectation, the wall was brought to completion in twenty days. It was thirty stades in length and of corresponding height, and the added strength of the wall made it impregnable to assault; for there were lofty towers at frequent intervals and it was constructed of stones four feet long and carefully joined.

### *How Cyrus led an army against his brother and was slain (19-31).*

**19.** At the close of the year Exaenetus was archon in Athens, and in Rome six military tribunes took over the consular magistracy, Publius Cornelius, Caeso Fabius, Spurius Nautius, Gaius Valerius, and Manius Sergius. At this time Cyrus, who was commander of the satrapies on the sea, had been planning for a long while to lead an army against his brother Artaxerxes; for the young man was full of ambition and had a keenness for the encounters of war that was not unrewarded. When an adequate force of mercenaries had been collected for him and all preparations for the campaign had been completed, he did not reveal the truth to the troops, but kept asserting that he was leading the army to Cilicia against the despots who were in rebellion against the King. He also dispatched ambassadors to the Lacedaemonians to recall to their minds the services he had rendered in their war against the Athenians and to urge them to join him as allies. The Lacedaemonians, thinking that the war would be to their advantage, decided to give aid to Cyrus and forthwith sent ambassadors to their admiral, named Samus, with instructions that he should carry out whatever Cyrus ordered. Samus had twenty-five triremes, and with these he sailed to Ephesus to Cyrus' admiral and was ready to co-operate with him in every respect. They also sent eight hundred infantry, giving the command to Cheirisophus. The commander of the barbarian fleet was Tamos, who had fifty triremes which had been fitted out at great expense; and after the Lacedaemonians had arrived, the fleets put out to sea, following a course for Cilicia.

Cyrus, after gathering to Sardis both the levies of Asia and thirteen thousand mercenaries, appointed Persians of his kindred to be governors of Lydia and Phrygia, but of Ionia, Aeolis, and the neighbouring territories, his trusted friend Tamos, who was a native of Memphis; then he with his army advanced in the direction of Cilicia and Pisidia, spreading the report that certain peoples of those regions were in revolt. From Asia he had in all seventy thousand troops, of whom three thousand were cavalry, and from the Peloponnesus and the rest of Greece thirteen thousand mercenaries. The soldiers from the Peloponnesus, with the exception of the Achaeans, were commanded by Clearchus the Lacedaemonian, those from Boeotia by Proxenus the Theban, the Achaeans by Socrates the Achaean, and those from Thessaly by Menon of Larissa. The officers of the barbarians, in minor commands, were Persians, and of the whole army Cyrus himself was commander-in-chief. He had disclosed to the commanders that he was marching against his brother, but he kept this hid from the troops for fear that they would leave his enterprise stranded because of the scale of his expedition. Consequently along the march, by way of providing for the coming occasion, he curried favour with the troops by affability and by providing abundant supplies of provisions.

**20.** After Cyrus had traversed Lydia and Phrygia as well as the regions bordering on Cappadocia, he arrived at the boundaries of Cilicia and the entrance at the Cilician Gates. This pass is narrow and precipitous, twenty stades in length, and bordering it on both sides are exceedingly high and inaccessible mountains; and walls stretch down on each side from the mountains as far as the roadway, where gates have been built across it. Leading his army through these gates, Cyrus entered a plain which in beauty yields to no plain in Asia, and through which he advanced to Tarsus, the largest city of Cilicia, which he speedily mastered. When Syennesis, the lord of Cilicia, heard of the great size of the hostile army, he was at a great loss, since he was no match for it in battle. When he was summoned to Cyrus' presence and had been given pledges, he went to him, and on learning the truth about the war he agreed to join him as an ally against Artaxerxes; and he sent one of his two sons along with Cyrus, giving him also a strong contingent of Cilicians for his army. For Syennesis, being by nature unscrupulous and having adjusted himself to the uncertainty of Fortune, had dispatched his other son secretly to the King to reveal to him the armaments that had been gathered against him and to assure him that he took the part of Cyrus out of necessity, but that he was still faithful to the King and, when the opportunity arose, would desert Cyrus and join the army of the King.

Cyrus rested his army twenty days in Tarsus, and after this, when he would have resumed the march, the troops suspected that the campaign was against Artaxerxes, and as each man reckoned up the length of the distances entailed and the multitude of hostile peoples through whom they would have to pass, he was filled with the deepest anxiety; for the word had got about that it was a four months' march for an army to Bactria and that a force of more than four hundred thousand soldiers had been mustered for the King. Consequently the soldiers became most fearful and vexed, and in anger at their commanders they attempted to kill them on the ground that the commanders had betrayed them. But when Cyrus entreated one and all of them and assured them that he was leading the army, not against Artaxerxes, but against a certain satrap of Syria, the soldiers yielded, and when they had received an increase in pay, they resumed their former loyalty to him.

**21.** As Cyrus marched through Cilicia he arrived at Issus, which lies on the sea and is the last city of Cilicia. At the same time the fleet of the Lacedaemonians also put in at the city, and the commanders went ashore, met with Cyrus, and reported the goodwill of the Spartans toward him; and they disembarked and turned over to him the eight hundred infantry under the command of Cheirisophus. The pretence was that these mercenaries were sent by the friends of Cyrus, but in fact everything was done with the consent of the ephors. The Lacedaemonians had not yet openly entered upon the war, but were concealing their purpose, awaiting the turn of the war.

Cyrus set out with his army, travelling toward Syria, and ordered the admirals to accompany him by sea with all the ships. When he arrived at the Gates, as they are called, and found the place clear of guards, he was elated, for he was greatly concerned lest troops might have occupied them before his arrival. The place is narrow and precipitous in character, so that it can be easily guarded by few troops. For two mountains lie against each other, the one jagged and with great crags, and the other beginning right at the road itself, and it is the largest in those regions, bearing the name Amanus and extending along Phoenicia; and the space between the mountains, some three stades in length, has walls running its whole length and gates closed to make a narrow passage. Now, after passing through the Gates without a fight, Cyrus sent off that part of the fleet that was still with him to make the return voyage to Ephesus, since it was of no further use to him now that he would be travelling inland. After a march of twenty days he arrived at the city of Thapsacus, which lies on the Euphrates River. Here he remained five days, and after winning the army to himself both by abundant supplies and by booty from foraging, he summoned it to an assembly and disclosed the truth about his campaign. When the soldiers received his words unfavourably, he besought them, one and all, not to leave him in the lurch, promising, besides other great rewards, that, when they came to Babylon, he would give every man of them five minas of silver. The soldiers, accordingly, soaring in their expectations, were prevailed upon to follow him. When Cyrus crossed the Euphrates with his army, he pressed on the way without making any halt, and as soon as he reached the borders of Babylonia he rested his troops.

**22.** King Artaxerxes had learned some time before from Pharnabazus that Cyrus was secretly collecting an army to lead against him, and when he now learned that he was on the march, he summoned his armaments from every place to Ecbatana in Media. When the contingents from the Indians and certain other peoples were delayed because of the remoteness of those regions, he set out to meet Cyrus with the army that had been assembled. He had in all not less than four hundred thousand soldiers, including cavalry, as Ephorus states. When he arrived on the plain of Babylonia, he pitched a camp beside the Euphrates, intending to leave his baggage in it; for he had learned that the enemy was not far distant and he was apprehensive of their reckless daring. Accordingly he dug a trench sixty feet wide and ten deep and encircled the camp with the baggage-wagons of his train like a wall. Having left behind in the camp the baggage and the attendants who were of no use in the battle, he appointed an adequate guard for it, and leading forward in person his army unencumbered, he advanced to meet the enemy which was near at hand.

When Cyrus saw the King's army advancing, he at once drew up his own force in battle order. The right wing, which rested on the Euphrates, was held by infantry composed of Lacedaemonians and some of the mercenaries, all under the command of Clearchus the Lacedaemonian, and helping him in the fight were the cavalry brought from Paphlagonia, more than a thousand. The left wing was held by the troops from Phrygia and Lydia and about a thousand of the cavalry, under the command of Aridaeus. Cyrus himself had taken a station in the centre of the battle-line, together with the choicest troops gathered from Persians and the other barbarians, about ten thousand strong; and leading the van before him were the finest-equipped cavalry, a thousand, armed with Greek breastplates and swords. Artaxerxes stationed before the length of his battle line scythe-bearing chariots in no small number, and the wings he put under command of Persians, while he himself took his position in the centre with no less than fifty thousand elite troops.

**23.** [Battle of Cunaxa] When the armies were about three stades apart, the Greeks struck up the paean and at first advanced at a slow pace, but as soon as they were within range of missiles they began to run at great speed. Clearchus the Lacedaemonian had given orders for them to do this, for by not running from a great distance he had in mind to keep the fighters fresh in body for the fray, while if they advanced on the run when at close quarters, this, it was thought, would cause the missiles shot by bows and other means to fly over their heads. When the troops with Cyrus approached the King's army, such a multitude of missiles was hurled upon them as one could expect to be discharged from a host of four hundred thousand. Nevertheless, they fought but an altogether short time with javelins and then for the remainder of the battle closed hand to hand.

The Lacedaemonians and the rest of the mercenaries at the very first contact struck terror into the opposing barbarians both by the splendour of their arms and by the skill they displayed. For the barbarians were protected by small shields and their divisions were for the most part equipped with light arms; and, furthermore, they were without trial in the perils of war, whereas the Greeks had been in constant battle by reason of the length of the Peloponnesian War and were far superior in experience. Consequently they straightway put their opponents to flight, pushed after them in pursuit, and slew many of the barbarians. In the centre of the lines, it so happened, were stationed both the men who were contending for the kingship. Consequently, becoming aware of this fact, they made at each other, being eagerly desirous of deciding the issue of the battle by their own hands; for Fortune, it appears, brought the rivalry of the brothers over the throne to culmination in a duel as if in imitation of that ancient rash combat of Eteocles and Polyneices so celebrated in tragedy. Cyrus was the first to hurl his javelin from a distance, and striking the King, brought him to the ground; but the King's attendants speedily snatched him away and carried him out of the battle. Tissaphernes, a Persian noble, now succeeded to the supreme command held by the King, and not only rallied the troops but fought himself in splendid fashion; and retrieving the reverse involved in the wounding of the

## Book XIV

King and arriving on the scene everywhere with his elite troops, he slew great numbers of the enemy, so that his presence was conspicuous from afar. Cyrus, being elated by the success of his forces, rushed boldly into the midst of the enemy and at first slew numbers of them as he set no bounds to his daring; but later, as he fought too imprudently, he was struck by a common Persian and fell mortally wounded. Upon his death the King's soldiers gained confidence for the battle and in the end, by virtue of numbers and daring, wore down their opponents.

24. On the other wing Aridaeus, who was second in command to Cyrus, at first withstood stoutly the charge of the barbarians, but later, since he was being encircled by the far-extended line of the enemy and had learned of Cyrus' death, he turned in flight with the soldiers under his command to one of the stations where he had once stopped, which was not unsuited as a place for retreat. Clearchus, when he observed that both the centre of his allies and the other parts as well had been routed, stopped his pursuit, and calling back the soldiers, set them in order; for he feared that if the entire army should turn on the Greeks, they would be surrounded and slain to a man. The King's troops, after they had put their opponents to flight, first plundered Cyrus' baggage-train and then, when night had come on, gathered in force and set upon the Greeks; but when the Greeks met the attack valiantly, the barbarians withstood them only a short while and after a little turned in flight, being overcome by their deeds of valour and skill. The troops of Clearchus, when they had slain great numbers of the barbarians, since it was already night, returned to the battlefield and set up a trophy, and about the second watch got safe to their camp. Such was the outcome of the battle, and of the army of the King more than fifteen thousand were slain, most of whom fell at the hands of the Lacedaemonians and mercenaries under the command of Clearchus. On the other side some three thousand of Cyrus' soldiers fell, while of the Greeks, we are told, not a man was slain, though a few were wounded.

When the night was past, Aridaeus, who had fled to the stopping-place, dispatched messengers to Clearchus, urging him to lead his soldiers to him and to join him in making a safe return to the regions on the sea. For now that Cyrus had been slain and the King's armaments held the advantage, deep concern had seized those who had dared to take the field to unseat Artaxerxes from the throne.

25. Clearchus called together both the generals and commanders and took counsel with them on the situation. While they were discussing it, there came ambassadors from the King, the chief of whom was a man of Greece, Phalynus by name, who was a Zacynthian. They were introduced to the gathering and spoke as follows: "King Artaxerxes says: Since I have defeated and slain Cyrus, do you surrender your arms, come to my doors, and seek how you may appease me and gain some favour." To these words each general gave a reply much like that which Leonides made when he was guarding the Pass of Thermopylae, and Xerxes sent messengers ordering him to lay down his arms. For Leonides at that time instructed the messengers to report to the King: "We believe that if we become friends of Xerxes, we shall be better allies if we keep our arms, and if we are forced to wage war against him, we shall fight the better if we keep

them." When Clearchus had made a somewhat similar reply to the message, Proxenus the Theban said, "As things now stand, we have lost practically everything else, and all that is left to us is our valour and our arms. It is my opinion, therefore, that if we guard our arms, our valour also will be useful to us, but if we give them up, then not even our valour will be of any help to us." Consequently he gave them this message to the King: "If you are plotting some evil against us, with our arms we will fight against you for your own possessions." We are told that also Sophilus, one of the commanders, said, "I am surprised at the words of the King; for if he believes that he is stronger than the Greeks, let him come with his army and take our arms away from us; but if he wishes to use persuasion, let him say what favour of equal worth he will grant us in exchange for them." After these speakers Socrates the Achaean said, "The King is certainly acting toward us in a most astounding fashion; for what he wishes to take from us he requires at once, while what will be given us in return he commands us to request of him at a later time. In a word, if it is in ignorance of who are the victors that he orders us to obey his command as though we had been defeated, let him come with his numerous host and find out on whose side the victory lies; but if, knowing well enough that we are the victors, he uses lying words, how shall we trust his later promises?"

After the messengers had received these replies, they departed; and Clearchus marched to the stopping-place whither the troops had retired who had escaped from the battle. When the entire force had gathered in the same place, they counselled together how they should make their way back to the sea and what route they should take. Now it was agreed that they should not return by the same way they had come, since much of it was waste country where they could not expect provisions to be available with a hostile army on their heels. They resolved, therefore, to make toward Paphlagonia, and set out in that direction with the army, proceeding at a leisurely pace, since they gathered provisions as they marched.

**26.** The King was recovering from his wound, and when he learned that his opponents were withdrawing, he believed that they were in flight and set out in haste after them with his army. As soon as he had overtaken them because of their slow progress, for the moment, since it was night, he went into camp near them, and when day came and the Greeks were drawing up their army for battle, he sent messengers to them and for the time being agreed upon a truce of three days. During this period they reached the following agreement: The King would see that his territory was friendly to them; he would provide them guides for their journey to the sea and would supply them with provisions on the way; the mercenaries under Clearchus and all the troops under Aridaeus should pass through his territory without doing any injury. After this they started on their journey, and the King led his army off to Babylon. In that city he accorded fitting honours to everyone who had performed deeds of courage in the battle and judged Tissaphernes to have been the bravest of all. Consequently he honoured him with rich gifts, gave him his own daughter in marriage, and henceforth continued to hold him as his most trusted friend; and he also gave him the command which Cyrus had held over the satrapies on the sea.

Tissaphernes, seeing that the King was angered at the Greeks, promised him that he would destroy them one and all, if the King would supply him with armaments and come to terms with Aridaeus, for he believed that Aridaeus would betray the Greeks to him in the course of the march. The King readily accepted this suggestion and allowed him to select from his entire army as many of the best troops as he chose. (When Tissaphernes caught up with the Greeks he sent word for Clearchus and the [lacuna] rest of the commanders to come to him and hear what he had to say in person. Consequently, practically all the generals, together with Clearchus and some twenty captains, went to Tissaphernes, and of the common soldiers about two hundred, who wanted to go to market, accompanied them. Tissaphernes invited the generals into his tent and the captains waited at the entrance. And after a little, at the raising of a red flag from Tissaphernes' tent, he seized the generals within, certain appointed troops fell upon the captains and slew them, and others killed the soldiers who had come to the market. Of the last, one made his escape to his camp and disclosed the disaster that had befallen them.

**27.** When the soldiers learned what had taken place, at the moment they were panic-stricken and all rushed to arms in great disorder, since there was no one to command; but after this, since no one disturbed them, they elected a number of generals and put the supreme command in the hands of one, Cheirisophus the Lacedaemonian. The generals organised the army for the march on the route they thought best and proceeded toward Paphlagonia. Tissaphernes sent the generals in chains to Artaxerxes, who executed the others but spared Menon alone, since he alone, because of a quarrel with his allies, was thought to be ready to betray the Greeks. Tissaphernes, following with his army, clung to the Greeks, but he did not dare to meet them in battle face to face, fearing as he did the courage and recklessness of desperate men; and although he harassed them in places well suited for that purpose, he was unable to do them any great harm, but he followed them, causing slight difficulties, as far as the country of the people known as the Carduchi.

Since Tissaphernes was unable to accomplish anything further, he set out with his army for Ionia; and the Greeks made their way for seven days through the mountains of the Carduchi, suffering greatly at the hands of the natives, who were a warlike people and well acquainted with the region. They were enemies of the King and a free people who practised the arts of war, and they especially trained themselves in hurling the largest stones they could with slings and in the use of enormous arrows, with which missiles they inflicted wounds on the Greeks from advantageous positions, slaying many and seriously injuring not a few. For the arrows were more than two cubits long and pierced both the shields and breastplates, so that no armour could withstand their force; and these arrows they used were so large, we are told, that the Greeks wound thongs about those that, had been shot and used them as javelins to hurl back. Now after they had traversed with difficulty the country we have mentioned, they arrived at the river Centrites, which they crossed, and entered Armenia. The satrap here was Tiribazus, with whom they made a truce and passed through his territory as friends.

**28.** As they made their way through the mountains of Armenia they encountered a heavy snow and the entire army came near to perishing. What happened was this. At first, when the air was stirred, the snow began to fall in light quantities from the heavens, so that the marchers experienced no trouble in their advance; but after this a wind arose and it came down heavier and heavier and so covered the ground that not only the road but even the peculiarities of the region could no longer be seen at all. Consequently despondency and fear seized the army, which was unwilling to turn back to certain destruction and unable to advance because of the heavy snow. As the storm increased in intensity, there came a great wind and heavy hail which beat in gusts on their faces and forced the entire army to come to a halt; for everyone, being unable to endure the hardship entailed in a further advance, was forced to remain wherever he happened to be. Although without supplies of any kind, they stuck it out under the open sky that day and the following night, beset by many hardships; for because of the heavy snow which kept continually falling, all their arms were covered and their bodies were completely chilled by the frost in the air. The hardships they endured were so great that they got no sleep the entire night. Some lighted fires and got some help from them, and some, whose bodies were invaded by the frost, gave up all hope of succour, since practically all their fingers and toes were mortifying. Accordingly, when the night was past, it was found that most of the baggage animals had perished, and of the soldiers many were dead and not a few, though still conscious, could not move their bodies because of the frost; and the eyes of some were blinded by reason of the cold and the glare from the snow. Every man would certainly have perished had they not gone on a little farther and found villages full of supplies. These villages had entrances for the beasts of burden which were tunnelled under the ground and others for the human inhabitants who descended into them by ladders . . . and in the houses the animals were supplied with hay, while the human inhabitants enjoyed a great abundance of all the necessities of life.

**29.** After they had remained in the villages eight days, they went on to the river Phasis. Here they passed four days and then made their way through the territory of the Chaoi [Taochians?] and the Phasians. When the natives attacked them, they defeated them in battle, slaying great numbers of them, seized their farms, which abounded in provisions, and spent fifteen days on them. Continuing their advance from here, they then traversed the territory of the Chaldaeans, as they are called, in seven days and arrived at the river named Harpagus, which was four plethra wide. From here their advance brought them through the territory of the Scytini by a road across a plain, on which they refreshed themselves for three days, enjoying all the necessities of life in plenty. After this they set out and on the fourth day arrived at a large city which bore the name of Gymnasia. Here the ruler of these regions concluded a truce with them and furnished them guides to lead them to the sea. Arriving in fifteen days at Mt. Chenium, when the men marching in the van caught sight of the sea, they were overjoyed and raised such a cry that the men in the rear, assuming that there was an attack by enemies, rushed to arms. When they had all got up to the place from which the sea could be seen, they raised their hands to the gods and gave thanks, believing they had now come through to safety; and gathering together into one spot a great number of stones, they formed from them great cairns on which they set up as a dedication spoils taken from the barbarians, wishing to leave an eternal memorial of their expedition. To the guide they gave as presents a silver bowl and a suit of Persian raiment; and he, after pointing out to them the road to the Macronians, took his departure. The Greeks then entered the territory of the Macronians, with whom they concluded a truce, receiving from them as a pledge of good faith a spear used by these barbarians and giving them in return a Greek one; for the barbarians declared that such an exchange had been handed down to them from their forefathers as the surest pledge of good faith. When they had crossed the boundaries of this people, they arrived at the territory of the Colchians. When the natives gathered here against them, the Greeks overcame them in battle and slew great numbers of them, and then, seizing a strong position on a hill, they pillaged the territory, gathered their booty on the hill, and refreshed themselves plentifully.

**30.** There were found in the regions great numbers of beehives which yielded valuable honey. But as many as partook of it succumbed to a strange affliction; for those who ate it lost consciousness, and falling on the ground were like dead men. Since many consumed the honey because of the pleasure its sweetness afforded, such a number had soon fallen to the ground as if they had suffered a rout in war. Now during that day the army was disheartened, terrified as it was at both the strange happening and the great number of the unfortunates; but on the next day at about the same hour all came to themselves, gradually recovered their senses, and rose up from the ground, and their physical state was like that of men recovered after a dose of a drug.

When they had refreshed themselves for three days, they marched on to the Greek city of Trapezus, [Trebizond] which is a colony of the Sinopians and lies in the territory of the Colchians. Here they spent thirty days, during which they were most magnificently entertained by the inhabitants; and they offered sacrifices to Heracles and to Zeus the Deliverer and held a gymnastic contest at the place at which, men say, the Argo put in with Jason and his men. From here they dispatched Cheirisophus their commander to Byzantium to get transports and triremes, since he claimed to be a friend of Anaxibius, the admiral of the Byzantians. The Greeks sent him off on a light boat, and then, receiving from the Trapezians two small boats equipped with oars, they plundered the neighbouring barbarians both by land and by sea. Now for thirty days they waited for the return of Cheirisophus, and when he still delayed and provisions for the troops were running low, they set out from Trapezus and arrived on the third day at the Greek city of Cerasus, a colony of the Sinopians. Here they spent some days and then came to the people of the Mosynoecians. When the barbarians assembled against them, the Greeks defeated them in battle, slaying great numbers of them, and when they fled for refuge to a stronghold where they had their dwelling and which they defended with wooden towers seven stories high, the Greeks launched successive assaults upon it and took it by storm. This stronghold was the capitol of all the other walled communities and in it, in the loftiest part, their king had his dwelling. A custom, handed down from their fathers, is followed that the king must remain for his entire life in the stronghold and from it issue his commands to the people. This was the most barbarous nation, the soldiers said, that they passed through: the men have intercourse with the women in the sight of all; the children of the wealthiest are nourished on boiled nuts; and they are all from their youth tattooed in various colours on both their back and breast. This territory they passed through in eight days and the next country, called Tibarene, in three.

31. From there they arrived at Cotyora, a Greek city and a colony of the Sinopians. Here they spent fifty days, plundering both the neighbouring peoples of Paphlagonia and the other barbarians. The citizens of Heracleia and Sinopê sent them vessels on which both the soldiers and their pack-animals were conveyed across. Sinopê was a colony founded by the Milesians, and situated as it was in Paphlagonia, it held first place among the cities of those regions; and it was in this city that in our day Mithridates, who went to war with the Romans, had his largest palace. At that city also arrived Cheirisophus, who had been dispatched without success to get triremes. Nevertheless, the Sinopians entertained them in kindly fashion and sent them on their way by sea to Heracleia, a colony of the Megartans; and the entire fleet came to anchor at the peninsula of Acherusia, where, we are told, Heracles led up Cerberus from Hades. As they proceeded from there on foot through Bithynia they fell among perils, as the natives skirmished with them along their route. So they barely made their way to safety to Chrysopolis in Chalcedonia, eight thousand three hundred surviving of the original ten thousand. From there some of the Greeks got back in safety, without further trouble, to their native lands, and the rest banded together around the Chersonesus and laid waste the adjoining territory of the Thracians.

Such, then, was the outcome of the campaign of Cyrus against Artaxerxes.

32. In Athens the Thirty Tyrants, who were in supreme control, made no end of daily exiling some citizens and putting to death others. When the Thebans were displeased at what was taking place and extended kindly hospitality to the exiles, Thrasybulus of the deme of Stiria, as he was called, who was an Athenian and had been exiled by the Thirty, with the secret aid of the Thebans seized a stronghold in Attica called Phyle. This was an outpost, which was not only very strong but was also only one hundred stades distant from Athens, so that it afforded them many advantages for attack. The Thirty Tyrants, on learning of this act, at first led forth their troops against the band with the intention of laying siege to the stronghold, but while they were encamped near Phyle there came a heavy snow, and when some set to work to shift their encampment, the majority of the soldiers assumed that they were taking to flight and that a hostile force was at hand; and the uproar which men call Panic struck the army and they removed their camp to another place.

The Thirty, seeing that those citizens of Athens who enjoyed no political rights in the government of the three thousand were elated at the prospect of the overthrow of their control of the state, transferred them to the Peiraeus and maintained their control of the city by means of mercenary troops; and accusing the Eleusians and Salaminians of siding with the exiles, they put them all to death. While these things were being done, many of the exiles flocked to Thrasybulus; (and the Thirty dispatched ambassadors to Thrasybulus) publicly to treat with him about some prisoners, but privately to advise him to dissolve the band of exiles and to associate himself with the Thirty in the rule of the city, taking the place of Theramenes; and they promised further that he could have licence to restore to their native land any ten exiles he chose. Thrasybulus replied that he preferred his own state of exile to the rule of the Thirty and that he would not end the war unless all the citizens returned from exile and the people got back the form of government they had received from their fathers. The Thirty, seeing many revolting from them because of hatred and the exiles growing ever more numerous, dispatched ambassadors to Sparta for aid, and meanwhile themselves gathered as many troops as they could and pitched a camp in the open country near Acharnae, as it is called.

33. Thrasybulus, leaving behind an adequate guard at Phyle, led forth the exiles, twelve hundred in number, and delivering an unexpected attack by night on the camp of his opponents, he slew a large number of them, struck terror into the rest by his unexpected move, and forced them to flee to Athens. After the battle Thrasybulus set out straightway for the Peiraeus and seized Munychia, which was an uninhabited and strong hill; and the Tyrants with all the troops at their disposal went down to the Peiraeus and attacked Munychia, under the command of Critias. In the sharp battle which continued for a long time the Thirty held the advantage in numbers and the exiles in the strength of their position. At last, however, when Critias fell, the troops of the Thirty were dismayed and fled for safety to more level ground, the exiles not daring to come down against them. When after this great numbers went over to the exiles, Thrasybulus made an unexpected attack upon his opponents, defeated them in battle, and became master of the Peiraeus. At once many of the inhabitants of Athens who wished to be rid of the tyranny flocked to the Peiraeus and all the exiles who were scattered throughout the cities of Greece, on hearing of the successes of Thrasybulus, came to the Peiraeus, so that from now on the exiles were far superior in force. In consequence they began to lay siege to the city.

The remaining citizens in Athens now removed the Thirty from office and sent them out of the city, and then they elected ten men with supreme power first and foremost to put an end to the war, in any way possible, on friendly terms. But these men, as soon as they had succeeded to office, paid no attention to these orders, but established themselves as tyrants and sent to Lacedaemon for forty warships and a thousand soldiers, under the command of Lysander, but Pausanias, the king of the Lacedaemonians, being jealous of Lysander and observing that Sparta was in ill repute among the Greeks, marched forth with a strong army and on his arrival in Athens brought about a reconciliation between the men in the city and the exiles. As a result the Athenians got back their country and henceforth conducted their government under laws of their own making; and the men who lived in fear of punishment for their unbroken series of past crimes they allowed to make their home in Eleusis.

34. The Eleians, because they stood in fear of the superior strength of the Lacedaemonians, brought the war with them to an end, agreeing that they would surrender their triremes to the Lacedaemonians and let the neighbouring cities go free. And the Lacedaemonians, now that they had brought their wars to an end and were no longer concerned with them, advanced with their army against the Messenians, of whom, some were settled in an outpost on Cephallenia and others in Naupactus, which the Athenians had given them, among the western Locrians.

Driving the Messenians from these regions, they returned the one outpost to the inhabitants of Cephallenia and the other to the Locrians. The Messenians, being now driven from every place because of their ancient hatred of the Spartans, departed with their arms from Greece, and some of them, sailing to Sicily, took service as mercenaries with Dionysius, while others, about three thousand in number, sailed to Cyrene and joined the forces of exiles there. For at that time disorder had broken out among the Cyrenaeans, since Ariston, together with certain others, had seized the city. Of the Cyrenaeans, five hundred of the most influential citizens had recently been put to death and the most respected among the survivors had been banished. The exiles now added the Messenians to their number and joined battle with the men who had seized the city, and many of the Cyrenaeans were slain on both sides, but the Messenians were killed almost to a man. After the battle the Cyrenaeans negotiated with each other and agreed to be reconciled, and they immediately swore oaths not to remember past injuries and lived together as one body in the city.

At this same time the Romans increased the number of colonists in the city known as Velitrae.

### How the Lacedaemonians came to the aid of the Greeks of Asia (35-36).

**35.** At the close of this year, in Athens [400] Laches was archon and in Rome the consulship was administered by military tribunes, Manius Claudius, Marcus Quinctius, Lucius Julius, Marcus Furius, and Lucius Valerius; and the Ninety-fifth Olympiad was held, that in which Minos of Athens won the stadion. This year Artaxerxes, the King of Asia, after his defeat of Cyrus, had dispatched Tissaphernes to take over all the satrapies which bordered on the sea. Consequently the satraps and cities which had allied themselves with Cyrus were in great suspense, lest they should be punished for their offences against the King. Now all the other satraps, sending ambassadors to Tissaphernes, paid court to him and in every way possible arranged their affairs to suit him; but Tamōs, the most powerful satrap, who commanded Ionia, put on triremes his possessions and all his sons except one whose name was Glōs and who became later commander of the King's armaments. Tamōs then, in fear of Tissaphernes, sailed off with his fleet to Egypt and sought safety with Psammetichus, the king of the Egyptians, who was a descendant of the famous Psammetichus [664-10]. Because of a good turn he had done the king in the past, Tamōs believed that he would find in him a haven, as it were, from the perils he faced from the King of Persia. But Psammetichus, completely ignoring both the good turn and the hallowed obligation due to suppliants, put to the sword the man who was his suppliant and friend, together with his children, in order to take for his own both Tamōs' possessions and his fleet.

When the Greek cities of Asia learned that Tissaphernes was on his way, they were deeply concerned for their future and dispatched ambassadors to the Lacedaemonians, begging them not to allow the cities to be laid waste by the barbarians. The Lacedaemonians promised to come to their aid and sent ambassadors to Tissaphernes to warn him not to commit any acts of aggression against the Greek cities. Tissaphernes, however, advancing with his army against the city of the Cymaeans first, both plundered its entire territory and got possession of many captives; after this he laid siege to the Cymaeans, but on the approach of winter, since he was unable to capture the city, he released the captives for a heavy ransom and raised the siege.

36. The Lacedaemonians appointed Thibron commander of the war against the King, gave him a thousand soldiers from their own citizens, ordered him to enlist as many troops from their allies as he should think desirable. Thibron, after going to Corinth and summoning soldiers from the allies to that city, set sail for Ephesus with not more than five thousand troops. Here he enrolled some two thousand soldiers from his own and other cities and then marched forth with a total force of over seven thousand. Advancing some one hundred and twenty stades, he came to Magnesia which was under the government of Tissaphernes; taking this city at the first assault, he then advanced speedily to Tralles in Ionia and began to lay siege to the city, but when he was unable to achieve any success because of its strong position, he turned back to Magnesia. And since the city was unwalled and Thibron therefore feared that at his departure Tissaphernes would get control of it, he transferred it to a neighbouring hill which men call Thorax; then Thibron, invading the territory of the enemy, glutted his soldiers with booty of every kind. But when Tissaphernes arrived with strong cavalry forces, he withdrew for security to Ephesus.

### *The founding of Adranum in Sicily and the death of Socrates the philosopher (37).*

37. At this same time a group of the soldiers who had served in the campaign with Cyrus and had got back safe to Greece went off each to his own country, but the larger part of them, about five thousand in number, since they had become accustomed to the life of a soldier, chose Xenophon for their general, and Xenophon with this army set out to make war on the Thracians who dwell around Salmydessus. The territory of this city, which lies on the left side of the Pontus, stretches for a great distance and is the cause of many shipwrecks. Accordingly the Thracians made it their practice to lie in wait in those parts and seize the merchants who were cast ashore as prisoners. Xenophon with the troops he had gathered invaded their territory, defeated them in battle, and burned most of their villages. After this, when Thibron sent for the soldiers with the promise to hire them, they withdrew to join him and made war with the Lacedaemonians against the Persians.

While these events were taking place, Dionysius founded in Sicily a city just below the crest of Mount Aetne and named it Adranum, after a certain famous temple. In Macedonia King Archelaüs was unintentionally struck while hunting by Craterus, whom he loved, and met his end, after a reign of seven years [418-399]. He was succeeded on the throne by Orestes, who was still a boy and was slain by Aeropus, his guardian, who held the throne for six years. In Athens Socrates the philosopher, who was accused by Anytus and Meletus of impiety and of corrupting the youth, was condemned to death and met his end by drinking the hemlock. But since the accusation had been undeserved, the people repented, considering that so great a man had been put to death; consequently they were angered at the accusers and ultimately put them to death without trial.

## The construction of the wall on the Chersonesus (38).

**38.** At the end of the year in Athens [399] Aristocrates entered the office of archon and in Rome the consular magistracy was taken over by six military tribunes; Gaius Servilius, Lucius Verginius, Quintus Sulpicius, Aulus Mutilius, and Manius Sergius. After these magistrates had entered office the Lacedaemonians, learning that Thibron was conducting the war inefficiently, dispatched Dercylidas as general to Asia; and he took over the army and advanced against the cities in the Troad. Now Hamaxitus and Colonae and Arisba he took at the first assault, then Ilium and Cerbenia and all the rest of the cities of the Troad, occupying some by craft and conquering the others by force. After this he concluded an armistice of eight months with Pharnabazus and advanced against the Thracians who were dwelling at that time in Bithynia; and after laying waste their territory he led his army off into winter quarters.

In Trachinian Heracleia civil discord had arisen and the Lacedaemonians sent Herippidas there to restore order. As soon as Herippidas arrived in Heracleia he called an assembly of the people, and surrounding them with his hoplites, he arrested the authors of the discord and put them all to death, some five hundred in number. And since the inhabitants about Oete had revolted, he made war on them, subjected them to many hardships, and forced them to leave their land. The majority of them, together with their children and wives, fled into Thessaly, from where they were restored to their homes five years later by the Boeotians.

While these events were taking place, the Thracians s invaded the Chersonesus in great multitudes, laid waste the whole region, and held its cities beleaguered. The inhabitants of the Chersonesus, being hard pressed in the war, sent for the Lacedaemonian Dercylidas to come from Asia. He, crossing over with his army, drove the Thracians out of the country and shut off the Chersonesus by a wall which he ran from sea to sea. By this act he prevented any future descent of the Thracians; and after being honoured with great gifts he transported his army to Asia.

**39.** Pharnabazus, after the truce had been made with the Lacedaemonians, went back to the King and won him over to the plan of preparing a fleet and appointing Conon the Athenian as its admiral; for Conon was experienced in the encounters of war and especially in combat with the present enemy, and although he excelled in warfare, he was at the time in Cyprus at the court of Evagoras the king. After the King had been persuaded, Pharnabazus took five hundred talents of silver and prepared to fit out a naval force. Sailing across to Cyprus, he ordered the kings there to make ready a hundred triremes and then, after discussions with Conon about the command of the fleet, he appointed him supreme commander at sea, giving indications in the name of the King of great hopes Conon might entertain. Conon, in the hope not only that he would recover the leadership in Greece for his native country if the Lacedaemonians were subdued in war but also that he would himself win great renown, accepted the command. Before the entire fleet had been made ready, he took the forty ships which were at hand and sailed across to Cilicia, where he began preparations for the war.

Pharnabazus and Tissaphernes gathered soldiers from their own satrapies and marched out, making their way towards Ephesus, since the enemy had their

## BOOK XIV

forces in that city. The army accompanying them numbered twenty thousand infantry and ten thousand cavalry. On hearing of the approach of the Persians Dercylidas, the commander of the Lacedaemonians, led out his army, having in all not more than seven thousand men, but when the forces drew near each other, they concluded a truce and set a period of time during which Pharnabazus should send word to the King regarding the terms of the treaty, should he be ready to end the war, and Dercylidas should explain the matter to the Spartans. So upon this understanding the commanders dispersed their armies.

**40.** The inhabitants of Rhegium, who were colonists of Chalcis, were angered to see the growing power of Dionysius. For he had sold into slavery the Naxians and Catanians, their kinsmen, and to the Rhegians, because they were of the same blood as these unfortunate peoples, this act was the cause of no ordinary concern, since all feared the same disaster would befall them. They therefore decided to take the field speedily against the tyrant before he became entirely secure. Their decision upon war was forthwith supported strongly also by the Syracusans who had been exiled by Dionysius, for most of them were at that time resident in Rhegium and were continually discussing the matter and pointing out that all the Syracusans would seize the occasion to join in an attack. In the end the Rhegians appointed generals and sent out with them six thousand infantry, six hundred cavalry, and fifty triremes. The generals crossed the strait and induced the generals of the Messenians to join in the war, declaring that it would be a terrible thing for them to stand idly by when Greek cities, and their neighbours, had been totally destroyed by the tyrant. Now the generals were won over by the Rhegians and, without obtaining a vote of the people, led forth their forces which consisted of four thousand infantry, four hundred cavalry, and thirty triremes. When the armaments we have mentioned had advanced as far as the borders of Messenê, opposition broke out among the soldiers due to a harangue delivered by the Messenian Laomedon; for he advised them not to begin a war against Dionysius who had done them no wrong. Accordingly the Messenian troops, since the people had not approved the war, followed his advice at once, and, deserting their generals, turned back home; and the Rhegians, since they were not strong enough alone for a battle, when they saw that the Messenians were disbanding their army, also turned back speedily to Rhegium. At the outset Dionysius had led out his army to the border of the Syracusan territory, awaiting the attack of the enemy; but when he learned of their retirement, he led his forces back to Syracuse. When the Rhegians and Messenians sent ambassadors to treat upon terms of peace, he decided that it was to his advantage to put an end to enmity against these states and concluded peace.

*The preparations made by Dionysius for the war against the Carthaginians and his manufacture of arms, in connection with which he invented the missile hurled by a catapult (41-44).*

**41.** When Dionysius observed that some of the Greeks were deserting to the Carthaginian domain, taking with them their cities and their estates, he concluded that so long as he was at peace with the Carthaginians many of his subjects would be wanting to join their defection, whereas, if there were war, all who had been enslaved by the Carthaginians would revolt to him. He also heard that many Carthaginians in Libya had fallen victims to a plague which had raged among them. Thinking for these reasons, then, that he had a favourable occasion for war, he decided that preparation should first be effected; for he assumed that the war would be a great and protracted one since he was entering a struggle with the most powerful people of Europe. At once, therefore, he gathered skilled workmen, commandeering them from the cities under his control and attracting them by high wages from Italy and Greece as well as Carthaginian territory. For his purpose was to make weapons in great numbers and every kind of missile, and also quadriremes and quinqueremes, no ship of the latter size having yet been built at that time. After collecting many skilled workmen, he divided them into groups in accordance with their skills, and appointed over them the most conspicuous citizens, offering great bounties to any who created a supply of arms. As for the armour, he distributed among them models of each kind, because he had gathered his mercenaries from many nations; for he was eager to have every one of his soldiers armed with the weapons of his people, conceiving that by such armour his army would, for this very reason, cause great consternation, and that in battle all of his soldiers would fight to best effect in armour to which they were accustomed. And since the Syracusans enthusiastically supported the policy of Dionysius, it came to pass that rivalry rose high to manufacture the arms. For not only was every space, such as the porticoes and back rooms of the temples as well as the gymnasia and colonnades of the market place, crowded with workers, but the making of great quantities of arms went on, apart from such public places, in the most distinguished homes.

**42.** In fact the catapult was invented at this time in Syracuse, since the ablest skilled workmen had been gathered from everywhere into one place. The high wages as well as the numerous prizes offered the workmen who were judged to be the best stimulated their zeal. Over and above these factors, Dionysius circulated daily among the workers, conversed with them in kindly fashion, and rewarded the most zealous with gifts and invited them to his table. Consequently the workmen brought unsurpassable devotion to the devising of many missiles and engines of war that were strange and capable of rendering great service. He also began the construction of quadriremes and quinqueremes, being the first to think of the construction of such ships. For, hearing that triremes had first been built in Corinth, he was intent, in his city that had been settled by a colony from there, on increasing the scale of naval construction. After obtaining leave to transport timber from Italy he dispatched half of his woodmen to Mount Aetne, on which there were heavy stands at that time of both excellent fir and pine, while the other half he dispatched to Italy, where he got ready teams to convey the timber to the sea, as well as boats and crews to bring the worked wood speedily to Syracuse. When Dionysius had collected an adequate supply of wood, he began at one and the same time to build more than two hundred ships and to refit the one hundred and ten he already had; and he also constructed all about the Great Harbour, as it is now called, one hundred and sixty costly shipsheds, most of which could accommodate two vessels, and repaired the one hundred and fifty which were already there.

**43.** With so many arms and ships under construction at one place the beholder was filled with utter wonder at the sight. For whenever a man gazed at the eagerness shown in the building of the ships, he thought that every Greek in

Sicily was engaged on their construction; and when, on the other hand, he visited the places where men were making arms and engines of war, he thought that all available labour was engaged in this alone. Moreover, despite the unsurpassable zeal devoted to the products we have mentioned, there were made one hundred and forty thousand shields and a like number of daggers and helmets; and in addition corselets were made ready, of every design and wrought with utmost art, more than fourteen thousand in number. These Dionysius expected to distribute to his cavalry and the commanders of the infantry, as well as to the mercenaries who were to form his bodyguard. He also had catapults made of every style and a large number of the other missiles. For half of the ships of war which were prepared, the pilots, officers at the bow, and rowers were drawn from citizens, while for the rest of the vessels Dionysius hired mercenaries. When the building of the ships and the making of arms were completed, Dionysius turned his attention to the gathering of soldiers; for he believed it advantageous not to hire them far in advance in order to avoid heavy expenses.

In this year Astydamas, the writer of tragedies, produced his first play; and he lived sixty years.

The Romans were besieging Veii, and when a sortie was made from the city, some of the Romans were cut to pieces by the Veientes and others escaped by shameful flight.

**44.** When this year had come to an end, Ithycles was archon in Athens [398] and in Rome five military tribunes were established in place of the consuls, Lucius Julius, Marcus Furius, Marcus Aemilius, Gaius Cornelius, and Caeso Fabius. Dionysius, the tyrant of the Syracusans, as soon as the major part of the task of making arms and building a fleet was completed, turned at once to the gathering of soldiers. From the Syracusans he enrolled those who were fit for military service in companies and from the cities subject to him he summoned their able men. He also gathered mercenaries from Greece, and especially from the Lacedaemonians, for they, in order to aid him in building up his power, gave him permission to enlist as many mercenaries from them as he might wish. Speaking generally, since he made a point of gathering his mercenary force from many nations and promised high pay, he found men who were responsive. Since Dionysius was going to raise up a great war, he addressed himself to the cities of Sicily with courtesy, eliciting their goodwill. He saw that the Rhegians and Messenians who dwelt on the Strait had a strong army mobilised and he feared that, when the Carthaginians crossed over to Sicily, they would join the Carthaginians; for these cities would add no little weight to the side with which they allied themselves for the war. Since these considerations were the cause of great concern to Dionysius, he made a present to the Messenians of a large piece of territory on their borders, binding them to him by such a benefaction; and to the Rhegians he dispatched ambassadors, urging them to form a connection by marriage and to give him in marriage a maiden who was a citizen of theirs; and he promised that he would win for them a large section of neighbouring territory and do all that was in his power to add to the strength of their city. For since his wife, the daughter of Hermocrates, had been slain at the time the cavalry revolted, he was eager to beget children, in the belief that the loyalty of his offspring would be the strongest safeguard of his tyrannical power. Nevertheless, when an assembly of the people was held in Rhegium to consider Dionysius' proposal, after much discussion the Rhegians voted not to accept the marriage connection. Now that Dionysius had failed of this design, he dispatched his ambassadors for the same purpose to the people of the [Epizephyrian] Locrians. When they voted to approve the marriage connection, Dionysius sued for the hand of Doris, the daughter of Xenetus, who at that time was their most esteemed citizen. A few days before the marriage he sent to Locri a quinquereme, the first one he had built, embellished with silver and gold furnishings; on this he had the maiden conveyed to Syracuse, where he led her into the acropolis. And he also sought in marriage from among the people of his city the most notable maiden among them, Aristomache [daughter of Hipparinus, sister of Dion], for whom he dispatched a chariot drawn by four white horses to bring her to his own home.

### How war broke out between the Carthaginians and Dionysius (45-47).

**45.** After Dionysius had taken in marriage both maidens at the same time, he gave a series of public dinners for the soldiers and the larger part of the citizens; for he now renounced the oppressive aspect of his tyranny, and changing to a course of equitable dealing, he ruled over his subjects in more humane fashion, no more putting them to death or banishing them, as had been his practice. After his marriages he let a few days pass and then called an assembly of the Syracusans and urged them to make war against the Carthaginians, declaring that they were most hostile to all Greeks generally and that they had designs at every opportunity on the Greeks of Sicily in particular. For the present, he pointed out, the Carthaginians were inactive because of the plague which had broken out among them and had destroyed the larger part of the inhabitants of Libya, but when they had recovered their strength, they would not refrain from attacking the Sicilian Greeks, against whom they had been plotting from the earliest time. It was therefore preferable, he continued, to wage a decisive war upon them while they were weak than to wait and compete when they were strong. At the same time he pointed out how terrible a thing it was to allow the Greek cities to be enslaved by barbarians, and that these cities would the more zealously join in the war, the more eagerly they desired to obtain their freedom. After speaking at length in support of his policy he speedily won the approval of the Syracusans. Indeed they were no less eager than he for war, first of all because of their hatred of the Carthaginians who were the cause of their being compelled to take orders from the tyrant; secondly, because they hoped that Dionysius would treat them in more humane fashion because of his fear of the enemy and of an attack upon him by the citizens he had enslaved; but most of all, because they hoped that once they had got weapons in their hand, they could strike for their liberty, let Fortune but give them the opportunity.

**46.** After the meeting of the assembly the Syracusans, with the permission of Dionysius, seized as plunder the property of the Phoenicians; for no small number of Carthaginians had their homes in Syracuse and rich possessions, and many also of their merchants had vessels in the harbour loaded with goods, all of which the Syracusans plundered. Similarly the rest of the Sicilian Greeks drove out the Phoenicians who dwelt among them and plundered their possessions; for although they hated the tyranny of Dionysius, they were still glad to join in the

## Book XIV

war against the Carthaginians because of the cruelty of that people. For the very same reasons, too, the inhabitants of the Greek cities under the rule of the Carthaginians, as soon as Dionysius publicly enacted war, made open display of their hatred of the Phoenicians; for not only did they seize their property as plunder, but they also laid hands on their persons and subjected them to every kind of physical torture and outrage, remembering what they had themselves suffered during the time of their captivity. So far did they go in the vengeance they wreaked on the Phoenicians both at this time and subsequently, that the Carthaginians were taught the lesson no more to transgress the law in their treatment of conquered peoples; for they did not fail to realise, learning as they did by very deeds, that in war Fortune is impartial to both combatants and in defeat both sides must suffer the same sort of thing that they themselves have done to those who were unfortunate.

Now when Dionysius had made ready all his preparations for the war, he determined to send messengers to Carthage with the announcement: The Syracusans declare war upon the Carthaginians unless they restore freedom to the Greek cities that they have enslaved.

Dionysius, then, was engaged in the affairs we have discussed.

Ctesias the historian ended with this year his *History of the Persians,* which began with Ninus and Semiramis. And in this year the most distinguished composers of dithyrambs were in their prime, Philoxenus of Cythera, Timotheiis of Miletus, Telestus of Selinus, and Polyeidus, who was also expert in the arts of painting and music.

**47.** At the close of the year, in Athens [397] Lysiades [Suniades?] became archon, and in Rome six military tribunes administered the office of consul, Popilius Mallius, Publius Maelius, Spurius Furius, and Lucius Publius. When Dionysius, the tyrant of the Syracusans, had completed all his preparations for the war according to his personal design, he sent a herald to Carthage, having given him a letter to the senate, which contained the statement that the Syracusans had resolved to make war upon the Carthaginians unless they withdrew from the Greek cities. The herald accordingly, pursuant to his orders, sailed to Libya and delivered the letter to the senate. When it had been read in the council and subsequently before the people, it came about that the Carthaginians were not a little distressed at the thought of war; for the plague had killed great numbers of them, and they were also totally unprepared.

Nevertheless, they waited for the Syracusans to take the initiative and dispatched members of the senate with large sums of money to recruit mercenaries in Europe.

Dionysius with the Syracusans, the mercenaries, and his allies marched forth from Syracuse and made his way towards Eryx. For not far from this hill lay the city of Motyê, a Carthaginian colony, which they used as their chief base of operations against Sicily; and Dionysius hoped that with this city in his power he would have no small advantage over his enemies. In the course of his march he received from time to time the contingents from the Greek cities, supplying the full levy of each with arms; for they were all eager to join his campaign, hating as they did the heavy hand of Phoenician domination and relishing the prospect at last of freedom. He received first the levy from Camarina, then those of Gela and Acragas; and after these he sent for the Himeraeans, whose home was on the other side of Sicily, and after adding the men of Selinus, as he passed by, he arrived at Motyê with all his army. He had eighty thousand infantry, well over three thousand cavalry, and a little less than two hundred warships, and he was accompanied by not less than five hundred merchantmen loaded with great numbers of engines of war and all the other supplies needed.

### How Dionysius reduced by siege Motyê, a notable city of the Carthaginians (48-53).

**48.** Since the armament was on the great scale we have described, the people of Eryx were awed by the magnitude of the force and, hating the Carthaginians as they did, came over to Dionysius. The inhabitants of Motyê, however, expecting aid from the Carthaginians, were not dismayed at Dionysius' armament, but made ready to withstand a siege; for they were not unaware that the Syracusans would make Motyê the first city to sack, because it was most loyal to the Carthaginians. This city was situated on an island lying six stades off Sicily, and was embellished artistically to the last degree with numerous fine houses, thanks to the prosperity of the inhabitants. It also had a narrow artificial causeway extending to the shore of Sicily, which the Motyans breached at this time, in order that the enemy should have no approach against them.

Dionysius, after reconnoitring the area, together with his engineers, began to construct moles leading to Motyê, hauled the warships up on land at the entrance of the harbour, and moored the merchantmen along the beach. After this he left his brother Leptines admiral in command of the works, while he himself set out with the infantry of his army against the cities that were allies of the Carthaginians. Now the Sicani, fearing the great size of the army, all went over to the Syracusans, and of the rest of the cities only five remained loyal to the Carthaginians, these being Halicyae, Solus, Aegesta, Panormus, and Entella. Hence Dionysius plundered the territory of Solus and Panormus, and that also of Halicyae, and cut down the trees on it, but he laid siege to Aegesta and Entella with strong forces and launched continuous attacks upon them, seeking to get control of them by force. Such was the state of the affairs of Dionysius.

**49.** Himilcon, the general of the Carthaginians, being himself busy with the mustering of the armaments and other preparations, dispatched his admiral with ten triremes under orders to sail speedily in secret against the Syracusans, enter the harbour by night, and destroy the shipping left behind there. This he did, expecting to cause a diversion and force Dionysius to send part of his fleet back to the Syracusans. The admiral who had been dispatched carried out his orders with promptness and entered the harbour of the Syracusans by night while everyone was ignorant of what had taken place. Attacking unawares, he rammed the vessels lying at anchor along the shore, sank practically all of them, and then returned to Carthage. Dionysius, after ravaging all the territory held by the Carthaginians and forcing the enemy to take refuge behind walls, led all his army against Motyê; for he hoped that when this city had been reduced by siege, all the others would forthwith surrender themselves to him. Accordingly, he at once put many times more men on the task of filling up the strait between the city and the coast, and, as the mole was extended, advanced his engines of war little by little toward the walls.

## Book XIV

**50.** Meanwhile Himilcon, the admiral of the Carthaginians, hearing that Dionysius had hauled his warships up on land, manned at once his hundred best triremes; for he assumed that if he appeared unexpectedly, he should easily seize the vessels which were hauled up on land in the harbour, since he would be master of the sea. Once he succeeded in this, he believed, he would not only relieve the siege of Motyê but also transfer the war to the city of the Syracusans. Sailing forth, therefore, with one hundred ships, he arrived during the night at the territory of Selinus, skirted the promontory of Lilybaeum, and arrived at daybreak at Motyê. Since his appearance took the enemy by surprise, he disabled some of the vessels anchored along the shore by ramming and others by burning, for Dionysius was unable to come to their defence. After this he sailed into the harbour and drew up his ships as if to attack the vessels which the enemy had drawn up on land. Dionysius now massed his army at the entrance of the harbour; but when he saw that the enemy was lying in wait to attack as the ships left the harbour, he refused to risk launching his ships within the harbour, since he realised that the narrow entrance compelled a few ships to match themselves against an enemy many times more numerous. Consequently, using the multitude of his soldiers, he hauled his vessels over the land with no difficulty and launched them safely in the sea outside the harbour. Himilcon attacked the first ships, but was held back by the multitude of missiles; for Dionysius had manned the ships with a great number of archers and slingers, and the Syracusans slew many of the enemy by using from the land the catapults which shot sharp pointed missiles. Indeed this weapon created great dismay, because it was a new invention at this time. As a result, Himilcon was unable to achieve his design and sailed away to Libya, believing that a sea-battle would serve no end, since the enemy's ships were double his in number.

**51.** After Dionysius had completed the mole by employing a large force of labourers, he advanced war engines of every kind against the walls and kept hammering the towers with his battering-rams, while with the catapults he kept down the fighters on the battlements; and he also advanced against the walls his wheeled towers, six stories high, which he had built to equal the height of the houses. The inhabitants of Motyê, now that the threat was at hand-grips, were nevertheless not dismayed by the armament of Dionysius, even though they had for the moment no allies to help them. Surpassing the besiegers in thirst for glory, they in the first place raised up men in crow's-nests resting on yard-arms suspended from the highest possible masts, and these from their lofty positions hurled lighted fire-brands and burning tow with pitch on the enemies' siege engines. The flame quickly caught the wood, but the Sicilian Greeks, dashing to the rescue, swiftly quenched it; and meantime the frequent blows of the battering-rams broke down a section of the wall. Since now both sides rushed with one accord to the place, the battle that ensued grew furious. For the Sicilian Greeks, believing that the city was already in their hands, spared no effort in retaliating upon the Phoenicians for former injuries they had suffered at their hands, while the people of the city, envisioning the terrible fate of a life of captivity and seeing no possibility of flight either by land or by sea, faced death stoutly. And finding themselves shorn of the defence of the walls, they barricaded the narrow lanes and made the last houses provide a lavishly constructed wall. From this came even greater difficulties for the troops of

Dionysius. For after they had burst through the wall and seemed to be already masters of the city, they were raked by missiles from men posted in superior positions. Nevertheless, they advanced the wooden towers to the first houses and provided them with gangways; and since the siege machines were equal in height to the dwellings, the rest of the struggle was fought hand to hand. For the Sicilian Greeks would launch the gangways and force a passage by them on to the houses.

**52.** The Motyans, as they took account of the magnitude of the peril, and with their wives and children before their eyes, fought the more fiercely out of fear for their fate. There were some whose parents stood by entreating them not to let them be surrendered to the lawless will of victors, who were thus wrought to a pitch where they set no value on life; others, as they heard the laments of their wives and helpless children, sought to die like men rather than to see their children led into captivity. Flight of course from the city was impossible, since it was entirely surrounded by the sea, which was controlled by the enemy. Most appalling for the Phoenicians and the greatest cause of their despair was the thought how cruelly they had used their Greek captives and the prospect of their suffering the same treatment. Indeed there was nothing left for them but, fighting bravely, either to conquer or die. When such an obstinate mood filled the souls of the besieged, the Sicilian Greeks found themselves in a very difficult position, for fighting as they were from the suspended wooden bridges, they suffered grievously both because of the narrow quarters and because of the desperate resistance of their opponents, who had abandoned hope of life. As a result, some perished in hand-to-hand encounter as they gave and received wounds, and others, pressed back by the Motyans and tumbling from the wooden bridges, fell to their death on the ground. In the end, while the kind of siege we have described had lasted some days, Dionysius made it his practice always toward evening to sound the trumpet for the recall of the fighters and break off the siege. When he had accustomed the Motyans to such a practice, the combatants on both sides retiring, he dispatched Archylus of Thurii with the elite troops, who, when night had fallen, placed ladders against the fallen houses, and mounting by them, seized an advantageous spot where he admitted Dionysius' troops. The Motyans, when they perceived what had taken place, at once rushed to the rescue with all eagerness, and although they were too late, none the less faced the struggle. The battle grew fierce and abundant reinforcements climbed the ladders, until at last the Sicilian Greeks wore down their opponents by weight of numbers.

**53.** Straightway Dionysius' entire army burst into the city, coming also by the mole, and now every spot was a scene of mass slaughter; for the Sicilian Greeks, eager to return cruelty for cruelty, slew everyone they encountered, sparing without distinction not a child, not a woman, not an elder. Dionysius, wishing to sell the inhabitants into slavery for the money he could gather, at first attempted to restrain the soldiers from murdering the captives, but when no one paid any attention to him and he saw that the fury of the Sicilian Greeks was not to be controlled, he stationed heralds to cry aloud and tell the Motyans to take refuge in the temples which were revered by the Greeks. When this was done, the soldiers ceased their slaughter and turned to looting the property; and the plunder yielded much silver and not a little gold, as well as costly raiment and an abundance of every other product of felicity. The city was given over by Dionysius to the soldiers to plunder, since he wished to whet their appetites for future encounters. After this success he rewarded Archylus, who had been the first to mount the wall, with one hundred minas, and honoured according to their merits all others who had performed deeds of valour; he also sold as booty the Motyans who survived, but he crucified Daïmenes and other Greeks who had fought on the side of the Carthaginians and had been taken captive. After this Dionysius stationed guards in the city whom he put under the command of Biton of Syracuse; and the garrison was composed largely of Siceli. He ordered Leptines his admiral with one hundred and twenty ships to lie in wait for any attempt by the Carthaginians to cross to Sicily; and he also assigned to him the siege of Aegesta and Entella, in accordance with his original plan to sack them. Then, since the summer was already coming to a close, he marched back to Syracuse with his army.

In Athens Sophocles, the son of Sophocles, began to produce tragedies and won the first prize twelve times.

### *How the Aegestaeans set fire to the camp of Dionysius (54).*

**54.** When the year had come to an end, in Athens [396] Phormion assumed the archonship and in Rome six military tribunes took the place of the consuls, Gnaeus Genucius, Lucius Atilius, Marcus Pomponius, Gaius Duilius, Marcus Veturius, and Valerius Publilius; and the Ninety-sixth Olympiad was celebrated, that in which Eupolis of Elis was the victor. In the year when these magistrates entered office Dionysius, the tyrant of the Syracusans, set out from Syracuse with his entire army and invaded the domain of the Carthaginians. While he was laying waste the countryside, the Halicyaeans in dismay sent an embassy to him and concluded an alliance, but the Aegestaeans, falling unexpectedly by night on their besiegers and setting fire to the tents where they were camped, threw the men in the encampment into great confusion; for since the flames spread over a large area and the fire could not be brought under control, a few of the soldiers who came to the rescue lost their lives and most of the horses were burned, together with the tents. Now Dionysius ravaged the Carthaginian territory without meeting any opposition, and Leptines his admiral from his quarters in Motyê kept watch against any approach of the enemy by sea.

The Carthaginians, when they learned of the magnitude of the armament of Dionysius, resolved far to surpass him in their preparations. Consequently, lawfully according Himilcon sovereign power, they gathered armaments from all Libya as well as from Iberia, summoning some from their allies and in other cases hiring mercenaries. In the end they collected more than three hundred thousand infantry, four thousand cavalry in addition to chariots, which numbered four hundred, four hundred ships of war, and over six hundred other vessels to convey food and engines of war and other supplies. These are the numbers stated by Ephorus. Timaeus, on the other hand, says that the troops transported from Libya did not exceed one hundred thousand and declares that an additional thirty thousand were enlisted in Sicily.

## How the Carthaginians crossed over to Sicily with three hundred thousand soldiers and made war upon Dionysius and the retreat of Dionysius to Syracuse (55).

55. Himilcon gave sealed orders to all the pilots with commands to open them after they had sailed and to carry out the instructions. He devised this scheme in order that no spy should be able to report to Dionysius where they would put in; and the orders read for them to put in at Panormus. When a favourable wind arose, all the vessels cast off their cables and the transports put out to open sea, but the triremes sailed into the Libyan Sea and skirted the land. The wind continued favourable, and as soon as the leading vessels of the transports were visible from Sicily, Dionysius dispatched Leptines with thirty triremes under orders to ram and destroy all he could intercept. Leptines sailed forth promptly and straightway sank, together with their men, the first ships he encountered, but the rest, having all canvas spread and catching the wind with their sails, easily made their escape. Nevertheless, fifty ships were sunk, together with five thousand soldiers and two hundred chariots.

After Himilcon had put in at Panormus and disembarked his army, he advanced toward the enemy, ordering the triremes to sail along beside him; and having himself taken Eryx by treachery as he passed, he took up quarters before Motyê. Since Dionysius and his army were during this time at Aegeste, Himilcon reduced Motyê by siege. Although the Sicilian Greeks were eager for a battle, Dionysius conceived it to be better, both because he was widely separated from his allied cities and because the transport of his food supplies was reduced, to renew the war in other areas. Having decided, therefore, to break camp, he proposed to the Sicani to abandon their cities for the present and to join him in the campaign; and in return he promised to give them richer territory of about equal size and, at the conclusion of the war, to return to their native cities any who so wished. Of the Sicani only a few, fearing that, if they refused, they would be plundered by the soldiers, agreed to Dionysius' offer. The Halicyaeans similarly deserted him and sent ambassadors to the Carthaginian camp and concluded an alliance with them. And Dionysius set out for Syracuse, laying waste the territory through which he led his army.

## The Carthaginian expedition to the Straits and the capture of Messenê (56-58).

56. Himilcon, now that his affairs were proceeding as he wished, made preparations to lead his army against Messenê, being anxious to get control of the city because of its favourable facilities; for it had an excellent harbour, capable of accommodating all his ships, which numbered more than six hundred, and Himilcon also hoped that by getting possession of the straits he would be able to bar any aid from the Italian Greeks and hold in check the fleets that might come from the Peloponnesus. With this programme in mind, he formed relations of friendship with the Himeraeans and the dwellers in the fort of Cephaloedium, and seizing the city of Lipara, he exacted thirty talents from the inhabitants of the island. Then he set out in person with his entire army toward Messenê, his ships sailing along the coast beside him. Completing the distance in a brief time, he pitched his camp at Peloris, at a distance of one hundred stades from Messenê. When the inhabitants of this city learned that the enemy was at hand, they could

not agree among themselves about the war. One party, when they heard reports of the great size of the enemy's army and observed that they themselves were without any allies - what is more, that their own cavalry were at Syracuse - were fully convinced that nothing could save them from capture. What contributed most to their despair was the fact that their walls had fallen down and that the situation allowed no time for their repair. Consequently they removed from the city their children and wives and most valuable possessions to neighbouring cities. Another party of the Messenians, however, hearing of a certain ancient oracle of theirs which ran, "Carthaginians must be bearers of water in Messenê," interpreted the utterance to their advantage, believing that the Carthaginians would serve as slaves in Messenê. Consequently not only were they in a hopeful mood, but they made many others eager to face battle for their freedom. At once, then, they selected the ablest troops from among their young men and dispatched them to Peloris to prevent the enemy from entering their territory.

**57.** While the Messenians were busied in this way, Himilcon, seeing that they had sallied against his place of landing, dispatched two hundred ships against the city, for he hoped, as well he might, that while the soldiers were trying to prevent his landing, the crews of the ships would easily seize Messenê, stripped of defenders as it was. A north wind sprang up and the ships with all canvas spread entered the harbour, while the Messenians who were on guard at Peloris, in spite of their hurried return, failed to arrive before the ships. Consequently the Carthaginians invested Messenê, forced their way through the fallen walls, and made themselves masters of the city. Of the Messenians, some were slain as they put up a gallant fight, others fled to the nearest cities, but the great mass of the common people took to flight through the surrounding mountains and scattered among the fortresses of the territory; of the rest, some were captured by the enemy and some, who had been cut off in the area near the harbour, hurled themselves into the sea in hopes of swimming across the intervening strait. These numbered more than two hundred and most of them were overcome by the current, only fifty making their way in safety to Italy. Himilcon now brought his entire army into the city and at first set to work to reduce the forts over the countryside; but since they were strongly situated and the men who had fled to them put up gallant struggles, he retired to the city, having found himself unable to master them. After this he refreshed his army and made preparations to advance against Syracuse.

**58.** The Siceli, who had hated Dionysius from of old and now had an opportunity to revolt, went over in a body, with the exception of the people of Assorus, to the Carthaginians. In Syracuse Dionysius set free the slaves and manned sixty ships from their numbers; he also summoned over a thousand mercenaries from the Lacedaemonians, and went about the countryside strengthening the fortresses and storing them with provisions. He was most concerned, however, to fortify the citadels of the Leontines and to store in them the harvest from the plains. He also persuaded the Campanians who were dwelling in Catane to move to Aetne, as it is now called, since it was an exceptionally strong fortress. After this he led forth his entire army one hundred and sixty stades from Syracuse and encamped near Taurus, as it is called. He had at that time thirty thousand infantry, more than three thousand cavalry, and one hundred and eighty ships of war, of which only a few were triremes.

Himilcon threw down the walls of Messenê and issued orders to his soldiers to raze to the ground the dwellings, and to leave not a tile or timber or anything else but either to burn or break them. When the many hands of the soldiers speedily accomplished this task, no one would have known that the site had been occupied. For, reflecting that the place was far separated from the cities which were his allies and yet was the most strategically situated of any in Sicily, he had determined that he would see either that it was kept uninhabited or that it was an arduous and prolonged task to rebuild it.

### The great sea-battle between the Carthaginians and Dionysius and the victory of the Carthaginians (59-62).

59. After Himilcon had exhibited his hatred for the Greeks by the calamity he visited upon the Messenians, he dispatched Magon his admiral with his naval armament under orders to sail to the peak known as Taurus [Tauromenium]. This area had been taken by Siceli in large numbers, who, however, had no leader. They had formerly been given by Dionysius the territory of the Naxians, but at this time, having been induced by Himilcon's offers, they occupied this peak. Since it was a strong position, both at this time and subsequent to the war, they made it their home, throwing a wall about it, and since those who gathered remained (*meneiri*) upon Taurus, they named the city Tauromenium.

Himilcon, advancing with his land forces, made so rapid a march that he arrived at the place we have mentioned in the territory of Naxos at the same time as Magon put in there by sea. Since there had recently been a fiery eruption from Mt. Aetne as far as the sea, it was no longer possible for the land forces to advance in the company of the ships as they sailed beside them; for the regions along the sea were laid waste by the lava, as it is called, so that the land army had to take its way around the peak of Aetne. Consequently he gave orders to Magon to come to port at Catane, while he himself advanced speedily through the heart of the country with the intention of joining the ships on the Catanaean shore; for he was concerned lest, when his forces were divided, the Sicilian Greeks should fight a battle with Magon at sea, and this is what actually took place. For Dionysius, when he realised that Magon had a short sail, whereas the route of the land forces was toilsome and long, hastened to Catane with the object of attacking Magon by sea before the arrival of Himilcon. His hope was that his land forces lined up along the coast would embolden his own troops while the enemy would be the more fearful, and, what was the most important consideration, that if he should suffer a reverse of some kind, the ships in distress would be able to take refuge in the camp of the land forces. With this purpose in mind, he dispatched Leptines with his whole fleet under orders to engage with his ships in close order, and not to break his line lest he be endangered by the great numbers of his opponents; for, including merchantmen and oared vessels with brazen beaks, Magon had no less than five hundred ships.

60. When the Carthaginians saw the shore thronged with infantry and the ships of the Greeks bearing down on them, they were at once not a little alarmed and began to make for the land; but later, when they realised the risk they ran of destruction in giving battle at the same time both to the fleet and to the infantry,

they quickly changed their mind. Deciding, therefore, to face the battle at sea, they drew up their ships and awaited the approach of the enemy. Leptines advanced with his thirty best vessels far ahead of the rest and joined battle, in no cowardly fashion, but without prudence. Attacking forthwith the leading ships of the Carthaginians, at the outset he sank no small number of the opposing triremes; but when Magon's massed ships crowded about the thirty, the forces of Leptines surpassed in valour, but the Carthaginians in numbers. Consequently, as the battle grew fiercer, the steersmen laid their ships broadside in the fighting and the struggle came to resemble conflicts on land. For they did not drive upon the opposing ships from a distance in order to ram them, but the vessels were locked together and the fighting was hand to hand. Some, as they leaped for the enemy's ships, fell into the sea, and others, who succeeded in their attempt, continued the struggle on the opponents' ships. In the end Leptines was driven off and compelled to flee to the open sea, and his remaining ships, attacking without order, were overcome by the Carthaginians; for the defeat suffered by the admiral raised the spirits of the Phoenicians and markedly discouraged the Sicilian Greeks.

After the battle had ended in the manner we have described, the Carthaginians pursued with even greater ardour the enemy who were fleeing in disorder and destroyed more than one hundred of their ships, and stationing their lighter craft along the shore, they slew any of the sailors who were swimming toward the land army. As they perished in great numbers not far from the land, while the troops of Dionysius were unable to help them in any way, the whole region was full of corpses and wreckage. There perished in the sea battle no small number of Carthaginians, but the loss of the Sicilian Greeks amounted to more than one hundred ships and over twenty thousand men. After the battle the Phoenicians anchored their triremes in the harbour of Catane, took in tow the ships they had captured, and when; they had brought them in, repaired them, so that they made the greatness of their success not only a tale for the ears but also a sight for the eyes of the Carthaginians.

**61.** The Sicilian Greeks made their way toward Syracuse, but as they reflected that they would certainly be invested and forced to endure a laborious siege, they urged Dionysius to seek an immediate encounter with Himilcon because of his past victory; for, they said, perhaps their unexpected appearance would strike terror into the barbarians and they could repair their late reverse. Dionysius was at first won over by these advisers and ready to lead his army against Himilcon, but when some of his friends told him that he ran the risk of losing the city if Magon should set out with his entire fleet against Syracuse, he quickly changed his mind; and in fact he knew that Messenê had fallen to the hands of the barbarians in a similar manner. So, believing that it was not safe to strip the city of defenders, he set out for Syracuse. The majority of the Sicilian Greeks, being angered at his unwillingness to encounter the enemy, deserted Dionysius, some of them departing to their own countries and others to fortresses in the neighbourhood.

Himilcon, who had reached in two days the coast of the Catanaeans, hauled all the ships up on land, since a strong wind had arisen, and, while resting his forces for some days, sent ambassadors to the Campanians who held Aetne, urging them to revolt from Dionysius. He promised both to give them a large amount of territory and to let them share in the spoils of the war; he also informed them that the Campanians dwelling in Entella found no fault with the Carthaginians and took their side against the Sicilian Greeks, and he pointed out that as a general thing the Greeks as a race are the enemies of all other peoples. but since the Campanians had given hostages to Dionysius and had sent their choicest troops to Syracuse, they were compelled to maintain the alliance with Dionysius, although they would gladly have joined the Carthaginians.

**62.** After this Dionysius, who was in terror of the Carthaginians, sent his brother-in-law Polyxenus as ambassador both to the Greeks in Italy and to the Lacedaemonians, as well as the Corinthians, begging them to come to his aid and not to suffer the Greek cities of Sicily to be utterly destroyed. He also sent to the Peloponnesus men with ample funds to recruit mercenaries, ordering them to enlist as many soldiers as they could without regard to economy. Himilcon decked his ships with the spoils taken from the enemy and put in at the great harbour of the Syracusans, and he caused great dismay among the inhabitants of the city. For two hundred and fifty ships of war entered the harbour, with oars flashing in order and richly decked with the spoils of war; then came the merchantmen, in excess of three thousand, laden with more than five hundred . . .; and the whole fleet numbered some two thousand vessels. The result was that the harbour of the Syracusans, despite its great size, was blocked up by the vessels and it was almost entirely concealed from view by the sails. The ships had just come to anchor when at once from the other side the land army advanced, consisting, as some have reported, of three hundred thousand infantry and three thousand cavalry. The general of the armaments, Himilcon, took up his quarters in the temple of Zeus and the rest of the multitude encamped in the neighbourhood twelve stades from the city. After this Himilcon led out the entire army and drew up his troops in battle order before the walls, challenging the Syracusans to battle; and he also sailed up to the harbours with a hundred of his finest ships in order to strike terror into the inhabitants of the city and to force them to concede that they were inferior at sea as well. But when no one ventured to come out against him, for the time being he withdrew his troops to the camp and then for thirty days overran the countryside, cutting down the trees and laying it all waste, in order not only to satisfy the soldiers with every kind of plunder, but also to reduce the besieged to despair.

*The plundering by the Carthaginians of the temples of both Demeter and Corê (63).*

*The retribution by the gods upon the plunderers of the temples and the destruction of the Carthaginian host by a pestilence (63, 70-71).*

**63.** Himilcon seized the suburb of Achradine; and he also plundered the temples of both Demeter and Core, for which acts of impiety against the divinity he quickly suffered a fitting penalty. For his fortune quickly worsened from day to day, and whenever Dionysius made bold to skirmish with him, the Syracusans had the better of it. Also at night unaccountable tumults would arise in the camp and the soldiers would rush to arms, thinking that the enemy was attacking the palisade. To this was added a plague which was the cause of every kind of

# Book XIV

suffering. Of this we shall speak a little later, in order that our account may not anticipate the proper time.

Now when he threw a wall about the camp, Himilcon destroyed practically all the tombs in the area, among which was that of Gelon and his wife Demarete, of costly construction. He also built three forts along the sea, one at Plemmyrium, one at the middle of the harbour, and one by the temple of Zeus, and into them he brought wine and grain and all other provisions, believing that the siege would continue a long time. He also dispatched merchant ships to Sardinia and Libya to secure grain and every kind of food. Polyxenus, the brother-in-law of Dionysius, arrived from the Peloponnesus and Italy, bringing thirty warships from his allies, with Pharacidas the Lacedaemonian as admiral.

### The sea-battle between the Syracusans and the Carthaginians and the victory of the Syracusans (64).

**64.** After this Dionysius and Leptines had set out with warships to escort a supply of provisions; and the Syracusans, who were thus left to themselves, seeing by chance a vessel approaching laden with food, sailed out against it with five ships, seized it, and brought it to the city. The Carthaginians put out against them with forty ships, whereupon the Syracusans manned all their ships and in the ensuing battle both captured the flag-ship and destroyed twenty-four of the remainder; and then, pursuing the fleeing ships as far as the enemy's anchorage, they challenged the Carthaginians to battle. When the latter, confused at the unexpected turn of events, made no move, the Syracusans took the captured ships in tow and brought them to the city. Elated at their success and thinking how often Dionysius had met defeat, whereas they, without his presence, had won a victory over the Carthaginians, they were now puffed up with pride. And as they gathered in groups they talked together about how they took no steps to end their slavery to Dionysius, even though they had an opportunity to depose him; for up until then they had been without arms, but now because of the war they had weapons at their command. Even while discussions of this kind were taking place, Dionysius sailed into the harbour and, calling an assembly, praised the Syracusans and urged them to be of good courage, promising that he would speedily put an end to the war. And he was on the point of dismissing the assembly when Theodorus, a Syracusan, who was held in high esteem among the cavalry and was considered a man of action, made bold to speak as follows in regard to their liberty.

### The speech in the assembly on freedom by Theodoras (65-69).

**65.** "Although Dionysius has introduced some falsehoods, the last statement he made was true: that he would speedily put an end to the war. He could accomplish this if he were no longer our commander. for he has often been defeated, but had returned to the citizens the freedom their fathers enjoyed. As things are, no one of us faces battle with good courage so long as victory differs not a whit from defeat; for if conquered, we shall have to obey the commands of the Carthaginians, and if conquerors, to have in Dionysius a harsher master than they would be. For even should the Carthaginians defeat us in war, they would only impose a fixed tribute and would not prevent us from governing the city in accordance with our ancient laws; but this man has plundered our temples, has taken the property of private citizens together with the lives of their owners, and pays a wage to servants to secure the enslavement of their masters. Such horrors as attend the storming of cities are perpetrated by him in time of peace, yet he promises to put an end to the war with the Carthaginians. But it behooves us, fellow citizens, to put an end not only to the Phoenician war but to the tyrant within our walls. For the acropolis, which is guarded by the weapons of slaves, is a hostile redoubt in our city; the multitude of mercenaries has been gathered to hold the Syracusans in slavery; and he lords it over the city, not like a magistrate dispensing justice on equal terms, but like a dictator who by policy makes all decisions for his own advantage. For the time being the enemy possess a small portion of our territory, but Dionysius has devastated it all and given it to those who join in increasing his tyranny.

"How long, then, are we to be patient though we suffer such abuses as brave men endure to die rather than experience them? In battle against the Carthaginians we bravely face the final sacrifice, but against a harsh tyrant, in behalf of freedom and our fatherland, even in speech we no longer dare to raise our voices; we face in battle so many myriads of the enemy, but we stand in shivering fear of a single ruler, who has not the manliness of a superior slave.

**66.** "Surely no one would think of comparing Dionysius with Gelon of old. For Gelon, by reason of his own high character, together with the Syracusans and the rest of the Sicilian Greeks, set free the whole of Sicily, whereas this man, who found the cities free, has delivered all the rest of them over to the lordship of the enemy and has himself enslaved his native state. Gelon fought so far forward in behalf of Sicily that he never let his allies in the cities even catch sight of the enemy, whereas this man, after fleeing from Motyê through the entire length of the island, has cooped himself up within our walls, full of confidence against his fellow citizens, but unable to bear even the sight of the enemy. As a consequence Gelon, by reason both of his high character and of his great deeds, received the leadership by the free will not only of the Syracusans but also of the Sicilian Greeks, while, as for this man whose generalship has led to the destruction of his allies and the enslavement of his fellow citizens, how can he escape the just hatred of all? For not only is he unworthy of leadership but, if justice were done, would die ten thousand deaths. Because of him Gela and Camarina were subdued, Messenê lies in total ruin, twenty thousand allies are perished in a sea-battle, and, in a word, we have been enclosed in one city and all the other Greek cities throughout Sicily have been destroyed. For in addition to his other malefactions he sold into slavery Naxos and Catane; he has completely destroyed cities that were allies, cities whose existence was opportune. With the Carthaginians he has fought two battles and has come out vanquished in each. Yet when he was entrusted with a generalship by the citizens but one time, he speedily robbed them of their freedom, slaying those who spoke openly on behalf of the laws and exiling the more wealthy; he gave the wives of the banished in marriage to slaves and to a motley throng; he put the weapons of citizens in the hands of barbarians and foreigners. These deeds, O Zeus and all the gods, were the work of a public clerk, of a desperate man.

**67.** "Where, then, is the Syracusans' love of freedom? Where the deeds of our ancestors? I say nothing of the three hundred thousand Carthaginians who were totally destroyed at Himera; I pass by the overthrow of the tyrants who followed Gelon, but only yesterday, as it were, when the Athenians attacked Syracuse with such great armaments, our fathers left not a man free to carry back word of the disaster. Shall we, who have such great examples of our fathers' valour, take orders from Dionysius, especially when we have weapons in our hands? Surely some divine providence has gathered us here, with allies about us and weapons in our hands, for the purpose of recovering our freedom, and it is within our power this day to play the part of brave men and rid ourselves with one accord of our heavy yoke. Hitherto, while we were disarmed and without allies and guarded by a multitude of mercenaries, we have, I dare say, yielded to the pressure of circumstances; but now, since we have arms in our hands and allies to give us aid as well as bear witness of our bravery, let us not yield but make it clear that it was circumstances, not cowardice, that made us submit to slavery. Are we not ashamed that we should have as commander in our wars the man who has plundered the temples of our city and that we choose as representative in such important matters a person to whom no man of good sense would entrust the management of his private affairs? And though all other peoples in times of war, because of the great perils they face, observe with the greatest care their obligations to the gods, do we expect that a man of such notorious impiety will put an end to the war?

**68.** "In fact, if a man cares to put a finer point on it, he will find that Dionysius is as wary of peace as he is of war. For he believes that, as matters stand, the Syracusans, because of their fear of the enemy, will not attempt anything against him, but that once the Carthaginians have been defeated they will claim their freedom, since they will have weapons in their hands and will be proudly conscious of their deeds. Indeed this is the reason, in my opinion, why in the first war he betrayed Gela and Camarina and made these cities desolate, and why in his negotiations he agreed that most of the Greek cities should be given over to the enemy. After this he broke faith in time of peace with Naxos and Catane and sold the inhabitants into slavery, razing one to the ground and giving the other to the Campanians from Italy to dwell in. And when, after the destruction of these peoples, the rest of Sicily made many attempts to overthrow his tyranny, he again declared war upon the Carthaginians; for his scruple against breaking his agreement in violation of the oaths he had taken was not so great as his fear of the surviving concentrations of the Sicilian Greeks.

"Moreover, it is obvious that he has been at all times on the alert to effect their destruction. First of all at Panormus, when the enemy were disembarking and were in bad physical condition after the stormy passage, he could have offered battle, but did not choose to do so. After that he stood idly by and sent no help to Messenê, a city strategically situated and of great size, but allowed it to be razed, not only in order that the greatest possible number of Sicilian Greeks should perish, but also that the Carthaginians might intercept the reinforcements from Italy and the fleets from the Peloponnesus. Last of all, he joined battle offshore at Catane, careless of the advantage of pitching battle near the city, where the vanquished could find safety in their own harbours. After the battle, when strong winds sprang up and the Carthaginians were forced to haul their fleet up on land, he had a most favourable opportunity for victory; for the land forces of the enemy had not yet arrived and the violent storm was driving the enemy's ships on the shore. At that time, if we had all attacked on land, the only outcomes left the enemy would have been, either to be captured with ease, if they left their ships, or to strew the coast with: wreckage, if they matched their strength against the waves.

**69.** "But to lodge accusations against Dionysius at greater length among Syracusans is, I should judge, not necessary. For if men who have suffered in very deed such irretrievable ruin are not roused to rage, will they, forsooth, be moved by words to wreak vengeance upon him, men too who have seen his behaviour as the worst of citizens, the harshest of tyrants, the most ignoble of all generals? For as often as we have stood in line of battle under his command, so often have we been defeated, whereas but just now, when we fought independently, we defeated with a few ships the enemy's entire force. We should, therefore, seek out another leader, to avoid fighting under a general who has pillaged the shrines of the gods and so finding ourselves engaged in a war against the gods; for it is manifest that heaven opposes those who have selected the worst enemy of religion to be their commander. Noting that when he is present our armies in full force suffer defeat, whereas, when he is absent, even a small detachment is sufficient to defeat the Carthaginians, should not all men see in this the visible presence of the gods? Therefore, fellow citizens, if he is willing to lay down his office of his own accord, let us allow him to leave the city with his possessions; but if he does not choose to do so, we have at the present moment the fairest opportunity to assert our freedom. We are all gathered together; we have weapons in our hands; we have allies about us, not only the Greeks from Italy but also those from the Peloponnesus. The chief command must be given, according to the laws, either to citizens, or to the Corinthians who dwell in our mother-city, or to the Spartans who are the first power in Greece."

### The retribution by the gods upon the plunderers of the temples and the destruction of the Carthaginian host by a pestilence (70-71).

**70.** After this speech by Theodoras the Syracusans were in high spirits and kept their eyes fixed on their allies; and when Pharacidas the Lacedaemonian, the admiral of the allies, stepped up to the platform, all expected that he would take the lead for liberty. But he was on friendly terms with the tyrant and declared that the Lacedaemonians had dispatched him to aid the Syracusans and Dionysius against the Carthaginians, not to overthrow the rule of Dionysius. At this statement so contrary to expectation the mercenaries flocked about Dionysius, and the Syracusans in dismay made no move, although they called down many curses on the Spartans. On a previous occasion Aretes [Aristus] the Lacedaemonian, at the time that he was asserting the right of the Syracusans to freedom, had betrayed them, and now at this time Pharacidas vetoed the movement of the Syracusans. For the moment Dionysius was in great fear and dissolved the assembly, but later he won the favour of the multitude by kindly words, honouring some of them with gifts and inviting some to general banquets.

After the Carthaginians had seized the suburb and pillaged the temple of Demeter and Core, a plague struck the army. Over and above the disaster sent by influence of the deity, there were contributing causes: that myriads of people were gathered together, that it was the time of the year which is most productive of plagues, and that the particular summer had brought unusually hot weather. It also seems likely that the place itself was responsible for the excessive extent of the disaster; for on a former occasion the Athenians too, who occupied the same camp, had perished in great numbers from the plague, since the terrain was marshy and in a hollow. First, before sunrise, because of the cold from the breeze over the waters, their bodies were struck with chills, but in the middle of the day the heat was stifling, as must be the case when so great a multitude is gathered together in a narrow place.

**71.** Now the plague first attacked the Libyans, and, as many of them perished, at first they buried the dead, but later, both because of the multitude of corpses and because those who tended the sick were seized by the plague, no one dared approach the suffering. When even nursing was thus omitted, there was no remedy for the disaster. For by reason of the stench of the unburied and the miasma from the marshes, the plague began with a catarrh; then came a swelling in the throat; gradually burning sensations ensued, pains in the sinews of the back, and a heavy feeling in the limbs; then dysentery supervened and pustules upon the whole surface of the body. In most cases this was the course of the disease; but some became mad and totally lost their memory; they circulated through the camp, out of their mind, and struck at anyone they met. In general, as it turned out, even help by physicians was of no avail both because of the severity of the disease and the swiftness of the death; for death came on the fifth day or on the sixth at the latest, amidst such terrible tortures that all looked upon those who had fallen in the war as blessed. In fact all who watched beside the sick were struck by the plague, and thus the lot of the ill was miserable, since no one was willing to minister to the unfortunate. For not only did any not akin abandon one another, but even brothers were forced to desert brothers, friends to sacrifice friends out of fear for their own lives.

*How Dionysius outgeneralled the thousand most turbulent mercenaries of his and caused them to be massacred (72).*

*How Dionysius laid siege to the outposts and camp of the Carthaginians (72).*

**72.** When Dionysius heard of the disaster that had struck the Carthaginians, he manned eighty ships and ordered Pharacidas and Leptines the admirals to attack the enemy's ships at daybreak, while he himself, profiting by a moonless night, made a circuit with his army and, passing by the temple of Cyane, arrived near the camp of the enemy at daybreak before they were aware of it. The cavalry and a thousand infantry from the mercenaries were dispatched in advance against that part of the Carthaginian encampment which extended toward the interior. These mercenaries were the most hostile, beyond all others, to Dionysius and had engaged time and again in factional quarrels and uproars. Consequently Dionysius had issued orders to the cavalry that as soon as they came to blows with the enemy they should flee and leave the mercenaries in the lurch; when this order had been carried out and the mercenaries had been slain to a man, Dionysius set about laying siege to both the camp and the forts. While the barbarians were still dismayed at the unexpected attack and bringing up reinforcements in disorderly fashion, he on his part took by storm the fort known as Polichna; and on the opposite side the cavalry, aided in an attack by some of the triremes, stormed the area around Dascon. At once all the warships joined in the attack, and when the army raised the war-cry at the taking of the forts, the barbarians were in a state of panic. For at the outset they had rushed in a body against the land troops in order to ward off the assailants of the camp; but when they saw the fleet also coming up to attack, they turned back to give help to the naval station. The swift course of events, however, outstripped them and their haste was without result. For even as they were mounting the decks and manning the triremes, the enemy's vessels, driven on by rowers, struck the ships athwart in many cases. Now one well-delivered blow would sink a damaged ship; but blows in repeated ramming, which broke through the nailed timbers, struck terrible dismay into the opponents. Since all about the mightiest ships were being shattered, the rending of the vessels by the crushing blows raised a great noise and the shore extending along the scene of the battle was strewn with corpses.

### How Dionysius reduced the Carthaginians by siege and set fire to many ships of the enemy (73).

73. The Syracusans, eagerly co-operating in their success, rivalled one another in great zeal to be the first to board the enemy's ships, and surrounding the barbarians, who were terror-stricken at the magnitude of the peril they faced, put them to death. Nor did the infantry who were attacking the naval station show less zeal than the others, and among them, it so happened, was Dionysius himself, who had ridden on horseback to the section about Dascon. Finding there forty ships of fifty oars, which had been drawn up on the beach, and beside them merchant ships and some triremes at anchor, they set fire to them. Quickly the flame leaped up into the sky and, spreading over a large area, caught the shipping, and none of the merchants or owners was able to bring any help because of the violence of the blaze. Since a strong wind arose, the fire was carried from the ships drawn up on land to the merchantmen lying at anchor. When the crews dived into the water from fear of suffocation and the anchor cables were burnt off, the ships came into collision because of the rough seas, some of them being destroyed as they struck one another, and others as the wind drove them about, but the majority of them were victims of the fire. Thereupon, as the flames swept up through the sails of the merchant-ships and consumed the yard-arms, the sight was like a scene from the theatre to the inhabitants of the city and the destruction of the barbarians resembled that of men struck by lightning from heaven for their impiety.

### The defeat of the Carthaginians by land and also by sea (74).

74. Forthwith, elated by the Syracusan successes, both the oldest youths and such aged men as were not yet entirely incapacitated by years manned lighters, and approaching without order all together made for the ships in the harbour. Those which the fire had ruined they plundered, stripping them of anything that could be saved, and such as were undamaged they took in tow and brought to the city. Thus even those who by age were exempt from war duties were unable to restrain themselves, but in their excessive joy their ardent spirit prevailed over their age. When the news of the victory ran through the city, children and women, together with their households, left their homes, everyone hurrying to the walls, and the whole extent was crowded with spectators. Of these some raised their hands to heaven and returned thanks to the gods, and others declared

## Book XIV

that the barbarians had suffered the punishment of heaven for their plundering of the temples. For from a distance the sight resembled a battle with the gods, such a number of ships going up in fire, the flames leaping aloft among the sails, the Greeks applauding every success with great shouting, and the barbarians in their consternation at the disaster keeping up a great uproar and confused crying. But as night came the battle ceased for the time, and Dionysius kept to the field against the barbarians, pitching a camp near the temple of Zeus.

### The flight of the Carthaginians by night, Dionysius having co-operated with them without the knowledge of the Syracusans for a bribe of four hundred talents (75).

**75.** Now that the Carthaginians had suffered defeat on land as well as on sea, they entered into negotiations with Dionysius without the knowledge of the Syracusans. They asked him to allow their remaining troops to cross back to Libya and promised to give him the three hundred talents which they had there in their camp. Dionysius replied that he would not be able to allow the whole army to escape, but he consented to their citizen troops alone withdrawing secretly at night by sea; for he knew that the Syracusans and their allies would not allow him to make any such terms with the enemy. Dionysius acted as he did to avoid the total destruction of the Carthaginian army, in order that the Syracusans, by reason of their fear of the Carthaginians, should never find a time of ease to assert their freedom. Accordingly Dionysius agreed that the flight of the Carthaginians should take place by night on the fourth day hence and led his army back into the city.

Himilcon during the night conveyed the three hundred talents to the acropolis and delivered them to the persons stationed on the island by the tyrant, and then himself, when the time agreed upon had arrived, manned forty triremes during the night with the citizens of Carthage and began his flight, abandoning all the rest of his army. He had already made his way across the harbour, when some of the Corinthians observed his flight and speedily reported it to Dionysius. Since Dionysius took his time in calling the soldiers to arms and gathering the commanders, the Corinthians did not wait for him but speedily put out to sea against the Carthaginians, and vying with each other in their rowing they caught up with the last Phoenician ships, which they shattered with their rams and sent to the bottom. After this Dionysius led out the army, but the Siceli, who were serving in the army of the Carthaginians, forestalling the Syracusans, fled through the interior and, almost to a man, made their way in safety to their native homes. Dionysius stationed guards at intervals along the roads and then led his army against the enemy's camp, while it was still night. The barbarians, abandoned as they were by their general, by the Carthaginians, and by the Siceli as well, were dispirited and fled in dismay. Some were taken captive as they fell in with the guards on the roads, but the majority threw down their arms, surrendered themselves, and asked only that their lives be spared. Some Iberians alone massed together with their arms and dispatched a herald to treat about taking service with him. Dionysius made peace with the Iberians and enrolled them in his mercenaries, but the rest of the multitude he made captive and whatever remained of the baggage he turned over to the soldiers to plunder.

## The difficulties which befell the Carthaginians because of their impiety against the deity (76-77).

**76.** With such swiftness did Fortune work a change in the affairs of the Carthaginians, and point out to all mankind that those who become elated above due measure quickly give proof of their own weakness. For they who had in their hands practically all the cities of Sicily with the exception of Syracuse and expected its capture, of a sudden were forced to be anxious for their own fatherland; they who overthrew the tombs of the Syracusans gazed upon one hundred and fifty thousand dead lying in heaps and unburied because of the plague; they who wasted with fire the territory of the Syracusans now in their turn saw their own fleet of a sudden go up in flames; they who so arrogantly sailed with their whole armada into the harbour and flaunted their successes before the Syracusans had little thought that they were to steal away by night and leave their allies at the mercy of their enemy. The general himself, who had taken the temple of Zeus for his headquarters and the pillaged wealth of the sanctuaries for his own possession, slipped away in disgrace to Carthage with a few survivors, in order that he might not by dying and paying a debt to nature go unscathed for his acts of impiety, but should in his native land lead a life that was notorious, while reproaches were heaped on him on every hand. Indeed, so calamitous was his lot that he went about the temples of the city in the cheapest clothing, charging himself with impiety and offering acknowledged retribution to heaven for his sins against the gods. In the end he passed sentence of death upon himself and starved himself to death. He bequeathed to his fellow citizens a deep respect for religion, for straightway Fortune heaped upon them the other calamities of war as well.

**77.** When the news of the Carthaginian disaster had spread throughout Libya, their allies, who had long hated the oppressive rule of the Carthaginians and even more at this time because of the betrayal of the soldiers at Syracuse, were inflamed against them. Consequently, being led on partly by anger and partly by contempt for them because of the disaster they had suffered, they endeavoured to assert their independence. After exchanging messages with one another they collected an army, moved forward, and pitched camp in the open. Since they were speedily joined not only by freemen but also by slaves, there was gathered in a short time a body of two hundred thousand men. Seizing Tynes, a city situated not far from Carthage, they based their line of battle on it, and since they had the better of the fighting, they confined the Phoenicians within their walls. The Carthaginians, against whom the gods were clearly fighting, at first gathered in small groups and in great confusion and besought the deity to put an end to its wrath; thereupon the entire city was seized by superstitious fear and dread, as every man anticipated in imagination the enslavement of the city. Consequently they voted by every means to propitiate the gods who had been sinned against. Since they had included neither Core nor Demeter in their rites, they appointed their most renowned citizens to be priests of these goddesses, and consecrating statues of them with all solemnity, they conducted their rites, following the ritual used by the Greeks. They also chose out the most prominent Greeks who lived among them and assigned them to the service of the goddesses. After this they constructed ships and made careful provision of supplies for the war.

## Book XIV

Meanwhile the revolters, who were a motley mass, possessed no capable commanders, and what was of first importance, they were short of provisions because they were so numerous, while the Carthaginians brought supplies by sea from Sardinia. Furthermore, they quarrelled among themselves over the supreme command and some of them were bought off with Carthaginian money and deserted the common cause. As a result, both because of the lack of provisions and because of treachery on the part of some, they broke up and scattered to their native lands, thus relieving the Carthaginians of the greatest fear.

Such was the state of affairs in Libya at this time.

### The merging of the cities of Sicily which had been laid waste (78).

### How Dionysius reduced by siege certain of the cities of Sicily and brought others into an alliance and how he established relations of friendship with the rulers Agyris of Agyrium and Nicodemus [Damon] of Centuripae (78).

78. Dionysius, seeing that the mercenaries were most hostile to him and fearing that they might depose him, first of all arrested Aristotle, their commander. At this, when the body of them ran together under arms and demanded their pay with some sharpness, Dionysius declared that he was sending Aristotle to Lacedaemon to face trial among his fellow citizens, and offered to the mercenaries, who numbered about ten thousand, in lieu of their pay the city and territory of the Leontines. To this they gladly agreed because the territory was good land, and after portioning it out in allotments they made their home in Leontini. Dionysius then recruited other mercenaries and trusted in them and his freed-men to maintain the government.

After the disaster which the Carthaginians had suffered, the survivors from the cities of Sicily that had been enslaved gathered together, gained back their native lands, and revived their strength. Dionysius settled in Messenê a thousand Locrians, four thousand Medmaeans [Medma in Bruttium], and six hundred Messenians from the Peloponnesus who were exiles from Zacynthus and Naupactus. But when he observed that the Lacedaemonians were offended that the Messenians whom they had driven out were settled in a renowned city, he removed them from Messenê, and giving them a place on the sea, he cut off some of the area of Abacaene and annexed it to their territory. The Messenians named their city Tyndaris, and by living in concord together and admitting many to citizenship, they speedily came to number more than five thousand citizens.

After this Dionysius waged a number of campaigns against the territory of the Siceli, in the course of which he took Menaenum and Morgantinum and struck a treaty with Agyris, the tyrant of the Agyrinaeans, and Damon, the lord of the Centoripans, as well as with the Herbitaeans and the Assorini. He also gained by treachery Cephaloedium, Solus, and Enna, and made peace besides with the Herbessini.

Such was the state of affairs in Sicily at this time.

### How Agesilaüs, the Spartan king, crossed over into Asia with an army and laid waste the territory which was subject to the Persians (79).

**79.** In Greece the Lacedaemonians, foreseeing how great their war with the Persians would be, put one of the two kings, Agesilaüs, in command. After he had levied six thousand soldiers and constituted a council of thirty of his foremost fellow citizens, he transported the armament from Aulis to Ephesus. Here he enlisted four thousand soldiers and took the field with his army, which numbered ten thousand infantry and four hundred cavalry. They were also accompanied by a throng of no less number which provided a market and was intent upon plunder. He traversed the Plain of Cayster and laid waste the territory held by the Persians until he arrived at Cymê. From this as his base he spent the larger part of the summer ravaging Phrygia and neighbouring territory; and after sating his army with pillage he returned toward the beginning of autumn to Ephesus. While these events were taking place, the Lacedaemonians dispatched ambassadors to Nephereus, the king of Egypt, to conclude an alliance; he, in place of the aid requested, made the Spartans a gift of equipment for one hundred triremes and five hundred thousand measures of grain. Pharax, the Lacedaemonian admiral, sailing from Rhodes with one hundred and twenty ships, put in at Sasanda in Caria, a fortress one hundred and fifty stades from Caunus. From this as his base he laid siege to Caunus and blockaded Conon, who was commander of the King's fleet and lay at Caunus with forty ships. But when Artaphernes and Pharnabazus came with strong forces to the aid of the Caunians, Pharax lifted the siege and sailed off to Rhodes with the entire fleet. After this Conon gathered eighty triremes and sailed to the Chersonesus, and the Rhodians, having expelled the Peloponnesian fleet, revolted from the Lacedaemonians and received Conon, together with his entire fleet, into their city. Now the Lacedaemonians, who were bringing the gift of grain from Egypt, being unaware of the defection of the Rhodians, approached the island in full confidence; but the Rhodians and Conon, the Persian admiral, brought the ships into the harbours and stored the city with grain. There also came to Conon ninety triremes, ten of them from Cilicia and eighty from Phoenicia, under the command of the lord of the Sidonians.

### How Agesilaüs defeated in battle the Persians, who were commanded by Pharnabazus (80).

**80.** After this Agesilaüs led forth his army into the Plain of Cayster and the country around Sipylus and ravaged the possessions of the inhabitants. Tissaphernes, gathering ten thousand cavalry and fifty thousand infantry, followed close on the Lacedaemonians and cut down any who became separated from the main body while plundering. Agesilaüs formed his soldiers in a square and clung to the foothills of Mt. Sipylus, awaiting a favourable opportunity to attack the enemy. He overran the countryside as far as Sardis and ravaged the orchards and the pleasure-park belonging to Tissaphernes, which had been artistically laid out at great expense with plants and all other things that contribute to luxury and the enjoyment in peace of the good things of life. He then turned back, and when he was midway between Sardis and Thybarnae, he dispatched by night the Spartan Xenocles with fourteen hundred soldiers to a thickly wooded place to set an ambush for the barbarians. Then Agesilaüs himself moved at daybreak along the way with his army. When he had passed the place of ambush and the barbarians were advancing upon him without battle order and harassing his rearguard, to their surprise he suddenly turned about on the Persians. When a sharp battle followed, he raised the signal to the soldiers in ambush and they, chanting the battle song, charged the enemy. The Persians, seeing that they were caught between the forces, were struck with dismay and turned at once in flight. Pursuing them for some distance, Agesilaüs slew over six thousand of them, gathered a great multitude of prisoners, and pillaged their camp which was stored with goods of many sorts. Tissaphernes, thunderstruck at the daring of the Lacedaemonians, withdrew from the battle to Sardis, and Agesilaüs was about to attack the satrapies farther inland, but led his army back to the sea when he could not obtain favourable omens from the sacrifices.

When Artaxerxes, the King of Asia, learned of the defeats, being alarmed by the war with the Greeks, he was angry at Tissaphernes, since he considered him to be responsible for the war. He had also been asked by his mother, Parysatis, to grant her revenge upon Tissaphernes, for she hated him for denouncing her son Cyrus, when he made his attack upon his brother. Accordingly Artaxerxes appointed Tithraustes commander with orders to arrest Tissaphernes and sent letters to the cities and the satraps that all should perform whatever he commanded. Tithraustes, on arriving at Colossae in Phrygia, with the aid of Ariaeus, a satrap, arrested Tissaphernes while he was in the bath, cut off his head, and sent it to the King. Then he persuaded Agesilaüs to enter into negotiations and concluded with him a truce of six months.

### On the Boeotian War and the actions comprised in it (81).

### How Conon was appointed general by the Persians and rebuilt the walls of the Athenians (81, 85).

**81.** While affairs in Asia were handled as we have described, the Phocians went to war with the Boeotians because of certain grievances and persuaded the Lacedaemonians to join them against the Boeotians. At first they sent Lysander to them with a few soldiers, who, on entering Phocis, gathered an army; but later the king, Pausanias, was dispatched there with six thousand soldiers. The Boeotians persuaded the Athenians to take part with them in the war, but at the time they took the field alone and found Haliartus under siege by Lysander and the Phocians. In the battle which followed Lysander fell together with many Lacedaemonians and their allies. The entire body of other Boeotians speedily turned back from the pursuit, but some two hundred Thebans advanced rather rashly into rugged terrain and were slain. This was called the Boeotian War. Pausanias, the king of the Lacedaemonians, on learning of the defeat, concluded a truce with the Boeotians and led his army back to the Peloponnesus.

Conon, the admiral of the Persians, put the Athenians Hieronymus and Nicodemus in charge of the fleet and himself set forth with intent to interview the King. He sailed along the coast of Cilicia, and when he had gone on to Thapsacus in Syria, he then took boat by the Euphrates river to Babylon. Here he met the King and promised that he would destroy the Lacedaemonians' naval power if the King would furnish him with such money and other supplies as his plan required. Artaxerxes approved Conon, honoured him with rich gifts, and appointed a paymaster who should supply funds in abundance as Conon might assign them. He also gave him authority to take as his associate leader for the war any Persian he might choose. Conon selected the satrap Pharnabazus and then returned to the sea, having arranged everything to suit his purpose.

**82.** At the close of this year, in Athens [395] Diophantus entered upon the archonship, and in Rome, in place of consuls, the consular magistracy was exercised by six military tribunes, Lucius Valerius, Marcus Furius, Quintus Servilius, and Quintus Sulpicius. After these men had assumed their magistracies the Boeotians and Athenians, together with the Corinthians and the Argives, concluded an alliance with each other. It was their thought that, since the Lacedaemonians were hated by their allies because of their harsh rule, it would be an easy matter to overthrow their supremacy, given that the strongest states were of one mind. First of all, they set up a common Council in Corinth to which they sent representatives to form plans, and worked out in common the arrangements for the war. Then they dispatched ambassadors to the cities and caused many allies of the Lacedaemonians to withdraw from them; for at once all of Euboea and the Leucadians joined them, as well as the Acarnanians, Ambraciots, and the Chalcidians of Thrace. They also attempted to persuade the inhabitants of the Peloponnesus to revolt from the Lacedaemonians, but no one listened to them; for Sparta, lying as it does along the side of it, was a kind of citadel and fortress of the entire Peloponnesus.

Medius, the lord of Larissa in Thessaly, was at war with Lycophron, the tyrant of Pherae, and when he asked for aid to be sent him, the Council dispatched to him two thousand soldiers. After the troops had arrived Medius seized Pharsalus, in which there was a garrison of Lacedaemonians, and sold the inhabitants as booty. After this the Boeotians and Argives, parting company with Medius, seized Heracleia in Trachis; and on being admitted at night within the walls by certain persons, they put to the sword the Lacedaemonians whom they seized but allowed the other Peloponnesians to leave with their possessions. They then summoned to the city the Trachinians whom the Lacedaemonians had banished from their homes, and gave them the city as their dwelling place; and indeed they were the most ancient settlers of this territory. After this Ismenias, the leader of the Boeotians, left the Argives in the city to serve as its garrison and himself persuaded the Aenianians and the Athamanians to revolt from the Lacedaemonians and gathered soldiers from among them and their allies. After he had recruited a little less than six thousand men, he took the field against the Phocians. While he was taking up quarters in Naryx in Locris, which men say was the birthplace of Ajax, the people of the Phocians came against him in arms under the command of Alcisthenes the Laconian. A sharp and protracted battle followed, in which the Boeotians were the victors. Pursuing the fugitives until nightfall, they slew not many less than a thousand, but lost of their own troops in the battle about five hundred. After the pitched battle both sides dismissed their armies to their native lands, and the members of the Council in Corinth, since affairs were progressing as they desired, gathered to Corinth soldiers from all the cities, more than fifteen thousand infantry and about five hundred cavalry.

**83.** When the Lacedaemonians saw that the greatest cities of Greece were uniting against them, they voted to summon Agesilaüs and his army from Asia.

## Book XIV

In the meantime they gathered from their own levy and their allies twenty-three thousand infantry and five hundred cavalry and advanced to meet the enemy. The battle took place along the river Nemea, lasting until nightfall, and parts of both armies had the advantage, but of the Lacedaemonians and their allies eleven hundred men fell, while of the Boeotians and their allies about twenty-eight hundred.

After Agesilaüs had conveyed his army across from Asia to Europe, at first he was opposed by certain Thracians with a large force; these he defeated in battle, slaying the larger number of the barbarians. Then he made his way through Macedonia, passing through the same country as Xerxes did when he made his campaign against the Greeks. When Agesilaüs had traversed Macedonia and Thessaly and made his way through the pass of Thermopylae, he continued. . . .

Conon the Athenian and Pharnabazus were in command of the King's fleet and were tarrying in Loryma of the Chersonesus with more than ninety triremes. When they learned that the enemy's naval forces were at Cnidus, they made preparations for battle. Peisander, the Lacedaemonian admiral, set out from Cnidus with eighty-five triremes and put in at Physcus of the Chersonesus. On sailing from there he fell in with the King's fleet, and engaging the leading ships, he won the advantage over them; but when the Persians came to give aid with their triremes in close formation, all his allies fled to the land. Peisander turned his own ship against them, believing ignoble flight to be disgraceful and unworthy of Sparta. After fighting brilliantly and slaying many of the enemy, in the end he was overcome, battling in a manner worthy of his native land. Conon pursued the Lacedaemonians as far as the land and captured fifty of their triremes. As for the crews, most of them leaped overboard and escaped by land, but about five hundred were captured. The rest of the triremes found safety at Cnidus.

**84.** Agesilaüs enlisted more soldiers from the Peloponnesus and then advanced with his army against Boeotia, whereupon the Boeotians, together with their allies, at once set out to Coroneia to meet him. In the battle which followed the Thebans defeated the forces opposed to them and pursued them as far as their camp, but the others held out only a short time and then were forced by Agesilaüs and his troops to take to flight. Therefore the Lacedaemonians, looking upon themselves as conquerors, set up a trophy and gave back the dead to the enemy under a truce. There fell of the Boeotians and their allies more than six hundred, but of the Lacedaemonians and their associates three hundred and fifty. Agesilaüs, who had suffered many wounds, was taken to Delphi, where he looked after his physical needs.

After the sea-fight Pharnabazus and Conon put out to sea with all their ships against the allies of the Lacedaemonians. First of all they induced the people of Cos to secede, and then those of Nisyros and of Teos. After this the Chians expelled their garrison and joined Conon, and similarly the Mitylenaeans and Ephesians and Erythraeans changed sides. Something like the same eagerness for change infected all the cities, of which some expelled their Lacedaemonian garrisons and maintained their freedom, while others attached themselves to Conon. As for the Lacedaemonians, from this time they lost the sovereignty of the sea. Conon, having decided to sail with the entire fleet to Attica, put out to sea, and after bringing over to his cause the islands of the Cyclades, he sailed against the island of Cythera. Mastering it at once on the first assault, he sent the Cytherians under a truce to Laconia, left an adequate garrison for the city, and sailed for Corinth. After putting in there he discussed with the members of the Council such points as they wished, made an alliance with them, left them money, and then sailed off to Asia.

At this time Aeropus, the king of the Macedonians, died of illness after a reign of six years, and was succeeded in the sovereignty by his son Pausanias, who ruled for one year. Theopompus of Chios ended with this year and the battle of Cnidus his *Hellenic History,* which he wrote in twelve books. This historian began with the battle of Cynossema, with which Thucydides ended his work, and covered in his account a period of seventeen years [410-194].

### How Conon was appointed general by the Persians and rebuilt the walls of the Athenians (85).

85. At the conclusion of the year, in Athens [394] Eubulides was archon and in Rome the consular magistracy was administered by six military tribunes, Lucius Sergius, Aulus Postumius, Publius Cornelius, and Quintus Manlius. At this time Conon, who held the command of the King's fleet, put in at the Peiraeus with eighty triremes and promised the citizens to rebuild the fortifications of the city; for the walls of the Peiraeus and the long walls had been destroyed in accordance with the terms the Athenians had concluded with the Lacedaemonians when they were reduced in the Peloponnesian War. Accordingly Conon hired a multitude of skilled workers, and putting at their service the general run of his crews, he speedily rebuilt the larger part of the wall. For the Thebans too sent five hundred skilled workers and masons, and some other cities also gave assistance. Tiribazus, who commanded the land forces in Asia, was envious of Conon's successes, and on the plea that Conon was using the King's armaments to win the cities for the Athenians, he lured him to Sardis, where he arrested him, threw him in chains, and remanded him to custody.

### How the Lacedaemonians defeated the Boeotians near Corinth and this war was called the Corinthian (86).

86. In Corinth certain men who favoured a democracy, banding together while contests were being held in the theatre, instituted a slaughter and filled the city with civil strife; and when the Argives gave them their support in their venture, they put to the sword one hundred and twenty of the citizens and drove five hundred into exile. While the Lacedaemonians were making preparations to restore the exiles and gathering an army, the Athenians and Boeotians came to the aid of the murderers, in order that they might secure the adhesion of the city. The exiles, together with the Lacedaemonians and their allies, attacked Lechaeum [Corinth's harbour on the Corinthian Gulf, connected by long walls] and the dock-yard by night and seized them by storm; and on the next day, when the troops of the city, which Iphicrates commanded, came out against them, a battle followed in which the Lacedaemonians were victorious and slew no small number of their opponents. After this the Boeotians and Athenians, and with them the Argives and Corinthians, came with all their forces to Lechaeum, and at the outset they laid siege to the place and forced their way into the corridor

## Book XIV

between the walls; but afterward the Lacedaemonians and the exiles put up a brilliant fight and forced out the Boeotians and all who were with them. They then, having lost about a thousand soldiers, returned to the city. And since the Isthmian Games were now at hand, there was a quarrel over who should conduct them. After much contention the Lacedaemonians had their way and saw to it that the exiles conducted the festival. Since the severe fighting in the war took place for the most part about Corinth, it was called the Corinthian War, and it continued for eight years.

### How Dionysius forced his way with much fighting into Tauromenium and then was driven out (87-88).

**87.** In Sicily the people of Rhegium, bringing the charge against Dionysius that in fortifying Messenê he was making preparations against them, first of all offered asylum to those who were expelled by Dionysius and were active against him, and then settled in Mylae the surviving Naxians and Catanians, prepared an army, and dispatched as its general Heloris to lay siege to Messenê. When Heloris made a reckless attack upon the acropolis, the Messenians and the mercenaries of Dionysius, who were holding the city, closed ranks and advanced against him. In the battle that followed the Messenians were victorious and slew more than five hundred of their opponents. Marching straightway against Mylae, they seized the city and let the Naxians who had been settled there go free under a truce. These, accordingly, departed to the Siceli and the Greek cities and made their dwelling some in one place and others in another. Dionysius, now that the regions about the Straits had been brought to friendly terms with him, planned to lead an army against Rhegium, but he had trouble with the Siceli who held Tauromenium. Deciding, therefore, that it would be to his advantage to attack them first, he led out his forces against them, pitched a camp on the side toward Naxos, and persisted in the siege during the winter, in the belief that the Siceli would desert the hill since they had not been dwelling there long.

**88.** The Siceli, however, had an ancient tradition, handed down from their ancestors, that these parts of the island had been the possession of the Siceli, when Greeks first landed there and founded Naxos, expelling from that very hill the Siceli who were then dwelling on it. Maintaining, therefore, that they had only recovered territory that belonged to their fathers and were justly righting the wrongs which the Greeks had committed against their ancestors, they put forth every effort to hold the hill. While extraordinary rivalry was being displayed on both sides, the winter solstice occurred, and because of the consequent winter storms the area about the acropolis was filled with snow. Thereupon Dionysius, who had discovered that the Siceli were careless in their guard of the acropolis because of its strength and the unusual height of the wall, advanced on a moonless and stormy night against the loftiest sectors. After many difficulties both because of the obstacles offered by the crags and because of the great depth of the snow he occupied one peak, although his face was frosted and his vision impaired by the cold. After this he broke through to the other side and led his army into the city., but when the Siceli came up in a body, the troops of Dionysius were thrust out and Dionysius himself was struck on the corslet in the flight, sent scrambling, and barely escaped being taken alive. Since the Siceli pressed upon them from superior ground, more than six hundred of Dionysius' troops were slain and most of them lost their complete armour, while Dionysius himself saved only his corslet. After this disaster the Acragantini and Messenians banished the partisans of Dionysius, asserted their freedom, and renounced their alliance with the tyrant.

89. Pausanias, the king of the Lacedaemonians, was accused by his fellow citizens and went into exile after a reign of fourteen years, and his son Agesipolis succeeded to the kingship and reigned for the same length of time as his father. Pausanias too, the king of the Macedonians, died after a reign of one year, being assassinated by Amyntas, who seized the kingship and reigned twenty-four years.

### How the Carthaginians were defeated near the city of Bacaena [Abacaene] by Dionysius (90).

90. At the conclusion of this year, in Athens [393] Demostratus took over the archonship, and in Rome the consular magistracy was administered by six military tribunes, Lucius Titinius, Publius Licinius, Publius Melaeus, Quintus Mallius, Gnaeus Genycius, and Lucius Atilius. After these magistrates had entered office, Magon, the Carthaginian general, was stationed in Sicily. He set about retrieving the Carthaginian cause after the disaster they had suffered, for he showed kindness to the subject cities and received the victims of Dionysius' wars. He also formed alliances with most of the Siceli and, after gathering armaments, launched an attack upon the territory of Messenê. After ravaging the countryside and seizing much booty he marched from that place and went into camp near the city of Abacaene, which was his ally. When Dionysius came up with his army, the forces drew up for battle, and after a sharp engagement Dionysius was the victor. The Carthaginians fled into the city after a loss of more than eight hundred men, while Dionysius withdrew for the time being to Syracuse; but after a few days he manned one hundred triremes and set out against the Rhegians. Arriving unexpectedly by night before the city, he put fire to the gates and set ladders against the walls. The Rhegians, coming up in defence as they did at first in small numbers, endeavoured to put out the flames, but later, when their general Heloris arrived and advised them to do just the opposite, they saved the city. For if they had put out the fire, they would not have been strong enough to prevent Dionysius from entering, being far too small a number; but by bringing firewood and timbers from the neighbouring houses they made the flames higher, until the main body of their troops could assemble in arms and come to the defence. Dionysius, who had failed of his design, traversed the countryside, wasting it in flames and cutting down orchards, and then concluded a truce for a year and sailed off to Syracuse.

91. The Greek inhabitants of Italy, when they saw the encroachments of Dionysius advancing as far as their own lands, formed an alliance among themselves and established a Council. It was their hope to defend themselves with ease against Dionysius and to resist the neighbouring Leucani; for these last were also at war with them at this time.

The exiles who held Lechaeum in Corinthian territory, being admitted into the city [Corinth] in the night, endeavoured to get possession of the walls, but when the troops of Iphicrates came up against them, they lost three hundred of their number and fled back to the ship station. Some days later a contingent of the Lacedaemonian army was passing through Corinthian territory, when Iphicrates and some of the allies in Corinth fell on them and slew the larger number. Iphicrates with his peltasts advanced against the territory of Phlius, and joining battle with the men of the city, he slew more than three hundred of them. Then, when he advanced against Sicyon, the Sicyonians offered battle before their walls but lost about five hundred men and found refuge within their city.

**92.** After these events had taken place, the Argives took up arms in full force and marched against Corinth, and after seizing the acropolis and securing the city for themselves, they made the Corinthian territory Argive. The Athenian Iphicrates also had the design to seize the city, since it was advantageous for the control of Greece; but when the Athenian people opposed it, he resigned his position. The Athenians appointed Chabrias general in his place and sent him to Corinth.

In Macedonia Amyntas, the father of Philip, was driven from his country by Illyrians who invaded Macedonia, and giving up hope for his crown, he made a present to the Olynthians of his territory which bordered on theirs. For the time being he lost his kingdom, but shortly he was restored by the Thessalians, recovered his crown, and ruled for twenty-four years. Some say, however, that after the expulsion of Amyntas the Macedonians were ruled by Argaeus for a period of two years, and that it was after that time that Amyntas recovered the kingship.

**93.** The same year Satyrus, the son of Spartacus and king of Bosporus, died after a reign of forty years, and his son Leucon succeeded him in the rulership for a period of forty years.

In Italy the Romans, who were in the eleventh year of their siege of the Veians, appointed Marcus Furius to be dictator and Publius Cornelius to be master of the horse. These restored the spirit of the troops and captured Veii by constructing an underground passage; the city they reduced to slavery, selling the inhabitants with the other booty. The dictator then celebrated a triumph, and the Roman people, taking a tenth of the spoil, made a gold bowl and dedicated it to the oracle at Delphi.

The ambassadors who were taking it fell in with pirates from the Lipari islands, were all taken prisoners, and brought to Lipara. But Timasitheüs, the general of the Liparaeans, on learning what had taken place, rescued the ambassadors, gave them back the vessel of gold, and sent them on their way to Delphi. The men who were conveying the bowl dedicated it in the Treasury of the Massalians and returned to Rome. Consequently the Roman people, when they learned of this generous act of Timasitheus, honoured him at once by conferring the right to public hospitality, and one hundred and thirty-seven years later, when they took Lipara from the Carthaginians, they relieved the descendants of Timasitheus of the payment of taxes and gave them freedom.

**94.** When the year had ended, in Athens [392] Philocles became archon, and in Rome the consular magistracy was assumed by six military tribunes, Publius and Cornelius, Caeso Fabius, Lucius Furius, Quintus Servilius, and Marcus Valerius; and this year the Ninety-seventh Olympiad was celebrated, that in which Terires was victor. In this year the Athenians chose Thrasybulus general and sent him to sea with forty triremes. He sailed to Ionia, collected funds from the allies, and proceeded on his way; and while tarrying at the Chersonesus he made allies of Medocus and Scuthes, the kings of the Thracians. After some time he sailed from the Hellespont to Lesbos and anchored off the coast at Eresus. Strong winds arose and twenty-three triremes were lost. Getting off safe with the other ships he advanced against the cities of Lesbos, with the intention of winning them over; for they had all revolted with the exception of Mitylenê. First he appeared before Methymna and joined battle with the men of the city, who were commanded by the Spartan Therimachus. In a brilliant fight he slew not only Therimachus himself but no small number of the Methymnaeans and shut up the rest of them within their walls; he also ravaged the territory of the Methymnaeans and received the surrender of Eresus and Antissa. After this he gathered ships from the Chian and Mitylenaean allies and sailed to Rhodes.

## The expedition of the Carthaginians to Sicily and the settlement of the war (95-96).

**95.** The Carthaginians, after a slow recovery from the disaster they had suffered at Syracuse, resolved to keep their hand in Sicilian affairs. Having decided upon war, they crossed over with only a few warships, but brought together troops from Libya and Sardinia as well as from the barbarians of Italy. The soldiers were all carefully supplied with equipment to which they were accustomed and brought over to Sicily, being no less than eighty thousand in number and under the command of Magon. This commander accordingly made his way through the Siceli, detaching most of the cities from Dionysius, and went into camp in the territory of the Agyrinaeans on the banks of the Chrysas River near the road that leads to Morgantina. For since he was unable to bring the Agyrinaeans to enter an alliance with him, he refrained from marching farther, since he had news that the enemy had set out from Syracuse.

Dionysius, on learning that the Carthaginians were making their way through the interior, speedily collected as many Syracusans and mercenaries as he could and set forth, having in all not less than twenty thousand soldiers. When he came near the enemy he sent an embassy to Agyris, the lord of the Agyrinaeans. This man possessed the strongest armament of any of the tyrants of Sicily at that time after Dionysius, since he was lord of practically all the neighbouring fortified communities and ruled the city of the Agyrinaeans which was well peopled at that time, for it had no less than twenty thousand citizens. There was also laid up on the acropolis for this multitude which had been gathered together in the city a large store of money which Agyris had collected after he had murdered the wealthiest citizens. Dionysius, after entering the city with a small company, persuaded Agyris to join him as a genuine ally and promised to make him a present of a large portion of neighbouring territory if the war ended successfully. At the outset, then, Agyris readily provided the entire army of Dionysius with food and whatever else it needed, led forth his troops in a body, joined with Dionysius in the campaign, and fought together with him in the war against the Carthaginians.

**96.** Magon, since he was encamped in hostile territory and was ever more and more in want of supplies, was at no little disadvantage; for the troops of Agyris, being familiar with the territory, held the advantage in laying ambushes and were continually cutting off the enemy's supplies. The Syracusans were for deciding the issue by battle as soon as possible, but Dionysius opposed them, saying that time and want would ruin the barbarians without fighting. Provoked to anger at this the Syracusans deserted him. In his first concern Dionysius proclaimed freedom for the slaves, but later, when the Carthaginians sent embassies to discuss peace, he negotiated with them, sent back the slaves to their masters, and made peace with the Carthaginians. The conditions were like the former except that the Siceli were to be subject to Dionysius and that he was to receive Tauromenium. After the conclusion of the treaty Magon sailed off, and Dionysius, on taking possession of Tauromenium, banished most of the Siceli who were in it and selected and settled there the most suitable members of his own mercenary troops.

Such was the state of affairs in Sicily; and in Italy the Romans pillaged the city of Faliscus of the tribe of the Falisci.

**97.** At the close of this year, in Athens [391] Nicoteles was archon, and in Rome the consular magistracy was administered by three military tribunes, Marcus Furius and Gaius Aemilius. After these magistrates had entered office, the philo-Lacedaemonians among the Rhodians rose up against the party of the people and expelled from the city the partisans of the Athenians. When these banded together under arms and endeavoured to maintain their interests, the allies of the Lacedaemonians got the upper hand, slaughtered many, and formally banished those who escaped. They also at once sent ambassadors to Lacedaemon to get aid, fearing that some of the citizens would rise in revolt. The Lacedaemonians dispatched to them seven triremes and three men to take charge of affairs, Eudocimus, Philodocus, and Diphilas. They first reached Samos and brought that city over from the Athenians, and then they put in at Rhodes and assumed the oversight of affairs there. The Lacedaemonians, now that their affairs were prospering, resolved to get control of the sea, and after gathering a naval force they again little by little began to get the upper hand over their allies. So they put in at Samos and Cnidus and Rhodes; and gathering ships from every place and enrolling the choicest marines, they equipped lavishly twenty-seven triremes.

Agesilaüs, the king of the Lacedaemonians, on hearing that the Argives were engaged about Corinth, led forth the Lacedaemonians in full force with the exception of one regiment. He visited every part of Argolis, pillaged the homesteads, cut down the trees over the countryside, and then returned to Sparta.

**98.** In Cyprus Evagoras of Salamis, who was of most noble birth, since he was descended from the founders of the city, but had previously been banished because of some factional quarrels and had later returned in company with a small group, drove out Abdemon of Tyre, who was lord of the city and a friend of the King of the Persians. When he took control of the city, Evagoras was at first king only of Salamis, the largest and strongest of the cities of Cyprus; but when he soon acquired great resources and mobilised an army, he set out to make the whole island his own. Some of the cities he subdued by force and others he won over by persuasion. While he easily gained control of the other cities, the peoples of Amathus, Soli, and Citium resisted him with arms and dispatched ambassadors to Artaxerxes the King of the Persians to get his aid. They accused Evagoras of having slain King Agyris, an ally of the Persians, and promised to join the King in acquiring the island for him. The King, not only because he did not wish Evagoras to grow any stronger, but also because he appreciated the strategic position of Cyprus and its great naval strength whereby it would be able to protect Asia in front, decided to accept the alliance. He dismissed the ambassadors and for himself sent letters to the cities situated on the sea and to their commanding satraps to construct triremes and with all speed to make ready everything the fleet might need; and he commanded Hecatomnus, the ruler of Caria, to make war upon Evagoras. Hecatomnus traversed the cities of the upper satrapies and crossed over to Cyprus in strong force.

Such was the state of affairs in Asia. In Italy the Romans concluded peace with the Falisci and waged war for the fourth time on the Aequi; they also sent a colony to Sutrium but were expelled by the enemy from the city of Verrugo.

## How Thibrus, [Thibron] the Lacedaemonian general, was defeated by the Persians and slain (99).

**99.** At the close of this year Demostratus was archon in Athens,[390] and in Rome the consuls Lucius Lucretius and Servilius took office. At this time Artaxerxes sent Struthas as general to the coast with an army to make war on the Lacedaemonians, and the Spartans, when they learned of his arrival, dispatched Thibron as general to Asia. Thibron seized the stronghold of Ionda [Isinda] and a high mountain, Cornissus [Solmissus?], forty stades from Ephesus. He then advanced with eight thousand soldiers together with the troops gathered from Asia, pillaging the King's territory. Struthas, with a strong force of barbarian cavalry, five thousand hoplites, and more than twenty thousand light-armed troops, pitched his camp not far from the Lacedaemonians. Eventually, when Thibron once set out with a detachment of his troops and had seized much booty, Struthas attacked and slew him in battle, killed the larger number of his troops, and took captive others. A few found safety in Cnidinium, an outpost.

Thrasybulus, the Athenian general, went with his fleet from Lesbos to Aspendus and moored his triremes in the Eurymedon River. Although he had received contributions from the Aspendians, some of the soldiers, nevertheless, pillaged the countryside. When night came, the Aspendians, angered at such unfairness, attacked the Athenians and slew both Thrasybulus and a number of the others; whereupon the captains of the Athenian vessels, greatly alarmed, speedily manned the ships and sailed off to Rhodes. Since this city was in revolt, they joined the exiles who had seized a certain outpost and waged war on the men who held the city. When the Athenians learned of the death of their general Thrasybulus, they sent out Agyrius as general.

Such was the state of affairs in Asia.

**100.** In Sicily Dionysius, the tyrant of the Syracusans, with intent to annex the Greeks of Italy as well to the overlordship that he held in the island, postponed the general war against them to another time. He judged rather that it was good policy to attack first the city of the Rhegians, because it was the advanced bastion of Italy, and so set out from Syracuse with his army. He had twenty thousand infantry, a thousand cavalry, and one hundred and twenty ships of war. He crossed with his troops to the borders of Locris and from there made his way through the interior, cutting down the trees and burning and destroying

## Book XIV

the territory of the Rhegians. His fleet sailed along to the other districts upon the sea and he encamped with his entire army at the Strait. When the Italians learned that Dionysius had crossed the sea to attack Rhegium, they dispatched sixty ships from Croton, with intent to hand them over to the Rhegians. While this fleet was cruising on the high sea, Dionysius sailed against them with fifty ships, and when the fleet fled to land, he pressed his attack no less vigorously and began to make fast and haul off the ships that were lying off-shore. Since the sixty triremes were in danger of being captured, the Rhegians came to their aid in full force and held Dionysius off from the land by the multitude of their missiles. When a heavy storm arose, the Rhegians hauled up the ships high and dry on the land, but Dionysius lost seven ships in the heavy gale and together with them no fewer than fifteen hundred men. Since the sailors were cast ashore together with their ships on Rhegian territory, many of them were taken prisoner by the Rhegians. Dionysius, who was on a quinquereme and many times narrowly escaped foundering, about midnight barely found safety in the harbour of Messenê. Since the winter season had already come, he drew up terms of alliance with the Leucani and led his forces back to Syracuse.

**101.** After this, when the Leucanians overran the territory of Thurii, the Thurians sent word to their allies to gather to them speedily under arms. For the Greek cities of Italy had an agreement among themselves to the effect that if any city's territory was being plundered by the Leucanians, they should all come to its aid, and that if any city's army did not take up a position to give aid, the generals of that city should be put to death. Consequently, when the Thurians dispatched messengers to the cities to tell of the approach of the enemy, they all made ready to march. The Thurians, who were first off the mark in their actions, did not wait for the troops of their allies, but set forth against the Leucanians with above fourteen thousand infantry and about one thousand cavalry. The Leucanians, on hearing of the approach of the enemy, withdrew to their own territory, and the Thurians, falling in haste upon Leucania, captured the first outpost and gathered much booty, thus taking the bait, as it were, for their own destruction. For having become puffed with pride at their success, they advanced with light concern through some narrow and sheer paths, in order to lay siege to the prosperous city of Laüs. When they had arrived at a certain plain surrounded by lofty hills and precipitous cliffs, thereupon the Leucanians with their entire army cut them off from retreat to their native soil. Making their appearance, which was quite unexpected and unconcealed, on the height, they filled the Greeks with dismay, both because of the great size of the army and because of the difficulty of the terrain; for the Leucanians had at the time thirty thousand infantry and no less than four thousand cavalry.

**102.** When the Greeks were to their surprise caught in such hopeless peril as we have described, the barbarians descended into the plain. A battle took place and there fell of the Italian Greeks overwhelmed as they were by the multitude of the Leucanians, more than ten thousand men, since the Leucanians gave orders to save no one alive. Of the survivors some fled to a height on the sea, and others, seeing warships sailing toward them and thinking they belonged to the Rhegians, fled in a body to the sea and swam out to the triremes. The approaching fleet belonged to Dionysius the tyrant, under command of his brother Leptines, and had been sent to the aid of the Leucanians. Leptines received the swimmers kindly, set them on land, and persuaded the Leucanians to accept a mina of silver for each captive, the number of whom was over a thousand. Leptines went surety for the ransom money, reconciled the Italian Greeks with the Leucanians, and persuaded them to conclude peace. He won great acclaim among the Italian Greeks, having settled the war, as he had, to his own advantage, but without any profit to Dionysius. For Dionysius hoped that, if the Italian Greeks were embroiled in war with the Leucanians, he might appear and easily make himself master of affairs in Italy, but if they were rid of such a dangerous war, his success would be difficult. Consequently he relieved Leptines of his command and appointed Thearides, his other brother, commander of the fleet.

Subsequent to these events the Romans portioned out in allotments the territory of the Veians, giving each holder four plethra, but according to other accounts, twenty-eight. The Romans were at war with the Aequi and took by storm the city of Liphlus; and they began war upon the people of Velitrae, who had revolted. Satricum also revolted from the Romans; and they dispatched a colony to Cercii.

### How the Greeks of Italy joined to form a single political group and took the field against Dionysius (103).

103. When the year had ended, in Athens [389] Antipater was archon, and in Rome Lucius Valerius and Aulus Mallius administered the consular magistracy. This year Dionysius, the lord of the Syracusans, openly indicated his design of an attack on Italy and set forth from Syracuse with a most formidable force. He had more than twenty thousand infantry, some three thousand cavalry, forty ships of war, and not less than three hundred vessels transporting food supplies. On arriving at Messenê on the fifth day he rested his troops in the city, while he dispatched his brother Thearides with thirty ships to the islands of the Liparaeans, since he had learned that ten ships of the Rhegians were in those waters. Thearides, sailing forth and coming upon the ten Rhegian ships in a place favourable to his purpose, seized the ships together with their crews and speedily returned to Dionysius at Messenê. Dionysius threw the prisoners in chains and turned them over to the custody of the Messenians; then he transported his army to Caulonia, laid siege to the city, advanced his siege-engines, and launched frequent assaults.

When the Greeks of Italy learned that the armaments of Dionysius were starting to move across the strait which separated them, they in turn mustered their forces. Since the city of the Crotoniates was the most heavily populated and had the largest number of exiles from Syracuse, they gave over to them the command of the war, and the people of Croton gathered troops from every quarter and chose as general Heloris the Syracusan. Since this man had been banished by Dionysius and was considered by all to possess action and enterprise, it was believed that he could be best trusted, because of his hatred, to lead a war against the tyrant. When all the allies had gathered in Croton, Heloris disposed them to his liking and advanced with the entire army toward Caulonia. He calculated that he would by his appearance at the same time both relieve the siege and also be in combat with the enemy worn out by their daily assaults. In all he had about twenty-five thousand infantry and two thousand cavalry.

104. The Italian Greeks had accomplished the major part of their march and were encamped on the Eleporus River, when Dionysius drew off from the city and advanced to meet them. Now Heloris was in the van of his army with five hundred of his choicest troops and Dionysius, as it happened, was encamped forty stades from the enemy. On learning from his scouts that the enemy was near, he roused his army at early light and led it forward. Meeting at daybreak the troops of Heloris, who were few in number, he engaged them in unexpected battle, and since he had his army ready for combat, he gave the enemy not a moment to recover themselves. Though Heloris found himself in desperate straits, he withstood the attackers with what troops he had, while he sent some of his friends to the camp, urging them to rush up the main body of soldiers. These speedily carried out their orders, and when the Italian Greeks learned of the danger facing their general and his troops, they came to their aid on the run. Meanwhile Dionysius, with his troops in close order, surrounded Heloris and his men and slew them almost to a man, though they offered a gallant resistance. Since the Italian Greeks in their haste entered the fighting in scattered groups, the Sicilian Greeks, who kept their lines intact, experienced no difficulty in overcoming the enemy. Nevertheless, the Greeks of Italy maintained the fight for some time, although they saw their comrades falling in great numbers. But when they learned of the death of their general, while being greatly hampered as they fell foul of one another in their confusion, then at last they completely lost spirit and turned in flight.

*How Dionysius, although he had been victorious in battle and had taken ten thousand prisoners, let them go without requiring ransom and allowed the cities to live under their own laws (105).*

105. Many were killed in their rout across the plain; but the main body made a safe retreat to a hill, which was strong enough to withstand a siege but had no water and could be easily contained by the enemy. Dionysius invested the hill and bivouacked under arms that day and through the night, giving careful attention to the watches. The next day the beleaguered suffered severely from the heat and lack of water. They then sent a herald to Dionysius inviting him to accept ransom; he, however, did not preserve moderation in his success but ordered them to lay down their arms and put themselves at the disposal of their conqueror. This was a harsh order and they held out for some time; but when they were overborne by physical necessity, they surrendered about the eighth hour, their bodies being now weakened. Dionysius took a staff and struck it on the ground while numbering the prisoners as they descended, and they amounted to more than ten thousand. All men were apprehensive of his brutality, but on the contrary he showed himself most kindly; for he let the prisoners go subject to no authority without ransom, concluded peace with most of the cities, and left them independent. In return for this he received the approval of those he had favoured and was honoured with gold crowns; and men believed that this would probably be the finest act of his life.

## The capture and razing of Caulonia and Hipponium and the removal of their inhabitants to Syracuse (106-107).

**106.** Dionysius now advanced against Rhegium and prepared to lay siege to the city with his army because of the slight he had received in connection with his offer of marriage. Deep distress gripped the Rhegians, since they had neither allies nor an army that was a match for him in battle, and they knew, furthermore, that if the city were taken, neither pity nor entreaty would be left them. Therefore they decided to dispatch ambassadors to entreat him to deal moderately with them and to urge him to make no decision against them beyond what be came a human being. Dionysius required three hundred talents of them, took all their ships, which amounted to seventy, and ordered the delivery of one hundred hostages. When all these had been turned over, he set out against Caulonia. The inhabitants of this city he transplanted to Syracuse, gave them citizenship, and allowed them exemption from taxes for five years; he then levelled the city to the ground and gave the territory of the Cauloniates to the Locrians.

The Romans, after taking the city of Liphoecua from the people of the Aequi, held, in accordance with the vows of the consuls, great games in honour of Zeus.

**107.** At the close of this year, in Athens [388] Pyrgion was archon and in Rome four military tribunes took over the consular magistracy, Lucius Lucretius, Servius Sulpicius, Gaius Aemilius, and Gaius Rufus, and the Ninety-eighth Olympiad was celebrated, that in which Sosippus of Athens was the victor. When these men had entered office, Dionysius, the lord of the Syracusans, advanced with his army to Hipponium, removed its inhabitants to Syracuse, razed the city to the ground, and apportioned its territory to the Locrians. For he was continuously set upon doing the Locrians favours for the marriage they had agreed to, whereas he studied revenge upon the Rhegians for their affront with respect to the offer of kinship. On the occasion when he sent ambassadors to them to ask them to grant him in marriage a maiden of their city, the Rhegians replied to the ambassadors by action of the people, we are told, that the only maiden they would agree to his marrying would be the daughter of their public executioner. Angered because of this and believing that he had been grossly insulted, he was bent on getting revenge upon them. Indeed the peace he had concluded with them in the preceding year had come from no hankering on his part for friendly relations, but was designed to strip them of their naval power, which consisted of seventy triremes. For he believed that if the city were cut off from aid by sea he could easily reduce it by siege. Consequently, while loitering in Italy, he kept seeking a plausible excuse whereby he might seem to have broken the truce without prejudice to his own standing.

## How Dionysius laid siege to Rhegium (108, 111).

**108.** Dionysius now led his forces to the Strait and made preparations to cross over. First he asked the Rhegians to provide him with supplies for sale, promising that he would promptly return from Syracuse what they had given. He made this request in order that men should think that, if they did not provide the food, he would be justified in seizing the city, whereas if they did, he believed their food would run out and by sitting down before the city he would speedily master it by starvation. The Rhegians, suspecting nothing of this, at first supplied them lavishly with food for several days; but when he kept extending his stay, at one time claiming illness and at another offering other excuses, they suspected what he had in mind and no longer furnished his army with supplies. Dionysius, pretending now to be angered at this, returned the hostages to the Rhegians, laid siege to the city, and launched daily assaults upon it. He also constructed a great multitude of siege weapons of unbelievable size by which he rocked the walls in his determination to take the city by storm. The Rhegians chose Phyton as general, armed all who could bear arms, gave close concern to their watches, and, as opportunity arose, sallied out and burned the enemy's siege engines. Fighting brilliantly as they did for their fatherland on many occasions before the walls, they roused the anger of the enemy, and although they lost many of their own troops, they also slew no small number of the Sicilian Greeks. And it happened that Dionysius himself was struck by a lance in the groin and barely escaped death, recovering with difficulty from the wound. The siege wore on because of the unsurpassable zeal the Rhegians displayed to maintain their freedom; but Dionysius held his armaments to the daily assaults and would not give up the task he had originally proposed to himself.

**109.** The Olympic Games were at hand and Dionysius dispatched to the contest several four-horse teams, which far surpassed all others in swiftness, and also pavilions for the festive occasion, which were interwoven with gold and embellished with expensive cloth of gay and varied colours. He also sent the best professional reciters that they might present his poems in the gathering and thus win glory for the name of Dionysius, for he was madly addicted to poetry. In charge of all this he sent along his brother Thearides. When Thearides arrived at the gathering, he was a centre of attraction for the beauty of the pavilions and the large number of four-horse teams; and when the reciters began to present the poems of Dionysius, at first the multitude thronged together because of the pleasing voices of the actors and all were filled with wonder, but on second consideration, when they observed how poor his verses were, they laughed Dionysius to scorn and went so far in their rejection that some of them even ventured to rifle the tents. Indeed the orator Lysias, who was at that time in Olympia, urged the multitude not to admit to the sacred festival the representatives from a most impious tyranny; and at this time he delivered his *Olympiacus*. In the course of the contest chance brought it about that some of Dionysius' chariots the course and others collided among themselves and were wrecked. Likewise the ship which was on its way to Sicily carrying the representatives from the games was wrecked by strong winds near Taras [Tarentum] in Italy. Consequently the sailors who got safe to Syracuse spread the story throughout the city, we are told, that the badness of the verses caused the ill-success, not only of the reciters, but of the teams and of the ship with them. When Dionysius learned of the ridicule that had been heaped upon his verses, his flatterers told him that every fair accomplishment is first an object of envy and then of admiration. He therefore did not give up his devotion to writing.

The Romans fought a battle at Gurasium with the Volscians and slew great numbers of the enemy.

## How the Greeks concluded the Peace of Antalcidas with Artaxerxes (110).

110. At the conclusion of these events the year came to an end, and among the Athenians [387] Theodotus was archon and in Rome the consular magistracy was held by six military tribunes, Quintus Caeso Sulpicius, Aenus Caeso Fabius, Quintus Servilius, and Publius Cornelius. After these men had entered office, the Lacedaemonians, who were hard put to it by their double war, that against the Greeks and that against the Persians, dispatched their admiral Antalcidas to Artaxerxes to treat for peace. Antalcidas discussed as well as he could the circumstances of his mission and the King agreed to make peace on the following terms: "The Greek cities of Asia are subject to the King, but all the other Greeks shall be independent; and upon those who refuse compliance and do not accept these terms I shall make war through the aid of those who consent to them." Now the Lacedaemonians consented to the terms and offered no opposition, but the Athenians and Thebans and some of the other Greeks were deeply concerned that the cities of Asia should be left in the lurch, but since they were not by themselves a match in war, they consented of necessity and accepted the peace.

The King, now that his difference with the Greeks was settled, made ready his armaments for the war against Cyprus. For Evagoras had got possession of almost the whole of Cyprus and gathered strong armaments, because Artaxerxes was distracted by the war against the Greeks.

## How Dionysius laid siege to Rhegium, the capture of Rhegium, and the disasters suffered by the city (111-112).

111. It was about the eleventh month of Dionysius' siege of Rhegium, and since he had cut off relief from every direction, the inhabitants of the city were faced by a terrible dearth of the necessities of life. We are told, indeed, that at the time a medimnus of wheat among the Rhegians cost five minas. So reduced were they by lack of food that at first they ate their horses and other beasts of burden, then fed upon boiled skins and leather, and finally they would go out from the city and eat the grass near the walls like so many cattle. To such an extent did the demand of nature compel the wants of man to turn for their satisfaction to the food of dumb animals. When Dionysius learned what was taking place, far from showing mercy to those who were perforce suffering beyond man's endurance, on the contrary he brought in cattle to clear the place of the green stuff, with the result that it was completely stripped. Consequently the Rhegians, overcome by their excessive hardships, surrendered their city to the tyrant, giving him complete power over their lives. Within the city Dionysius found heaps of dead who had perished from lack of food, and the living too whom he captured were like dead men and weakened in body. He got together more than six thousand captives and the multitude he sent off to Syracuse with orders that those who could pay as ransom a mina of silver should be freed, but to sell as slaves those who were unable to raise that sum.

112. Dionysius seized Phyton, the general of the Rhegians, and drowned his son in the sea, but Phyton himself he at first bound on his loftiest siege engines, wreaking a vengeance upon him such as is to be seen upon the stage of tragedy. He also sent one of his servants to him to tell him that Dionysius had drowned his son in the sea the day before; to whom Phyton replied, "He has been more

fortunate than his father by one day." After this Dionysius had him led about the city under flogging and subjected to every indignity, a herald accompanying him and announcing that Dionysius was inflicting this unusual vengeance upon the man because he had persuaded the city to undertake the war. Phyton, who had shown himself a brave general during the siege and had won approval for all his other qualities, endured his mortal punishment with no low-born spirit. Rather he preserved his spirit undaunted and cried out that he was punished because he would not betray the city to Dionysius, and that heaven would soon visit such punishment upon Dionysius himself. The courage of the man aroused sympathy even among the soldiers of Dionysius, and some of them began to protest. Dionysius, fearing that some of the soldiers might make bold to snatch Phyton out of his hands, ceased to punish him and drowned the unfortunate man at sea together with his near of kin. So this man suffered monstrous tortures unworthy of his merits. He won many of the Greeks to grieve for him at the time and many poets to lament the sad story of his reversal of fortune thereafter.

**113.** At the time that Dionysius was besieging Rhegium, the Celts who had their homes in the regions beyond the Alps streamed through the passes in great strength and seized the territory that lay between the Apennine mountains and the Alps, expelling the Tyrrhenians who dwelt there. These, according to some, were colonists from the twelve cities of Tyrrhenia; but others state that before the Trojan War Pelasgians fled from Thessaly to escape the flood of Deucalion's time and settled in this region. Now it happened, when the Celts divided up the territory by tribes, that those known as the Sennones received the area which lay farthest from the mountains and along the sea. But since this region was scorching hot, they were distressed and eager to move; hence they armed their younger men and sent them out to seek a territory where they might settle. Now they invaded Tyrrhenia, and being in number some thirty thousand they sacked the territory of the Clusini.

At this very time the Roman people sent ambassadors into Tyrrhenia to spy out the army of the Celts. The ambassadors arrived at Clusium, and when they saw that a battle had been joined, with more valour than wisdom they joined the men of Clusium against their besiegers, and one [Quintus Fabius Ambustus] of the ambassadors was successful in killing a rather important commander. When the Celts learned of this, they dispatched ambassadors to Rome to demand the person of the envoy who had thus commenced an unjust war. The senate at first sought to persuade the envoys of the Celts to accept money in satisfaction of the injury, but when they would not consider this, it voted to surrender the accused. The father of the man to be surrendered, who was also one of the military tribunes with consular power, appealed the judgement to the people, and since he was a man of influence among the masses, he persuaded them to void the decision of the senate. Now in the times previous to this the people had followed the senate in all matters; with this occasion they first began to rescind decisions of that body.

### The capture of Rome, except for the Capitoline, by the Gauls (114-117).

**114.** The ambassadors of the Celts returned to their camp and reported the reply of the Romans. At this they were greatly angered and, adding an army from their fellow tribesmen, they marched swiftly upon Rome itself, numbering more than seventy thousand men. The military tribunes of the Romans, exercising their special power, when they heard of the advance of the Celts, armed all the men of military age. They then marched out in full force and, crossing the Tiber, led their troops for eighty stades along the river; and at news of the approach of the Galatians they drew up the army for battle. Their best troops, to the number of twenty-four thousand, they set in a line from the river as far as the hills and on the highest hills they stationed the weakest. The Celts deployed their troops in a long line and, whether by fortune or design, stationed their choicest troops on the hills. The trumpets on both sides sounded the charge at the same time and the armies joined in battle with great clamour. The elite troops of the Celts, who were opposed to the weakest soldiers of the Romans, easily drove them from the hills. Consequently, as these fled in masses to the Romans on the plain, the ranks were thrown into confusion and fled in dismay before the attack of the Celts. Since the bulk of the Romans fled along the river and impeded one another by reason of their disorder, the Celts were not behindhand in slaying again and again those who were last in line. Hence the entire plain was strewn with dead. Of the men who fled to the river the bravest attempted to swim across with their arms, prizing their armour as highly as their lives; but since the stream ran strong, some of them were borne down to their death by the weight of the arms, and some, after being carried along for some distance, finally and after great effort got off safe. Since the enemy pressed them hard and was making a great slaughter along the river, most of the survivors threw away their arms and swam across the Tiber.

**115.** The Celts, though they had slain great numbers on the bank of the river, nevertheless did not desist from the zest for glory but showered javelins upon the swimmers; and since many missiles were hurled and men were massed in the river, those who threw did not miss their mark. So it was that some died at once from mortal blows, and others, who were wounded only, were carried off unconscious because of loss of blood and the swift current. When such disaster befell, the greater part of the Romans who escaped occupied the city of Veii, which had lately been razed by them, fortified the place as well as they could, and received the survivors of the rout. A few of those who had swum the river fled without their arms to Rome and reported that the whole army had perished. When word of such misfortunes as we have described was brought to those who had been left behind in the city, everyone fell into despair; for they saw no possibility of resistance, now that all their youth had perished, and to flee with their children and wives was fraught with the greatest danger since the enemy were close at hand. Now many private citizens fled with their households to neighbouring cities, but the city magistrates, encouraging the populace, issued orders for them to bring speedily to the Capitoline grain and every other necessity. When this had been done, both the acropolis and the Capitoline were stored not only with supplies of food but with silver and gold and the costliest raiment, since the precious possessions had been gathered from over the whole city into one place. They gathered such valuables as they could and fortified the place we have mentioned during a respite of three days. For the Celts spent the first day cutting off, according to their custom, the heads of the dead. For two days they lay encamped before the city, for when they saw the walls deserted and yet heard the noise made by those who were transferring their most useful

# Book XIV

possessions to the acropolis, they suspected that the Romans were planning a trap for them. On the fourth day, after they had learned the true state of affairs, they broke down the gates and pillaged the city except for a few dwellings on the Palatine. After this they delivered daily assaults on strong positions, without, however, inflicting any serious hurt upon their opponents and with the loss of many of their own troops. Nevertheless, they did not relax their ardour, expecting that, even if they did not conquer by force, they would wear down the enemy in the course of time, when the necessities of life had entirely given out.

**116.** While the Romans were in such throes, the neighbouring Tyrrhenians advanced and made a raid with a strong army on the territory of the Romans, capturing many prisoners and not a small amount of booty. But the Romans who had fled to Veii, falling unexpectedly upon the Tyrrhenians, put them to flight, took back the booty, and captured their camp. Having got possession of arms in abundance, they distributed them among the unarmed, and they also gathered men from the countryside and armed them, since they intended to relieve the siege of the soldiers who had taken refuge on the Capitoline. While they were at a loss how they might reveal their plans to the besieged, since the Celts had surrounded them with strong forces, a certain Cominius Pontius undertook to get the cheerful news to the men on the Capitoline. Starting out alone and swimming the river by night, he got unseen to a cliff of the Capitoline that was hard to climb and, hauling himself up it with difficulty, told the soldiers on the Capitoline about the troops that had been collected in Veii and how they were watching for an opportunity and would attack the Celts. Then, descending by the way he had mounted and swimming the Tiber, he returned to Veii. The Celts, when they observed the tracks of one who had recently climbed up, made plans to ascend at night by the same cliff. Consequently about the middle of the night, while the guards were neglectful of their watch because of the strength of the place, some Celts started an ascent of the cliff. They escaped detection by the guards, but the sacred geese of Hera, which were kept there, noticed the climbers and set up a cackling. The guards rushed to the place and the Celts deterred did not dare proceed farther. A certain Marcus Mallius, a man held in high esteem, rushing to the defence of the place, cut off the hand of the climber with his sword and, striking him on the breast with his shield, rolled him from the cliff. In like manner the second climber met his death, whereupon the rest all quickly turned in flight. Since the cliff was precipitous they were all hurled headlong and perished. As a result of this, when the Romans sent ambassadors to negotiate a peace, they were persuaded, upon receipt of one thousand pounds of gold, to leave the city and to withdraw from Roman territory.

The Romans, now that their houses had been razed to the ground and the majority of their citizens slain, gave permission to anyone who wished to build a home in any place he chose, and supplied him at state expense with roof-tiles; and up to the present time these are known as "public tiles." Since every man naturally built his home where it suited his fancy, the result was that the streets of the city were narrow and crooked; consequently, when the population increased in later days, it was impossible to straighten the streets. Some also say that the Roman matrons, because they contributed their gold ornaments to the common safety, received from the people as a reward the right to ride through the city in chariots.

**117.** While the Romans were in a weakened condition because of the misfortune we have described, the Volscians went to war against them. Accordingly the Roman military tribunes enrolled soldiers, took the field with their army, and pitched camp on the Campus Martius, as it is called, two hundred stades distant from Rome. Since the Volscians lay over against them with a larger force and were assaulting the camp, the citizens in Rome, fearing for the safety of those in the encampment, appointed Marcus Furius dictator. . . . These armed all the men of military age and marched out during the night. At day-break they caught the Volscians as they were assaulting the camp, and appearing on their rear easily put them to flight. When the troops in the camp then sallied forth, the Volscians were caught in the middle and cut down almost to a man. Thus a people that passed for powerful in former days was by this disaster reduced to the weakest among the neighbouring tribes.

After the battle the dictator, on hearing that Bola was being besieged by the Aeculani [Aequi], who are now called the Aequicoli, led forth his troops and slew most of the besieging army. From here he marched to the territory of Sutrium, a Roman colony, which the Tyrrhenians had forcibly occupied. Falling unexpectedly upon the Tyrrhenians, he slew many of them and recovered the city for the people of Sutrium.

The Gauls on their way from Rome laid siege to the city of Veascium which was an ally of the Romans. The dictator attacked them, slew the larger number of them, and got possession of all their baggage, included in which was the gold which they had received for Rome and practically all the booty which they had gathered in the seizure of the city. Despite the accomplishment of such great deeds, envy on the part of the tribunes prevented his celebrating a triumph. There are some, however, who state that he celebrated a triumph for his victory over the Tuscans in a chariot drawn by four white horses, for which the people two years later fined him a large sum of money. But we shall recur to this in the appropriate period of time. Those Celts who had passed into Iapygia turned back through the territory of the Romans; but soon thereafter the Cerii made a crafty attack on them by night and cut all of them to pieces in the Trausian Plain.

The historian Callisthenes began his history with the peace of this year between the Greeks and Artaxerxes, the King of the Persians. His account embraced a period of thirty years in ten Books and he closed the last Book of his history with the seizure of the Temple of Delphi by Philomelus the Phocian. But for our part, since we have arrived at the peace between the Greeks and Artaxerxes, and at the threat to Rome offered by the Gauls, we shall make this the end of this Book, as we proposed at the beginning.

# MAPS

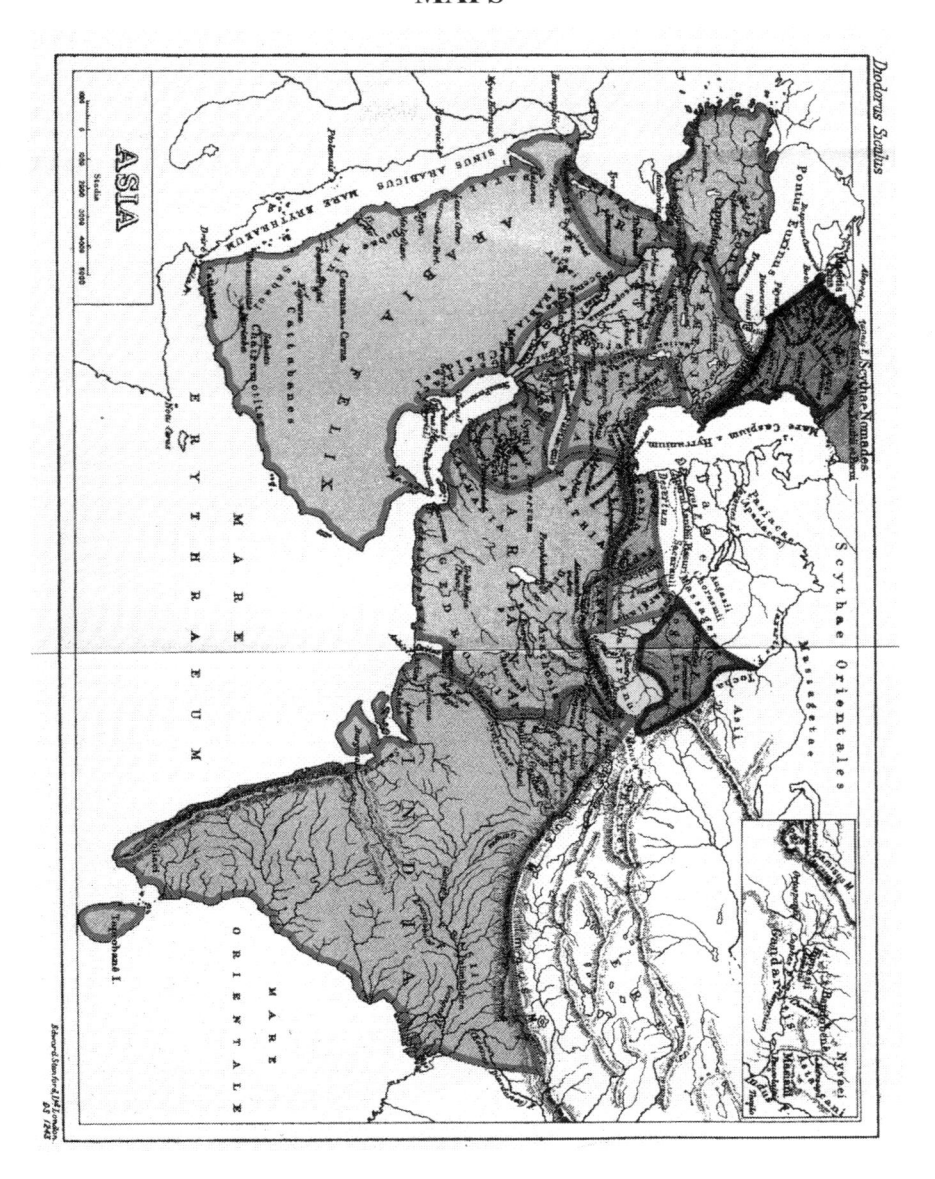

Maps

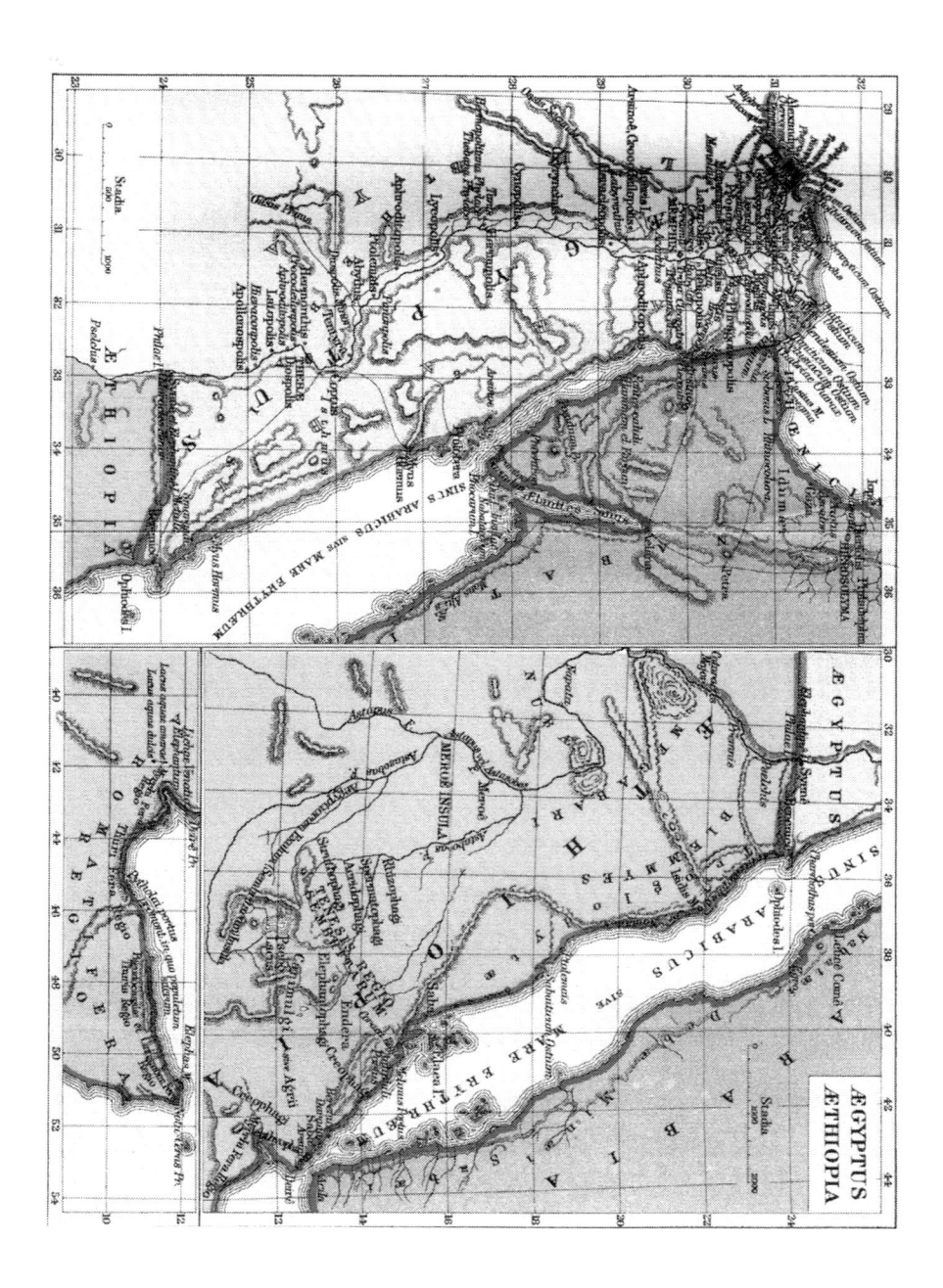

# Maps

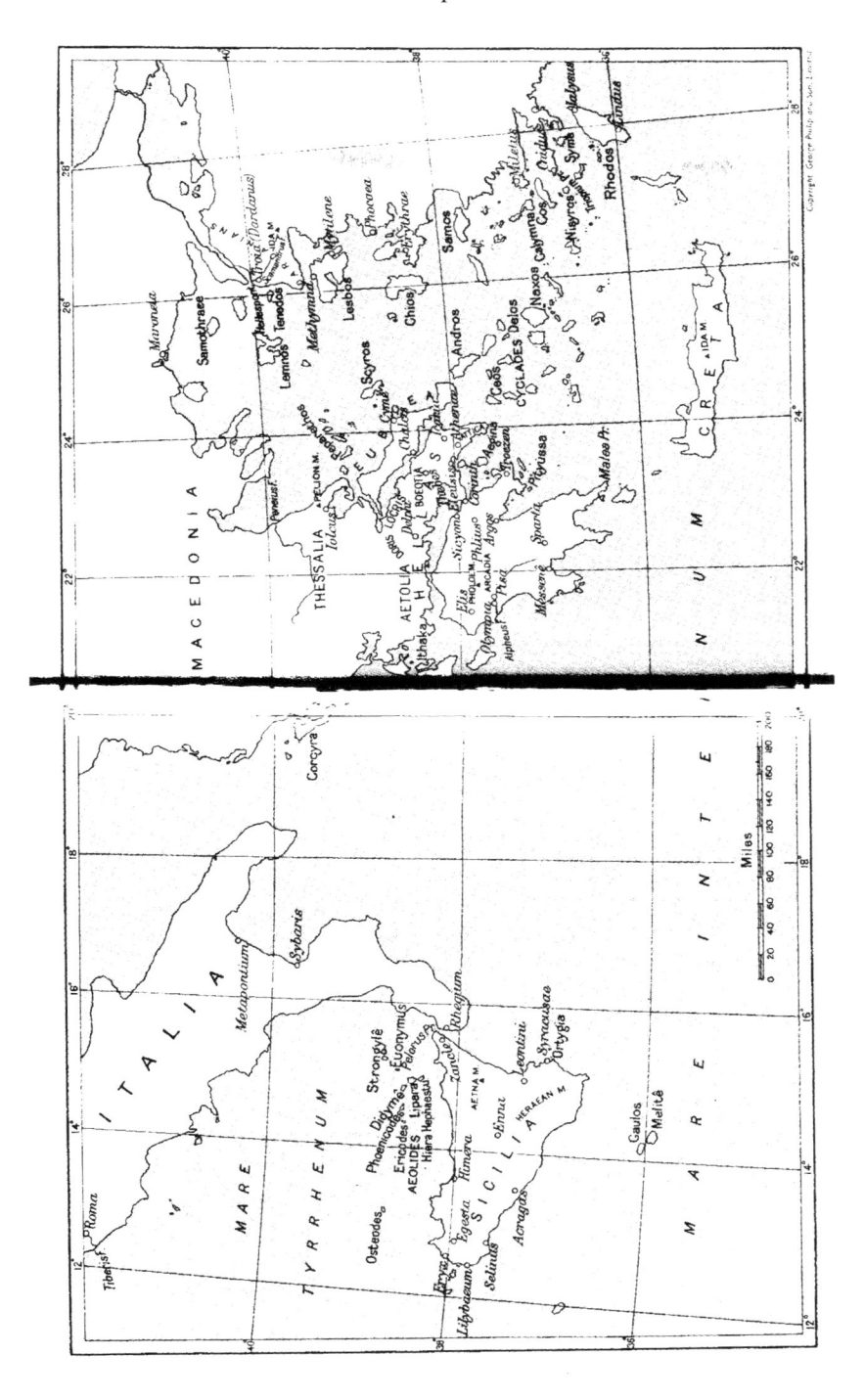

# Maps

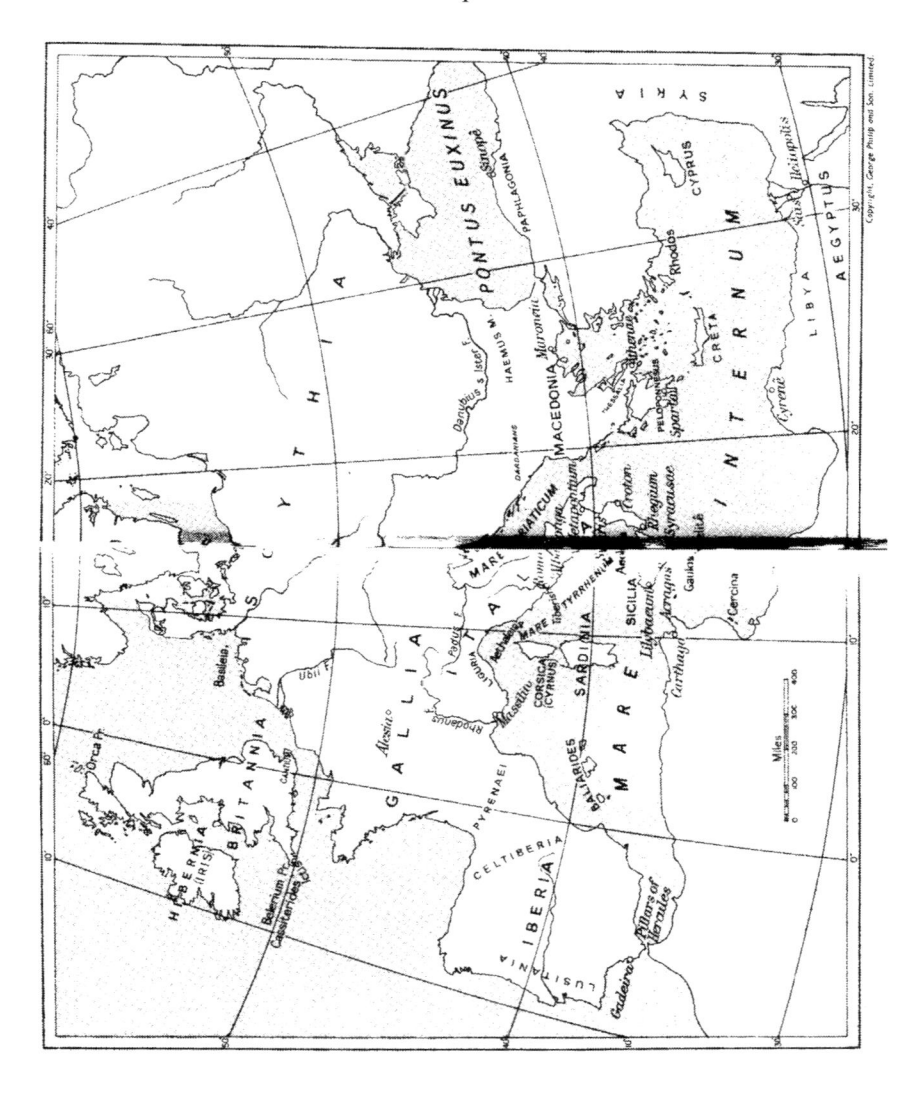

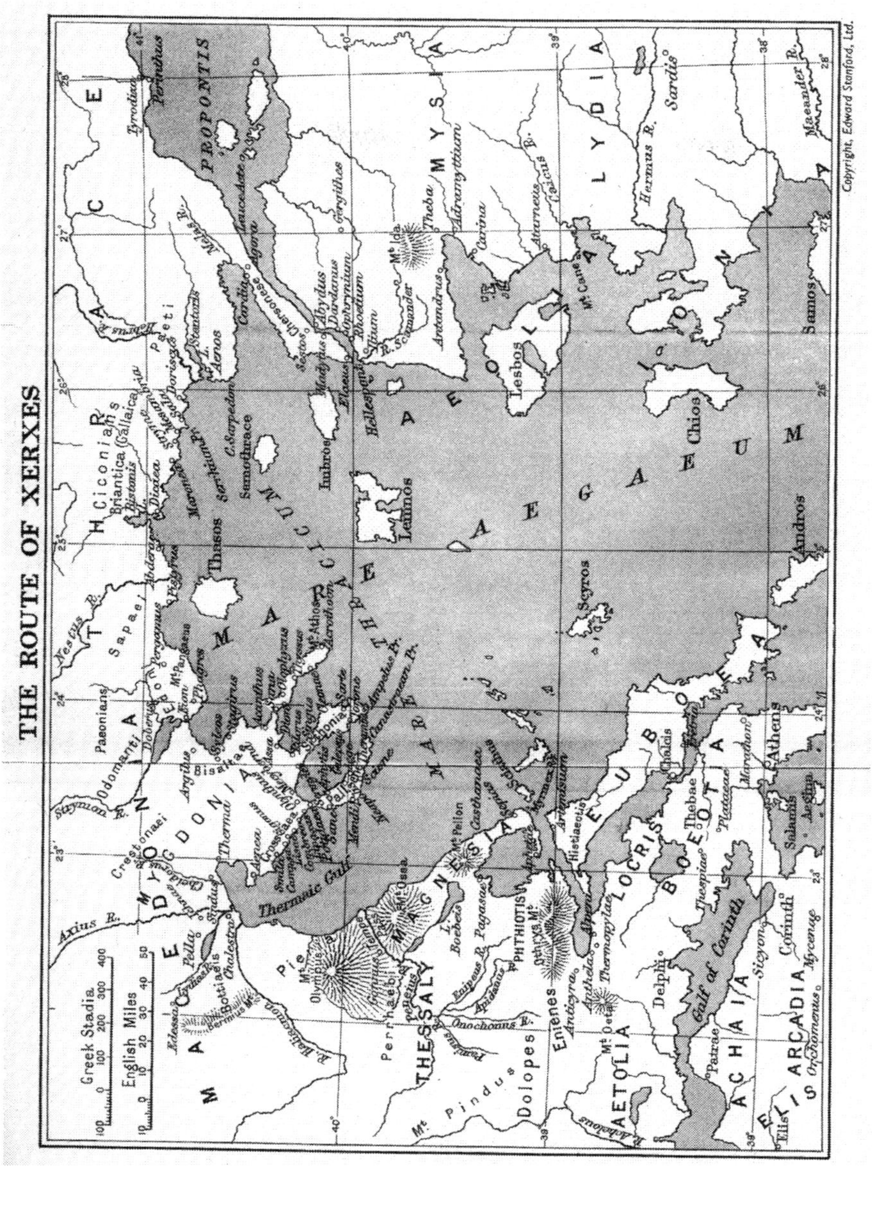
THE ROUTE OF XERXES
Greek Stadia
English Miles
PROPONTIS
MARE AEGAEUM
Thermaic Gulf
Gulf of Corinth
Thasos
Samothrace
Imbros
Lemnos
Lesbos
Chios
Samos
Andros
Scyros
Athens
Thebae
Delphi
Corinth
Salamis
Sardis
Abydus
Sestos
Cardia
Mt Ida
Mt Athos
Mt Olympus
Mt Pindus
Mt Oeta
Thermopylae
THESSALY
MAGNESIA
AETOLIA
ACHAIA
ARCADIA
Copyright, Edward Stanford, Ltd.

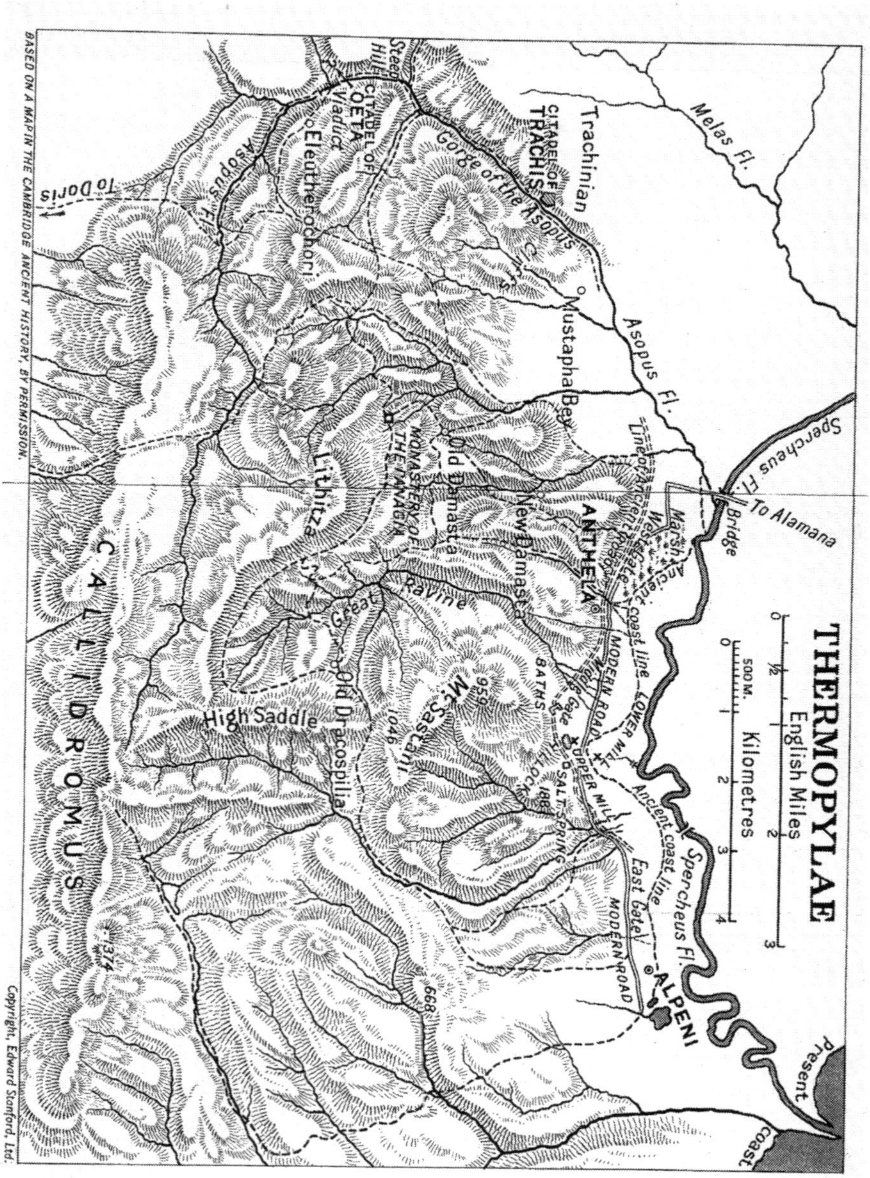
THERMOPYLAE
English Miles
Kilometres
Melas Fl.
Spercheus Fl.
To Alamana
Bridge
Asopus Fl.
Trachinian
CITADEL OF TRACHIS
Gorge of the Asopus
Steep Hill
CITADEL OF OETA
Viaduct
Eleutherochori
To Doris
Mustapha Bey
Marsh
Ancient coast line
West Gate
ANTHELA
Old Damasta
New Damasta
MONASTERY OF THE PANAGIA
Lithitza
Great Ravine
Old Dracospilia
High Saddle
Mt. Sastani
BATHS
MODERN ROAD
LOWER MILL
UPPER MILL
SALT SPRING
Modern Road
East Gate
ALPENI
Present Coast
CALLIDROMUS
BASED ON A MAP IN THE CAMBRIDGE ANCIENT HISTORY, BY PERMISSION.
Copyright, Edward Stanford, Ltd.

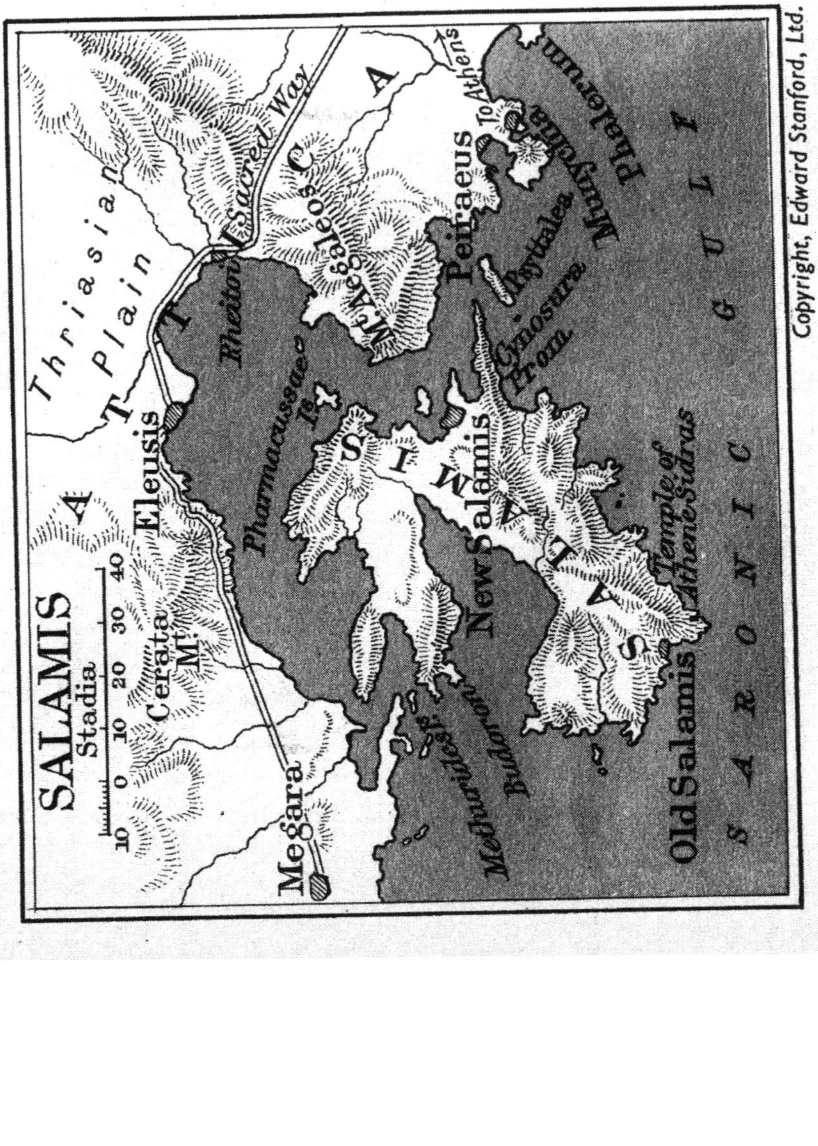
SALAMIS
Stadia
10 0 10 20 30 40
Thriasian Plain
ATTICA
Eleusis
Cerata Mt.
Megara
Sacred Way
Rheitoi
Mt. Aegaleos
Pharmacussae Is.
Peiraeus
To Athens
Munychia
Phalerum
Psyttalea
Cynosura Prom.
SALAMIS
New Salamis
Budorum
Methurides Is.
Temple of Athene Sciras
Old Salamis
SARONIC GULF
Copyright, Edward Stanford, Ltd.

## Maps

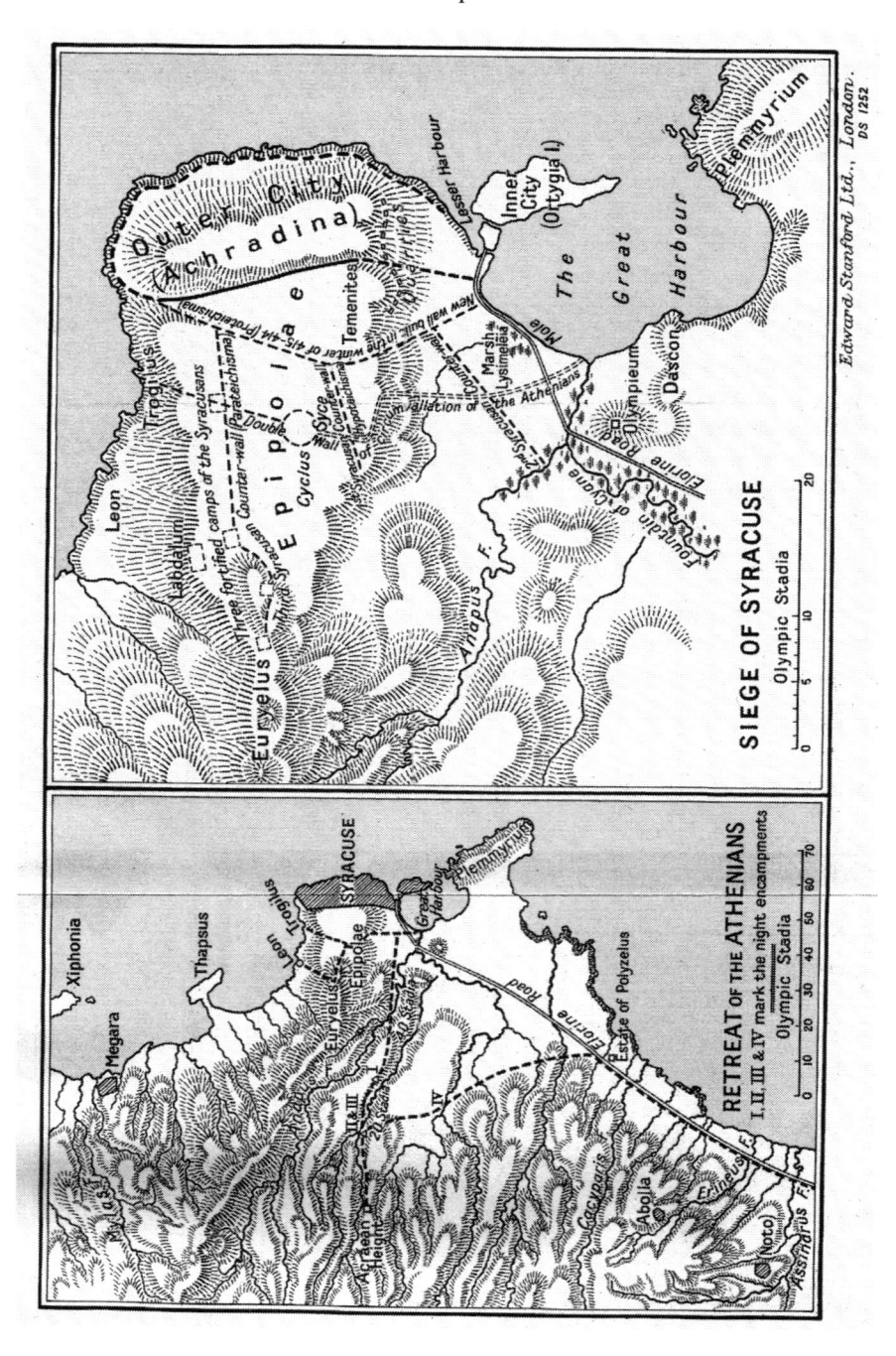

**SIEGE OF SYRACUSE**

**RETREAT OF THE ATHENIANS**
I, II, III & IV mark the night encampments

## Maps

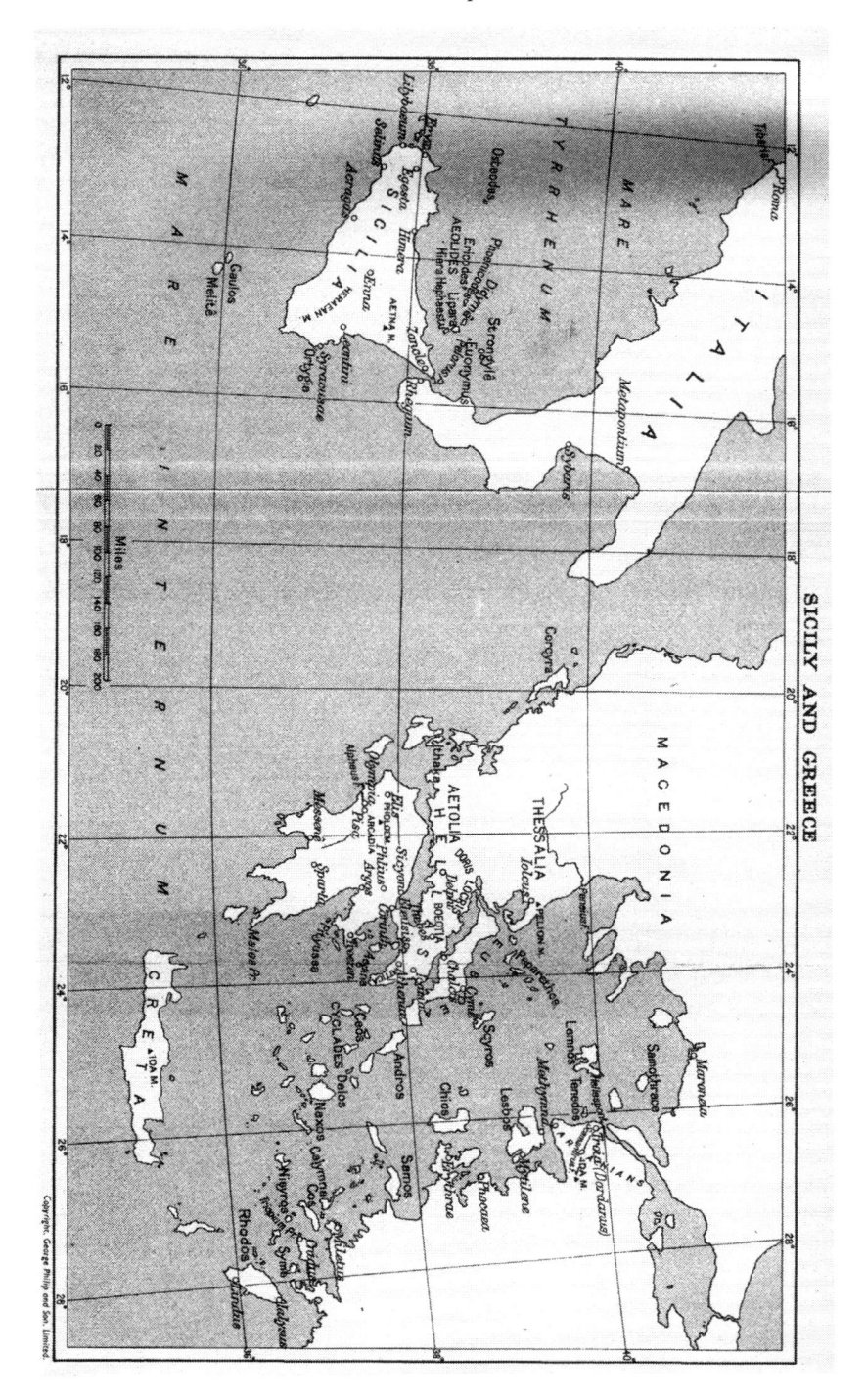

# Maps

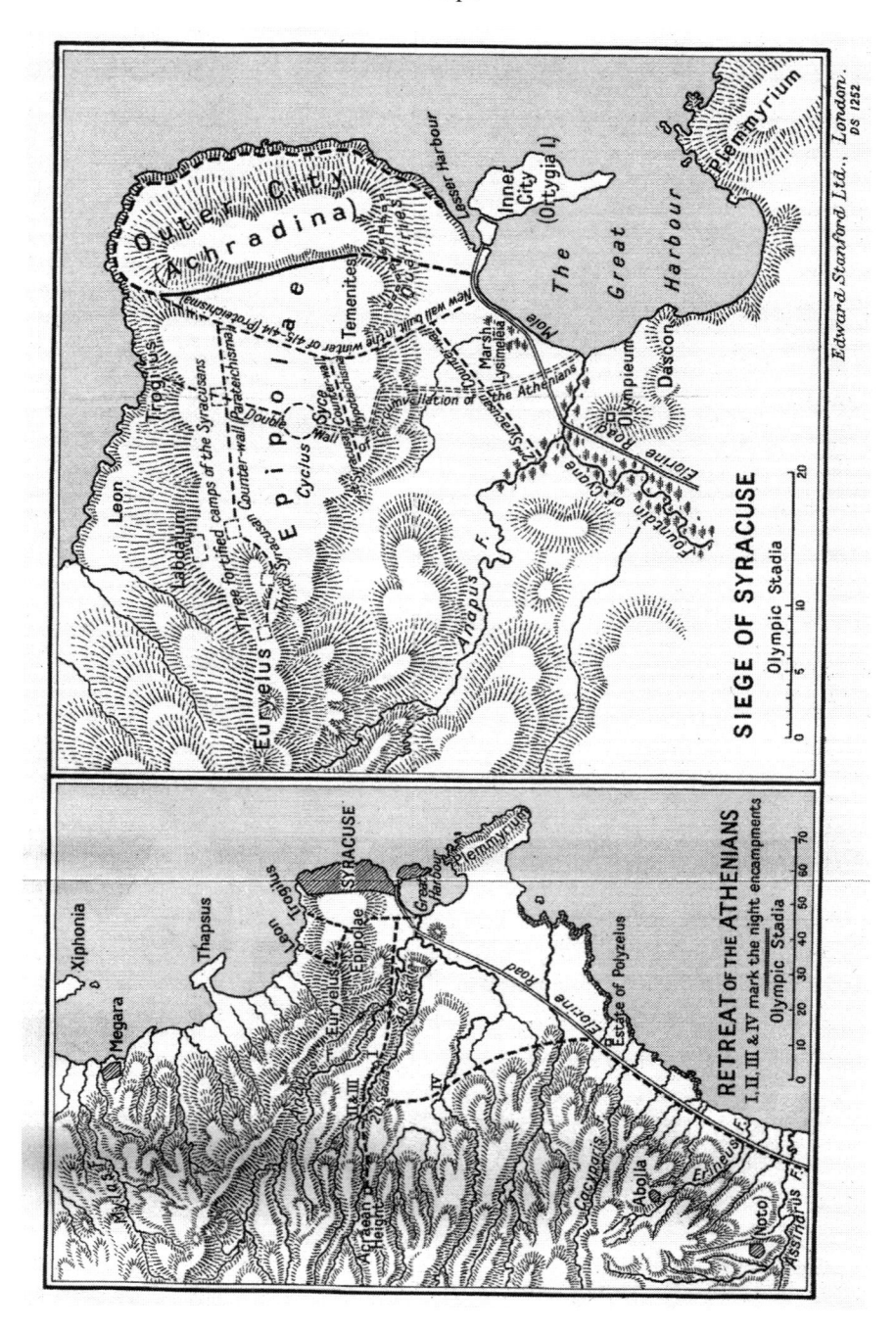

590

# SOPHRON CATALOGUE

## 2014

**Caesar's Commentaries: The Complete Gallic War. Revised.** 8vo., xxiv,507 pp.; Introduction, Latin text of all eight Books, Notes, Companion, Grammar, Exercises, Vocabularies, 17 Maps, illus. all based on Francis W. Kelsey.     ISBN 978-0-9850811 1 9 . . . . . . . .$19.95

**Virgil's Aeneid Complete, Books I-XII.** With Introduction, Latin text and Notes by W. D. Williams. 8vo., xxviii, 739 pp., 2 maps, Glossary, Index.     ISBN 978-0-9850811 6 4 . . . . . . . .$27.95

*Praxis Grammatica.* **A New Edition.** John Harmer. 12 mo., xviii, 116 pp.; Introduction by Mark Riley.     ISBN 978-0-9850811 2 6.  $3.95

**The *Other* Trojan War. Dictys & Dares.** 12 mo., xxii,397 pp.; Latin/English Parallel Texts; Frazer's Introduction & Notes, Index.     ISBN 978-0-9850811 5 7. . . . . . . $14.95

**The Stoic's Bible:** *a Florilegium for the Good Life. EXPANDED.* Giles Laurén. 8vo., xxvi,653 pp., 2 illus., Introduction, Bibliography.     ISBN 978-0-9850811-0-2. . . . . . . . $24.95

**Why Don't We Learn from History?** B. H. Liddell Hart. 12 mo., 126 pp.     ISBN 978-0-9850811 3 3. . . . . . . .$4.95

**Quintilian. Institutionis Oratoriae. Liber Decimus.** Text, Notes & Introductory Essays by W. Peterson. Foreword by James J. Murphy. 8vo., cvi,291 pp., Harleian MS facsimile, Indexes.     ISBN 978-0-9850811-8-8 . . . . . . . $19.95

**Schools of Hellas.** Kenneth Freeman. 12 mo., xxi,279 pp., illus., Indexes.     ISBN 978-0-9850811-9-5 . . . . . . . $14.95

**Cornelius Nepos Vitae.** 12 mo., xviii,314 pp., 3 maps, notes, exercises, & vocabulary by John Rolf.     ISBN 978-0-9850811-7-1 $14.95

**Greek Reader.** Mark Riley. Based on the selection of Wilamowitz-Moellendorff, with notes and a vocabulary. 12 mo., vi,286 pp.
     ISBN 978-0-9897836-0-6 . . . . . . . $12.95

**Quintilian**: *A Roman Educator and his Quest for the Perfect Orator*. Revised Edition, George A. Kennedy. 12 mo., 188 pp. Index.
ISBN 978-0-9897836-1-3 . . . . . . . . $9.95

**Diodorus Siculus**. I *The Library of History in Forty Books.* Vol. I. (books I-XIV). 8vo., xxvii,590 pp., frontis., maps.
ISBN 978-0-9897836-2-0 . . . . . . .$19.95

**Diodorus Siculus**. II *The Library of History.* Vol. II., 8vo., xiv,493 pp., maps          ISBN 978-0-9897836-3-7          $19.95

**Foulquié, Paul.** *La Dialectique.* in-8, 160 pp.,
ISBN 978-1-4954688-3-4          $7.40

Available from SOPHRON EDITOR (CreateSpace and Amazon worldwide)

*In Preparation*:
  Isocrates by Richard Enos.
  Horace *Opera*